Adobe®

Premiere® Pro 2.0

STUDIO TECHNIQUES

Jacob Rosenberg

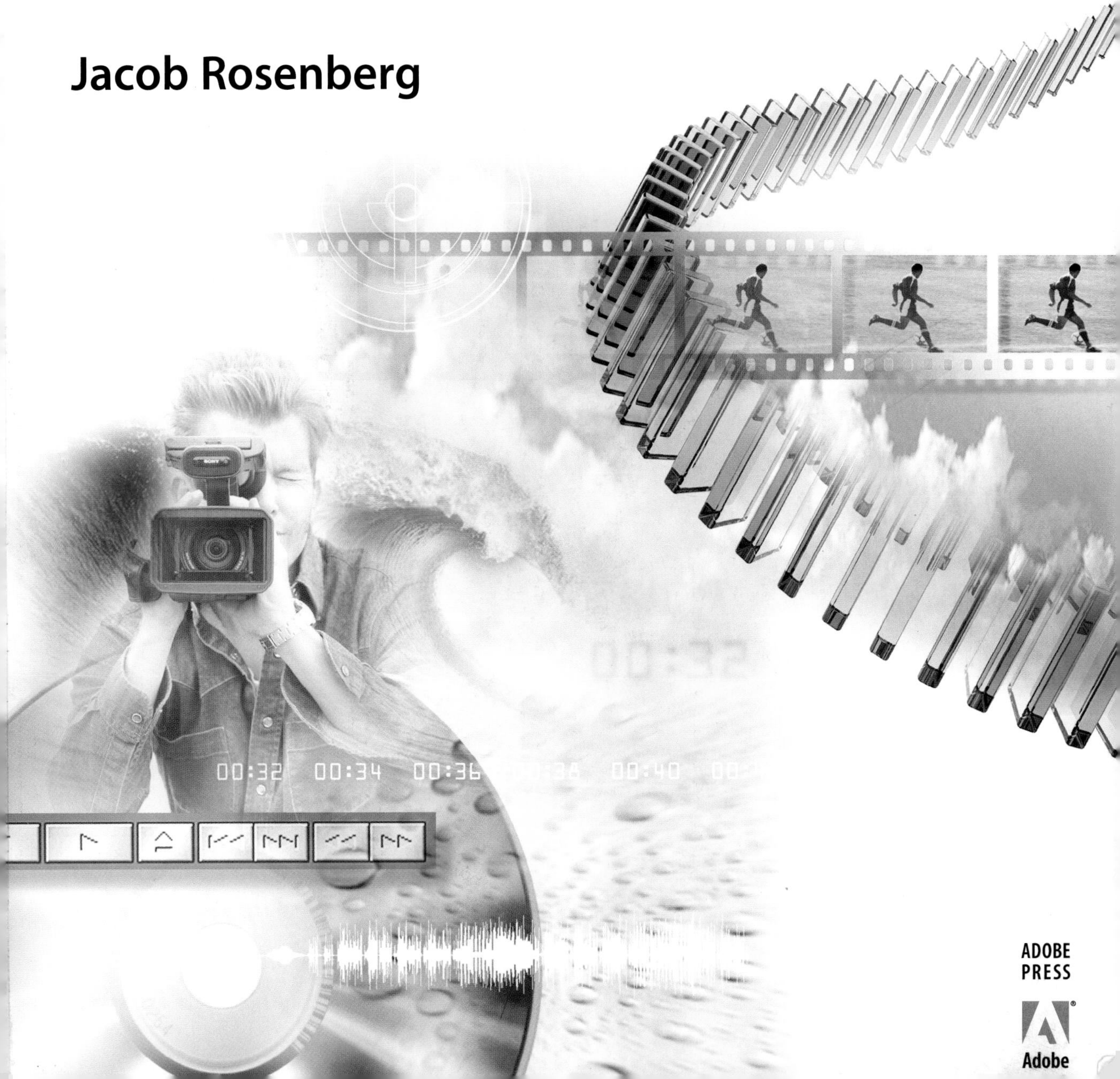

ADOBE PRESS

Adobe

Adobe Premiere Pro 2.0 Studio Techniques

Jacob Rosenberg

This Adobe Press book is published by Peachpit. For information on Adobe Press books, contact:

Peachpit
1249 Eighth Street
Berkeley, CA 94710
(510) 524-2178
Fax: (510) 524-2221

http://www.adobepress.com
To report errors, please send a note to errata@peachpit.com

Peachpit Press is a division of Pearson Education
Project Editor: Karen Reichstein
Development and Copy Editor: Linda Laflamme
Production Editor: Myrna Vladic
Technical Editor: Charles Liss
Proofreader: Liz Welch
Compositors: Diana Van Winkle, Van Winkle Design; Joan Keyes, Dovetail Publishing Services
Indexer: Karin Arrigoni
Cover design: Charlene Charles-Will
Cover illustration: Alicia Buelow

Notice of Rights

Notice of Liability

Trademarks

ISBN 0-321-38547-0

9 8 7 6 5 4 3 2 1

Contents

DVD Contents

Dedication

I would like to continue dedicating this book to my friend Michael Anthony Ternasky and to my father, Joel Rosenberg.

My mentor Michael "MT" Ternasky was killed in an automobile accident shortly before I started film school. Mike was the impetus for my pursuing that dream and for naming my production company Formika Films. I dedicate the work I do to his memory.

Mike grew up as a rebel with a passion to be the best at whatever he did. When I first met him, he ran a skateboard company called H-Street, and he ran it to top capacity. When Mike died, he had formed his own "super" skateboard company, Plan B, which pooled together the best skateboarders in the world and produced some of the most ground-breaking and influential skateboard videos to date. I was fortunate enough to be a part of those videos and to have been educated in the "MT Filming and Editing School of Hard Knocks" under his direction.

In dealing with the grief that followed Mike's death, I became close friends with his older brother Joe who, at the time, worked at Adobe Systems. Knowing that my editing skills were strong, Joe suggested that I try my hand at testing Adobe editing software. After I was turned down as a tester for the Quality Assurance Team (no college degree at the time, and no formal computer experience), Joe got me an interview with the engineering team that wrote the code for Adobe Premiere. Nick Schlott (then the engineering manager) took a gamble and hired me to test the program from an editor's perspective. I was to communicate directly with the engineers about what wasn't working and what needed changing. That was almost twelve years ago, and my relationship with Adobe continues to this day.

I tell this story as a means of showing the amazing and positive twists and turns that can come from a tragic event. By acknowledging the impact of someone's life and death on my own life, I am able to keep pushing forward.

At age 67, my father sets a precedent for enthusiasm, energy, and passion. Riding a few hundred miles a week on his bicycle and challenging himself daily, he continually aspires to do more and learn more about the world. My father has contributed greatly to the person I am today by teaching me the power of communication and the overwhelming value of educating and inspiring the people around you. This past year my father and I rode in a fundraiser riding from San Francisco to Los Angeles in an effort to raise money for HIV/AIDS. Taking a week of my life and devoting it to such a task and such an experience was a chance of a lifetime and I am grateful my father inspired me to participate with him and make a difference.

I dedicate this book to my two friends and two fathers. Thank you for your knowledge, passion, and guidance.

About the Author

Jacob Rosenberg is a Los Angeles-based filmmaker and Adobe Premiere expert. Jacob has worked extensively with the Premiere software development team for over ten years. Over the last two years, Jacob has made a name for himself in the post-production community spearheading cutting-edge high definition workflows using desktop computers and Adobe software. Jacob served as the online editor and online supervisor for the feature film *Dust to Glory,* which utilized an all-Adobe workflow and generated a 35mm film print from an HD Premiere project. Currently, Jacob serves as the online editor and digital intermediate supervisor for the independent film *Lbs.* Jacob also recently directed a music video for singer/songwriter John Gold, shot and edited in high-definition video using the software included in Adobe Production Studio.

Jacob got his start in high school by filming and editing skateboard videos. After graduating from Emerson College, Jacob moved to L.A. and began his film career. Today, he is an accomplished independent filmmaker having directed national commercials, music videos, and several short films. Jacob moonlights as the host of an acclaimed DVD training series, *Total Training for Adobe Premiere Pro.*

About the Technical Editor

With more than ten years experience in the graphics and video industry, **Charles Liss** has worked for such companies as Adobe Systems and Canopus Corporation. Charles has made Premiere Pro the cornerstone of his work for the last six years, touching on almost all parts of the product. Currently a test automation engineer, he continues to work with Adobe and the Premiere team, always working to find new ways to make this product better. He lives in the heart of Silicon Valley with his wife Kimberly and their two dogs.

Acknowledgments

I first need to acknowledge the people who first gave me the opportunity to work with Adobe Systems year after year:

Joe Ternasky, for getting my back, lobbying for me, and getting me the second interview. Nick Schlott, for taking a chance and hiring me. Greg Gilley, for continuing to have me back, again and again and again. Marianne Deaton, for helping to ensure that everything was in order for me to keep coming back. Steve Warner, for hiring me again and again and again. Bruce Bowman, for the tradeshow work, friendship and opportunities that he helped create, and some last-minute tech-editing duties. Richard Townhill, for his trust and the opportunities he extended to me. Dave Trescot, who not only extended me opportunities, but also encouraged me to take my training and education skills a bit further and build a relationship with Total Training. His guidance has been invaluable. And where would I be had John Warnock and Chuck Geschke not been rebels themselves and created such a sound company?

So many people have been instrumental in bringing the Premiere product to life. I want to at least thank the good folks on the ninth floor in San Jose who work hard to give users a product they can rely on. Production Studio is a great leap forward, and the lead that Premiere Pro has taken should be noted. To the tech support folks in Seattle, I also thank you for being there and being on top of your game.

I again feel very privileged to have had such great support in putting this book together. Thank you to Jeffrey Warnock, who first suggested the idea and put me in touch with Peachpit. To my editor, Linda Laflamme, it's difficult to write a good book without a good editor and on the second trip, I am glad it's the same you! A very special nod of appreciation to Charles Liss who singlehandedly juggled the tech edit while releasing a product and learning to fly! He ensured that the details and jargon that I tossed around were very well-grounded in fact. To my project editor, Karen Reichstein, I appreciate that you kept the book's and reader's best interest in mind, staying on top of all the things necessary to get the book done. A late edition special thanks to Michael McCarthy who helped me update the appendices; your technical knowledge is much appreciated and admired.

I know it's like a movie credit roll, but I want to make sure these people know I appreciate their support. In no particular order: Mitch Wood, Kristan Jiles, Jason Levine, David Kuspa, Paul E. Young, Terry Ragan, Andrew Huebscher, Addison Liu, Mike Kanfer'no, Jason Woliner, Giles Baker, Mark Cokes, Brad Pillow, Mike Berry, Zachary Lam, Maryann MacGregor, Bob Currier, MT, Ganoush, Robert F., Lorbs, Al Tse, the Stratton family, Matt Toledo & family, Michelle Love-Escobar, Wally & Patty (and fam), Scott Waugh, Dana Brown, Mouse McCoy, Rich Wilson, and the D2G group, thanks for the opportunity. Rob Legato, Ron Ames and Adam Gerstel, thanks for the education. Sample Digital: Josh Kline, Cone, Matt "Shart" Reason, and Marlowe, thanks for the office space. Matt Dowling @

Blackmagic Designs, David Newman and David Taylor @ CineForm, Wes @ Automatic Duck, Tim Smith @ Canon, Dan Restuccio @ Post Magazine, Cynthia Wisehart @ Millimeter Magazine, John Gold. To the folks at Laser Pacific, Leon Silverman and Tom Vice, thanks for your support with all my tests and projects. And here's a special thanks to those I forgot to mention.

And finally, I would like to thank my family for their patience with such an enthusiastic and hyper-curious child who was allowed to explore all of the things that interested him. If not for their patience, I have no clue what my life would look like today. I have been blessed with a tight family that supported my growth and individuality even when it wasn't comfortable for them. Mom, Dad, and Jessica, thank you.

To my love and soulmate, Lilit, I am forever grateful we finally found each other.

Foreword

In the past two years since the initial release of this book, Jacob Rosenberg has risen to the forefront of high-definition workflows using Premiere Pro to go places not traveled before. From the film *Dust to Glory* to the music video "Cactusflower" and, most recently, to the film, *Lbs.*, Jacob continues to immerse himself in cutting-edge projects. Whether directing, editing, or supervising a project, Jacob's quest for knowledge and experience continues. I have known Jacob for most of his life, and I can truly say that he has a creative spark and passion for video and filmmaking.

For over ten years, he has tracked the development of Adobe Premiere as a tester, consultant, user, and critic. He has extensive experience with Premiere, Premiere Pro, and other Adobe products from both inside and outside Adobe.

What most impresses me about Jacob is that he is a smart, sensitive, and artistic filmmaker who demands that the tools he uses live up to the vision he has for his projects. This combination of artistic drive and extreme technical competence makes Jacob the perfect person to guide you through the ins and outs of Adobe Premiere Pro 2.0.

In this book, you will find that Premiere Pro has grown even more since its last release. With a new interface, loads of new features, and an emphasis on integration with the other video applications, Premiere Pro 2.0 has come into its own. You will find new DVD features, newly integrated Adobe Clip Notes, new multi-cam support, and new color correction features. Best of all, while reading this book, you will see Premiere Pro through the eyes of someone who lives his life with the product. I am sure you will find the journey rewarding.

John Warnock

I

Introduction

So here we are at version 2.0 of Adobe Premiere Pro. For those of you keeping track, this is the 12th version of the product. When I finished the previous edition of this book, I did not anticipate the grand vision the Premiere product team at Adobe had in mind. They revamped the entire interface to unify it with the other video products and then added a lot of new features.

For *Adobe Premiere Pro 2.0 Studio Techniques*, I revisited every chapter and every lesson with 2.0's latest features in mind. In a few instances, the lessons are not much changed. In others, such as multi-cam, color correction, track mattes, and DVD authoring, it's a whole new ballgame.

A Real Tool for Real Work

A lot of changes in my professional life are also reflected in the restructuring and in the content of some lessons. My expertise with Premiere Pro led to my involvement with the feature film, *Dust to Glory*. I conformed *Dust to Glory* in Premiere Pro and supervised the assembling of an HD project (Digital Intermediate) that served as the source for the final film output of the movie. The workflow that I designed and the lessons that I learned were invaluable. *Dust to Glory* was made during the development of cycle of 2.0, so many of the issues we encountered in the editing room were addressed in this latest version of the software. Coming off of *Dust to Glory* I have new-found admiration for the capabilities of Premiere Pro and a lot more personal experience using it in the most demanding situations.

Today all the work I do is in high definition. If you haven't done so already, you should start to explore for yourself the potential that HD video offers you as an editor/producer/

director/photographer. Superior quality video clips are now within reach at a consumer price point. It's time to start digging in to maximize that potential.

At the end of the day, it all comes down to money and a budget. Sure, you can pay high prices and get great integrated editing systems, but throughout its history Premiere and its diverse feature set have offered a high value for a relatively low price. Think about it: You can digitize video, add titles, apply effects, fine-tune audio, and export directly to a DVD without having to use any other software—that's fantastic. With the new advances in hardware, cameras, and processors, now is as good of a time as ever to invest in a simple editing solution. In this book, you will find lots of lessons and tons of tips that will help you make the most of your investment.

Who Should Read This Book?

Adobe Premiere Pro 2.0 Studio Techniques is for anyone who wants to get more out of using Adobe Premiere Pro—from new users to old hands.

If you are new to Premiere, the "Fundamentals of Premiere Pro" section and bonus appendices on the accompanying DVD will give you a good foundation to build on.

If you're looking for step-by-step lessons to help you hone your skills, the "Advanced" sections will give you plenty of resources to mine. Jump to the subject you desire and dig in. The step-by-step lessons are derived from real-world examples and techniques that I have used and developed during my own work, and many include some of my original video and audio files. The best way to learn editing is with real material, such as shots that make up a scene that must be tailored into a whole.

Being a visual person, I sometimes need to *see* exactly what a feature does in order to understand it. Video tutorials on the DVD supplement the discussions in the book. Watch the short video clips to learn more about difficult, technical, or purely visual concepts. Notes in the book's text will direct you to the clips at the appropriate time. You'll find the tutorials very conversational and direct.

What's in This Book?

Adobe Premiere Pro 2.0 Studio Techniques is composed of seven sections. Here's a quick preview of what you'll find where.

- **I: Fundamentals of Premiere Pro.** Here you will find almost every Premiere Pro feature, window, and button explained in simple terms and clear illustrations. New to this section are Chapter 1, "The New Premiere Pro Workspace: How It Works and What's New," Chapter 10, "Titler Basics," Chapter 11, "DVD Basics," and Chapter 12, "Adobe Bridge and Adobe Production Studio."
- **II: Advanced Graphics and Titling.** After the overview come the hands-on lessons. In this section, you will learn how to properly import layered Photoshop files, nest sequences to build more controllable effects, create custom image pan effects with presets, and get better results from the Titler. The lessons here culminate in the creation of a custom menu-based DVD using the latest DVD authoring tools, with the all-new Chapter 16, "Custom DVD Design."
- **III: Advanced Audio Techniques.** Imagery is only half of your project, and this section shines the spotlight on the other half: audio. After a complete overview of fine-tuning your system's audio settings, you will learn to record a voiceover, edit it, add effects, and mix it all down. New to this section is Chapter 21, "5.1 Surround Sound Mixing," which explains how to convert a stereo project to a surround sound one.
- **IV: Advanced Effect Techniques.** Focusing on several of Premiere Pro's most important effects, this section provides plenty of real-world examples. Chapters 22, "New Color Correction Tools," and 23, "Advanced Color Correction: Three-Way Color Corrector," reveal two of the new color correction tools and take you further than before in understanding how to properly white balancing your footage, create a custom color look, and apply secondary color corrections. In this section, you will also investigate track mattes, key green-screen material, and create a good-looking picture-in-picture effect.

- **V: Advanced Editing.** Here you will work with professional footage from a short film and some music videos too. You will refine your timeline editing and trimming skills, and learn the brand-new multi-cam editing workflow.
- **VI: Professional Workflows.** These three new chapters, located on the book's DVD, were too big to fit in the printed book. You'll learn about Adobe's new Clip Notes feature; encoding into Flash, H.264, and Windows Media using the Adobe Media Encoder; and getting a complete workout with HDV and HD. By the end your brain should be full of new ideas about the best ways to work now and in the future.

What's on the DVD?

Accompanying this book is a DVD chock full of additional chapters, lesson files, video tutorials, plug-ins, and tryout versions of Adobe Premiere Pro 2.0 and Adobe Audition 2.0. Copy its entire contents to your hard drive, then drag and drop all the folders of the APPST2 disc directly onto one of your video drives (preferably not your root drive). The APPST2 Lesson Files folder contains lessons for each chapter.

Throughout the book, you will be directed to the Video Tutorials folder when a tutorial exists to explain or illustrate something in the chapter. The video tutorials are arranged by the name of the technique shown. For example, Titler_Workout.wmv is a short clip that shows how to rearrange the Titler panels. I have also included additional tutorials not referenced in the book that highlight a few cool features that I couldn't squeeze into the book.

The Third-Party Plug-Ins folder is full of trial versions and demo copies of plug-ins that add extra functionality to Premiere Pro. Documentation and installation instructions for using each of the plug-ins are also provided.

If you have a question that isn't answered elsewhere, consult the Appendices folder. The appendices are formatted as PDF files. You can copy them to your system and read them using Acrobat Reader.

- **Before You Edit.** These appendices define the terms, technical presets, and system settings you need to review before and during your initial launch of Premiere Pro. You'll learn about all the nuts and bolts that go into creating a DV system from the ground up, as well as definitions of common digital video terms. Most importantly, you'll learn the proper settings for your system and Premiere Pro to keep them working together at their best.
- **While You Edit.** To make way for new material, we removed a few lessons from the previous edition. Appendix D updates the Color Match technique and explains the Auto effects. Appendix E is updated from the previous version, as well, discussing EDLs and AAF file import and export. If you are having technical difficulties while you edit, consult Appendix F, "Troubleshooting."

Where Do I Go Beyond This Book?

If you want to continue your quest for Premiere Pro knowledge and experience beyond this book, consider looking into my Premiere DVD training series from Total Training. These DVDs contain alternate real-world lessons, examples, and additional footage. For more details, explore the Premiere Pro/Digital Video links at www.totaltraining.com. Other good resources are *Adobe Premiere Pro 2.0 Classroom in a Book* (Adobe Press) and Aanarav Sareen's podcasts for CreativeCow.net.

Check out my Web site at www.formikafilms.com for info on the films, music videos, and productions that keep me busy. If you want to stay current with my Adobe Premiere Pro work, visit www.premiereprotraining.com. You can also email me at studiotech@premiereprotraining.com.

Fundamentals of Premiere Pro

CHAPTER

1

The New Premiere Pro Workspace: How It Works and What's New

What's new in 2.0? It's the question on everyone's minds; it's also a key topic of this first chapter. Here you'll learn about Premiere Pro's new workspace features and terminology, as well as how to rearrange and customize your desktop layout. Whether you're new to Premiere Pro or just to 2.0, you'll be working more efficiently by the end of this chapter.

Panels = Windows

With the release of the Adobe Production Studio, Adobe revealed a unified interface design that better ties together Premiere Pro 2.0, After Effects 7.0, Audition 2.0, and Encore DVD 2.0. What we formerly referred to as windows are now called *panels*. You can dock, move, and resize these panels with greater ease and more uniformity than was possible with the former window-based layout.

Every window is now a self-contained panel; for example, the former Monitor window which held both the Source Monitor and Program Monitor, is gone. The Source Monitor is its own panel as is the Program Monitor. These two can be docked together (see **Figure 1.1**) or separated; the choice is yours.

You can easily resize one panel by dragging any of its edges outward; 2.0 automatically decreases the size of the adjacent panels to keep them fully visible (see **Figure 1.2**). In former versions of Premiere, you had to readjust all window sizes manually to avoid overlapping.

Figure 1.1 In Premiere Pro 2.0, your workspace is now arranged in dockable panels instead of windows. For example, you can now dock the Source and Program monitors in the same frame, allowing for a more efficient workspace for effects feedback. In previous versions of Premiere, the single monitor layout would not allow you to actively toggle between Source and Program; only opening associated media would let you do that.

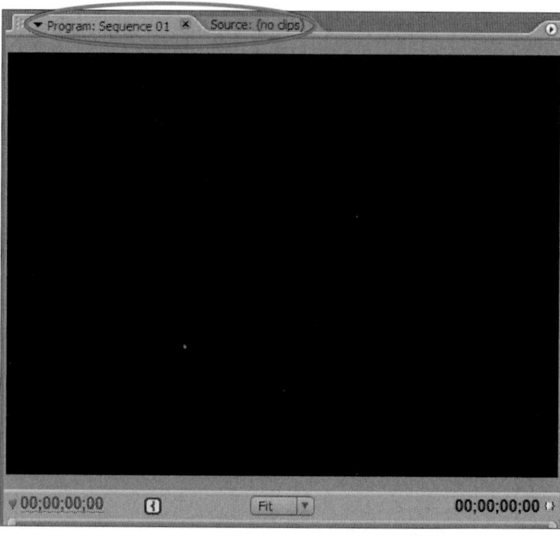

Figure 1.2 The new panel-based interface allows you to dynamically resize your panels as you work. Increasing the size of one panel decreases the size of the others without creating blank space or overlap in your workspace.

Frames and Panes

Another advantage of panels over windows is that every panel can be docked into any of the existing frames in the interface. Because there is no longer blank or empty space in the new interface whenever a panel occupies a defined region of the interface, that region is referred to as a *frame* or a *pane* (**Figure 1.3**).

Figure 1.3 This layout contains seven frames. Despite their size, technically the Audio Master Meters and Tools panels are both frames and you could dock other panels in their spaces.

Think of a frame much like a picture frame and a panel as the picture. More than one picture can be stacked in that frame, or you could split the frame up to show more pictures at once. This is what Premiere Pro 2.0 does, making complete use of the available desktop space for

a

b

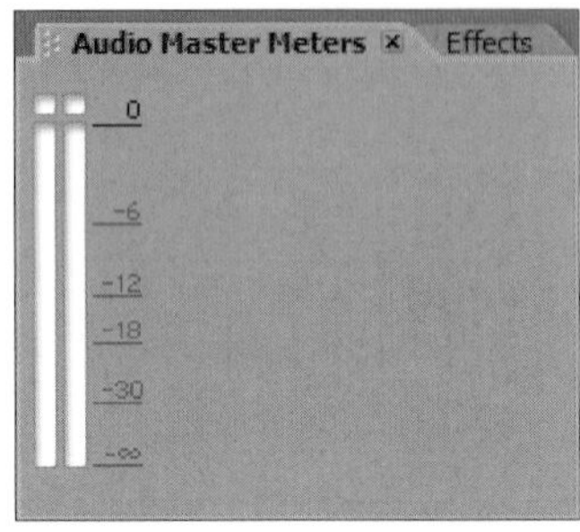

c

Figures 1.4a, b, and c The Audio Master Meters panel (a) is considered a legitimate frame. Because the frame is so small, however, it's hard to have another panel docked into it that is not of equal size. Here, even the Effects panel needs the frame to be larger to display properly (b). Once you enlarge the frame, the other panels docked in the frame now fill that same size (c).

editing (**Figures 1.4a, b,** and **c**). The trick to making a more efficient workspace is knowing which panes take up less space, which take up more, and then which are used most often for what tasks.

The 2.0 Panels

So what are the available panels in 2.0, and what are they used for? This section takes a closer look at each one, introducing you to some new panels and reminding you of some familiar ones.

The Project Panel

Formerly called the Project window, the Project panel houses all your project media and sequences for your project (**Figure 1.5**). The only change here is the name; no features were added or taken away since the last product release.

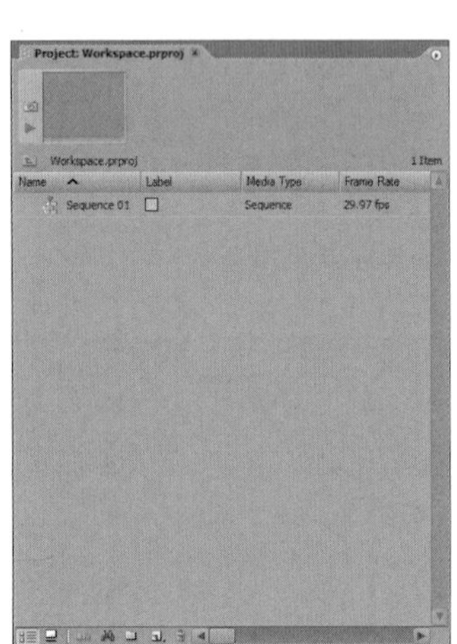

Figure 1.5 This is the Project panel, where all your project files, sequences, and media are stored while you work.

Chapter 3, "Using the Project Panel," focuses on the Project panel's functions.

The Source Monitor and Program Monitor Panels

The Source Monitor is used to preview and select source material for your sequences. The Program Monitor is used to preview, edit, and play the edited sequences. As a result of the windows-to-panels conversion (**Figure 1.6**), the Source and Program Monitor panels can dock together into the same frame or exist independently, and both be open at the same time. When editing with HD, I tend to work with one Monitor frame that has both the Source Monitor and Program Monitor docked into it.

NOTES

You may notice this chapter does not contain coverage of the Capture panel. Because it is not typically a panel that you would leave open and integrate with various workspace layouts, I've left discussion of the Capture panel to Chapter 2, "Capturing Video."

Figures 1.6 You can dock the Source Monitor and Program Monitor separately or together in a single frame.

The Source and Program Monitors are fully explored in Chapter 4, "Playing Back and Viewing Your Media."

You can access two additional panels from the Program Monitor as well: the Trim panel and the new Multi-Cam Monitor panel.

The Trim and Multi-Cam Panels

The Trim panel and the Multi-Cam Monitor are specialized panels used for specific editing tasks. With the Trim panel you can make precise edit adjustments at exact cut points in a simple visually based monitor (**Figure 1.7**). Chapter 26, "Advanced Editing: Creating your Cut," explains the Trim panel's uses. The Multi-Cam Monitor panel is a new Monitor panel that enables you to edit multiple camera shot material (**Figure 1.8**). Chapter 27, "Advanced Editing: The New Multi-Cam Workflow," explores the Multi-Cam Monitor panel in its entirety.

Figures 1.7 With the Trim panel you can adjust and fine-tune the exact cut points between two clips in the timeline.

Figures 1.8 With the Multi-Cam Monitor panel you can execute, refine, and view multiple camera material.

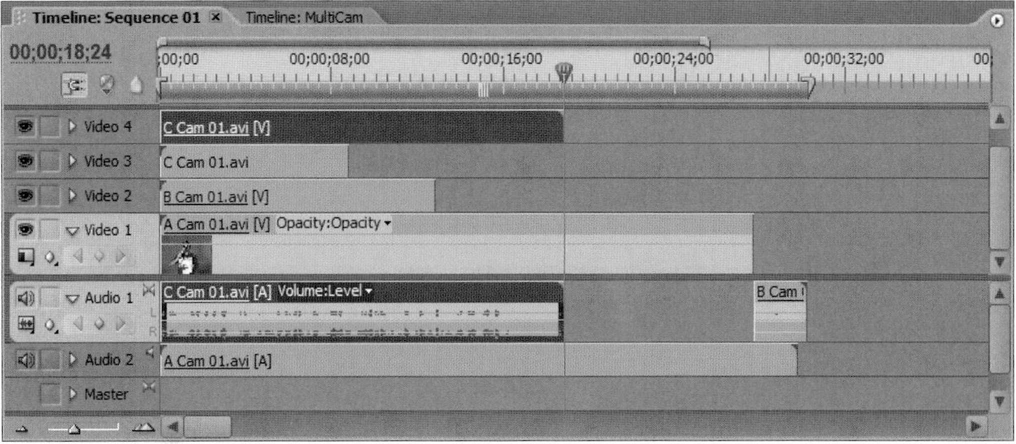

Figure 1.9 Here the Timeline panel has two sequences docked in it, Sequence 01 and Multi-Cam.

The Timeline Panel

In the Timeline panel you physically assemble, modify, and create your edited sequence (**Figure 1.9**). With 2.0, any panel can be docked into the frame that holds your Timeline panel; however, typically you will just have more sequences docked in the frame.

You can have more than one Timeline panel open so that you could in essence look at two sequences without switching back and forth using the tabs. The Timeline panel is explored in Chapter 5, "The Timeline Panel."

The Audio Mixer and Audio Master Meters Panels

Former versions of Premiere Pro could display a fully expanded Audio Mixer and an abridged output meters-only version (**Figures 1.10a** and **b**). Premiere Pro 2.0 preserves the Audio Mixer panel as it was in 1.5, plus it adds a new separate panel that always displays the master VU Meters from the Audio Mixer. This new panel is called the Audio Master Meters.

The Audio Mixer and the Audio Master Meters are discussed in more detail in Section III, "Advanced Audio Techniques."

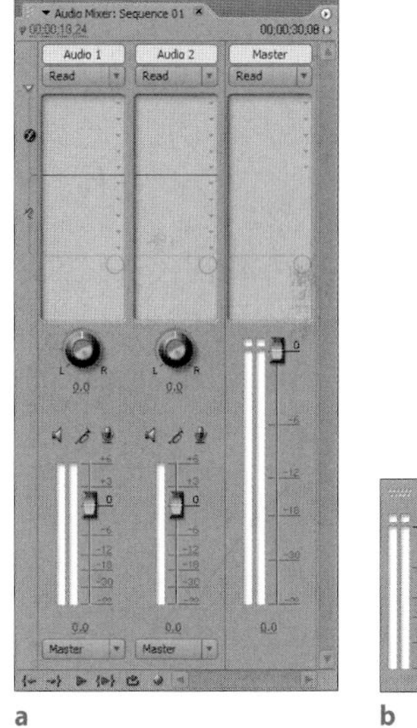

Figures 1.10a and b The familiar Audio Mixer (a) is now joined by the Audio Master Meters panel (b), which is much smaller and contains only the necessary meters to monitor the decibel level of the output sound.

DVD Layout Panel

A brand-new panel for 2.0, the DVD Layout panel (**Figure 1.11**) assists in the process of customizing an interactive, menu-based DVD.

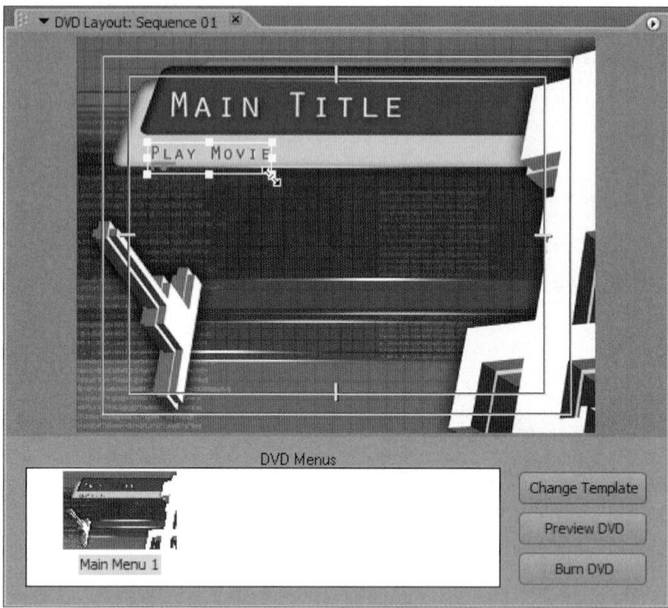

Figure 1.11 In the New DVD Layout panel you can click, drag, and adjust various elements associated with a custom DVD.

Chapter 11, "DVD Basics," introduces the basics of this panel and its functions, while Chapter 16, "Custom DVD Design," takes the discussion one big step further. When using the DVD Layout panel, you can adjust the properties of the panel and its associated elements using the Effect Controls panel.

The Effect Controls Panel

Whenever you adjust an effect property or want to see the value of certain settings for an applied effect, head to the Effect Controls panel to extract or modify that information (**Figure 1.12**).

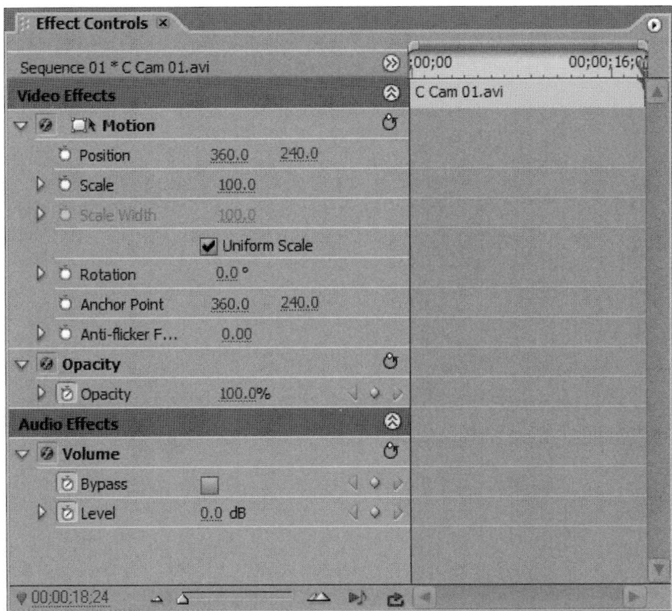

Figure 1.12 In the Effect Controls panel, you adjust and modify a clip effect parameter that has been applied to a clip in your sequences. Additionally, you can use the Effect Controls panel with the DVD Layout panel to modify DVD Menu elements.

Chapter 7, "Transition Basics," introduces the Effect Controls panel, while Chapter 8, "Effect Controls Basics," fully explores it.

The Effects Panel

The Effects panel hasn't changed with 2.0. Whether you're applying video effects, audio clip effects, video transitions, or audio transitions, the Effects panel is where all the effects and transitions are housed (**Figure 1.13**).

The Effects panel also holds custom effects that you created by exporting the effect properties of any effect applied to a clip in your sequence. Custom effect presets are stored in the Presets folder.

Figure 1.13 The Effects panel holds all the effects and transitions that can be used in your project. Additionally, the Effects panel can hold custom-made effect presets, which you can access from the Presets folder.

The Titler Panels

The Adobe Title Designer, now known as the Titler in Premiere Pro 2.0, was remodeled as five different panels to conform to the new 2.0 interface (**Figure 1.14**). The five panels that make up the Titler are Titler, Tools, Styles, Actions, and Properties.

Although you can open the Titler panels individually, your desktop layout is better served if you to open them and create a workspace that has them all together. Chapter 10, "Titler Basics" introduces and explores these panels, then Chapter 15, "Advanced Titling: Styles and Templates," will deepen your understanding of the Titler.

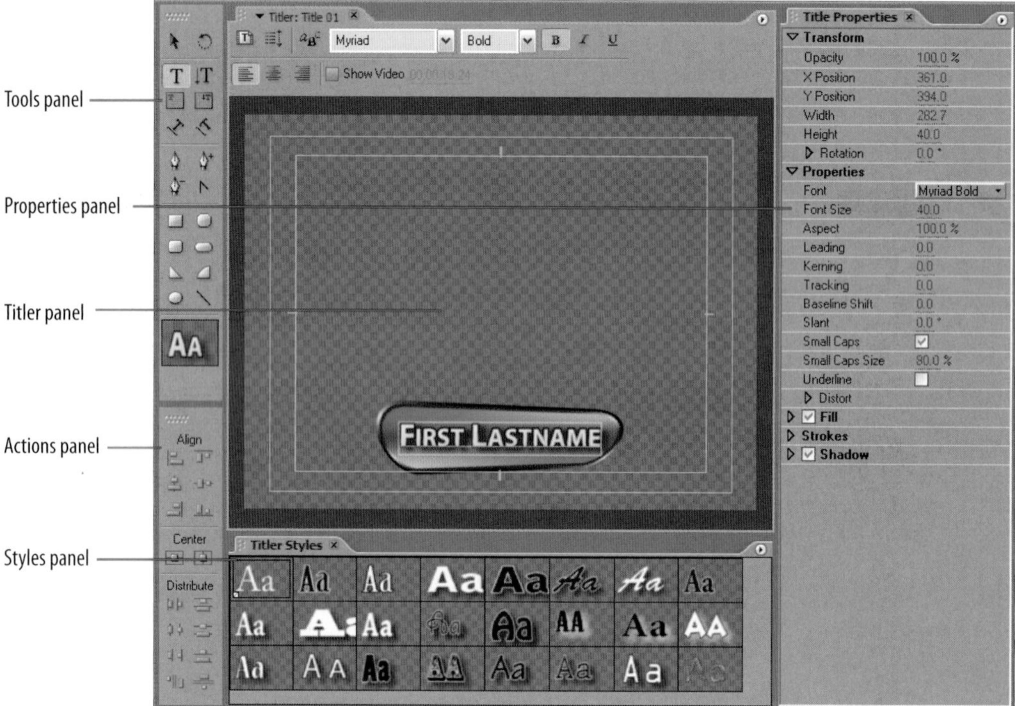

Figure 1.14 The Titler, Tools, Styles, Actions, and Properties panels are the group of panels that comprise 2.0's Titler.

The Tools Panel

Called the Tool Box in 1.5, the Tools panel (**Figure 1.15**) holds all the tools that assist in timeline editing or Program Monitor adjustments. In 2.0, you can drop the Tools panel either vertically or horizontally into any region of your workspace. Consult Chapter 6, "The Editing Workflow," for more details on this panel's tools.

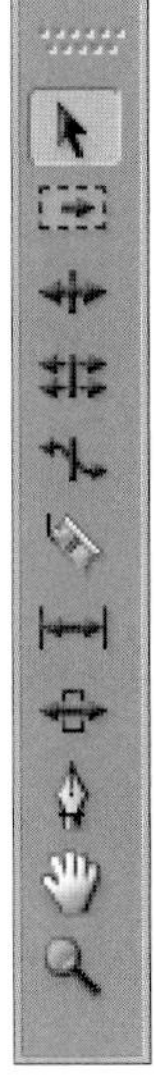

Figure 1.15 Vertically or horizontally the Tools panel doesn't need too much space to reveal its tools.

The History, Events, and Info Panels

What used to be the primary Tab palettes from Premiere Pro 1.5 are now panels just like rest of the former "windows." The History panel logs every step that you take in Premiere Pro, and you can use it to back up any number of steps or undo previously completed tasks (**Figure 1.16**). The Events panel keeps track of errors and warnings. If something doesn't seem to be working right or you want to look back at a warning you saw, you can look at the events listed in the Events panel. Finally, the Info panel displays feedback relevant to the panel or region of the application you are working in. If you selected a clip in the Timeline or Project panel, information specific to the selection appears in the Info panel.

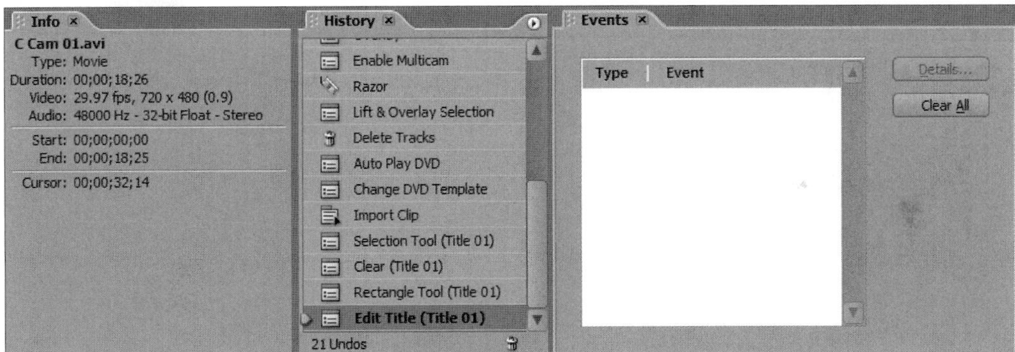

Figure 1.16 When you select a clip in the Timeline panel, the properties of the selected clip appear in the Info panel. The History panel shows a listing of all the actions recently taken. By clicking on a previous action, you can back up to that point and undo what was done between the current time and that previous point. The Events panel lists any error or warning messages and allows you to select the message and display its details. Hopefully your Events panel remains empty like mine.

These panels are referenced throughout the book and there is not one dedicated chapter devoted to any of them in particular.

Now that you have seen the different panels, let's focus on selecting a panel, rearranging the panels in your workspace, and resizing a frame.

To view a short video tutorial on navigating and rearranging your workspace, see the Workspace_Workout.wmv clip in the Video Tutorials folder on the book's DVD.

Selecting, Resizing, and Rearranging

When it comes to organizing your workspaces, a picture is worth more than a thousand words. This section illustrates how to rearrange and resize your panels. In all cases, the first step is selecting a panel. A selected panel has an orange outline around its edges inside its frame. In all the figures to come, when I reference the "selected" panel, I mean the panel with the orange outline. When a panel is selected, all corresponding menu items and keyboard shortcuts that are assigned to the panel become active. For instance, if you select the Effect Controls panel, the Clip > Audio Options menu is not available. If your Source Monitor is selected with an audio clip open in it, however, Clip > Audio Options becomes active and available.

Rearranging Your Panels

Now dig in so you can start understanding how to manipulate panels. **Figures 1.17** through **1.19** focus on three different methods of re-arranging the panels in your desktop.

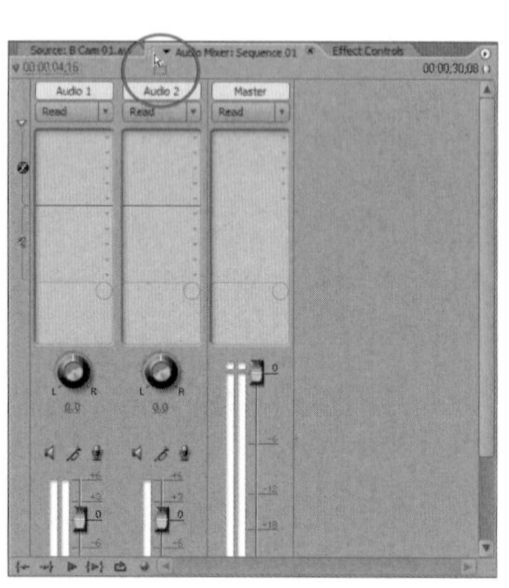

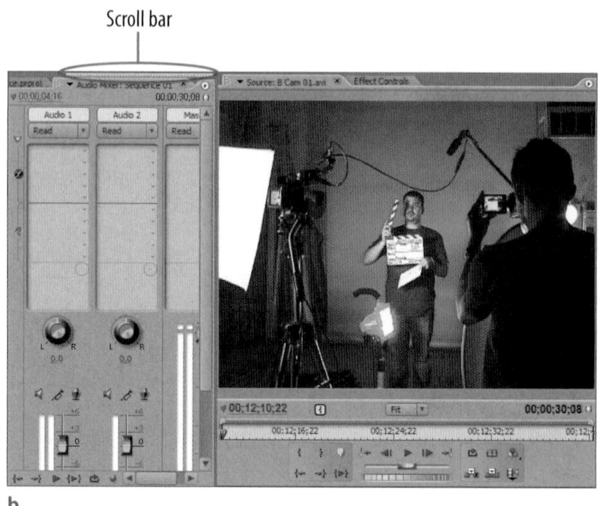

Figures 1.17a and b You can pull the tab for a panel, such as the Audio Mixer, from the current frame (a). Figure 1.17b shows the Project panel frame with the Audio Mixer docked into it. Notice how there is a scroll bar at the top of the frame to scroll between the Project panel tab and the Audio Mixer tab.

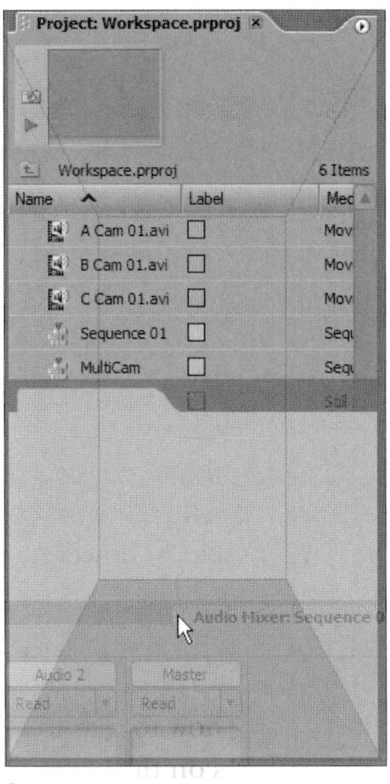

a

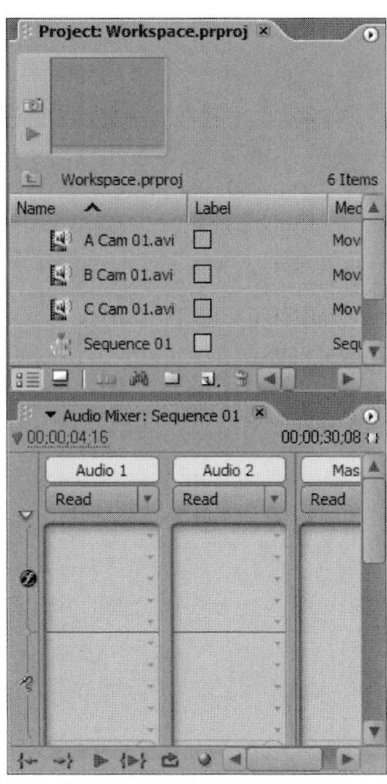

b

Figures 1.18a and b In these figures, I am moving the Audio Mixer into the frame of the Project panel and trying to make a new frame for it in the existing Project panel frame. When you drop a panel into a new frame, the portion of the grid that darkens is where the panel will be split to create the new frame. Notice how once you drop the panel at the bottom of the Project panel frame, the overall size of the original frame is exactly the same. Once you drop the panel into a new frame, you can manually resize it. (To see how to resize this workspace, check out Figure 1.21.)

Figure 1.19 Anytime you drag beyond the edges of an outer frame so that you are on the very edge of the desktop, you can create a new frame that spans the entire height or width of the desktop. Here the Audio Mixer is dropped to the far left of the desktop and can easily be resized and expanded to its full height.

Figure 1.20 When you press the Ctrl key, the panel becomes a transparent preview of what it will ultimately look like (left). When you release the Ctrl key you have a floating panel to which you can add additional panels (right).

Figure 1.20 shows how you can move a panel and reposition it as its own "floating" panel on top of the desktop.

To move a panel from its current frame, simply grab the panel's tab portion and drag the panel to another region of the desktop. If you position it inside another existing frame, you can dock it into the current frame (Figures 1.17a and b).

If you pull your panel from its current frame and then decide not to move the panel, simply press the Esc key while still holding down the mouse to deactivate your selection of the panel. If you want your panel to exist as a "floating" panel on top of the application window and desktop, hold down the Ctrl key when you release the mouse button and drop the panel on top of the interface (**Figure 1.20**).

Resizing Your Panels

You can select and rearrange, now try resizing. Once again, images do the best job of explaining here. **Figures 1.21a** through **c** assume that you want to increase the overall size of the Project panel frame from the Editing workspace (Windows > Workspace > Editing).

To resize a frame, drag any of its inner edges away from the center of the frame. As you make a size adjustment, the adjacent frames reduce in size accordingly. Frames have

a

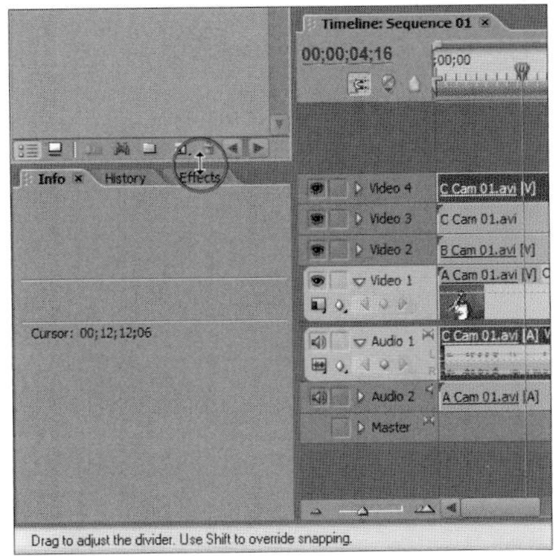

b

c

Figures 1.21a through c Consider the Editing workspace at various stages: the right edge of the Project panel frame being dragged right to make it wider (a), the bottom of the Project panel frame being dragged downwards (b) to make it taller, and the corner of the Project panel frame being selected (notice the tool updates to have four arrows) and dragged diagonally downwards and to the right to increase the height and width simultaneously (c).

snapping points for their horizontal and vertical alignment. When you try to resize a frame, by default you can get only so close to the snapping point before you snap into perfect alignment. If you want to resize a frame and not have it snap to the alignment of adjacent frames, hold down the Shift key while you adjust the frame so that you override the snapping behavior.

It takes a little while to get the rhythm down with resizing. Keep in mind that every size adjustment of one frame affects the current size on another adjacent frame. When creating new frames, also take into account that many of the surrounding frames need to be resized to accommodate the spatial distribution of the frames and their preferred sizes.

Things to Remember

The most valuable things to take away from this chapter are familiarity with the new terminology and the expected responsiveness to how to drop and replace panels. When you get to Chapter 15 there's a little quiz waiting for you to see how easy of a time you have building a custom workspace for the Titler.

A great feature to remember is the Custom Workspaces menu listing and the ability to load preexisting workspaces and to customize your own. For a number of lessons in this book, you will rely on existing workspaces and in a couple of instances I have provided a few of my own. If you find yourself in a resizing downward spiral, simply go up to your Window > Workspace menu and select any of the preexisting workspaces to get back to square one. If you have created a workspace that you want to keep, go to Window > Workspace > Save Workspace and then name the current workspace configuration so that it becomes selectable from the Window > Workspace menu.

It is not a simple task to understand the workspace revisions right out of the new 2.0 box, but once you get used to the layout functionality, you'll find that your work in the application and the allocation of panel space and sizes is much more efficient.

In the next chapter I will introduce the Capture panel, which is a specialized panel that is your interface to recording audio and video for usage inside of Premiere Pro.

CHAPTER

2

Capturing Video

Video capture is at the heart of Premiere Pro—you can't do much until you have some clips to work with. To get the clips you want at the best quality with the most information for your project, you'll need to understand the Capture panel, as well as capturing fundamentals, such as logging your tapes and striping your DV tapes with timecode. This chapter will take you on a tour of what's new and what's necessary, examining, for example, how Premiere Pro's Capture panel is integrated with your open project. Along the way, you will learn a workflow that provides better media management and long-term project stability. Because Premiere Pro 2.0 supports a handful of new video formats (SD, HDV, and HD) this chapter will also give you guidelines for system requirements and the file sizes you should expect for your captured clips.

Scratch Disks and Device Control

Before you get to the Capture panel, you need to make sure your Scratch Disk and Device Control preferences are set correctly. These help establish where your captured files are recorded and which method Premiere uses to communicate with the attached video device (a camera or deck).

For capturing any format, I recommend that you do not use your root disk (C:) as the primary scratch disk. Instead, create a unique folder to which you target your captured files on your scratch or capture disk. The storage size and read/write speed of your scratch disk should relate directly to the format you are capturing. A scratch disk for capturing HD is likely to be both larger (because you have much more data) and faster (because you have higher data rates) than a drive used for capturing DV. For capturing HD, you need striped disks with some form of data redundancy.

To assign your scratch disks, choose Edit > Preferences > Scratch Disks and specify the disks you want (**Figure 2.1**). If you want the captured media from separate projects to be captured into separate subfolders, you must create and target those subfolders separately for each project before you start capturing. You can always change your scratch disks before you capture a clip, and this can be done quite easily in the Capture panel.

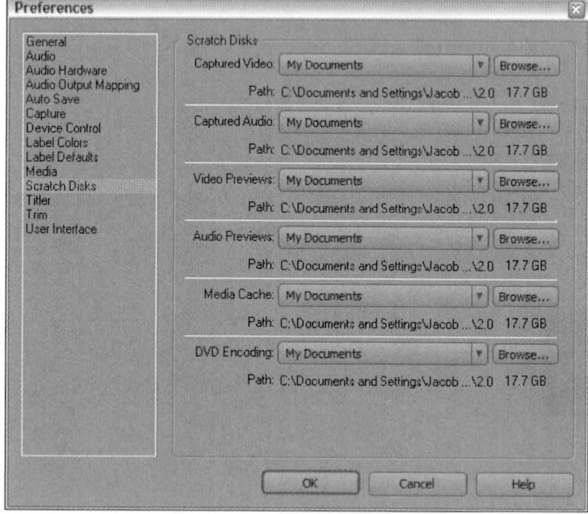

Figure 2.1 In the Preferences dialog, you assign your scratch disks that relate to capturing video and audio.

Daisy chaining is the linking together of multiple external drives. Typically, FireWire drives have two input/output ports. If your computer has only one available FireWire port, you could daisy-chain two drives so your computer could recognize both. The first drive (E:) would connect to your computer via FireWire, and the second drive (F:), using the extra FireWire port on the first, would connect to drive E: and be recognized as an additional drive on your system. Although it is fine to configure drives in this manner, the DV specifications do not support this configuration for capturing DV footage from a DV device.

DV/HDV Capturing

For capturing all video formats, make sure that your drives have the proper spin rate (7200 rpm minimum). If you are capturing DV or HDV to external FireWire drives, make sure they are not daisy-chained together (**Figure 2.2**).

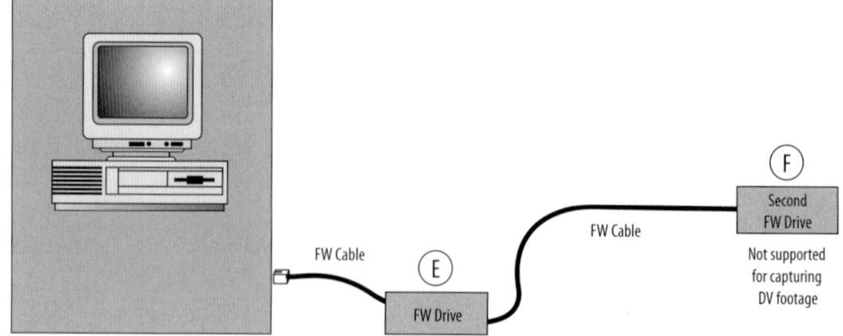

Figure 2.2 The FireWire drive E: is connected to the computer with a FireWire cable, and then drive F: is daisy-chained to E: with a FireWire cable. Drive F: is not supported for capture and playback with a DV device, but can be used for additional storage.

Because Premiere Pro 2.0 supports both DV and HDV capture and editing via FireWire, there is a new single Device Control driver: DV/HDV Device Control. To load DV/HDV Device Control, choose Edit > Preferences > Device Control. In the Device Control pane of the Preferences dialog (**Figure 2.3a**), select the device control method from the Devices drop-down menu, then manually adjust those controls by clicking the Options button and entering the information that matches the device you are using (**Figure 2.3b**). Each camera or deck has its own unique protocol and method of communicating using device control, and it's important that you set the options before you start capturing.

Out of habit from my earliest Premiere days, I always turn on my camera and connect the FireWire cable before I launch Premiere Pro. Because Windows XP supports hot plugging of external devices (it loads the drivers and activates the device without having to reboot), you can power on your camera at any time during your Premiere session. I don't recommend turning your camera on and off while you work, but if your battery dies or you want to turn your camera off, it's okay. The application will be all right and so will you. If you do power up your camera in the middle of a session, you may have to wait 10 to 20 seconds for the drivers to load and communication and transmission to be engaged.

a

b

Figures 2.3a and b You can assign your device control settings in the Preferences dialog (a). Clicking Options reveals the DV/HDV Device Control Options. In the Options dialog (b), you specify your device's video standard, brand, and type. Click the Check Status button to find out whether the device is communicating with Premiere Pro. Offline means there is no communication; Online means there is.

Capturing uncompressed HD footage requires multiple striped disks, due to both the large file size of HD clips and the higher data rate of HD video. Because of the size issues, you must use striped (RAID 0) hard drives to capture the video. Striping the drives enables the large files to be written in smaller, more accessible segments on each separate drive. A RAID controller is the device that manages how the segments are distributed and read from the drives. Because drives can fail and data has the potential to be lost, some form of data redundancy (back up) is highly recommended. You can create data-redundant RAID 3 or RAID 5 arrays at the price of one extra disk (for the redundant data) and a better RAID controller (to process the redundant data). This additional drive will protect your data in the event of failure from any drive in the array.

A RAID controller is an interface that efficiently distributes and manages the shared data between the drives of an array. RAID controllers come in the form of PCI cards or are directly integrated onto your motherboard. Typically, large and fast arrays use PCI-X based RAID controllers managing four to ten disks. These disks can be housed in both internal and external drive cages and require a workstation class (Dual Xeon/Opteron) motherboard to process the data.

With the recent advent of faster SATA hard drives and RAID controllers, prohibitively expensive SCSI drive systems are no longer the only option for real-time HD performance.

SD/SDI and HD/SDI Capturing

Premiere Pro 2.0 now natively supports capturing standard definition (SD) video and high definition (HD) video using the AJA Xena HS video capture card. This means that if you install both Premiere Pro 2.0 and an AJA Xena HS, you will be able to capture SD or HD video using the Xena card as long as your computer supports the data rates of those formats. The Xena card captures from SD and HD source decks using an SDI (Serial Digital Interface) connection. Typical SD/SDI and HD/SDI source formats are

- **DigiBeta** (SD)
- **HDCAM** (HD, more compressed)
- **D5** (HD, less compressed)
- **HDCAM SR** (HD, least compressed tape-based HD format)

Capturing SD and HD using the Xena HS card does not always follow the same drive requirements as specified for DV and HDV. With SD and HD capture, for example, you are not able to capture to a FireWire drive. Because the native support for SD and HD captures the files into an uncompressed AVI format, you not only need a lot more disk space to capture these files, you also need faster drives, faster access time, and in the case of uncompressed HD, you need *really* fast drives and an even faster card to accelerate the communication and management of the data while you capture and playback.

Table 2.1 lists the data rate of the natively supported 2.0 formats, as well as the amount of drive space you need to allocate for one hour of their respective content. As you can see, you have a lot of formats and obviously the bigger the frame size, the bigger the data rate. In the "Advanced Editing" and "Professional Workflows" sections of this book, you will learn to load and manipulate a number of files in these formats. Unfortunately (depending on how you look at it), once you start working in HD you won't want to go back to SD. And thus your journey down the road of the six-million-dollar system will begin (actually, it will be a heck of a lot cheaper than that).

Table 2.1 Data rate of 2.0 supported formats

Format	Data Rate (Megabytes per Second)	Gigabytes of Storage (per Hour of Content)
DV/HDV	3.4 MBps	13 GBph
SD (30i) 8-bit	30.0 MBps	105 GBph
SD (30i) 10-bit	37.5 MBps	132 GBph
SD (25i) 8-bit	25.0 MBps	88 GBph
SD (25i) 10-bit	31.2 MBps	110 GBph
HD 720p (60i) 8-bit	105.5 MBps	371 GBph
HD 720p (60i) 10-bit	131.8 MBps	463 GBph
HD 1080p (24) 8-bit	94.9 MBps	334 GBph
HD 1080p (24) 10-bit	118.6 MBps	417 GBph
HD 1080i (25) 8-bit	98.9 MBps	348 GBph
HD 1080i (25) 10-bit	123.6 MBps	435 GBph
HD 1080i (29.97) 8-bit	118.6 MBps	417 GBph
HD 1080i (29.97) 10-bit	148.3 MBps	521 GBph

TIP

Larger stripe sizes are preferable for arrays used primarily for video editing. This means that when you create your array select the largest available stripe size from the RAID controller.

Serial Device Control

Because SD/SDI and HD/SDI support hinges on communicating with specific types of playback devices, the DV/HDV Device Control plug-in doesn't cut the mustard when it comes to deck control of non-DV devices. In previous versions of Premiere Pro, the solution came from a third-party plug-in, Pipeline Digital's ProVTR. This plug-in is now integrated into Premiere Pro 2.0 and available via the Device Control dialog. To select and use Serial Device Control, go to Edit > Preference > Device Control and for Devices select Serial Device Control. The Options button functions in a same manner as with DV/HDV Device Control; clicking it opens a dialog that allows you to specify deck-related settings (**Figure 2.4**).

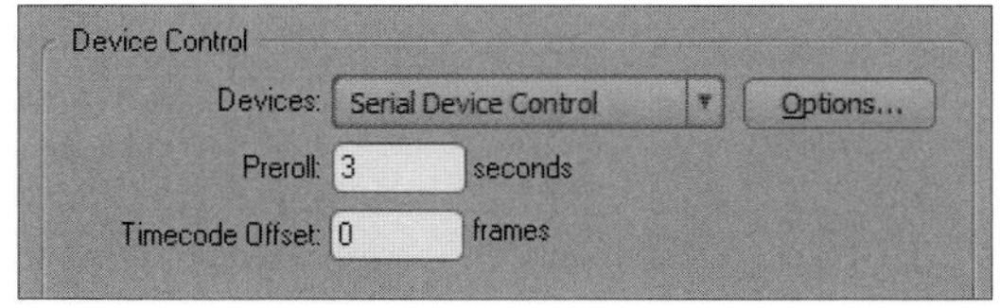

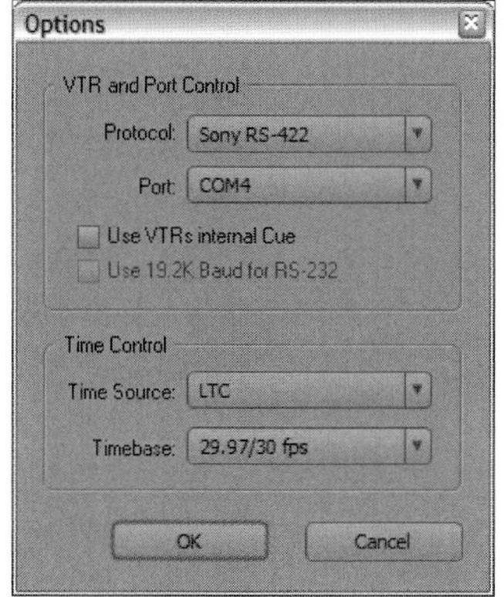

Figure 2.4 Serial Device Control is a new Device driver for Premiere Pro 2.0. Its options should be adjusted specifically to the source device (deck/VTR) from which you are capturing.

The Serial Device Control Options are broken into two parts, VTR and Port Control and Time Control. The VTR and Port Control options relate directly to the protocol in which you are communicating with the deck and the port to and from the communication is directed. Time Control relates to the source format of the timecode on your source tape and the frame rate (timebase) to which the tape adheres.

To begin working with Serial Device Control, you first assign the Device Control Protocol, whether the deck is Sony RS-422, Panasonic RS-232, or something else. Your deck will have a port on the back that accepts one of the protocol standards; if the protocol isn't obvious, you can always look it up in the manual or online. Next, you assign the physical COM port that the serial cable from your source deck is plugged into on your machine. A check box for Use VTR's Internal Cue allows you to toggle on the VTR's internal cueing for more accurate seeking to specific timecode values on the source. If you have trouble with a deck rewinding endlessly or not finding a timecode you are searching for, you may want to select this check box. The check box below this, Use 19.2K Baud for RS-232, refers to the communication method used with RS-232 source decks. Again, if your deck calls for this method, you can select the check box.

Two simple drop-down menus, Time Source and Timebase, handle time control. When timecode is written onto a tape the signal is written in either the LTC (longitudinal timecode) or VITC (vertical interval timecode) format. LTC is the standard format (signal) in which you will find most timecode; VITC, however, allows for additional information to be added and extracted from the timecode track. You will often find source material with VITC timecode. On most decks as you play the video, you can easily identify whether the timecode track is LTC or VITC. Once you know the source format of the timecode, you can assign it in the Time Source drop-down. If you are unsure of the timecode source format, select LTC+VITC. The final drop-down menu that you can select is Timebase. The timebase is quite simply the frame rate of your source tape. **Table 2.2** provides the proper settings for various types of source.

Table 2.2 Timebase settings

Source Material	Setting
1080p	23.976 fps
NTSC 1080i	59.94/60 fps
PAL 1080i	50 fps
NTSC	29.97/30 fps
PAL	25 fps

In almost all cases, the deck will tell you what frame rate it is playing at in some part of its interface.

Exploring Capture

Beyond the new format support and new device control drivers, 2.0 has only a few other new features relating to capture, leaving the previous functionality and behavior intact. Let's take a look at the Capture panel in the context of capturing DV or HDV video from your FireWire port. To open the Capture panel, choose File > Capture or press F5 (**Figure 2.5**). On the left side of the panel is your viewing area for the signal that is being transmitted to your Capture panel. The top bar always contains feedback as to what the Capture panel is doing—rewinding, playing back, batch capturing clips, and so on. Below the viewing area is the timecode feedback area, which displays (from the left) the current timecode, marked In timecode, marked Out timecode, and duration of In/Out. Below the timecode are

The Serial Device Control integration was long overdue, but there is one catch: To use it as your device control, you *must* use one of two serial cables to connect and communicate with your deck properly: ProVTR (www.thepipe.com) or Addenda (www.addenda.com). If you do not use one of these cables, Serial Device Control does not behave properly or engage in any playback or device control functions.

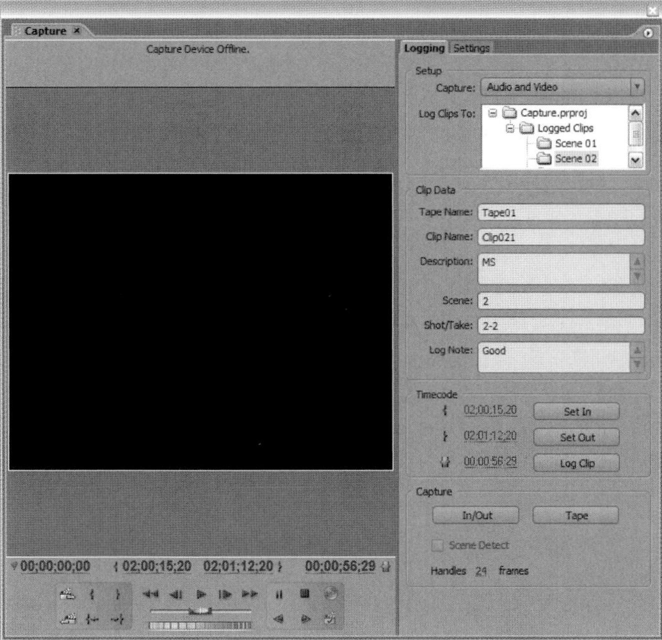

Figure 2.5 The Capture panel offers full shuttle and deck control, advanced logging functionality, and scene detection.

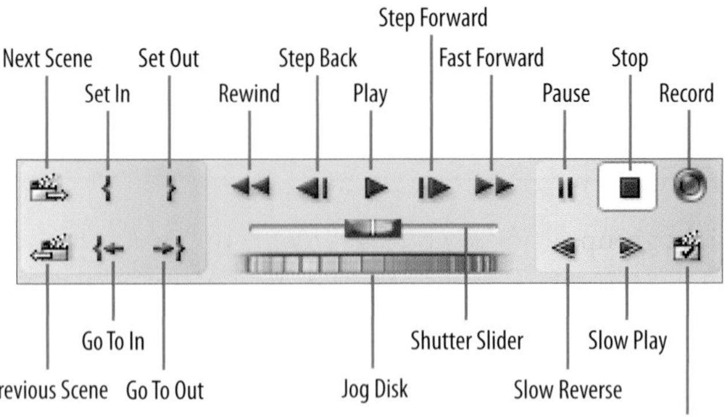

Figure 2.6 The Transport controls consist of three group boxes: left, center, and right.

your transport controls, which are made up of three group boxes (**Figure 2.6**).

Transport Controls

The left group box oftransport controls begins with the Next Scene (top) and Previous Scene (bottom) buttons. The number of times you click these buttons determines how many scenes you advance forward or backwards: two clicks moves two scenes. The viewing area displays a message as it is rewinding back the number of scenes you specified. If you click Previous Scene twice, for example, it displays "Searching 2 Scenes Back." The next buttons are quite straightforward and common to most of the transport areas in the other Monitor panels. The top row holds Set In Point and Set Out Point, while the bottom row contains Go To In Point and Go To Out Point. If you have an In or Out point marked, clicking the Go To buttons advances your tape to the specified point.

In the top row of the center group box, you'll find the familiar tape controls: Rewind, Step Back (one frame increment), Play, Step Forward (one frame increment), and Fast Forward. Below is the shuttle slider, which dynamically changes the forward or backward playback speed. Pull the shuttle right to change the forward speed, and pull it left left to change backward playback speed. The farther away from the center you move the shuttle, the faster playback will be. Dragging the shuttle all the way to the right is the equivalent of fast forward, while dragging just a hair to the right increases the speed only slightly. At the bottom of the center box is the jog disk, which steps through frame by frame. You can just roll your mouse over the jog to keep it going. The nice thing about the jog is that once you start scrubbing it, your mouse doesn't get lost off screen left or right. It stays centered on the wheel so you can scrub, scrub, scrub to your heart's content.

The right group box has the Pause, Stop, and Record buttons in the top row. The Slow Reverse button, the Slow Play button, and the Scene Detect toggle are on the bottom. Although all of these controls are here for your clicking, I capture more efficiently with the keyboard alone.

J, K, and L: More Than Three Letters

J, K, and L are critical keys whenever you are playing back in a Monitor panel or the Capture panel. Here's how these shortcuts can help you:

- **J** Plays in reverse at normal speed, press again for double speed, and again for quadruple speed
- **K** Stop
- **Spacebar** Toggles between pausing and playing
- **L** Plays forward at normal speed; press again for double speed, and again for quadruple speed
- **R** Rewind
- **F** Fast forward
- **G** Capture

When you are paused at a specific tape location, the instant you click the Capture button, the camera plays and starts recording at the same time.

Say you're stepping through your tape doing normal captures (or logging). Press L to start playing, if you want to fast forward at the highest speed while still seeing your video, press F to play very fast with the video still visible. If you see something you like, press the spacebar to pause, then maybe press J twice to rewind, L to play, and finally G to capture. Once you're happy with the capture, press G again (or Esc or spacebar) to end the capture. Name your file, and move on. If you want to fast forward at the camera's fastest speed, press K to stop, then press F to engage fast forward again while the camera is in Stop mode to have the fastest forward speed possible. The same is true for R (rewinding). So, navigate with J, K, L, F, and R. When you see the shot you want, press pause (spacebar). If you want to step frame by frame, use the Left and Right Arrow

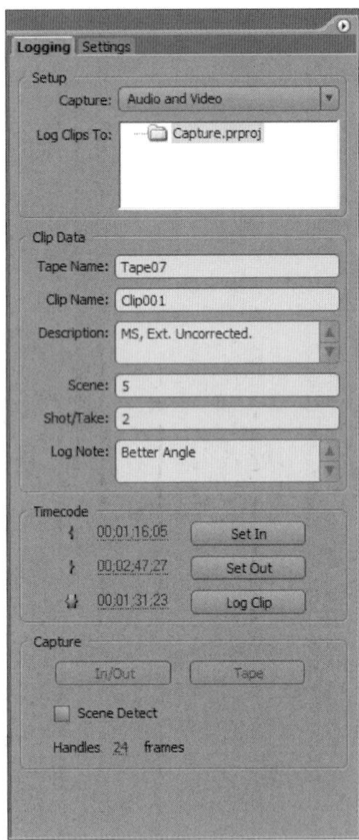

Figure 2.7 The wealth of information that you manually enter in the Capture panel's Logging tab will be attached to the logged offline file or captured clip.

keys to go forward or backwards (right and left respectively); one press moves one frame, two moves two frames, and so on. Shift+Arrow steps at five-frame increments. When you have finished with your tape, press K to stop, then E to eject the tape. Pop a new one in and continue.

Logging and the Logging Tab

My advice is to always log your videotapes before you begin editing with them. You will spare yourself a lot of hassles this way.

Logging a tape consists of scanning through your tape, noting the timecode In and Out points of specific instances, then assigning these instances a unique name and various descriptions. Logging a tape is beneficial, because it provides a running description with exact timecode locations for every shot on the tape.

You will log your tapes using the Logging tab (**Figure 2.7**), which is the default tab that is open on the right side of the Capture panel. It is critical to managing your captured media that you become familiar with this tab's fields.

When you log your clips, you are defining parameters of the media. Because you can define a number of specific values, it is very easy for Premiere Pro to make an *offline file* that respects all of these parameters (**Figure 2.8**).

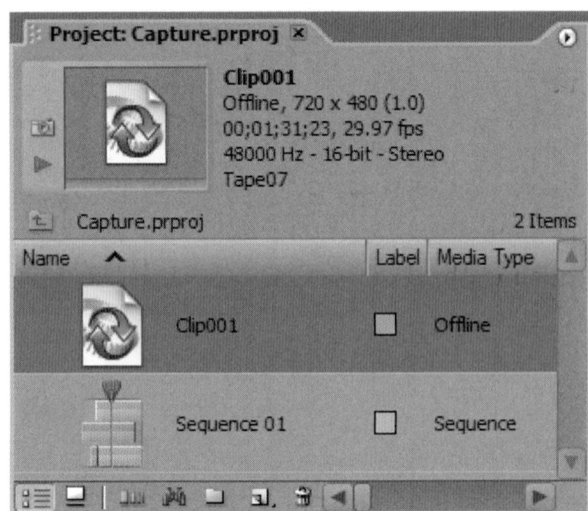

Figure 2.8 Once a clip is logged directly to the Project panel, it appears offline. An offline file simulates the physical clips with all its properties, but no video or audio.

For example, when you log an audio and video clip named Clip01 that has a duration of ten seconds between the In and Out points, Premiere Pro creates an offline file in your Project panel with the same parameters and filename. In fact, there will be a tangible ten-second offline that you can edit in your timeline.

"Offline file" is a term for media that is not detected on your system, while the parameters of the media still exist in your Project panel. If a file is accidentally deleted from your system, the icon and information for the file will still exist in your project (Figure 2.8), but be listed as offline. Additionally, if you were to log a clip to your Project panel but did not yet capture it, the logged clip would be offline until you captured it and the media was added to your computer.

If you are logging only, there will be no media linked to the logged clip. The filename, the tape name, the timecode In and Out points, descriptions, and so on are all attached to the file. To give the clip online status, simply choose File > Batch Capture. Because you have all the parameters logged, Premiere Pro knows exactly which tape the file comes from, where it is on that tape, and what you want to name it. If you choose not to batch capture the clip, you can still use the clip within your project, but Premiere Pro will display the message "Media Offline" instead of playing that clip back.

The power of this feature is that you can edit right away after logging, even if you have not captured any media. Even if you lose all of your media and retain only your project file, as long as you digitized and logged your footage properly, you will only have to batch capture the missing clips to get your project back into its former shape. Label your tapes clearly, and you can rescue your project from disaster.

Setup

The Setup area has two parameters:

- **Capture.** Defines the properties of the capture you want to log. From the drop-down list, choose Video, Audio, or Audio and Video.
- **Log Clips To.** Specifies the location to which you are logging your clips. Because you log directly to the Project panel, you can target a specific bin in which to place the logged clips.

In the initial release of Premiere Pro, once you log a clip as Video, you cannot open that log file and change it to Audio and Video. You cannot reload the logged instance back into the Capture panel. Certain parameters can be updated, but the capture properties (audio and video, only audio, or only video) are locked once you log the file.

a

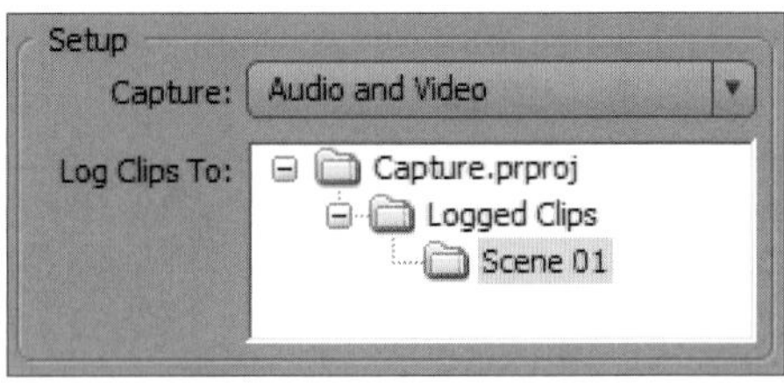

b

Figures 2.9a and b The bin structure of the Project panel (a) is the same as in the Log Clips To field of the Setup group box (b). The bin you select in the Log Clips To field is the bin in which the logged or captured clips will be added to the project.

Your entire project bin structure will be revealed in the Log Clips To field (**Figures 2.9a** and **b**). I always make a unique folder called Logged Clips that I log into. Once I capture my files, I copy or move them to a new, more appropriate folder.

Clip Data

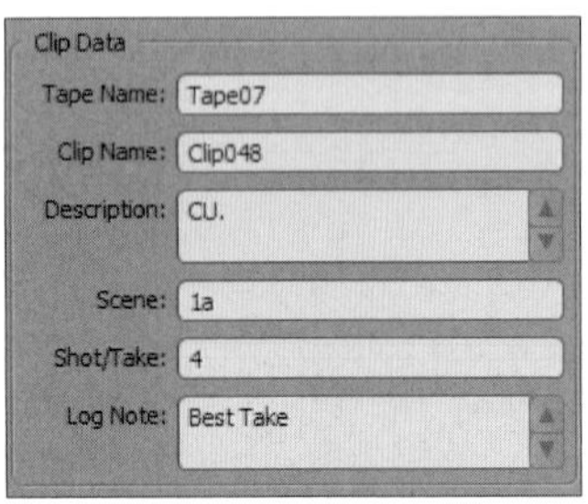

Figure 2.10 The Clip Data fields are where you can add all the details regarding your logged or to be captured clip.

Ahh, the most important fields are right here in the Clip Data section (**Figure 2.10**). If your tapes are labeled clearly this should be simple. The parameters are

- **Tape Name.** The name of the tape currently in your camera. You should change this only when you put a new tape in and begin logging from the new tape.
- **Clip Name.** The name you apply to the clip that you are logging. Premiere Pro auto-increments your names with a +01 numbering system. If you name your first clip Dad_Party and click Log Clip, for example, Premiere logs the clip and displays the name Dad_Party01 in the Capture panel. This is helpful, but not always what you need. Fortunately, all your logged data gets verified before you physically create the logged clip in the Project panel.
- **Description.** Details you want to remember about the file. I always name my files something plain and then save the specifics for the Description and Log Notes.

For Dad_Party, the Description might be: "Jessica arrives with Joshua, early."

- **Scene and Shot/Take.** A scene number and a shot number, respectively. Use these only if they apply to your clip.
- **Log Note.** Details about the file that will actually be written into the captured file itself. A file's Description, Scene, and Shot/Take are associated with it in your project only. If you were to open the file in another editing application, you would not know it was scene 3, shot 2, you would just see the tape name, filename, and log note. If you think that your captured clips will be used in separate projects, then use the Log Notes field to duplicate your Description, Scene, and Shot/Take information. For the Dad_Party example shot, I would write, "Dark and out of focus when Jessica talks to Joshua, Use only at the end." This is a description and note about my thoughts during the log and a suggestion for the editor (myself or someone else).

All of these fields will be persistent, meaning once you enter information into the Description, for example, that information stays in the field for the next clip that you log. You can, of course, clear a field before you confirm the logging of any clip. Only the Clip Name auto-increments.

NOTES

I cannot emphasize enough the importance of properly logging a tape's name, at the very least.

Timecode

The Timecode fields are pretty slick. Not only is this area another place to click a button to set your timecode In and Out points, but also the Timecode fields are displayed as hot-text fields so modifying them is simple (**Figure 2.11**). Instead of having to reset a misplaced In or Out point from scratch, you can very easily click and drag the timecode display left or right to reduce or add to the marked point. Click the Set In (or Set Out) button when you're satisfied. After defining the In and Out points, you can see the duration. To the right of the duration is the Log Clip button, which puts all of the data from the entire Log tab into a dialog for you to verify. Click OK to add a new clip as an offline file to the destination log folder you specified.

Figure 2.11 You can easily modify the timecode values by clicking on them and dragging to the left or right.

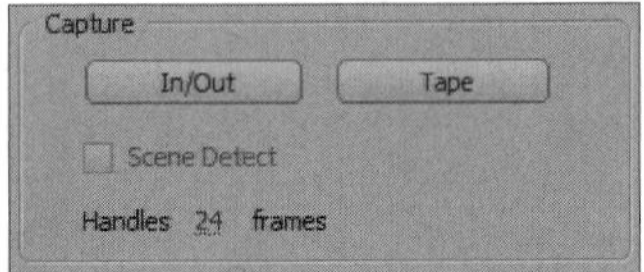

Figure 2.12 The Logging tab's Capture controls enable you to capture the current In/Out instance or to engage Scene Detect capture of the entire tape starting at the current position. Use Handles to define how many extra frames before and after your In/Out instance to record.

Capture and Scene Detection

To capture a clip you just logged, go to the Capture panel's Logging tab and click the In/Out button (**Figure 2.12**). This button instructs the program to capture from the Capture panel's current In point to its current Out point.

If you need to capture an entire tape, however, consider Premiere Pro's powerful new Scene Detect feature. Because your DV camera records data to the tape, it writes time and date stamps to the tape every time you stop and start recording. If you were to look through the data of the tape, you could find every unique shot based on the changes in the time and date stamps. Additionally, using scene detection, you can advance forward or backward at specific increments. You use the Scene Detect feature in conjunction with the Tape button.

Selecting the Scene Detect check box puts capturing into Scene Detect mode. This does not affect logging. When you click the Tape button with Scene Detect turned on, however, Premiere Pro starts capturing your tape from the current position and continues to the end of the tape using scene detection. Premiere Pro rolls through your tape in one pass, treating each time/date stamp instance as an individual clip. While it appears that Premiere Pro is recording one long file, every time/date stamp instance results in an individual captured clip. When I don't have the time to log a tape or I am not sure which portions I want to use, I capture the entire tape using Scene Detect and Tape, drop all the clips in the timeline, and just delete those I don't want.

A free record does not rely on timecode In and Out instances; it just captures what is being played from the time you click Record until you stop playback or stop capture. Free recording uses the tape name, filename, timecode values, description, and other metafields that are active when you first press Record. After you stop recording, you can then verify or adjust the fields before saving the captured file.

In Scene Detect mode, Premiere Pro uses the Tape Name in the Clip Data area and then it uses the active Clip Name with auto-incrementing for each individual capture. You cannot give each file a unique name as you record; you have to modify that later in the Project panel.

The final setting in the Capture area is Handles. This is one of the few enhanced features of the 2.0 Capture panel. Handles are extra frames at the beginning and end of your capture. If you have an In point of 1;01;20 and an Out point of 1;05;10 and Handles is set to 20 frames, your captured clip will start at 1;01;00 and end at 1;06;00. When you open that clip in your project, the In and Out points will still be 1;01;20 and 1;05;10, but you will have an extra 20 frames. I always set Handles at 15 to 30 frames so that I never have to recapture additional material to get my shots right. Handles are assigned to all capture In/Out instances as well as batch captures and Scene Detect captures. If you do a *free record* capture, no handles will be assigned. In previous versions of Premiere Pro, the handles were added during the logging. In 2.0, the handles are added during the execution of the previously listed record methods. The new handles' functionality is very useful when you import a batch list or EDL and want to capture more frames than the list or EDL defines.

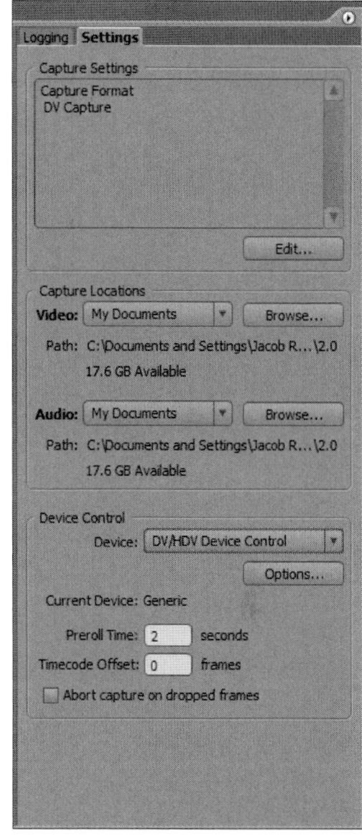

Figure 2.13 The Settings tab provides you with quick access to Capture Settings, Capture Locations (scratch disks), and Device Control. There is no need to open your preferences. Just activate the Settings tab.

Settings Tab

The Capture panel's Settings tab (**Figure 2.13**) allows access to a number of typically buried presets and preferences related to your capture settings, the capture location, and device control.

Capture Settings

The Settings tab's Capture Settings area displays the Capture Format (here called the Recorder) you specified for your project. To change it, click the Edit button. The Capture pane of the Project Settings dialog opens; click on the Capture Format drop-down list to select a capture module. For all of the DV presets, the capture module is DV Capture, for HDV it is HDV Capture, and for SD/SDI and HD/SDI it is Adobe HD-SDI Capture. If you have a third-party capture card installed, you will have other choices listed.

Capture Locations

The Capture Locations area (**Figure 2.14**) displays the Scratch Disks Preferences you set for capturing video and audio. As you capture, it also updates the amount of disk space available on your assigned scratch disks. You can change them as you capture. Click the appropriate Browse button (Video or Audio) and navigate to the folder you need, and then choose Custom from the drop-down menu.

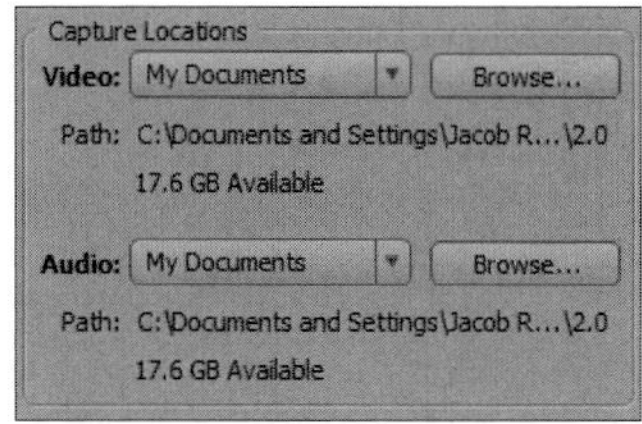

Figure 2.14 In the Capture Locations area, you can assign your scratch disks, which are the paths to which your captured video and audio media is automatically saved.

For a shortcut to Premiere Pro's default document folder, choose My Documents from the drop-down list, or choose Same as Project to capture to the folder you specified as a Scratch Disk Preference. If you have a project where you want different tapes captured to different folders, capture your first tape, make a change in Capture Locations, then capture your second tape, and so on.

If you have your DV camera turned on and connected, but you are unable to transmit and communicate with it, check the device status in your DV Device Control Options dialog first. Go to Edit > Preferences > Device Control, then click Options. If the device is listed as online but you cannot transmit to it, power off the device and then power it back on. When it powers off you should hear the Windows Device Management bell chime off; then when the device powers back on, the bell sound should chime on. I typically check all FireWire insertion points and reinsert the cable. Also, check your own internal process, and make sure you aren't turning on the camera in Camera mode as opposed to VCR or VTR.

Device Control

The Device Control field is a shortcut to your Device Control Preferences. You can change all these values as you would if you accessed them from Edit > Preferences > Device Control. Additionally, your device type (if you specified one) will be revealed in the Current Device field. If your camera is not responding, you can switch to the Settings tab, click Options in the Device Control section, and verify your settings in the DV/HDV Device Control Options. If your DV camera does go offline, a message to that effect appears in the Capture panel above the display area. When using Serial Device Control there is no online or offline prompt. If the transport controls in the Capture panel turn gray and cannot be selected, however, there is likely to be a communication conflict with the device to which you are connected.

Capture Wing Menu

Just about every panel in Premiere Pro has a wing menu (**Figure 2.15**). The wing menu is a shortcut area to certain features and modes. Because Premiere Pro has a fully customizable keyboard, putting functions in the wing menus

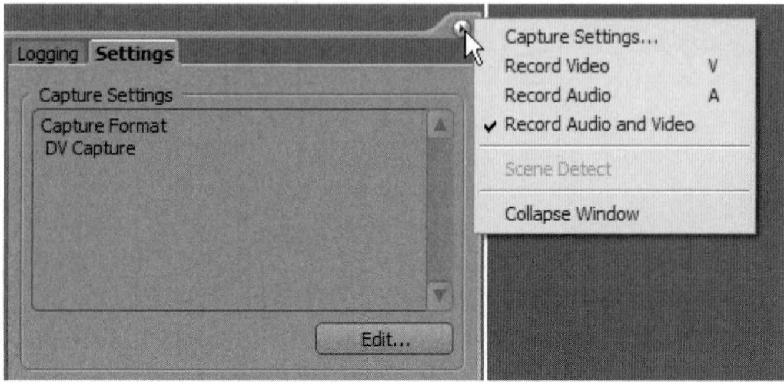

Figure 2.15 The wing menu provides access to a few shortcuts. Because the shortcuts populate the menu, they can be assigned as keyboard shortcuts.

allows these functions to be mapped to the keyboard. From the wing menu, you can access your capture settings, set your capture mode, turn scene detection on or off, and collapse the Capture panel.

New Capture Preferences

Premiere Pro 2.0 offers a new Preference that allows you to define a few settings specific to capturing. Select Edit > Preferences > Capture to go to the Capture Preference. Its check boxes are pretty straightforward (**Figure 2.16**). For example, you have the option to automatically abort any capture that drops a frame. This means that if you are capturing to disk and a frame is dropped, instead of continuing with the capture Premiere automatically aborts the current capture. If the check box for Report Dropped Frames is checked, then you get feedback as to whether any frames were dropped during capture. When the option Generate Batch Logfile Only on Unsuccessful Completion is enabled, if you execute a batch capture and capture fails for some reason, Premiere Pro adds a physical log file to your Project panel calling out the clip that failed to capture so that you can recapture it again. The final check box is a new to the application before: Use Device Control

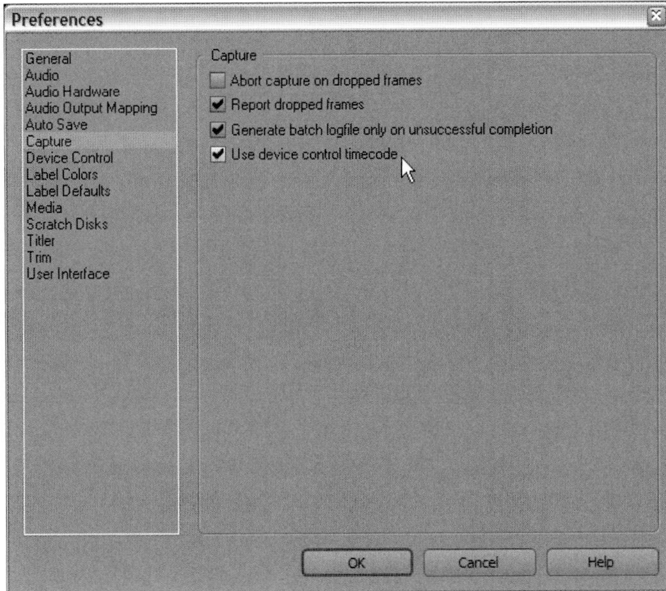

Figure 2.16 The Capture Preferences allows you to select options to ensure that no media is captured with dropped frames and that if frames are dropped, an error log reports it. Additionally, in the Capture Preference you can choose to stamp the timecode coming from the device control driver onto your captured clips.

Timecode. When this is turned on, Premiere Pro uses the timecode from the device control as the timecode reference that it writes into the captured file. This means that if you are capturing through with FireWire but controlling your source deck with Serial Device Control, the timecode stream being read by the serial device control will be the timecode stamped onto the captured FireWire clip. Anytime you are using Serial Device Controls, the check box should be selected.

The Right Workflow

Knowing what the capture parameters and controls are and what they do is only half the equation. Following an efficient workflow is vital. For DV and HDV users, striping and labeling your tapes should be your first task (**Figure 2.17**).

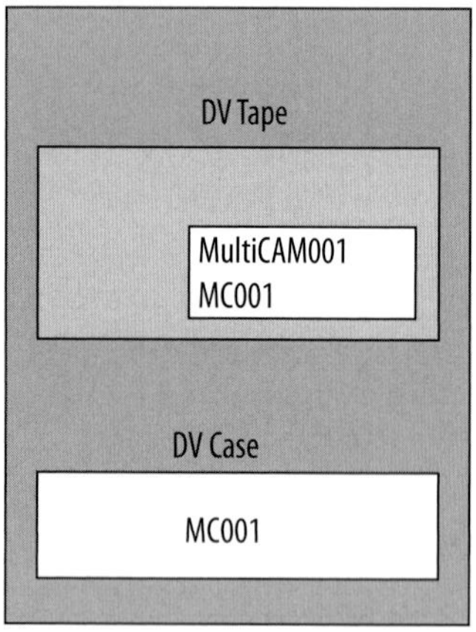

Figure 2.17 Make sure your tape and its case have the same name. This may feel like basic stuff, but it goes a long way toward better organizing your library of footage. Here the tape label has a descriptive name and a shortened name used for logging and capturing (MC001).

Timecode and Striping Your Tapes

When using Premiere in a DV/HDV environment, do not underestimate the benefit of *striping* your MiniDV Tapes. The timecode format for MiniDV is such that if the camera detects blank tape (static) and you begin recording, the timecode always begins at 00;00;00;00. This can cause trouble.

Say you record for ten minutes, then you watch your last shot. You try to press Stop exactly at the shot's end, but inadvertently stop in the blank space just after it. When you next press Record, the timecode starts all over again at 00;00;00;00. You then record for another 50 minutes and finish the tape. Technically, you now have two identical timecode values on different portions of your tape—which can make logging and batch capturing with this tape a nightmare.

Or, you may play through and mark In and Out points, passing the brief blank space not knowing that it is there. When batch capturing, Premiere Pro automatically captures all the clips you logged. Because the first recorded instance has ten minutes of content and then blank space, as soon as the batch capture hits the stoppage, Premiere will seek for three seconds looking for new timecode. If

Premiere does not find any new timecode in those three seconds, it assumes it has hit the end of the tape and it stops. Of course, with a MiniDV tape, you might not actually be at the end of your tape. (**Figure 2.18.**)

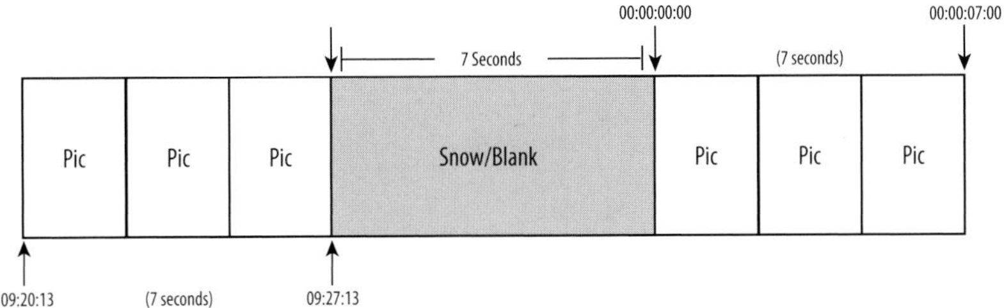

Figure 2.18 In this diagram, the strip represents 21 seconds of your DV tape and the timecode represents the timecode value for the associated frames of video. Because there is no recorded video in the snow/blank section, timecode starts all over again at 00;00;00;00 when recording reengages.

To properly prepare and to work more efficiently with MiniDV, I recommend two steps before your shoot with your camera:

1. Stripe your tape with a full recording pass so that there is a continuous run of timecode and data on your tape from beginning to end. It will not damage the tape or affect future recordings on that tape.
2. Label your tape clearly and with an alpha+numeric value, such as Bleach001 (ProjectName+NumericValue). If you pre-label your tapes, you can find specific tapes more easily once you start logging. You can also add the description of the tape after you record.

Capturing Best Practices

With your DV/HDV video recorded, it's time to capture. Pop your tape in, set the camera to VTR mode, and press F5 to open your Capture panel. Before I try my first capture, I like to press Play (L) to make sure my timecode numbers are being transmitted and I am seeing my video. The basic steps for a capture are

1. Cue up your tape, and then specify the parameters of what you're logging. I usually create a new folder in my

Project panel and name it Logged Clips, then select it from the Log Clip To field.

2. Enter the name of your tape in the Tape Name field. If you have a good sense of what the filenames will be, enter that for the Clip Name. For example, I might use Bleach_BTS (*Bleach* is my short film, and BTS means behind the scenes).
3. Press L to start playing back.
4. When you find the first In point, press I to set it.
5. You can keep playing if your shot is long and enter the description as it plays back. If you do click within a text field while playback is engaged, you cannot access your keyboard shortcuts (because of text conflicts) until you click out of the field.
6. Enter any additional metadata, set your Out point, then click Log Clip. All of the data you entered will appear in a dialog that you can modify.
7. Click OK, and Premiere adds a new offline file to your chosen bin. For me, that's the Logged Clips bin.

From there, you can continue logging one tape or switch to any others that you need to log. Because Premiere Pro supports offline files, you need not capture immediately after you have logged. At any time, you can select individual or groups of offline files to batch capture and get the media online.

Offline Files

Once you have successfully logged clips to your Project panel, you do not have to capture them immediately to use them in your project. Clips with no media linked will be displayed as offline files. If you scroll through the columns of the Project panel, you can see all the data associated with the file that you logged. Offline files can be edited and used in your project, as would any normal media file (**Figure 2.19**). They do not, however, display any media that would be associated with them. You can edit, trim, and adjust offline files. Once you batch capture or link media to them, the media will show up exactly as you edited it.

Figure 2.19 Offline files can be opened in the Source Monitor and edited in the timeline. In all these panels, the timecode properties and audio/video attributes are represented and a graphic placeholder is open to let you know that files are offline.

Batch Capturing

Premiere Pro builds on Premiere's earlier batch list capturing features. Now, not only can you create and import traditional text batch lists, but your project can also act as a master batch list enabling Premiere Pro to log your clips (captured or not) directly into the open project (into a bin you define). There is no batch list functionality lost with Pro: You can still import and export individual batch lists in a comma-delimited format. Instead, a highly intuitive method has been added that makes your project file more valuable and much deeper. Logging directly to the Project panel saves the clip data into the project file (**Figure 2.20**). As long as you don't delete the clip reference from your Project panel, you will always be able to recapture, based on the original logged parameters.

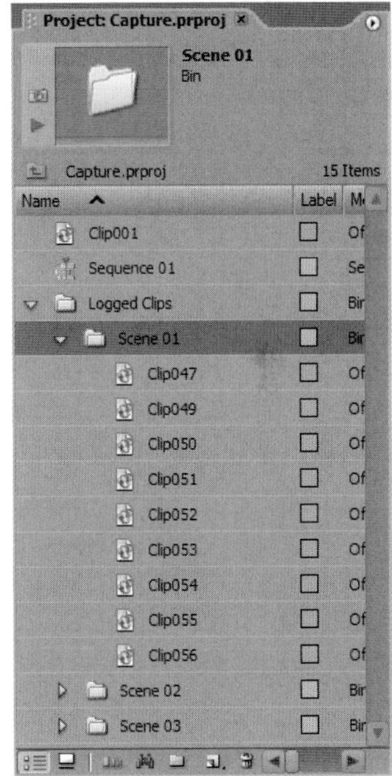

Figure 2.20 Depending on which columns you choose to view and in which order, you have access to all the metadata that was logged to the clips. Additionally, you can see a number of other details and add comments into custom fields.

With all your clips logged and a bin of offline files, you can do a couple of different things to specify what you want to capture. If you select File > Batch Capture with the Log Clips bin selected from your Master Project view, all of the offline files in that folder that have proper tape, name, and timecode In/Out information will be captured. If you have one specific file selected, Premiere will batch capture only that file.

If you need several clips, Ctrl-click to select multiple files within a folder. Premiere Pro will batch captures only those

Not all DV devices automatically eject the tape when capture is complete. You can expect DV decks to always eject, but not all DV cameras support the automatic eject feature. Once capturing from a tape is complete, while the dialog is open telling you to insert another tape, you safely can manually press eject and then insert the new tape.

selected files. The program first asks you to put into your camera the first tape associated with your media; then it engages playback and captures all the specified clips that are on that tape. When finished with a tape, it ejects the tape and prompts you to put in a new one. You insert the next tape, and then click OK to continue batch capturing.

For error reporting, I recommend that you turn on Generate Batch Log File Only on Unsuccessful Completion so that if there are any errors with your batch captures, a file listing the errors will be waiting for you in the same bin location as the offline files.

Linking Your Media

Because your project file holds all the metadata associated with each captured clip, you can unlink and delete the media that is currently linked (associated) with your clips. When you unlink a file, you can break the link with files on the disk, or you can break the link and delete the media file on disk. In both cases, the clip reference in the Project panel would still be preserved. If you are trying to free space on your system, for example, you can break the links and delete all the unused files in your project. These files would remain visible, but be offline. If you decide you need them after all, select them and choose Batch Capture to bring them back online (**Figure 2.21**).

Figure 2.21 With a bin full of offline files, you can right-click on the bin and choose Link Media from the context menu to relink every file in descending order. If you choose Batch Capture, Premiere will execute a batch capture of all the offline clips in the bin.

This reinforces the importance of using a consistent naming convention for your tapes and files: Doing so makes relinking and recapturing quite easy, which in turn makes your project more mobile and more flexible. If you want to give your project to someone else, send your tapes with the project file (which compresses down to a very small size). When the project is opened, all of the files will show up offline. All your friend needs to do is run Batch Capture and insert the proper tapes when instructed.

If you moved a file and Premiere Pro cannot find it, select the offline file and choose Clip > Link Audio and Video (assuming you need both media types). Whatever you link to then associates itself with the file in your project.

Microsoft Excel - Batch_List.csv

	A	B	C	D	E	F	G	H
1	MC001	00;00;04;20	00;00;07;06	MultiCam_A	Not fluid stumble on words.	Green Screen Master shot		
2	MC001	00;00;16;13	00;00;46;09	MultiCam_A 01	Good take won't use	Green Screen Master shot	1	1
3	MC001	00;00;48;01	00;01;08;10	MultiCam_A 02	Better shot should be the one	Green Screen Master shot	1	2
4	MC001	00;01;31;02	00;01;57;04	MultiCam_A 03	Best!	Green Screen Master shot	1	3
5	MC001	00;02;07;13	00;02;33;07	MultiCam_A 04	Bad lighting	Green Screen Master shot	1	4
6	MC001	00;02;29;25	00;03;06;22	MultiCam_A 05	Good shot audio level too low	Green Screen Master shot	1	5
7	MC001	00;03;00;27	00;03;37;28	MultiCam_A 06	Good Shot cuts early.	Green Screen Master shot	1	6
8	MC001	00;03;33;00	00;03;55;20	MultiCam_A 07	Unusable	Green Screen Master shot	1	7

Figure 2.22 In this batch list file, you can see how each of the fields correlate with fields from Premiere Pro: A is Tape Name, B is In Point, C is Out Point, D is Clip Name, E is Log Comment, F is Description, G is Scene, and H is Take.

Exporting and Importing Batch Lists

To make sure the logged files from your tapes exist in a portable format, you have the ability to create and export batch lists or import existing batch lists. To export a text batch list, select the folder, clip, or clips that you want to make the batch list from and then choose Project > Export Batch List. Premiere Pro creates a comma-delimited text document that honors the data associated with the clips (**Figure 2.22**).

Importing a batch list is pretty cool. You choose Project > Import Batch List, target the batch list that you want, then click OK. Premiere Pro creates a new folder in your project that has the same name as the batch list. Inside that folder are offline clip instances of all the items in the batch list. A text file that becomes physical clip instances—Premiere Pro has definitely entered the new millennium.

Manual Captures, No Device Control

If you have a camera connected that does not support device control or if you are using an RCA to DV converter box (called a *bridge*), which takes an analog signal and converts it to a DV stream of data on a FireWire cable, then you should turn off DV Device Control. In the Capture panel's Settings tab, choose None from the Device drop-down list. You will still be using the DV Capture Recorder because you do have a signal into your FireWire port, but you will not have device control for that signal (**Figure 2.23**).

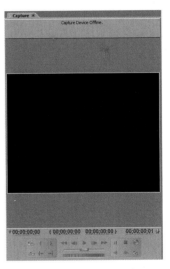

Figure 2.23 With the capture device offline, you are unable to access any of the transport controls because Device Control cannot be initialized.

If you have a VCR wired through a DV converter, for example, you just press the VCR's Play, Pause, Fast Forward, and Rewind buttons to find the segment that you want to capture. Press G on your keyboard (or click Record in

Background Capture
A feature that arrived with Premiere Pro 1.5 is the capability to capture in the background. You begin capturing, then minimize Premiere. The program will continue capturing while you are doing other things on your computer.

the Capture panel) to begin capturing, and then press G or Esc to stop (or click the Stop button). In the Capture panel's Clip Data area, you can enter a tape name and filename, as well as the other metadata that you want associated with the captured file. After you click OK to confirm the data in these fields, Premiere adds the newly captured clip to your project.

Clips captured via FireWire using a converter box have a timecode value starting at 00;00;00;00 for frame 1. Because the FireWire port does not detect any timecode information on the cable, it starts timecode from zero.

If you have captured clips without device control and thus without timecode, think carefully before deleting the media and making those files offline. Because there is no absolute method of ensuring that you can recapture these files with exactly the same In and Out points, your edit will change if you have to recapture your media.

Things to Remember

Striping and labeling your tapes is fundamentally the most important part of the capture process. It ensures that your media can be found with relative ease if any problems arise. Additionally, you can back up a text batch list of all the clips in your project. This list can be used as a reference or it can be imported into another separate project.

Traditional issues relating to capture usually entail problems with your tapes, such as discontinuous timecode or mislabeling. If you have good timecode and proper naming conventions, then all you need to observe is your camera habits and the temperament of DV device issues on your system. The lessons from this chapter provide the groundwork of where to go and what to do to capture and log properly into Premiere Pro.

The next chapter will help you work more efficiently with the clips once they are captured, introducing the display views and functionality of the Project panel.

CHAPTER

3

Using the Project Panel

The Project panel is the center of the universe for Premiere Pro. Every element that is used in your edited sequence first must be imported and opened in your project. All video clips, audio files, still images, and sequences have icons and instances that you can access in your Project window (**Figures 3.1a** and **b**). Although, depending on how much content you have imported and saved, your project size can get pretty large (four to ten megs), if you need to email it, it will zip into an incredibly small file, because the project file format is XML based. Over the course of this chapter, I will give you an overview of the Project panel's functions, features, and behaviors.

Because so many of these functions relate to clip handling, it's important to understand how Premiere Pro manages clips. When you first import a file into your project, that file is referred to as a *master clip*. It is the master file from which all edited and used instances will come. If clip01 is edited into a sequence using only half of its duration, the edited instance of clip01 in the sequence is referred to as a *subclip* or a *child* of the master clip. This subclip, if opened separately, can access all the information of the master clip, while honoring its assigned In/Out points and duration. Deleting an edited subclip does not delete the master clip. Deleting a master clip from your project will delete all of the subclips, because the subclips point to the master clip to get their information. Because Premiere Pro supports offline files in the timeline, if you accidentally delete a master clip from your hard drive, all project clip instances will remain intact with the media appearing offline.

To get a better sense of clip handling, take a look at how to import and open your media.

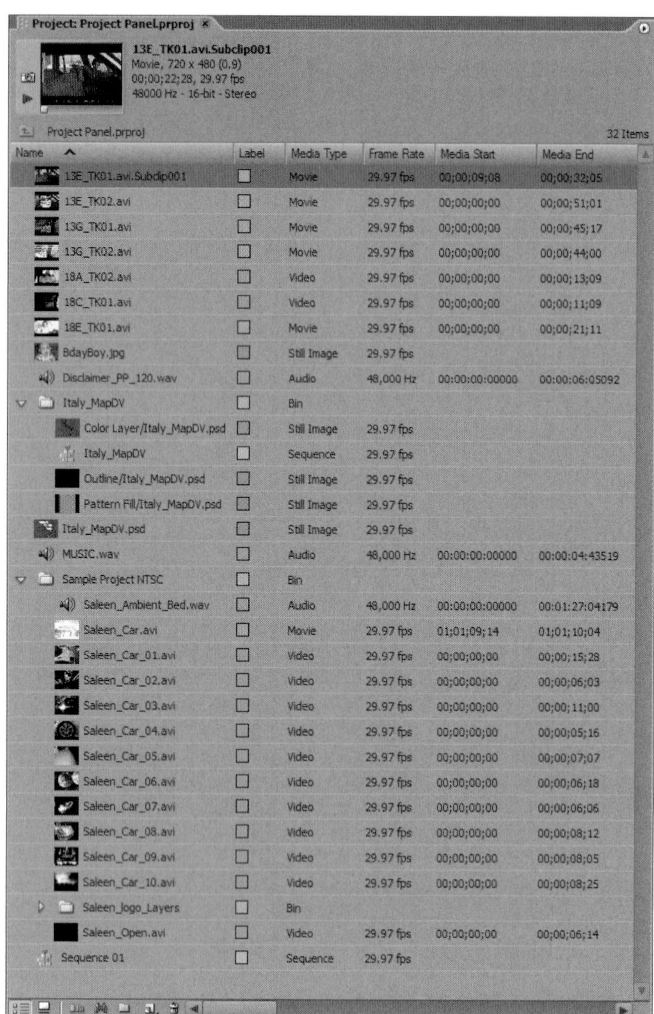

a

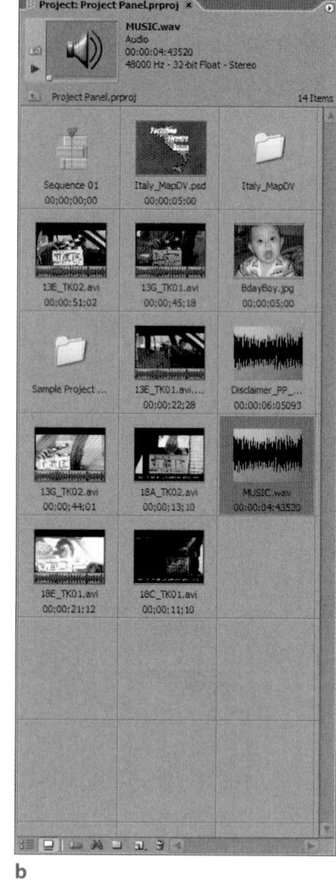

b

Figures 3.1a and b The Project panel can display its contents in Icon view (above) or List view with icons turned on (left).

Importing Files

Premiere Pro 2.0 made some important additions and changes to subclips. I'll discuss these in detail in Chapter 4, "Playing Back and Viewing your Media."

If you wanted to open and look at a clip in previous versions of Premiere, you would select File > Open and then target the video clip. The video clip would open in your Source Monitor, but would not be added to your project until you either dragged it into the Project window or dropped it in the edit of your timeline. With Premiere Pro, the only things you can *open* are other projects. You can, however, *import* files into the Project window to examine them before adding them to the timeline. To add or open any media files, you must import them. You can access the Import dialog (**Figure 3.2**) by

- Choosing File > Import
- Double-clicking in the blank space of the Project panel
- Right-clicking in the blank space of the Project panel and selecting Import
- Pressing Ctrl+I

Then simply click and select the file you wish to import.

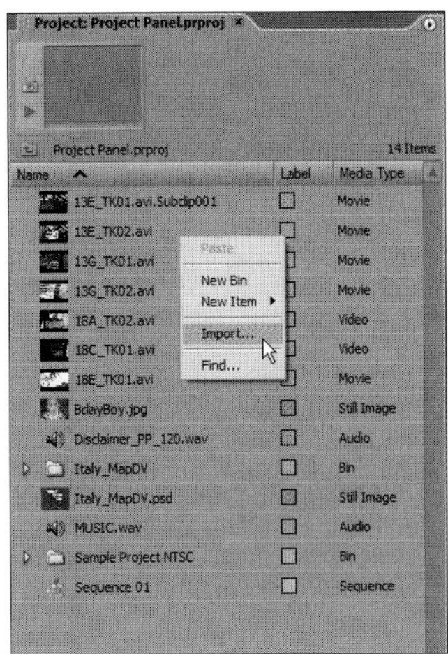

Figure 3.2 You can access the Import dialog in multiple ways. You can right-click in the empty space of the Project panel, then choose Import from the context menu, for example; or you can double-click in the empty space of the Project window to immediately open the Import dialog.

To import multiple items, select them using the Shift or Ctrl modifier keys when targeting the files (**Figure 3.3**). To import a folder full of files, click on the folder listing that the files reside in and click the Import Folder button. Premiere Pro then creates a new folder in your project that includes all the files in that folder. When importing, be aware that each media type has some importing specifics as well.

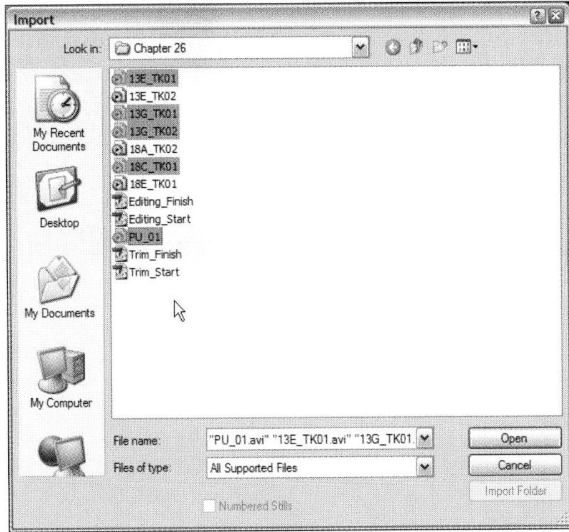

Figure 3.3 By holding down the Ctrl key, you can click and target the files you want to import. Here, multiple media files are selected for importing.

A cousin of the HTML format, XML is a self-describing file format that is used to transfer information from one place to the next. None of the XML file data is compressed, and it is not written in a binary language. Instead, XML files contain readable human language and data followed by descriptions of the data. XML files can be read and opened in word processing applications, making it easy to search for specific fields of information.

Video

A new feature for Premiere Pro 2.0 is the option to have all your video, including stills, scaled to your project dimensions upon importing. Say that you have project settings of 720 × 480 using DV as your editing mode. If you import a

To reset a file to its original dimensions, select the file in the Project panel and choose Clip > Video Options > Scale to Frame Size and then uncheck "Scale to Frame Size." If the file is already in the timeline, you can right-click on it to access the same feature.

small, 320 × 240 QuickTime clip, you can use a new Preference check box (Default Scale to Frame Size) to apply a scale adjustment to the smaller clip, enlarging it to match your project's dimensions when you drop it into any of the project sequences (**Figure 3.4**). If you do not want to auto-scale imported items, either turn off the Preference check box or select the auto-scaled file in the Project panel and turn off auto-scaling. Remember, however, this setting affects auto-scaling only when you add that file into a sequence. If you want to do dynamic scale adjustments, zooms, and other manipulations, be sure to turn off the Preference.

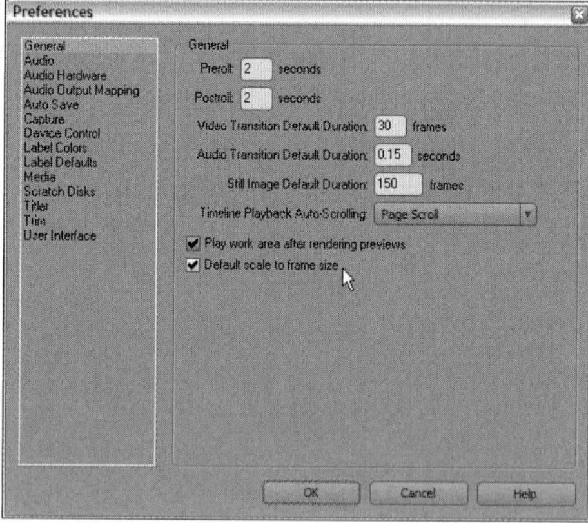

Figure 3.4 In the General area of the Preferences dialog you can choose to enable scaling of clips to the project frame size (Default Scale to Frame Size). The media files import at their full size but are resized to the project frame size when you add them to a sequence.

Audio

Importing audio is slightly different, and 2.0 added another new feature to ease the process. To reduce access time and increase the details to be extracted from your audio files, Premiere Pro may convert your audio when it is imported into your project; this process is called *conforming* (**Figure 3.5**).

You can import all sorts of audio files—WAVs, MP3s, AIFFs, and so on—but the most important settings to remember are your project's sample rate and whether or not the

Figure 3.5 In the bottom-right corner of the application window, a small conforming progress bar displays the name of the file being conformed and the file's progress.

imported audio is compressed. If you import a compressed audio file (MP3, WAV, or AIFF), Premiere Pro will conform the audio of that file to match the sample rate of your project. If you import an uncompressed audio file such a WAV, AVI, or AIFF, Premiere Pro will not have to conform the audio in most cases. Adobe refined the rules for conforming to result in better overall performance; however, the details and rules as to what is conformed are tedious.

Your audio project settings are commonly expressed as 16-bit 48kHz. The bit value (bit depth) reflects the resolution of your audio file. The more bits, the clearer the detail in the audio file. Premiere Pro supports up to 32 bits. The kHz value is your sample rate, also known as your Hertz rate (1kHz equals 1000 Hertz). The sample rate reflects the number of samples in your audio file. For example, 48kHz means your audio file has 48000 audio samples per second. Premiere Pro supports up to 96kHz or 96000 samples per second.

Conforming

A lot of high-end audio editing and video editing applications adjust their imported media, conforming it to a format that accurately matches their settings and can be accessed easily. Although Premiere Pro can extract plenty of information from a standard WAV, MP3, or AIFF audio file, by conforming a file Premiere creates a standard audio file format optimized for access time, waveform display, playback, and effect application. The downside to audio conforming is that the process consumes time and disk space when you import files. The upside is that everything sounds better, and 2.0 offers some new ways of managing the conforming files.

Premiere's rules for what audio gets conformed are quite specific and not too easy to wrap your head around: 32kHz and 48kHz audio files, such as DV AVI, AVI, and AIFF with uncompressed audio will not be conformed when imported into projects with a 1:1 (equal), 1:2, or 2:3 ratio sample rate. This means that 32kHz uncompressed audio is not conformed in a 32kHz project (1:1) or a 48kHz project (2:3). The same 32kHz uncompressed audio *is* conformed when imported into a 44.1kHz project. Conversely, 48kHz audio is conformed when imported into a 32kHz (3:2) project.

The higher the bit depth, the more dynamic the range of the audio file is. A fixed-bit format has a ceiling, or limit, to its range. A floating-bit format is a way of expanding the bit depth to provide a much more dynamic range for applying effects. The bit depth is called *floating*, because once the effect is applied at the floating bit depth, the file is reduced back to the preset bit depth for playback. Although 24 bits is the ceiling for audio files in Premiere Pro, all of your conformed audio files will be conformed at a floating 32-bit depth. The benefit is that effects and clip adjustments are assigned on the 32-bit floating file, which results in much more accurate and higher quality adjustments.

I don't make the rules here, so don't shoot the messenger! Keep in mind that uncompressed audio follows the 1:1, 1:2, and 2:3 rules, and compressed audio files are conformed no matter what the kHz rate.

So, if you set your project's audio sample rate to 48kHz, all of your compressed audio will be conformed to 48kHz. Additionally, the newly conformed audio files will alter the bit depth to a floating bit rate of 32. Traditional DV audio has a bit depth of 16.

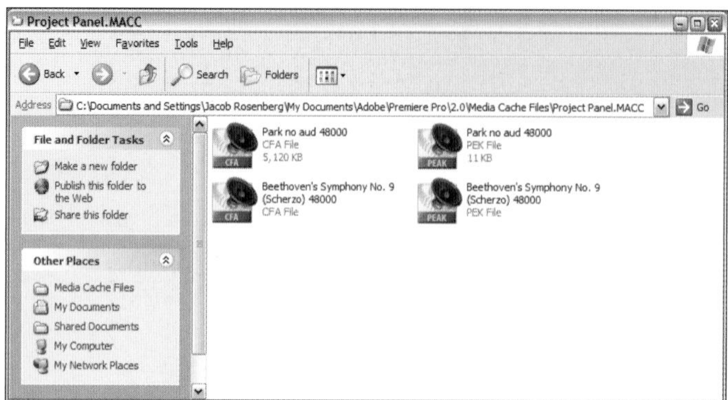

Figure 3.6 The new Media Cache folder contains reference files that your project uses and a subfolder for each Premiere project. In these subfolders you can find all the CFA (conformed audio) and PEK (Peak) files relating to the project's; media. Deleting these files will not disrupt any of your created projects, instead when a project is opened without a necessary conform file, Premiere Pro automatically generates a new one.

When Premiere Pro conforms your audio, it creates two unique files that associate themselves with the original audio file in your project. One of the files has a .cfa extension, the other a .pek extension. In 2.0, these two files are created in a project-specific subfolder in your Media Cache folder. The Media Cache folder contains files relating to all the projects you have created (**Figure 3.6**). You can delete these files at any time, and Premiere Pro automatically regenerates the ones it needs on a project-by-project basis. After conforming an audio file, Premiere Pro notes the resulting sample rate and references the conform file when you import that audio into a new project. With this architecture, an audio file is conformed only once. Whenever you import the file into a new project, that project references the existing conform and peak files already in the Media Cache subfolder. Using the Media Cache Database you can manage what has been conformed and what hasn't (**Figure 3.7**). The Media Cache Database collects information on which files have been imported into all your projects and where their associated conform or peak files reside. Choose Edit > Preferences > Media to access the Media Cache Database file or change its location. If you delete media from your disk and want to delete the associated conform and peak files, use the Clean button.

NOTES

Peak files contain visual waveform information for their associated CFA files. Because the PEK file stores the waveform information, anytime you display or zoom into the waveform of an audio file, the results are almost instantaneous. If a PEK file is deleted, it will be created again the next time the waveform display is called upon for a selected audio file. It will take a moment to build the PEK, but once it's created, the visual feedback will be almost instantaneous.

Keep in mind that if you move or rename a file that is referenced in the database it will break the link to the existing conformed and peak files.

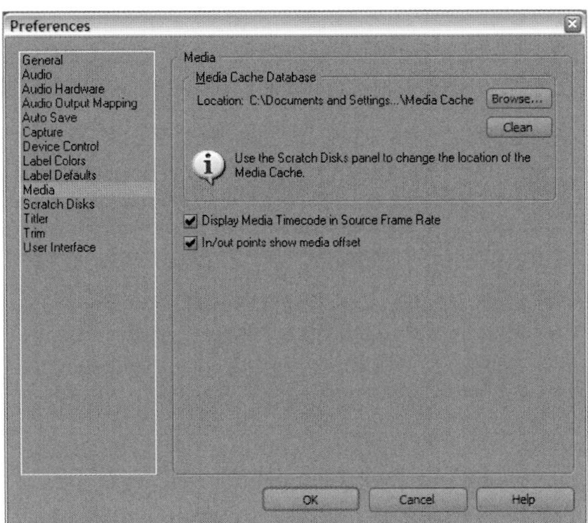

Figure 3.7 The new Media Cache Database keeps track of all the files that have been imported into Premiere Pro projects and where the conformed audio and peak files for each of the files exists. You can pick an exact location for the database to be stored, and more importantly, you can easily clean your system of orphaned conform files by clicking the Clean button. Because the database keeps track of file paths for source media and file paths for their respective CFA and PEK files, when you choose to clean the database, Premiere searches each path in the database. If it does not find the physical file specified, it deletes the associated CFA and PEK files that were created.

Consider a typical conforming process: You start a project with a sample rate of 48kHz, and you import a DV AVI clip that has an audio setting of 16 bits, 32kHz. As Premiere Pro adds the clip to your project, it does not conform the audio, but it does generate a PEK file and stores it in the Media Cache folder specific to your new project. This PEK file is essentially a snapshot of the waveform information in the audio file so that you can have immediate feedback when zooming in, enlarging, and looking at the physical waveform of the audio in the Source Monitor, Program Monitor, or Timeline panel. Suppose you next import an MP3 file to serve as your music track for your DV project. The moment you select to import the file Premiere starts to conform the audio and make the peak file. In the lower-right corner of the application window, you will see a conform audio progress bar (Figure 3.5). In all cases you can still play back the audio of a file that is being conformed or is waiting to be conformed, but you may not be able to see the waveform information if the PEK file hasn't been generated. In the same Media Cache folder that contains the DV AVI PEK file, there will now be two additional files, a CFA and PEK for MP3 file.

Why conform? Conforming allows more efficient audio processing because real-time conversion is not needed on conform files. By conforming the file, the audio now exists in a format that Premiere Pro can access, display, and adjust much more quickly. Once you start to make tweaks and adjustments, you are referencing the conformed file that has the audio converted to match your project settings; additionally you have the conformed files with a higher bit depth so their processing is even more accurate.

Although conforming will pause if you do certain actions, you can safely work with an audio file in Premiere Pro 2.0 before its conforming is complete.

To avoid conforming, import and use DV AVI files, AVI files with uncompressed audio, or AIFF files with uncompressed audio that fits either the 1:1, 1:2, or 2:3 sample rate ratio. Remember that any WMA, MP3, QuickTime file, or other compressed audio format will be conformed the first time you import it into Premiere Pro 2.0. Finally, as long as you don't move your source files you should only have to conform them once.

Stills

Another aspect of Premiere to get a makeover is its interpretation of still images. When Premiere Pro imports a still image that is larger than the current frame size of your project, it retains the image's full dimensions by default. If you prefer, however, you can turn on an automatic scale preference to resize the still to the frame size of your project. This is the same feature specified in the previous video section. A still image that is 2000 × 1000 imports at that size; if you check the Default Scale to Frame Size preference, however, Premiere Pro will re-rasterize a scaled version of the still at your current project frame size for use in the project. Because you can modify this scale setting before or after importing, the still's original size can be accessed anytime you want. This behavior is different than in previous versions of Premiere.

The new rule of thumb (and this will be explored more heavily in Chapter 14, "Working with Stills: Motion and Advanced Keyframing") is that if you want to do any pans, zooms, or dynamic scale adjustments make sure Default Scale to Frame Size is off (**Figure 3.8**).

Figure 3.8 In the Source Monitor, the Still Rome01 is open and you can view its full frame. When this file is added to the timeline and default scaling is unchecked, you can see only a small portion of the image in the video frame. In the Program Monitor, the viewing scale is set to 25%, and you can see the full size of the still image represented by the thin gray lined square in the Program Monitor.

A frame of video has 72 dots per inch, but a still image can have many, many more. When you are creating stills for use in Premiere Pro, I recommend modifying them to 72dpi. Make their frame size as big as you want, but reduce the dpi when you can. This speeds up the process in which Premiere Pro samples your image. Anytime you have a filter or effect on your still image, Premiere Pro looks at the entire image (sampling), then does the math and processing of the effect. A higher dpi setting creates more work for the sampling and processing. Having a large frame size with 72dpi yields a faster response from the application.

Photoshop Documents

Being part of the Adobe family, Photoshop and Premiere Pro have an enhanced functionality between them, particularly when importing and using native Photoshop documents (PSD files) in Premiere Pro. Because you can have multiple sequences in your project, you have the option to import a layered Photoshop file as a unique sequence with all its layers stacked one on top of the other, respecting the hierarchy of the original document (**Figure 3.9**). This is a powerful feature, because it makes it quite easy to add motion to what was originally a static document.

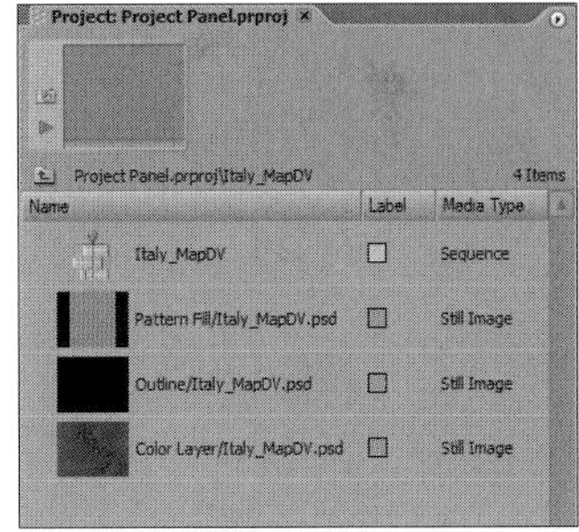

Figure 3.9 When you import a Photoshop file with all its layers, a bin is created with the same name as the imported PSD, in this case Italy_MapDV. Premiere Pro then creates a unique still for each layer of the Photoshop file. Because this PSD was imported as a sequence, Premiere Pro also creates a sequence that is named for the PSD and holds all the layers on separate tracks.

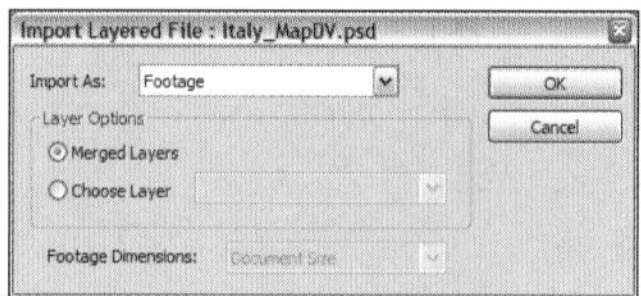

Figure 3.10 When you import a layered Photoshop file as a single merged file, Premiere Pro creates a single clip to represent the composite of all the layers. This appears as an option when you select to Import as Footage.

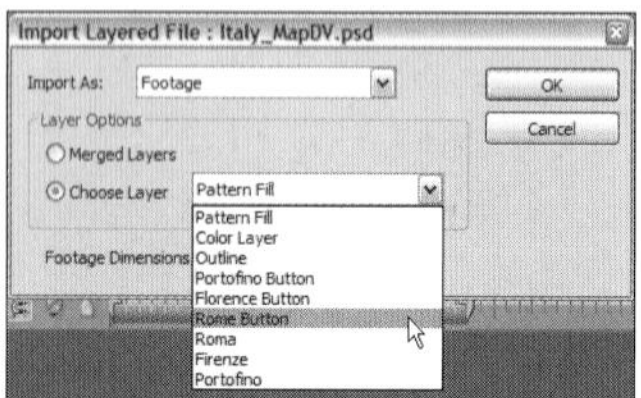

Figure 3.11 When you select Choose Layer, Premiere Pro imports only the chosen layer and adds it to your project file. Again, the option to import a single layer is available only when you choose to import the PSD as Footage.

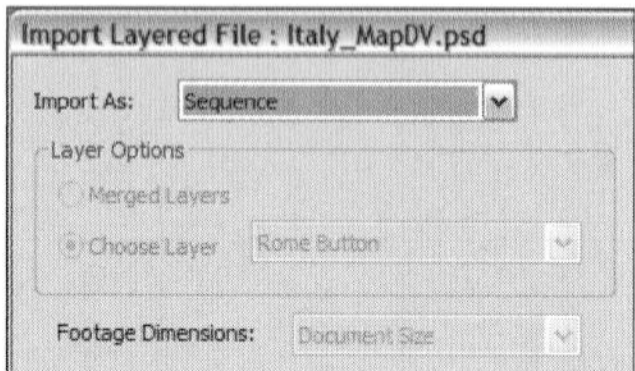

Figure 3.12 Importing a layered PSD as a sequence yields no additional options, because all layers will be imported to accurately represent the original PSD.

When the program imports layered PSDs, every layer of the Photoshop file can be imported as a separate still image, and all the stills are stacked directly on top of each other in separate video tracks to provide an accurate reflection of the original layered PSD. When you import a PSD with layers you get three choices:

- **Import as a single still image with all the layers merged.** This gives you a single still image that has the same name as the Photoshop file (**Figure 3.10**).
- **Import just one of the layers as a still image.** This imports the selected layer as a single still image with the name of the layer/name of the PSD as its filename. For example, with the PSD file named Italy_MapDV and a chosen layer named Portofino, the imported layer name would be Portofino/Italy_MapDV.psd (**Figure 3.11**).
- **Import as a sequence with all layers.** This option does a lot more: It creates a new folder in your project that is named with the exact name of the PSD file. In that folder are still images and a sequence. Each still represents a unique layer of the file, named in the form layer name/filename. Finally, the created sequence is named after the imported PSD. If you open it, it will contain all of the layers stacked on unique tracks, thus representing the original file (**Figure 3.12**).

Because of the proper importation of Photoshop files, it is a breeze to animate and add motion to even the most simple logo. The only trick to remember when you are creating your Photoshop file is to use different layers for different image elements. You'll get to animate this layered Photoshop document in Chapter 13, "Working with Photoshop Files: Nesting and Animating."

Old Projects

Premiere Pro still supports the opening of legacy projects (from former versions both Mac and PC). All you need to do is select your .ppj files from the Import dialog. When you import an old project, Premiere Pro creates a new bin in your current project. The bin is named for the project and inside of that bin is all the media associated with that project plus a new sequence that reflects the edited timeline of the old project. Virtual clips from legacy projects are created as unique sequences inside of this folder, and your older title files can be opened and saved anew in the new Adobe Title Designer. There are two methods of opening old projects.

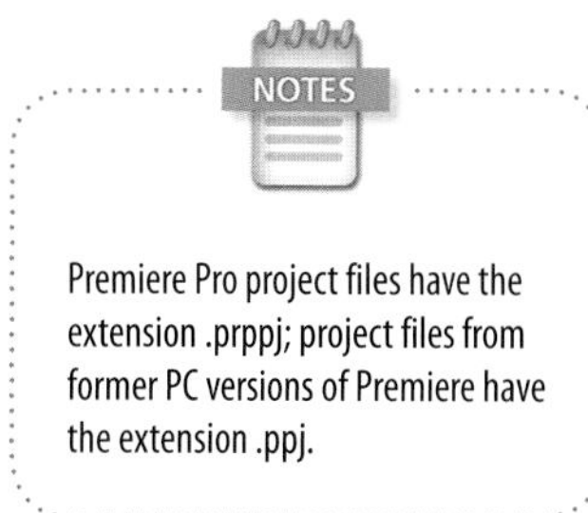

Premiere Pro project files have the extension .prppj; project files from former PC versions of Premiere have the extension .ppj.

If you double-click on the project file icon for a project created with a former version of Premiere, Premiere Pro prompts you with a dialog that tells you the project is from a former version and needs to be updated to Premiere Pro's file format (**Figure 3.13**). To save a new version of the file and not overwrite the original, the dialog gives you the option to rename the updated project file. Once you have properly named the file, the project will open inside of Premiere Pro.

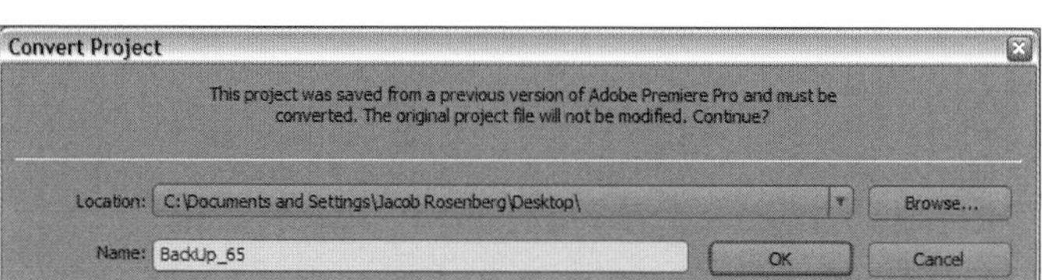

Figure 3.13 When opening an older project, you can automatically rename the file so that the Premiere Pro version does not overwrite the original.

The second method of opening a former Premiere project is by importing it into an open Premiere Pro project. When you import a legacy Premiere project into an open project, Premiere Pro creates a new bin using the name of the imported project file. Inside of the bin will be the entire bin structure of the legacy project with a sequence that reflects the edited timeline of the project (**Figure 3.14**).

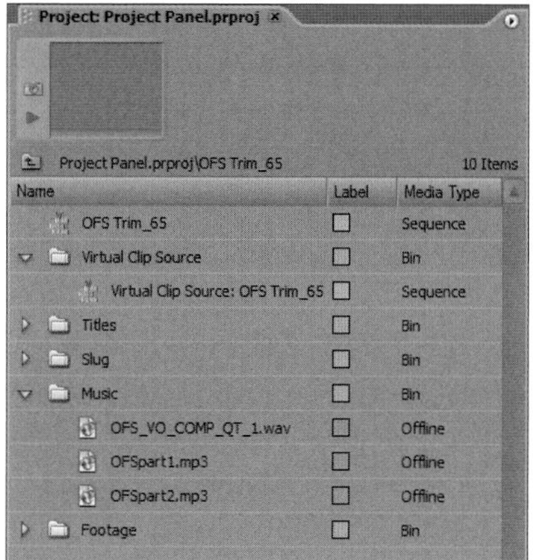

Figure 3.14 When I imported an old Premiere 6.5 project into Premiere Pro 2.0, Premiere Pro created a new bin named for the original project file. Inside that bin is the exact content of the old project with a new sequence file that reflects the timeline of the old project. Here you can see that the OFS TRIM_65 sequence at the top of the window matches the name of the imported project. Also notice that because my old project had a virtual clip instance, a separate sequence was created to reflect that. Virtual clips have been replaced with the nesting functionality.

Project Views

With your project full of media, you have a few choices in how to view the contents of your project. Former versions of Premiere offered three views: List, Icon, and Thumbnail. For Premiere Pro, List and Thumbnail were unified into the new List view and Icon view was added for storyboard elements. The two icons in the lower-left corner of the Project window toggle between List view (the left icon) and Icon view (the right icon).

List View

List view not only accommodates smaller icon sizes, it also uses a number of columns from which you can organize and order your project. In List view, the project name is always on the left. To the right of the name column are the columns you can reorganize and customize. When displaying items and bins in List view, Premiere Pro follows the standard Windows Folder view functionality. Twirling down a bin to open it reveals its contents within the window, and double-clicking on a bin causes the bin's contents to fill the entire Project window view. To navigate back up one level, you must click the Up Folder button (**Figure 3.15**).

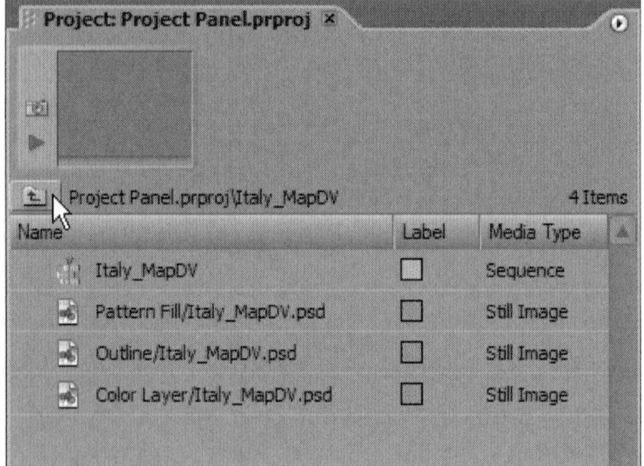

Figure 3.15 When you double-click on a bin, it assumes the full display of the Project panel. When you are inside of a bin and want to go up one level of bins or back out to the root project bin view, click the Up Folder button. Here you can see that the Italy_MapDV bin is currently active in the Project panel. Pressing the Up Folder button, you would be at the root level of the project and could see the other items in the project.

List View Columns

You can customize and sort the information columns in List view and use them for a number of different tasks. If you don't care for the default listing of columns, change their order by clicking and dragging on the column headings to

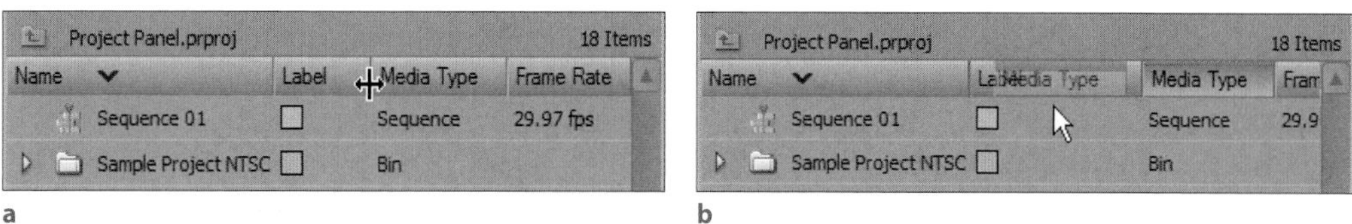

Figures 3.16a and b You can easily resize the width of a column (a) or drag and drop a column to change its horizontal position (b). Notice the thin blue vertical line on the left edge of the Label column; that is the position into which the Media Type column will be moved.

move them around. You can also increase or decrease their size to a set amount by dragging from either of a heading's edges (**Figures 3.16a** and **b**).

Certain columns can yield information that can be adjusted. By using the hot text interface, you can change the In point of clip within the Project panel by scrubbing for the listed in the Video In Point column. You can do the same with the Video Out Point and Video Duration columns (**Figure 3.17**).

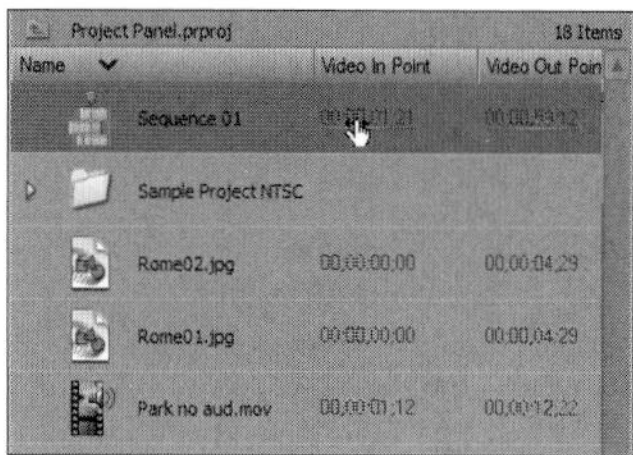

Figure 3.17 You can adjust any of the blue hot text fields by clicking and scrubbing on the numbers.

Custom Columns

You can create custom columns and turn on or off specific columns by choosing Edit Columns from the wing menu. In the Edit Columns dialog, choose the check boxes for the columns you want listed. You can change the order by selecting an item and moving it up or down within the dialog's list.

Most importantly, in this dialog you can create your own custom columns. Clicking the Add button creates a new column. You can create two types of columns:

- **Text columns.** These have fields to which text can be written. If you need additional space to make notes for your media in your Project panel, you can create a custom column called My Notes. In that column, you will be able to click and write any text information. You can sort the information by highlighting (clicking on) the My Notes column heading and then clicking again to sort based on an ascending or descending order. This is helpful if you have an alternative order in which you want your files to be edited. I will make a custom column and then enter number values, such as 01, 05, 07, and a comment after. If I want to edit based on this order, I just select the column and choose my sort order.

- **Boolean columns.** These are check box columns. Use these to create a custom column in which you can easily identify an attribute with a check. When I edit photo montages, I usually want to know whether the picture is a portrait (vertical) or landscape (horizontal). I create a new Boolean column and name it Portrait, then click in the check box for every image that is a portrait. If I want to list all my portraits together, I click on the Portrait column name to sort based on that criteria, either ascending or descending.

In addition to a flexible column structure, List view has multiple display modes.

List Display Modes

In List view you can decide how you want to view listed items by clicking on the wing menu (**Figure 3.18**). Choose View > List or View > Icon to toggle the view from List to Icon, and choose the Thumbnails submenu to change the size of the icons in the Thumbnail Preview area or turn it off entirely. If you do not want to see an icon for your video clip, but instead want to see a thumbnail displaying the poster frame, you can uncheck the Off item and then select the size that you want the thumbnails to be. The bigger the size, the fewer items you will see within your viewing area of the Project panel. I always use the small size and toggle thumbnails on or off. The thumbnails settings are global, so there is no way to turn off thumbnails for one folder in your project and leave them on for another.

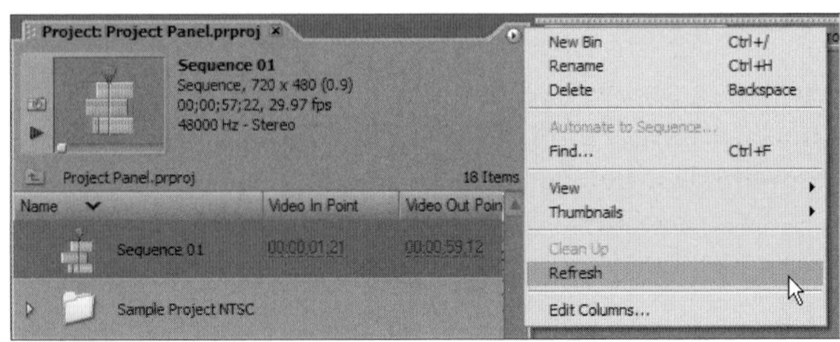

Figure 3.18 The Project panel wing menu offers a bunch of quick access features. By having items in this menu, you can assign them as unique keyboard shortcut items.

Personally, I prefer to use List view with thumbnails off. This is always the fastest (because it does not have to display the thumbnails) and offers the most space (vertically) to display your project files.

Icon View

I am a bit critical of Icon view (shown in Figure 3.1a), because I don't think it is a very intuitive or completely developed view mode. The Storyboard window in older versions of Premiere, which does not exist in Premiere Pro, was a pretty straightforward window with a sequential grid to which all of the items would snap. The grid was only as wide as your window size, and if you made the window larger, the grid would fill the space and still keep the sequential order of the items in the window. The Icon view in Premiere Pro follows a similar grid format, but it does not have a defined size. Additionally, if you resize your window or move items, they do not snap to a set sequential order.

I find the Icon view helpful when working with still images, because you can create an order of items that is not as easy to create in List view. Because List view (shown in Figure 3.1b) presents your items based on an ascending or descending order, you can't just drag your items into a different order within List view. With Icon view, you can drag them anywhere you want and the respected order will be left to right, top to bottom. Icon view is best used in conjunction with the Automate to Timeline function (bottom button bar), which allows you to automatically edit a sequence of clips using their listed or sorted order in a Project panel.

Viewing and Adjusting

After you import files into your project, you can extract a lot of information from them and make a number of adjustments to the files before you edit with them. You know the List view contains a ton of columns that reveal all the data associated with each file. Now I want to show you some additional functions and features that make working with the files a bit easier.

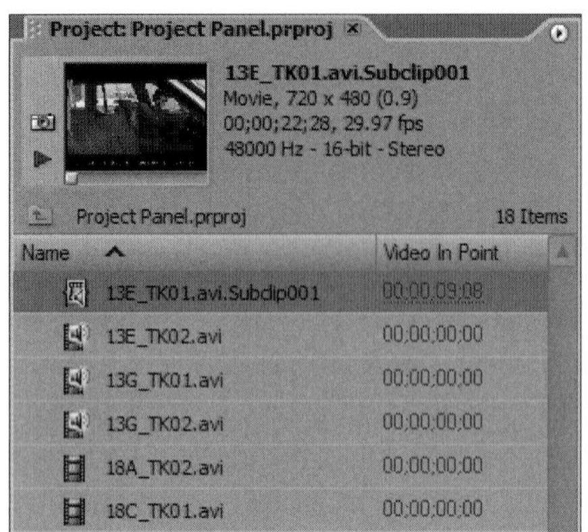

Figure 3.19 With any clip selected in the Project panel, the Thumbnail Preview area (top-left corner) displays a preview with some additional details about the file. Not only can you turn off this area to give more space to the contents of your project, you can also play back and assign poster frames for any of the selected media. With the List view set to thumbnails off, you can always click on a file and see the thumbnail for it in the Thumbnail Preview area.

Thumbnail Preview Area

In the top left corner of the Project panel, the Thumbnail Preview area provides a preview of and some information about the selected item in your Project panel (**Figure 3.19**). If you click once on an audio, video, or sequence file, you will get the associated thumbnail and a little transport control to play that file. If you are editing DV files in DV mode, they will play on your FireWire device as well as in the Thumbnail Preview area. I love the fact that you can play back a sequence in this area without having to open it in the Timeline panel.

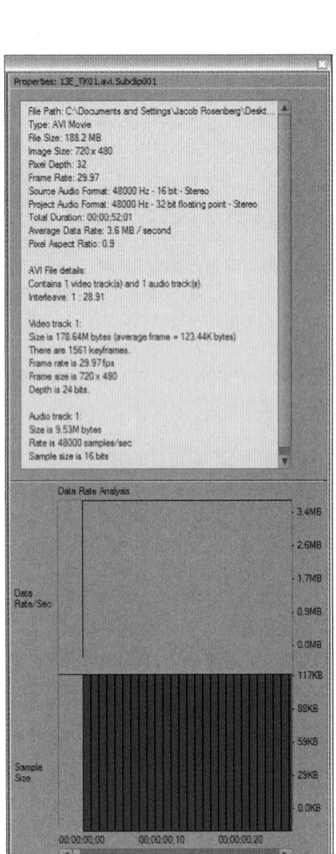

Figure 3.20 The Properties dialog not only gives you details of the selected file's audio, video, and timecode attributes, but also a graphic analysis of the data rate.

Properties

You can view properties for the selected file in two different places. Although you will get a brief bit of information in the Thumbnail Preview area, if you right-click on a file in the Project panel and choose Properties, you will get a lot more. In addition, you can access this function by choosing File > Get Properties for > File/Selection.

Viewing your properties is the way to verify certain settings and parameters associated with your file (**Figure 3.20**). If you are unclear which compressor is used with an imported video clip, for example, the compressor will be revealed when you get properties for the clip.

Project Settings

To access your Project Settings once your project is open, go to Project > Project Settings and then choose the area you want to adjust or change. Because the project has already been created and is open, certain parameters will be locked.

Clip Settings

You can adjust and access a few settings for certain selected media in your Project panel. For example, if you want to switch the incorrect field order of a video clip, you can access the field order from the Clip menu once you have your video clip selected in the Project panel.

Adjusting your clips within the Project panel keeps you one step ahead of your edit. If you have a clip that you want to use in slow motion only, you don't have to always adjust its speed in the Timeline panel; you can preset the speed to the master clip directly in the Project panel (**Figure 3.21**).

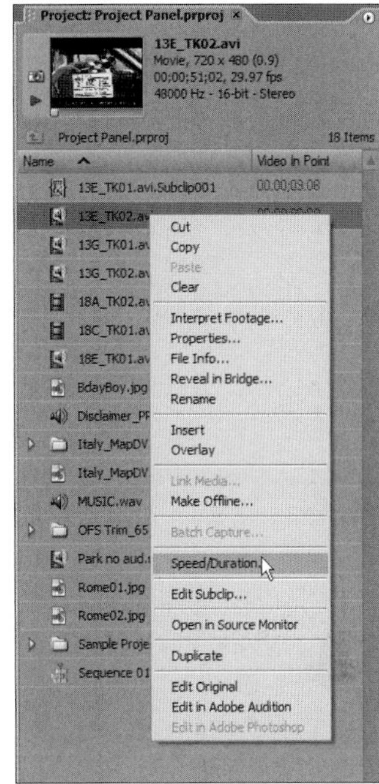

Figure 3.21 Right-clicking on any file in the Project panel reveals a context menu of options for that file. For example, you can adjust the speed of a clip within the Project panel before it is added to your sequence.

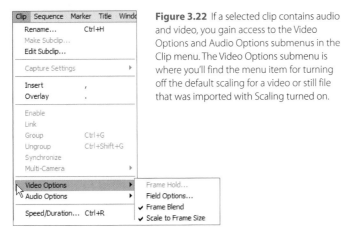

Video Clip Menu

With a video clip selected, the Clip menu reveals a handful of functions that you can apply to the clip (**Figure 3.22**). Rename allows you to change the alias for the file in the Project panel. It does not modify the linked file on disk, but just the displayed file in the project. You can edit your clip directly to the Timeline panel by using Insert and Overlay. Choose Clip > Video Options > Field Options. From the resulting Field Options dialog, you can change any of the field settings associated with your clip. The last Clip menu choice is to modify the speed or duration of the file.

Figure 3.22 If a selected clip contains audio and video, you gain access to the Video Options and Audio Options submenus in the Clip menu. The Video Options submenu is where you'll find the menu item for turning off the default scaling for a video or still file that was imported with Scaling turned on.

If you modify a master clip in the Project panel, it affects all edited instances from that modification point forward. If you previously edited five instances from one master clip, then changed its speed to 50%, those five instances would not change to 50%.

Audio Clip Menu

With audio files selected, a number of very important features are available in the Clip > Audio Options submenu: Audio Gain, Source Channel Mappings, and Extract. Breakout To is still in there too, but it's not as important as it used to be.

Audio Gain and Normalizing Your Audio

When you import an audio file, it has a set volume level associated with it. Once you edit the audio file into your timeline, its volume can be increased or decreased a number of ways. An incredibly powerful feature that is somewhat hidden, Audio Gain allows you to perfect the audio level of your master clip so that you do not need to make constant adjustments of the edited subclips. Adjusting your Audio Gain setting allows you adjust your audio level based on an increase or decrease in decibels (dBs).

If you have an audio clip selected or a video clip with audio, go to Clip > Audio Options > Audio Gain. The Gain dialog allows you to either increase or decrease the dB of your selected clip. The Normalize button takes this one step further (**Figures 3.23**).

Within the range of audio volume levels, there are some decibel ratings that don't register any sound at all (low) and others that register sounds too loud (high). If sound

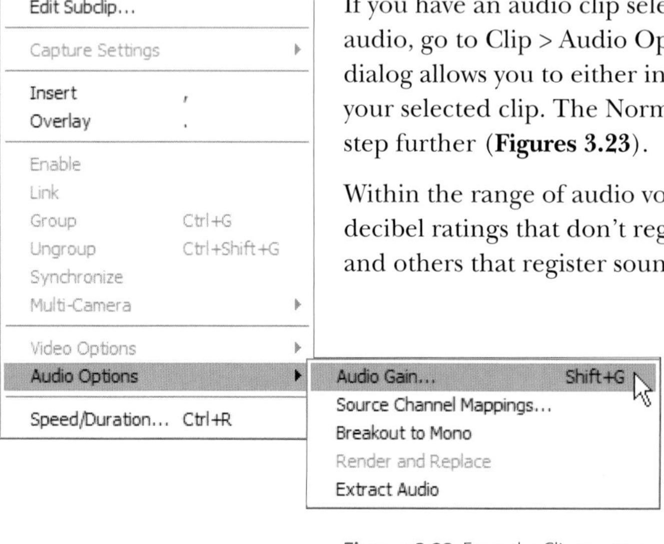

Figures 3.23 From the Clip menu, you can access the Clip Gain dialog, which allows you to normalize your clip gain level.

levels register too high, you will usually get pops, crackles, or distortions. If your original recording has pops, crackles, and distortions, there is not too much you can do to remove those sounds as you cannot undo the audio that was recorded. If the volume for the audio file you import is too low or too high once it arrives in Premiere Pro, however, you can make a uniform adjustment to compensate for that.

Normalize is an intelligent, automated function that looks at your entire audio file, at the peaks and valleys (highs and lows), then recommends the gain setting that will give you the best volume adjustment value without exceeding the proper ceiling of 0dB during playback. Normalize gives you a positive or negative dB value that will bring your volume to a safe overall level where there is no distortion. Normalize saves a ton of your time tinkering to find the right level. Normalizing in the Project window on the master file ensures that all of the master clip's associated subclips will honor that level adjustment.

I recommend that when you import audio clips and audio/video clips you first normalize their levels to get them to the best dB setting. You can worry about specific instances where you want to make minor adjustments later.

Source Channel Mappings

It's funny how a small feature can demand such enthusiasm, but the arrival of Source Channel Mappings in 2.0 has generated a great deal of excitement. Choosing Clip > Audio Options > Source Channel Mappings enables you, for example, to remap the stereo audio of a DV clip so that two mono audio files are attached to the video instead. Although the clip appears exactly the same in the Project panel, when you edit with it in the Timeline panel, the video is linked to two separate mono files, each reflecting the left and right channels of the source stereo file.

The Source Channel Mappings dialog is very straightforward. Here you can turn off channels, swap channels, and remap stereo, mono, and 5.1 audio files into any of the three formats (**Figures 3.24a** and **b**). Additionally, if you wanted to break a stereo clip into a pair of mono tracks, but keep them recognized as stereo, you can select Mono as Stereo. Mono as Stereo breaks the Left and Right channels of a stereo clip into two separate Stereo channels; each individual channel is then filled with a stereo version of the Left or Right channel.

A previous (1.5) feature, Treat as Stereo, has been replaced by Source Channel Mappings as well. If you want to make a mono file appear and play as stereo, you just select the file and go to Clip > Audio Options > Source Channel Mappings. In the resulting dialog, click Stereo, and then OK.

Breakout To

With the introduction of Source Channel Mappings, the Breakout To feature is no longer as significant, especially because Breakout To tends to clutter your Project panel

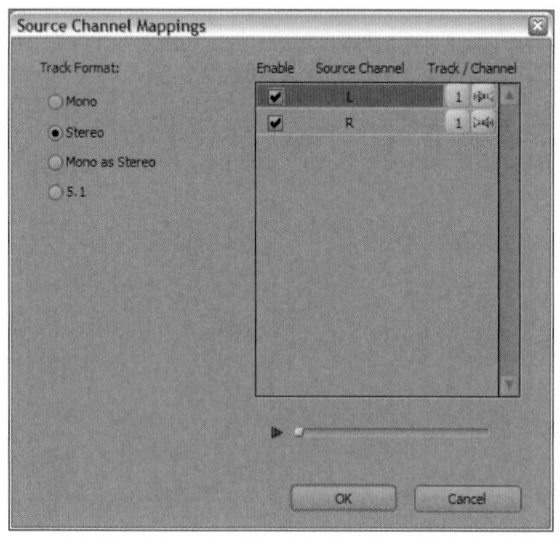

a

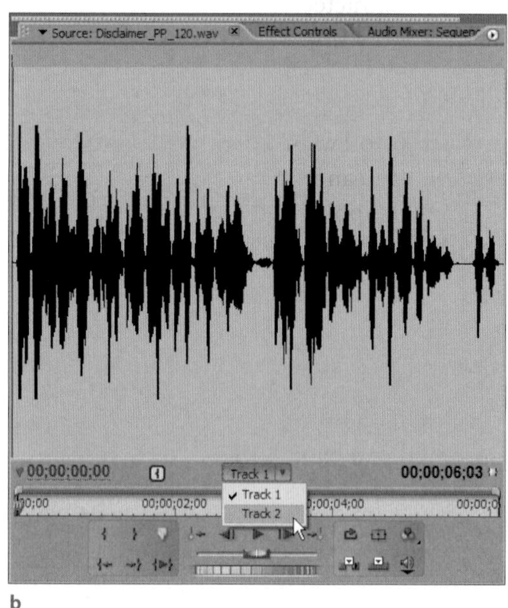

b

Figures 3.24a and b This long overdue audio feature enables Premiere Pro editors to edit stereo audio clips as a linked pair of mono clips. While the feature Breakout to Mono creates a physical pair of new mono files in your Project panel, the Source Channel Mappings dialog (a) allows you to remap a stereo clip as mono without adding any extra clutter to your Project panel. Additionally, when you open a stereo audio clip that has been remapped as mono in the Source Monitor, you can toggle between the two channels via a drop-down menu at the bottom of the viewing area (b).

with additional files that don't have the same linked property as source channel mapped files. Just as Source Channel Mappings allows you to remap a stereo file as a mono pair using the same single clip in Project panel, Breakout To allows you physically break a stereo file (or 5.1) into two individual mono clips that appear as separate mono audio files in the Project panel (**Figure 3.25**).

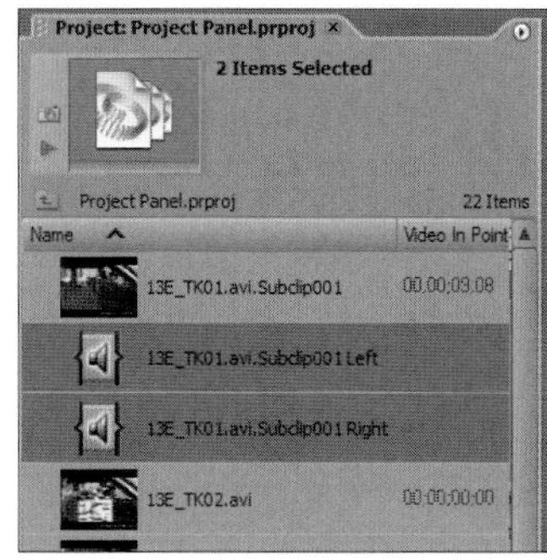

Figure 3.25 When you select Clip > Audio Options > Breakout to Mono Clips for a video clip with a stereo track, Premiere Pro duplicates the source audio and creates left and right mono audio clips that have the same timecode value as the master video clip.

In my eyes, Breakout To was a workaround for the absence of Source Channel Mappings. Now that we have the new feature, Breakout To is not as practical as it once was.

Extract

Have you ever had an audio/video clip and wanted to just use the audio only? Have you ever had a DV file and wanted to edit its audio in Adobe Audition? If the answer to either of these questions is yes, then you will be happy about the new Extract audio feature. Extract quite simply enables you to select a clip that contains audio and video and extract only the audio, whether it be stereo, mono, or 5.1. The extracted audio clip displays as a single file in the Project panel using its current audio format. Using Extract is simple; you select the file you want to extract audio from in the Project panel, then choose Clip > Audio Options > Extract. If you want to change to the extracted clip's format, you can remap it using, you guessed it, Source Channel Mappings. If you want to re-edit the file directly in Adobe Audition, select the extracted file in your Project panel and choose Edit > Edit in Audition.

Creating New Elements

The last territory I want to discuss is the bottom bar area of the Project panel (**Figure 3.26**). Here you can perform several tasks and create numerous items for your project.

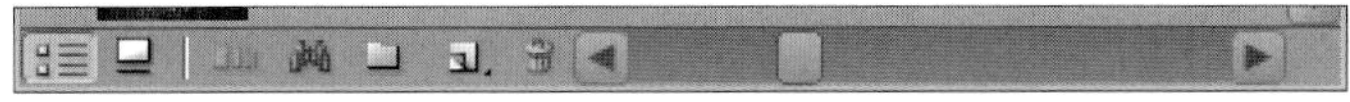

Figure 3.26 From the left, the icons in the bottom menu bar of the Project window are List View, Icon View, Automate to Timeline, Search, New Bin, New Item, and Trash.

From the left, the icons are:

- **List View and Icon View.** Click these icons to toggle between the Project panel's two views.
- **Automate to Timeline.** Click the third icon to automatically edit a selection of clips by having them placed back to back with the option of having transitions between them. This function is explored completely in Chapter 14.
- **Search.** Click the binoculars to bring up a search tool that allows you to search the Project panel from any column based on a number of criteria: Column is which column you want to search in, Operator is the criterion, and Find What is the area where you type the characters you are looking for. Case Sensitive ensures the search respects upper- and lowercase character values.
- **New Bin.** Click this icon to create a new bin that has its name field selected so that you can type the new name immediately. Whatever bin is selected or has the focus of the Project panel is where the new bin will be created.
- **New Item.** Click the New Item button to open a list of choices: Sequence, Offline Files, Titles, Bars and Tone, Black Video, Color Matte, and Universal Counting Leader. Simply choose the type of item you'd like to create. You will learn the appropriate uses for each of these items as you step through the lessons in later chapters.
- **Trash.** Select the items to delete, then click the Trash. If your selected clip has been used in a sequence, you will be warned before you can delete the file. If the selected clip has not been used, there will be no warnings.

To delete a file from your project and from your disk, select the file either from the Project menu or from the right-click context menu and select Unlink Media. In the Unlink dialog, click the file that you want deleted. You will be warned, Premiere will delete the file from disk, then you can delete the clip instances from your project.

Remember that the selection in the Project panel may be affected by the tasks that you execute from the bottom button bar. If a bin is selected and you create a new bin, for example, the new bin will be created inside of the selected bin. In addition, you should keep a few other organizational tips in mind.

Organizational Tips

The Project panel is where you can organize and make life easier for yourself. I try to use a lot of bins that are labeled for their intended usage. Instead of populating my project with 250 different files in one view, I try to create specific bins for specific files. I typically use the following bin structure for my projects:

- **Logged Clips:** Holds all offline, logged files
- **Video:** Holds online video clips and may have subfolders to identify different groups of the clips
- **Audio:** Holds additional audio-only files
- **Music:** Used only if a project has music or soundtrack files
- **Voice-Over:** Used only if a project has voice-over files
- **Graphics:** Holds all Photoshop or computer-generated graphic files
- **Titles:** Holds all Adobe Title Designer titles
- **Stills:** Holds pictures or still photographs
- **Sequences:** Holds all of the sequences for the open project

Creating a bin structure in your Project window that is similar to the folder structure on your hard drive makes it easier to find and move items in your project. If you always put your titles in a Title folder on your drive and you always create a Title bin in any new project that you create, it will be easy to find any older title and use it in a new project.

Things to Remember

The most important concepts to take away from this chapter are how to add, work with, and manipulate media in the Project panel. Combine these with the lessons you learned about logging and capturing in the last chapter, and you begin to see the power of Premiere Pro.

Many of the features presented in this chapter will be more fully explored in the projects to come, but already you can anticipate which features are most helpful and will be used often in your editing workflow. The Video Options submenu, Audio Options submenu, and importing layered Photoshop files are just a few examples.

In the next chapter, you will move forward to playing media in the Monitor panels, exploring the differences and similarities between the Source and Program Monitors.

CHAPTER

Playing Back and Viewing Your Media

I like to think of the Project panel as the container for all of your media. The Source Monitor is where you can view that media in detail and decide which portions you want to work with. As you'll see in the next chapter, the Timeline panel and Program Monitor are your virtual videotape or canvas where you arrange, manipulate, and create your edit.

With Premiere Pro 2.0, the Source Monitor and Program Monitor are now separate panels (**Figure 4.1**). In the Source Monitor, you open source material and pick the portions you want to incorporate into your sequence. In the Program Monitor, you open and view the sequences that you are editing. Although their buttons and transport controls are almost identical, the function of each window is quite different, as you'll see.

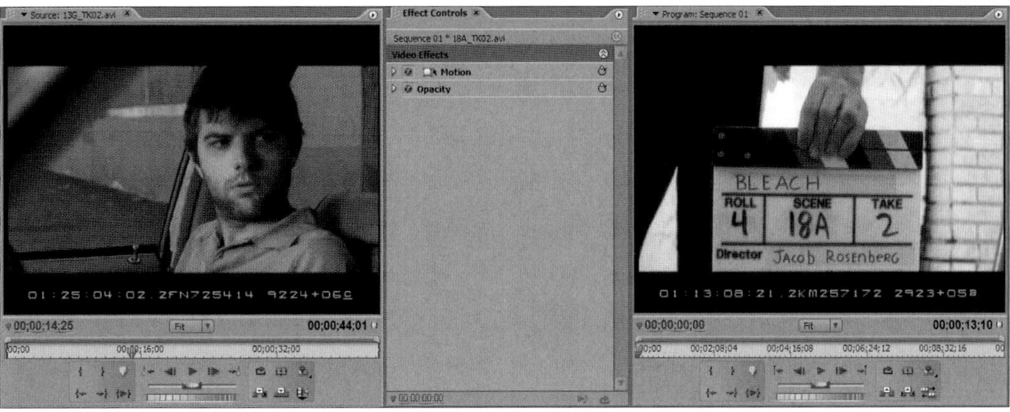

Figure 4.1 In Premiere Pro 2.0's new layout the Source Monitor is the panel on the far left; the Program Monitor is a separate panel on the far right.

The Source Monitor

In older versions of Premiere, the Source Monitor was called the Clip window and it was not attached to the Program Monitor. The windows were recombined in Premiere Pro 1.0, but Premiere Pro 2.0 finally breaks that attachment. You can still think of the Source Monitor as a clip window, because it is the only window where you can open and play individual clips. You use the Source Monitor to open and review media that you wish to edit and incorporate into your sequences (**Figure 4.2**).

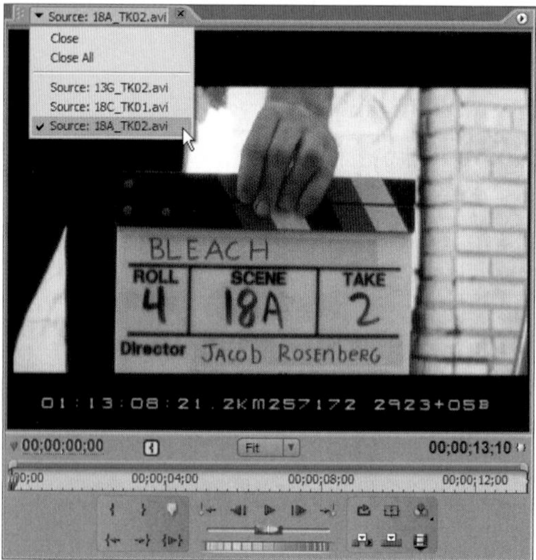

Figure 4.2 The Source Monitor features a drop-down menu and wing menu (right corner), as well as timecode fields, a time navigation area, transport controls, and editing group boxes.

What You Can Open

In the Source Monitor you will be able to open and view

- Video clips
- Audio clips
- Audio and video clips
- Stills
- Sequences

Additionally, you can open synthetic media, such as

- Color mattes
- Black video

- Offline files
- Bars and tone
- The Universal Counting Leader

When you drag media from the Project panel into the Source Monitor, you open the media for viewing and playback (even offline files). If you double-click on media in your Project panel, it will load it into the Source Monitor. However, not all media opens for viewing when double-clicked on. With sequences, a standard double-click opens the sequence in the Timeline panel, and a Ctrl+double-click opens the sequence in the Source Monitor. With offline files, a double-click opens an offline file's properties; dragging it into the Source Monitor opens it as a clip to scrub in.

Monitor Layout

As shown in Figure 4.2, the Source Monitor has a few distinct regions that display information and give you access to transport controls and features. Although the Source Monitor has a tab area, media does not open as separate tabs. Media opens and is listed within the Source Monitor tab.

To the right of the tab area is the wing menu (**Figure 4.3**), which has physical links to some of the button options

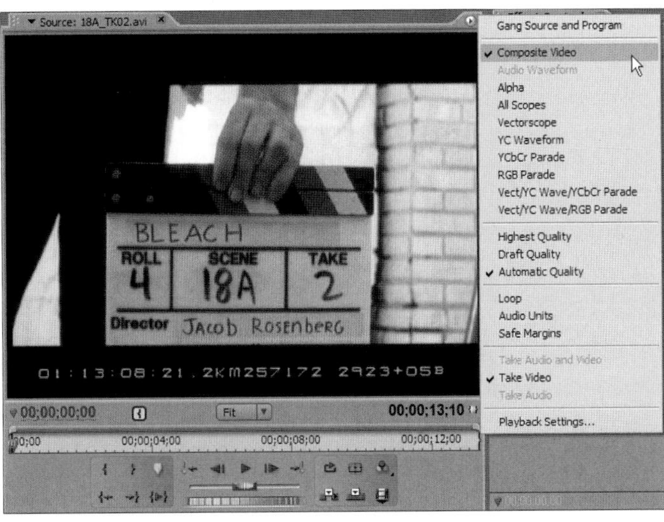

Figure 4.3 Like all panels, the Source Monitor has a wing menu that allows direct access to features that can be routed to customized keyboard shortcuts.

at the bottom of the window. These physical links can be assigned to unique keyboard shortcuts using the Keyboard Customization function.

The center of the Source Monitor is the viewing area, where media plays back. You can load multiple items into the Source Monitor by dragging multiple selections or folders into its viewing area. Dragging a folder full of items loads all of the items into the Source Monitor. To open an individual item once it is loaded, select it from the drop-drown menu. You can close the open media from the window by selecting Close from the drop-down menu. You can also close all the listed items by selecting Close All.

Below the viewing area, you have the timecode display, time ruler, viewing area bar, and the transport controls arranged in three separate groups, similar to the Capture window.

To watch a tutorial that discusses how Premiere Pro 2.0 handles clip time-codes, open the Timecode_Review .wmv file, located in the Video Tutorials folder on the book's DVD. When the file loads in Windows Media Player, press Alt+Enter to play it back at full-screen size.

Timecode and the Time Navigation Controls

When you open media in the Source Monitor, the lower left text area reveals the timecode value of the current frame that is being played or scrubbed on in the monitor. The timecode value to the right is the total duration of the media in the window. Once you start modifying the In and Out points, the duration updates dynamically.

If you find that the correct timecode does not display when you open a clip, there are two new preferences that you should check (**Figure 4.4**). To ensure you are viewing your source clip's captured timecode, confirm that both the Edit > Preferences > Media > Display Media Timecode in Source Frame Rate and In/Out Points Show Media Offset check boxes are selected.

The time ruler is basically a visual counter for your open media that can be scrubbed in and zoomed into and out from (**Figure 4.5**). Time is delineated by tick marks that represent the Timebase specified in your Project Settings. Any markers, In points, and Out points assigned in your clip also are visually represented in the time ruler. Above the time ruler is the viewing area bar, which you stretch and drag to zoom into and navigate through portions of

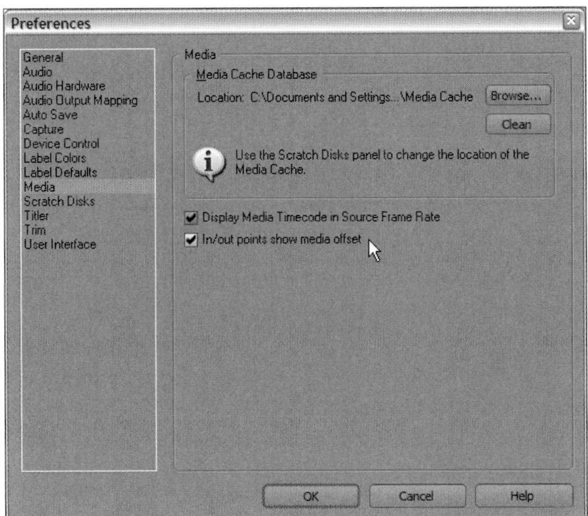

Figure 4.4 Using 2.0's new preferences, you can specify what timecode displays when a clip opens. If you turn on the first check box, when you add a non-drop frame clip to a drop frame project, the clip's timecode displays as non-drop frame instead of the project's drop frame. Checking the second box means that when you open a clip it does not show its In/Out counter value from 00;00;00;00 to the end of the clip; instead it displays the physical timecode that was captured with the clip, such as 01:01:00:00.

your open media. In the time ruler, the blue playback head that you click and drag around to scrub through your media is called the Current Time Indicator (CTI). The CTI also exists in the timeline where it is referred to as the CTI or Edit Line.

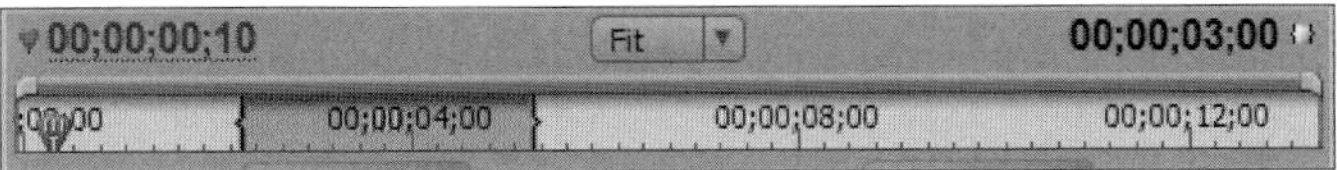

Figure 4.5 The blue timecode value reflects the current position of the CTI. The black timecode value reflects the duration of the In/Out instance visible in the time ruler. You can resize the gray viewing area bar to zoom in and out of the time ruler.

Scrubbing through a one-hour clip frame by frame would be difficult, for example, if you did not have the capability to zoom into a specific area of the time ruler. By being able to zoom in (dragging inward from the edges of bar), you can get down to whatever magnification you want. Once you are zoomed in, you can click and drag from the center of the bar to reveal different areas of the open clip. The viewing area bar does have an intelligent zoom: If the CTI is within view, the viewing area bar will zoom in and out around the CTI position.

Buttons and Transport Controls

Below the time ruler are your transport controls and various buttons associated with marking and navigating to In and Out points in the source media. These buttons and controls are broken up into three separate group boxes (**Figure 4.6**). The left group assigns and navigates to In and Out points for your open media. The center group holds the transport controls for playing back your media. The right group contains buttons specific to the editing tasks of the Source Monitor window.

Figure 4.6 The Transport area of the Source Monitor contains three group boxes of controls. The left group manages In and Out points, the center group handles playing back your media, and the right group houses editing-related buttons.

If you hold down the Alt key, Play In to Out becomes the Play Edit button.

Although some buttons do not have keyboard shortcuts assigned to them, you can search the Edit > Keyboard Customization > Windows > Monitor and Trim Windows to see which keyboard shortcuts are available to be assigned.

Holding the Shift key when clicking Step Back steps back five frames at a time. Likewise, holding the Shift key when pressing Step Forward steps forward in five-frame increments.

In the left group are six buttons (and one hidden one):

- **In Point** (shortcut key: I). Marks an In point at the current CTI position.
- **Out Point** (shortcut key: O). Marks current CTI position.
- **Set Unnumbered Marker** (shortcut key: * on the number pad). Assigns an unnumbered marker at the current CTI position.
- **Go to In** (shortcut key: Q). Automatically moves the CTI from its current position to the assigned In point.
- **Go to Out** (shortcut key: W). Automatically moves the CTI from its current position to the assigned Out point.
- **Play In to Out.** Automatically plays back your media from your assigned In point to your assigned Out point.
- **Play Edit.** When you press the Alt key, the Play In to Out button becomes the Play Edit button. Plays back from the current CTI position using General Preferences.

The center group houses your primary transport controls, which are (from the left):

- **Go to Previous Marker.** Moves the CTI from its current position to the position of the nearest assigned marker prior to it.

- **Step Back** (shortcut key: Left Arrow). Moves the CTI back one frame at a time. You must click every time you want to step; holding down this button will not continuously step.
- **Play/Stop Toggle** (shortcut key: Spacebar). Plays or stops the media in the viewing area. This toggle has it to engage playback. When you are playing a clip, the Stop icon displays. When you press it, playback stops.
- **Step Forward** (shortcut key: Right Arrow). Moves the CTI one frame forward with each click. You cannot hold down this button to have the CTI continuously step.
- **Go to Next Marker.** Updates the CTI position to the next assigned marker nearest to the CTI's current position.
- **Shuttle slider.** Allows you to dynamically throw the Monitor into variable playback speeds. The farther from the center, left, or right the slider is, the faster playback will be. The closer to the center you drag, the slower playback will be. The shuttle is great for watching in slow motion as it will play beautifully without stuttering.
- **Jog disk.** Enables you to scrub through your media, either forward or backward, with greater detail. Jogging is like scrubbing through your clip in slow motion; you can control the scrubbing by dragging. While the shuttle controls variable playback speeds, the jog disk steps through your media at a constant frame-by-frame rate.

On the right, the third group has specific functions unique to the Source Monitor:

- **Loop.** Activates a state of playback. If you have Loop pressed, whenever you engage playback you will be in Loop mode, meaning when the CTI hits the end of the media or an Out point, it continues playing from the beginning or In point of the clip.
- **Safe Margins.** A display state for the Source Monitor. When you click Safe Margins, they will be visible in your Source Monitor (**Figure 4.7**), adhering to the value assigned for them in your General Project Settings. Safe Margins are best used when trying to make sure graphics, stills, and clips have action within the television safe area of the video frame.

Figure 4.7 With Safe Margins turned on, the gray overlaid boxes reflect the Title Safe (inner box) and Action Safe (outer box) areas.

- **Output.** Refers to what is being output or displayed in your Source Monitor panel. The first group of choices in the drop-down menu includes all your vectorscope and waveform monitors, and the second group includes the output display quality (**Figure 4.8**). Briefly, if you were to select YC Waveform for your output display, your same media would play back in the Source Monitor, only it would be displayed as if it was being output to a waveform monitor. Using difference scope views allows you to gauge color and brightness values of your media. It is very helpful to use these scopes when performing such tasks as color correction.

Figure 4.8 From the Output button's drop-down menu you can specify the Source Monitor's viewing mode. Additionally, you can toggle the display quality between Highest, Draft, and Automatic.

The quality settings are Highest, Draft, and Automatic. Highest displays the media in the Source Monitor at its full resolution. Draft displays media at quarter resolution. Automatic plays your media at full resolution when it does not detect instances with filtering or effects (which require rendering). If Automatic mode detects an instance that needs to be rendered, it switches to quarter resolution for that instance, then back to full resolution when finished with the instance. The changes in sizes will affect playback performance. If you have a sequence with a lot of effects open in your Source Monitor, you may not experience excellent real-time playback if you are set to Highest quality, because it will try to render the sequence in real-time at high quality, which requires a lot processing. Leave your Source Monitor in Automatic mode, instead.

- **Insert** (shortcut key: ,). Inserts selected media from the Source Monitor into the timeline at either an assigned In point or the CTI (if you don't have an assigned In point). An insert edit does not overwrite media in the timeline. An Insert edit splits and shifts whatever media is in the timeline so that your shot can be placed without replacing or overwriting any other media.
- **Overlay** (shortcut key: .). Overlays the selected media from the Source Monitor into the timeline at an assigned In point or the CTI (if you don't have an assigned In point). An Overlay edit is the opposite of an Insert: It overwrites the material that it is being edited over. With an Insert edit, if you inserted a five-second clip in the middle of your timeline, the overall duration of the timeline would increase by five seconds. Using the same example with an Overlay edit, the duration would not change; you would have replaced five seconds of your edit with a different five seconds of material.
- **Toggle Take Audio and Video.** Determines which elements of your media will be edited into your timeline. If you have a clip with both audio and video, you have the option of adding the video only, audio only, or audio and video together to your timeline. Clicking the toggle activates the different states of the button to give you

the proper feedback for each state. If the toggle is in Audio mode, only the audio portion of your clip will be used for edits (**Figure 4.9**). Video mode means only video will be used, and Audio and Video mode means audio and video both will be used.

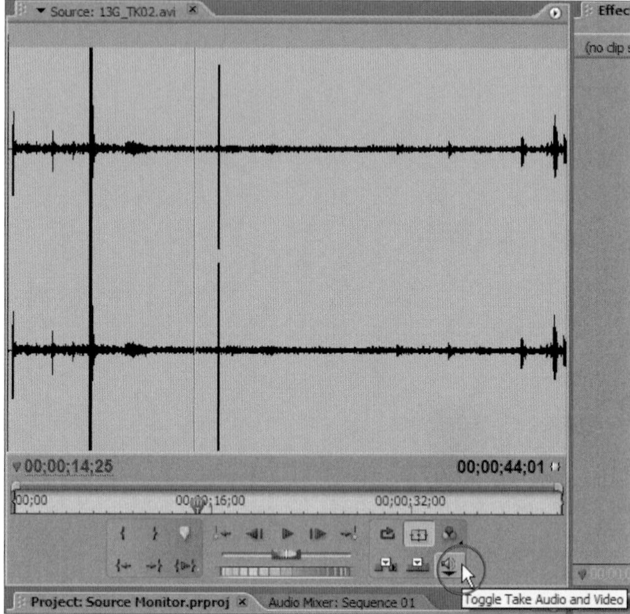

Figure 4.9 When the Toggle Take Audio and Video is Audio mode, the Source Monitor displays the audio waveform for the active clip and will edit only the audio attributes into the timeline.

The Source Monitor group boxes contain all the tools necessary for navigating and defining which portions and attributes of the open media will be added to your sequence. Once media is added to your sequence, you can continue to use the Source Monitor to edit material from the active sequence.

Editing Functions

In the Source Monitor, you can perform edits using the Insert and Overlay buttons, or you can drag and drop from the Source Monitor into the Timeline window. The usual workflow is to open the media in the Source Monitor, to determine the In/Out instance of the media, then to add it into the Timeline window (**Figure 4.10**).

Additionally, a clip instance edited into the Timeline window can be opened in the Source Monitor by double-clicking on the clip in the timeline (**Figure 4.11**). The

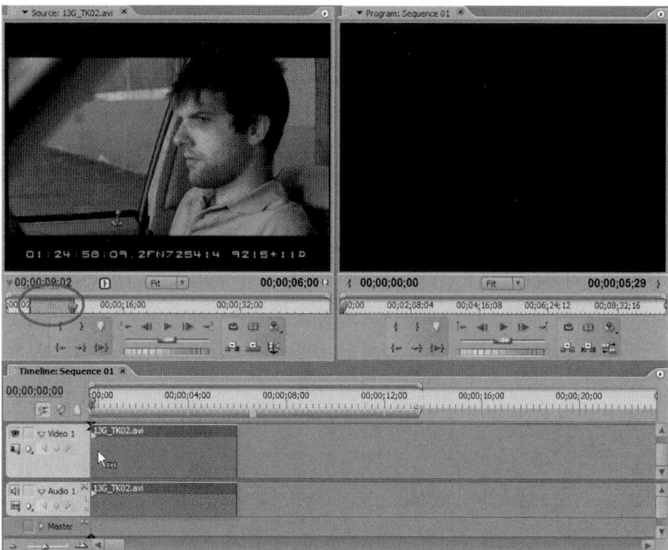

Figure 4.10 You can designate a subclip instance within the source material by assigning In and Out points (notice the dark gray region in the time ruler). You then can drag that subclip from the Source Monitor and drop it in the timeline.

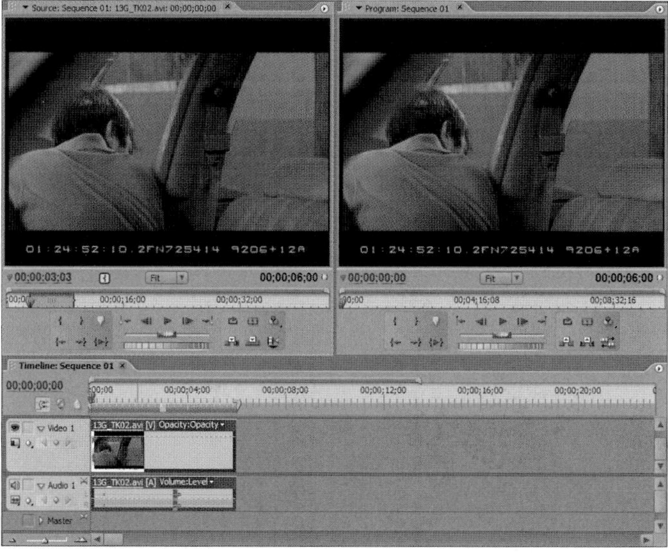

Figure 4.11 Double-clicking on the subclip instance from the timeline does not open the master clip from which the In/Out was assigned. Instead, it opens the subclip as its own clip instance in the Source Monitor. Any modifications made to this subclip's In or Out points in the Source Monitor immediately affects the clip instance in the timeline. Notice that the clip name in the top of the Source Monitor reflects that of the timeline instance (Sequence Name: Clip Name and timecode) that was opened as opposed to the master clip from which it originated (Clip Name only as seen in Figure 4.10).

clip opens as a subclip in the Source Monitor window, and any adjustments to its In point or Out point automatically update the clip instance in the timeline.

Although the technical name for a clip instance dropped down into the timeline is a subclip, there is also a powerful Subclip feature that is new for 2.0.

For a quick review of creating and working with subclips in Premiere Pro 2.0, open the Subclip_Review .wmv tutorial, located in the Video Tutorials folder on the book's DVD. When the file loads in Windows Media Player, press Alt+Enter to play it back at full-screen size.

Creating a Subclip

New to Premiere Pro 2.0 is the ability to create individual subclips for your Project panel. Dragging and dropping clips into your sequences might be fine for most work, but if you work with long or diverse content-oriented clips then you might want to break the master clips up into smaller more defined subclips with individual names. If you want to create a unique subclip instance that references only a small portion of a master clip, you first open the master clip from the Project panel in the Source Monitor and define an In/Out instance. Now, instead of dragging the clip into the timeline, drag the clip directly into the Project panel (**Figure 4.12**). After you drop the clip into the Project panel, Premiere prompts you to rename it. Do so, and a new subclip instance appears (specific icon and all) in the Project panel, ready for use in any of your sequences.

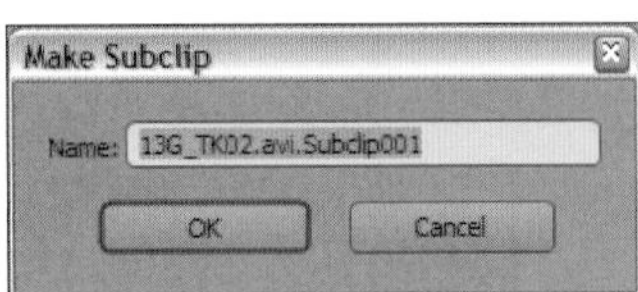

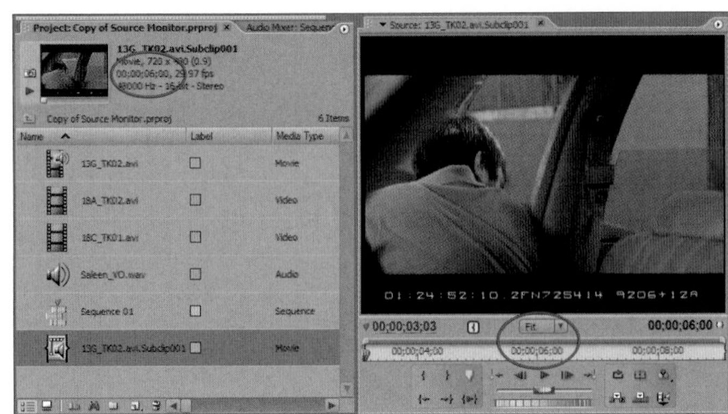

Figure 4.12 With the same In/Out instance from the master clip in Figure 4.10, notice how the cursor updates when you drag the source clip into the Project panel. Once the subclip is named, when it is opened in the Source Monitor notice that the entire range of the clip is defined by the In and Out points previously assigned when creating the subclip. Note that the duration of the clip in both the Project panel and Source Monitor is 6;00.

With Project panel subclips, as long as the source media for the master clip is not deleted from your disk, you can view the media for subclip. This means you can remove the master clips from your project, to reduce clutter, and continue editing only with the custom-created subclips.

Wing Menu Options

The Source Monitor's wing menu is where you can choose features or viewing modes specific to the window. Most of the choices are self-explanatory, but two important functions aren't that obvious:

- **Gang Source and Program.** Gang Source and Program means that you are locking certain transport controls together. If you gang the two monitors, all scrubbing in the Source Monitor will be mimicked in the Program Monitor. If you step one frame forward in the Program, you will step one frame forward in the Source. Although this does not seem like an obvious and useful function, it proves very powerful for certain workflows such as color correction and multicam editing.
- **Audio Units.** Because you now have conformed audio files of greater bit depth and detail, you may want to zoom in, scrub, and assign In or Out points at the subframe level (**Figure 4.13**). To switch your counter display from Video Frames to Audio Units, simply select Audio Units from the wing menu. Remember, once you switch

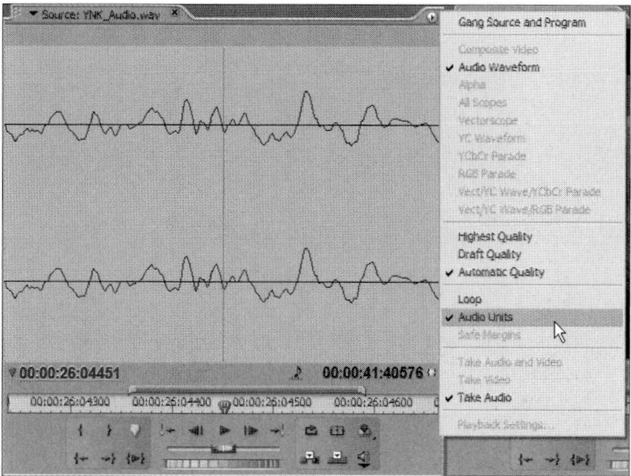

Figure 4.13 With the Source Monitor set to display audio units, you zoom closer into audio files. In addition, the timecode reflects time in 1/100000ths units so that you can isolate, identify, and edit an exact sample of audio.

to Audio Units, the Step Forward button will step one sample at a time and that will barely register any sound. Although there is an increase in detail, you may have to do a bit more physical scrubbing and clicking within the scrub area to navigate to your desired locations.

Magnification

Finally, you can magnify the viewable area of your open media, by choosing the Source Monitor's drop-down Magnification menu, between the timecode displays. Clicking it reveals a list of zoom states. The default choice, Fit, considers the current size of the window and then resizes the media so that the entire frame fits inside the window. You will notice that if you set your magnification to Fit, any resizing of the window results in dynamic automatic resizing of the media. If you choose 25% from the Magnification menu, the media takes up a quarter of its normal full-sized space. If your Source Monitor window is larger than the 25% size, there will be gray space surrounding the edge of the media. If you select a size that is greater than the size of the Source Monitor window, the edges of the clip exceed the edges of the Source Monitor window (**Figures 4.14a** and **b**).

a

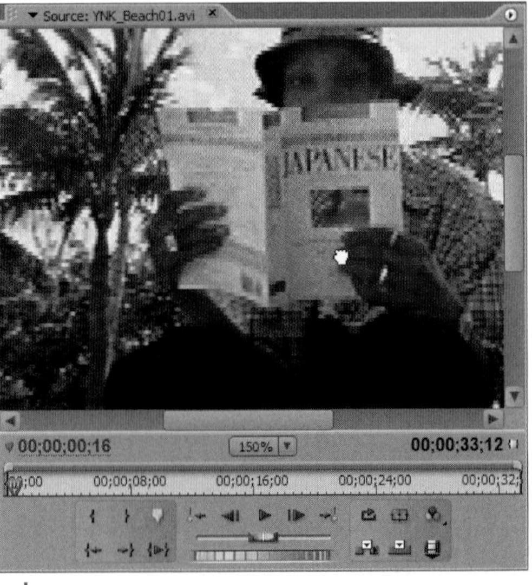

b

Figures 4.14a and b Two zoom states for the Source Monitor: Fit (a) always fits the image as large as possible into the current window size. If you are zoomed in close (b), you can use the Hand tool to drag the frame inside the view area to look at a different region of the image.

The Program Monitor

The Program Monitor is your television screen for the timeline's edited sequences. From the Program Monitor, you can make edits and adjustments to the open sequences, as well as preview or manipulate the creation of video effects. The Program Monitor has almost the same buttons and features as the Source Monitor; the difference is that the Program Monitor refers to sequences, not source material (**Figure 4.15**). For example, the In Point, Out Point, Markers, and Edits buttons are applied to whatever active sequence is open in the Program Monitor, not to individual clips. Because of the button similarities, this section will cover only those transport buttons unique to the Program Monitor.

Figure 4.15 The Program Monitor always displays an open sequence, enabling you to navigate through the sequence and to make adjustments to specific areas of your edit. Similar to the Source Monitor it contains a drop-down menu that allows you to open other sequences from your Timeline panel. Notice how the Timeline panel contains the same two sequences that the Program Monitor reveals from its drop-down menu.

When you are making an edit from the Source Monitor to the timeline and you are using the editing buttons, the position of the CTI or the In point in the Program Monitor is where your edit will be performed. These windows work hand in hand, so it's important to pay attention to what you are doing in both windows.

What You Can Open

In the Program Monitor you can open any and all sequences in your project—whether the sequence is open in the timeline or not. Double-clicking on a sequence from your Project panel activates it in the timeline, as well as activating it in the Program Monitor. Whatever sequence is active in the Timeline window will also be active in the Program Monitor and vice versa.

Monitor Layout

The panel for the Program Monitor has the same structure as the Source Monitor, but all the timecode data and information listed reflect the active sequence, as opposed to an active item of media. The CTI position reflects the location of the CTI within the boundaries of your sequence.

The tab area of the Program Monitor allows you to activate or close any open sequences. Because the Program Monitor is merely a monitor for sequences, activating a sequence opens it in the Timeline panel, thus allowing you to play back, edit, and manipulate it. To close a sequence from the Program Monitor, click the drop-down menu with the sequence active and choose Close. This does not delete the sequence; it just closes it from view. Closing a sequence in the Timeline panel also closes the associated listing in the Program Monitor.

Timecode and Time Navigation Controls

A sequence can have a total duration of 23 hours, 59 minutes, 59 seconds, and 29 frames, which is just enough time to use all the timecode values that exist. When you scrub within the Program Monitor's time ruler you will be scrubbing through whatever sequence is open in your Program Monitor. If you scrub in the timeline's time ruler, the CTI in your Program Monitor will update and scrub. The Program Monitor's timecode field always displays the current value that the CTI is on in the active sequence.

Zooming in and out with Program Monitor's viewing area bar enables you to zoom in the Program Monitor only and not in the sequence in the Timeline window. This is a nice feature as your view does not update in the timeline when you want to zoom in for greater detail in the Program Monitor. The same goes for moving the viewing area bar to work in a different area of the sequence. In each of these instances, when you scrub in the new view or different area, the CTI updates in both panels.

Buttons and Transport Controls

Although the Program Monitor has buttons that perform the same tasks as those in the Source Monitor, it also has a few different ones. For example, the first and last buttons of the center group's top row are unique to the Source Monitor:

- **Go to Previous Edit Point** (shortcut key: Page Up). Enables you to snap the CTI to the left to the nearest edit or cut point. An edit point is considered any clip end or cut from one clip to the next.
- **Go to Next Edit Point** (shortcut key: Page Down). Snaps the CTI position to the nearest edit point to the right of the current CTI position.

The right group has three buttons only available in the Program Monitor. You'll find them on the button row, starting from the left:

- **Lift** (shortcut key: ;). The opposite of Overlay. If you have determined an In and Out point instance in your sequence and you would like to remove the material from that position, click Lift. Lift removes the material from the In/Out instance and preserves the space it took up.
- **Extract** (shortcut key: '). The opposite of Insert. Determine an In/Out instance in your sequence and choose Extract to remove the material *and* the space that the material took up in your timeline. For example, if you choose a five-second section and click Extract, your overall sequence duration would be reduced by five seconds.
- **Trim** (shortcut keys: Ctrl+T). Opens the Trim panel, which is a Monitor panel used for viewing and adjusting edit points in the Timeline. You can also open the Trim panel from the Program Monitor's wing menu.

The Lift and Extract buttons are the basis for editing sequences in the Program Monitor.

Editing Functions

Used in conjunction with Insert and Overlay, Lift and Extract make up the powerful framework for performing complex edits with very simple keystrokes. As you work through the book, you will encounter these editing functions often. Be aware, however, that Program Monitor editing functions cannot be applied to every track of video at the same time. To lift or extract material you must first *target* the tracks that you wish to perform edits on, which is covered in depth Chapter 5, "The Timeline Panel." You can target only one video and audio track at time, or you can target just video or just audio.

When I am editing with the Program Monitor, I often use the Page Up and Page Down keys to navigate and snap to edit points in the timeline. From these edit points, I either move the clips physically or with keystrokes to modify and create my edit. If you have no In point or Out point selected in the Program Monitor, edits from the Source Monitor will be executed at the current position of the CTI.

Wing Menu Options

From the Program Monitor's wing menu (**Figure 4.16**), you can gang Source to Program, adjust your monitor output, set the display quality, toggle to audio units, and choose the view mode for your monitor. There are a few choices that deserve a closer look:

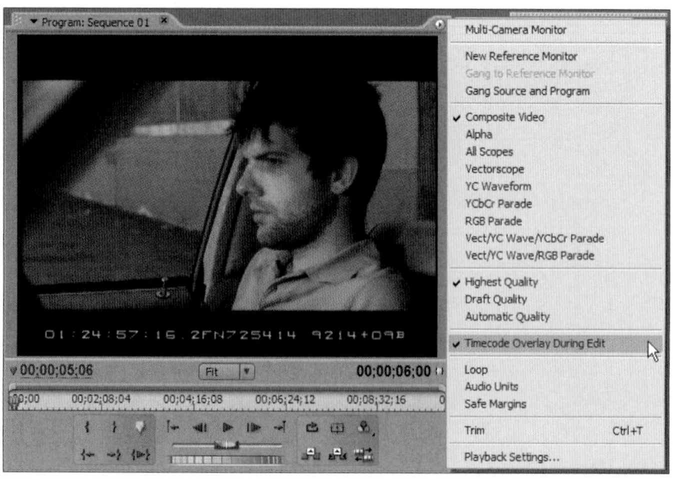

Figure 4.16 The Program Monitor's wing menu adds two new choices in 2.0—Multi-Camera Monitor and Timecode Overlay During Editing—to the familiar list.

- **Multi-Camera Monitor.** The Multi-Camera Monitor can be opened and docked into any pane in 2.0 and it is accessed through the wing menu of the Program Monitor. The Monitor and its powerful new features will be explored in great detail in Chapter 27, "Advanced Editing: The New Multi-Cam Workflow."
- **New Reference Monitor.** To create a New Reference Monitor, simply select this option from the wing menu. When you open a new Reference Monitor you are creating a duplicate Monitor window from which you can view the active sequence (**Figure 4.17**). By default with 2.0 a new Reference Monitor is ganged to the Program Monitor. To turn this off, uncheck the listing in the Program Monitor or Reference Monitor wing menu or click off the Gang button.

Figure 4.17 Opening a new Reference Monitor creates a new monitor that can reference whatever the active sequence was when the command was executed. Here you have Sequence 01 displayed in both the Program and Reference Monitor (which is docked into the same frame as the Source Monitor panel). This is useful for color correction: If you open the Reference Monitor and set the output mode to Waveform, you can simultaneously monitor the literal waveform value adjustments in the Reference Monitor and the image being adjusted in the Program Monitor.

- **Timecode Overlay During Edit.** While you are editing clips in the Timeline panel, it is often useful to see the source timecode of the clip you are trimming while you are adjusting it. If this wing menu option is checked (**Figure 4.18**) then a semi-transparent overlay of the currently edited clip's timecode will appear while you work with it. If the check mark is turned off, no overlay will appear. The timecode that appears corresponds directly to the Source Timecode for the frame you are referencing in your edit.

The Reference Monitor references only the active sequence when it is created. If you were to open another sequence or click on a different timeline, the Reference Monitor would not update to display the active sequence; it would continue to reference the sequence with which it was opened. (More on Reference Monitors in Chapter 22, "New Color Correction Tools: Fast Color Correction.")

Figure 4.18 With Timecode Overlay During Edit checked, anytime you trim or physically edit a clip in the timeline, the source timecode of the affected clip(s) is displayed on top of the clip in the Program Monitor. In the figure, I have extended the Out point of the clip by 1;08. The current frame of the clip that I have revealed through this edit has a precise timecode value of 00;00;10;10.

- **Playback Settings.** The Playback Settings option is your wing menu shortcut to Project > Project Settings > General > Editing Mode > Playback Settings (**Figure 4.19**). The Playback Settings dialog is where you can toggle on or off the communication between Premiere Pro and

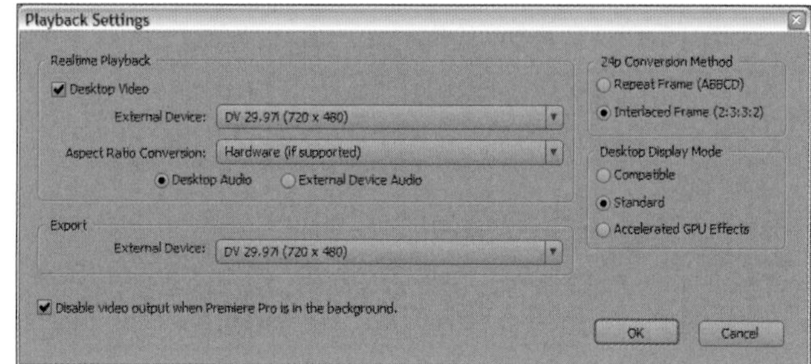

Figure 4.19 The Playback Settings dialog, which is accessible from the Program and Source Monitor wing menus, can help scale back the processing power needed to playback your video either by toggling on or off desktop display of your projects video or disabling Premiere Pro's communication with an external device (your connected DV device or video card). The dialog also offers settings for dealing with 24P playback and new settings for defining your Desktop Display mode.

your DV hardware for various playback circumstances. Additionally, you can define whether or not you want to accelerate desktop previewing and display by choosing to use your graphics card's GPU processor. If you have a robust graphics card, such as an NVidia GeForce card or an ATI X800, then you can set the Desktop Display setting to Accelerated GPU Effects. Otherwise, most users should leave the setting at Standard.

Although the Reference Monitor is primarily used in very specific instances (color correction and track matting), having quick access to your Playback Settings can be very helpful when trying to focus your real-time playback performance to desktop only or an external device only.

Effect Editing and the Program Monitor

The Program Monitor is also used in conjunction with the Effect Controls panel. While you are assigning and adjusting effects, the Program Monitor displays a preview of the effect. The relationship between the Program Monitor and Effect Controls panel will be explored in Chapter 8, "Effect Controls Basics."

Things to Remember

The easiest way to think about the Source and Program Monitors is that the Source Monitor views source material yet to be edited, and the Program Monitor views sequences and edited material. They both perform the same task of navigating through media; they just look to different places for media to view. The Source Monitor finds the clips and identifies the sections you want to add to your sequences. Picking the location to add the clips and then navigating through the edited sequence of clips is what the Program Monitor handles.

New features such as unique Sub-Clips and the ability to display a Timecode Overlay During Edit allow for less clutter and more precision when using these panels.

This chapter has focused on the specific features and functions of both Monitor panels, but you have yet to explore the workflow for editing. To establish a workflow, you need to understand one more piece: the Timeline panel. The next chapter will tackle that task, then Chapter 6, "The Editing Workflow," will unify these windows during a proper walk-through of the editing process.

CHAPTER

5

The Timeline Panel

The Timeline panel is where you will spend the most time in Adobe Premiere Pro. The Timeline panel is the interface in which you can see the physical representation of your video clips and edit them together. I like to think of the Timeline panel as a canvas or videotape, which slowly takes shape and definition as you work. For the original release of Premiere Pro, Adobe completely revamped not only the Timeline panel's design, but also its editing functionality (**Figure 5.1**). Perhaps the biggest advancement is support for multiple sequences.

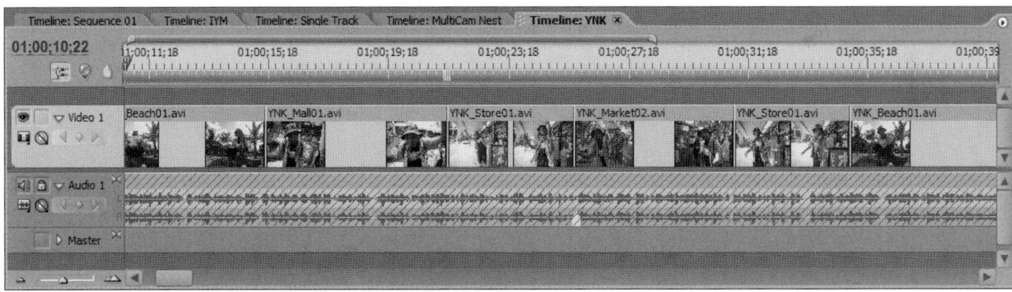

Figure 5.1 The Timeline panel in Premiere Pro supports a great editing workflow and a host of powerful features, such as multiple, nestable sequences and multi-cam editing.

Sequences and Layout

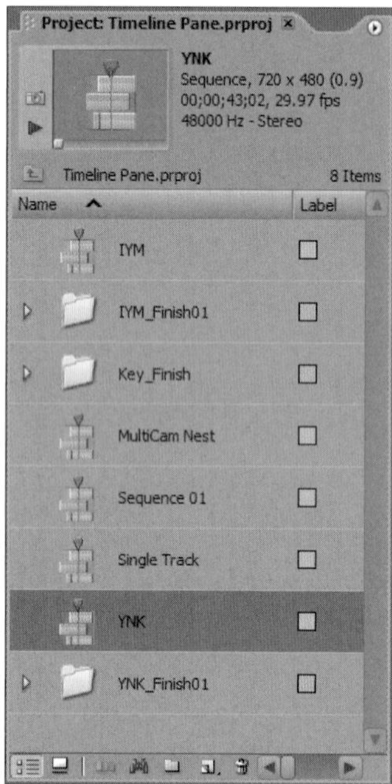

Figure 5.2 Notice that Figure 5.1's sequences have icons that reflect them in the Project panel. Double-clicking a sequence icon opens the sequence in the Timeline panel.

In previous versions of Premiere, your Project panel was tied directly to your Timeline panel—one project meant one timeline. In Premiere Pro, the Project and Timeline panels are still related, but now both can open and support multiple sequences (**Figure 5.2**).

To create a sequence, you select File > New Sequence or click on the Create Item > Sequence button in the Project panel. To open a sequence in the Timeline panel, you double-click on the icon from the Project panel. (Ctrl+double-click to open the sequence in the Source Monitor.) When opened, the sequences load into the Timeline panel, and each has a tab associated with it. The more sequences loaded, the more tabs visible in the Timeline panel. If the number of tabs exceeds the visible space in the panel, a slider bar appears at the top of the tab area enabling you to navigate to the other tabbed sequences.

By clicking on the tab for a loaded sequence, you bring it to the front of the view. Once a sequence is in view, you can edit and work inside of it. The active sequence in the Timeline panel also will be the active sequence viewed in the Program Monitor and viceversa. Although sequences may have varying numbers of total tracks, different track heights, and different master audio settings, the editing behavior of all sequences is the same.

If you click and drag a sequence out of the Timeline panel and into empty space in your layout, you will create a new Timeline panel with that sequence open inside it. As long as you have the screen real estate to display them, you can have multiple Timeline panels and multiple sequences open (**Figure 5.3**).

The Timeline panel's real estate can be broken down into four main parts (**Figure 5.4**):

- **Tab dock area.** Here you toggle between your loaded sequences.
- **Time navigation controls area.** Here you scrub the CTI, adjust the viewing area bar, get visual feedback for In

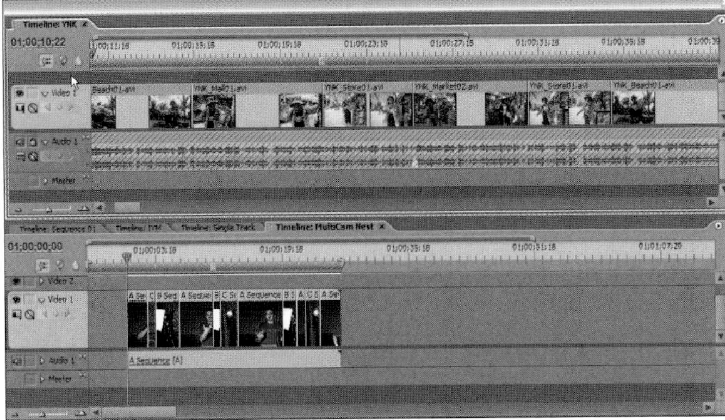

Figure 5.3 By grabbing a sequence from its tab, you can pull it from its current timeline. Holding down the Ctrl key, you can place it on top of your existing layout or just dock it into a pane as you would move any other panel, dropping it into the blank space of the panel where a new Timeline panel will be created, holding the sequence.

points, Out points, markers, and selections, as well as decide the size and area of the timeline you wish to view.

- **Track header area.** Here you can decide what each track displays and the mode it is in. This space contains all the details for each track that is displayed in the track content area.
- **Track content area.** Here audio and video tracks are displayed at the settings and parameters you dictate in the track header.

The tab dock area's function should be clear, but the other sections of the panel deserve a closer look.

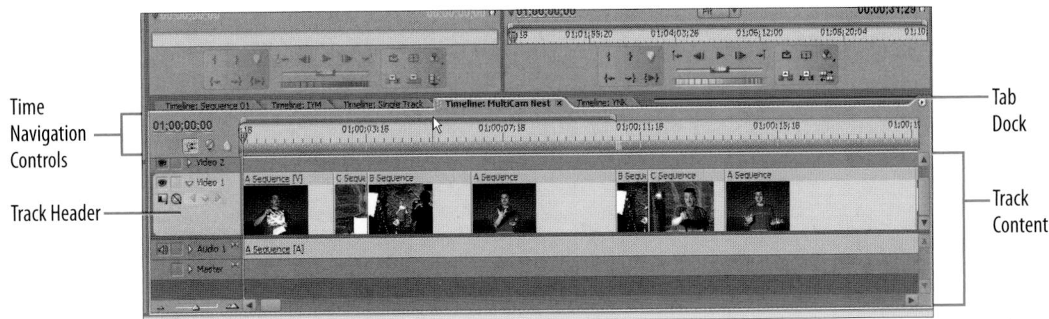

Figure 5.4 The Timeline panel is made up of four primary areas.

Time Navigation Controls Area

The time navigation controls area is at the top of the track content area portion of the Timeline panel (**Figure 5.5**). It is composed of the following:

- Viewing area bar
- Time ruler
- Work area and work area bar
- Timecode area

Start at the top with the viewing area bar.

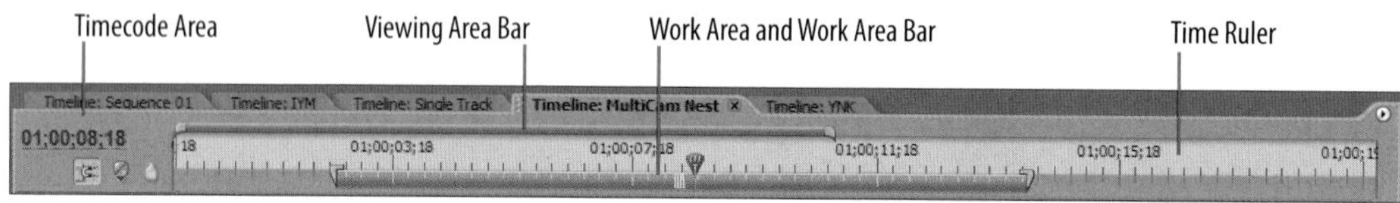

Figure 5.5 The time navigation controls area is made up of four components.

The Viewing Area Bar

The Timeline panel's viewing area bar functions the same as the one in the Monitor panels. By decreasing its size, you zoom in the timeline's view. Expand the bar to zoom out. If the CTI is within the visible area of the Timeline panel, adjusting the viewing area bar intelligently keeps the CTI centered within the panel. You can also drag the bar left or right to focus on a particular portion of the timeline.

The Time Ruler

The time ruler is the gray bar delineated by tick marks that represent the timecode values for the active sequence. Clicking and scrubbing in this area activates the CTI to update and play back the video underneath the area being scrubbed. The timecode values displayed on the time ruler increase or decrease, respectively, when you zoom in or out your current view. In the time ruler, In points and Out points are shown as a dark gray point between brackets. You can assign In and Out points here, as well as view them.

Work Area and Work Area Bar

The work area is the dark gray area at the bottom of the time ruler. Here the lighter colored work area bar and the markers are visible. To assign markers, press one of the marker buttons at the top of the track header area. In the timeline, a marker will be assigned to whatever frame the CTI is on.

The work area bar dictates the area you want to preview, play, or export in the timeline. The work area bar helps you define smaller areas to preview and export as you can either export the entire sequence or just the work area.

Below the work area, you may see either a red or green line. The color tells you whether or not rendering preview files is necessary or completed (**Figures 5.6a** and **b**). When you work in the timeline and apply an effect to a clip, a red bar displays above that clip signifying that its data must be reprocessed and preview files need to be created in order to properly play the clip back with the effect. Using the work area bar, you define the areas over which you want preview files created. If you set the work area bar above the clip and press Enter, Premiere will render preview files for the clip. Once you create the preview file, the red bar turns green.

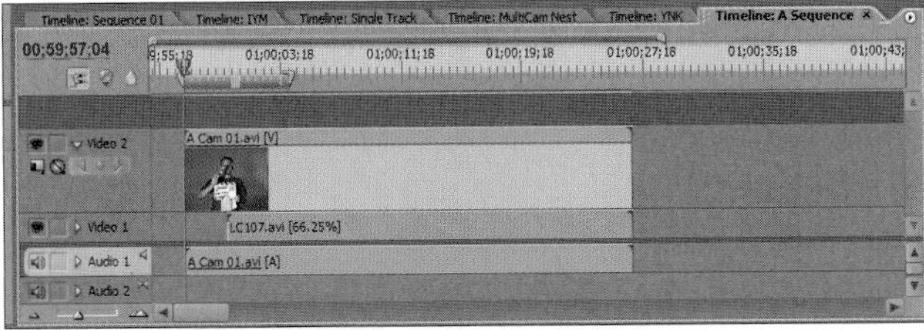

a

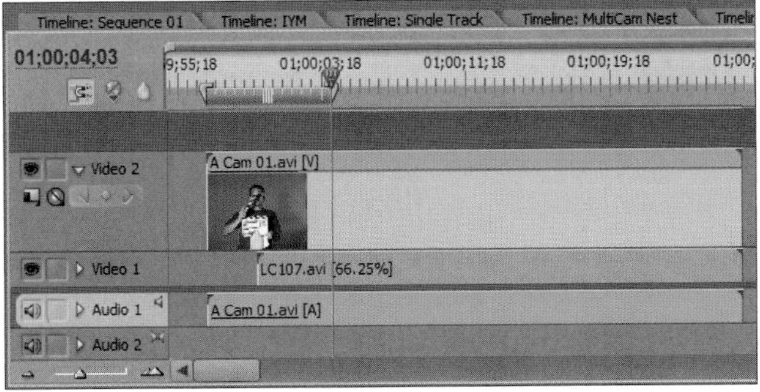

b

Figures 5.6a and b When you apply an effect to a clip, a purple line appears on it as an indicator (a). Above the track content area and below the work area bar, the red bar specifies that this clip needs rendering to play back at full resolution. When you press Enter, Premiere creates preview files for only the portion of the clip that is covered by the work area bar (b).

The important thing to remember is that the work area bar allows you to define specific areas to export or for which to build preview files.

In the 2.0 Edit > Preferences > General dialog box, you'll find a brand new check box that relates to the work area. To play back only the work area after building preview files, check the Play Work Area After Rendering Previews check box (**Figure 5.7**). In former versions of Premiere Pro if your work area defined a portion of your timeline, say in the middle of a 20-minute sequence, Premiere Pro would render the necessary preview files and then play back your timeline from the beginning of the entire sequence. With the new check box turned on, you can concentrate on just the area you're adjusting.

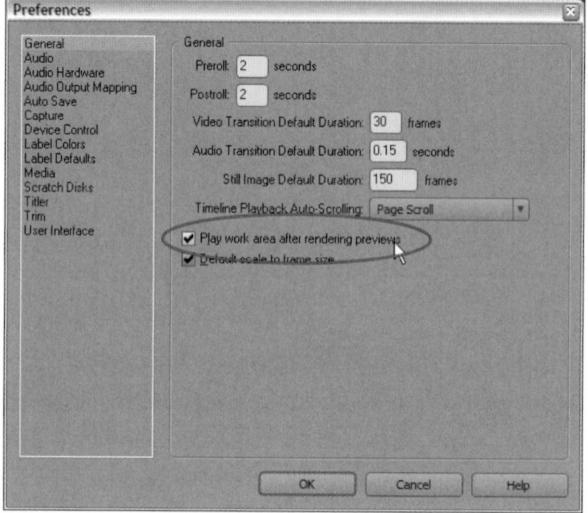

Figure 5.7 This is one of those check boxes that I recommend leaving checked. It's a head scratcher to find a scenario where you would want to have this turned off. It's just as easy to expand your work area bar to cover your sequence as it is to open the Preference and uncheck the box.

Timecode Area

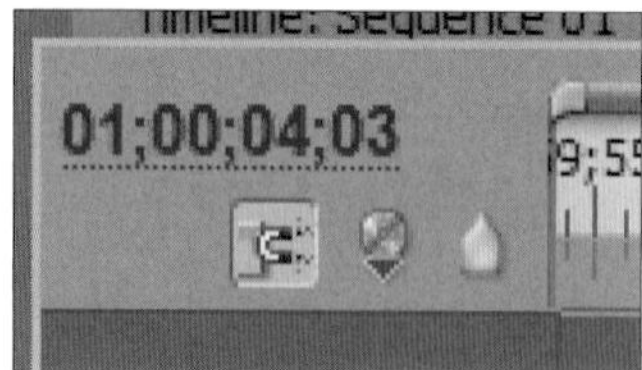

Figure 5.8 The Timecode area houses the timecode display (in blue), the Snapping button (left), the Set DVD Marker, and Set Unnumbered Marker buttons (right).

Next to the work area reside three important controls (**Figure 5.8**):

- **Timecode display.** Shows the timecode number that corresponds to the position of the CTI in the timeline. Click in this hot text field, type a timecode value, and press Enter to snap to that position. If you type +5 and then press Enter, you will advance five frames to the right of your current CTI position. Typing a negative number moves you back the specified number of frames. You can use the hot text box to scrub through the timeline as well.

- **Snapping button.** Toggles Snapping mode on and off. When Snapping is on (the default) and you move a clip in the timeline, the clip jumps to align to the nearest clip edge or marker. This is very helpful when you don't want any gaps or blank spaces created when you add clips to the timeline. Turning Snapping off enables you to drag and drop clips without them automatically moving to any edges. Snapping to an edge usually occurs when the clip being dragged is within about ten pixels of another clip edge or marker. If you are trying to make minor adjustment to the position of a clip that is within the snapping range, you will want to turn off Snapping and then make the move.
- **Set DVD Marker.** New for 2.0, this button adds one of three different DVD markers for creating custom DVD menu elements. Clicking this button opens a dialog that allows you to define the type of marker that gets assigned to the current CTI position (**Figure 5.9**).

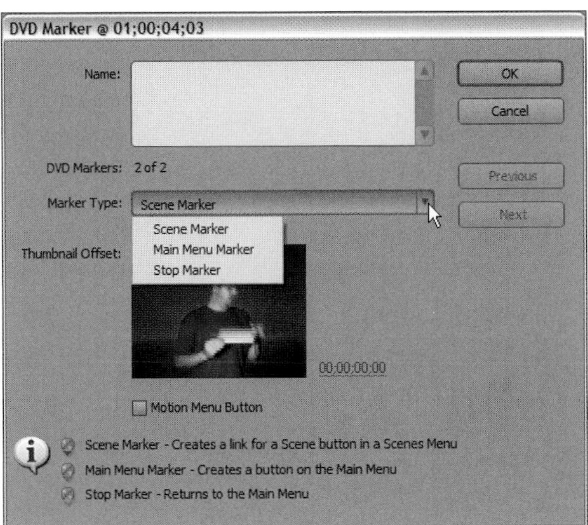

Figure 5.9 New for Premiere Pro 2.0 is the ability to assign custom DVD menu markers to specific points in your edited sequences.

- **Add Marker button.** Adds a marker at the current position of the CTI. Double-clicking on a marker icon in the work area reveals the Marker dialog box, in which you can update a number of related fields with information regarding the marker (**Figure 5.10**).

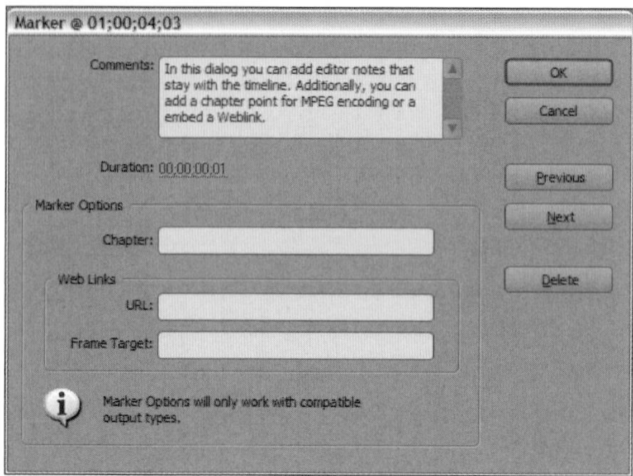

Figure 5.10 Double-click on a marker in the timeline to access the Marker dialog. Here you can add comments, assign duration, add chapter marks, and add web links to the selected marker.

You'll learn more about markers and Snapping mode in several lessons later in the book, as they are very helpful with lining up shots and arranging your edits with precision. There is also plenty more to explore and learn about building your own custom DVD menus, as you'll see in Chapter 11, "DVD Basics."

Track Header Area

At the left of the Timeline panel, the track header area is where you toggle settings, display modes, and viewing modes for your tracks. Although you can drag and resize the panel as much as you like, the track header area cannot be made smaller than its default size.

Each track in the timeline has its own header with the track's name and track-related controls. You can rename a track by right-clicking anywhere in its header box and choosing Rename. Track headers come in two sizes: collapsed and expanded. You toggle between the two using the triangular icon next to the track's name. In their collapsed state (triangular icon points right), all track headers include an Output button and a Track Lock button. Audio tracks also have one extra icon, because mono, stereo, and 5.1 tracks look exactly the same. To tell the number of channels an audio track has, look for the icon of one

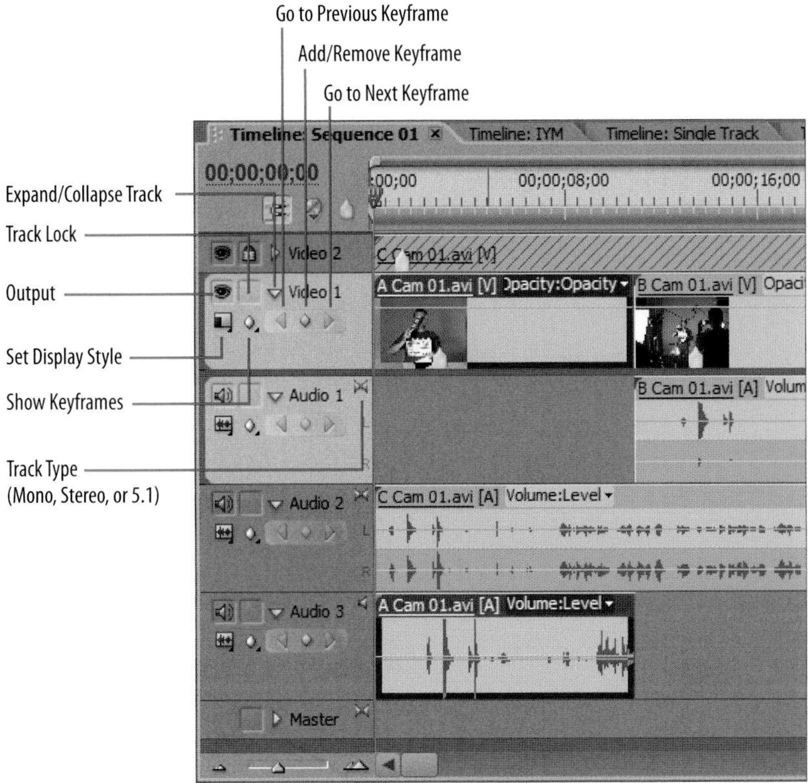

Figure 5.11 In the track header, you can you view and assign many different features to the content of the tracks. The Video 2 is collapsed and locked, for example. Video 1 is targeted (light gray) and expanded. Audio 1 is an expanded stereo track that is targeted. Audio 2 is also expanded, and Audio 3 is an expanded mono track. The Master track is collapsed and set to stereo.

speaker (mono), two speakers (stereo), or 5.1 (5.1) in the track header's top-right corner (**Figure 5.11**).

Click the triangular icon to expand, or *twirl down*, an audio or video track header (the icon now points down), and you gain several more button controls: Display Style, Show Keyframes, Next Keyframe, and Previous Keyframe. Take a closer look.

Output Button

For both audio and video tracks, the Output button turns the track's output functions on and off. If there is an eye (for video) or speaker (for audio) shown in this box, then Output is turned on. If the box is empty, then the track will not be seen or heard when you play the sequence.

For example, you might toggle off output for a music track, while you edit other audio tracks, instead of trying to decipher them while the music is playing.

Track Lock

Clicking the Track Lock icon toggles the locking feature, which prohibits changes to the track. If you lock a track, hash marks appear within the boundaries of the track in the track content area. When the hash marks are visible, you are unable to click, select, or drag any media on to or off of the locked track. Locked tracks can be output with the rest of the sequence, however. To unlock a track, simply click the button again.

Locking is very helpful when you have placed items that you do not want to move, such as titles, music, or audio effects. Lock the track, and no matter what edits are made on other tracks, all your media will remain in the same place.

Display Style

Expanding a track gives you much more room to look at the track's contents. It also gives you additional controls, such as the Display Style icon, which lets you customize the track's look. Each video clip that is added to the timeline has associated with it frames that are played back in the Program Monitor. If you would like to get a sample of those frames within the boundaries of the clip in the track content area, click Set Display Style then choose: Show Head and Tail, Show Head Only, Show Frames, or Show Name Only. Most pro editors typically display the name only. When you are first learning Premiere Pro, however, Show Head and Tail is best, because it shows you the first frame and also the last frame of each clip. If you are zoomed into the timeline enough, the name of the clip will show between the first and last frame.

If you set your display to Show Frames, zooming and navigating in your timeline may take a bit longer. The delay results from small preview frames being loaded into each view. These are needed to display all frames properly. Loading the frame is not instantaneous. Having additional RAM will help speed up this process, because the frames will be loaded into the RAM and accessed much quicker.

For audio tracks, Display Styles offers two choices: Show Waveform, which displays a graphic representation of your audio file, and Show Name Only.

Show Keyframes

In Premiere Pro, you can modify and add effect keyframes within the boundaries of a clip in the Timeline panel. Say you want to zoom in on a video clip from your normal view, 100%, to 150%. To do this properly, you use the Motion tool, scale from 100% to 150%, and assign 100% and 150% values to certain frames (called *keyframes*) of the clip so that Premiere can calculate the difference between them. The result will be a dynamic zoom into your video clip, the speed of the zoom will be dictated by the time between the specified keyframes. The longer the time, the slower the zoom, and the shorter, the faster.

To add and adjust keyframes, you need to be in the display mode to view them. By default Premiere Pro 2.0 has Show Keyframes > Opacity as the default Video Track keyframe mode. This way if you want to fade a shot in or out, the value for you to adjust is right in from of you.

To explore the other keyframe options, click the Show Keyframes icon, then choose the mode you want.

Video Keyframes

For video tracks, the Show Keyframes icon offers three choices: Show Keyframes, Show Opacity Handles, or Hide Keyframes.

Show Keyframes enables you to see the keyframes associated with each clip in the timeline. It also gives you access to a drop-down keyframes menu in the body of a clip (**Figure 5.12**). With it, you can switch between the various keyframes of a single clip.

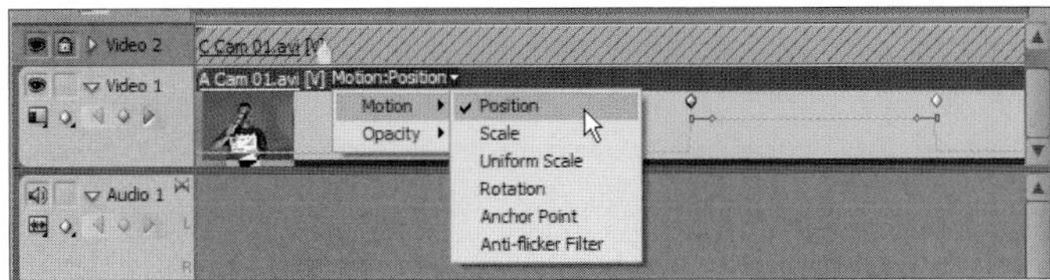

Figure 5.12 Having assigned position keyframes in the Motion effect for this selected clip, you can access and adjust those keyframes in the track area by putting the track in Keyframe Display mode then choosing Motion > Position. If you are zoomed in and cannot see the Effect drop-down menu, right-click on the clip with the keyframed effect. Remember that to view effect keyframes, you must first set the track to Show Keyframes in the track header.

Every video track has an Opacity value that is the transparency associated with the clip (**Figure 5.13**). A setting of 100% Opacity means that the file is completely visible with no transparency. A setting of 50% Opacity is half visibility. You can adjust the clip's opacity in either its default keyframe display mode or by switching your display to Show Opacity Handles. Because 2.0 has its new default display mode, the Show Opacity Handles mode is redundant.

Figure 5.13 In Premiere Pro 2.0, by default, your track display shows Keyframes:Opacity. Opacity is represented by a yellow line that defines the Opacity value for each clip in the track. At the top of the clip, the line indicates 100% opacity. At the bottom, it indicates 0% opacity or complete transparency. To adjust Opacity, press the P key to access the Pen tool and drag the line up or down. The ramp in this clip shows a fade up of opacity.

Hide Keyframes displays only the clip name and associated display style.

Audio

For audio tracks, Show Keyframe offers more options, because with these you can display two different keyframe properties: clip or track. Your choices are:

- Show Clip Keyframes
- Show Track Keyframes
- Show Clip Volume
- Show Track Volume
- Hide Keyframes

Premiere Pro supports both clip-based and track-based audio effects. Clip-based effects can be assigned to unique clip instances in the timeline. Track-based effects can be assigned to an entire track. A track-based effect affects all the media in the track in which it is assigned. Show Clip Keyframes displays the keyframes assigned for clip-based effects. Show Track Keyframes displays keyframes assigned for track-based effects (**Figure 5.14**).

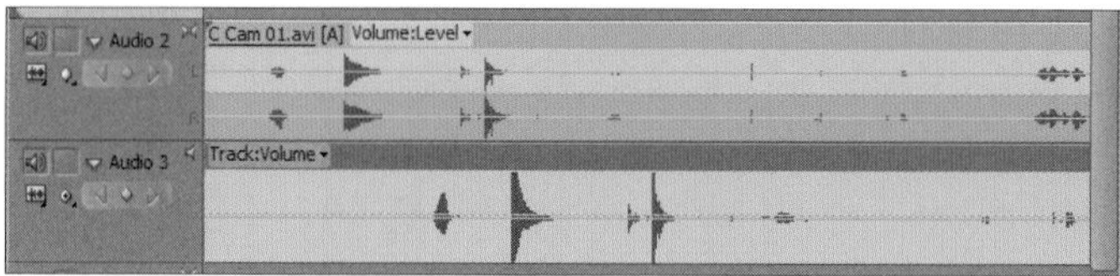

Figure 5.14 Audio 2 is set to display clip keyframes, and you can see the drop-down effect menu visible within the boundary of the clip. Audio 3 is set to display track keyframes, so the top of Audio 3's track content area is gray and its icon for the Show Keyframes mode has a small dot in the center of the keyframe.

Volume is the audio equivalent of video's opacity setting. With audio, if the volume is turned off, then you won't hear any sound; if a video track's opacity is zero, then you won't see any image. To remain consistent with 2.0's new display mode, the default display for all audio tracks is Show Clip Keyframes > Volume. With this setting, if you want to turn a clip's volume up or down, the controls are right there in the track waiting for you to adjust them.

Toggling between Show Clip Volume and Show Track Volume displays the assigned values of either individual clips or the overall tracks. Each of these parameters will be explored in later lessons. For now, just remember that individual audio clips have their own volume adjustments and effect settings. Plus, each individual track can have its own volume adjustments and effect settings. It is usually wise to first assign the clip adjustments, then make track adjustments when necessary.

Keyframe Navigation

While in a keyframe display mode, you can navigate through the assigned keyframes, using the Go To Previous and Go To Next Keyframe buttons. Go To Previous Keyframe moves the CTI backward one keyframe, and Go To Next Keyframe moves it forward one.

In the middle of the left-and right-pointing navigation buttons is the Add/Remove Keyframe button. To delete a keyframe, position the CTI's red Edit Line on it, then click the Add/Remove Keyframe button. If there is no keyframe under the Edit Line and you click the Add/Remove Keyframe button, Premiere adds a keyframe at that spot.

To navigate between clip keyframes, you must have a clip selected and have the CTI within the boundaries of the clip to go to the next or previous keyframe. This is not an issue when displaying track-based keyframes; the track keyframe area is for the entire track, not just one clip instance.

The red line that extends into the track content area from the CTI in the time ruler is commonly referred to as the Edit Line, because edit functions will occur at its position. When working in the timeline, keep in mind that the terms "CTI" and "Edit Line" are often used interchangeably.

Track Header Extras

Besides housing the control icons, the track header area has a few other important functions.

Targeting Tracks

When you are using the edit commands in the Source or Program Monitor, you must dictate which tracks the edits should be performed on. You must *target* the tracks. To target a track, click in any spot in the header that is not a

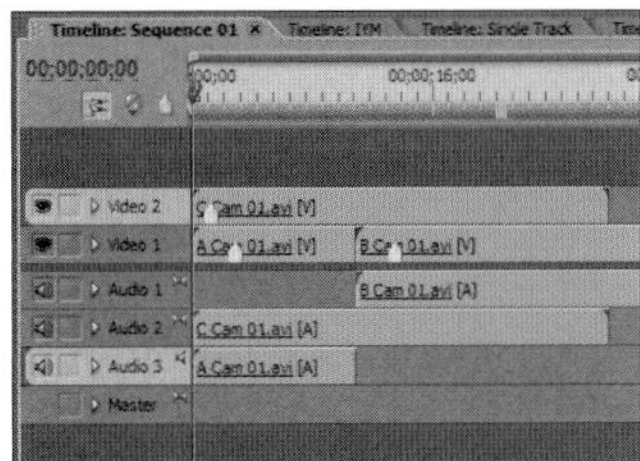

Figure 5.15 Video 2 and Audio 3 are the targeted tracks. Notice the light gray color and the dark gray bracket that is on the left edge of the track header. Targeting tracks is necessary for assigning edits with the Monitor panels and applying default transitions.

Figure 5.16 The Add Tracks dialog allows you to add video, audio, and audio submix tracks. You also can specify the position of the new tracks.

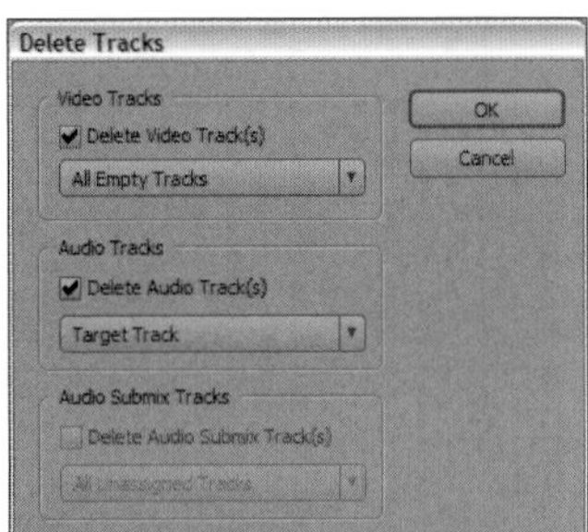

Figure 5.17 The Delete Tracks dialog lets you delete all of the separate track types in one dialog. You can either delete empty tracks or specific targeted tracks.

box, button, or text field. Alternately, you can use keyboard shortcuts to target tracks:

- **Target Next Video Track Above:** Ctrl+plus sign (+)
- **Target Next Video Track Below:** Ctrl+hyphen (-)
- **Target Audio Above:** Ctrl+Shift+plus sign (+)
- **Target Audio Below:** Ctrl+Shift+hyphen (-)

A targeted track has a dark gray bracket on its left side and is a bit brighter in color than the others listed (**Figure 5.15**). Locked tracks cannot be targeted.

In certain instances you will want to target audio only or video only. To turn targeting of a track off, click again within the boundaries of a targeted track.

Adding and Deleting Tracks

To create new tracks or delete existing tracks from your sequence, right-click within the track header area and choose the Add Tracks or Delete Tracks from the context menu.

Choosing Add Tracks from the context menu (or choosing Sequence > Add Tracks from the main menu bar) brings up the Add Tracks dialog. Here, you can specify whether to add video, audio, or audio submix tracks. You can specify the audio track type (mono, stereo, or 5.1), as well as its newly created placement in relation to the other tracks: before the first track, after the target track, or after the last track (**Figure 5.16**).

When you choose Delete Tracks from the context or sequence menu, you get the Delete Tracks dialog, which presents the same three track types, just with slightly different criteria (**Figure 5.17**). After you select the track type, you can choose to delete the target video track, all empty audio or video tracks, or all unassigned audio submix tracks.

For example, if you wanted to get rid of an extra empty video track, you could delete it by targeting it, choosing Sequences > Delete Tracks, checking Delete Video Track(s), and selecting Target Track from the list box.

To clean up a project once you are finished working in it, you can check Delete Video Track(s) and Delete Audio Track(s) in the Delete Tracks dialog, choosing All Empty Tracks from both drop-down menus.

You can create new tracks by dragging and dropping a clip to the gray area (the pasteboard) just above the last video or audio tracks. Drag and drop a video clip to the pasteboard above the video tracks to create a new video track, or drag and drop an audio-only clip to the pasteboard just below the last audio track to create a new audio track.

Resizing Tracks

To customize your Timeline panel, you can change the height of individual tracks. To adjust a video track, expand the track, position the pointer over the top edge of the track's header (the pointer transforms into the track height adjustment tool), then click and drag. For an audio track, click and drag the bottom. Once you find the right height, it will persist whenever you expanded the track. All tracks have the same collapsed size, but once they are expanded, every track can be its own unique size.

If you hold the Shift key down while making an adjustment to an expanded track's size, you automatically increase or decrease the size of all expanded tracks of the same type (**Figures 5.18a** and **b**). If you adjust an expanded video track, for example, only other expanded video tracks are affected. You would have to adjust the audio tracks separately. Collapsed tracks are not affected, either.

a

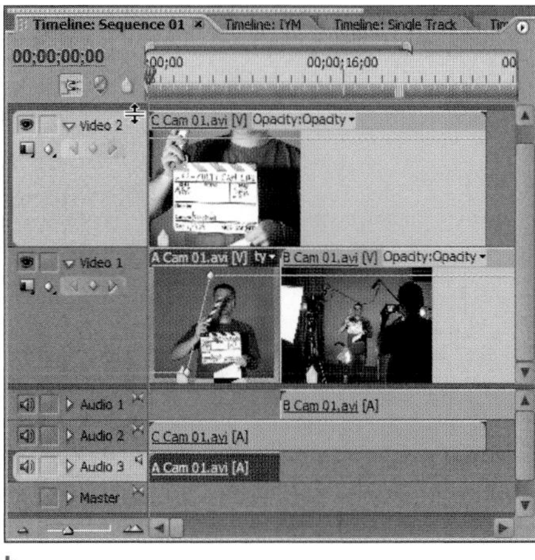

b

Figures 5.18a and b When you grab the outer edge of a track, the small track size adjustment tool appears (a). If you hold down the Shift key and increase the track's size, all expanded tracks of that type increase (b).

Adjusting Your Timeline Track View

If you want your Timeline panel to emphasize audio tracks more than video tracks, you can click and drag the center line in the track header. The thick center line separates the audio and video tracks; clicking and dragging it automatically adjusts the balance between the displayed audio and video tracks.

Track Content Area

To the right of the track headers is the track content area, where all your editing work gets done. As you remember, the track header area determines how the track content area looks and what tracks are targeted for editing. Your video tracks are above the center gray line, and the audio tracks are below.

At the right edge of the timeline are two scroll bars—one for video and another for audio—so you can scroll your video and audio tracks separately. Below the tracks, the horizontal scroll bar helps you navigate to different points in your sequence (**Figure 5.19**).

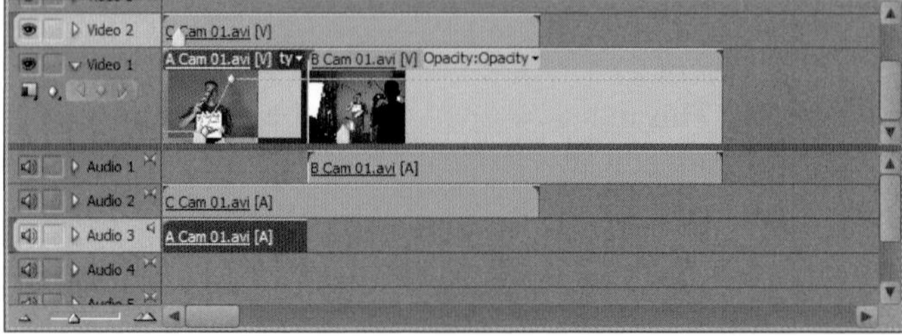

Figure 5.19 The track content area is surrounded by the horizontal scroll bar on the bottom, the vertical track scroll bars on the right, and the zoom controls just below the track header.

To zoom in or out of your tracks, use the zoom controls in the lower-left corner of the Timeline panel. Clicking on the small mountains zooms out, while clicking on the big mountains zooms in. Dragging the slider in the direction of either mountain achieves the same result. Pressing the + or – key also zooms in and out, respectively. Every zoom keystroke updates the feedback of the zoom view as well.

Now it's time to move into the primary content area of the Timeline panel. The best place to start is with the behavior of video tracks.

Figure 5.20 You can display your tracks in four different views. Video 1 displays the clip's name only. Video 2 displays frames. Video 3 is set to Head Only and its keyframes are set to Motion:Scale. Video 4 has Show Head and Tail. All three tracks except Video 3 are displaying the default Keyframes:Opacity video.

Video Tracks

Your track view, display style, and keyframe viewing mode dictate what is seen in each video track. **Figure 5.20** shows the results of different view settings.

All video tracks have the same video properties with unique adjustable opacity and motion settings, which was not the case in previous versions of Premiere.

You can have unlimited video tracks in a sequence and the hierarchy of what's visible goes from the top of the stack down. This means that although the Video 1 track is your primary editing track, if you place a clip above Video 1 on the Video 2 track 2, it will cover the content on Video 1. Titles will go on Video 2, and the edited clips will be beneath the titles on Video 1. If you stack clips and wish to expose what's beneath, reduce the opacity of the top clips to reveal the lower ones. In Figure 5.20, only Video 4 is visible in the stack, because they are all on top of each other. If you were to reduce the opacity of Video 4, you would start to see Video 3 beneath it.

Another new track feature in Premiere Pro is the ability to add transitions to every track of audio and video. If you want to fade in a title on Video 2, you would place a one-sided cross dissolve transition on the head of the title. Because black is the blank space color of the timeline, if there is nothing beneath the title on Video 1, the title would fade

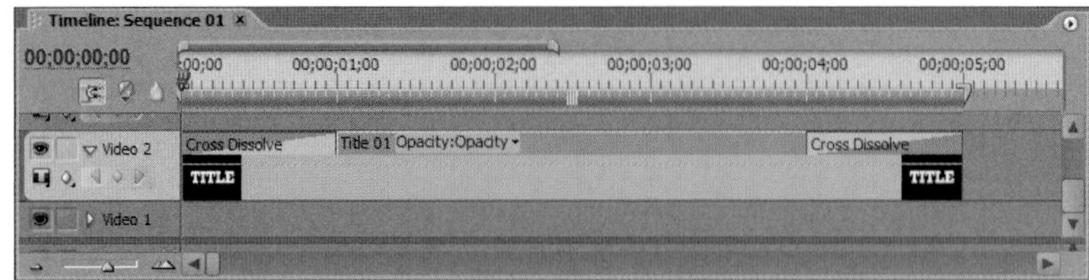

Figure 5.21 The title on Video 2 has two transitions: one at its head and one at its tail. With nothing beneath the title, the sequence will transition from black to the title then back to black at the end.

up from black (**Figure 5.21**). If there is a clip of media beneath the title, the title will fade up on top of the media.

The look of a track in the content area can tell you a lot. The next sections examine a number of indicators found in the content area.

Locked Tracks

Locked tracks have a hash mark indicator throughout the entire track (**Figure 5.22**). No media can be moved, selected, or added to a locked track.

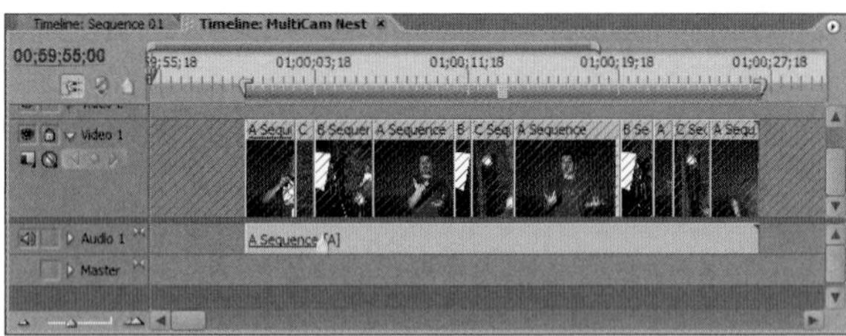

Figure 5.22 Video 1 is locked. You cannot apply edits to it, target it, or select or move clips in it.

Out of Sync

If the audio portion of an audio and video clip becomes shifted out of sync with the video portion (or viceversa), a red indicator box appears in the corner of the clip (**Figure 5.23**). The indicator box tells you how many seconds and frames out of sync the media is.

Figure 5.23 The red indicator for the linked audio and video states that the clips are out of sync.

Right-click in the box to reveal two options: Move Into Sync and Slip Into Sync (**Figures 5.24a** through **d**). Moving into sync physically moves the clip back to the position where the media was originally. Slip into Sync attempts to shift the media. Although the media will be offset physically still, Premiere updates the material in the audio and video so that it is back in sync but separated.

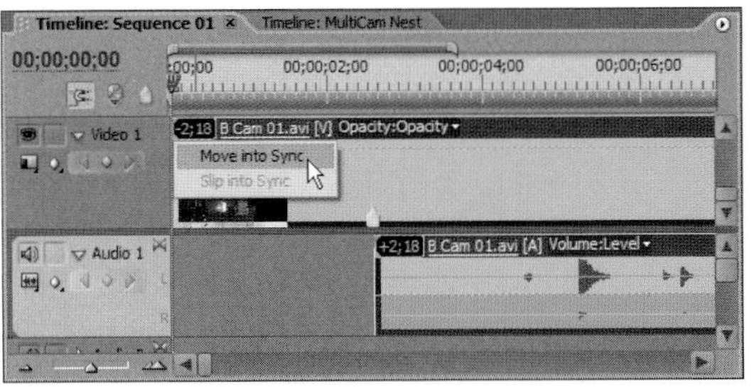

a

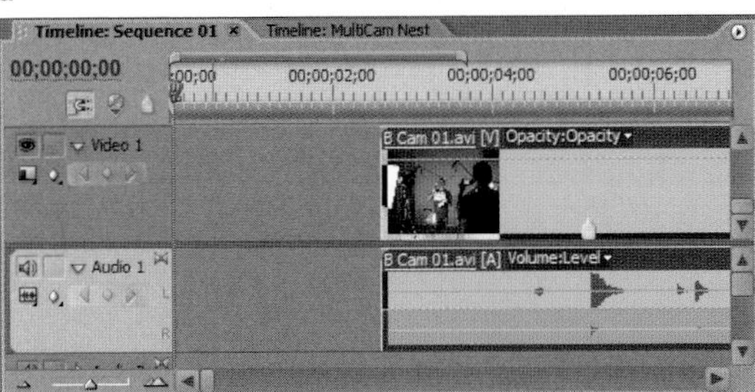

b

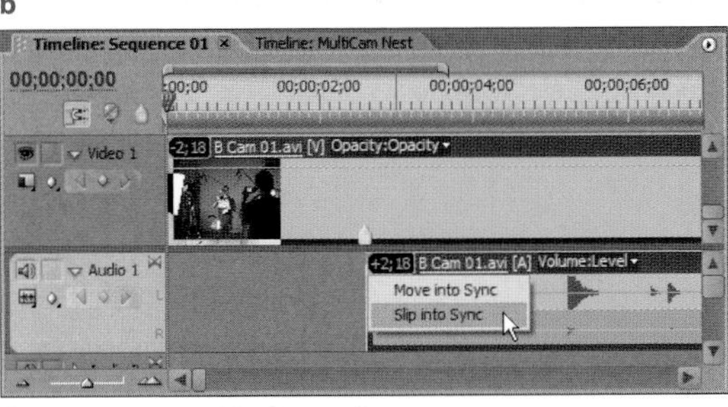

c

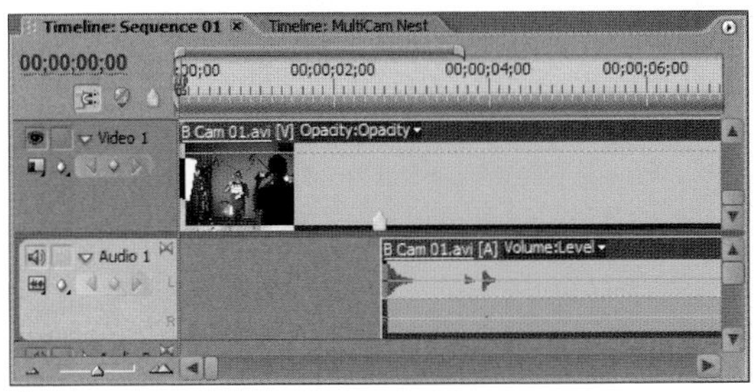

d

Figures 5.24a through d If you choose Move Into Sync, Premiere slides the media over to realign it and get back into sync (a and b). Choosing Slip Into Sync preserves the timeline postion by slipping the source material in the clip into sync (c and d). To perform a slip edit, you must have additional head and/or tail clip material than what has been edited with the clip into the timeline.

When you capture a clip with both audio and video from your DV device, the clip plays back in the Source Monitor with both audio and video synchronously. When you drag an instance of the clip into the timeline using both the audio and video, the audio and video are "linked" together so that the audio is in sync with the video. You easily can find linked audio and video clips because the color of both clips is the same. If either the audio or video portion of the clip changes independently, then an icon displays revealing their sync status.

Clip Effect Keyframes

If you expand a track and turn on keyframe viewing, all clips will have a little drop-down Effects menu within the body of the clip. The drop-down menu displays the name of the selected effect parameter. This drop-down menu lets you toggle between the different effects and their parameters, so that you can decide which keyframes you want to view.

Because you can have multiple effects assigned to one clip, you navigate between the effects and their keyframable parameters from this menu.

All clips that have additional effects applied to them will have a purple line beneath the name area.

Clip Markers

Clip markers appear as upward arrows in the boundary of a clip when a track is expanded. When you are dragging clips in the Timeline panel, clip markers will be identified as an edge that can be snapped to. This is very helpful when you are building your edit, as you can place markers in the exact positions where you want media added. When you add your media with Snapping on, you can place the media exactly where you initially determined.

You cannot double-click on clip markers in the timeline to assign marker settings; only timeline markers can have assigned comments, chapter numbers, and so on.

Media Boundaries

When you open a clip in the Source Monitor, it can have up to four defined parameters: Media In and Media Out, which are the first and last frames of the media, as well as Video In and Video Out, which correspond to assigned In and Out points. Sometimes your Media In and Video In will be the same value, because you started capturing at exactly the first frame you wanted to use in your edit.

In the track content area, a clip that begins at its Media In has a darkened upper-left edge. A clip that ends at its Media Out has a darkened upper-right edge (**Figure 5.25**). These darkened edges are known as *dog ears*. The dog ears mean that you cannot extend or drag left or right to reveal more material from the clip because more material does not exist.

Figure 5.25 As the dog ears on the clip's head and tail indicate, this timeline clip instance is using the entire duration of the master clip it references.

Audio Tracks

Audio tracks can be one of three different types: mono, stereo, and 5.1 surround. You can place audio files into a track with matching settings only. In other words, place only stereo clips in stereo tracks, mono in mono tracks, and 5.1 in 5.1 tracks. If you drop a mono clip into a project with only stereo tracks, you must drag it to the gray pasteboard area at the bottom of the panel; Premiere will create a new mono track.

In regards to viewing audio track content, where video tracks display icons of video frames, audio tracks display the waveform values of the audio in the track.

Audio Display Modes

Audio tracks display the corresponding channel information of the clips they contain. Mono tracks reveal single-channel waveform files, stereo tracks show dual-channel files, and 5.1 surround has six-channel files. Because stereo and 5.1 require a lot of space to display their waveform information, you will often find yourself expanding these tracks and shifting the timeline view emphasis to focus more on audio (**Figure 5.26**). You can accommodate this workflow quickly by creating a Workspace layout that moves your panels accordingly. Waveforms will either be on or off for your audio track.

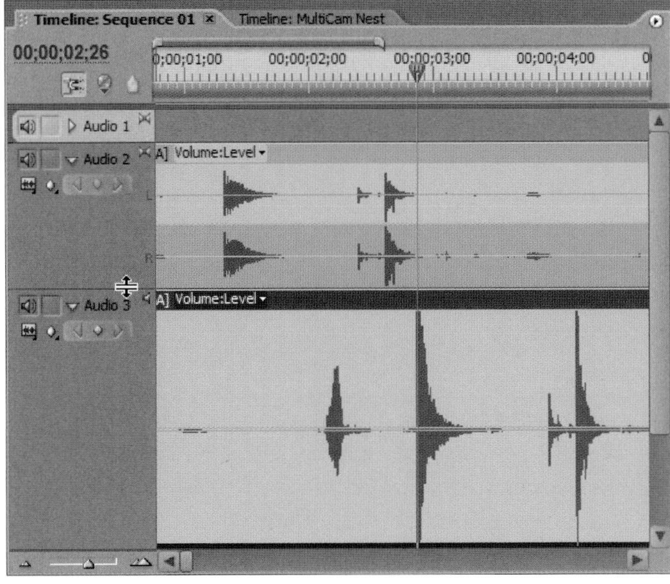

Figure 5.26 Just because audio tracks have only two display modes (waveforms on and off) doesn't mean that they can't be resized independently! It is far more appropriate to increase your audio track sizes and zoom in on each to get as much detail as possible from your waveform image.

Audio: Clip Versus Track

With audio tracks, you have the ability to look at clip effects and keyframes at either the clip level or the track level. Selecting Clip reveals the same drop-down effects menu as it does with video. Selecting track-based keyframes reveals a thick gray bar at the top of the track with a drop-down effect menu listing the parameters. The drop-down menu resides at the head of the track so you must navigate back to the beginning to define the parameter that you wish to view or adjust.

Audio Volume

The volume setting will be a thin orange wire that sits somewhere around the middle of your waveform. The wire sits in the middle because that is where the 0dB setting is. Raising the wire increases the volume, and lowering it reduces the volume (**Figure 5.27**). (More on editing and adjustable audio parameters in Section III, "Advanced Audio Techniques.")

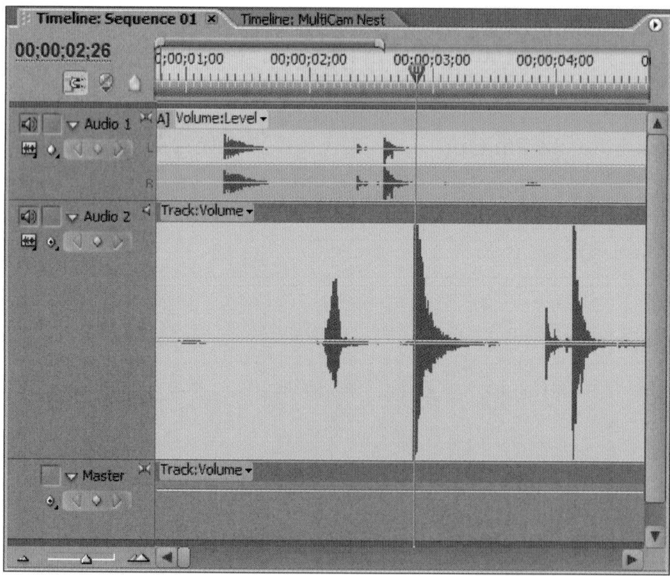

Figure 5.27 Audio 1 displays the clip volume; Audio 2 displays track volume. Because clip content cannot be added to the Master track, it also reveals an orange track volume wire.

Master Track

The audio Master track is not a track into which clips can be placed. The Master track is strictly for raising, lowering, or adding effects to the master mix down of your audio tracks (**Figure 5.28**).

Figure 5.28 Because the Master track is track based, you can choose between viewing the track volume and the track (effect) keyframes.

Because transitions can be applied to all tracks of audio and video, you should use the audio cross fade transitions to fade your audio up and down. Instead of fiddling with volume keyframes, just drop the transition on the beginning or end of the clip and adjust its duration.

If you expand the Master track, you will notice that it only allows you to display track-based keyframe parameters. Think of all your audio tracks as being funneled into the Master track that then turns things up, turns them down, and adds a reverb or any other effect. The final mix of your audio will pass through your Master track, which can always be monitored by looking at the levels in the VU Meters of the Audio Mixer panel.

No matter what type of tracks your sequence contains—mono, stereo, or 5.1 surround—it will always be mixed down and played back in whatever channel type the Master track is set to.

Wing Menu

The Timeline panel's wing menu contains two important settings:

- **Audio Units.** Changes the counter setting from video frames to audio units. This feature functions the same as it does in the Monitor panels, allowing greater zooming power and more detail from the audio files in the timeline. To remove clicks and pops or to make sure you are editing at the right spot, switch to Audio Units,

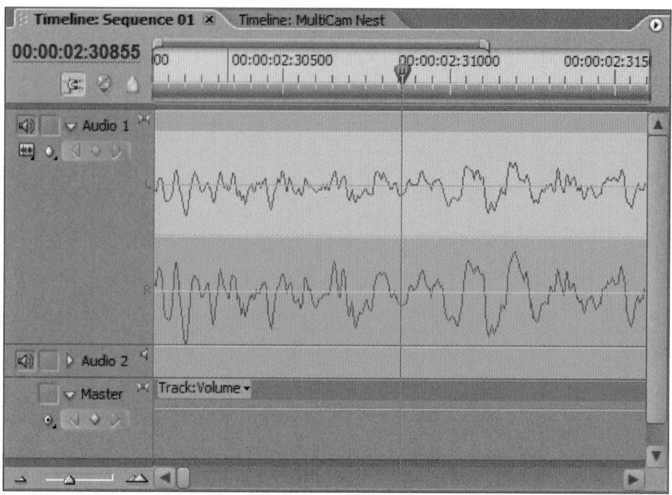

Figure 5.29 With the display set to Audio Units, you can zoom into the timeline at a subframe level. Doing this helps you extract more details from your audio file to clip out, remove, or cut on exact samples.

zoom in, and find the proper place to make your edit (**Figure 5.29**).

- **Sequence Zero Point.** Opens a dialog that enables you to reassign the starting timecode value of your current sequence. This is very helpful with multi-camera editing techniques. It is also helpful if you are creating a project that matches back to another tape with its own specific timecode. Whatever value you enter will reflect the displayed timecode value of frame 1 in your sequence. Even though these options are tucked away in a wing menu, they can still be assigned as keyboard shortcuts from Edit > Keyboard Customization > Windows > Timeline Window > Timeline Window Menu.

Playback Scrolling

Premiere Pro 2.0 offers a new preference for the playback scroll mode for the track content area of your timeline. To access the preference go to Edit > Preferences > General and click on the drop-down menu for Timeline Playback Auto-Scrolling (**Figure 5.30**).

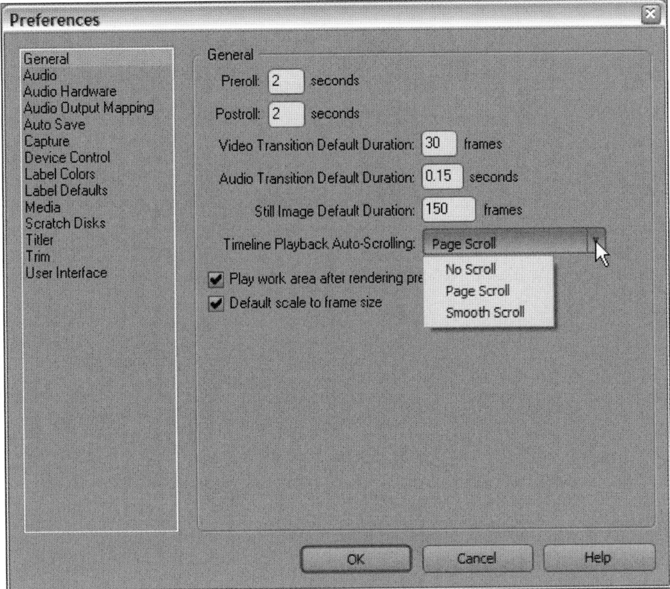

Figure 5.30 The new Timeline Playback Auto-Scrolling preference gives you three new choices for how you want your timeline to update as you play it back.

The three available methods of scrolling are

- **No Scroll.** When the CTI/playback head plays beyond the current viewed area of your timeline and it stops, the view of the timeline will not update to show its current position; instead the viewing area remains.
- **Page Scroll.** When the CTI/playback head plays beyond the current viewed area of your timeline, the timeline view updates to show the next area being played through. When the CTI/Playback head reaches the end of that viewed area, it updates to the next one.
- **Smooth Scroll.** In this mode, the CTI/playback head is positioned in the center of your timeline viewing area and the timeline smoothly scrolls past it until playback stops or is stopped.

I use Page Scroll and Smooth Scroll most. Smooth scroll always keeps your playback head in the center of the sequence, but it can be dizzying to watch it move past, especially if you are zoomed in to a high magnitude.

Things to Remember

The most important things to remember in regards to the Timeline panel are what you are viewing and which mode you are in. If you are editing audio clip keyframes and you are set to display track keyframes, you will start hitting your head against the wall! Don't do that; just look and see if the track has a gray bar on top. If it does, then you are working on the track level.

Let's say you find that your real-time preview responsiveness is not good enough when displaying a title that has motion and effects on top of a video clip that you are editing. In this case, you can turn off the output of the title track, tweak the edit beneath it and then, when you want to see the title, turn its track back on.

The last thing to remember is to use transitions to fade both audio and video in and out. Although it is a much different workflow than for former versions of Premiere, it makes the adjustments and workflow much faster to drop the cross dissolve and keep going.

The basics are behind you; now it's time to edit. In the next chapter, you will explore dragging, dropping, moving, and editing with the Monitor and Timeline panels.

CHAPTER 6

The Editing Workflow

Editing in Premiere Pro is far more intuitive and efficient than it has ever been. Whether you are using the Source Monitor to trim your clips or dropping all your clips to the timeline and then adjusting, Premiere Pro offers a host of tools and techniques to make the editing process less cumbersome.

I like to have a workflow when I edit, a structure and rhythm that I follow so that it is easy to make changes to what has been edited and so I can also decipher my work very clearly.

This chapter will guide you through a basic workflow and explain the rules and functions of editing in Premiere Pro. After a quick overview of the editing terms and basics, you will explore the program's functions within the context of a workflow.

Editing Basics

In former versions of Premiere, it was easy to get confused and accidentally change the flow or sync of your timeline. Every editing task you perform in Premiere Pro, however, has some sort of interface response, so you know what you are doing as you do it. To understand what is going on, look at the cursor and the bottom of the application window. The cursor (Selection tool) updates and changes its appearance based on which tool you are using (see **Figure 6.1**). At the bottom of the application window, text suggestions will help guide you through your editing decisions. The text line offers ideas for tools and keystrokes that perform tasks associated with what you are doing. As you go through this chapter, pay attention to the feedback. Try to anticipate what it will say and what the results will be if you were to perform a suggested task.

Figure 6.1 With the Selection tool hovering over the edge of a clip, it automatically turns into the edge trimming tool.

Six actions are the fundamentals of editing in the timeline:

- **Trim.** To adjust the In and Out points of media in the timeline.
- **Ripple.** To shift media to make room for added media or delete space created by removed media.
- **Insert.** To add media to the timeline by rippling and shifting media to make room for the added clips.
- **Overlay.** To add media to the timeline by placing the new clip on top of whatever media is beneath it in the track. Replaces the existing media with the new clip.
- **Lift.** To remove media from the timeline while preserving the space that the removed media occupied in the track. The opposite of Overlay.
- **Extract.** To remove media from the timeline by lifting the media, then rippling the surrounding media so that the space occupied by the removed clip is deleted. The opposite of Insert.

You'll hear these words often in this chapter. Your fingers also will become very familiar with two keys: Ctrl and Alt. These two keys are the modification keys that toggle not only the state of the selected tool, but also the editing mode when you are dragging and dropping media.

Because the Insert, Overlay, Lift, and Extract functions are just a modification key away, you can very easily perform complex edits. From shifting the order of edited shots to keeping your edit free of unnecessary gaps and empty spaces, these editing functions are quite powerful.

Learn the rules, then expect results. This is the key to being comfortable with the workflow. Knowing the tools and their exact behavior makes the editing process that much easier. You should also be aware of a major change from previous versions: Premiere Pro no longer supports A/B editing, in which the edit combines two subtracks of video into one Master track. Instead it offers single-track editing. This approach may take some getting used to, but once you free your mind from its AB shackles and see the new light, it's beautiful!

Single-Track Editing

Because Premiere Pro is a single-track editing application, all of your edits between clips occur on a single video track in the timeline (**Figure 6.2**). Because of the single-track design, Premiere Pro offers a number of tools to modify your clips after they have been placed. If you come from an AB background, you may have a few puzzling moments, but it's very likely that all of your problems can be solved by finding the right tool to use. When you get to the advanced editing techniques in Section V, you will learn the proper tool for specific problems and explore various editing methods.

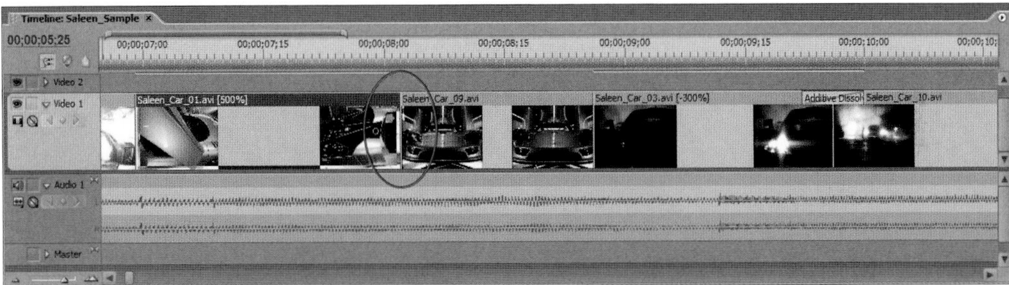

Figure 6.2 Premiere Pro is based on a single-track editing model. No longer is there a visual A and B roll in Premiere Pro; there's only a single track of video where transitions appear as virtual Band-Aids, joining two clips together.

For example, the Ripple Edit tool enables you to easily trim In and Out points while keeping the surrounding clips adjacent to the adjusted clip (**Figure 6.3**). The Slip tool is helpful because you can slide the In and Out points within the boundaries of the clip instance that is already placed in the timeline.

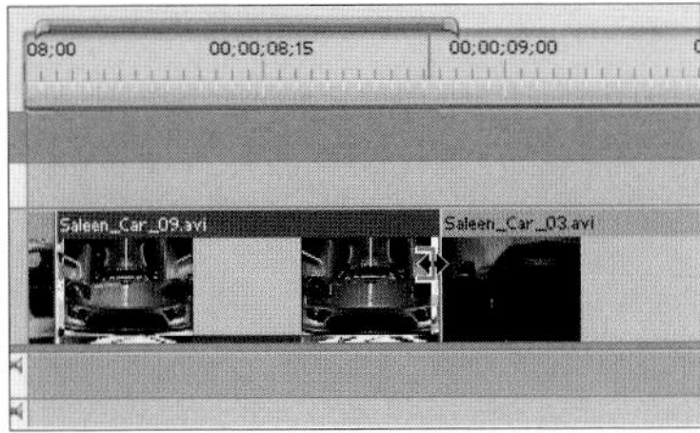

Figure 6.3 When you trim the tail of a clip with the Ripple Edit tool, the adjacent clip remains butted up against the newly adjusted clip. The Ripple Edit tool automatically deletes the blank space created by the edit and slides the media left so that there is no space between the cuts.

Editing with the Source Monitor

The most straightforward and intuitive way to start the editing workflow is to open a clip from the Project panel into the Source Monitor. Once the clip is open in the Source Monitor, navigate through the clip and mark your In and Out points around the portion of the clip that you wish to use. Drag the clip down to the timeline and place it in its desired location. Of course, there's a little more to it than that.

Drag and Drop, Insert and Overlay

As long as your mouse button is pressed, you have control of the clip and can move it. While holding the clip in the track that you want to add it to, find the downward arrow between two lines that's to the right of the cursor. This tells you the method in which the clip will be added to the timeline (**Figure 6.4**).

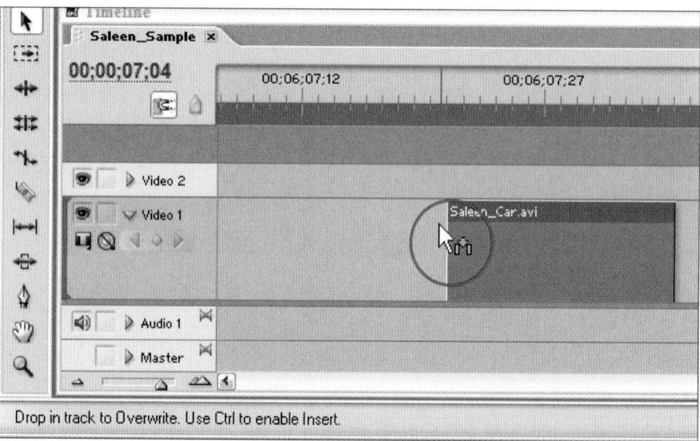

Figure 6.4 When you drag a clip or item into the timeline, Premiere will edit to the timeline in Overlay mode (the default). The cursor updates to indicate an Overlay edit as you drop the media. Notice the text in the bottom-left corner of the screen that gives you additional tips and information.

A downward arrow means the default method, which is an Overlay edit for Premiere Pro (a change from earlier versions of the program). In an Overlay edit, the clip will be placed directly on top of and replace the material underneath when you drop it in the timeline. A right-facing arrow means an Insert edit (more on that later).

Additionally, as you are editing there will be text feedback as to the mode you are editing in and the available keyboard modification keys. While you have a clip held, the bottom bar of the application displays helpful text.

Releasing the mouse releases the clip wherever your pointer is located, adding it to the timeline using your chosen method of placement: Overlay or Insert.

Overlay Edits

To better understand overlay edits, try a short exercise. You can use the Sample Project in the APPST2 Lesson Files folder or substitute your own video clips.

1. Open the APPST2 Lesson Files/Sample Project NTSC folder and double-click on the Sample_NTSC.prproj icon inside the folder to open the project.
2. Choose File > New > Sequence to create a new sequence in the project. Name the Sequence OVERLAY and assign it two video tracks and two stereo audio tracks. Double-click on the Sample Media folder in the Project panel; you will use these clips to edit with.
3. Click on the menu bar of the Timeline window to make it active. Zoom in to the timeline by dragging the zoom toward the large mountains. In the timecode area, be sure that Snapping is turned on (**Figure 6.5**). (Clicking the Snap to Edges button or pressing S toggles Snapping on and off.)

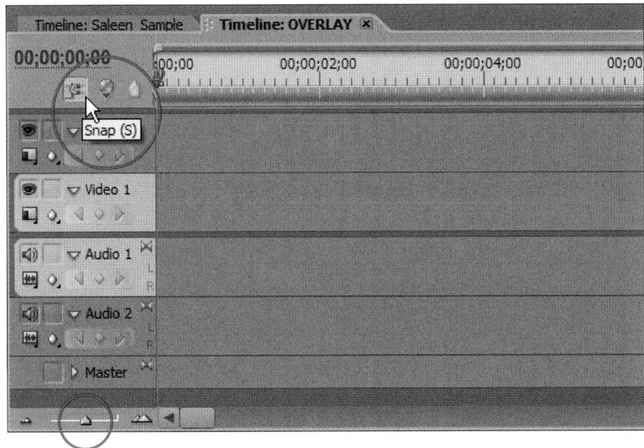

Figure 6.5 With the Timeline panel active, notice how the selected sequence has a yellow rim on it; this is the active sequence. The Snap to Edge button is turned on, and you are zoomed in about halfway through the zoom scale.

4. Select the clip Saleen_Car_01.avi from the Project panel, drag it down into the timeline, and slowly move it to the left toward the start of the timeline. Notice how it snaps to the far left side; this is the effect of Snapping mode (**Figure 6.6**). When it's on, you can add media to the timeline without creating gaps or unwanted spaces. Also notice that the cursor icon indicates an Overlay edit.

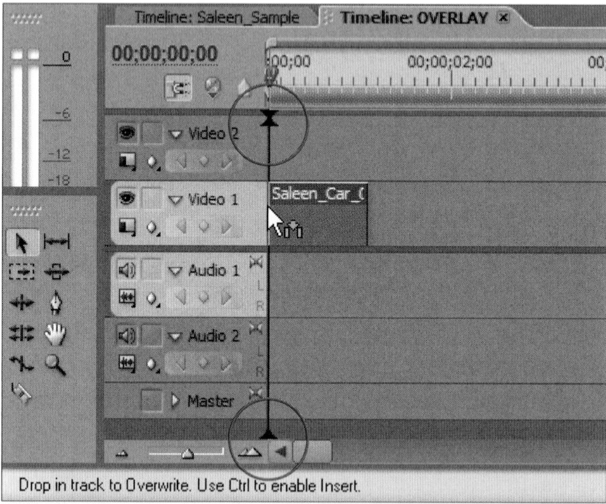

Figure 6.6 When Snapping is turned on, you see a thick black line with arrow on its top and bottom specifying where the clip will snap to. Here, the clip snaps to the head of the timeline in an Overlay edit.

5. Grab the Saleen_Car_02.avi clip, and place it immediately after the first clip on the same track. You should be able to easily drop this clip at the end of the other first clip; it should snap to the end. In fact, this clip can snap to either the start of the timeline or the Out-point edge of the first clip.

6. With two clips back to back in the timeline, drag the Saleen_Car_03.avi clip directly on top of Saleen_Car_02 (**Figures 6.7a** and **b**) so that it snaps to the cut between the two clips. When you release Saleen_Car_03, it will be added to the timeline in the position you determined, replacing the content that was beneath it.

When you add media to the timeline using an Overlay edit, it *replaces* whatever media was beneath it when you release the clip. The newly added clip replaces only the content that it covers. Because Saleen_Car_02 is longer than Saleen_Car_03, the remainder of Car_02 stays in the timeline. If you don't want the remainder of Car_02 in the timeline, you can select the remaining instance of it and delete it. (If there is media to the right, say Saleen_Car_04, you can use the Ripple Delete command to delete the clip and the space it occupies.)

a

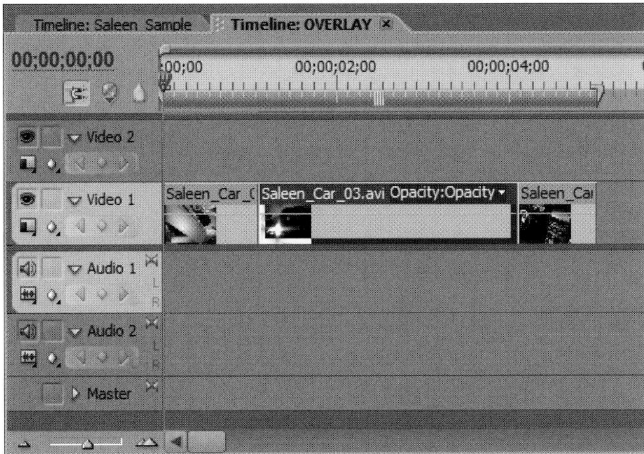

b

Figures 6.7a and b When you snap to the cut between the first two clips (top), notice how the Saleen_Car_03 clip is somewhat transparent, revealing what the Overlay edit will be replacing (the track instance of Saleen_Car_02) beneath it. Once the mouse is released (bottom), the Car_03 clip replaces the beginning of Car_02, leaving its tail after the end of the Car_03 instance.

Don't like the way an edit turns out? Press Ctrl+Z to back up one step. The next short lesson looks at Insert edits. If you get confused by all of this, be sure to notice the feedback of the cursor and the text feedback in the bottom program bar. So, pay attention to the cursor icon and read the associated text.

Insert Edits and the Ctrl Key

Premiere Pro's second type of edit is the Insert edit. Instead of replacing and overlaying the content of the timeline, an Insert edit splits the content beneath the clip and inserts the clip in between.

Here's how it works.

1. Make a new sequence and name it INSERT. Arrange the Saleen_Car_01 and Saleen_Car_02 clips back to back in the Video 1 track of your new INSERT sequence. Remember to zoom in with the slider control or + key.
2. Click and drag Saleen_Car_03 from the Project window down to the same cut point that you edited it at in the last lesson. Snap the clip to the edit point and continue holding the mouse down.
3. Instead of releasing the clip as you did before, press the Ctrl key while holding your mouse. Notice that when you press the Ctrl key, the cursor changes from the downward arrow of an Overlay edit to the right arrow of an Insert edit (**Figures 6.8a** and **b**). Additionally, there will be right-facing teeth marks that appear on your other tracks. These teeth marks signify which tracks the Insert edit will be applied to. Notice that the text in the bottom bar updates to confirm the Insert mode and its behavior.

   In an Insert edit, Premiere Pro "pushes" all the media to the right of your cursor position, leaving enough free space for the new clip. The new clip is inserted between the existing clips and nothing is overwritten. The Insert edit will occur on all those tracks displaying the teeth marks, meaning that space will be allocated for the selected clips on all those tracks. If a specific track is locked, it will not have an insert tooth and you cannot perform Insert edits on it.

When using Insert edits, remember that track items shift positions. Unless a track is locked, a standard Insert edit (Ctrl) inserts onto all tracks. An Insert on Target Track Only edit (Ctrl+Alt) limits the track shifting to only the track to which you are adding the media.

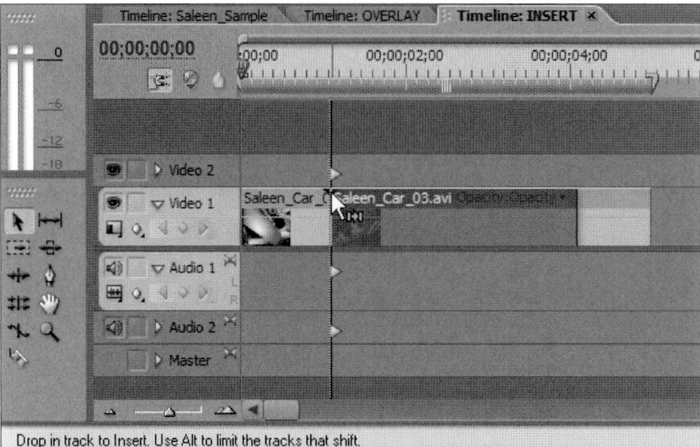

a

b

Figures 6.8a and b Press the Ctrl key while dragging and dropping a clip to toggle to Insert editing mode (a). The cursor icon updates to a right-pointing arrow, indicating that the clip will push the current media to the right to make room for itself in the timeline (b).

4. With the Ctrl key pressed, release the mouse to drop the clip. Be sure not to release Ctrl before the mouse. Saleen_Car_03 inserts itself before Car_02, shifting the timeline material to the right.
5. Drag the clip Saleen_Car_04 from the Project window, and drop it onto Video 2 above the cut between Car_03 and Car_02.

6. Pressing Ctrl, drag Saleen_Car_05 from the Project panel and drop it at the middle of Car_04 on Video 2 (**Figure 6.9**). It splits the media in half on *both* Video 1 and Video 2, because insert editing by default makes space for the inserted clip on all tracks.

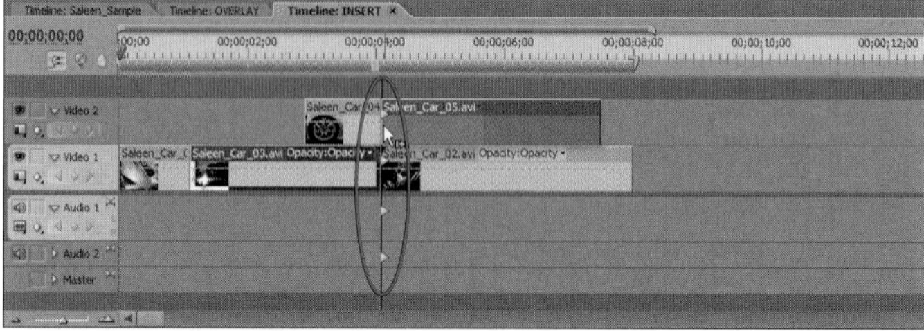

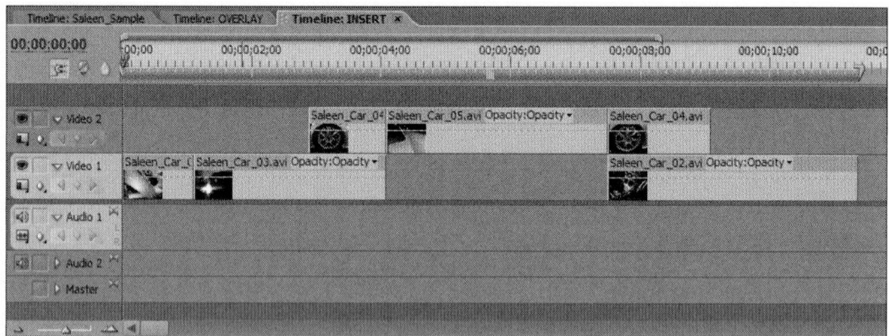

Figure 6.9 With the teeth marks identifying the tracks being inserted onto, inserting Saleen_Car_05 into Car_04 on Video 2 splits the content of Video 1 in half as well.

7. Press Ctrl+Z to undo the last edit, then try another variation of the Insert edit. While pressing Ctrl and Alt, drag Saleen_Car_05 to the same cut point in as the last step, then release the mouse (**Figures 6.10a** and **b**). This edit is called an Insert Only on Target Track. Notice how it affects only the target track and there are no teeth marks on the tracks other than where your media is being added.

All Insert edits place the media based on the location of the inserted clip's first frame. To find this spot, look for the dotted line that displays as you hold down the Ctrl key. The dropped clip will begin at the point on the timeline under this dotted line. You can also see that the Program Monitor has a two-up display that shows the start frame of the clip being added and the exact frame in the timeline where the clip will be edited.

When you drag and drop media from the Source Monitor into the timeline, Overlay and Insert editing functions similarly. The big difference is that the Source Monitor allows you to make adjustments to the In and Out points for your source material before adding the media to the timeline.

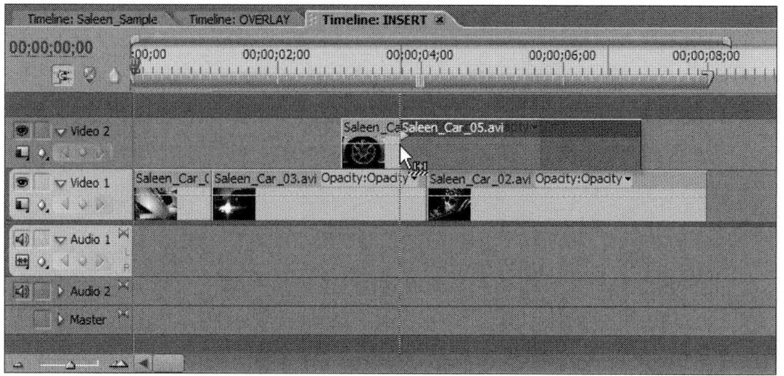

a

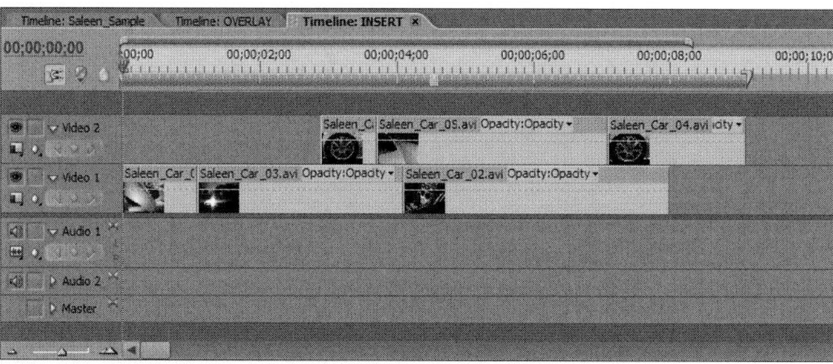

b

Figures 6.10a and b When you press Ctrl+Alt while dragging and dropping, the cursor indicates an Insert Only on Target Track edit (a). Now Premiere shifts only the media on Video 2; Video 1 remains intact (b).

NOTES

When assembling your initial edit, try adding all your clips to the timeline to establish the basic order of shots. If you open a clip that you want to add earlier in the cut, use an Insert edit (press the Ctrl key while dragging and dropping) to place the shot where you like.

Edit Functions and the CTI

An alternative workflow for editing from the Source Monitor is to use the Insert and Overlay buttons with an open clip. Look in the right group of transport controls, bottom row. The Insert button depicts a clip being inserted into another that is separated; Overlay shows one clip being dropped directly on top of another. If you prefer keyboard shortcuts, use the comma (,) to insert and the period (.) to overlay.

Editing with the buttons or shortcuts is a bit more rigid than the freedom of dragging and dropping with your mouse. For example, there is no button to insert only on a target track, the equivalent of Ctrl+Alt. Dragging and dropping with the mouse allows you to drop your added media wherever you define in the timeline. Using the edit

NOTES

To target video tracks you can use the keyboard shortcuts as well. Ctrl+plus sign (+) targets the track above the current targeted track, and Ctrl+hyphen (-) targets the track below the currently targeted track. For audio tracks, use Ctrl+Shift+plus sign to target the audio track above (closest to bottom) or Ctrl+Shift+hyphen to target the track below (closer to the video tracks).

controls adds the media to the timeline in the location of either the CTI/Edit Line or an assigned In point from the Program Monitor.

To understand the edit buttons, try another method of editing the clips from Premiere Pro's Sample Project.

1. Create a new sequence, and name it SOURCE EDIT.
2. To edit properly from the Source Monitor, you need to specify the tracks on which you want your edit to occur by targeting your tracks. To target a track, click within the empty space of the track header area. The area around the track header when targeted will turn a lighter gray and the left edge will become darkened and rounded.
3. Use the range select method (click and drag over the clips with the cursor) in the Project panel to select two clips (Saleen_Car_01 and Saleen_Car_02). Drag them into the targeted track so that they start at the beginning of the timeline. Notice how the multiselected clips are placed one immediately after the other in the track. You will most likely have to zoom in again; press the \ key to snap your zoom to fit the current clips within the boundary of the window.
4. Click and scrub in the time ruler area of the timeline to move the CTI/Edit Line to 02;12. With the CTI on this frame, press I to add an In point to the timeline at the position of the CTI.

   When you execute either the Insert or Overlay editing command using the Source Monitor's edit buttons, Premiere first looks for an assigned In point at which to perform the edit. If no In point is assigned, Premiere performs the edit at the Edit Line's position.
5. Double-click on the Saleen_Car_03 clip from the Project panel to open it in the Source Monitor. (Notice that clip has a previously assigned In/Out point. This is fine.) Press the Insert Edit button to insert the clip from the Source Monitor into the timeline at the In point you specified on the targeted track (**Figure 6.11**).

Figure 6.11 With Target Video 1 in the Timeline, assign an In point at 02;12 in the Source Monitor, then click the Source Monitor's Insert button to execute an Insert edit of the source material down into the timeline. Take note that when the edit is executed, the CTI snaps to the end of the added clip and the previously marked In point is cleared.

6. Press Ctrl+Z to undo, then click the Overlay button to see that an Overlay edit differs from an Insert edit. This time, the source material replaces the underlying clip material instead of pushing it out of the way to the right. Keep this sequence as it is; you will be using it for the next short lesson.

Using the editing commands is excellent for instances when you are either defining a specific region to which you want to edit (as in the three- and four-point editing techniques coming up), or if you have found an exact frame at which you want to insert or overlay. Instead of dragging and dropping, you just execute the desired edit at precisely the position you desire. It certainly ensures position accuracy, and used in conjunction with the Program Monitor's timeline transport controls, it can be a quick and efficient way to navigate and edit.

NOTES

When you are dragging and dropping in the timeline or trimming the edges of a clip, watch the Program Monitor for feedback as to the frames you are editing. For example, when you are dropping a clip into the timeline, the Program Monitor shows you the last frame of the media before your inserted or overlaid shot and the first of media after the last frame of your inserted or overlaid shot (**Figure 6.12**).

Timeline Editing

Once you have added clips to your timeline, Premiere Pro offers lots of features to help you organize and arrange them. When you are editing and rearranging in the Timeline panel, you drag media from its current position and drop it where you want it to be. The same way you can choose to overlay or insert when you drop a clip, you can lift or extract a clip when you drag it within the Timeline panel. The opposite of overlaying, lifting is the default behavior. Extracting is the Ctrl-modified behavior, and it is the opposite of inserting.

Figure 6.12 For Insert and Overlay edits, the Program Monitor's two-up display tells you the last frame before your cut and the first frame after your cut. Because I am performing an Insert edit, notice that the two-up frames are consecutive. My Insert edit will occur between the value of 00;00;02;03 and 00;00;02;04 for the clip in the timeline.

Lifting and Extracting

In addition to Overlay and Insert, which are functions for dropping media *in* the timeline, Premiere Pro has two unique functions for moving and dragging media *from* its timeline position: Lift and Extract. To understand how they work, continue working with the SOURCE EDIT sequence.

1. Select the center clip, Saleen_Car_02 and drag it up to Video 2 (**Figure 6.13**).

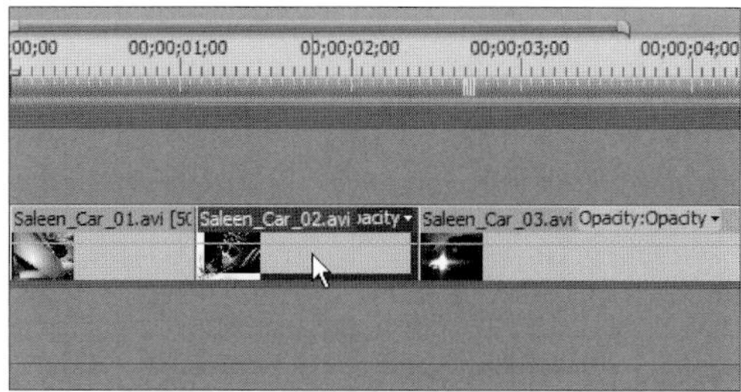

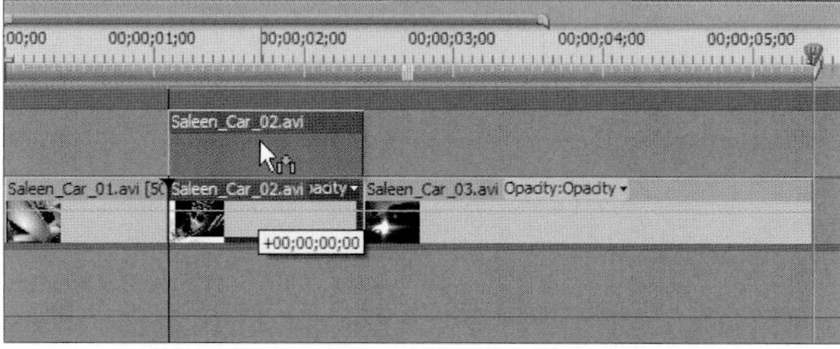

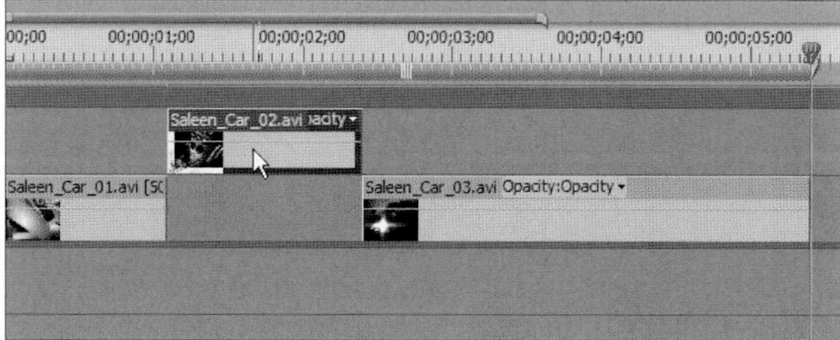

Figure 6.13 Premiere's default move for dragging clips is the Lift, which moves the clip from its current position and preserves the position of all other media in the timeline. Notice that once the clip is lifted, when it is being dropped it displays the Overlay icon.

Notice that the space that Car_02 occupied on Video 1 is now empty. This is the default Lift behavior: You drag a clip from its position—lifting the media from its original spot—and the space defined by the clip's former boundaries remains open and preserved in the timeline. Like overlaying, lifting does not disturb or modify any elements surrounding the clips that you are lifting. Although Premiere does not give you any feedback to indicate you are in Lift mode, it is the default for dragging and moving a clip.

2. Press Ctrl+Z to undo your Lift edit so you can try an Extract edit.

3. Hold your mouse over Saleen_Car_02, then press and hold down the Ctrl key. To perform an Extract edit, you must hold down the Ctrl modifier *before* you click on a clip to select it (**Figures 6.14a**, **b**, and **c**). With the Ctrl key pressed, the icon next to the cursor is now a left-pointing arrow to indicate you're in Extract mode. The text in the bottom status bar tells you as well.

Figures 6.14a, b, and c Before you click and move the clip from its current position, hold the Ctrl key down to put the cursor into Extract mode (a). Before you release the clip and drop it onto Video 2, you can release the Ctrl key to drop the clip back in Overlay mode (b). Now, because this clip was extracted from Video 1 and then overlaid on Video 2, the space it occupied on Video 1 is ripple deleted and the clip overlays above the other clips on Video 2 (c).

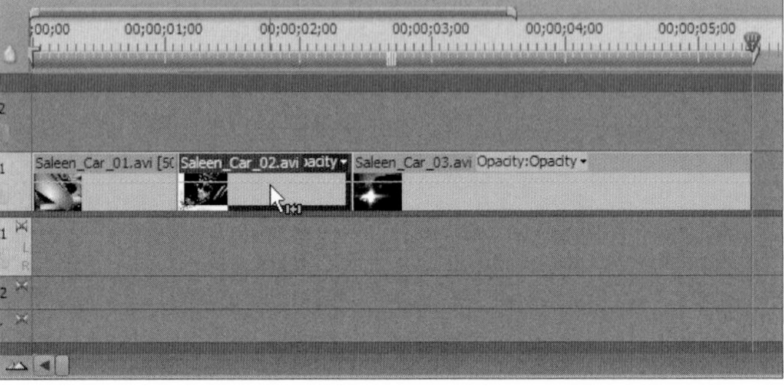

s

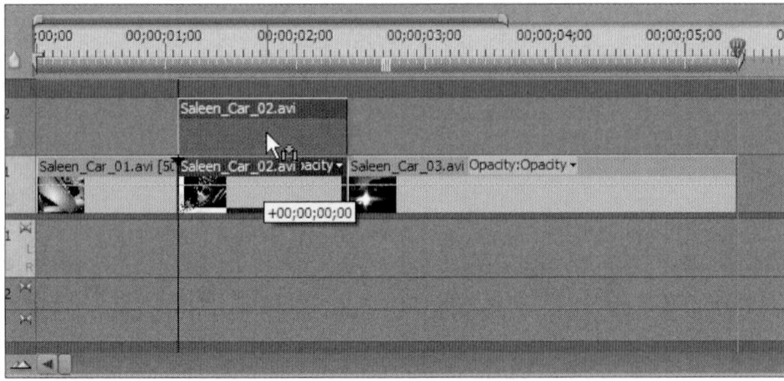

b

c

4. With the Ctrl key and mouse button held down, drag Car_02 to a new position on Video 2. First release the Ctrl key, *then* release the mouse. If you are still holding Ctrl when you release the clip after your move, you are immediately thrown into Insert mode. If you release Ctrl before the clip, you are in Overlay mode. Because you were in Overlay mode here, no shifting of track contents occurred.

These are the fundamental functions of dragging clips in the timeline. Use Lift to preserve the space the dragged media occupied and Extract to ripple delete the space that it occupied. When you link both the dragging (Lift and Extract) and dropping (Overlay and Insert) editing modes together, you will get a taste for what makes the editing workflow so powerful in Premiere Pro.

One Move, Four Choices

I want to take a few moments to reiterate the last step of the last lesson. Once you decide the dragging method (Lift or Extract) for moving your clip from its current timeline position, you can choose not only a new location for the clip, but also how you want to drop it in (Insert or Overlay). Realizing this was my epiphany about the new power of Premiere Pro. Never before have Premiere's timeline editing tools offered such powerful options. Remember, as long as you hold down your mouse button while dragging a clip, you can decide whether to perform an Overlay edit or to press Ctrl to perform an Insert edit.

Consider a sequence of five clips arranged 1-2-3-4-5. Say you want to reorder the clips 4-1-2-3-5. In former versions of Premiere, you would have to perform about four steps to achieve what you can now do in one: Press the Ctrl key and drag Clip 4 from its current position (Extract) to the left. Your cursor snaps to the head (beginning) of the timeline with Clip 4 covering Clip 1. Press the Ctrl key and release the mouse and Clip 4 (Insert edit). Because you performed an Extract, Premiere closed the space formerly occupied by Clip 4, cutting Clip 3 directly to 5. Because you toggled to Insert mode, Premiere slides Clip 1 to the right to make room for Clip 4 at the beginning of the timeline before Clip 1. This is a monumental moment in the Premiere Pro editing experience.

Editing with the Program Monitor

Overlay and Insert apply to source material; Lift and Extract apply to timeline material. Just as you can overlay and insert using buttons in the Source Monitor, you can also lift and extract in the Program Monitor using the Lift and Extract buttons or their keyboard shortcuts (; for Lift and ' for Extract). Give it a try.

1. Create a new sequence named PROGRAM EDIT, and arrange the Saleen_Car_01 through Saleen_Car_04 clips back to back on Video 1.
2. With Video 1 targeted, mark an In point at 02:28 and an Out point at 06;11 (**Figure 6.15**). This space specifies in which portion of the timeline you want your edit to occur.

Figure 6.15 As with Source Monitor editing, the Program Monitor relies on targeting tracks and In/Out points to determine which portion of the timeline gets edited. Notice the In/Out instance in the Program Monitor and the blue highlight area in the Timeline panel. This blue area indicates the track location where your Program Monitor edit will occur.

After you define your In and Out points, Premiere displays a dark gray instance surrounded by the In/Out brackets in the timeline's time ruler. Additionally, a light blue highlight/outline in the targeted track helps you identify the duration of the In/Out location specified for your edit.

3. Click the button for the type of edit you want. First, try the Lift button, which removes the material but leaves a gap in the timeline, preserving the space it took up. Press Ctrl+Z to undo, then click the Extract button to remove the material and close the gap that it occupied (**Figures 6.16a** and **b**).

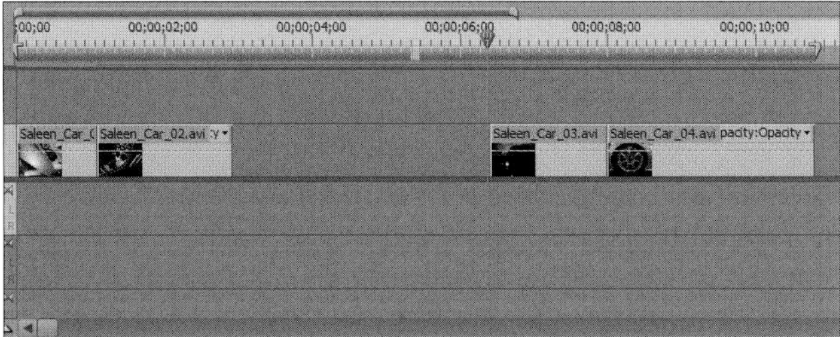

a

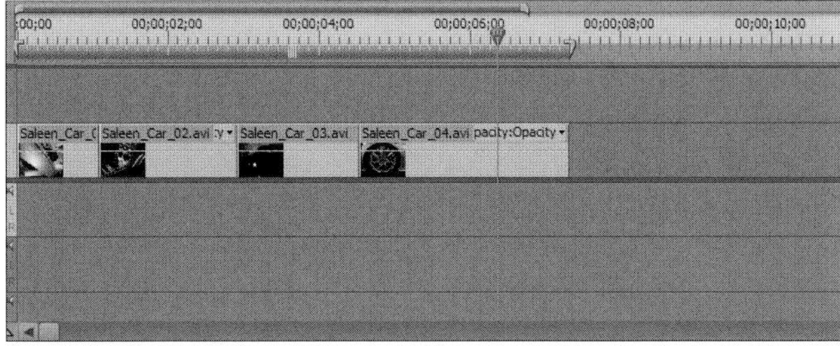

b

Figures 6.16a and b The Lift function (a) removes the material from the timeline entirely, leaving a gap at its former position. An Extract edit (b) removes the material and also closes the gap with a ripple edit.

The primary benefit to using these Lift and Extract commands is that they remove the media from the timeline completely. Notice that when you lift or extract with the mouse, the selected material still has physical properties in the timeline and you have to decide where you want to put it. You can't just lift with the mouse and drag it out of the window to remove it; you have to find a new home for your dragged material. This is not the case with the Lift and Extract commands, which permanently remove the material from your timeline. Sounds mischievous, but it's really quite a practical alternative to the mouse moves.

Three- and Four-Point Editing

When the Program Monitor is used in conjunction with the Source Monitor, it can edit instances with exact precision thanks to three- and four-point editing.

Say your source clip has an In point and an Out point defined; that's two points. If you define an In point in your timeline with your Program Monitor, that's considered a third editing point. A three-point edit is any edit that uses a combination of three edit points. Because the Insert and Overlay commands execute their edits to any assigned In point in the timeline, you can pick an exact instance in a source clip and place it starting at an exact point in the timeline.

If your source material has an assigned In and Out point and the timeline also has a proper In and Out point, you have four points.

By now, you should know your way around creating a sequence and editing material together. Try following along with clips of your own choice. This technique universally applies to a variation of three-point edits:

1. Create a new sequence in your project and add four clips to Video Track 1.
2. Double-click on a new clip from the Project window to open it in the Source Monitor. Define an In point where you want the new clip to start and an Out point where you want the clip to end. That's two points.
3. In the Program Monitor, move the CTI to a specific location of the timeline where you want to add your open source clip. Once you are in position, press I or click the In point button to add an In point at the specified location. That's your third point.
4. Click either the Insert or Overlay button in the Source Monitor to add your exact source clip instance (two edit points) to the exact timeline position you assigned (one edit point).

Figure 6.17 With an In point assigned in the timeline and a source clip with both an In and Out point, clicking the Overlay button (or pressing the period key) executes a three-point Overlay edit starting at the marked timeline In point.

Congratulations, you have just performed a three-point edit (**Figure 6.17**). To try another variation, you need to isolate a portion of the timeline that you want filled with alternate material.

1. With the same sequence open, reposition the CTI in the Program Monitor and assign an In and Out point to a section of the timeline that you want to replace (two edit points). Be aware of which tracks are targeted.

   Here you are creating an In/Out instance on Video Track 1 in which you defined the boundaries of your edit.

2. Open a new clip in the Source Monitor. This time, define just an In point where you want the clip to start when it is added to the timeline (one edit point).

   Look for a clip with content that can fill the space defined in step 1. The In point you set defines where you want the clip to start when you add it to the timeline. You do not need to assign an Out point for the source clip, because the timeline In/Out points define the boundaries that the clip will fill.

3. Be sure you are targeting the track in which the material that you wish to replace resides. Click the Overlay button (**Figure 6.18**).

   If you were to click the Insert button, Premiere would insert the clip within the boundary and shift all the material to the right. By clicking Overlay, you are physically replacing the exact media defined by your three-point edit.

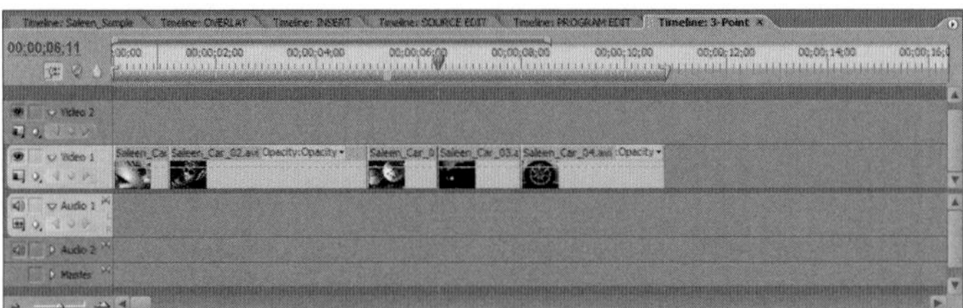

Figure 6.18 Working the opposite way, you filled a space in your timeline with specific source material. Another three-point edit!

In a four-point edit, you define the boundaries of the timeline area you wish to edit (In/Out) and the exact source material (In/Out) that you wish to place between those boundaries. The primary difficulty with four-point edits is that the In/Out duration of the source clip must match the In/Out duration of the timeline boundaries; otherwise the Fit Clip dialog will appear warning you of the mismatch and asking you to speed or slow the source clip when adding it to the timeline. If the source clip's In/Out duration is longer than the space you wish to fit it in, you must increase the speed of the clip so that when it is added to the timeline the defined In/Out points will still be respected. Choose to slow the clip speed to make the clip longer if there is not enough source content to reach the Out boundary.

Three- and four-point edits are excellent when you want to fill a specific gap or fit certain content in an exact location. As you'll learn, three-point editing is usually the most efficient way of working in Premiere Pro. Four-point edits are useful when you are making an edit with a voice-over track and you need to insert a shot for an exact amount of time. If the speed of the shot is not an issue, you can pick exactly what you want to see and for exactly how much time.

Timeline Trimming

Although dragging and dropping lets you get your clips in place, other timeline tools enable you to fine-tune and trim your edit into shape. The two you will use most often to edit your clips are the Trim tool and the Ripple Edit tool.

The Trim tool is used to shave off and remove unwanted portions of clips that exist in the timeline. By clicking either on the beginning or the end of a clip you can add or take away from the material shown in the timeline. A variation of the Trim tool, the Ripple Edit tool allows you to add or subtract from clip instances while at the same time preserving the adjacent material so that no gaps are created.

When you are using the default cursor in the timeline (keyboard shortcut: V), it updates to the Trim tool when placed near the head or tail of a clip in the timeline, as shown back in Figure 6.1.

Sometimes you discover you want a little more or a little less of a clip after you've placed it in the timeline. You don't need to restart from scratch; just move your cursor and use it as the Trim tool instead.

To adjust a clip's In point, move your cursor over the start of the clip in the timeline. The cursor will change into the Trim-in icon, a left bracket. Clicking and dragging to the right trims off the material at the head of the clip, reducing its duration and changing the In point. If you click and drag to the left, it increases the overall duration of the clip and updates you with a new In point. The Program Monitor displays whatever frame the tool is trimming past, so that you can see exactly what frame your modification is set to. New in Premiere Pro 2.0 is a semitransparent timecode display of the current frame's source timecode.

Move your cursor over a clip's Out point to access the Trim-out tool (a right bracket). Click and drag the Trim-out icon to change the location of the clip's Out point.

Limitations occur when you have a clip that is surrounded by two other clips. For example, Clip 2 resides between Clips 1 and 3. You want to change the In point of Clip 2 to earlier in the clip, but you want to cut to the same spot in Clip 3. In this case, you want to extend the beginning of Clip 2 to the left so that you can start the clip earlier in the shot. There is already a clip immediately to the left, however, and if you use the Trim tool you cannot drag past the boundary of another clip.

In this case, if you do not see the Media Start "dog ear" indicator in the top-left corner, then you have additional material to the left of the current clip In point. While you can click and drag to the right to reduce the In point, if you are up against another clip you will not be able to use the Trim-in tool to adjust the In point of Clip 2 to the left. Adjusting the duration would require the media to the right of Clip 2 to be shifting to the right in order to make room for the extra material.

In former versions of Premiere, you would move Clips 2 and 3 to the right to make a gap between Clip 1 and 2, then extend the In point of Clip 2 to fill the gap so that the new material was added.

Premiere Pro now offers a quick and better solution: Use the Ctrl modifier key to access the Ripple Edit tool. The Ripple Edit tool intelligently makes adjustments by extending or retracting In or Out points and shifting the surrounding media left or right to keep everything held together.

Ripple Editing

One of the features of Insert and Extract edits is the shifting of the media left (Insert) or right (Extract). This intelligent shifting of the media is termed *rippling*, like small waves in a bathtub. The idea of ripple edits is that all your adjustments preserve the direct proximity of the adjacent media.

Go back to the OVERLAY sequence of three clips, one right after the other: Car_01-Car_03-Car_02. This time you want to increase the duration of the clip Car_03 by revealing more material before its timeline In point:

1. Position the Selection tool (V) at the head of the Saleen_Car_03 clip instance so that the brackets face right. Before you grab the edge of the clip, hold down the Ctrl key to toggle the Trim-in tool into the Ripple-in tool, which looks bigger and thicker than the Trim-in tool (**Figures 6.19a**, **b**, and **c**).

a

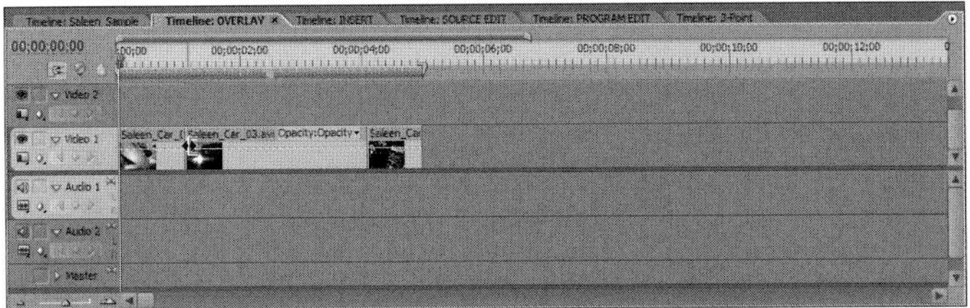

b

c

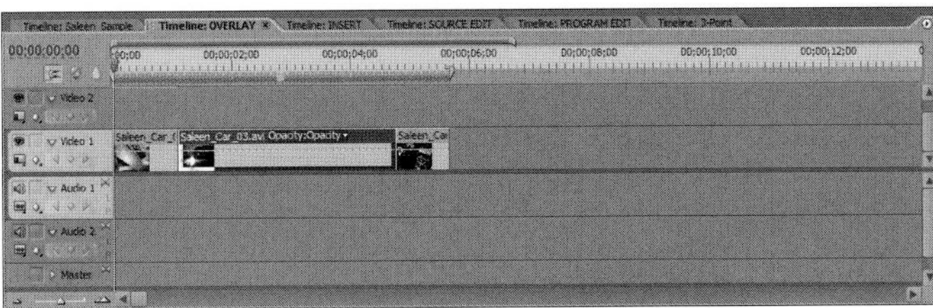

Figures 6.19a, b, and c Press Ctrl to toggle the Trim tool to the Ripple Edit tool (a). Drag to the left with the Ripple Edit tool to reveal new material (b). In this case, the shot has 20 frames added to its head. Note the timecode and two-up display in the Program Monitor revealing the outgoing frame from Car_01 and the new first frame of Car_03. In the final result (c), Car_01 is not adjusted at all; instead additional material is added to the head of Car_03, which ripples Car_02 further to the right down the timeline.

2. Continuing to hold down Ctrl, click and drag the In point left to reveal the new material and at the same time ripple (push) the material at the right of the edit down the timeline to the right. Using the Ripple Edit tool, you can trim and adjust the In and Out point of clip instances while at the same time preserving the cutting points of adjacent clips.

While you Ripple edit, the Program Monitor gives you a two-up display with the left frame revealing the last frame of Clip 1, before the cut, and the updating first frame of Clip 2, on the right, which you are dynamically changing as you continue to drag.

The Ripple-out tool works similarly on the tail end of clips. Although they may be hard to visualize, keeping four points in mind will help you master Ripple edits:

- Dragging the head of a clip left with Ripple-in lengthens the clip and pushes out (ripples) the material right.
- Dragging the head of a clip to the right with Ripple-in shortens the clip and takes in (ripples) material to the left.
- Dragging the tail of a clip right with Ripple-out increases the clip's duration and pushes out (ripples) material to the right.
- Dragging the tail of a clip to the left with Ripple-out reduces the duration and takes in (ripples) material left.

In all four of these examples, the cut points between the clip you are adjusting and its surrounding media will be preserved.

Ripple Delete

If you happen to have a blank gap or empty space in your timeline, you can right-click within the boundaries of the gap and select Ripple Delete. This will delete the gap by rippling material on the right side of the gap (taking it in) to the left to close the gap.

Just like Insert edits that shift all tracks, Ripple edits and Ripple Delete ripple all tracks left or right depending on what you are adjusting. Locked tracks, however, are not affected or moved. If you finally have everything lined up in your timeline only to discover an empty gap on Video 1, you probably should unlock all locked tracks and ripple the edit (**Figures 6.20a** and **b**).

a

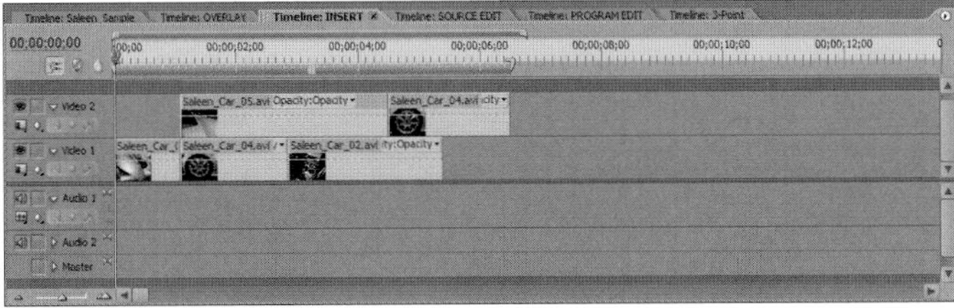

b

Figures 6.20a and b Whether ripple deleting an empty timeline space or clip, right-click on the selection and choose Ripple Delete from the context menu (a). In the bottom image (b), you can see that the ripple delete extracted the selected clip and shifted both tracks left to fill the space that the clip occupied.

Be warned, though, that not all tracks may be able to ripple the amount you desire and the edit may not be performed. If you ripple the Out point of a clip left and there are items on other tracks that prohibit movement to the left, Premiere Pro will not execute the edit. Unfortunately, the program does not throw up a warning to tell what is wrong and where. You will have to deduce some of the symptoms from experience and a keen eye. In any case, locking tracks that do not have the space to ripple will allow the other tracks to ripple properly.

Figure 6.21 From the top, the Tools panel's tools are: Selection, Track Select, Ripple Edit, Rolling Edit, Rate Stretch, Razor, Slip, Slide, Pen, Hand, and Zoom.

The Tools Panel

The Tools panel is your visual tool box from which you can click and choose tools that perform various powerful and helpful adjustments to your timeline (**Figure 6.21**). If you prefer not to click and select, each tool also has a keyboard shortcut. Once you have accessed a tool, your cursor updates with the appropriate icon for the selected tool. While a tool is selected, clicking and dragging in the timeline executes the tool's functions.

The Tools panel has a number of tools for editing and rearranging media in the Timeline panel. From top to bottom they are

- **Selection** (shortcut key: V). The standard cursor for selection. Press the Ctrl key to turn the Selection tool into the Ripple Edit tool.
- **Track Select** (shortcut key: M). Used to select all the content on one specific track. Pressing Shift turns this tool into the Multi-track Selection tool, which selects all tracks. Selection extends from where you click the tip of the tool to the right end of the timeline.
- **Ripple Edit** (shortcut key: B). Allows you to adjust the In or Out point of a clip instance in the timeline while rippling the media to its left or right, thus preserving the cuts.
- **Rolling Edit** (shortcut key: N). Enables you to dynamically roll the edit point between two clips, updating the Out point of the outgoing clip and the In point of the incoming clip at the same time.
- **Rate Stretch** (shortcut key: X). Lets you extend or reduce a clip's duration in the timeline by slowing down or increasing its speed, thus preserving its assigned In and Out points.
- **Razor** (shortcut key: C). Enables you to make incisions and cuts to individual media in the timeline. Holding the Shift key will make a cut through the entire timeline at the time position that you click.

- **Slip** (shortcut key: Y). Slides the visible media beneath the visible duration of the clip instance you are selecting, so that you can select a different portion of your clip to occupy the same space in the timeline. When you add a clip to the timeline, you may not be using all of the source material. If you were using only five seconds of a ten-second clip, then there is still five unused seconds somewhere beyond your In and Out points. Once a clip is edited into a sequence with adjacent material before and after it, use the Slip tool to shift the content of that clip within its timeline boundary. Slip the visible clip material left or right to display a different five-second section of the clip, without altering its timeline boundary.
- **Slide** (shortcut key: U). Allows you to slide the visible duration and selected content of a clip over the surrounding media. If you slide to the right, the clip to the left of the sliding clip will have its Out point increased to display its content. The clip to the right would get covered by the slide (and viceversa).
- **Pen** (shortcut key: P). Enables you to select and create keyframes in the Timeline window. Using the Ctrl key allows you to add keyframes. Using the Shift key allows you to click and select discontinuous keyframes and adjust them synchronously.
- **Hand** (shortcut key: H). An additional tool to click and drag the viewing area of the timeline left or right. It grabs at an anchor point where you click, and then moves left or right with your mouse.
- **Zoom** (shortcut key: Z). Zooms in and out of the timeline. Selecting and clicking zooms in. Holding Alt and clicking zooms out.

This brief overview of the editing tools for the timeline is intended to just whet your appetite. Section V, "Advanced Editing," and Section VI, "Professional Workflows," (located on the book's DVD) will serve up a full plate of details, presenting workflows for all the tools pointed out here.

Things to Remember

Don't be intimidated by the timeline editing behavior. Keep practicing, and it will click. The primary points to remember are the Ctrl key and the ripple behavior. Whether you are rippling an edit point or rippling timeline material for an Insert or Extract, the Ctrl key is the modifier for all Ripple functions. You use the Ctrl key modifier for extracting when dragging and for inserting when dropping. In addition, the Ctrl key modifier turns the standard Selection tool into the Ripple Edit tool so that your cuts remain seamless.

As you edit, pay attention to which tracks are locked and why; try to create an intuitive order to the media in your timeline. If you build your primary edit on the Video 1 track and get it as tight as possible before you start adding titles and transitions, you will save yourself the headache of inserting and shifting media around when you don't want to.

I have found a structure for building my sequences that works quite well. It usually entails editing all of my main video and audio content on specific tracks. All my titles, graphics, music, and additional sound effects have their own tracks, which I rename accordingly. Being able to quickly identify what is what within your edit will help you better manage your sequences and content. With nested sequences I also find that breaking an edit into working sections helps the managing project's process. If it is logical to break your project down into smaller pieces and separate sections, create a new sequence for each part. All of this discussion and all of these ideas are thrown into motion in the lessons found in the book's advanced techniques sections; this is just a reminder to get you thinking about your own workflow and structure.

So, get that primary edit in shape, then prepare for adding transitions and using the Effect Controls panel in the next chapter.

7

Transitions Basics

A transition is a segue from one moment to another, a change that connects two different things. In digital video editing, a transition is the visual method used to switch from one shot to the next. The type of transition you choose—from a simple cut to a dissolve to more elaborate effects—can play a large role in the mood and feel of your project.

For example, dissolves and wipes help articulate the passage of time, while straight cuts quicken the pace of a sequence. In a scene where someone is taking the entire morning to study a race program and handicap horses for a day's races, dissolves and wipes help articulate the passage of time. When your character is watching the climactic horse race, however, dissolves or wipes may destroy the continuity of action. Cuts from the race to the character and back will keep the pace tight and tense.

Whenever you are editing and choosing transitions, ask yourself: What am I trying to say, and who am I saying this to? In some cases, standard wipes and dissolves may not give your project the right look or feel. This chapter will show you how Premiere Pro's transitions behave, so you can better decide which effect is right for your project.

Single-Track Transition Basics

Previous versions of Premiere used AB editing: Transitions could be added only to a special track between the A and B tracks.

With its single-track editing approach, Premiere Pro handles transitions in a more streamlined and flexible manner (see **Figure 7.1**). You can place a transition on a clip's head, a clip's tail, or any cut point between two adjacent clips. This means that if you put two clips right next to each other, you can drag a transition from the Effects panel and drop it on the clips' cut point. Premiere Pro adds the appropriate media and uses it in the transition.

Check out the work of Japanese filmmaker Akira Kurosawa for some excellent examples of using wipes between shots to establish the passage of time between two moments.

Transitions can be placed between all media on all tracks, either audio or video. Finally, if you prefer the AB editing view, you can use the Effect Controls panel to look at the AB relationship between your transitions, as well as to access custom transition controls.

When you add a transition to media in the timeline, Premiere must render preview files for full-quality output of the transition instance. Red render bars appear over all instances of transitions until you render preview files by pressing Enter. Transitions on one or two DV clips should have no problem playing back in real time.

Figure 7.1 In Premiere Pro's single-track editing approach, small light purple transition "Band-Aids" connect adjacent clips on a single track in the timeline. When you click and select a transition, its properties and simulated AB roll appear in the Effect Controls panel. Here, the selected transition is a wipe, as seen in the Program Monitor.

The Effects Panel

The Effects panel is where all your audio and video effects and transitions live. To access it, choose Window > Effects or click the Effects tab in the Project panel. The panel has five master folders:

- Presets
- Audio Effects
- Audio Transitions
- Video Effects
- Video Transitions

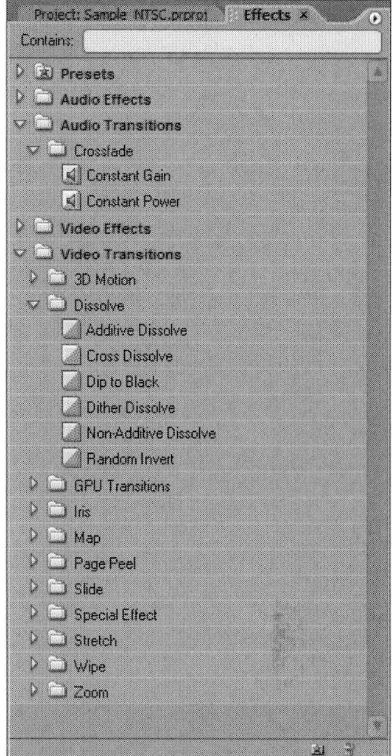

Figure 7.2 With both the Audio and Video Transitions folders expanded, you can see that your choice of audio transition boils down to two different fades. For video transitions, you have a lot more to choose from. Notice Constant Power and Cross Dissolve are the default transitions, as indicated by the red squares surrounding their icons.

Each contains subfolders in which effects or transitions are grouped by category. To find an effect, browse through the subfolders by twirling down their contents (**Figure 7.2**) or use the Contains field at the top of the window to search by name. As you type in the Contains field, Premiere expands folders to show items matching the search criteria. As you type the word "dissolve," for example, Premiere first displays all transitions and effects with "d" in their names, then only those with "di," and so on until displaying on those with "dissolve" in their names. Deleting letters backs you up through the displays of search results.

As you browse through your transitions, one audio and one video transition will look slightly different as their icons are surrounded with red squares. These are your default transition. *Default transitions* are the transitions used for automated tasks and quick placement with the keyboard shortcuts. (Chapter 8, "Effect Controls Basics," will discuss the contents of the Video and Audio Effects folders.)

Audio Transitions

The Audio Transitions folder contains a single subfolder called Crossfade, which contains two transitions: Constant Gain and Constant Power. Both transitions accommodate fading a clip up at its head, fading it down at its tail, and crossfading between two clips. The difference between

Constant Gain and Constant Power is subtle but distinct (**Figures 7.3a** and **b**).

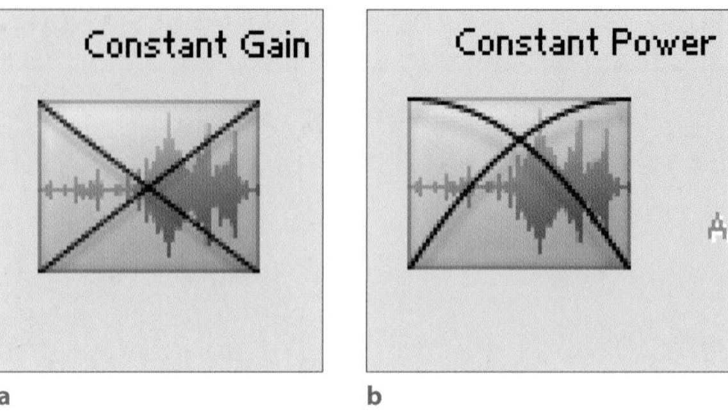

Figures 7.3a and b You can see the primary difference between the two audio transitions by comparing their icons: Constant Gain (a) increases volume uniformly, while Constant Power (b) adheres to more of a curve that rises faster to the full volume level.

Constant Gain always fades in a straight, diagonal rising or falling direction. When using Constant Gain to fade your audio up at the head of a shot, the audio volume starts at 0% at frame 1 and reaches the 100% level at the end of the transition. Along the way, the volume (the gain) constantly rises in a uniform fashion, like a straight rising line.

Constant Power is a bit different. When fading up, Constant Power increases your audio from 0% to 100% in a steeper curve that quickly gets the volume up, then climbs more slowly to its 100% limit. Instead of being at 50% halfway through your transition, Constant Power would be closer to 75% and then it would slowly level off to 100% from there.

Looking at the icon for each of these placed transitions will give you a good sense of how each works. For general fade purposes (fade in or out), I always use Constant Gain, which results in a progressive, simple fade. For cross-fades between two clips, I use Constant Power. With Constant Power transitioning two clips, instead of the audio dipping down halfway through the cross-dissolve the audio levels stay a bit higher and the sound level doesn't dip too low during the transition. In either case, you can quickly add the transition to your clips to fade their levels.

Video Transitions

The Video Transitions folder has ten subfolder categories:

- **3D Motion.** Contains transitions that have three-dimensional properties revealed over the course of the sequence—for example, a spinning cube with the first shot on one side and the second shot on a different side (**Figure 7.4**).

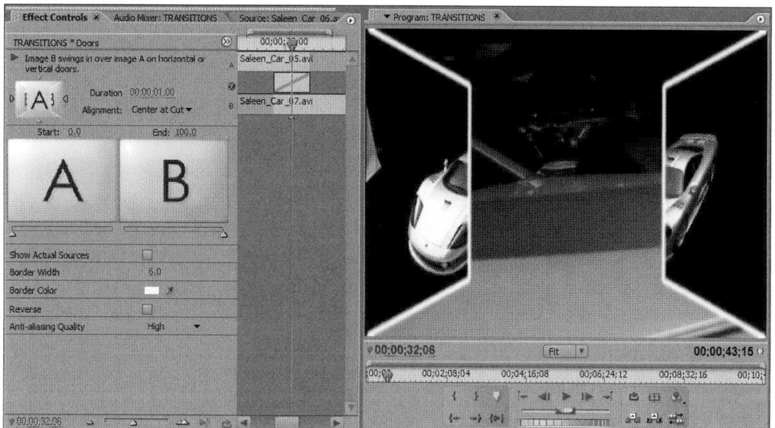

Figure 7.4 An example of a 3D Motion transition, the Doors transition opens or closes "doors" to reveal the incoming shot. Because the doors open or close, they allude to a third dimension or Z plane. You can add a border to the edge of the Doors effect and also anti-alias the border to make it more smooth.

- **Dissolve.** Contains methods of fading one shot into the other. This is the folder I draw from most often.
- **Iris.** Holds transitions that originate from an expanding centered shape, like the iris of a camera that dilates (**Figure 7.5**).

Figure 7.5 Using the Iris transitions you can pick from various shapes and have those shapes grow from nothing to reveal the incoming shot. Notice the description for this Iris Star transition in the top left of the Effect Controls panel.

- **Map.** Contains transitions that enable you to map certain image properties (luma and channel) to each other over the course of the transition. These transitions might be better termed as effects, because they overlap the two clips as opposed to creating a transition between the two (**Figures 7.6a** and **b**).

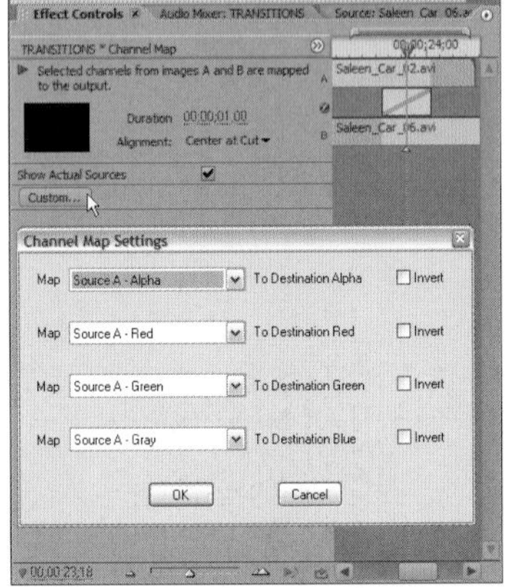

a

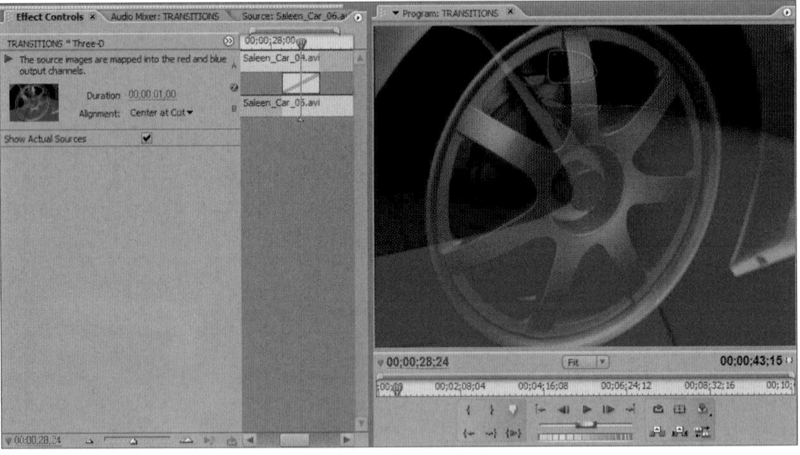

b

Figures 7.6a and b The Channel Map transition allows you to map specific color channels from one image to the channels of another image (a), causing them to show through. The result (b) can be an interesting effect, but not a useful transition.

- **Page Peel.** Includes transitions that peel away in different fashions, revealing another shot beneath.
- **Slide.** Holds transitions that slide one image on top of the other in various ways. There are also a number of band slides that look like strips of material that slide in separately and join together to make the new incoming shot.

- **Special Effect.** Contains more effect-like transitions. For example, Displace adds the image of the second shot to the first shot, not in a transitional way, but as an effect. Three-D maps the outgoing image to red and the incoming image to blue, like the effect of wearing red-and-blue 3D glasses. These are still considered transitions, because the effect requires two video sources (**Figures 7.7a** and **b**).

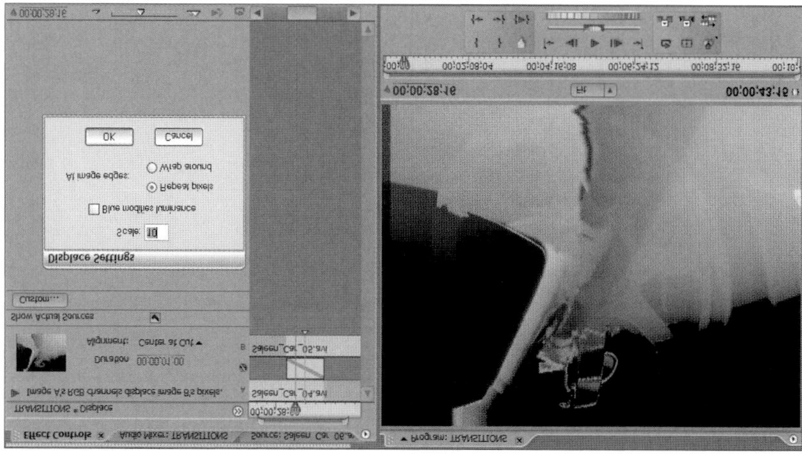

a

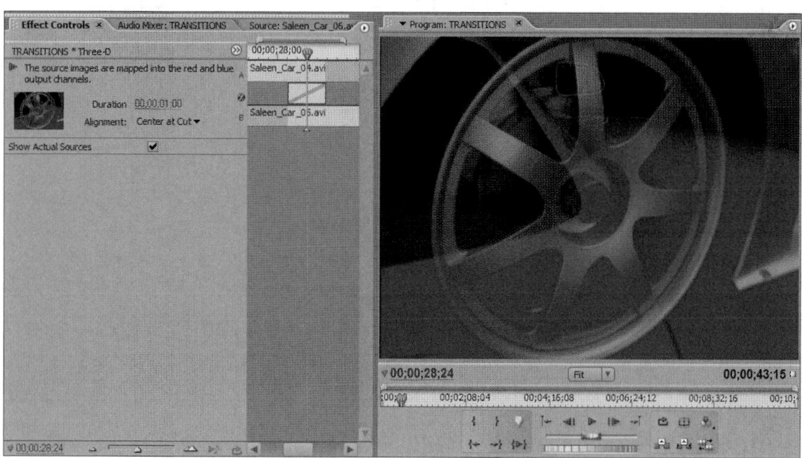

b

Figures 7.7a and b Displace (a) layers the two images, having the RGB color information of the outgoing clip A displace the pixels of the incoming clip B. The Three-D transition (b) produces a red/blue effect. In both cases these aren't really dynamic transitions; they are overlay effects.

While there are enough transitions here to get plenty of work done and have some creative choices, you can expand your transition options when you invest in a third-party capture card. Wedding and event videographers who need to have transitions with color, motion, and a bit more personality, for example, would benefit from more options than the standard transitions that come with Premiere Pro. Other editors, such as for film, TV, and music videos, and hobbyists certainly have enough transitions to choose from in Premiere Pro. Just be judicious in your selection of transitions, considering your audience and tone of the transition. A Star Iris Wipe might be flashier, for example, but perhaps a Cross Dissolve would better blend with your project's tone.

Figure 7.8 Set your default transition by right-clicking on a transition in the folder and selecting Set Selected as Default Transition.

- **Stretch.** Includes transitions in which the incoming images start at certain sizes and are stretched in different ways to reveal themselves.
- **Wipe.** Contains transitions that use the wiping technique of lines or shapes wiping in a set direction to reveal an incoming shot underneath. Wipes are another favorite of mine, because if you time a directional wipe with action that is moving in your shots, you can wipe with the action, hiding the edit more efficiently.
- **Zoom.** Contains transitions that magnify into and out of your images as a means of hiding the cuts between the shots. Cross Zoom, for example, focuses in very tightly on your outgoing image, cuts to a close-up view of your incoming image, and quickly pulls back to reveal the full image. The result is quick zoom in and out where one shot becomes another.

When editing in the timeline, if you reach the end of a shot that you would like to fade out or a cut where you want to apply a transition, it is only a keyboard shortcut away to add your default transition to the content at the current Edit Line position.

Default Transition

Out of the box, Premiere Pro's default video transition is Cross Dissolve, but perhaps you'd prefer another transition to be a keyboard shortcut away at all times. To choose or change the default transition, select the transition you want from the list in the Effects panel. With the transition highlighted, simply right-click on it and select Set Selected as Default Transition (**Figure 7.8**). The transition's icon now has a red border indicating it is assigned as your default. You can only have one audio and one video default transition.

You can quickly add the default audio and the default video transitions to the timeline using their keyboard shortcuts: Ctrl+D adds the default video transition, and Ctrl+Shift+D adds default audio transition. Once again, CTI position and targeted tracks are the keys to indicating where you want your transition added.

Default Durations

You can set a default duration for your transitions in your General Preferences. Choose Edit > Preferences > General, then input the desired number of frames for Video Default Transition Duration and the desired number of seconds for Audio Default Transition Duration (**Figure 7.9**). Whenever you add a transition to the timeline, it will automatically last the number of frames or seconds you specified.

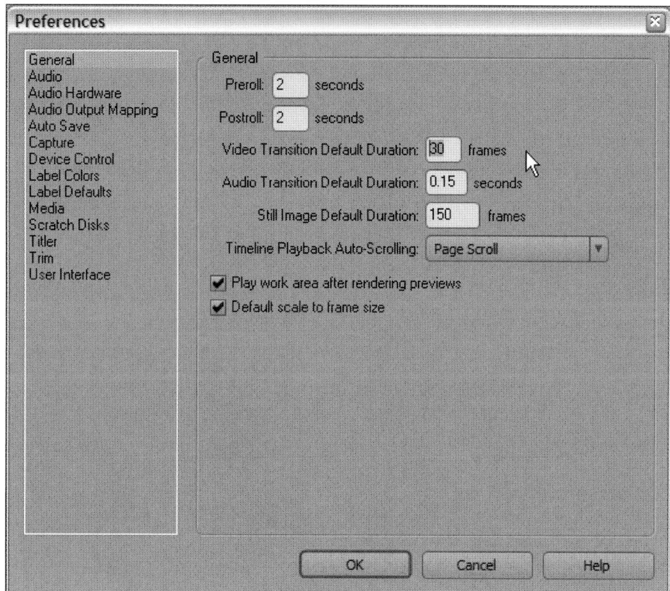

Figure 7.9 In the General Preferences dialog you can assign the default duration values for your video and audio transitions. Video transition durations are based on frames, while audio durations are based on milliseconds and can have subframe values. For example, 0.05 is a valid duration for a tiny audio transition.

If you need to change the setting while you work, choose Default Transition Duration from the Effects panel's wing menu. When I am adding a lot of audio transitions between clips so that there are no straight cuts, for example, I usually shorten the Audio Transition Default Duration to a bit less than one second. Sometimes a 0.10 second transition gets rid of the abrupt pop that exists when one audio clip cuts directly to the next. For fading both audio and video clips in and out, I find one second is usually enough, but that's simply a matter of timing, tempo, and personal taste.

Custom Bins

If you find that you use a specific group of transitions and you hate navigating to them every time, you can create a new bin in the Effects panel to hold your favorites. Choose New Custom Bin from the wing menu, or click the folder-shaped icon in the lower-right of the window.

Now you can drag the transitions or filters that you use most into the custom bin and rename it accordingly. Note that the transitions or effects do not move from their normal resting place; instead, Premiere places a shortcut to them in the custom folder for easy access. I recommend creating one custom bin for your favorite transitions and another for your favorite effects. Once you have your favorites organized for easy access, you're ready to drag and drop them into the timeline.

a

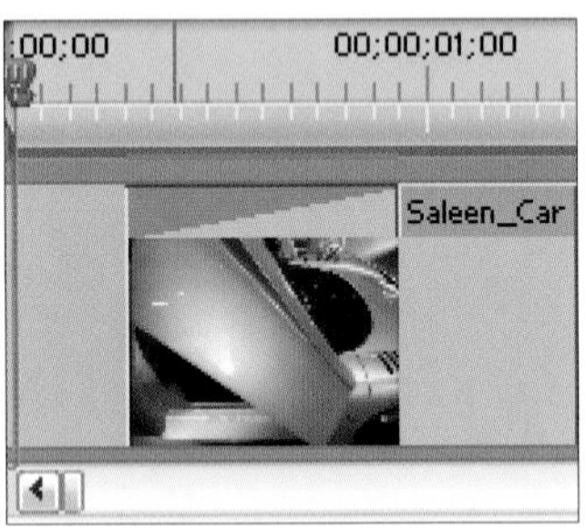

b

Figures 7.10a and b A single-sided transition is being added to the head of the clip (a). Because there is no material before the shot, the cursor displays the transition icon for starting at the cut. The darkened overlay area represents the content that the transition will cover. In 7.10b, you can see the results.

Dragging and Dropping Transitions

You can place transitions in the timeline in three different ways:

- Starting at the cut
- Ending at the cut
- Centered at the cut

The method used depends on the surrounding media and the mouse position when you release the transition.

Adding Transitions to a Single Clip

When you are working with a single clip, such as when you fade up a clip from black, you'll want to use the starting or ending at the cut methods. Starting at the cut means that when you drop a transition into the timeline, the transition will start from the cut point at which you inserted it.

For example, you want your project's first clip to fade up from black, so you need a transition to start at the cut—at the start of that initial clip (**Figures 7.10a** and **b**). Grab the Cross Dissolve (Video Transitions/Dissolve), and drag it to the head of that clip. Because there is no adjoining media to the left of the first clip, you see a blue line on the left, indicating the transition's start, and the transition icon to the right, indicating where the transition occurs. Notice the darkened area that appears when you hold the transition over the head of the shot. This shows you the transition's duration. Release the mouse to add the Cross Dissolve to the clip. The clip will now have the transition "Band-Aid" covering its head.

Ending at the cut is opposite of starting at the cut. To fade a clip out, for example, drag the transition to the right edge of the last clip (**Figure 7.11**). This time the blue line is on the right and the transition icon on the left, indicating the transition ends at the cut point onto which you drop the transition.

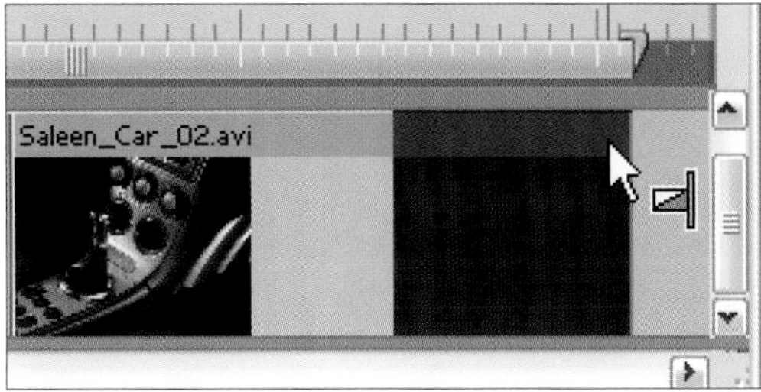

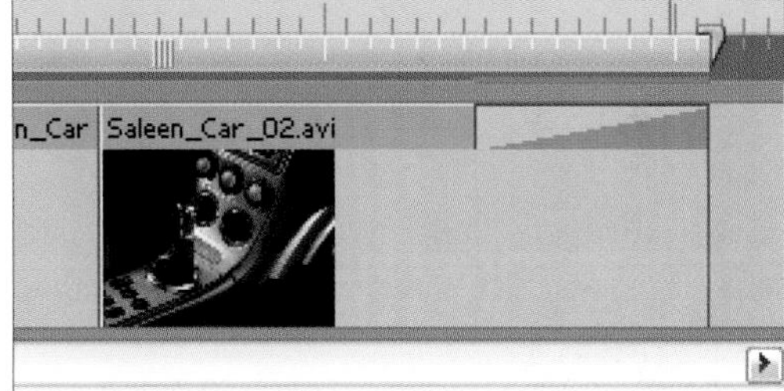

Figure 7.11 The opposite of Figure 7.10, this transition ends at the cut. The clip will fade down to the black empty space of the track.

Remember, to have a transition starting or ending at the cut, you cannot have any adjoining material near the clip. Any material directly to the left or right of the clip will be incorporated in the transition. For a clean starting or ending transition from or to black, for example, you need at least a one-frame gap of empty space to ensure the transition does not connect material.

Adding Transitions Between Two Shots

To create a balanced transition between two shots, center the transition at the cut. Centering is an option only when you are cutting between two shots. When you drag a transition over the cut point between two shots and hold the mouse directly over the center of the cut, the blue line appears in the middle of the transition icon. This means that the transition will have half of its duration on one side of the cut and half on the other (see **Figure 7.12**).

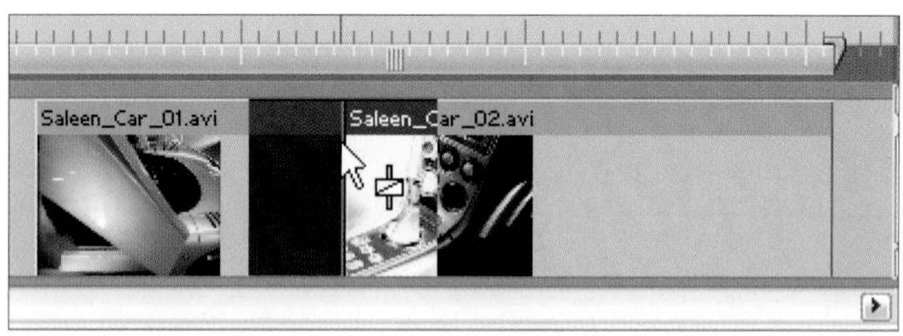

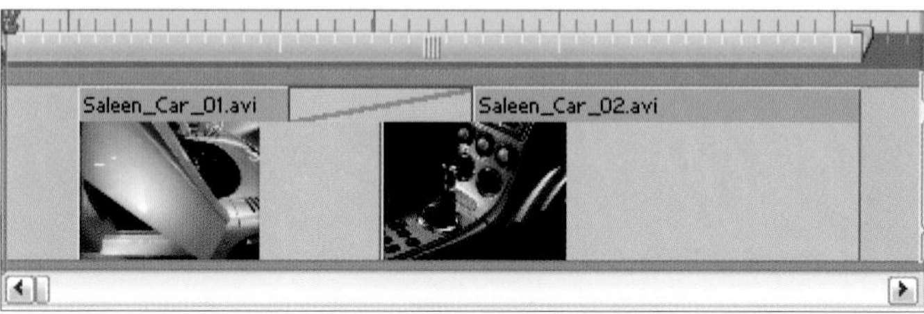

Figure 7.12 Drag and drop a transition directly over the cut point between two clips for a balanced, centered transition that connects the two shots.

Premiere uses an equal number of frames from each shot to display the transition properly. If you have a 30-frame transition centered on the cut between shots 1 and 2, Premiere needs 15 additional frames from the head of shot 2 and 15 frames from the tail of shot 1. If you only had 10 frames extra from shot 2, Premiere adjusts the transition duration to 20 frames and uses 10 extra frames from each shot to ensure the transition remains centered.

Sometimes you don't want or need such perfect symmetry in your transition, however, which brings us back to the techniques of starting and ending at the cut with two adjacent clips.

Drag a transition to the left side of a cut between two shots to get the icon for a transition that ends on the cut (**Figures 7.13a** and **b**). The current cut point between the shots will be the end of the transition when you add it to the timeline. Premiere adds additional material from the second shot so that the transition occurs properly. If you had a 30-frame transition ending on the cut from shot 1 to shot 2, for example, Premiere needs an additional 30 frames from the head of shot 2 for the transition to display properly. If there is not enough material, say you only had 20 frames, then Premiere assigns the transitions duration to be 20 frames instead.

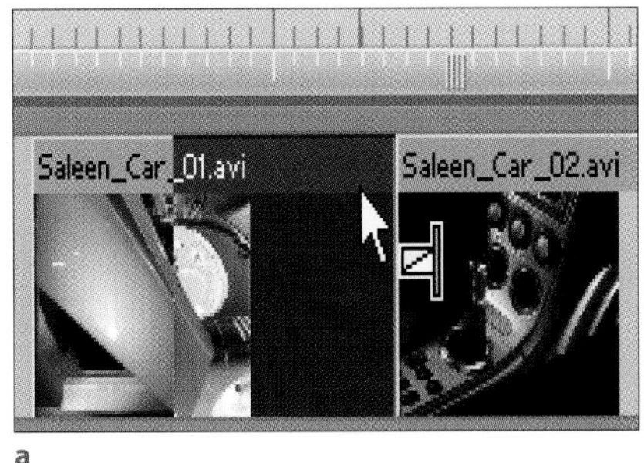

a

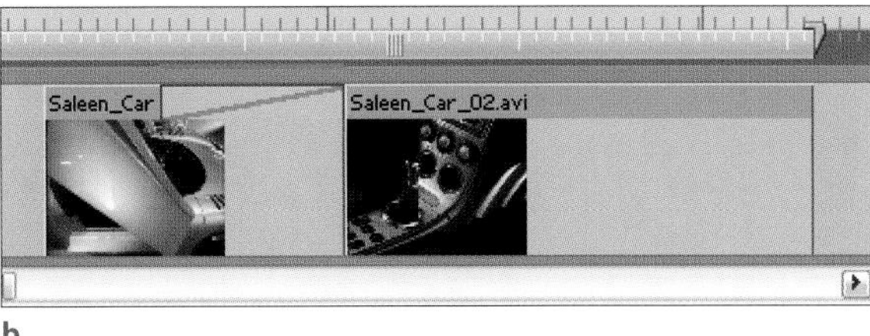

b

Figures 7.13a and b When you drag and drop a transition slightly to the left of the cut, you see the ending at the cut icon (a). The transition still applies to both clips and will complete at the current cut point with the image entirely focused on the incoming shot.

Drag just to the right of the cut between shots 1 and 2 to get the icon for a transition that starts on the cut (**Figure 7.14**). Using the default duration from the previous example, the transition would need 30 additional frames of tail material from shot 1 to start at the cut and transition to shot 2. Again, if fewer frames are available, Premiere will shorten the transition's duration accordingly.

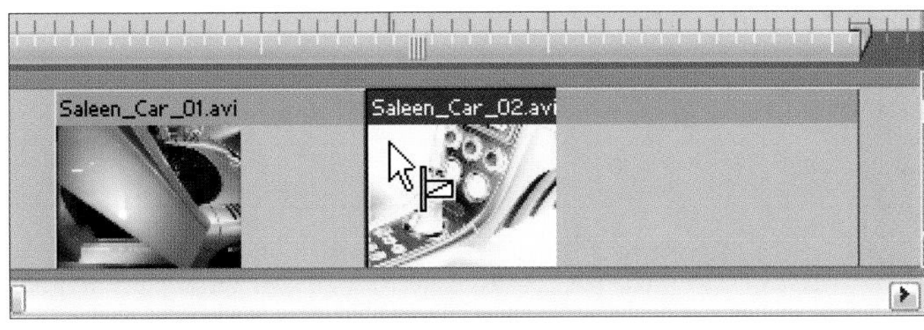

Figure 7.14 When you drag and drop just to the right of the cut between two clips, you see the icon for a transition that starts at the cut. With audio clips, transition placement functions the exact same way.

At some zoom magnifications, you may not have enough space to drag to the left or right of the cut to place a starting or ending at the cut transition. If you are zoomed out such that a few pixels are a few seconds, you will be able to target the center of the cut only. Not to worry, the Effect Controls panel can very easily adjust the alignment of a transition that has already been placed.

Keyboard Shortcuts and Adding Your Default Transitions

If all this dragging and dropping of transitions has your mouse a bit tired, you can assign your default transitions to the timeline with a few simple keystrokes: Ctrl+D to add a video transition, Ctrl+Shift+D to add an audio transition. To assign a default transition to the timeline, you must first target a track and then identify the location of placement using the position of the Edit Line.

For a transition to be properly added, the Edit Line must be resting over clip content on the targeted track and in close proximity to or exactly at a cut point. You can apply default transitions to both audio and video clips in only three basic ways:

- Starting at the cut at the single-sided head of a clip
- Ending at the cut at the single-sided tail of a clip
- Centered at the cut between two adjacent clips

Using the keyboard shortcut to advance to the next edit point (Page Up and Page Down), you can quickly navigate to a cut point and then press Ctrl+D to add a video transition or Ctrl+Shift+D to add an audio transition. Just pay attention to which tracks are targeted and where the Edit Line rests. Now that you know how to position transitions, take a look at the Effect Controls panel where you can adjust transitions that are already in the timeline.

Effect Controls Panel

You can adjust and assign all your effect and transition parameters in the Effect Controls panel (**Figure 7.15**). Double-click on a transition icon in the Timeline panel, and the selected transition opens in the Effect Controls panel for adjustments. You can also reach the Effect Controls panel by choosing Windows > Effect Controls or by clicking the Effect Controls tab in one of your workspace frames.

The Effect Controls panel is defined by two distinct areas: The left area is the Settings area and right area is the Navigation and Keyframe (for effects) area.

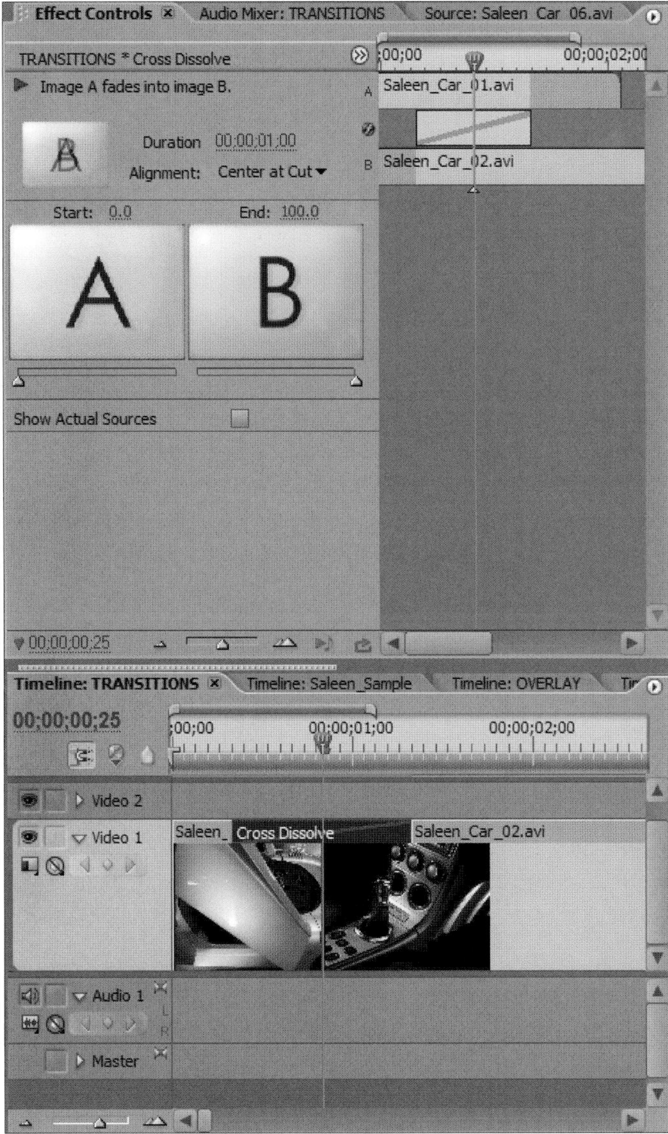

Figure 7.15 With a transition selected in the timeline, the Effect Controls panel reveals transition settings, parameters, and an AB roll track preview. The outgoing clip in the transition, Saleen_Car_01, appears on track A, and the incoming clip, Saleen_Car_02, appears on track B. The transition is the center track area.

The Settings area (see **Figure 7.16**) displays the name of the sequence you are working in and the type of transition that is open. A description of the transition appears below with a Preview Play button. Click it to loop a thumbnail playback of the applied transition. By default, the Thumbnail Preview window shows only icons to preview the transition. To see what the video in the timeline looks like, you must click on

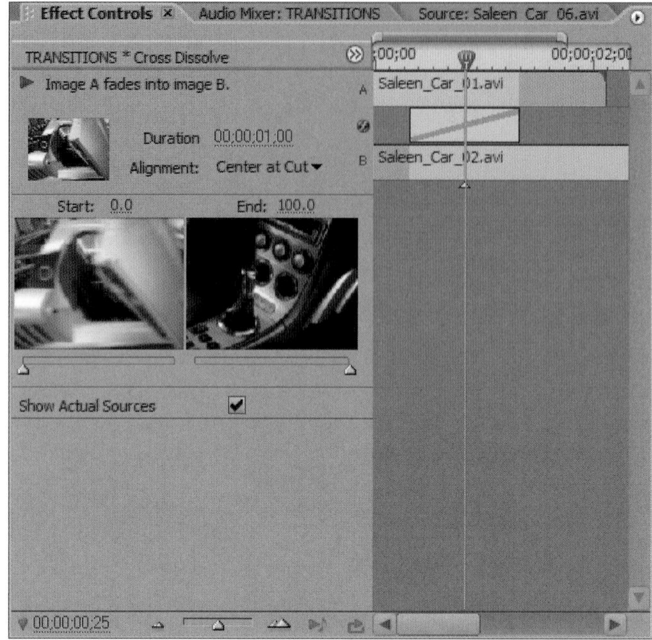

Figure 7.16 When you select a transition, the Settings area of the Effect Controls panel displays the sequence and transition names, a short description of the transition, previews, settings for Duration and Alignment, as well as the option to show the actual source frames.

the Show Actual Sources check box. The Duration hot text box enables you to dynamically scrub the value to either increase or decrease the duration of the transition. In the Alignment field, you choose a method of alignment from the drop-down list: Start at Cut, End at Cut, or Center at Cut. All three respect the original cut point that was assigned to your clips. The large Start and End preview windows allow you to customize the percentage value for which your transition will start from and end at, as well as reveal the flow of the transition, the A roll (start) to B roll (end) flow.

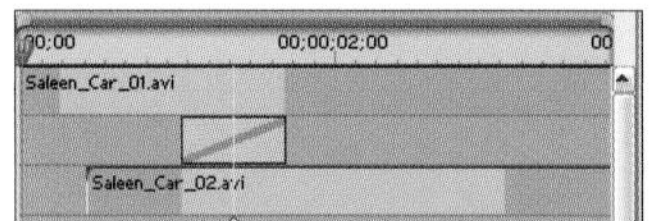

Figure 7.17 The entire Saleen_Car_01 clip is on the A track in the Navigation and Keyframe area of the Effect Controls panel. Only the light blue portion of the clip, however, will be visible in the sequence. The dark blue areas reflect additional clip material that is beyond the timeline frame boundaries of the used instance. With this view you can easily determine whether you have extra material to draw from when extending or contracting your clip material.

In the Navigation area to the right (**Figure 7.17**), you get to see a display of your transition and the material it covers in an AB editing mode. The clip on the top is A (note the icon), B is the bottom track, and the transition is in the middle. The bright colored portion of the clips signifies parts of the clips that are used and visible when playing back in the Timeline panel. Additional unused material, if any, is displayed as darkened material either after the transition on track A or before the transition on track B. Being able to see if there is additional material gives you the option of knowing which adjustments you can make to the transition.

The viewing area bar allows you to zoom in and out and navigate to different sections of your material. You can scrub the CTI from either the timeline or the Navigation area of the Effect Controls panel. To make adjustments to your transition and clip material, click, drag, and move the transition or clip edges using the various editing tools that reveal themselves depending on where you hold your mouse (**Figures 7.18a**, **b**, and **c**).

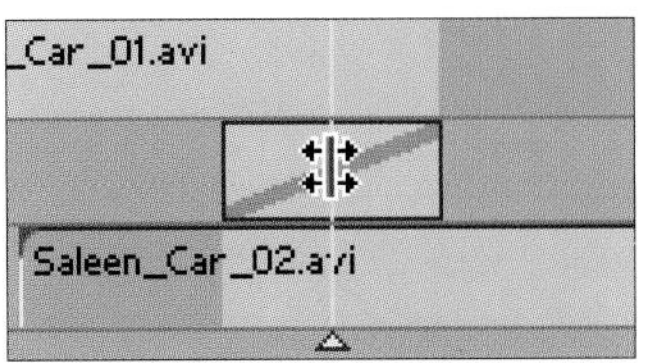

a

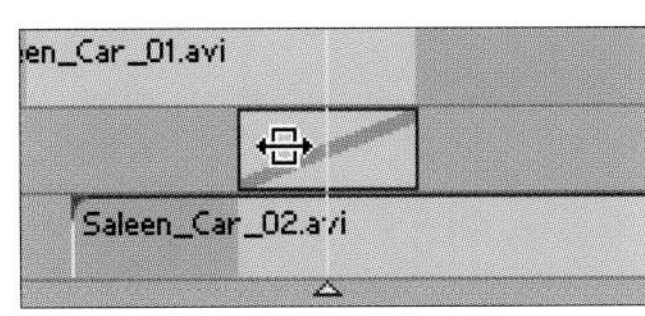

b

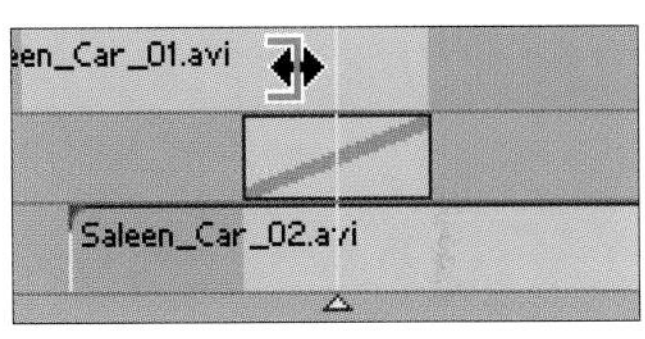

c

Figures 7.18a, b, and c Hold your mouse over the exact cut point of the two clips to get the Rolling Edit tool (a), which enables you to roll the edit point between the two clips while also sliding the entire transition. Hold your mouse over the transition to get the Slide tool (b), which allows you to preserve the cut point of the clips, but slide the transition in its exact duration to a different timeline position. Hold over either clip near the cut point to get the Ripple Edit tool (c), with which you can ripple edit the clip material, preserving the transition and the adjacent relationship of the clips.

Adjusting Your Transitions in the Effect Controls Panel

The white line in the middle of the tracks (**Figure 7.19**) signifies the original physical cut point between the two clips. If you toggle between Start at Cut, End at Cut, and Center at Cut, notice how the alignment of the transition is displayed in accordance with the cut point. To change your cut point, you can roll the white Edit Line back and forth. To properly change the cut point, hold the mouse over the Edit Line so that the cursor appears as the Rolling Edit tool. The Edit Line will update in the Timeline panel and a two-up display in the Program Monitor will reveal your updating cut point frames. When you roll the Edit Line, it's also nice to see that the duration and alignment of the transition is preserved. While you roll your edit, the two-up display in the Program Monitor reveals the last frame of your A roll on the left and the first frame of your B roll on the right.

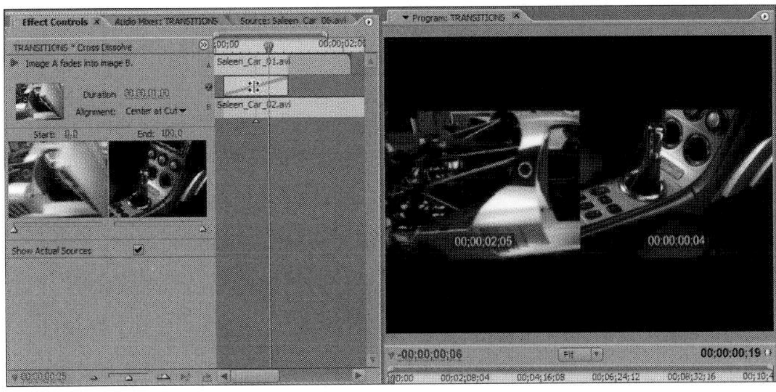

Figure 7.19 When you roll the edit point in the Transition view mode of the Effect Controls panel, the Program Monitor provides a two-up display of the new cut point, showing the outgoing frame on the left and incoming frame on the right. The frame count number in the bottom left corner of the Program Monitor tells you how many frames you have moved the edit. In the image, the CTI occupies the original position of the edit.

To update the position of the transition but preserve the original cut point, hold the mouse over the boundary of the transition so that the Slide tool icon appears. Now, slide the transition back and forth to move its entire position and preserve its duration. The two-up display shows the same last frame of A and first frame of B (**Figure 7.20**).

Figure 7.20 When you slide the transition itself, you get another two-up display that shows the first frame from the outgoing shot to be included in the transition on the left and the last frame of the incoming shot to be included on the right. The timecode feedback at the bottom of the Program Monitor shows the exact frame position of the sliding transition's In and Out points.

To extend either edge of the transition to make it longer or shorter, you need to hold the mouse over the edge of the transition so that you get the Edge Trim tool. Now, click and drag left or right to increase or reduce the duration of the transition. Dragging the right edge moves the incoming point from the B roll, so the right side of the two-up in the Program Monitor updates as you trim. Dragging the left edge updates the last frame of the A roll, so the left side of the Program Monitor's two-up updates.

To make ripple edits to clips under a transition, hold the mouse a tiny bit further inside the edge of the clip on A or B. Once you see the thick Ripple Edit tool (**Figures 7.21a** and **b**), any adjustment will ripple that clip's In or Out point, thus shifting all tracks in the timeline left or right appropriately. The two-up display will reveal the edge frame that is being adjusted, A on the left and B on the right.

a

b

Figures 7.21a and b By dragging the outgoing shot to the right, I reduced its overall duration by 10 frames (as shown in the feedback of 7.21a's Program Monitor). In 7.21b, I added 11 frames of material by sliding the B clip to the right. Notice how you can snap the head of the source material to the cut point, and Premiere indicates that there is no additional material to the left of the clip's head (see the dog ear).

The power of all these tools and the strength of Premiere Pro's new transition architecture is that although a transition may cover an edit point, you can still make editing adjustments to that point.

Timeline Adjustments

Outside of the Effect Controls panel you can still make adjustments to transitions in the Timeline panel. If the track is collapsed, you only will be able to edge trim the duration of the transition and slide it to a different position between the clips.

When the track is expanded, the transition reveals itself in the upper portion of the track with the cut point of the clips below. To make modifications to the transition, click and adjust within the boundary of the transition "Band-Aid." To make adjustments to the clip (ripple and rolling edits), select the appropriate tool or shortcut modifier, then click and drag below the transition in the clip cut point area.

Although you don't lose functionality in the timeline adjustments, you do not get to see the additional available material. So if you are dragging a transition edge in the timeline and it won't go any further, double-click the transition and look in the Effect Controls panel. You will find that there is no additional material to make up for the adjustment you want to apply.

Things to Remember

When you add a transition between two clips, you are defining a method through which one shot moves into another. Your transitions can start at, end at, or be centered on a cut point, plus they can be applied to all tracks. If there is content on Video 3 that can be enhanced by transitioning to another track, then by all means exploit that. The ability to have six titles fading one into the other and not have them populate two separate tracks (as in former versions of Premiere) is an excellent preservation of timeline real estate.

Although you don't need to completely understand all the adjustment tools in the Effect Controls panel just yet, I encourage you to experiment with some adjustments and get used to having the panel open while you work in the timeline. While you play, be sure to pay attention to the power and importance of the Ripple Edit tool, which is used to edge trim clip material when a transition is joining two clips together.

In the next chapter, you will explore the Effect Controls panel in a different context: effect adjustments.

CHAPTER

8

Effect Controls Basics

Working with Premiere Pro's many effects is similar to working with transitions. Like transitions, Premiere's Standard effects are grouped by type in the Effects panel. As you did with transitions, you add Standard effects to media by dragging them from the Effects panel and dropping them onto clips in the timeline. To fine-tune your effects, you use the Effect Controls panel (**Figure 8.1**). That's when Premiere Pro's power becomes evident.

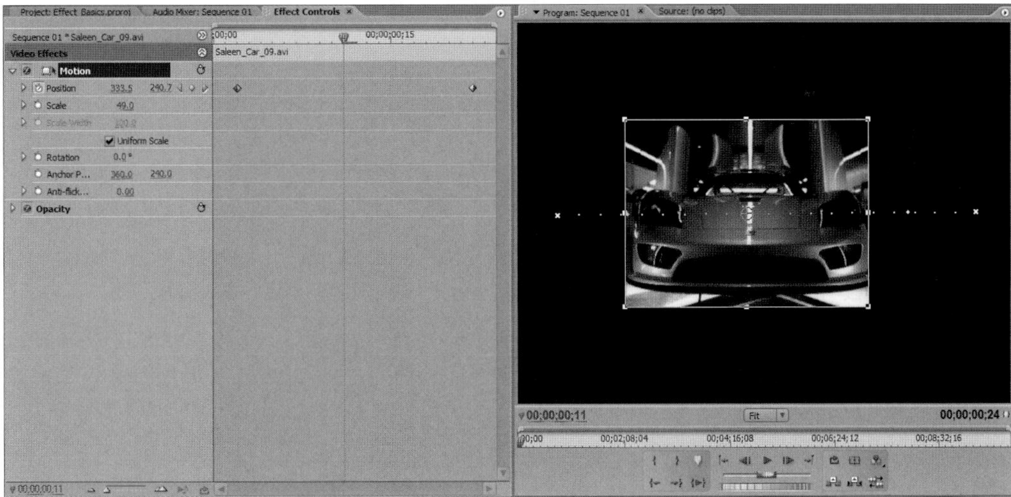

Figure 8.1 When a clip is selected from the timeline, the Effect Controls panel provides its effect settings for adjustment. The Program Monitor displays a keyframed motion path that was assigned in the Effect Controls panel.

If you're familiar with Adobe After Effects, the Effect Controls panel's design and implementation may seem familiar to you. In designing Premiere Pro, Adobe tried to bridge the few gaps between After Effects and Premiere. Because Adobe designed a number of Premiere Pro features similar to their After Effects counterparts, if you're familiar with one program, you will be comfortable with effect work in both. With 2.0, the inclusion of Value and Velocity graphs for individual effect parameters closes the effect gap even more between the two applications.

Standard Effects and Fixed Effects

Before you dive too deep into adjusting effects in the Effect Controls panel, you need to understand the two types of effects you can adjust: Standard effects and Fixed effects.

Standard effects are the effects that Premiere provides in the Effects panel's folders. You must manually apply them to your clips by dragging and dropping. *Fixed effects* are the basic properties that a clip has by default when it is placed on a track in the timeline. Video clips have two Fixed effects: Motion and Opacity. Audio clips have one: Volume (**Figure 8.2**).

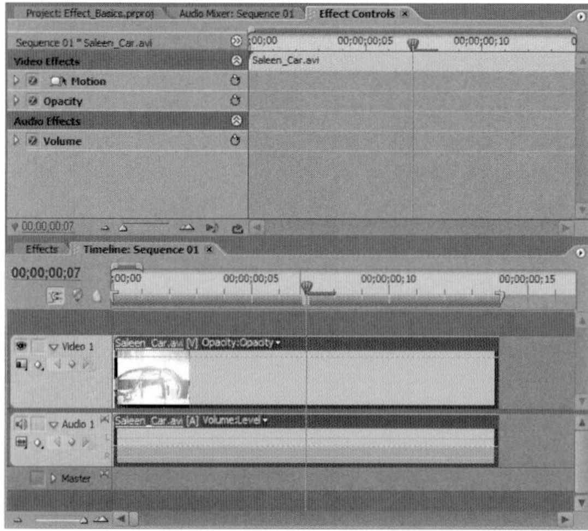

Figure 8.2 The selected clip has linked audio and video, so the three Fixed Effects—Motion, Opacity, and Volume—are immediately adjustable in the Effect Controls panel. Notice how the name of the selected clip and the open sequence is visible in the Effect Controls panel, as well as a display of the clip in the area to the right.

Video Fixed Effects: Motion

When you add a video clip in the timeline, you are placing it over a black, empty frame of space, whose size is defined by your Project Settings. You can use the Motion Fixed effect to reduce, enlarge, or move your clip within that frame of space. Combine the Motion effect with keyframes and you can pan and zoom around an image. The basic Motion parameters are

- **Position.** The physical location of the image inside or outside the frame. You can adjust the clip's X axis value, which moves it right or left, and Y axis value, which moves it up or down. To "hide" a portion of your clip, adjust Position so part of the clip is outside the boundary of the frame. Only the portion within the frame boundary will be visible (**Figure 8.3**).

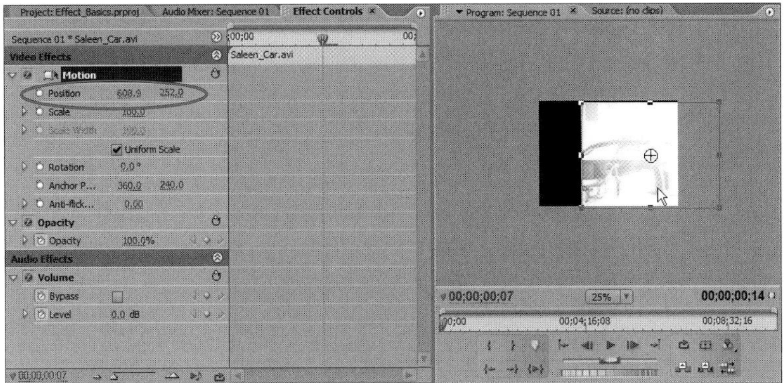

Figure 8.3 Clicking and dragging the clip updates its Position value in the Effect Controls panel. You can also modify the X and Y values directly. With the Monitor set to 25% view, you can see the visible frame area (black square) and the boundary of the clip being repositioned (wireframe).

- **Scale.** The overall size of your selected clip. 100% is the normal default value. You can adjust the Scale Height and Scale Width of a clip separately if you click off the check box for Uniform Scale. Leaving Uniform Scale checked ensures that all scaling adjustments are equal with the height and width (**Figure 8.4**).

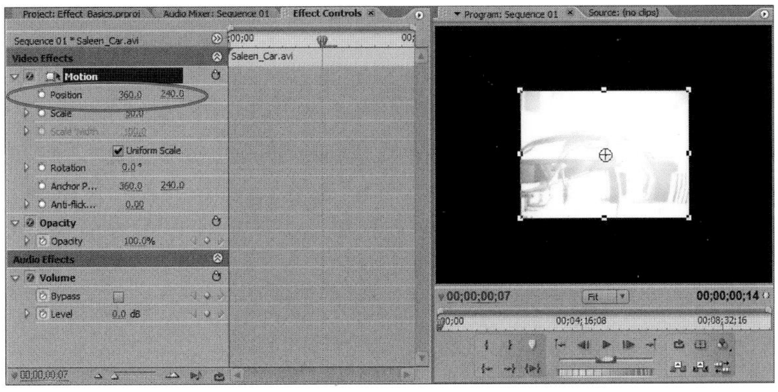

Figure 8.4 When you adjust the scale of your clip you can adjust the Height, the Width, or both together (Uniform). Here a 50% uniform scale adjustment results in the clip being half the size of its normal scale.

NOTES

Keyframing is a technique for which you assign changes in values to effect parameters at specific frames, called keyframes, in a clip. The job of the keyframes is to identify specific effect values at exact frames within the boundary of clip. For example, you set the first frame of your clip as a keyframe with the Scale effect set to 100%, and you set the last frame of the clip as a keyframe with Scale set to 200%. When Premiere plays back this clip, it dynamically increases the clip's scale from 100% to 200% over the duration of the clip, so the clip seems to smoothly zoom from 100% to 200%.

- **Rotation.** Defines the angle at which a clip spins (rotates). If keyframing is not turned on, you can change the rotation angle dynamically. To make your image rotate you must turn keyframing on and set at least two keyframes with different Rotation values. The clip will spin from the first keyframe's Rotation setting to the second's (**Figures 8.5** and **8.6**). If you want to rotate a full 360 degrees, the rotation value will be preceded by a prefix in the form "1x," with the number indicating how many full rotations have passed.

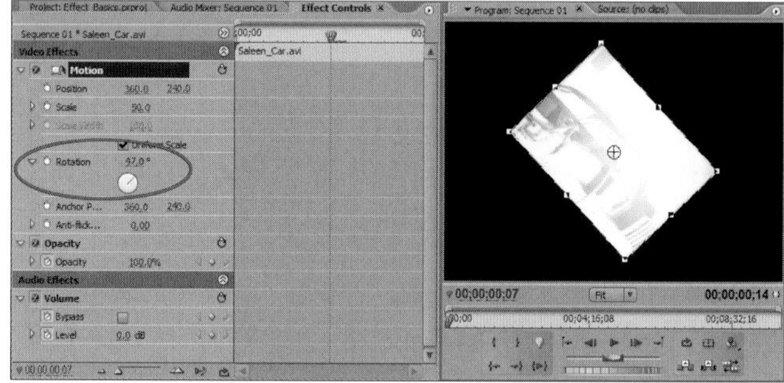

Figure 8.5 With the scale still at 50% it's easy to see a rotation adjustment applied to the clip. This rotation setting is at 47 degrees.

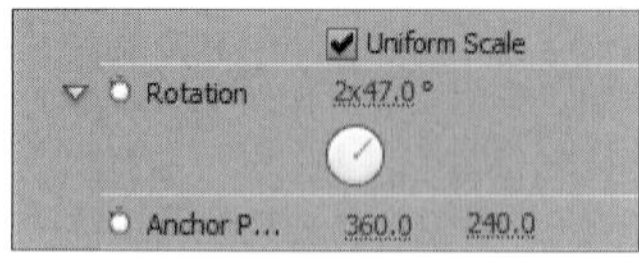

Figure 8.6 This rotation setting is set at 47 plus two spins.

- **Anchor Point.** The spot at which you choose to center your motion adjustments. Think of the anchor point as a tack through your image. If you move the anchor point to the bottom-right corner, any rotation would spin from the corner, not the center of the image (**Figure 8.7**).

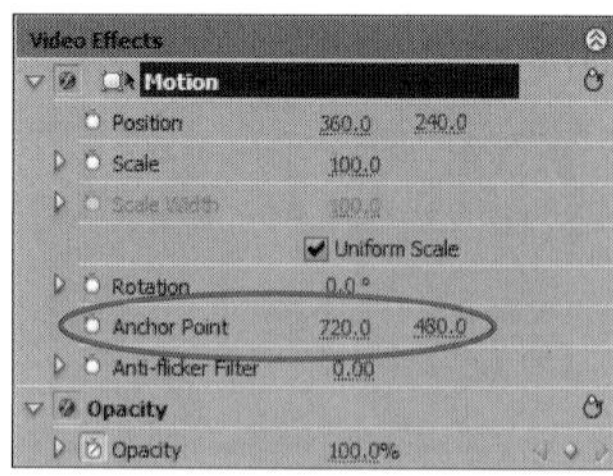

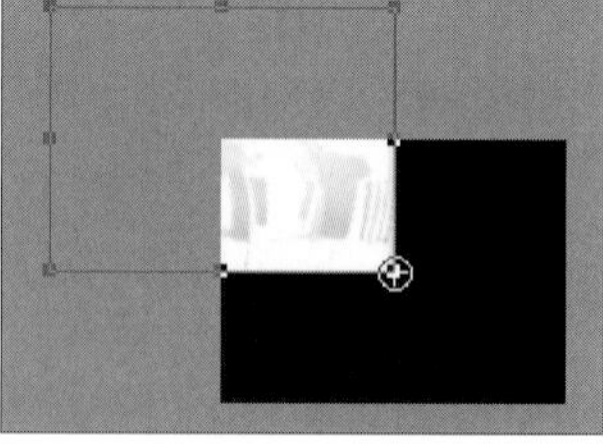

Figure 8.7 The anchor point here is defined as the lower-right corner of the frame, which has an exact coordinate value of 720×480. The anchor point and adjustments defines the point where effects and adjusts will apply symmetrically. If you were to apply rotation with this anchor point, the clip would spin and rotate around the lower-right corner.

- **Anti-flicker Filter.** When animating still images in recent versions of Premiere Pro, noticeable image flickers or a sort of unwanted shimmering effect often shows on the images when they are played back. This does not happen all the time, but it can occur. If, when animating a title or still image, you get a flickering/shimmering effect that you want to remove, try increasing the Anti-flicker Filter value (**Figure 8.8**).

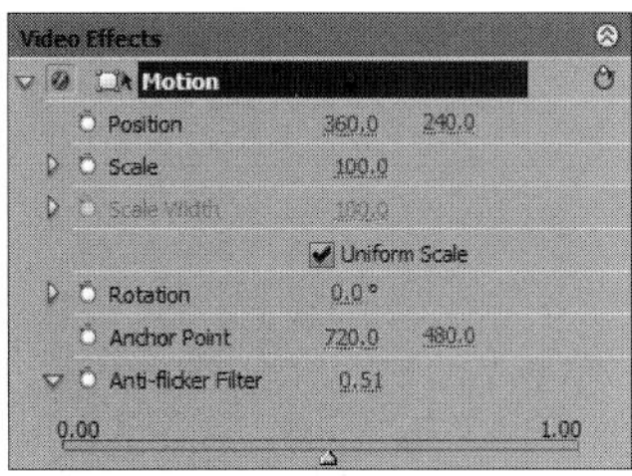

Figure 8.8 The Anti-flicker Filter is a new Fixed effect attribute that allows you to reduce any unwanted flickering or shimmering that might appear when animating still images in the timeline. Increasing the filter value reduces the presence of the flickering.

You can adjust the parameters for Motion, and other Fixed effects, in the Effect Controls panel (more on this coming up).

Video Fixed Effects: Opacity

The Opacity effect enables you to adjust the transparency of a clip so that you can see through it to varying degrees. In previous versions, Opacity was used to fade up titles, graphics, stills, and video clips on any track other than Video 1. Because Premiere Pro can use transitions on all tracks to fade in and out, you can now use Opacity for custom fades and overall opacity adjustments (**Figure 8.9**).

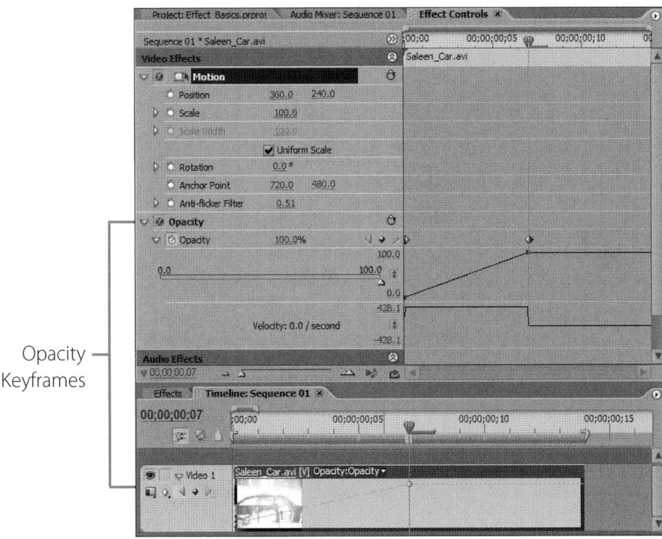

Figure 8.9 The two Opacity keyframes assigned in the Effect Controls panel are also visible in the timeline. Notice how the timeline keyframes have height positions that reflect their value going from 0 to 100% (a fade in). When you twirl down the Opacity effect listing not only can you see the ramp of the opacity, but you can also adjust the velocity of the ramp (more on this later). The keyframe value underneath the Edit Line in the Effect Controls panel has a value of 100. That is the same keyframe and Edit Line position as in the timeline.

Audio Fixed Effects: Volume

The single Fixed effect for audio clips is Volume, which has two parameters: Level and Bypass. Level adjusts the actual level of your audio clip either increasing it or decreasing it. Bypass enables you to turn off your level adjustments and use the default volume of the audio clip.

Adjusting an audio clip's Volume parameters affects the dB rating of the clip instance in the timeline. When keyframing is turned off, you are adjusting the overall volume of the entire clip. Turn keyframing on to dynamically fade up and fade down the volume levels of your audio clip (**Figure 8.10**).

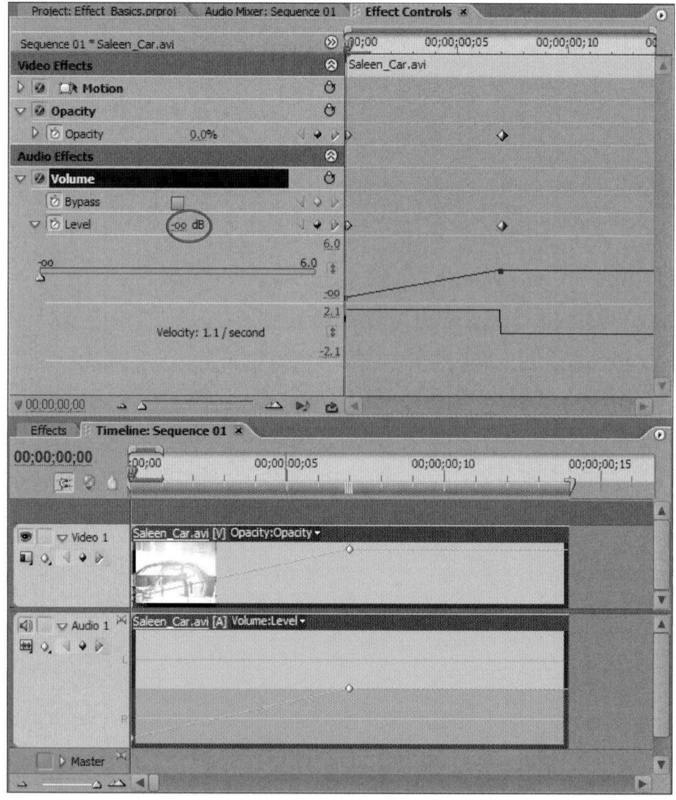

Figures 8.10 With the Edit Line on top of the first volume keyframe position, you can see that the start volume level is –0dB, which is the default normal level. This is a simple volume fade. To bypass any keyframed fade and play the audio at its original volume, you can turn on the Bypass Volume parameter.

Audio Standard Effects

The Audio Effects master folder in the Effects panel contains separate Mono, Stereo, and 5.1 subfolders, all of which contain the same Standard effects, customized by channel type. When adding these effects to your timeline, be sure to use the proper audio channel type. For example, mono clips would need Mono effects, stereo clips need effects from the Stereo folder, and 5.1 clips need those from the 5.1 folder. If you are ever unable to drop an audio effect on a clip, most likely you are trying to add an effect type that doesn't match the clip type.

As you may remember, you can modify a clip's gain before adding it to the timeline. Because clip gain is separate from clip volume, you will not see an adjustment to the displayed clip volume if you have adjusted the clip gain.

The Effect Controls Panel

In the last chapter, you learned the power of the Effect Controls panel for adjusting transitions. That panel takes on a different look and feel, however, when you adjust and manipulate clip effects. To start customizing your effect parameters, choose Window > Effect Controls. When you select a clip in the timeline, the left side of the Effect Controls panel lists the clip's Fixed and Standard effects and their parameters. The effects' associated keyframes appear on the right of the panel in a timeline view. Only when a clip is selected can you make adjustments to the effect parameters in the Effect Controls panel.

Depending on your preference, you can dock the Effect Controls panel in the Project panel frame, the Source Monitor frame, or you can leave it to float free as its own panel. To move from one frame to the other, click and drag the Effect Controls panel by its tab.

Effect Listings

Each effect listing has a twirl down triangle that enables you to expand the listing to reveal the effect's parameters or collapse it to view only the effect's name, on/off toggle, Reset button, and Direct Manipulation icon (**Figures 8.11a** and **b**).

The effect on/off toggle is at the far left of each listing. When the F is visible, the settings assigned within the effect will be applied to the selected clip. Click the F to turn off the effect for the selected clip. Turning an effect off deactivates it, but does not delete its parameters. This is useful when you're trying out multiple effects on the same clip. Disabling an effect also can improve real-time playback.

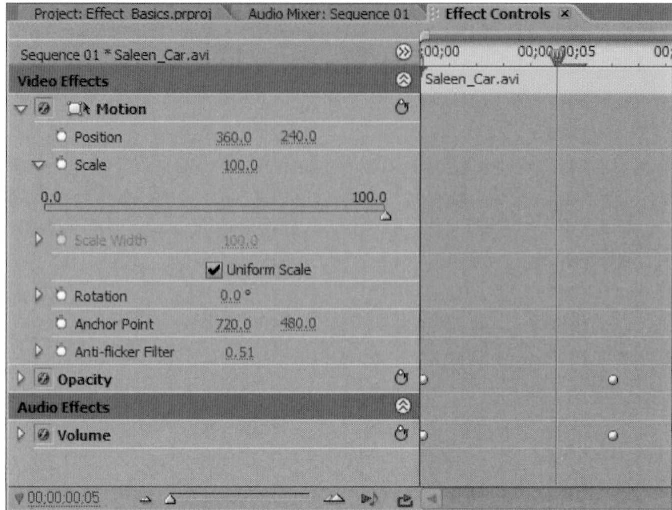

a

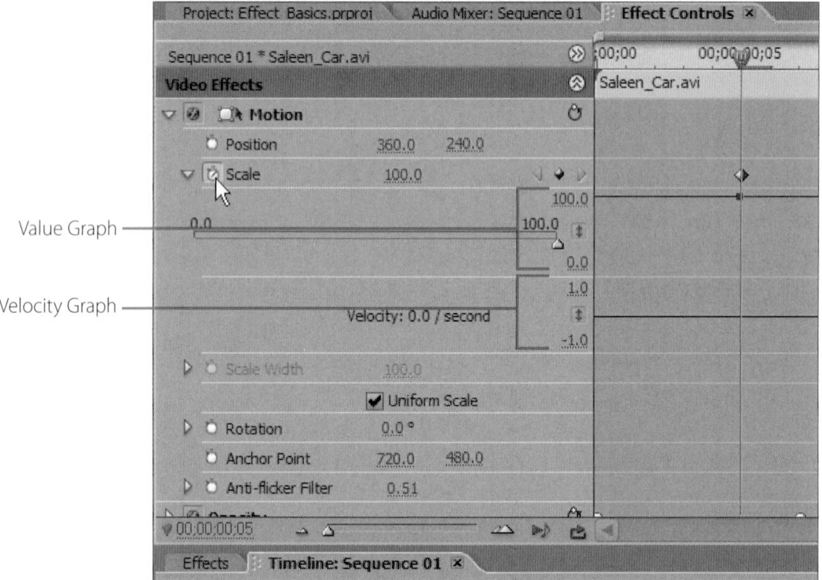

b

Figures 8.11a and b Twirling down the name of the effect reveals its effect parameters (Scale in the top image). Twirling down a parameter reveals, in most cases, an adjustment slider. To turn on keyframing for an individual parameter, click on the keyframe stopwatch for the parameter you want to adjust. Once you turn on keyframing, the effect listing expands further to show two keyframe graphs (Scale in the bottom image): The Value graph shows the effect value, and the Velocity graph shows the keyframe velocity between value keyframes.

On the opposite edge of the effect listing you'll find the Reset button. Click it to return the effect's parameters to their original state. Unfortunately, you cannot reset individual parameters, only the entire listing. Use Reset with caution on effects with multiple parameters: You can lose a lot of work very quickly. The Undo command may be a better choice.

Some effects, such as Motion, have the Direct Manipulation icon (a square with a mouse pointer next to it) before their names (**Figure 8.12**). Click on the effect name and the Program Monitor will display visible handles for you to grab and adjust. These handles directly manipulate a few specific parameters of the selected effect.

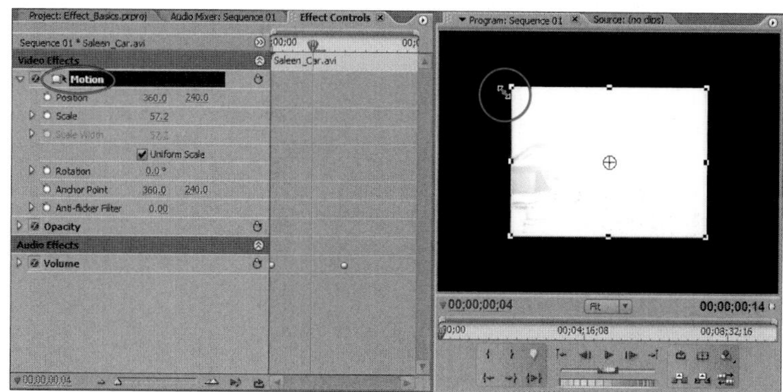

Figure 8.12 With direct manipulation turned on, you can click and drag from one of the corner handles to scale the selected clip. All your adjustments are dynamically updated into the settings area of the Effect Controls panel. In this figure I am adjusting the scale of the clip by dragging one of its corners inward.

Effect Parameters

To access an effect's parameters from the Effect Controls panel, twirl down the effect's listing. To the left of each parameter name is the Toggle Animation icon (a little stopwatch). Click it to enable or disable keyframe adjustments (see **Figures 8.13a**, **b**, and **c**). When the stopwatch is empty, keyframe adjustment is disabled. When the stopwatch has a box around it, you can adjust keyframes. Once you set keyframes, clicking the stopwatch off deletes all assigned keyframes for the parameter. In some cases, such as the Color Corrector, this deletes the effect. Premiere Pro

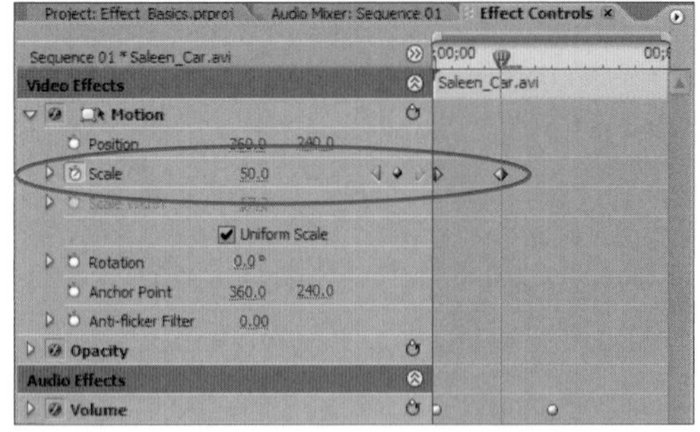

a

b

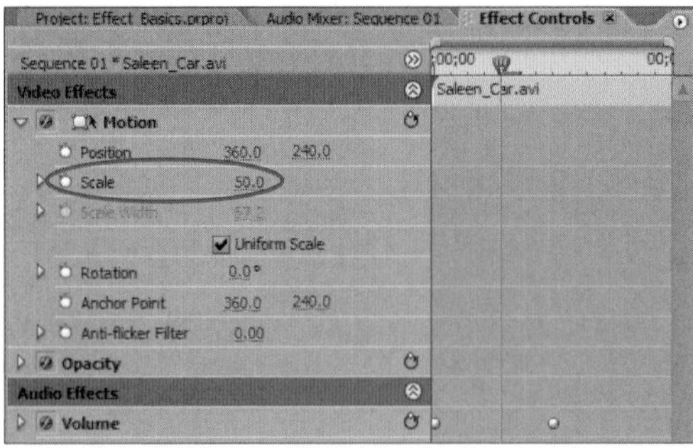

c

Figures 8.13a, b, and c If you have keyframes assigned (a) and you toggle the keyframing off, Premiere displays a warning (b), then deletes all keyframes (c). Notice that because the Edit Line was on top of the 10% scale keyframe when the keyframes were deleted, that became the static scale value.

displays a warning dialog asking you to confirm your action before deleting the keyframes.

You adjust the parameter using the hot text field to the right of its name. Scrub the field left or right to change its value. Holding down Ctrl while scrubbing adjusts the value at lower increments. Holding the Shift key and scrubbing adjusts the value at higher increments. Click in the hot text to manually enter the value you desire. If you prefer a more visual adjustment, click the twirl down triangle next to the parameter's name to access the slider control to change the parameter.

Docking the Effect Controls panel in the Project panel gives you a much wider panel, meaning you have more screen real estate devoted to viewing and adjusting keyframes. If you're less concerned with keyframes and need to view all the effect listings and their parameters in one glance, resize the Effect Controls panel to be very tall instead.

Timeline Viewing Area

The Effect Controls panel timeline viewing area displays the effect keyframes associated with the selected clip. To check the accuracy of the effect and keyframe placements, you can zoom and navigate through the clip using the panel's time ruler and viewing area bar. Scrubbing in the Effect Controls panel reveals the frames in the Program Monitor.

By default, the boundaries of the Effect Controls panel timeline viewing area are defined by the boundaries of the clip. Although this is the best view for most cases, you can extend the boundaries by toggling off Pin to Clip in the Effect Controls panel wing menu. If you turn off Pin to Clip, you can adjust the viewing area bar so that you can see beyond the edges of the clip in the Effect Controls panel timeline (**Figures 8.14a** and **b**). This view is not

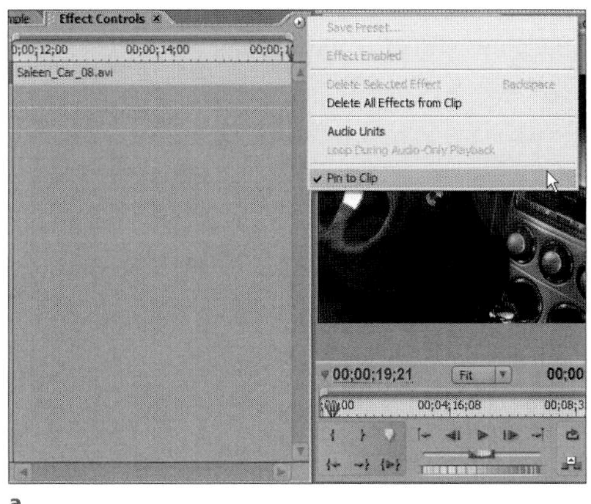

a

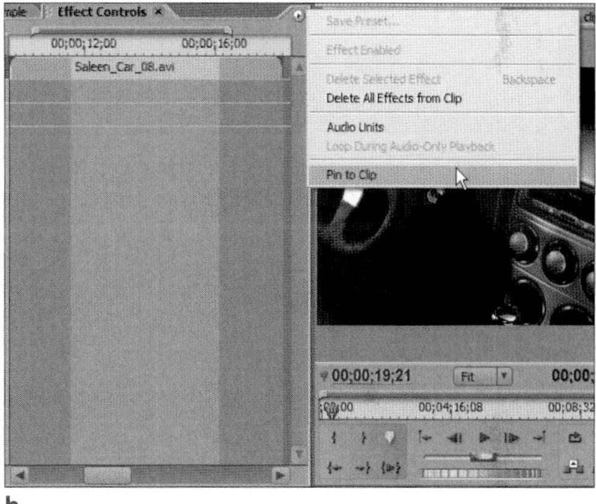

b

Figures 8.14a and b With Pin to Clip turned on (a) the boundaries of the Effect Controls panel Keyframe Navigation area are pinned to the edge of the clip's timeline instance. If you turn Pin to Clip off, you can see beyond the edge of the clip instance (dark blue area) to assign additional keyframes in this area.

recommended unless subtle or advanced keyframing is required that starts beyond the boundary of the clip.

Turn Pin to Clip off to place an effect keyframe outside the boundary of your clip. With this "extra" keyframe in place, you later can adjust the duration or extend the edge of your clip toward that keyframe without reapplying the effect.

Working with Keyframes

Working with keyframes is an important part of applying effects in Premiere Pro, so learning how to manipulate them is vital.

When you are assigning keyframes for an effect, first make sure that the clip associated with that effect is selected in the timeline and that the CTI is positioned between that clip's boundaries. Next, click the Toggle Animation button (the stopwatch) for the effect parameter that you wish to adjust or add keyframes. Now, any adjustment to the parameter adds a keyframe at the CTI's position with the setting in the parameter's hot text (**Figure 8.15**). If the CTI is over an existing keyframe, changing a parameter's setting changes the value for that keyframe. Clicking the Previous or Next Keyframe buttons snaps the CTI backward or forward one keyframe for the current parameter. This works exactly the same as it did when you went through the same steps in the timeline tracks.

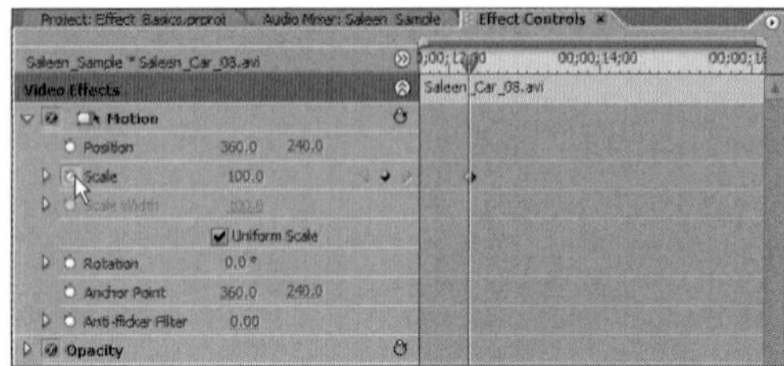

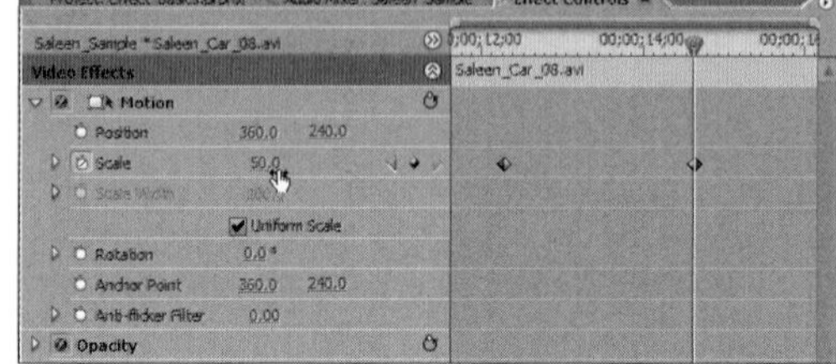

Figure 8.15 With the CTI positioned between the clip's boundary, turning on Toggle Animation assigns a start keyframe at the current Edit Line/CTI position. If the CTI is moved and the Scale is adjusted, a new keyframe is added at the new position to reflect the update.

If you wish to add a keyframe and adjust it later, move your CTI to the desired spot and click the Add Keyframe button at the right of the parameter name. If the CTI is positioned on top of a keyframe, the Add Keyframe button turns a dark gray and clicking it removes the current keyframe for that parameter.

To move a keyframe to a new location, select it and drag it in the Effect Controls panel timeline. Clicking and dragging a keyframe does not change its literal value, only its position. Using the Shift and Ctrl keys, you can select continuous or discontinuous keyframes to move them as a group. Clicking and dragging with the selection tool, you can marquee select a range of keyframes (**Figure 8.16**).

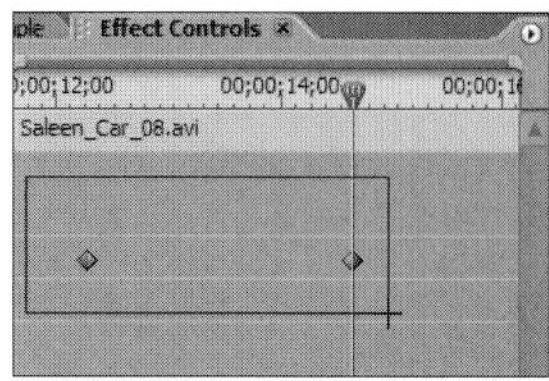

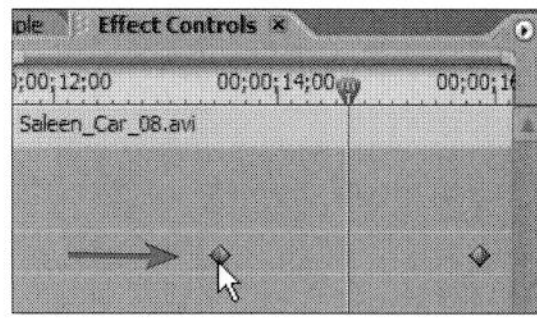

Figure 8.16 With the Selection tool, you can click and drag to marquee select multiple keyframes in the Effect Controls panel. Once those keyframes are selected, not only can you copy and paste them to other clips, but you can also drag them as an entire group.

Be sure to stay aware of the CTI's position in the Effect Controls panel as you work. As you scrub through a clip with multiple keyframes, the parameter values between keyframes update as you scrub. If you happen to park the CTI in a location without a keyframe and adjust a parameter that has Toggle Animation turned on, you will add a keyframe at that position (**Figures 8.17a** and **b**).

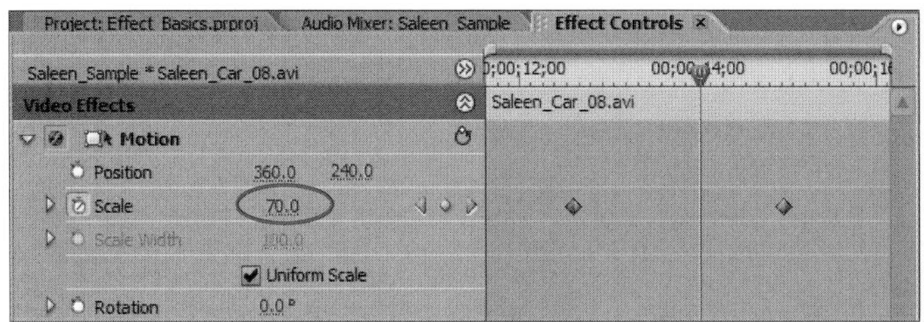

a

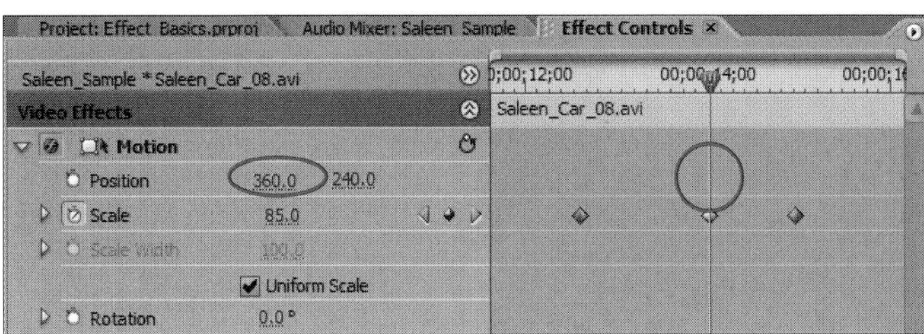

b

Figures 8.17a and b 8.17a shows a 100% Scale keyframe (left) and a 50% Scale keyframe (right). The current Scale value for the middle frame that the CTI is parked on is 70%. If you update that value to 85% (b), you decrease the amount of scaling for the same number of frames between the first and second keyframes and increase the amount of scaling necessary to get from the second to the third keyframe. Therefore, the Scale effect is much slower from the first to the second keyframe than it is from the second to the third.

Bezier Keyframes and Easing In and Out

There are a number of new keyframes features for Premiere Pro 2.0; however for this chapter, I want to focus on the basic support of Bezier curved keyframe handles. In Chapters 13 and 14, you will learn how to take keyframing to the next level.

Bezier curves enable you to make smooth paths by adjusting and pulling handles associated with specific points on a path. In Premiere Pro, those points are the keyframes that you assign. Say you apply a position adjustment to a clip and want the line between the two points to be slightly curved. You would assign one of the keyframes to have a Bezier handle, then adjust the handle of that keyframe so that there is a curve from that point (**Figures 8.18a** and **b**). In the timeline, you can further navigate and manipulate all the keyframes and their handles that you set in the Effect Controls panel; however, the new Value and Velocity graphs allow you more control without leaving the panel

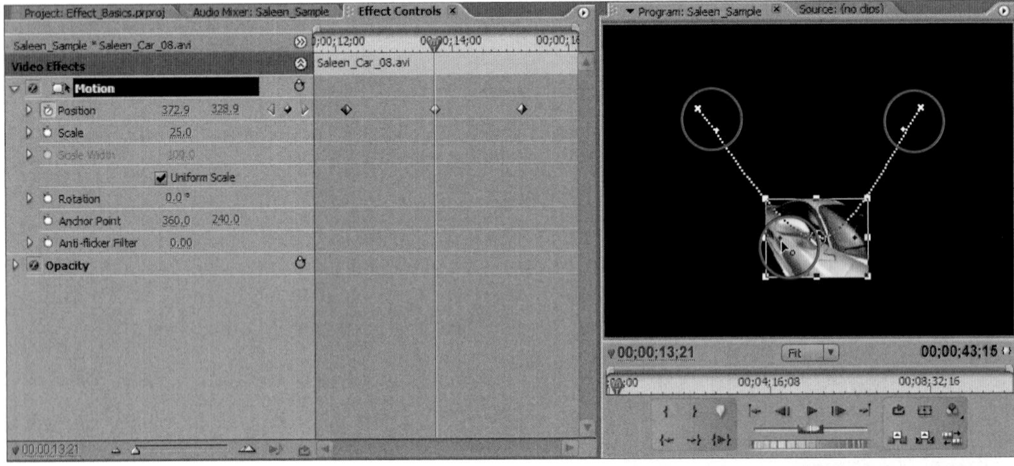

a

Figures 8.18a and b The initial motion path for this clip is a Continuous Bezier path, meaning that it smoothes the path between the position keyframes so that the movement between them is more fluid. Each of the position keyframes has a Bezier handle that can be tweaked to alter the curve around the selected keyframe (a). 8.17b shows the same path after the Bezier handles have been readjusted to alter the path even more. Notice how the selection tool becomes smaller and displays only its tip when it selects and adjusts Bezier handles.

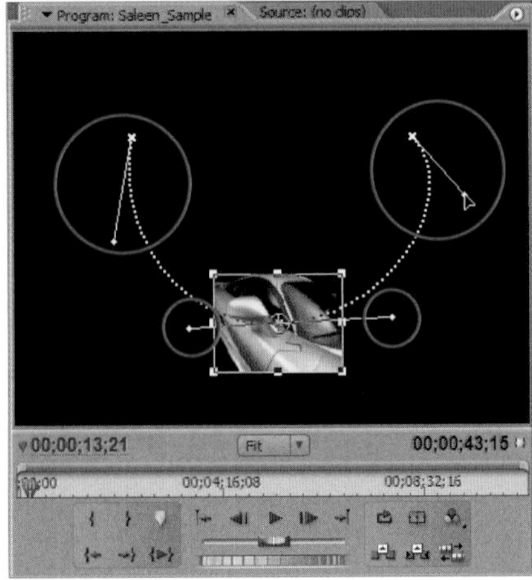

b

After you apply a keyframe, you can right-click on it and specify the type of handle or velocity setting that will be associated with its position (**Figure 8.19**). You have two main choices: Temporal Interpolation and Spatial Interpolation. Temporal Interpolation addresses the velocity and timing of getting to a keyframe frame value. Spatial Interpolation addresses the curve and path definition for the keyframe.

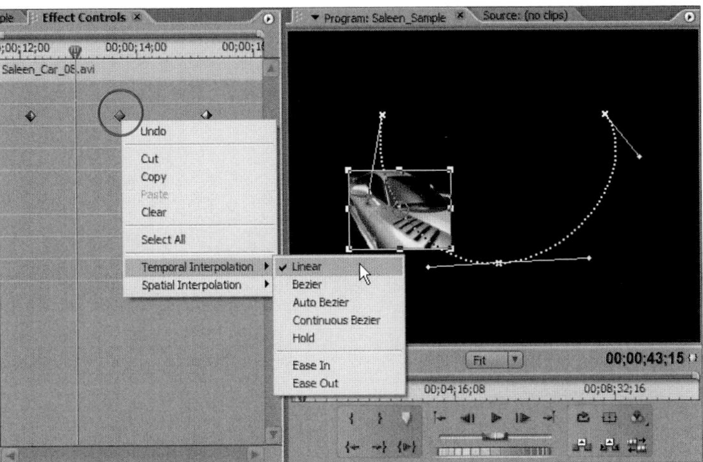

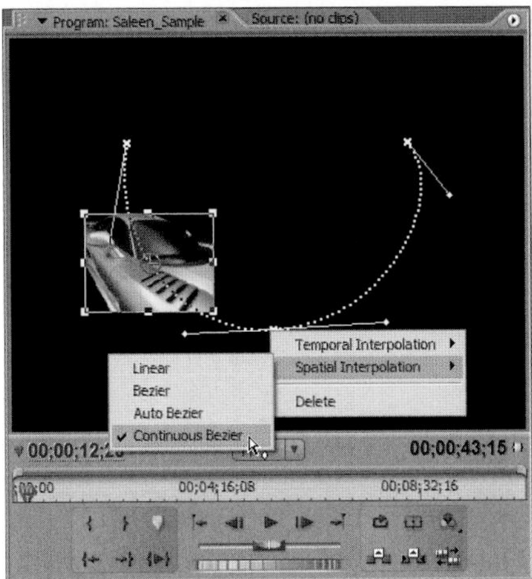

Figure 8.19 By right-clicking on the keyframe in the Effect Controls panel or on the keyframe handle with direct manipulation turned on, you can access the Temporal and Spatial submenus to assign your desired interpolation value.

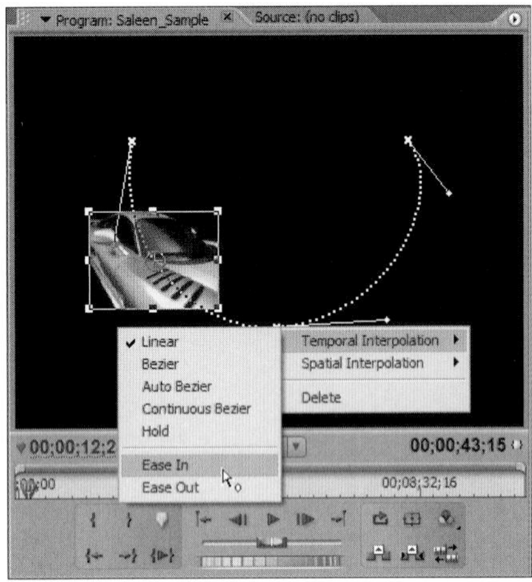

Figure 8.20 If you want a clip to slow slightly before arriving at a Position keyframe, turn on Ease In for the selected keyframe. The tightness of the keyframe path dots reflects the velocity of the clip on the path.

For Temporal Interpolation, you have seven options: Linear, Bezier, Auto Bezier, Continuous Bezier, Hold, Ease In, and Ease Out. Ease In and Ease Out are the most practical and most often used for Temporal Interpolation. The eases affect the speed and velocity of the effect arriving to or leaving from that keyframe (**Figure 8.20**).

With the new keyframe controls in Premiere Pro 2.0, you can adjust the spatial interpolation keyframes in the Program Monitor and the temporal interpolation keyframes in the new Velocity graph of the Effect Controls panel (**Figures 8.21a**, **b**, and **c**).

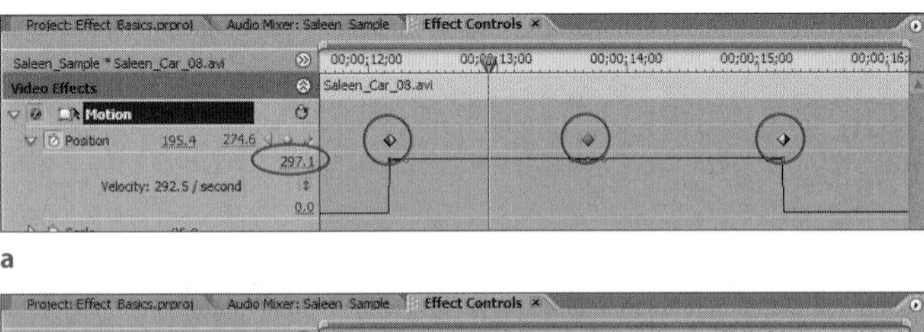

a

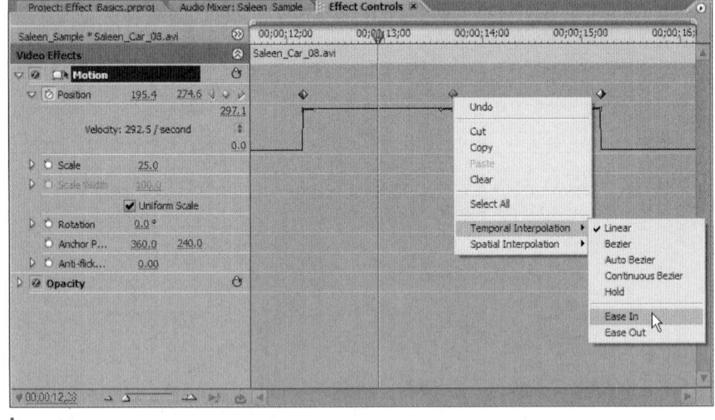

b

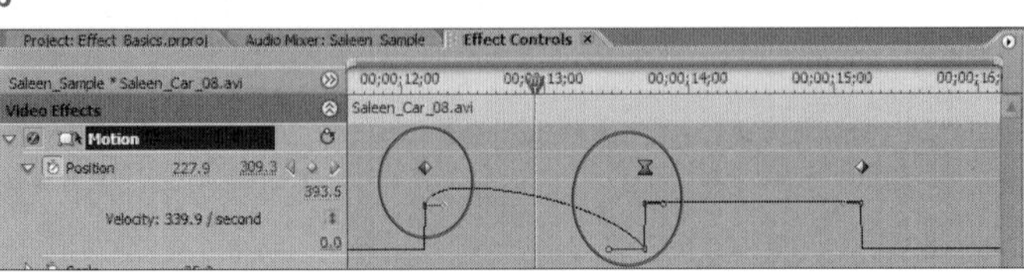

c

Figures 8.21a, b, and c The new Velocity graph in the Effect Controls panel lets you assign and adjust the temporal interpolation values. 8.20a shows a constant velocity value, but notice how each keyframe has a velocity point and Bezier handle for adjusting. Selecting Ease In as the Temporal Interpolation value for the middle (b) updates the Velocity graph. As a result, the graph shows the velocity slow down and reduce as it reaches the keyframe (c). To customize the ramp further you could grab any of the Bezier handles and adjust them as you would any other handle.

Viewing Keyframes in the Timeline

To view your keyframes in the Timeline panel, make sure you have Show Keyframes active from the display mode in the track header. A drop-down menu will then appear within the boundary of each clip. Click on the menu to see the effects associated with the clip. The submenus of each effect list all the associated parameters that make up your effect. Select a parameter to display its associated keyframes within the boundary of the clip in the track (**Figures 8.22a**, **b**, and **c**). The limitation of timeline keyframe viewing is that you can see only one keyframe parameter at a time; however, you can make your video track much taller than your new velocity and value graphs in the Effect Controls panel.

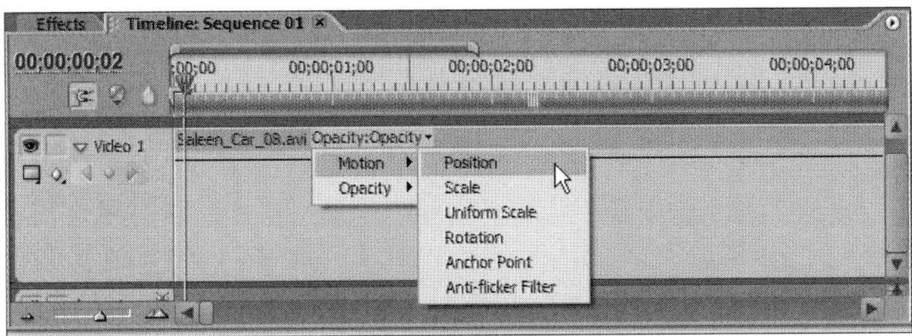

a

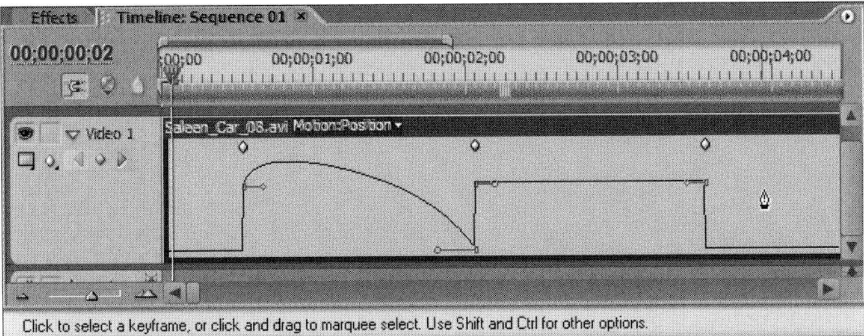

b

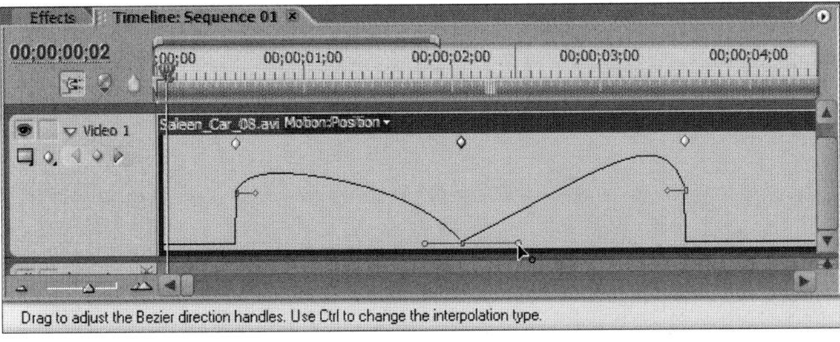

c

Figures 8.22a, b, and c 8.21a shows the drop-down menu and the display choices. 8.21b shows the same Position keyframes from the previous figure with the Temporal Interpolation value exhibited by the curved lines. In 8.21c, you can see that I am now adjusting the Bezier handle associated with the velocity coming from the second keyframe to the third. The bottom of the track is always a zero value; the higher you go up the track, the more the value increases. Take note of the feedback that is revealed in the bar below the panel.

The Pen Tool

To make selections and adjustments to the keyframes displayed in the Timeline panel, press P while the timeline is active to change your cursor into the Pen tool. Although you can make a few specific keyframe selections with the standard cursor tool, the Pen tool has many more important features.

One-dimension keyframes, such as Position (X and Y) and anchor points for Motion, cannot display Bezier keyframe handles in the timeline, because their values cannot be reflected within the single track.

To add keyframes to an effect parameter with the Pen tool, first make sure that the parameter has keyframing turned on in the Effect Controls panel. Back in the Timeline panel, hold the Ctrl key and click the Pen tool on the displayed wire to add a keyframe to the displayed parameter (**Figure 8.23**).

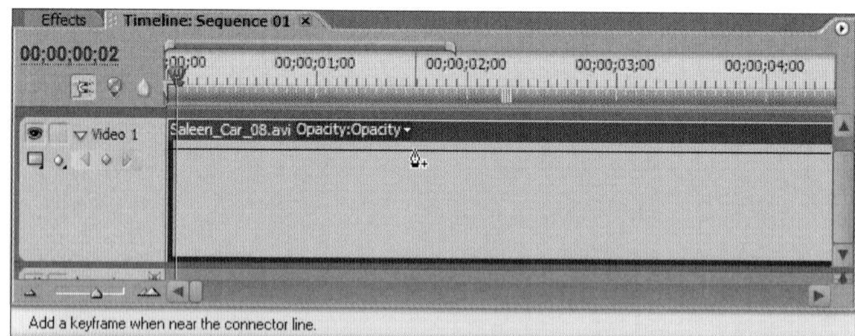

Figure 8.23 With the Pen tool, you can add a keyframe to the active parameter by holding down the Ctrl key and clicking on the connector line.

You also can modify displayed keyframes: Select the keyframe with the Pen tool and drag it up to increase the value of the parameter. Dragging the keyframe down reduces the parameter's value. Dragging a keyframe horizontally changes its position within the boundary of the clip.

Clicking and dragging over a group of keyframes with the Pen tool performs a range selection of the keyframes. With multiple keyframes selected, you can move or delete the entire selection (**Figures 8.24a** and **b**.) Range selection is one of the Pen tool's most powerful features.

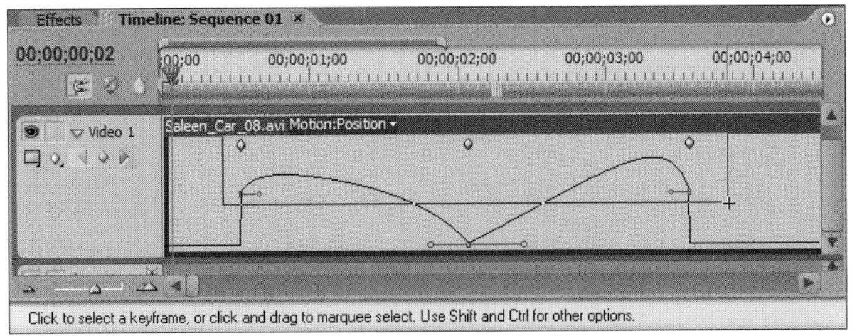

a

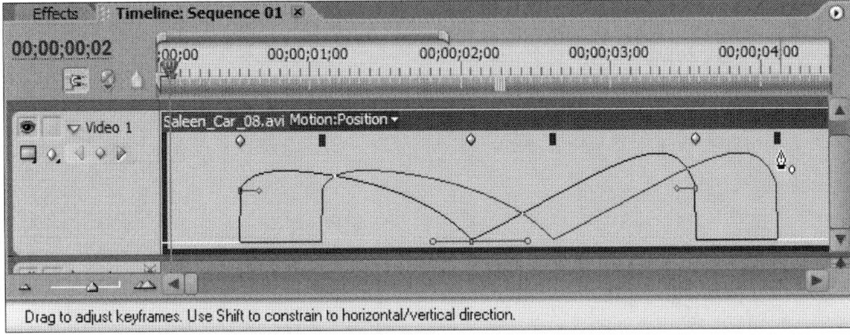

b

Figures 8.24a and b As you can in the Effect Controls panel, you can marquee select in the timeline (a). You then can shift and move the selected group of keyframes (b); notice the tool tip that displays the amount of time shift being applied to the keyframe shift.

Things to Remember

When adding and adjusting effects, always watch out for the keyframing states of the parameters and the position of the CTI. Often, if you are not paying close attention, you will get so involved in setting your parameters accurately that you will make three adjustments at different frames in your clip—but all will be moot because you forgot to turn on the keyframing stopwatch (the Toggle Animation button). Learn the rules, then expect results. Just as it is important for editing and viewing, the CTI position plays a vital role in the applying of effects.

The Effect Controls panel is always active, even when it is underneath another panel. The panel always displays the effect attributes of whatever clip is selected in the timeline. If you have the screen real estate luxury of being able to have your Effect Controls panel open at a big size, then by all means do it. The ease of jumping among your timeline, clips, and Effect Controls panel helps build a healthy workflow for adding and adjusting any effect.

You are down the home stretch in getting a basic understanding of the application. The next chapter reviews some of the important audio rules and introduces the Audio Mixer panel.

CHAPTER

9

Audio Basics

The way audio works in Premiere Pro is very different from the way it worked in previous versions. Adobe made three fundamental changes, all of which result in greater quality and better control over your audio. Premiere Pro supports:

- **An audio mixer.** More powerful and practical than previous versions, the audio mixer opens up the architecture to support both clip-based and track-based effects (**Figure 9.1**). This means that you can apply audio effects to individual clips or the entire content of specific tracks. You can also accomplish standard mixing practices, such as stemming, sends, and automation. The support for live mixing automation enables you to adjust volume faders and levels as you play your sequence back and have those fade adjustments saved to the sequence after a single pass.
- **VST plug-ins.** With the advantage of clip and track effects comes new compatibility for VST plug-ins. Premiere Pro ships with several professional VST plug-ins that support mono, stereo, and 5.1 source material (**Figure 9.2**), and many more of these audio effect plug-ins are available from third-party developers. (The VST plug-in format was originally developed for Steinberg's Cubase audio editing application.)
- **Creation of conformed audio and peak files.** Depending on the sample rate of the audio you bring into Premiere Pro, when you import and open files, Premiere Pro automatically converts them into proprietary format called *conformed audio files.* Although conforming converts audio with differing rates into the sample rate of your project, having conformed audio files increases the detail that can be extracted from the audio waveform and allows Premiere Pro to communicate and process audio files more efficiently. Because the conformed files have an increased resolution, Premiere can more accurately assign and play back added audio effects and filters. Regardless of whether you have to create conformed audio files, Premiere Pro always generates a *peak file* for

every imported audio file. This peak file is essentially a snapshot of the waveform information in the audio file so that when you open and look at the waveform in the various panels of the interface, you get instantaneous feedback showing the graph of the waveform.

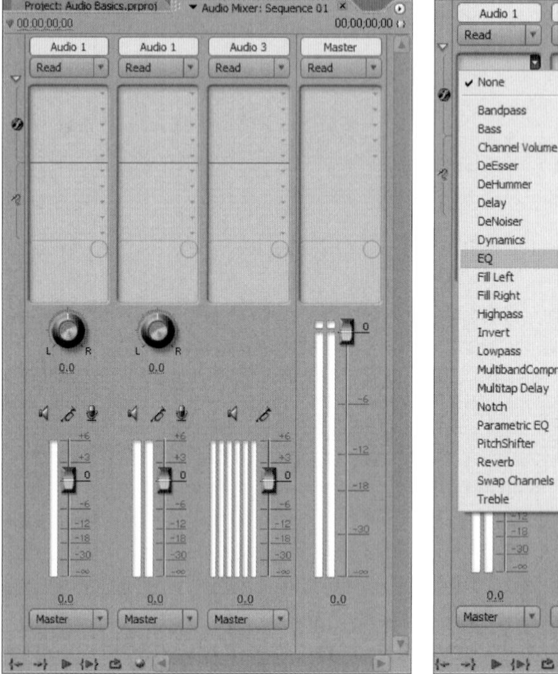

Figure 9.1 The full expanded Audio Mixer references the Audio sequence from the Timeline panel and displays three tracks: Audio 1 (mono), Audio 2 (stereo), and Audio 3 (5.1 surround). Each track has its own pan knob and volume fader. The Master fader on the right controls the volume for the entire sequence.

Figure 9.2 You access VST plug-ins from the Track Effects drop-down menu.

To better understand the importance of these changes, take a look at the flow of sound as it passes through Premiere Pro.

Importing and Conformed Audio Files

When you create a new project, one of the Project Settings you assign is the Sample Rate for audio—either 16-bit 48kHz or 16-bit 32kHz for standard DV. When you later import an audio file or an audio and video file, Premiere Pro looks at the audio's bit depth and sample rate and determines whether or not it needs to *conform* it to match your project's settings. The rules for conforming are as follows:

- Any audio that is compressed (MP3, AIFF, WAV, and so on) is always conformed regardless of the kHz setting.
- Uncompressed audio (WAV, AVI or AIFF) that has a ratio of 1:1, 1:2, or 2:3 to the project's sample rate is not conformed. This means that uncompressed 48kHz audio in a 48kHz project will not be conformed (1:1). Also, uncompressed 32kHz audio in a 48kHz project will not be conformed (2:3).

When the program creates conformed audio files, it increases the file to 32-bit resolution while increasing or decreasing the sample rate to match the project's kHz setting. Premiere then uses these conformed audio files along with the peak files to display the waveform information in the timeline and Source Monitor, to apply effects, and to play back the audio for the clip. Once you engage playback in Premiere Pro, if your DV camera is connected, the audio will always transmit at the proper bit and sample rate.

Conformed files are temporal, meaning that deleting them does not corrupt or destroy your project. If Premiere does not detect conformed files when opening the project, it creates new ones. When you import a file with audio, watch the conforming progress bar update in the bottom-right corner of the application's window. Once the bar completes, the conformed file is created and ready to use whenever you play back the audio clip. Fortunately, the management of conformed files is greatly improved in Premiere Pro 2.0 and that is all thanks to the Media Cache Database.

For the sake of drive performance and application responsiveness, keep your conformed audio files on a separate drive from your original source files. If your drive is slow, having to access both the source media and the conformed files from the same drive can create a bottleneck. You can specify your storage locations from Edit > Preferences > Scratch Disks.

Media Cache Database

In your Edit > Preferences > Media dialog, notice the section labeled Media Cache Database (**Figure 9. 3**). The Media Cache Database is a straightforward database file that manages and registers all the conformed audio files on your system. If you import a 48kHz audio file into a 32kHz project, you must conform the audio file down to 32kHz. When Premiere Pro performs the conforming, the program notes the action in the database. The database notes the source file that was conformed and the sample rate it was conformed into. The database tracks the location of each of these files. As long as you don't change the path or rename the original 48kHz file, if you were to import it into another 32kHz project, the database would not generate a new conform file, instead it would point the project to the previously conformed file and use that instead.

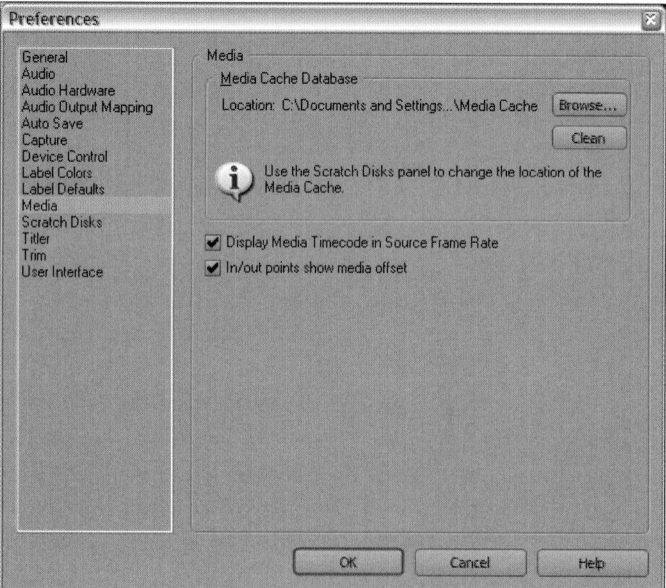

Figure 9.3 Your Media Cache Database is a powerful little tool for managing the conformed audio and peak files associated with your project media.

The Clean function of the database performs a system check and looks to see if all of the media that is registered in the database still resides on disk. If any files were moved from their previously registered paths or deleted, Premiere Pro automatically deletes their associated conformed files.

Fortunately, the latest version of Premiere Pro allows you to listen and edit your audio before or during any conforming. If the peak file hasn't been generated, however, you won't see any of the waveform information. Continuing on with listening to your audio, let's next discuss volume levels.

Understanding Volume Levels

When you first record or import an audio clip, it has audio information that is measured in decibels (dBs) when played back. Using the Audio Mixer's VU meters you can quickly see the waveform value for the audio or monitor the volume.

To monitor your audio clip with the waveform display, open the audio only clip in your Source Monitor. If the clip is a linked audio and video file, open it in the Source Monitor but toggle the Take Audio/Video button to Take Audio Only (**Figure 9.4**) so that only the waveform is displayed. To view the waveform for your audio files in the timeline, expand the audio track and be sure that the track is set to Show Waveforms. When looking at the waveform, tall waveforms denote stronger sound with a higher dB, and short waveforms reflect quieter sound with a lower dB.

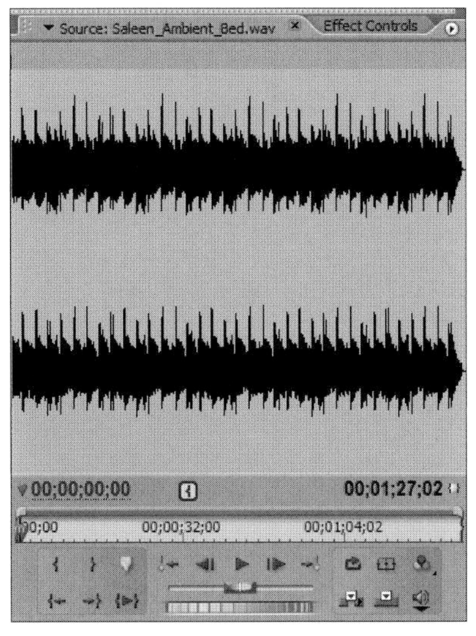

Figure 9.4 You can tell this audio clip is a stereo file, because the Source Monitor displays two waveform values.

Although the waveform is a nice visual representation, the VU meters give you more accuracy. To monitor your audio clip with VU meters, you must first add the clip to your sequence, then look at the VU meters registering in the Audio Mixer or the new Audio Master Meters panel (**Figure 9.5**).

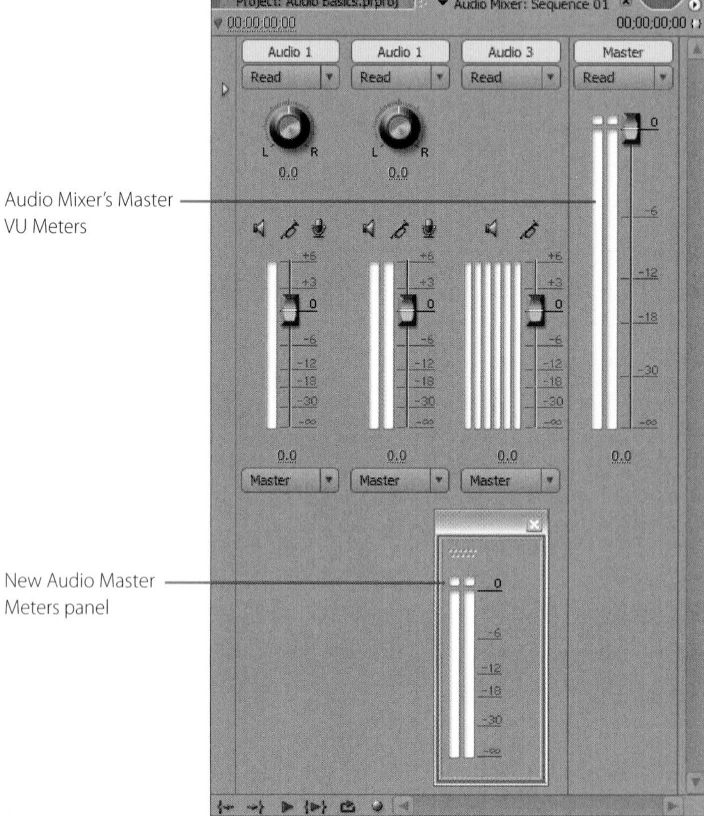

Figure 9.5 In Premiere Pro 2.0 you can see the VU meters two different ways: in the Audio Mixer panel or with the new meters-only Audio Mixer Meters panel. This new panel can be opened and docked into any frame of your workspace.

Loud audio registers close to 0dB, and quiet audio registers down around –18dB. The VU meters are essential for monitoring your audio levels so that they do not exceed their ceiling and begin to distort or degrade. If your audio is too loud (shown by red ticks in the VU meters), it will play back with clicks, pops, and other artifacts.

If your clip is too quiet, you might get your first clue in the waveform display: The clip doesn't have tall waveforms. When you monitor the clip more closely in the Audio Mixer's VU meters, you can see its exact dynamic dB levels as it plays back.

So, what do you do if your clip is too loud or too soft? You can alter the playback volume level from three controls:

- **Clip Gain.** For use on clips before adding them to a sequence. Gain adjustments are assigned to the master clip; whenever you use the clip the adjustments are preserved.
- **Clip Volume.** For use on clips already in a sequence. These adjustments stay with the clip even if it is moved to different tracks or copied from one sequence to another.
- **Track Volume.** For use on all clips in a single track. The volume adjustments are track specific and have no relation to specific clips in the track.

Keep in mind that when you make a Clip Volume or Clip Gain adjustment, Premiere does not alter the display of the file's waveform. Although your audio sounds louder after you adjust Clip Volume or Clip Gain, its waveform doesn't look any larger than it originally did. That's just how Premiere Pro works so far.

Clip Gain and Normalizing Your Audio

Before you add an audio clip to your sequence you can increase or reduce its volume by adjusting the Clip Gain. Say you import a quiet audio clip. Select the clip in the Project panel, then choose Clip > Audio Options > Audio Gain to access the Clip Gain dialog (**Figure 9.6**). For your quiet clip, increasing the dB setting (the Gain) boosts its audio signal accordingly. Setting the dialog's hot text to 5.0dB boosts the audio signal by 5.0dB. Clicking and dragging the hot text to the left reduces the Gain and trims audio levels by whatever negative value you assign. To apply your setting to the clip, click OK.

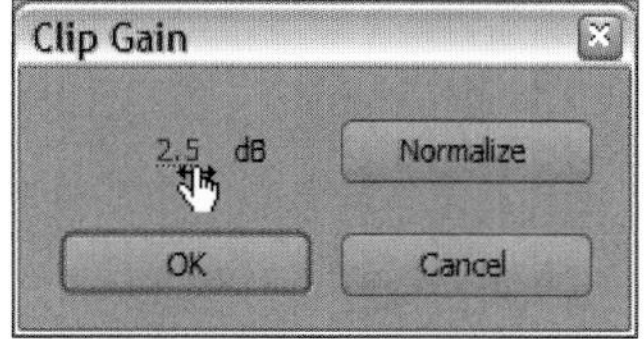

Figure 9.6 In the Clip Gain dialog, you can assign a positive or negative Gain value by adjusting the hot-text dB value. You can also apply an "intelligent gain" by clicking the Normalize button.

When normalizing a clip with dB levels that exceed 0dB, the Clip Gain dialog yields negative gain adjustment values so that you can reduce the strength of the signal. Remember that if your audio does exceed the 0dB ceiling, the source file probably is clipped and has some added artifacts. In these cases, lowering the volume doesn't make it sound better, just less noticeable. If you have damaged audio files, you can do a lot of fixing and adjusting in Adobe Audition.

Clicking the Clip Gain dialog's Normalize button achieves a very useful result: Premiere Pro provides a recommended Gain value for your clip. Premiere examines the entire dB value for the audio file selected, and it determines how much it can increase or decrease the dB so that the strongest signal does not peak or exceed the ceiling level (0dB) in any portion of the clip. Once you click Normalize, Premiere updates the Gain value in the hot-text field with a recommended value for proper adjustment. Click OK to apply the Gain value to the clip.

Although you can access the Clip Gain dialog when a clip is selected in the timeline, there is a major benefit to making Gain adjustments to the master clips in the Project panel. When you adjust the Clip Gain of the master clip, Premiere adheres to and respects that adjustment every time you add an instance of the clip to the timeline. Normalize your audio clips in the Project panel *before* adding them to the timeline. If you already have instances of a clip in the timeline and you adjust the master clip in the Project panel, the Gain value of the clips in the timeline does *not* update.

Clip Volume

In Premiere Pro, hold your mouse over a clip in your sequence to display that clip's information in the tool tip window. If gain adjustments have been made, you can see that information when holding the mouse over an audio clip in your active Timeline panel.

Say you need a track of bird sounds to accompany video of a flock of birds flying across a field and directly over the head of your subject in front of the camera. Your field recording came out at a low level, and when you import the clip into Premiere the birds sound as if they're miles away. To fix this, you first boost the Gain to increase the signal strength. Now when you add the clip to your sequence, you can lower the Clip Volume at the start of the sequence (so the birds sound as if they are at the far end of the field) and increase it at the end (so they sound as if they surround the viewer as well as the subject). These adjustments can be made by tweaking the clips' volume handles in the Timeline panel (**Figure 9.7**).

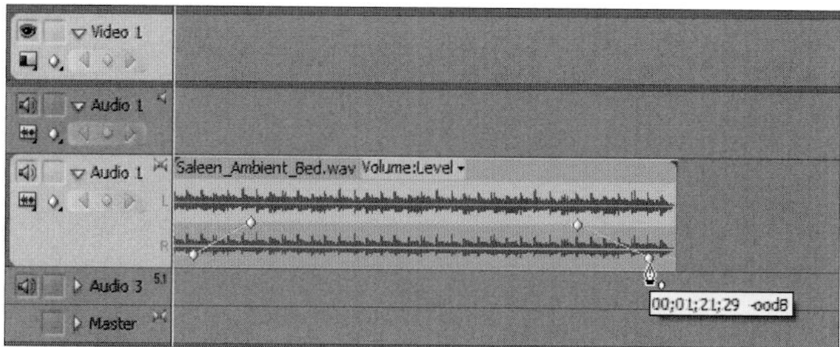

Figure 9.7 With the Audio 2 track showing the default Volume, the yellow volume line reflects the currently assigned levels. Using the Pen tool, you can click and add handles to the level to adjust the clip volume dynamically. Here the clip fades in to its normal 0dB clip volume, then fades out. Note the Pen tool and tool tip next to it that yields the –oodB value for the keyframe handle beneath it.

To review, Gain adjustments boost or reduce the basic signal level of your audio file, before and sometimes after it has been added to a sequence. Clip Volume is the means by which you adjust the volume level of a specific clip instance in a sequence.

Clip Gain is independent from the Clip Volume so Clip Gain adjustments do not affect a clip's Clip Volume setting. No matter what Gain settings you apply, a clip's Volume displays at the default of 0dB until you adjust Clip Volume. This independence also means, for example, you could increase the Gain to add strength to the audio signal, then bring the Volume down just a little.

Empty space on a video track is displayed as pure black. Empty space on an audio track registers as complete silence, or –oodB. The same way adding a cross dissolve to the head of a video clip fades it up from black, adding an audio dissolve to the head of an audio clip fades the audio up from complete silence to its assigned clip volume.

One way to increase the Volume of an audio clip in a sequence is to select the clip in the Timeline panel and open the Effect Controls panel. As you remember from Chapter 8, "Effect Controls Basics," Volume is a Fixed effect for audio clips. When you adjust the volume properties of a clip in the Effect Controls panel, position the CTI where you wish to make the change and twirl down the

Level slider for volume (**Figure 9.8**). To increase the entire clip's volume, make sure Toggle Animation (the stopwatch icon) is off, then make your adjustment. To keyframe volume fades and adjustments, turn Toggle Animation on and then assign keyframes with the desired Volume levels at the appropriate points in the clip's boundary.

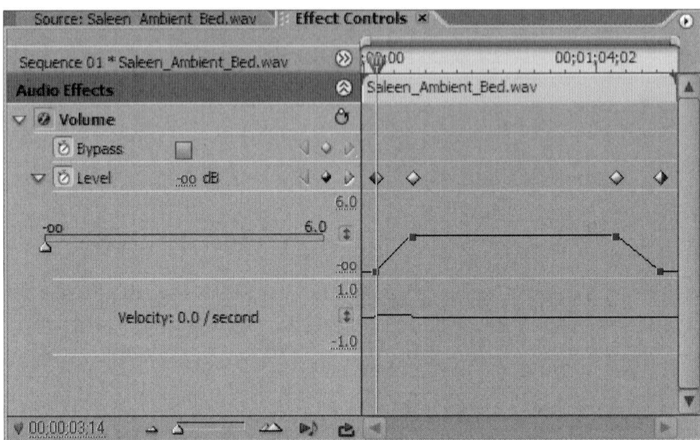

Figure 9.8 With the adjusted clip from Figure 9.7 selected from the timeline, its effects properties become available in the Effect Controls panel. Because the volume level has a number of handles with different values, the Toggle Animation button is active. With the CTI on top of the first keyframe handle, you can see that it has a value of –oodB, which is complete silence. Notice how the new Value graph in the timeline area of the Effect Controls panel mirrors the same fade levels as the Timeline panel from the previous figure.

If you prefer, you can adjust a clip's Volume in the Timeline panel with the Pen tool; press P with the timeline active (**Figures 9.9a** and **b**). First, toggle the audio track display to Show Clip Volume, and Premiere will display every clip's volume in that track. To adjust a static level, you can click and drag when the Pen tool displays the horizontal volume line. Dragging up increases the volume and down decreases. If you want to add keyframes with different level values, press the Ctrl key and click the Pen tool on the volume line to add a keyframe handle at the assigned position. Click on the keyframe, and drag it up or down to raise and lower the volume. Adjusting the Clip Volume level is useful for removing specific sections or unwanted sounds.

In the "Advanced Audio Techniques" section, Chapters 17 to 21, you will explore clip volume adjustments and much more.

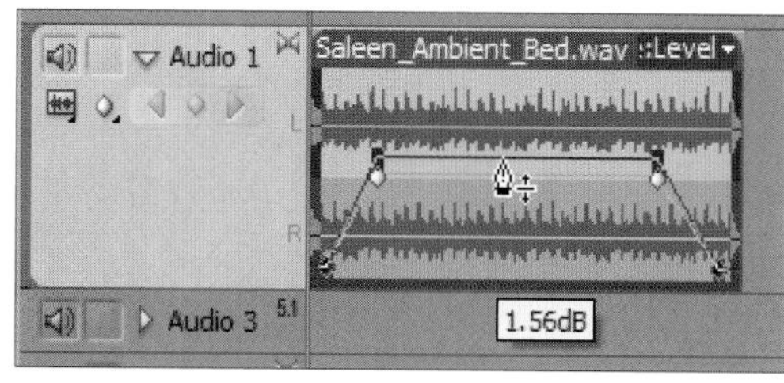

a

b

Figures 9.9a and b With the track displaying Show Clip Keyframes: Volume:Level, you can use the Pen tool to raise a static value between two volume handles (a) or click and modify a single keyframe handle (b). Notice how the tool tip tells you precisely how much you have increased or decreased the level.

Track Volume

Clip Gain and Clip Volume are specific to individual clips, but Track Volume adjusts the volume level of an entire track. You can adjust Track Volume from its default of 0dB in the Audio Mixer panel or the timeline. In the Audio Mixer panel, use the volume faders at the bottom of each track panel. The position of the fader reflects the level of the associated track. For a static adjustment, turn the Automation mode Off and then drag the fader up or down to increase or decrease the dB level (**Figure 9.10**).

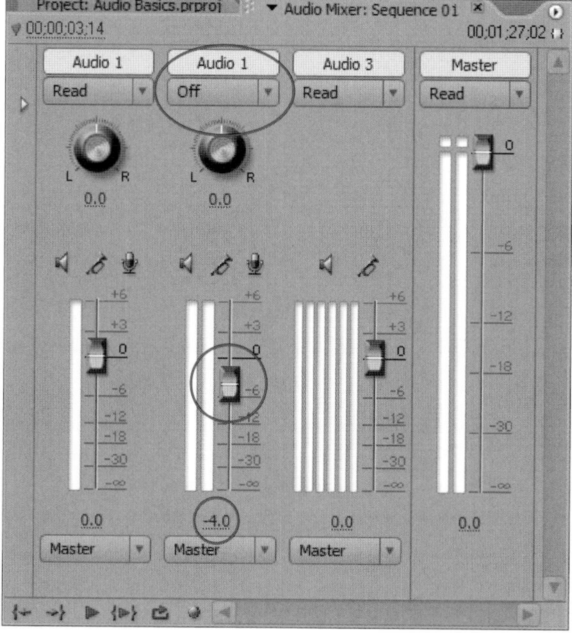

Figure 9.10 With the Automation mode for Audio 2 set to Off, you can make uniform track volume or panning adjustments that affect the entire track. Here the track volume for Audio 2 was turned down by 4dB, meaning all the audio in Audio 2, no matter how loud at the clip level, was reduced by 4.0dB at the track level.

Automation is the equivalent of keyframing effects, only it is done live as the audio tracks play. To fade the volume at specific points, switch the track into one of three Automation modes and press Play. Now, when the timeline plays back, you can make live adjustments to the audio track's parameters. Premiere saves these adjustments, writing them as keyframes to the adjusted parameter. Automation is very powerful as you can watch, listen, and make adjustments at the same time. You'll learn more about it in Chapter 20, "Mixing Your Audio."

Figure 9.11 The Master track displays at the bottom of the sequence and has only track-based display properties. The Master track does not contain specific clip information and it is always on. Notice that there is no Output button to mute the track.

Be careful: If you performed any Automation or if you keyframed track volume or effect values, setting the Automation mode to Off deletes all of the keyframes for the entire track.

To make adjustments to the track in the Timeline panel, toggle your audio track display to Show Track Volume or Show Track Keyframes and adjust accordingly with the Pen tool. Raising values above the center volume line increases the dB, and dragging below it decreases dB.

Audio Tracks

As mentioned earlier, you can have up to 99 audio tracks, including submix tracks, in any combination of mono, stereo, and 5.1 surround tracks. All of these 99 tracks get mixed together when you play back your sequence and their volume values are displayed in the VU meters of the Master track. By having all of your tracks mix down and then play out through the single Master track, you enable an added level of control for reducing, filtering, or adjusting the entire mix of your audio in one single track. Let's take a look at the Master track (**Figure 9.11**).

Master Track

When creating sequences, you have the ability to define your audio Master track as being mono, stereo, or 5.1. When you open the sequence, the Master track appears at the very bottom and cannot contain any clip information. In the Audio Mixer it is the track to the far right.

Think of the Master track as a siphon or a funnel. Although you may have all sorts of audio tracks in a sequence, they ultimately must be funneled down through the Master track and distributed accordingly. By placing a mono track in a stereo master, you gain a stereo mix down, which opens the possibilities of panning your mono audio to either the left or right channel or keeping it centered equally to both. If you place a stereo track in a sequence with a mono Master track, you lose the panning properties of the stereo track: The mix down would be to a single mono channel.

Because all of your sound is funneled through the Master track, adjusting the Master track's settings and parameters affects the overall sound of your sequence. For example, to reduce the volume for your entire sequence, simply turn down the Master volume slider in either the Audio Mixer or the track (displaying Track Volume). Similarly, say all of your audio had a specific frequency hiss or hum to it, you can apply the DeHummer effect to your entire sequence simply by adding the DeHummer effect to the Master track (**Figure 9.12**).

Figure 9.12 The Master track has a DeHummer effect applied from one of the Effects drop-down menus. You can also see that the Volume fader has been reduced to −2.0dB. These two adjustments will affect the entire mix and output of the sequence, so that all the audio has a DeHummer process on it and its volume lowered by −2.0dB.

Submix Tracks

As for the Master track, no clip content can physically be added or dragged onto submix tracks; you only can apply effects and make volume or pan adjustments. Similar to Master tracks, submix tracks act as pipelines. The workflow with submix tracks is to *send* a normal track to be processed through a submix track. This ability is especially useful when you want to apply the same effect to multiple tracks. When you apply one effect to a submix track and send multiple tracks to that submix track, all those tracks get processed with the effect from the submix (**Figure 9.13**).

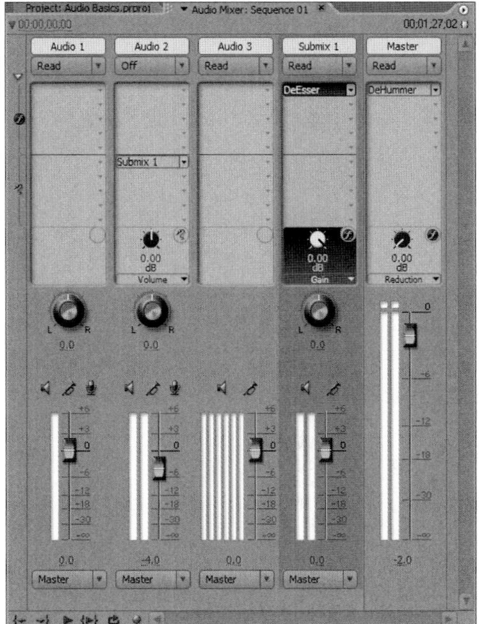

Figure 9.13 Here Audio 2 is sent to Submix 1. The Sends area is just below the Effects area of the Mixer panel. The DeEsser effect is assigned on Submix 1 and will be processed to the content of Audio 2, which is being sent to the submix track.

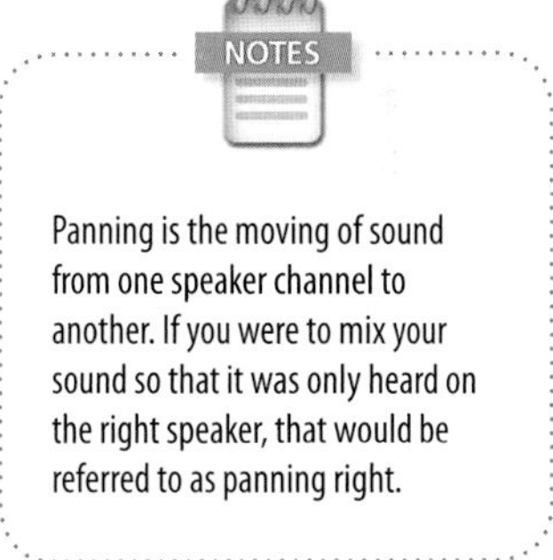

Panning is the moving of sound from one speaker channel to another. If you were to mix your sound so that it was only heard on the right speaker, that would be referred to as panning right.

For more on how submix tracks work, try the lessons in Chapter 20.

Clip Versus Track Effects

In Premiere Pro, you can apply audio effects at the clip or track level, just as you can assign clip and track volume. Like clip volume adjustments, clip effects apply to only one clip. Track effects, like track volume adjustments, apply to a specific track and not the individual track content. To add audio clip effects, you follow the same workflow as for video effects, with one exception. To decide which effect you want to use, you need to identify the type of clip you are adding the effect to: mono, stereo, or 5.1.

Clip Effects

As mentioned in Chapter 8, you must choose the proper type of clip Standard effect—Mono, Stereo, or 5.1—to match the clip to which you are applying it. As with video effects, you can adjust an audio effect by selecting a clip in the timeline and placing the CTI over the clip boundary. The clip's properties will appear in the Effect Controls panel (**Figure 9.14**).

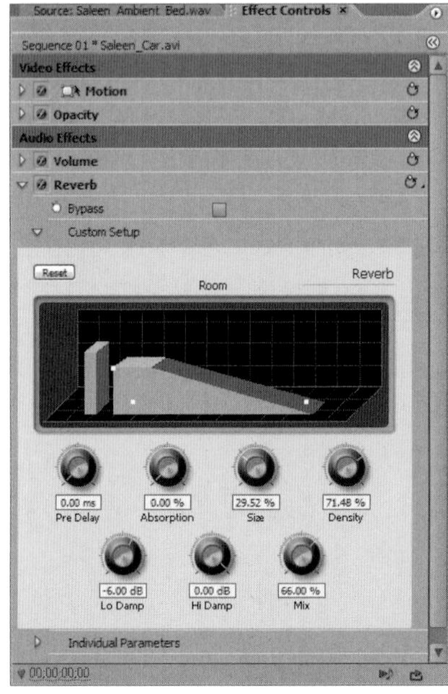

Figure 9.14 The Audio Effects listing is below the Video Effects listing in the Effect Controls panel. Here the Reverb effect listing has been expanded. Expanding the Custom Setup listing reveals a graphic interface that enables you to manipulate and adjust the reverb value.

A number of effects have the standard twirl down slider to adjust settings, but for others you must twirl down to access a custom setup display with a nice visually interactive adjustment area. As for video effects, you can add keyframes for audio effects only when the Toggle Animation button is switched on. When you move a clip with a keyframed effect applied, the keyframes preserve their position as the clip defines their boundary. Again as for video effects, you can view audio effects and their keyframes in the track area by setting the track display to Show Clip Keyframes.

Track Effects

Clip effects adjust only the clip instance, as it is visible in the sequence. Track effects are a means of adding effects to an *entire* track. Although you might want to change the pitch of one specific clip (using the PitchShifter clip effect), you may also want to add a reverb to an entire track.

Using the Audio Mixer, adding and adjusting track effects is quite simple. With the Audio Mixer open, you can view all of the tracks in your sequence; each has a unique panel in the mixer. Each panel has a name that corresponds to the associated track in the sequence. To add an effect to a track, you click on the top drop-down menu and select the effect from the list (see **Figure 9.15**). Once you select your effect, double-clicking on it brings up a dialog with visual parameters that you can adjust (see **Figure 9.16**). Right-clicking on the effect name reveals a drop-down menu of presets for that effect (see **Figure 9.17**).

Clip effect manipulation in the Audio Mixer leaves some features to be desired, because some audio effects do not have a visual display in which you can make adjustments. For these, you can make adjustments in a small area of the Audio Mixer's track panel (Figure 9.16). Highlight the added effect, and a drop-down list with the effect's name appears just above the radio buttons. Click on that drop-down list to reveal all of the parameters that you can adjust for the effect. To adjust the parameters, modify their value in the little box that appears above the list. With no keyframes or Automation applied, any effect adjustment will be static for the entire track. To apply effects, you can click and use the Pen tool in the timeline with Show Track Keyframes turned on, or you can set your track into an Automation mode and start adjusting.

With track-based effects (and mixing), keyframes have nothing to do with clip position and everything to do with track position. A track volume fade from 0dB to 4dB at 5 seconds into your timeline will persist no matter if there is clip media underneath the keyframes or not. If you have automated or added track-based keyframes, you may want to lock your track so that the mixing properties are preserved with the audio clips underneath.

You'll learn more about effects in the chapters of the "Advanced Audio Techniques" section.

Previewing and Playback

Depending on the effects and adjustments being made, Premiere Pro does not always need to create audio preview files. If you add a number of effects, however, Premiere Pro will render audio files when you press Enter to play your sequence back.

Powerful New Features

Premiere Pro 2.0 offers two excellent new audio features that you'll see used throughout the book: Source Channel Mappings and Extract Audio. Both of these new features are the type of forward thinking, workflow-oriented tools that make 2.0 superior to 1.5. Because of this, it is more powerful to teach them within the boundaries of a workflow. To preview their power, however, take a quick look at each now.

Source Channel Mappings

Say you capture a clip of an interview that has two channels of audio (Stereo). On one channel, the left, the audio was recorded from the microphone on your camera (ambient). On the other channel, the right, the audio was recorded with a directional microphone recording the subject of the interview. When you work with the clip, instead of having the audio for the clip appear as a single stereo file with

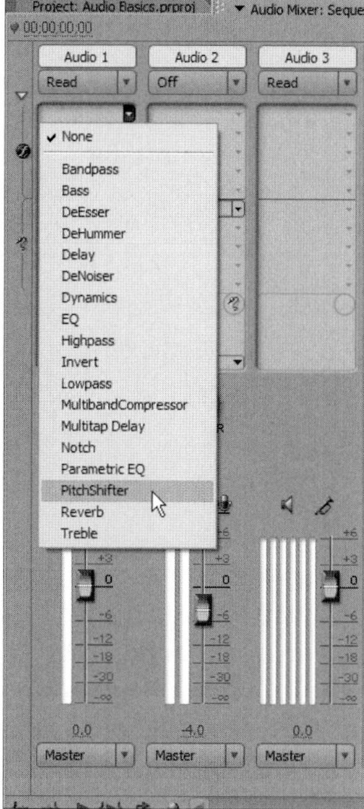

Figure 9.15 To assign a track effect in the Audio Mixer, click the Effects area of the desired track and select the effect from the drop-down menu.

Figure 9.16 Double-click on the PitchShifter, or any effect listing, to open its dialog and visually manipulate it. At the bottom of the Sends area, notice the control knob that reveals one of the PitchShifter's effect parameters.

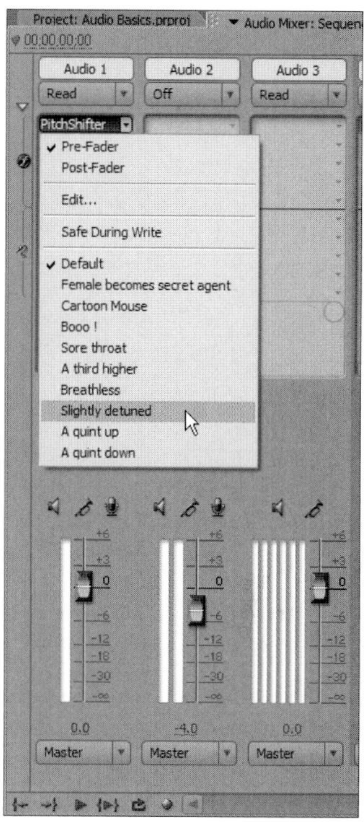

Figure 9.17 To access a custom preset, right-click on the effect and select the preset from the drop-down menu.

both channels on one stereo track, you can use the Source Channel Mappings feature to remap the audio of the clip to display in the timeline as two separate mono clips linked to the original file. This feature remaps the audio of the file so that the clip looks and acts exactly the same in the Project panel; when you add the clip to the timeline, however, it uses two mono tracks to display the remapped stereo audio. You will work with Source Channel Mappings in Chapter 27, "Advanced Editing: The New Multi-Cam Workflow."

Extract Audio

If you want to use the audio only of a clip and none of the video, or you want to use a section of audio only and not the video, you can now extract the audio from your audio and video clip so that in your Project panel you have a unique audio clip instance that is audio only with no video. This feature is very useful when you want to speed up the pace of your workflow so that you don't have to open the file in the Source Monitor and turn off the video of the file to use the audio only in the timeline. You will use Extract Audio in Chapter 16, "Custom DVD Design."

Things to Remember

At the end of the day you need your project to sound as good (or better) than it looks. Getting your audio to sound just right can go a long way toward enhancing the production value of your projects. Because you now know how to monitor your audio and because you know the three different ways to adjust it, your audio levels should now be in much better shape. Keep the overall levels of your tracks' audio adjusted so that the sound is loud enough, but not too loud.

It may help you to set your timeline to Audio Units display mode, which shows audio samples instead of video frames. The Audio Units display can help you zoom into your waveform in the monitors or timeline to see better what information is revealed.

Because you can assign clip and track effects separately, you can add more depth and diversity to the sound in your timeline.

The next chapter, on the other hand, will help you add more depth to your titles and graphics by introducing the Premiere Pro Titler.

CHAPTER

10

Titler Basics

Inside Premiere Pro is an incredibly useful titling tool: the Titler (formerly known as Title Designer in earlier versions of Premiere). Its straightforward and easy-to-use controls help make title creation quite simple. If you know Adobe Illustrator, some of Titler's tools, such as those for stacking and positioning items, will seem familiar. In this chapter, you will learn the basics of creating and using title styles, moving and arranging text and objects, as well as loading and saving templates.

In former versions of Premiere, title files were unique files that were saved to disk. In Premiere Pro 2.0, title files are saved into the project file rather than directly to disk. If you want to share files between projects, you can still export the title as its own file; you can also import older title files from previous versions into any project. To learn more about the latest incarnation of the Titler, you'll start by examining how 2.0's new panel layout affects the title panels. Then you will explore text and object creation, how to move these elements, and how to customize their appearance.

If it is important for you to preview specific characters in the Font Browser, go to Edit > Preferences > Titler. In the Titler Preferences panel, you can specify exactly which characters are displayed in the Font Browser.

Title Panels Overview

To open the Titler, press F9 or select File > New > Title. At the prompt, name the title that you are about to create. Using this name, Premiere Pro saves a placeholder for the title into your Project panel; as you work on the title, the file updates live.

The Titler is made up of five panels (**Figure 10.1**). The primary panel is the Titler panel. The Titler panel's top row of controls holds several function buttons for font types, text justifications, and specifying the type of title you want to create (still, roll, or crawl). You add objects and text to the drawing area (center section) with the Tools

Tools panel
Title Actions panel
Titler Styles panel
Titler panel
Titler styles
Title Properties panel

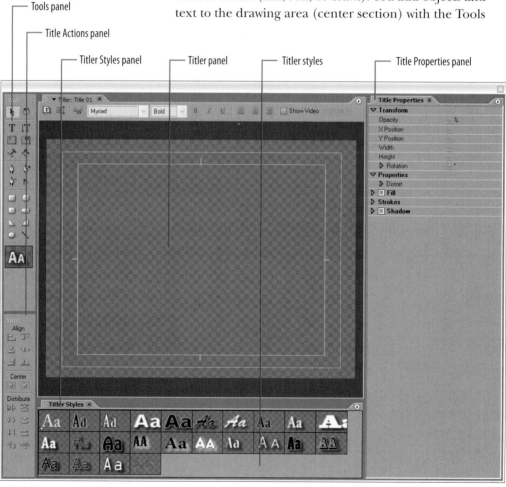

Figure 10.1 The Titler is composed of five panels.

panel. The Title Properties panel allows you to manipulate the text and object style, as well as adjust the position of the text or objects. From the Title Styles panel, you can add, select, and apply custom or default styles to objects and text. Finally, the Title Actions panel enables you to align and distribute text and objects within the boundaries of your title frame.

When the Titler is open, you have access to the Title menu in the main menu bar (**Figure 10.2**). The Title menu contains shortcuts and items that help arrange and adjust the open title or selection. You can assign keyboard shortcuts for most of the listed Title menu items. Premiere Pro 2.0 moves a number of buttons and shortcuts, such as the Templates function, from the Titler interface into the Title menu.

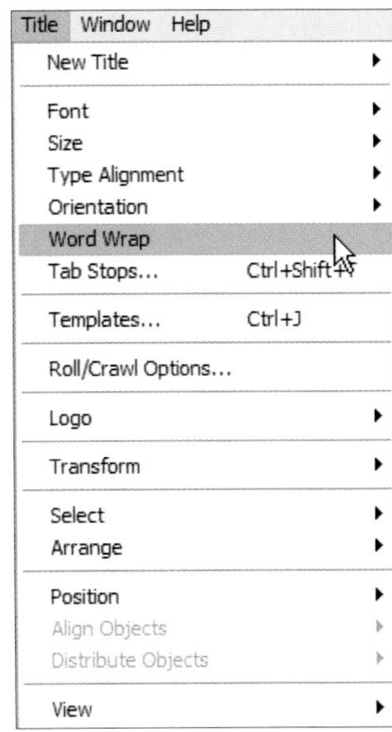

Figure 10.2 Some controls, such as Word Wrap, are available only from the Title menu. You can access a subset of the full Title menu by right-clicking in empty space of the drawing area.

The Titler Panel

The top row of controls in the Titler (**Figure 10.3**) begins with the Create New Title Based on Current Title button. This button is useful when you finish a title and want to create a duplicate with minor changes. Simply click the button, name the title, and get back to work on making the changes you want. The second button is the Roll/Crawl Options button. You can create three types of titles:

- **Still.** A static title that doesn't move
- **Roll.** A vertically moving, or rolling, title
- **Crawl.** A horizontally scrolling title

Figure 10.3 The top row of controls contains the Create New Title, Roll/Crawl option, Font Browser, and Font Style buttons as well as three Type Alignment buttons, the Show Video check box and a hot-text field for the background/sequence video timecode.

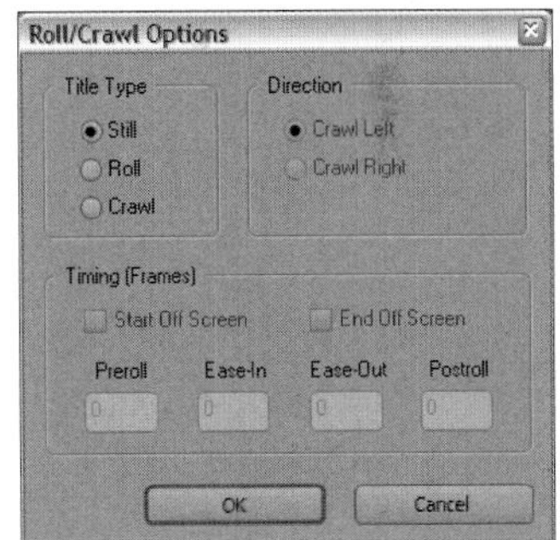

Figure 10.4 In the Roll/Crawl Options dialog you specify the type of title you want: Still, Roll, or Crawl. Click the Start Off Screen and End Off Screen check boxes to allow your rolling or crawling title to start completely out of view then roll (vertically) or crawl (horizontally) on and off screen. You can also adjust the direction of the crawl, either left or right.

When you click Roll/Crawl Options, you access a dialog where you can define what type of title you want (roll or crawl) as well as its dynamics. If you want your roll or crawl to start or end with the entire title off screen, check the appropriate box in the dialog (**Figure 10.4**). You then can assign frame values for how long you want the title to be off

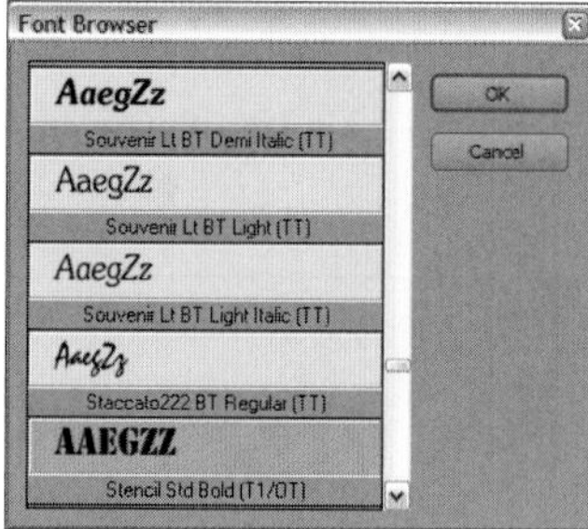

Figure 10.5 The Font Browser is a great interface for previewing what a font looks like and applying the font to your text.

Figure 10.6 The Font drop-down menu achieves the same results only the fonts display slightly smaller. Either way, using these options allows you to see a visual preview of the font you want to use.

screen before it comes on (Preroll), how long you want it to take to move to its center position (Ease-In), how long you want it to take to get back off screen (Ease-Out), and finally how long you want it to hold off screen (Postroll).

Next to the Roll/Crawl Options button is the Font Browser button. Select any text, click this button, and you can scroll through a list of font choices (**Figure 10.5**). Click on a font, and Premiere updates your text in a preview of the selected font. You also can use the Up and Down arrows to navigate to the next and previous fonts quickly. I really like the Font Browser, because it gives you an exact image of what each font looks like. From the enormous default list, you can see that Premiere Pro installs a ton of fonts for you. Next to the Font Browser button is a new drop-down Font menu that displays the same fonts as your browser, except slightly smaller and in a long menu (**Figure 10.6**).

The three buttons following the Font menu are self-explanatory, enabling you to make your selected text bold, italic, or underlined.

The next three buttons—Left, Center, and Right—are for assigning type alignment justification. With any paragraph or text item selected, clicking an alignment button will align the text to that setting.

The Show Video check box toggles on or off the Video Frame display from the open sequence. If the box is checked, you will see the associated video frame beneath your title. The hot text box to the right is tied to the timecode value in the open sequence. If you enter a timecode value or scrub the hot-text value, the displayed video frame updates to the frame in that timecode position. This is very helpful when you want to determine the exact positioning or proper color choices for a title. Checking Show Video and navigating with the timecode hot text enables you to see what your title looks like over any frame in your sequence.

If you want the displayed video frame to snap back to a special point in the sequence, position the CTI there. Now, click the Sync to Timeline Timecode button to move the title-over-video display to the CTI's position in the sequence.

Title Properties Panel

The Title Properties panel houses all of the adjustable style properties for both text and objects. Select any item created in the Titler to see its editable properties displayed in this panel (**Figure 10.7**).

Here you can move and adjust the position, rotation, and opacity for selected items in the Title Designer as well as add a Drop-Shadow or Stroke or change the Fill color(s) of your Text/Object. You will learn more about the Title Properties panel's controls later in the chapter.

Figure 10.7 With text selected in the drawing area, the fields of the Title Properties panel reflect all the settings associated with that text. Adjusting any of these fields dynamically updates the selection in the drawing area.

Tools and Actions Panels

The Tools panel houses text and object creation tools (see **Figure 10.8**), while the Actions Panel has buttons for aligning and distributing text or object elements. From the top, left to right the tools are

- **Selection** (shortcut key: V). For selecting, moving, and adjusting objects.
- **Rotation** (shortcut key: O). For grabbing and rotating text or objects.
- **Type** (shortcut key: T). For creating text.

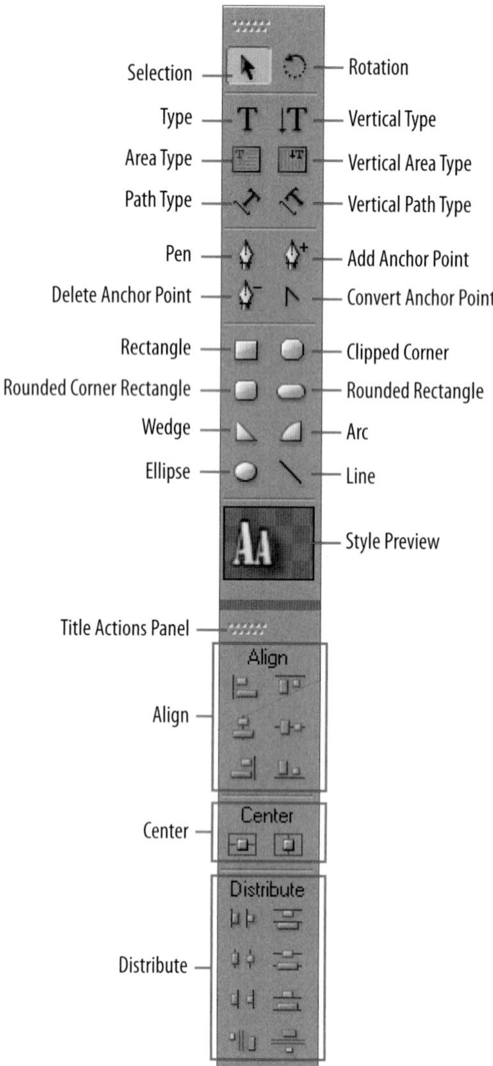

Figure 10.8 The Tools panel holds the Titler's object and text creation tools. The Actions panel contains buttons to align and distribute selected title elements.

- **Vertical Type** (shortcut key: C). For creating vertical text.
- **Area Type.** For defining a box in which to add horizontally oriented text; you specify the box size. Think of it as the text-in-a-box tool.
- **Vertical Area Type**. For defining a box in which to add vertically oriented text. Again, you specify the box size.
- **Path Type**. For writing text on a defined path.
- **Vertical Path Type**. For writing vertical text on a path.

Below the path type tools are the path adjustment tools:

- **Pen** (shortcut key: P). For creating and adjusting anchor points.
- **Add Anchor Point**. For adding anchor points on a path.
- **Delete Anchor Point**. For deleting or removing an anchor point on a path.
- **Convert Anchor Point**. For converting an anchor point into a smooth curve. Think of it as the Bezier adjustment tool.

The last group in the Tools panel is the object creation tools, which are pretty self-explanatory:

- Rectangle (shortcut key: R)
- Clipped Corner
- Two Rounded Corner Rectangles with different levels of curves with the corners
- Wedge (shortcut key: W)
- Arc (shortcut key: A)
- Ellipse (shortcut key: E)
- Line (shortcut key: L)

Below the Tools panel is the Actions panel that contains the Align, Center, and Distribute buttons, which enable you to align and distribute multiple selected objects. These buttons are active only when more than one title element is selected. If you want to align three items horizontally, for example, click and select the three objects and then choose the button for horizontal center alignment. As the tasks dictate in Chapter 15, "Advanced Titling: Styles and Templates," these buttons will be useful for aligning elements of your created titles.

The Styles Panel

The Styles panel is where you can load, save, and apply styles to selected objects and text in the drawing area (**Figure 10.9**). A small icon, or *swatch*, displays for each available style. As you create new styles, swatches for the styles are added and display in the primary area of the panel.

A style is a saved set of object properties (color, font, size, and so on) that you can use on any subsequent object or text item.

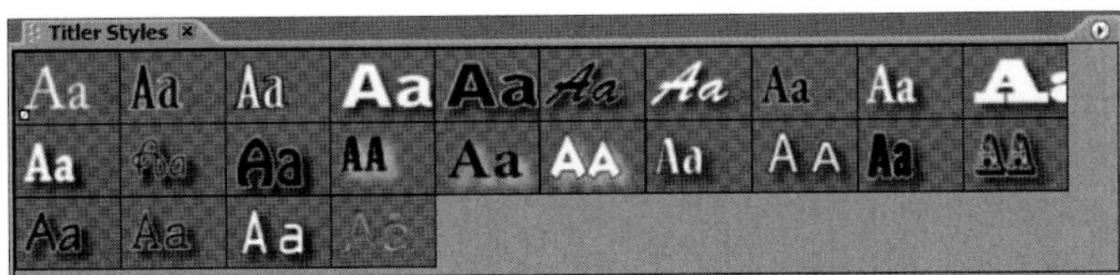

Figure 10.9 Preview the look of a style in the Styles panel, then click on the style to apply it to the selected items in your drawing area. Notice how the style in the first position has a little diamond on it; that means it is the default style that will be applied to newly created text or object in the Title panel.

When you create text or an object in the drawing area, Premiere Pro automatically applies the default style to it. Identified by a small diamond on the swatch, the default style swatch appears in the first position of the library (upper-left corner). To set a new style as the default style, right-click on the new style and choose Set Style as Default from the context menu. To change the style of text or an object, select it in the drawing area and click a style swatch to apply the associated style attributes to it. Although the style swatches that come with Premiere Pro are specifically designed for text, they can be applied to both text and objects.

To better understand style attributes, take a closer look at the details of creating and using styles with objects and text.

Creating an Object

To create an object, select an object creation tool, such as Rectangle, from the Tools panel, then click and drag in the drawing area. The farther you drag from the first click point, the larger your object. To conform the object to a 1:1 ratio, hold down Shift as you drag. If you want to make a perfect circle, for example, select the Ellipse tool, hold down the Shift key, and drag (**Figure 10.10**).

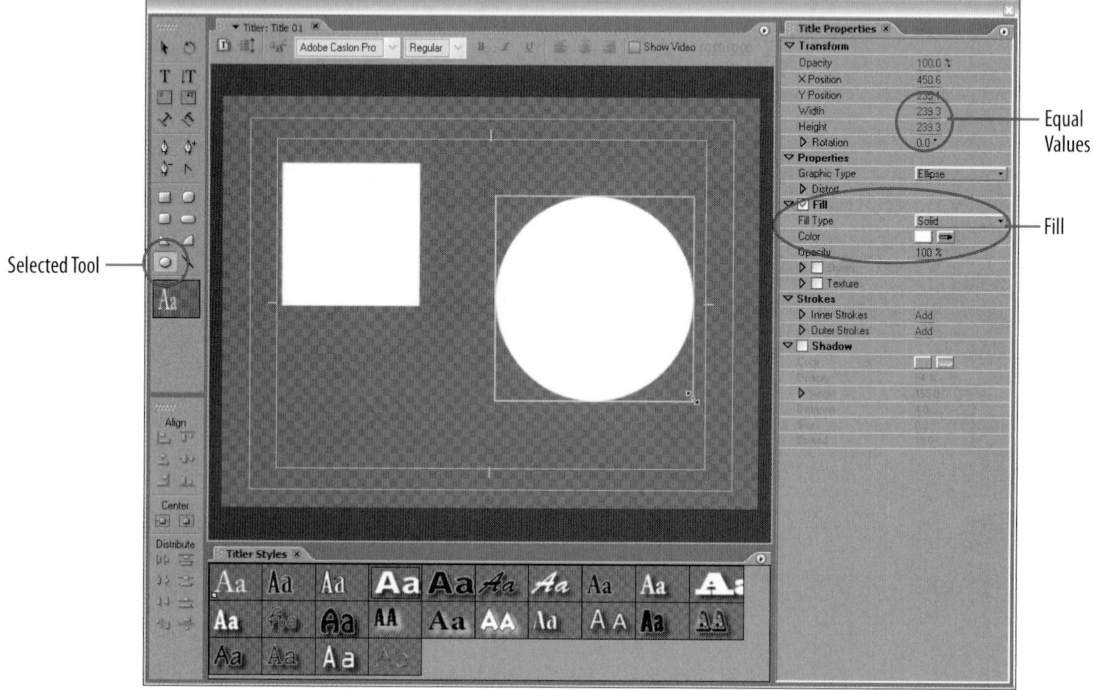

Figure 10.10 The first rectangle was created as a perfect square. The current 1:1 circle was created using the Ellipse tool and the Shift key to make sure it had a 1:1 aspect ratio. Its default style is solid white, as shown in the Title Properties panel.

When your cursor is in a Tool mode (one of the 15 text or object tools), its only function is to create the item associated with the tool. If you want to modify an object's dimensions, you must switch to the Selection tool (press V or click it in the Tools panel). With the Selection tool, you can click and drag the objects to move them. Pressing Alt while dragging duplicates an object.

Editing an Object's Physical Dimensions

Create a square or any object, then click on the Selection tool to activate it; you will see eight adjustment handles with which you can modify the object's dimensions. Clicking and dragging on the corner handles increases the object's size from the selected corner. Clicking and dragging from the side handle points adjusts the size of the object on the side that you are dragging. In both cases, holding the Shift key while dragging preserves the object's aspect ratio, meaning the object's size increases or decreases uniformly. When you hover over one of the corner handles, the cursor switches to the Rotation tool; grab the handles to rotate the selected item. Holding down the Shift key constrains rotation to exact 45-degree increments (**Figures 10.11a** and **b**).

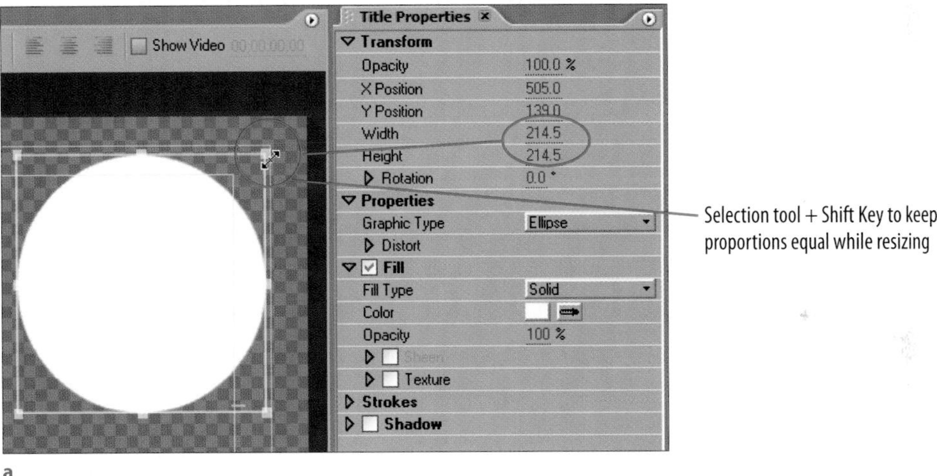

a

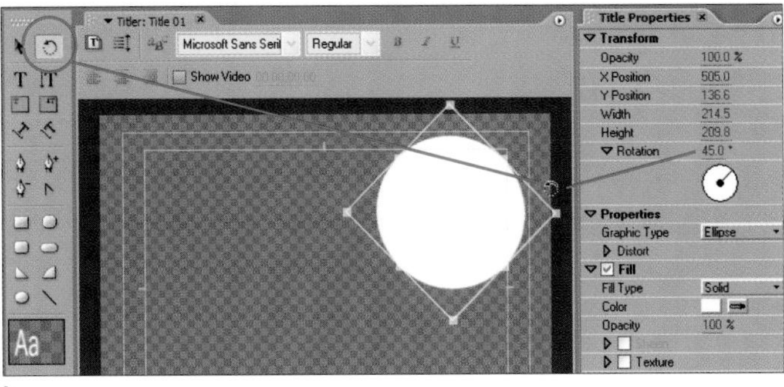

b

Figures 10.11a and b By clicking and dragging inward from one of the handles with the Selection tool (a), you can reduce the overall size of the circle while preserving its 1:1 dimensions. When you click and drag a corner handle with the Rotation tool (b), you can rotate the selected item. Note the Rotation tool and the feedback in the Properties panel.

For more detailed adjustments to specific dimensions, select the object and adjust it using the controls in the Transform panel (**Figure 10.12**). Here, you can adjust the object's location by specifying coordinates for X Position and Y Position, as well as set exact values for the object's Width and Height. You can also adjust the Opacity parameter, which determines the transparency of the object, and Rotation, which turns the object the number of degrees you specify, up to 360.

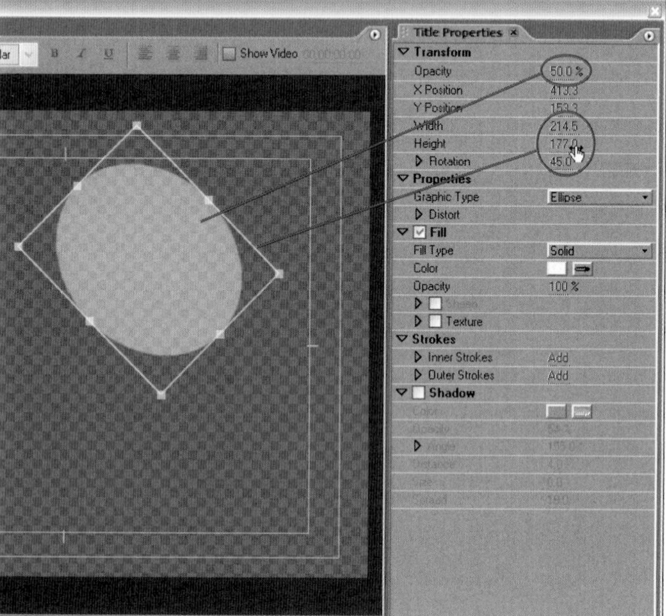

Figure 10.12 The Transform panel displays the exact Opacity, Position, Size, and Rotation values for the selected item. Because all of these fields are hot text, you can easily adjust any of them to exact settings.

Title Properties Panel

Although you can change an object's style simply by clicking on a different swatch in the Styles panel, the Properties panel provides more details about and adjustments for the chosen style. Five twirl down menus give you access to the necessary parameters: Transform, Properties, Fill, Strokes, and Shadow. Having covered the Transform function in the last section, let's now discuss the remaining parameters.

Properties

Select your object, then twirl down the Properties panel's Properties menu (**Figure 10.13**). The resulting Graphic Type drop-down menu lists the current object type and enables you to switch to a new type of object with the same dimensions as the original. Twirl down the Distort menu and adjust the X and Y values to add some x- and y-axis bending or distortion to your object. If you have text selected, an expanded drop-down menu appears revealing additional text-specific adjustment fields.

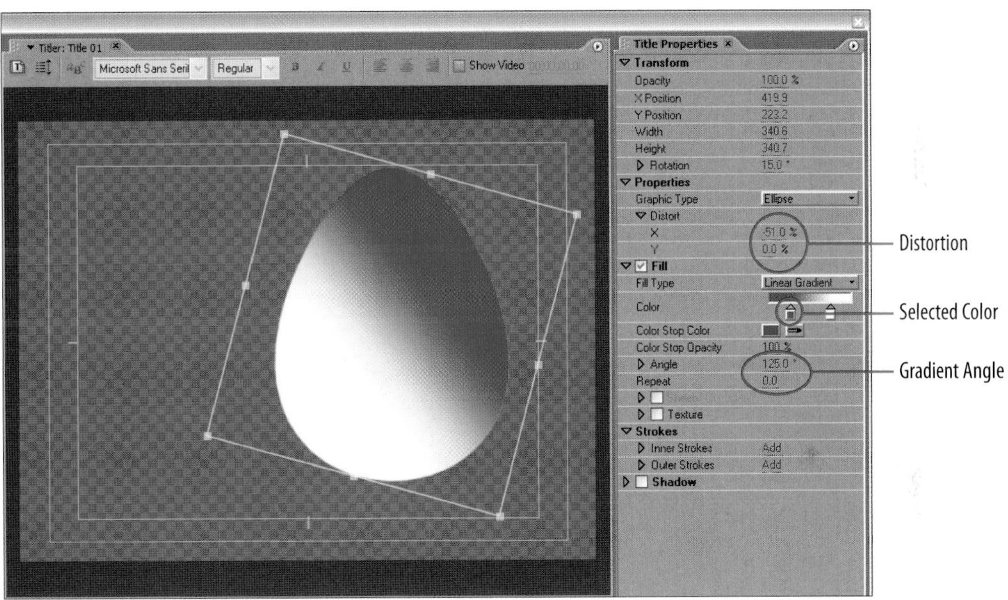

Figure 10.13 The Object Style reveals the style details associated with the selected ellipse. Notice that the X axis distortion has altered the shape of the circle and that the active Fill is using a linear gradient with the color split at a 125-degree angle. The embossed Color Picker for the blue portion of the gradient means that you can adjust and assign that color using the Color Stop Color controls below.

Fill

The Fill twirl down houses controls for adjusting the object's fill type, color, and more. For a transparent object, make sure the Fill check box is empty. Click the Fill check box on to access its controls. For example, the Fill Type drop-down menu enables you to specify the kind of fill you want: one solid color, two colors in a linear or radial gradient, four colors in a gradient, a bevel, Eliminate, which makes both an object's fill and shadow transparent, or Ghost, which removes the fill but keeps the shadow. You can specify the fill color in two ways: Click in the color box to access the Color Picker, or click and drag the eye-dropper over any color in your desktop window, then click again to set that color.

If you are assigning colors to a gradient, each color in the gradient has a box associated with it and an arrow pointing to where the color exists at its full value. To assign a color, click the box for the color that you want to change. The selected box becomes embossed and any adjustment you make using the eyedropper or Color Picker will update the selected gradient color. Clicking and dragging the boxes, you can increase or decrease the distance and positioning of the two colors.

Whether you are assigning one, two, or four fill colors, each fill color has an Opacity parameter that you can adjust. If you want one color of your two-color gradient to be a little bit transparent, select that color (by clicking the box), then adjust its Opacity value.

Sheen

Your fill can also have a *sheen*, which emulates a highlight on a shiny surface, like a chrome effect. To add a sheen to your object, click the Sheen check box and twirl down its parameters (**Figure 10.14**). A sheen's Color and Opacity settings work the same as those for a basic fill, and the rest of the sheen parameters are pretty self-explanatory. If you want a thin diagonal white stripe, for example, set Color to white, Size to 10, and Angle to 135. If you do not want the stripe centered, adjust Offset to shift it up or down. Chapter 12, "Advanced Titling: Styles and Templates" uses a sheen to help accentuate the shiny look of a lower third title.

Texture

Click the Texture check box on and twirl down its parameters to specify an external graphic to fill your text or object. Click inside the Texture box, and choose an image to load. Premiere automatically inserts it inside your object's fill area. Using the Flip with Object and Rotate with Object check boxes, you can lock the orientation of the fill image

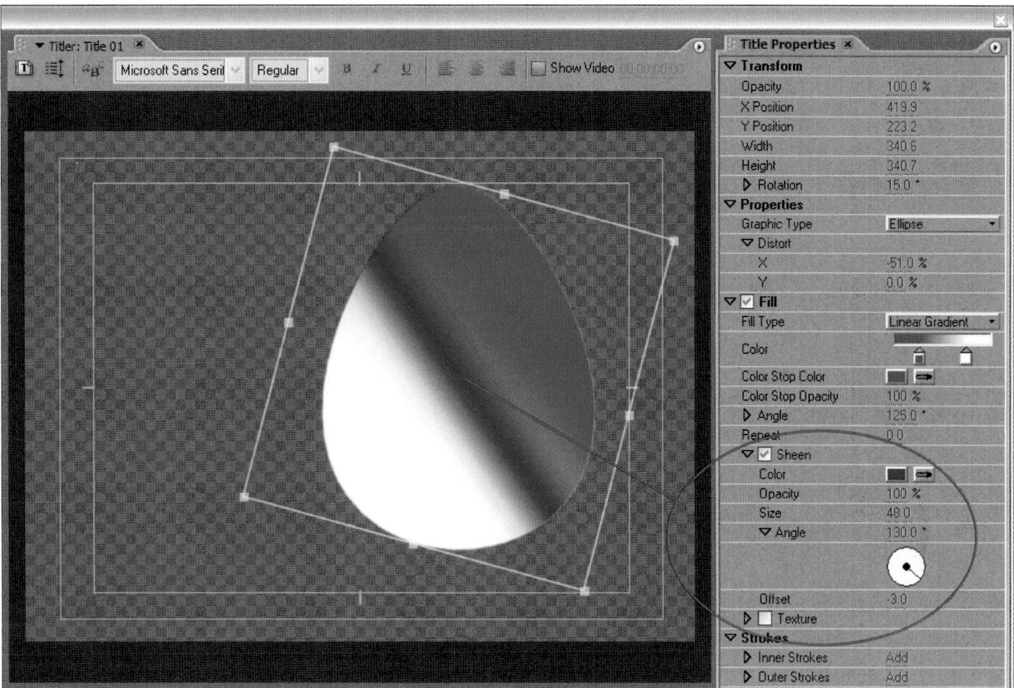

Figure 10.14 With the Sheen check box on in the Object Style panel, you can adjust the color, opacity, size, angle, and offset of this dark blue sheen.

(texture) to that of the object, so that if the object is flipped or rotated, then the texture flips or rotates accordingly.

The Scaling twirl down menu enables you to scale the size of the texture inside the object, while the Alignment twirl down lets you change the alignment of the texture image, moving it left or right, up or down inside the fill. Twirl down Blending to blend the texture with the fill color and more.

Strokes

Strokes are basically outlines (see **Figure 10.15**). They are not called outlines, because there are two types of strokes: inner strokes and outer strokes. An inner stroke is a line inside the defined edge of your object. When you increase the size of an inner stroke, it grows inward, closer to the center of your object. An outer stroke uses the edge of the object as its starting boundary and grows outward when you increase its size.

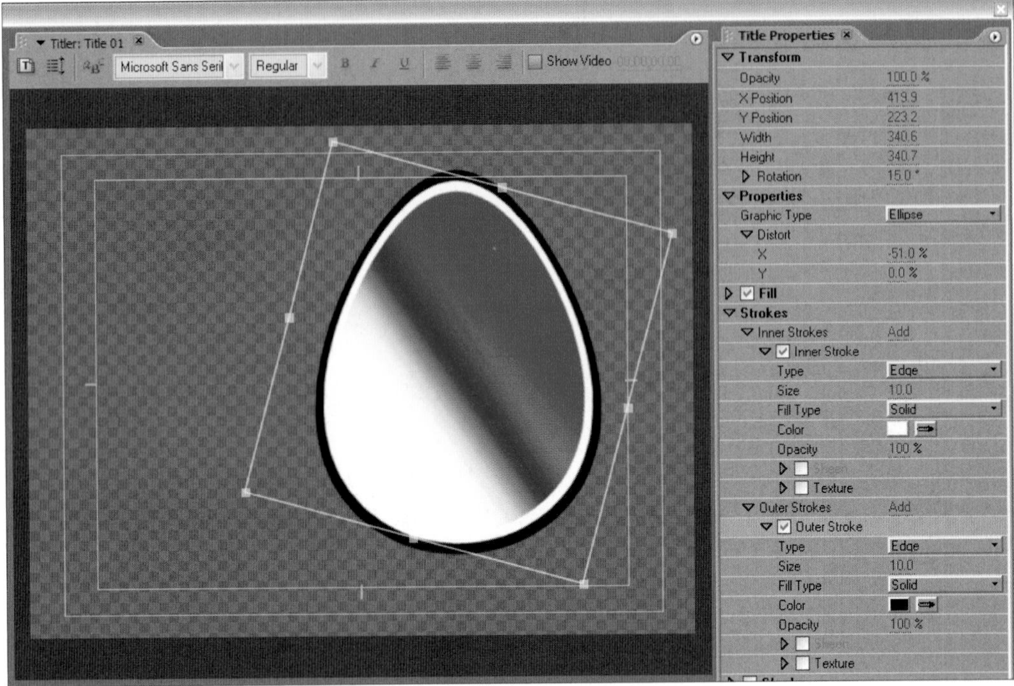

Figure 10.15 This object has both an inner stroke (white) and outer stroke (black). In addition to adjusting the stroke's default values, you can add a sheen or texture to the fill of the stroke.

To add and adjust an inner or outer stroke, twirl down the Strokes menu and click Add for the stroke you wish to create. You can create several inner and outer strokes, so get used to twirling down quite a bit to reveal the properties of each stroke.

Strokes can be one of three types:

- **Edge.** A basic line; the default type
- **Depth.** An angled edge on one side of your object that appears to add depth to the object (**Figure 10.16**)
- **Drop Face.** A copy of the object's size and dimensions that you can shift inside the object's boundaries for an inner stroke or outside for an outer stroke

Each stroke type has its own adjustments. For Edge strokes, you can set the line's size. For Depth strokes, you can adjust the angle and size. For Drop Face strokes, you can adjust the

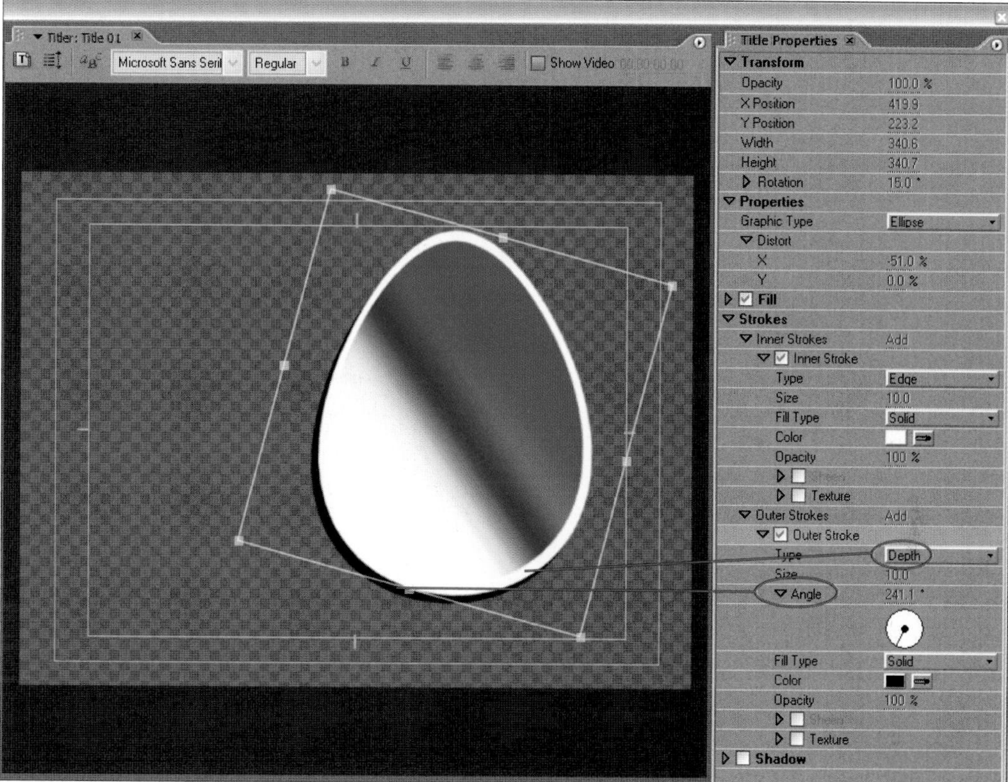

Figure 10.16 This time the object has Depth inner stroke. Notice how the depth appears on one side of the object, as if the object was viewed at an angle.

angle and magnitude of the stroke. The magnitude is the amount of shifting applied to the drop face of the object.

The controls for specifying fill type, choosing a color, setting opacity, and adding a sheen or texture mirror those for the Fill parameters.

Shadow

The final property attribute is Shadow (see **Figure 10.17**). Click the check box and twirl down to access the Shadow parameters: Color, Opacity, Angle, Distance, Size, and Spread. Color and Opacity operate as they do for Fill and Strokes. Angle dictates the angle from which the shadow falls. Distance measures the space between the object and the shadow—how close or how far away the shadow is from

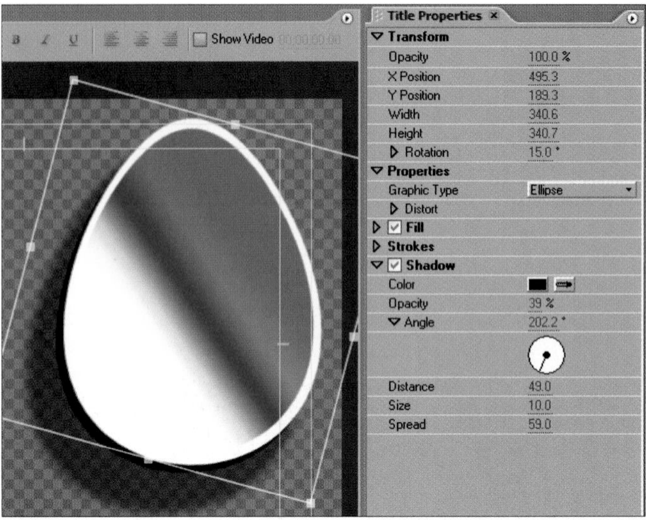

Figure 10.17 This shadow is a bit larger than its object (Size set to 10) and has a soft end edge (Spread set to 59). Its opacity is also reduced to make it more transparent.

the object. Size adjusts the shadow's overall size in accordance with the object: A value of 0.0 creates a shadow of equal size to the object, negative values create smaller shadows, and positive values result in larger shadows. Spread dithers or softens the edge of the shadow's color. Increasing the Spread value softens the shadows edges and gives the illusion of them disappearing into the other color, as opposed to dropping off.

Creating Text

Creating text is as simple as creating objects, with a few more functions and details thrown in. Decide on the orientation of your text—horizontal versus vertical, inside of a box or on a path—and click the associated text creation tool: Type, Vertical Type, Area Type, Vertical Area Type, Path Type, or Vertical Path Type. Click in the drawing area to create an instance for text to be added and begin typing. As you type, the text appears in the default style (**Figure 10.18**).

Text creation tools have two states: Create mode and Edit mode. Select a text creation tool and mouse over blank space in the drawing area. See the little dotted lines around the tool? These dotted lines tell you that when you click you will create a new instance where you can add

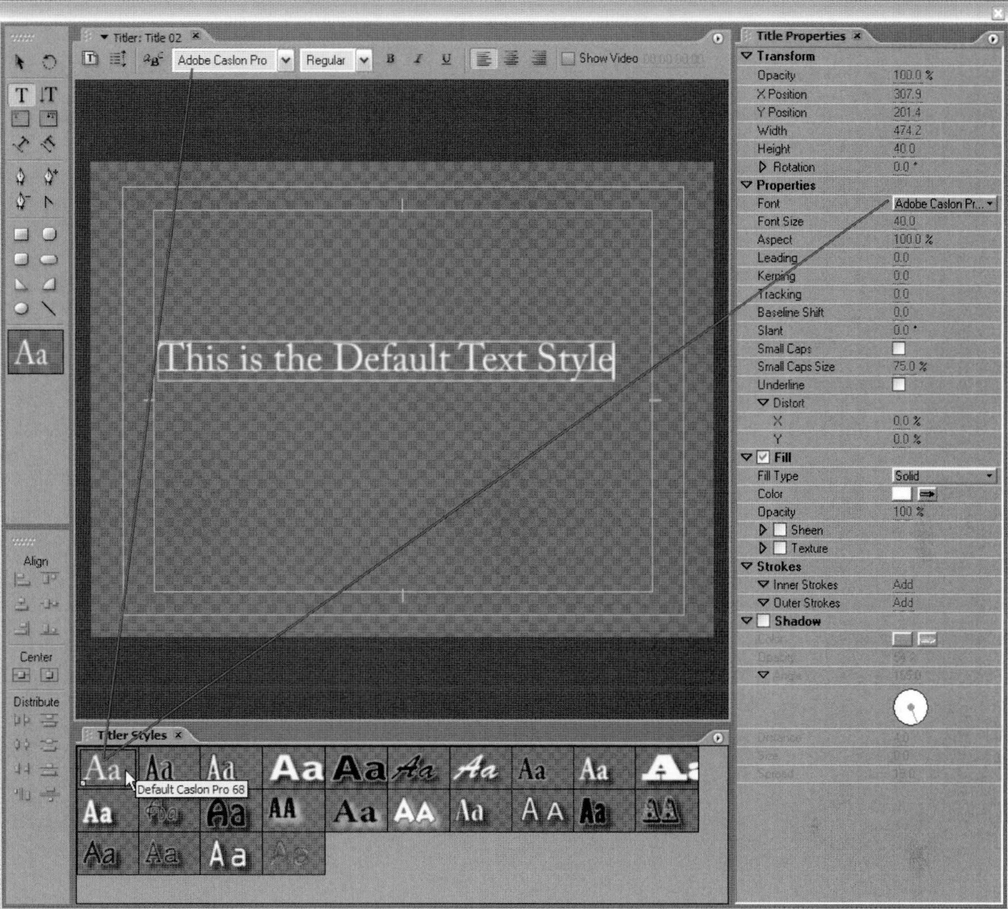

Figure 10.18 Using the Type tool, you can enter text in the drawing area by clicking with the tool and then typing. Notice that the text uses the default style, which is the swatch marked with the small diamond in the Styles panel. Also notice where the font for the style appears and the attributes in the Properties panel match the ones associated with the style.

text. With the same text tool selected, mouse over existing text: The dotted lines are gone. Click within the boundaries of existing text to select a specific character position to modify or add to. To select multiple words or characters, you need to click and drag inside the text area.

If you want to move text, either switch to the Selection tool and drag it or, with the current text active and the text tool still selected, move and adjust the text's position properties in the Transform panel (see **Figure 10.19**).

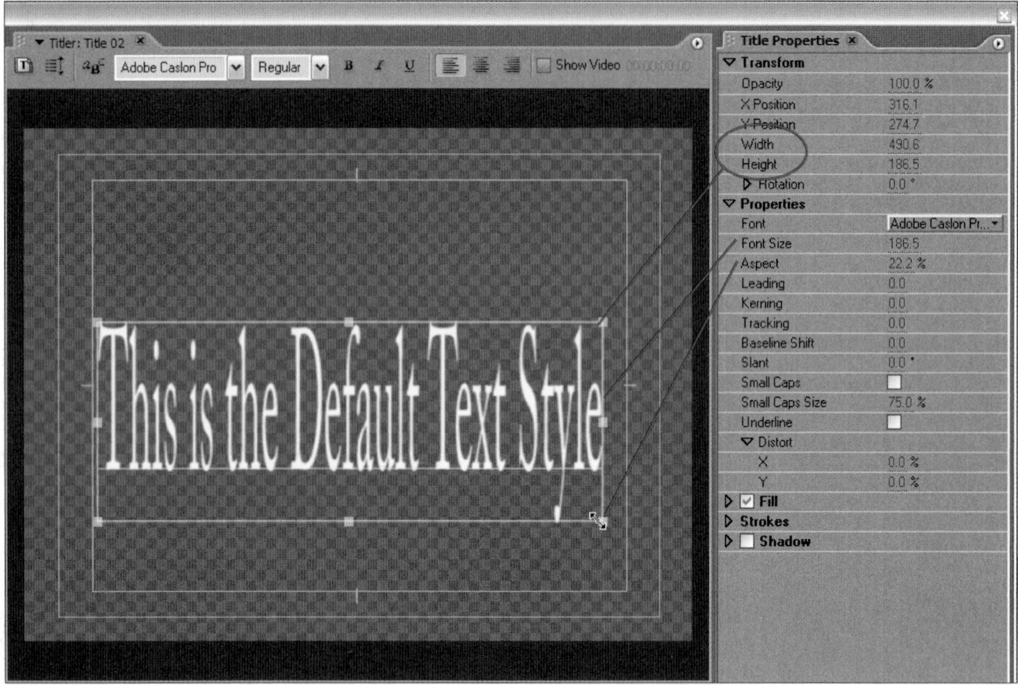

Figure 10.19 Use the Selection tool to select, resize, rotate, or move text. Hold down the Shift key and adjust the text's scale to change the font size dynamically without changing the aspect and distorting the font. Here, the Shift key is not pressed and the aspect of the font is changed along with the size. Height and Width update to display the rectangular dimension value of the text.

If you click on the Selection tool and select a text element, a box with handles appears around that text. Pulling the side or corner handles makes the same alterations as for objects. Holding the Shift key constrains the adjustment so that the text does not distort as you enlarge or shrink it.

Type Alignment

When entering text, you can specify how you would like it aligned: centered, left justified, or right justified. You can do this in a few different ways: Select the text box, and choose Title > Type Alignment from the main menu bar, then pick your alignment format (Left, Center, or Right). You can also right-click on a text selection and choose Type Alignment from the context menu that appears. Or, simply click one of the alignment buttons from the top row of controls.

Text Styles

You can apply styles to active text by clicking a swatch in the Styles Library. Once the style is activated for the selected text, you can fine-tune that style by adjusting the listed parameters in the Object Style panel. A key feature of applying styles to text is that you can select either entire words or individual letters and apply different styles (**Figures 10.20a, b,** and **c**).

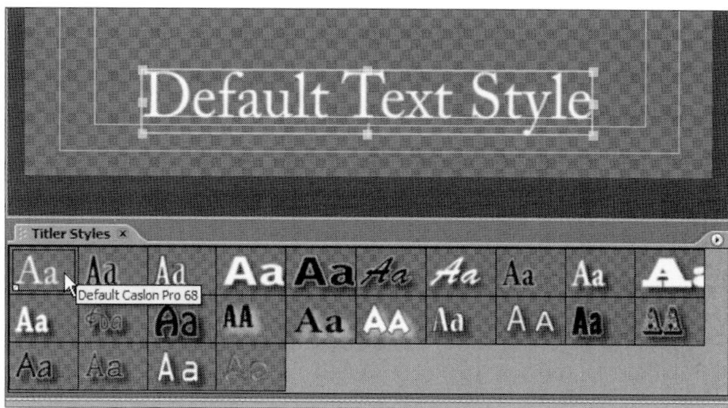

a

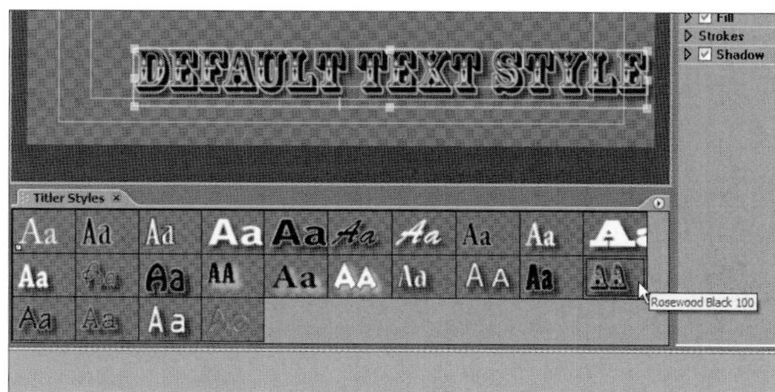

b

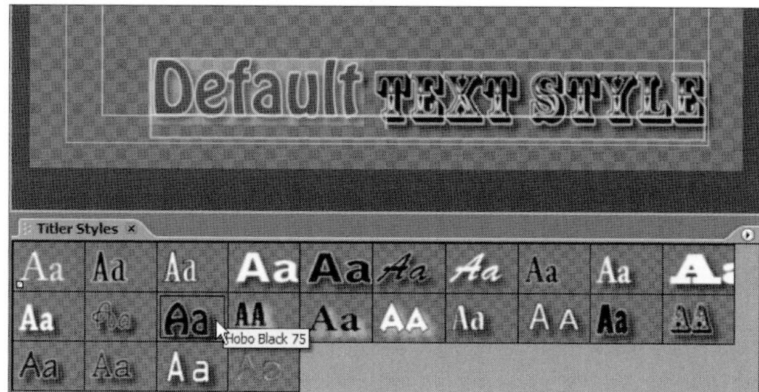

c

Figures 10.20a, b, and c When you first add text to the drawing area, it appears in the default style (a). Select all the text and click a swatch in the Styles panel to apply a new style (b), or select only a portion of the text and apply a new style to that (c).

The Properties panel's Fill, Strokes, and Shadow twirl downs for text are the same as for objects. The Properties twirl down for text, however, has 11 additional attributes to adjust. The first is the Font drop-down menu. To specify your text's font, choose one from the menu's list or click Browse to access the Font Browser. The text automatically updates to display the new font. Clicking and dragging the Font Size hot-text box dynamically and visually adjusts the size of the font. This is where I get jazzed about the Titler; most titlers force you to enter specific number values for text properties, then you have to wait for a preview of the property after you enter the value.

With the Aspect parameter, you can adjust the stretch of your text. Settings above 100% pull the text from its first character's position; settings below 100% squish the text closer together.

The Leading attribute adjusts the space between lines of text. Adding to the value creates more space between lines, and reducing brings the lines closer together (**Figure 10.21**).

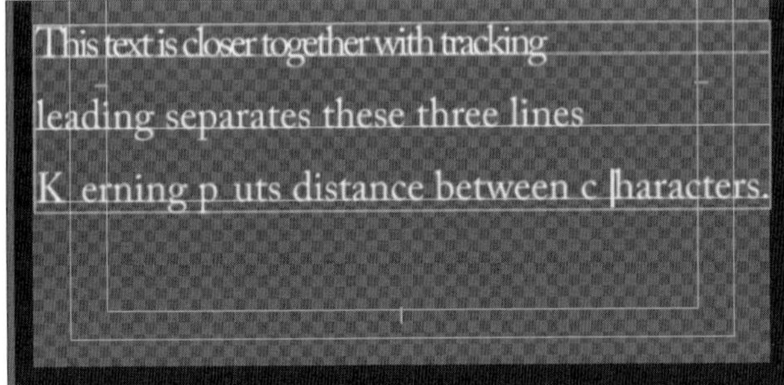

Figure 10.21 Reducing Tracking for the first line brought all the letters closer together. The extra spaces on the third line were created by clicking between pairs of characters and increasing Kerning. The Leading setting determined the distance between the lines.

To change the space between individual characters, use Kerning. Say you want a comma to fit more snugly next to the character on its left. With the Type tool, you would click between the letter and the comma, then change the Kerning setting to a negative value to bring the characters closer together. Positive Kerning values move characters farther apart (Figure 10.20).

The Tracking setting enables you to adjust the kerning for all characters equally. To add more space between every character of text, slide the Tracking hot text value to the right into positive numbers. Sliding left into negative numbers reduces the space between all characters (Figure 10.20).

The invisible line on which all your text is written is referred to as the *baseline.* To move the entire text or a specific character above or below the baseline, increase or decrease the Baseline Shift value, respectively. If you want something more creative than a flat horizontal line, use the Path Type tool or Vertical Path Type tool to define the line. Combining Kerning and Baseline Shift, you could very easily move that example comma closer to the character on its left and then up or down to an even better position.

The Slant attributes give you a pseudo italics look, slanting your characters based on the angle you choose.

The next attribute is very cool. The Small Caps check box enables you to convert all of your text to capital letters in one click (**Figure 10.22**). By keeping Small Caps Size set to less than 100%, you can preserve the text's original hierarchy of lowercase to capital letters. The default Small Caps Size is 75%, meaning that lowercase letters will be capitalized but their size will be 75% of the full size. Of course, your font must support lowercase letters for this to be most effective.

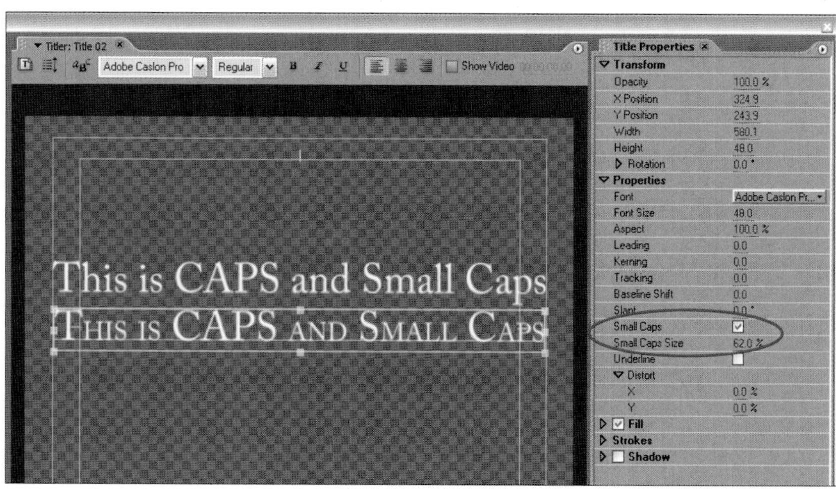

Figure 10.22 The second line of text is a duplicate of the first, but with Small Caps turned on and Small Caps Size set to 62%. Notice how Small Caps keeps the same proportions as in the sentence with both upper- and lowercase letters.

The last unique text property is Underline. Clicking on the Underline check box adds an underline beneath your text. The underline always respects the bottom of the character. In other words, if you add a baseline shift, the underline adheres to the bottom of the text, not the default baseline.

Although they apply distortion based on the X and Y axis for text as they do for objects, the Distort hot-text boxes are worth a mention. Although you can easily see distortion on large objects, the result is often very subtle on text. Playing with the Distort settings, however, can result in cool-looking characters. I encourage you to tinker with these, as well as fills, shadows, and strokes. Chapter 15 will guide you through some creative alterations on the way to making a custom style.

Moving and Arranging Text and Objects

Once you have items within the boundaries of your drawing area, you can select them using the click-and-drag method (Shift-click to select multiple items). After selecting items, you can move them around.

With the Properties panel's Transform controls you can adjust an item's opacity, position, overall size, and rotation (**Figure 10.23**). If you have multiple items selected and are using the Selection tool, the cursor updates to illustrate whether you are making a position (arrow) adjustment or rotation (Rotation tool) adjustment. This is the same as the selection behavior for modifying selected text or objects.

With one or more items selected, you can right-click on the selection and access the Position submenu's three options:

- **Horizontal Center.** Leaves the vertical position of your selection the same but centers the selection horizontally
- **Vertical Center.** Preserves the horizontal position of your selection and centers the selection vertically
- **Lower Third.** Preserves the horizontal position of your selection and moves the selection down to the lower third of the frame

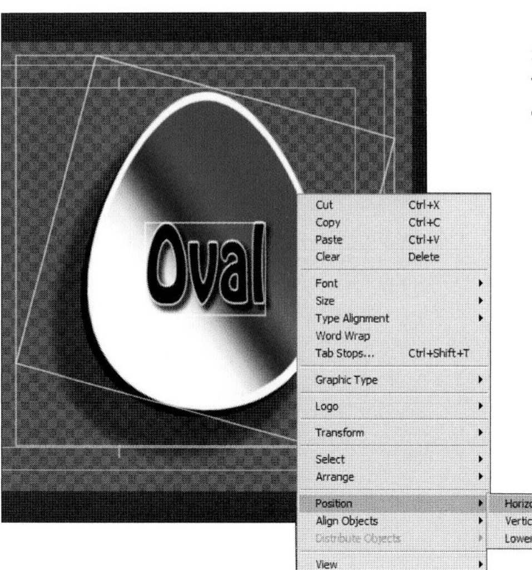

Figure 10.23 With both the text and object selected, you can still resize, rotate, and reposition the selected items as if they were one. Additionally, you can right-click on the selection to change the position of the selection within the drawing area.

If you have two items created on top of each other or you have text that you want to appear on top of an object, you may need to change the stacking order of these items. Right-click the item and choose Arrange > Send to Back to send it to the bottom of the stack, or right-click and choose Arrange > Bring to Front to bring it to the top of the stack. To bring an item forward (closer to the top) by one position, right-click and select Arrange > Bring Forward. To send an item backward one level (farther from the top), right-click and select Arrange > Send Backward. If you prefer working with the Title menu, select the item, then choose Title > Arrange and the direction you want to go.

Lower third refers to the lower-third portion of your frame. Typically news casts include a title that introduces a person with their name. This title resides in the lower third of the frame.

If all of the manipulating, shifting, and adjusting is too much, the Titler does offer some helpful ready-made templates that you can load and modify in a few simple steps.

Using Templates

Templates are pre-made title layouts that you can load and modify. Whether you're working on a video for your child's birthday, your family vacation, or another event, the odds are likely Premiere Pro offers a title template suited to your project. Templates provide integrated text and graphic elements that you can load and modify to add a bit more visual spice to your edited project (**Figure 10.24**).

Figure 10.24 From the Templates dialog, you can select and load ready-made title templates.

All of Premiere's built-in templates were created using the Titler. If you want to examine some title-making techniques, select a template and explore the Object Style and Transform panel settings for all the template's elements.

To load a template, press Ctrl+J on your keyboard, then select a template from the cascade of expanding folders in the Templates dialog. The dialog's right panel displays a preview of the selected template. Click OK to open the selected template inside of your drawing area. Be careful, however, when you load a template, it overwrites whatever items exist in your drawing area.

Modifying a Template

Once loaded, templates are pretty simple to modify. To modify a template or personalize it for your titling needs, select the Type tool and click within the boundaries of the text that you want to alter (**Figures 10.25a** and **b**). Making sure you do not see the dotted lines, click and select the text you want to change, then retype the text as you wish.

If you want to make your newly added text a little bit bigger or a different color, adjust the Properties panel attributes as you see fit. Likewise, you can click and select any object in the template to modify it.

a

b

Figures 10.25a and b When you are adding new text, the Type tool has dotted lines around it (a). When you load a template and hover the Type tool over a text element, note how the text gets highlighted with a box and the Type tool displays without the dotted lines (b). Clicking would allow you select and modify the highlighted text.

Saving Templates

You can save any custom text or object layout as a template for future use. The first step is to access the Templates dialog (select Title > Templates or press Ctrl+J). In the wing menu of the Templates dialog, choose Save <Titlename> as Template. You will be prompted to then name your custom template. Clicking OK saves a copy of the current layout in your Templates folder (on your root disk) with the name you specify, and adds an instance of it into your User Templates folder in the Template dialog's left panel. It's pretty easy and incredibly useful to create your own library of templates to suit unique project needs.

Chapter 15, "Advanced Titling: Styles and Templates," will add a few helpful templates to this folder.

Things to Remember

If you are feeling unsure about your title creation skills, I highly recommend loading some templates and modifying them to suit your needs. To create a simple new look, I typically load a lower-third template, then change the shape and color of the object, as well as the text's size and font. If I am happy with the results, I save the modified template as a new custom template.

If you want a different font for each letter in a word, for example, simply select each letter in turn, changing the font each time. The same goes for adjusting color, strokes, and shadows. With this in mind, you can create a diverse selection of titles and explore some wacky, but cool options.

As you make your adjustments, remember that with text you can make every property adjustment to either individual characters or entire text selections.

Ready to take your titling skills a step further? See Chapter 15, "Advanced Titling: Styles and Templates," to learn how to create custom title styles and templates that you can use over and over again for future projects.

CHAPTER

11

DVD Basics

With Premiere Pro 2.0, you can encode and burn DVDs directly from the timeline. Don't have a DVD burner on your system? No problem. When exporting to DVD, you have the option to either burn directly to a disc or to create files in folders that can be burned or authored to DVD later.

This chapter shows you the essentials and your choices for exporting from Premiere Pro to a DVD-ROM or to DVD files. You will explore exporting an auto-play DVD versus menu-based DVD, as well as get an overview of the MPEG encoding options in the Adobe Media Encoder.

Exporting to DVD is only available on a single sequence basis; you cannot make a single disc using two separate sequences as separate video tracks on the DVD. You can, however, place multiple video files on one timeline and designate each file with a different DVD marker, which enables you to create multiple, separate tracks on a DVD from a single timeline.

To export to DVD, it's quite simple. You just highlight the current timeline you wish to export and select File > Export > Export to DVD. From there, it's a matter of settings and choices. Before getting into those choices, however, you first need to differentiate between the two methods of authoring: auto-play and menu based.

Auto-Play vs. Menu-Based Authoring

When you choose Export to DVD from an active timeline, the default mode of authoring is called *Auto-play*, meaning the resulting disc will play automatically when inserted into a DVD player. With Auto-play, you cannot create a DVD with menus; you can only export a sequence and choose whether or not the created DVD plays in single-play mode or in a continuous loop. To create a menu-based DVD, you must open Premiere Pro's DVD Layout panel and click Change Template (**Figure 11.1a**).

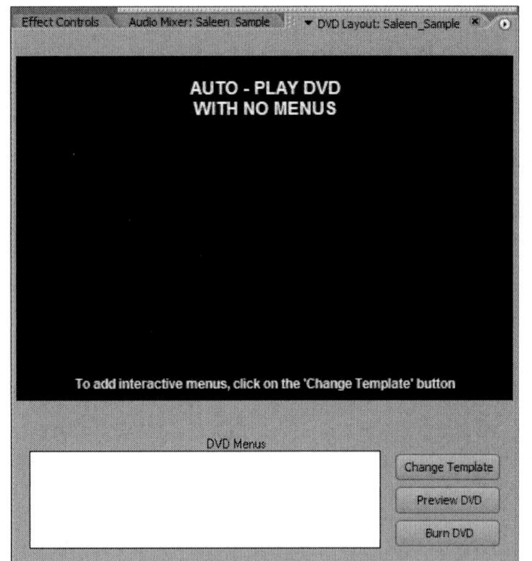

a

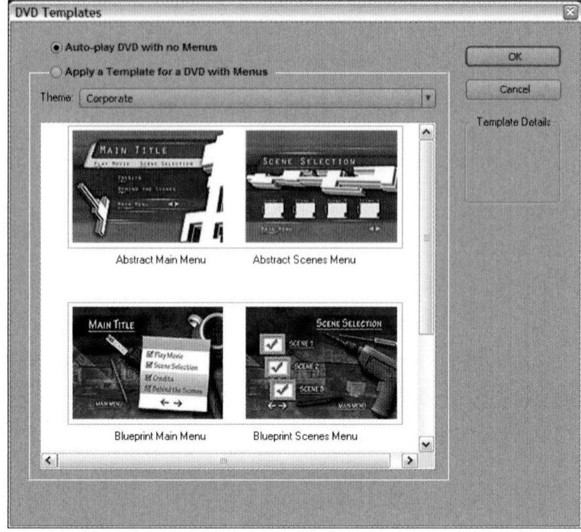

b

Figures 11.1a and b New to Premiere Pro 2.0 is the DVD Layout panel, where you can design and modify DVD menu templates. Because no template has been loaded for the selected sequence, Auto-play is the active Export to DVD mode (a). To load a menu template and turn off Auto-play, you must click the Change Template button and select one of the templates available in the DVD Templates dialog (b). On the contrary, if you had a menu structure built for a specific sequence and wanted to export to DVD in Auto-play mode, you would access this same dialog and click the button for Auto-play DVD with no Menus, thus disabling the menu-based output.

One of the top new features for 2.0 is the ability to create customizable and fully functioning menu-driven DVDs from your timeline. You'll learn the tips and trick to do just that in Chapter 16, "Custom DVD Design."

With the DVD Templates dialog box open (**Figure 11.1b**), click the radio button for Apply a Template for a DVD with Menus. You now can toggle between the different themes and select the appropriate template that you wish to load. Clicking OK applies the template to the active sequence from which you accessed the DVD templates. Once a template is loaded, the DVD Layout panel displays that template when opening its host sequence. If you were to create a new sequence, the DVD Layout panel would display the default Auto-play mode until you loaded a menu template and turned off Auto-play for the sequence.

No matter which type of DVD you wish to create, you have three choices for exporting when you write out the files of the DVD.

DVD Settings: One Export, Three Choices

When you choose Export to DVD, you access the Burn DVD dialog, which lets you control how you create the files for your DVD (**Figure 11.2**). The dialog is broken down into two basic sections: DVD Settings and Encoding. Although many of the choices in the DVD Settings area are straightforward, let's review them to understand exactly what they do. The first DVD Settings options specify where the files should be written, either to a disc, a folder, or an ISO image. The settings beneath—Burner Location, Copies, Status, and Export Range—all relate to the type of burn you will be exporting.

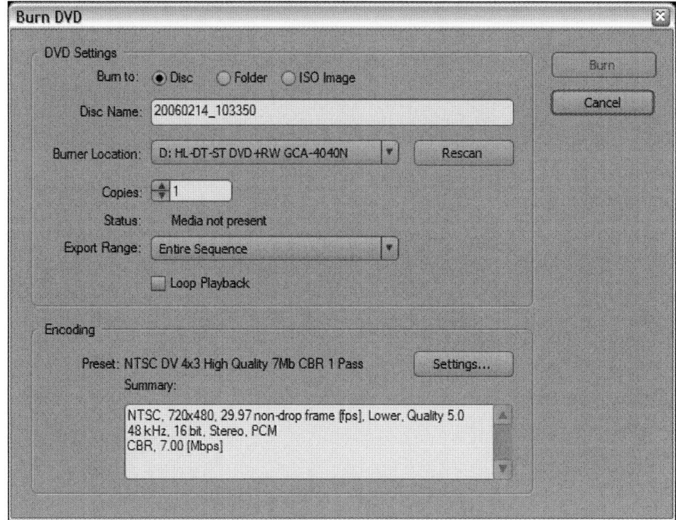

Figure 11.2 Select the File > Export > Export to DVD menu listing to open the Burn DVD dialog. Notice that at the top there are three choices for how you would like to process the files you are creating. Burn to Disc does just that and burns the files to a physical DVD, while Folder and ISO Image write the files to your hard drive.

Burn to Disc

Burning to disc is straightforward (assuming you have a DVD burner and disc installed) and produces a playable DVD in Auto-play or menu-based mode as the sequence dictates. When you choose Burn to Disc, the DVD Settings enable you to name the disc (Disc Name), define and scan the drive to which you will be burning (Burner Location), specify the number of copies you wish to burn (Copies), and get feedback as to whether or not Premiere Pro recognizes the drive and presence of media (Status).

In **Figure 11.3** you can see that my drive is detected but because there is no disc in the drive, I get the Status message "Media not Present."

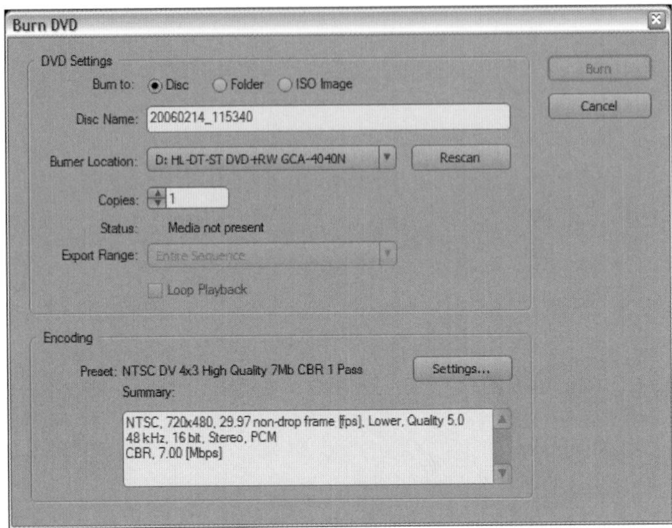

Figure 11.3 If you compare this figure to 11.2, you will notice one distinct difference in the DVD Settings area. The settings in Figure 11.2 are for a burn from an auto-play sequence, but these are for a burn of a menu-based sequence. When burning menu-based DVDs the Export Range and Loop Playback controls are disabled.

If you're burning an auto-play DVD, you have two additional decisions. In Auto-play mode, you must specify the Export Range setting, which determines whether you burn the entire sequence or only the portion under the work area bar. In addition, you can turn on Loop Playback, which creates a DVD that plays in a continual loop. Because DVD Markers distinguish the content of menu-based DVDs, there is no use for differentiating the work area or entire sequence when encoding; additionally a menu-based DVD does not have the ability to loop.

Burn to Folder

Choosing to burn to a folder is very valuable if you are considering backing up or repurposing the content of your DVD. When you burn to disc or an ISO image, Premiere Pro creates MPEG video files as well as various flavors of audio files and converts them into alternately named files (.VOB, and so on) in a structure that adheres to DVD architecture (AUDIO TS and VIDEO TS). If you want to collect all of the assets to be burned without the DVD formatting and renaming, however, choose Burn to Folder. When you select Burn to Folder, Premiere Pro asks for Folder Name and Folder Location settings (**Figure 11.4**). Provide these, and Premiere Pro encodes all the DVD files into that folder.

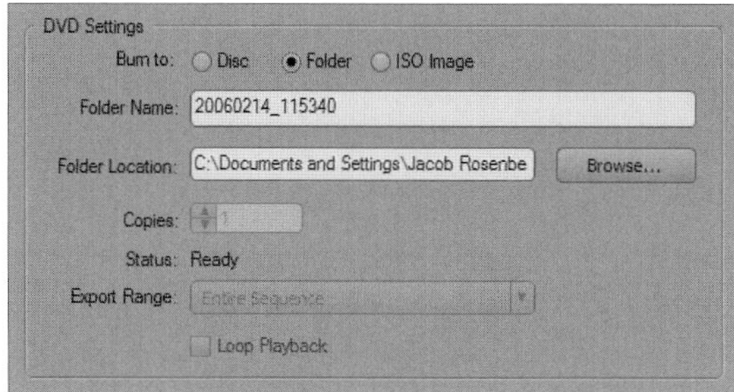

Figure 11.4 Notice that the DVD Settings change depending on what you are burning to. For a folder burn, you need only name the folder and define its location to write the desired files.

Exporting to a folder is a perfect workflow if you intend on authoring in another program such as Encore DVD. After you export the files to a folder you can open the files in Encore or any other DVD authoring application and further customize the DVD.

Burn to ISO Image

The final method is to burn to an ISO image. When you burn directly to a disc, Premiere Pro structures the files and stamps them on the disc in a standard way so that when you pop the disc into a player it knows how to play the disc and which files are available. This standard arrangement is called an *ISO image* (or disc image). When you choose Burn to ISO image, Premiere Pro writes the ISO image to your hard drive, saving it as a single file comprised of all the elements needed to author the DVD exactly as you designed it (see **Figure 11.5**). If you want to be able to burn discs from a separate application or send an image of the disc to someone else to burn from, select Burn to ISO Image.

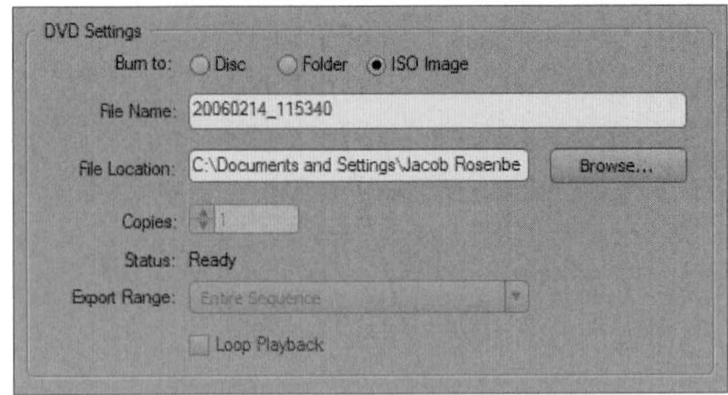

Figure 11.5 Instead of naming the disc or folder, burning to ISO Image asks you to name the ISO file and define the location in which the file will be written.

If you intended on making future copies of a disc, you could first burn to disc and then burn to ISO image. Later, you could load the ISO image in the disc burning utility and start burning new copies. An even faster method is to burn to an ISO image and use a separate utility to burn all your DVDs.

Encoding

As I briefly mentioned earlier, when you burn to disc or an ISO image Premiere Pro converts your audio and video into formats suitable for DVD players. This process is called *encoding*. The primary DVD encoding format is MPEG2. Like Windows Media, QuickTime, and Flash, MPEG2 is a form of compression that allows for high quality video to playback at low data rates. What makes MPEG2 different from other compression types is that instead of compressing each individual frame, it in essence takes "snapshots" of groups of frames, encoding the differences between the frames as opposed to the frames in their entirety. The number of frames used in a snapshot is commonly referred to as the *GOP (Groups of Pictures) size*. With various flavors of MPEG encoding you can have small GOP or large GOP sizes. Although MPEG compression makes a great playback format, because every frame is not individually and uniquely accounted for it can be a painful format in which to edit.

Regardless of whether you are burning to disc, folder, or ISO image, in every case you must determine the encoding settings and the amount of compression for your files. You modify your encoding settings using the Adobe Media Encoder (**Figure 11.6**). To access the Adobe Media

Figure 11.6 The Adobe Media Encoder has been overhauled for Premiere Pro 2.0. Take note of the Output area on the left side; this shows you a preview of the sequence being encoded from the settings you define on the right side. Using the time ruler at the bottom of the Output area; you can scrub to any frame in the sequence to see what it looks like. Under Export Settings on the right, notice that Format is locked as MPEG2-DVD. This setting is locked because you accessed the encoder from the Burn DVD dialog and Premiere Pro's DVD Authoring functions author in MPEG2-DVD only.

Encoder, click the Settings button in the Encoding section of the Export to DVD (Burn DVD) dialog box.

Instead of taking you on a complete tour of the Adobe Media Encoder, I will focus on the settings and functions commonly used to encode for DVD authoring. The Encoder can be broken into two areas: Source/Output (left side) and Export Settings (right side). Depending on the Export Settings to the right, the output or source content will update and preview on the left. Let's take a look at the Export Settings on the right.

If you are interested in going beyond the basics and exploring the Encoder in its entirely, check out Chapter 29, "Professional Workflows: Using the Adobe Media Encoder," which takes you on a tour of the encoder suggesting the best settings and formats for a number of different tasks.

Export Settings Area: Format and Presets

When you access the encoder to assign your DVD encoding settings from the Burn DVD dialog, the Adobe Media Encoder is locked into MPEG2-DVD as the export format.

When accessing the Encoder from the Burn DVD dialog, the only settings that the dialog needs are the parameters listed in the tabs below the Export Settings (**Figure 11.7**). These parameters can be customized or preloaded from a multitude of presets (**Figure 11.8**). In this case the Range setting does not apply to the encoding of the files for your DVD.

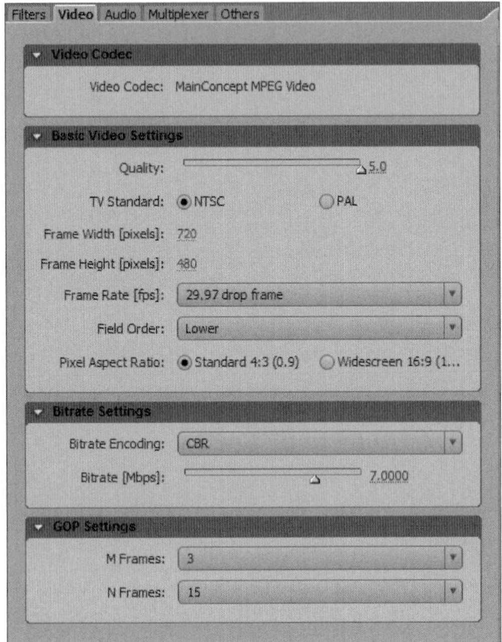

Figure 11.7 Below the Export Settings box are five tabs—Filters, Video, Audio, Multiplexer, and Others—featuring customizable settings that define exactly how the audio and video encodes in the selected MPEG2-DVD format. You can quickly load a preset from the Export Settings > Preset drop-down menu and then adjust any of the settings to your liking.

Choosing the right preset is as easy as understanding the video format of your source sequence. If you are editing with widescreen PAL MiniDV footage, you simply select one of the PAL DV 16×9 presets. If you are shooting widescreen NTSC DV 24p footage you can select from either of the NTSC Progressive 16×9 presets. If you aren't encoding widescreen footage, select from the 4×3 presets.

Once a preset is loaded, the Summary section (**Figure 11.9**) lists the settings for video (TV standard, frame size, frame rate, field dominance, and quality), audio (Hertz, bit depth, and format), and bitrate (encoding type, bitrate).

NTSC DV 16:9 High Quality 4Mb VBR 2 Pass
NTSC DV 16:9 High Quality 7Mb CBR 1 Pass
NTSC DV 16:9 High Quality 7Mb VBR 2 Pass SurCode for Dolby Digital 5.1
NTSC DV 16:9 Low Quality 3MB VBR 1 Pass
NTSC DV 16:9 Low Quality 3MB VBR 2 Pass
NTSC DV 16:9 Low Quality 4MB VBR 1 Pass
NTSC DV 16:9 Low Quality 4MB VBR 2 Pass
NTSC DV 16:9 Low Quality 6MB VBR 1 Pass
NTSC DV 16:9 Low Quality 6MB VBR 2 Pass
✔ NTSC DV 4:3 High Quality 7Mb CBR 1 Pass
NTSC DV 4:3 High Quality 7Mb VBR 2 Pass SurCode for Dolby Digital 5.1
NTSC DV 4:3 Low Quality 3MB VBR 1 Pass
NTSC DV 4:3 Low Quality 3MB VBR 2 Pass
NTSC DV 4:3 Low Quality 4MB VBR 2 Pass
NTSC DV 4:3 Low Quality 4MB VBR 1 Pass
NTSC DV 4:3 Low Quality 4Mb CBR 1 Pass
NTSC DV 4:3 Low Quality 6MB VBR 1 Pass
NTSC DV 4:3 Low Quality 6MB VBR 2 Pass
NTSC Progressive 16:9 High Quality 4Mb VBR 2 Pass
NTSC Progressive 16:9 High Quality 7Mb CBR 1 Pass
NTSC Progressive 4:3 High Quality 4Mb VBR 2 Pass
NTSC Progressive 4:3 High Quality 7Mb CBR 1 Pass
PAL DV 16:9 High Quality 4Mb VBR 2 Pass
PAL DV 16:9 High Quality 7Mb CBR 1 Pass
PAL DV 16:9 High Quality 7Mb VBR 2 Pass SurCode for Dolby Digital 5.1
PAL DV 16:9 Low Quality 3MB VBR 1 Pass
PAL DV 16:9 Low Quality 3MB VBR 2 Pass
PAL DV 16:9 Low Quality 4MB VBR 1 Pass
PAL DV 16:9 Low Quality 4MB VBR 2 Pass
PAL DV 16:9 Low Quality 6MB VBR 1 Pass
PAL DV 16:9 Low Quality 6MB VBR 2 Pass
PAL DV 4:3 High Quality 4Mb VBR 2 Pass
PAL DV 4:3 High Quality 7Mb CBR 1 Pass
PAL DV 4:3 High Quality 7Mb VBR 2 Pass SurCode for Dolby Digital 5.1
PAL DV 4:3 Low Quality 3MB VBR 1 Pass
PAL DV 4:3 Low Quality 3MB VBR 2 Pass
PAL DV 4:3 Low Quality 4MB VBR 1 Pass
PAL DV 4:3 Low Quality 4MB VBR 2 Pass
PAL DV 4:3 Low Quality 4Mb CBR 1 Pass
PAL DV 4:3 Low Quality 6MB VBR 1 Pass
PAL DV 4:3 Low Quality 6MB VBR 2 Pass
PAL Progressive 16:9 High Quality 4Mb VBR 2 Pass
PAL Progressive 16:9 High Quality 7Mb CBR 1 Pass
PAL Progressive 4:3 High Quality 4Mb VBR 2 Pass
PAL Progressive 4:3 High Quality 7Mb CBR 1 Pass

Figure 11.8 Premiere Pro offers many preset choices for the MPEG2-DVD format. If you are burning from an interlaced NTSC sequence, you can pick from any of the NTSC presets. If you are burning from a progressive NTSC sequence, select from the Progressive NTSC presets. In either case, once a preset is loaded you can modify the preset to change the settings further.

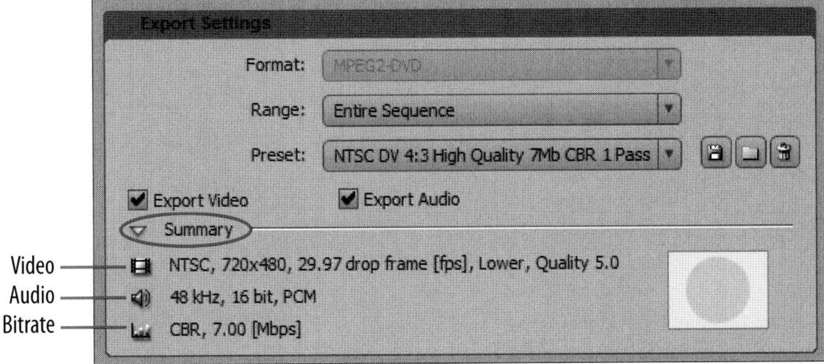

Figure 11.9 Below the check boxes for Exporting Audio and Video is a summary of the loaded preset that reflects the encoder settings. The top line is Video, the second is Audio and the third is the Bitrate Settings.

Table 11.1 File Sizes for 90 Minutes of CBR-Encoded Material

Constant Bitrate (in Megabits)	Resulting File Size (in Megabytes)
4 Mbps	2700 MB
5 Mbps	3375 MB
6 Mbps	4050 MB
7 Mbps	4735 MB

For most of the work I do, I tend to use a 4.5 Mbps constant bitrate when I have to burn a DVD for viewing purposes. Any source material with stereo audio and a duration of under two hours fits fine on a DVD, and the bitrate is large enough to ensure good quality.

CBR vs. VBR

When choosing a preset, note that all the listings are classified as either CBR or VBR. CBR (constant bit rate) applies the same amount of data to all of the source material when encoding, whereas VBR (variable bit rate) analyzes the source material and applies less data where it isn't needed and more data where it is needed. VBR functions best using two passes through the source material, the first pass to analyze and calculate the best bitrates and the second pass to write them out into the file. The quickest way to burn your DVD at the highest quality is to use the High Quality CBR presets, which write out the file in a single pass at a constant bit rate. The only drawback of high bitrate CBR encoding is that the file sizes tend to be larger and therefore less data can fit on a disc. **Table 11.1** details the results of various bitrates. When deciding which is right for your project, don't forget to add 1080 MB for PCM stereo audio as well.

Based on these results, a 5 Mbps Constant encode plus stereo audio will barely fit onto a standard DVD-5 disc. If you have a longer timeline and want to be more economical with file sizes, High Quality VBR 2 pass is the right choice. By doing two passes on your video you truly maximize the encoding process and allow the encoder to intelligently write more data where more data is needed and less data when it is not needed. If you have the time, two pass is always the best choice.

Presets vs. Customization

For most DVD burning, loading a preset is all you need to do, especially if you're encoding NTSC DV video. Standard NTSC DV is 29.97 fps, lower-field dominant, 720×480 with a 4×3 aspect ratio, and has stereo audio embedded in it. Although the majority of the encoder settings will match that of your source footage, you can customize some settings to give you better control and a higher quality encode. As you encode more and more video content you will pick up on which data rates offer the best results and which rates work better with which formats. If you are encoding standard definition video you might find that you need less data using two passes; by creating your own preset for each encode that you do, you ease the process of narrowing down and allowing quick access to the best settings for a specific encode.

If you decide to customize a preset, the next sections provide a tab-by-tab overview of what you can adjust and how it affects the encode. If you're encoding NTSC DV video for DVD authoring you can skip the Filters tab and head to the Video tab.

Video Tab

The Video tab houses two important group boxes: Basic Video Settings and Bitrate Settings (**Figure 11.10**). To help you keep track of their contents, as you hold your mouse over each drop-down menu or radio button Premiere Pro displays feedback on that setting at the bottom of the Video tab (just above OK and Cancel).

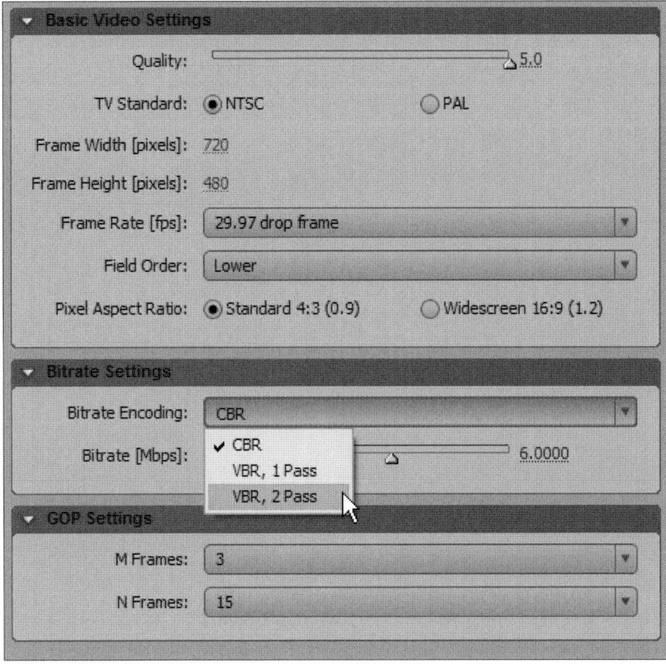

Figure 11.10 For all my MPEG encodes I leave Quality at 5.0; this adds some time to the encode, but it ensures greater accuracy to the compression of the source material.

The only setting that I recommend customizing in Basic Video Settings is the Quality slider. I always leave Quality at its top value of 5.0. Decreasing Quality speeds up encoding but at a detriment to accuracy because, in essence, the encoder uses less time to analyze the source material. The remaining options should always match the source footage you are encoding. For the 4×3 NTSC DV footage of our example, the settings in Figure 11.10 match perfectly.

The Bitrate Settings group box is where you can further customize your encode and decide whether or not you want a constant (CBR) or variable (VBR) encode. For CBR encodes, simply set the slider at your desired bitrate (**Figure 11.11a**) and you're ready to encode. VBR encodes require a little more thought (**Figure 11.11b**). For both encodes you need to look at the duration and format of what you are encoding in order to determine whether to use CBR or VBR. For DV footage under an hour you can use a high CBR value (refer to Table 11.1). For longer material from higher resolution sources (uncompressed HD or SD) you can use a VBR preset.

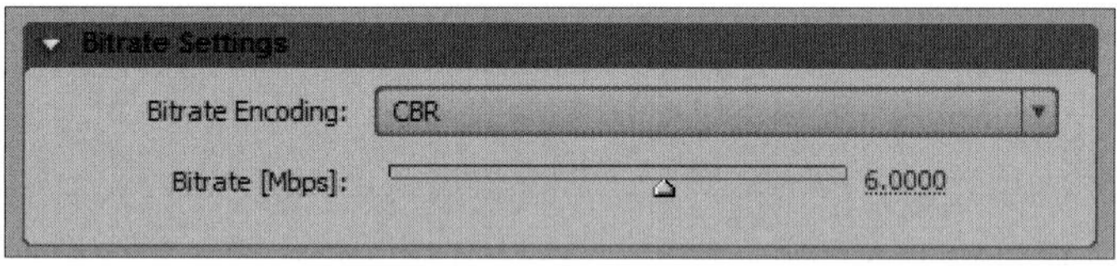

Figures 11.11a and b With CBR encoding, the Bitrate setting is straightforward; 6 Mbps is usually a good choice (a). A VBR, 2 Pass encode is a more complex setup with the Minimum, Target, and Maximum Bitrate each customized to a specific value (b). Typically, for a 90- to 120-minute video, the VBR settings in the figure are solid and will give you good results.

Bitrate Settings
Bitrate Encoding: CBR
Bitrate [Mbps]: 6.0000

a

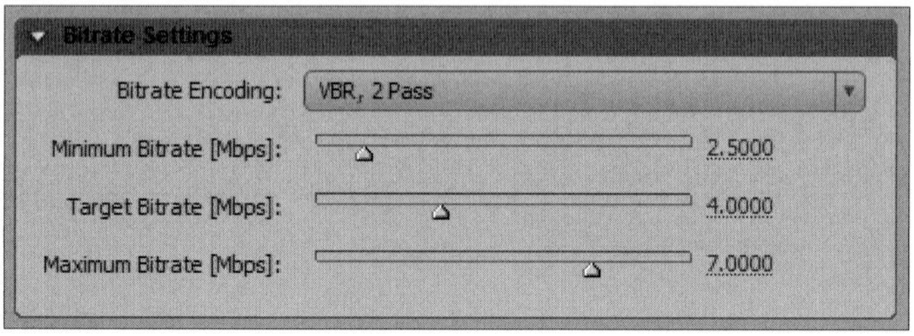

Bitrate Settings
Bitrate Encoding: VBR, 2 Pass
Minimum Bitrate [Mbps]: 2.5000
Target Bitrate [Mbps]: 4.0000
Maximum Bitrate [Mbps]: 7.0000

b

Because a VBR encode uses more data when more is needed and less when less is needed, you need to specify the Minimum Bitrate for the low areas, the Target Bitrate at which the encode should try to average out, and the Maximum Bitrate for the high areas that require more data. If you think about it, footage of a solid, single-color wall requires minimal data to encode; conversely, a shot from a hill overlooking colorful houses in San Francisco requires a great deal more data to represent the colors and details of the image. The wall would be a minimum bitrate section of your source, while the San Francisco shot might be a maximum. The only way to find out if your VBR values are set up right is to encode your video and pay attention to the compression throughout the video. If you find that in general the quality is lacking, bump up your minimum and target. If a couple of sections that have a lot of motion and lots of detail also have compression artifacts, then bump up your maximum.

Although the GOP Settings might look alternately enticing or intimidating, they do not make too much of a difference with basic DVD encoding.

For VBR encodes I tend to use a Minimum Bitrate ranging from 1.5 to 3.0, my Target is typically 4 to 5, and my Maximum Bitrate is 6.5 to 8. Keep in mind that as you increase the Minimum and Target you dramatically increase the file size of the encode. Typically the Maximum Bitrate is used less than the Minimum when encoding.

Audio Tab

The Audio tab has only one drop-down menu that yields valuable options for encoding the audio portion of your sequence. The Audio Format Settings drop-down gives you the choice of encoding your audio in PCM, MPEG, or Dolby Digital format (**Figures 11.12a**, **b**, and **c**).

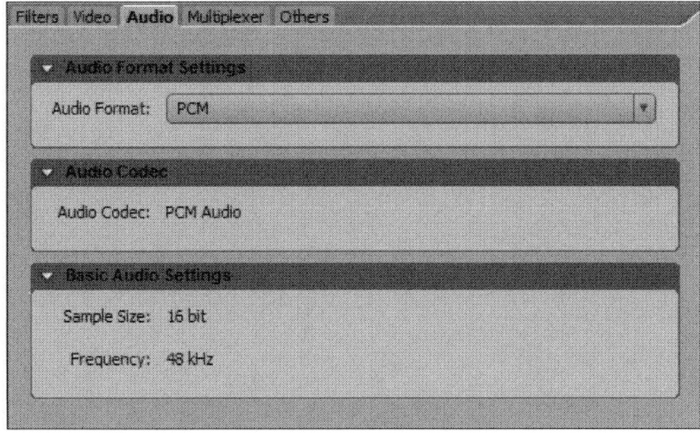

a

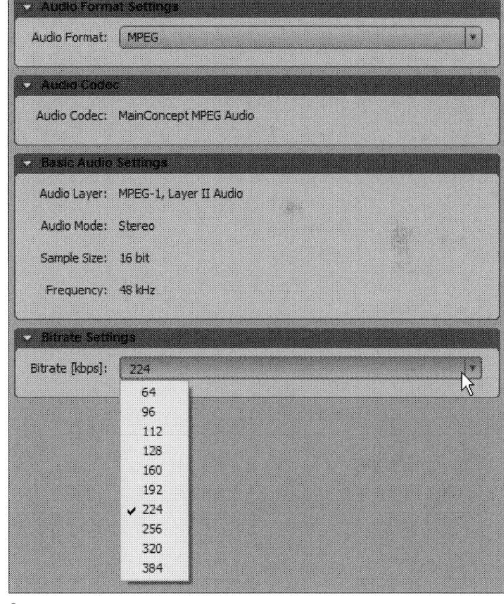

b

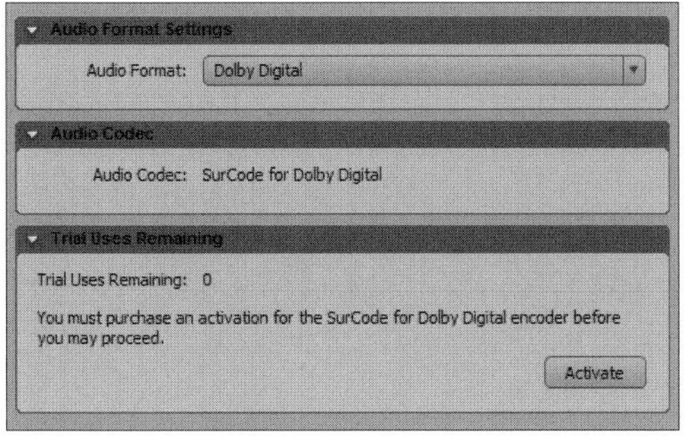

c

Figures 11.12a, b, and c The default audio format is PCM (a, top left). If you choose MPEG (layer 3, a.k.a. mp3), you have a choice of bitrates for encoding (b, top right). Select Dolby Digital (c, bottom left), and you will most likely use the SurCode for Dolby Digital codec (the Dolby Digital AC3 encoder comes at a fee of around $300).

Because DVD audio is supposed to be 16 bits at 48 kHz, the Basic Audio Settings are locked and reflect that value. Of course, audio can also be stereo or 5.1 at 16 bits 48 kHz. If you wish to encode in 5.1, you have to use the SurCode for Dolby Digital encoder for Audio Codec. Out of the box you get three free encodes with the SurCode for Dolby Digital encoder and then you have to buy a license to use it indefinitely.

If you are burning to files that will be authored later, you could choose MPEG for Audio Format, which makes the audio portion of your encode significantly smaller. Later, however, you would have to convert it to Dolby or PCM when authoring to DVD.

For most projects, you simply can leave your Audio tab with Audio Format set for PCM.

Multiplexer Tab

The last tab worth looking at is the Multiplexer tab. If you are authoring your DVD using Premiere Pro or Encore DVD, set the Multiplexer value to None. If you are authoring your DVD in another application that uses multiplexed files and you plan on using the files that you export from Premiere Pro as your source material, click the radio button for DVD.

A multiplexed encode for DVD writes both the audio and video into a single file as opposed to an MPEG video file and PCM audio file for each encoded clip.

For all Premiere Pro DVD authoring you can leave the Multiplexer button checked for None.

Saving Your Preset

When you finish customizing your Export Settings, you should save and name your custom preset for further use: Simply click the Save Preset button next to the Preset drop-down menu in the Adobe Media Encoder (**Figures 11.13a** and **b**).

Give the preset a descriptive name, then click OK, and Premiere saves it into the stack of presets that become available when you access the Encoder using MPEG2-DVD as your format.

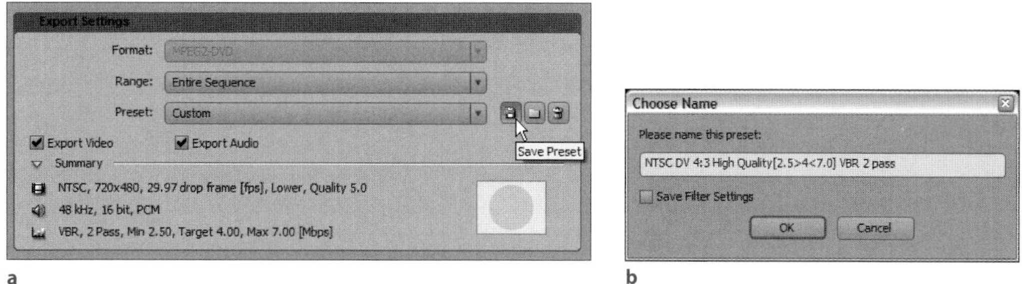

Figures 11.13a and b After you modify a preset, the Preset drop-down lists it as Custom (a). To save a Custom preset, click the Save button and then rename it as descriptively as possible so that you can know at a glance what the settings are (b).

Things to Remember

Keep in mind that the default Auto-play DVD setting does not provide any menu structuring; it simply plays whatever was exported from the moment you place the DVD in a DVD player. To create a menu-based DVD you must open the DVD Layout panel and choose Change Template to load a custom template that has menu structuring.

Because DV and HDV formats are already highly compressed you are likely to get visible artifacts and undesirable compression anomalies when using lower bitrates. When encoding DV footage to DVD, my quality settings are almost always maxed out with a bitrate of at least 5 to 6.0000 Mbps. Because DV is already highly compressed, throwing more bits at the DVD encode results in a better quality DVD. The previous bitrate range does not give you a full two hours of video on a DVD 5 (4.7 GB of space), but it certainly makes DV look great on a DVD.

When using 16×9 formats such as 1920×1080 HD, 1280×720 HD/HDV, or 1920×1080 HDV, you can easily make down-converted DVDs at 720×480 directly from your HD or HDV timeline. Because Premiere Pro does not offer HD DVD encoding, it will reduce the size of your video frame to fit in the 720×480 size that it encodes. Just remember to match the frame rate of your timeline with that of the preset you are using.

If you are using 24p HD material, use one of the High Quality 16×9 progressive presets. If you are using 1080i HDV (29.97), use one of the High Quality 16×9 DV presets and then *reverse* the field dominance from lower to upper (HDV is upper-field dominant).

And finally, although the presets are there for a reason, when you do decode to customize a preset take the time to save it so that if the encode is exactly what you want, you can reuse the settings time and time again.

In the next chapter, we'll look at Adobe Bridge and some of the new features that are available with Premiere Pro and the Adobe Production Studio.

12

Adobe Bridge and Adobe Production Studio

Coinciding with the release of Premiere Pro 2.0, Adobe released an entire suite of video-based products: Adobe Production Studio, which includes Premiere Pro 2.0, After Effects 7.0, Encore DVD 2.0, Audition 2.0, Photoshop CS2, and Illustrator CS2. Although it is an investment to purchase the full bundle, you won't need much additional software to complete your videos or films. You'll also have access to such extra features as Dynamic Link, which enables you to import an After Effects composition into Premiere Pro and have it update live in Premiere as you make changes to the source composition in After Effects. This chapter outlines a few of Production Studio's powerful integration features.

From every Production Studio application—whether purchased individually or in the bundle—you also can access another utility useful for integration: Adobe Bridge. First seen in the Adobe Creative Suite (Photoshop, Illustrator, and so on), Bridge is a file browsing tool that allows you to not only rearrange and search files on your system, but also add metadata to the files and run automated tasks. Whether you have the full Production Studio or Premiere Pro 2.0 only, Bridge can help you work more efficiently by enabling you to better organize, label, and run select automated tasks on batches of files. Production Studio operates on a creative level, touching all the tasks of film or video production, while Bridge operates on the file level, enabling you to edit metadata stored in any file so that you can search your system, share files, and preserve sensitive information, such as copyrights, intellectual property rights, photographer credits, and more.

To start this chapter, let's take a tour of Adobe Bridge, then I'll demonstrate the power of Production Studio.

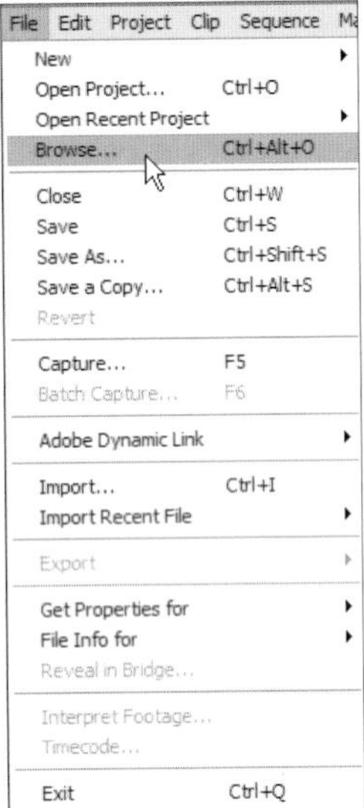

Figure 12.1 You can open Adobe Bridge from any Production Studio application by choosing File > Browse from the menu bar.

Adobe Bridge

To open Adobe Bridge from Premiere Pro 2.0 (or any other Production Studio application), choose File > Browse (**Figure 12.1**). You can also launch Adobe Bridge from the Program menu of Windows XP.

Calling Adobe Bridge a file browser does it a bit of a disservice because it offers so much more (which I'll discuss in a moment), but its browser functions are the first you see (**Figure 12.2**). When you open Bridge, the top-left tabs enable you to access either Favorites (pre-assigned folders and locations to navigate to) or Folders (List view showing your system's entire folder hierarchy). Above the tabs is a drop-down menu that shows the current folder; click on this menu to reveal the path of that folder as well as your Favorites folders and recently accessed folders.

When you select a folder from either of the navigation tabs or drop-down menu, the folder's contents displays in the content area.

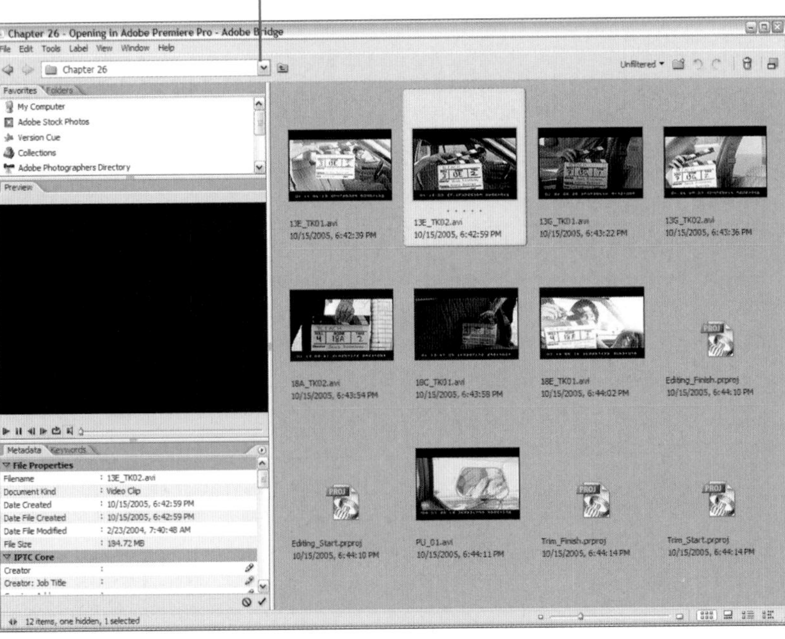

Figure 12.2 Here, Bridge displays the contents of the Chapter 26 folder of lesson files in Expanded mode. Notice the two tabs for Favorites and Folders (upper left). Below is a Preview tab, which enables you to play back, pause, and view any of the selected audio, video, or still image files revealed in the content area on the right. At the bottom left are two more important tabs: Metadata and Keywords.

Browsing and Displaying Your Files

Bridge has two display modes, Expanded (see Figure 12.2) or Compact (**Figure 12.3**). By default, Bridge opens in Expanded mode; click the Switch to Compact Mode button in the top-right corner (or press Ctrl+Enter) to reduce the window size and display only the content area with dramatically smaller icons.

Compact mode is great for those times when you need Bridge open, but don't want to obscure so much of your desktop. Because you can drag and drop files directly from Bridge into any open application, for example, you might need to see more of your host application behind Bridge.

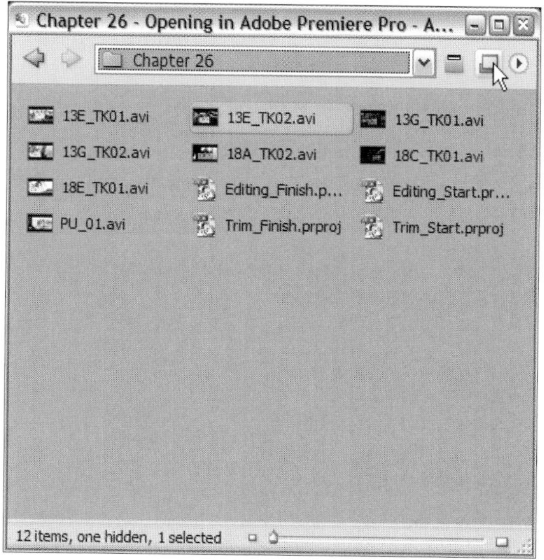

Figure 12.3 Compact mode reduces the size of Bridge and reveals the contents of only the selected folder in the smallest icon size. To expand Bridge, click the Expand button in the top-right corner (beneath the cursor in the image).

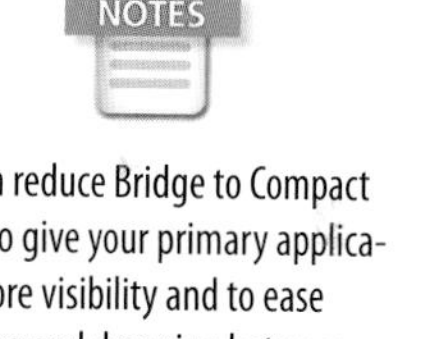

You can reduce Bridge to Compact mode to give your primary application more visibility and to ease dragging and dropping between applications. Just pres Ctrl+Enter to compact, then press Ctrl+Enter again to expand back to full size.

In addition to changing Bridge's overall display size, you can easily adjust the size of the icons displayed in the content area (see **Figures 12.4a** and **b**) as well as whether they're viewed in Thumbnail (the default), Filmstrip (vertically or horizontally oriented), Details, Versions, or Alternates view (see **Figure 12.5 a, b,** and **c**). You can easily toggle between these depending on how many files you're displaying and the way you like to work. I tend to work in either Thumbnails (when I want to see actual images from each file that I am browsing) or Details (when I am selecting and adjusting multiple files).

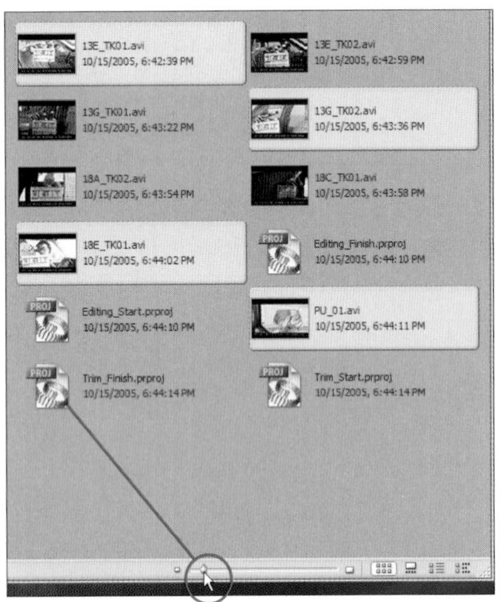

a

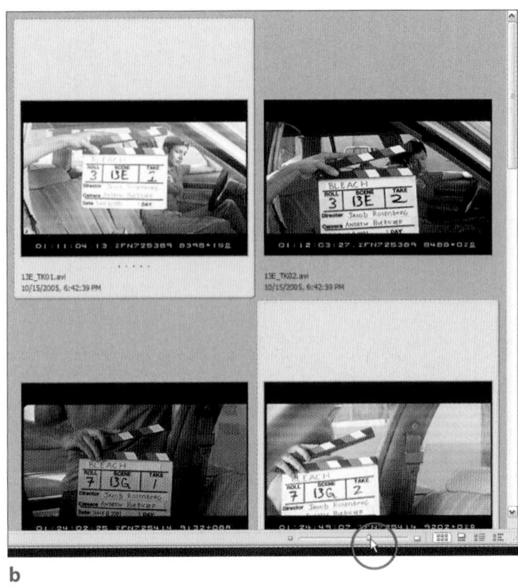

b

Figure 12.4a and b In Thumbnail mode, you can reduce the size of the content area's icons by dragging the icon scale slider to the left (a). Drag the slider right to enlarge the icons (b).

Your preferred viewing mode and icon size settings persist when you close and reopen Bridge. I find, however, it is often worth leaving Bridge open while you work in Production Studio applications to ease the importing and labeling of files.

TIP

Certain files, such as Write Only files, cannot have metadata added to them. If you were to try to add metadata to one of these files either through Bridge or through Premiere Pro's File > File Info menu item (which opens the same dialog), the entries on the right side of the dialog would be closed so that you could not click in them to add information into any of the fields. If a file is open and in use (busy) by another application you will not be able to add metadata to it either, so be sure the files you are editing are not open and active in any other applications.

Adding Metadata to Your Files

Beyond dragging and dropping files among applications, Bridge gives you the valuable ability to add and modify metadata embedded within the files on disk. Metadata can be almost anything: the name of the person who filmed a video file, copyright details, or logging notes, such as a tape name or log comment. In addition to adding or modifying a ton of information to the files, you can add searchable keyword tags and star ratings.

If detailed information about the file isn't articulated in the filename, adding metadata to the file is how you can stamp the information into it. Why is this important? Imagine a project for which you must share your source material with many other people. Adding metadata that

Orientation

a

13E_TK01.avi
Date Created: 10/15/2005, 6:42:39 PM
Date File Modified: Today, 11:45:34 AM
188.23 MB
Video Clip
Jacob Rosenberg

13E_TK02.avi
Date Created: 10/15/2005, 6:42:59 PM
Date File Modified: 2/23/2004, 7:40:48 AM
184.72 MB
Video Clip

13G_TK01.avi
Date Created: 10/15/2005, 6:43:22 PM
Date File Modified: 2/23/2004, 7:40:48 AM
164.95 MB
Video Clip

13G_TK02.avi
Date Created: 10/15/2005, 6:43:36 PM
Date File Modified: 2/27/2004, 12:37:58 PM
159.28 MB
Video Clip

18A_TK02.avi
Date Created: 10/15/2005, 6:43:54 PM
Date File Modified: 2/27/2004, 12:37:58 PM
45.79 MB
Video Clip

b

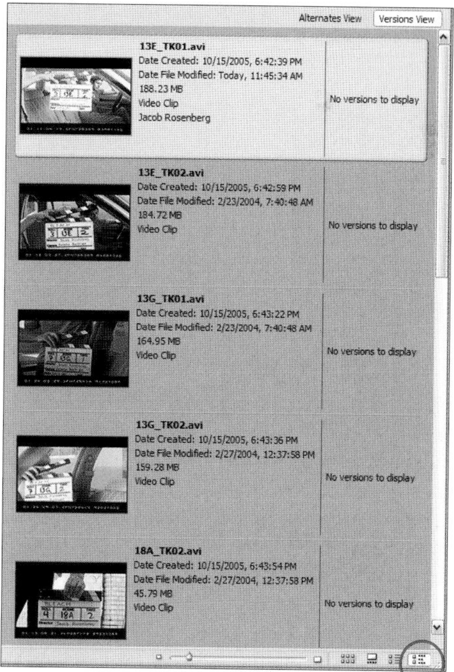

c

Figure 12.5a, b, and c Filmstrip view can be oriented horizontally or vertically (a). Details view provides vital statistics for each file (b), while Versions (c) and Alternates views show you your options.

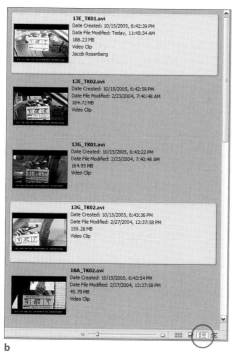

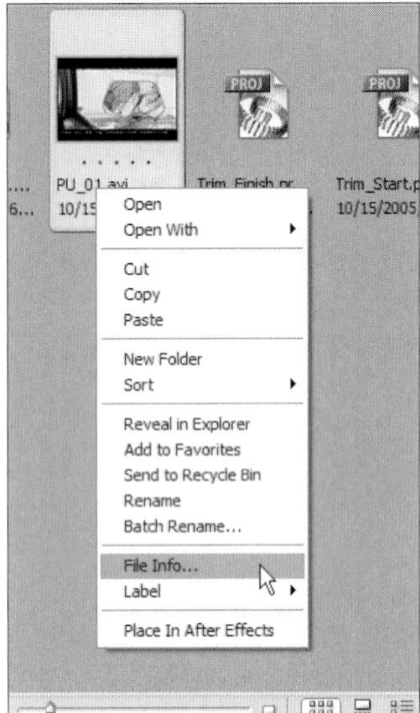

Figure 12.6 Right-click on a file in the contents area and select File Info to open the File Info dialog.

answers potential questions about the owner of the material, the content of the material, and intellectual property rights attributed to the material can clarify facts, credits, and details about the material quickly.

Although you can manually manipulate the Metadata tab by selecting a file in the content area and then adding information to the file's metadata fields, the easiest way to access a clip's full metadata is to right-click the file in the content area and choose File Info (**Figure 12.6**).

The left side of the resulting File Info dialog lists the categories of data you can modify and add to; the right side of the dialog holds the individual fields associated with the categories (**Figure 12.7**).

To add new data to a file, simply select the category and enter data into the appropriate field. Clicking OK adds the data into the file. Now any project to which the file is added will reference the newly added metadata.

If you need to add the same data to several files, you have two choices. The first method is to select multiple files in the content area and modify the metadata fields in the Metadata tab (**Figure 12.8**). The second method is to create and save a metadata template: Click on the File Info dialog's wing menu and choose Save Metadata Template

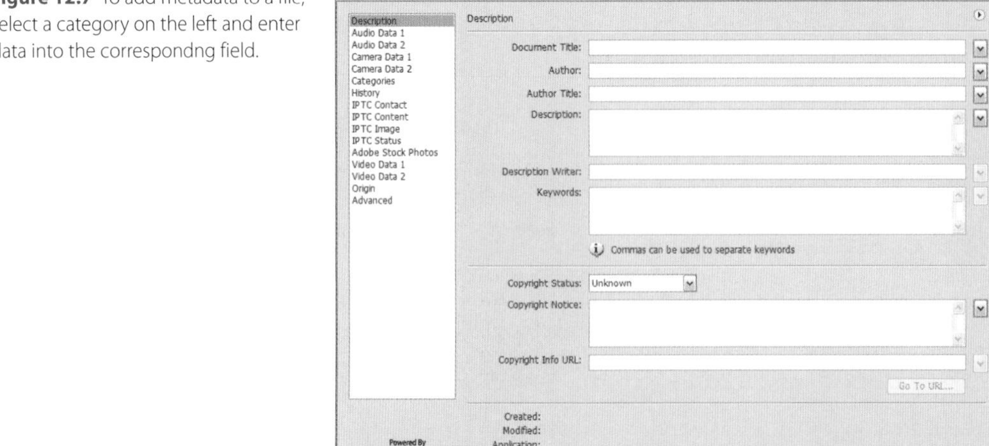

Figure 12.7 To add metadata to a file, select a category on the left and enter data into the correspondng field.

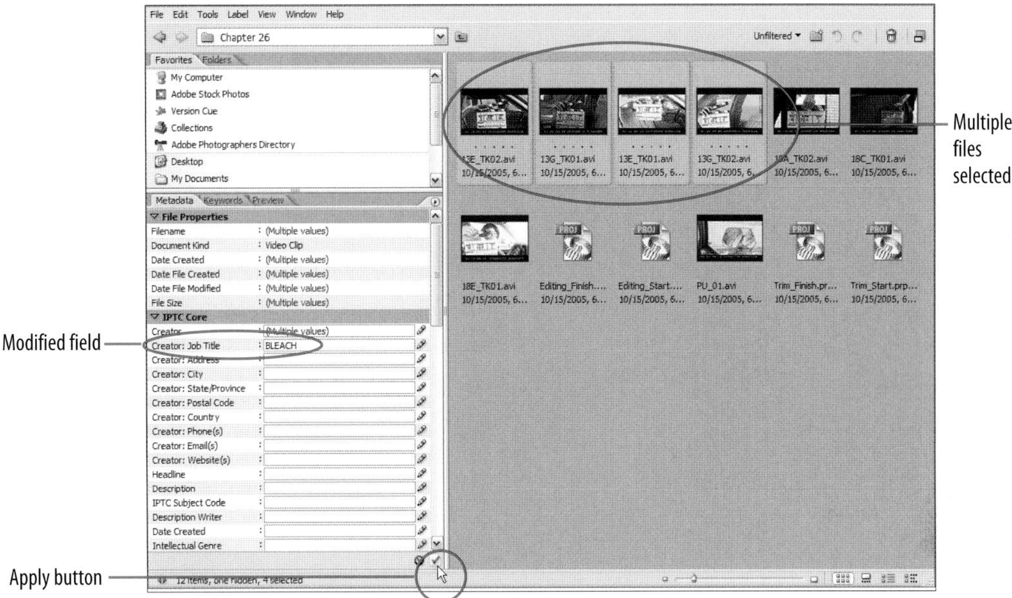

Figure 12.8 With multiple files selected, you can click on any of the metadata fields to modify their information. Here I named the Job Title for all of the files BLEACH, and then clicked the Apply button to apply the changes to the files.

(**Figure 12.9**). Premiere Pro asks you for a template name, then saves the metadata information in the active fields for further use later.

When you want to apply that saved template to other files, select them in the content area, choose Tools > Append Metadata or Replace Metadata, and select your template from the submenu (see **Figure 12.10**).

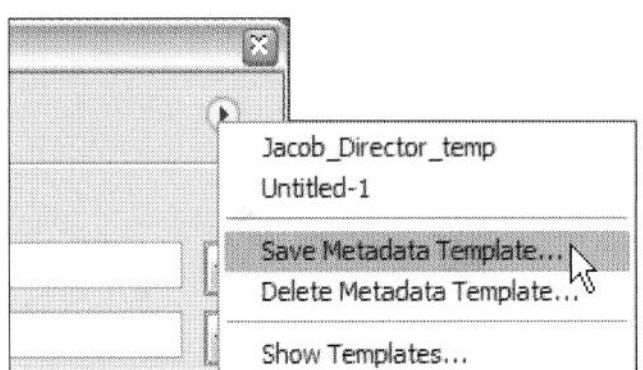

Figure 12.9 With metadata added to the File Info dialog, clicking on the wing menu allows you to save the current metadata as a template to be applied to other files.

Figure 12.10 Using the Append Metadata function, you can add the metadata from a saved template onto the four files selected in the content area. Append Metadata adds data to the files, while Replace Metadata replaces every field so that it matches the template exactly.

Because Replace Metadata replaces metadata already assigned to your file with the exact data from the template, I recommend using the Append Metadata function instead. Append Metadata adds all the data from your template into the file but keeps the original information intact.

Production Studio Integration

Bridge's benefits are clear, but what about Production Studio? Is it worth the upgrade? If you do a lot of work with Audition or After Effects as well as Premiere Pro, the answer is probably yes. Production Studio gives you the power of Premiere Pro's Edit in Adobe Audition feature for seamless transfer and editing of audio clips between Premiere and Audition, as well as Adobe Dynamic Link, which takes Premiere Pro and After Effects integration to a new level. With Dynamic Link you can create an After Effects composition from inside of Premiere Pro or import an existing After Effects composition into Premiere Pro and work in both applications simultaneously; the referenced comp from After Effects updates and displays accurately inside of Premiere Pro.

After I show you how to quickly and easily edit your audio files inside Adobe Audition 2.0 using Edit in Adobe Audition, I'll walk you through a practical example of using Dynamic Link to add animated text to a Premiere Pro sequence.

Editing in Adobe Audition

In past versions, if you were in Premiere Pro and wanted to edit or adjust the audio portion of a file in Adobe Audition, you had to export the audio as a separate file, edit it in Audition, save the Audition adjustments, and finally import the files back into Premiere. The 2.0 versions replace this cumbersome process with one simple menu choice: Edit > Edit in Adobe Audition.

With an audio/video or audio-only file selected in Premiere Pro 2.0's Timeline or Project panel, choose Edit > Edit in Adobe Audition to extract the audio from the file and open a temporary copy of that audio in Audition automatically. The original file in not overwritten or changed. When you finish modifying the audio in Audition, simply save it and the saved changes are dynamically updated to the referenced file in Premiere Pro. Because Premiere Pro makes a copy of the file when you select Edit in Adobe Audition, the most practical method of taking advantage of this feature is from a clip instance in the timeline.

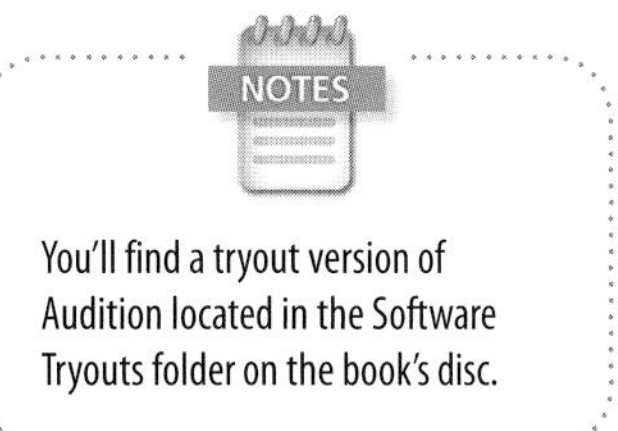

You'll find a tryout version of Audition located in the Software Tryouts folder on the book's disc.

To make things clearer, the next sections demonstrate two tasks that typically demand quality results. Using Edit in Adobe Audition for these will make your editing life easier and audible results better. If you have Audition 2.0 (or if you've installed the tryout version of Audition from this book's DVD), you can with these short lessons; otherwise the pictures will tell the story—and may convince you to look more closely at Audition or Production Studio.

The Amplify Effect

One of the most frustrating issues with displaying an audio waveform in Premiere Pro's timeline is that the amplitude of waveform often is not as dramatic or visually dynamic as you might desire (**Figure 12.11**). Even if you were to increase the gain of an audio file inside of Premiere Pro, the waveform display does not expand as the decibels of the audio are increased. Using the Edit in Adobe Audition

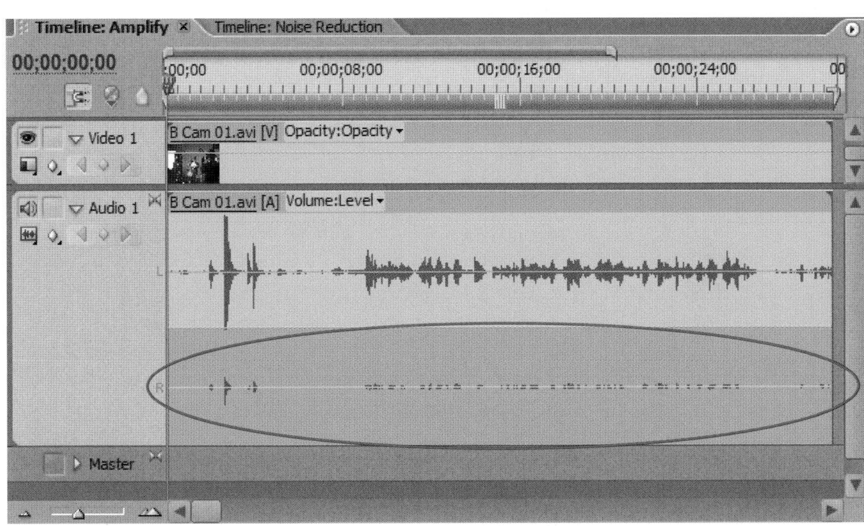

Figure 12.11 Even with Audio 1 expanded, the waveform information for the audio portion of the clip B Cam 01.avi is quite small. In general, this means that the audio is not that loud to begin with.

feature, you can increase and amplify the audio and waveform with a few quick steps.

1. Open the project file Edit_in_Audition.prproj from the APPST2 Lesson Files/Chapter 12 folder.
2. In the Amplify sequence, find the audio/video clip (B Cam 01.avi) that displays a weak or low amplitude waveform (Figure 12.11). Right-click on the audio portion of the file and choose Edit in Adobe Audition (**Figure 12.12**) to extract that audio from the selected file and open it in Audition.

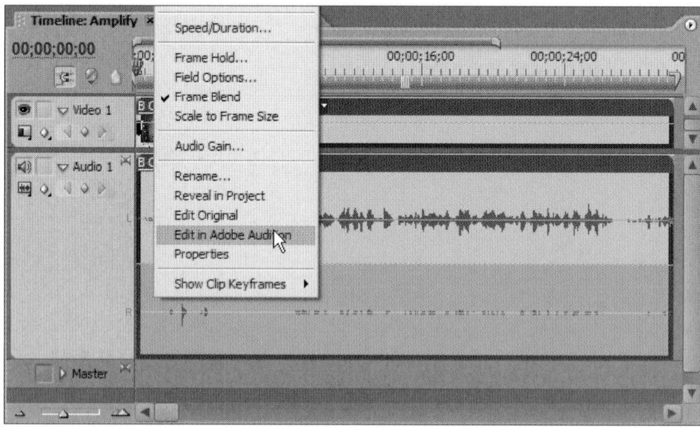

Figure 12.12 By right-clicking on the boundary of any audio clip in the timeline, you can access the Edit in Adobe Audition function.

When you choose Edit in Adobe Audition, Premiere Pro actually performs a Render and Replace, quickly creating a new clip instance of the audio file and replacing the previous timeline instance with this new one. This extracted audio file replaces the previously linked audio in the timeline so that instead of overwriting the source audio, you are now applying effects to a clip built from the source audio.

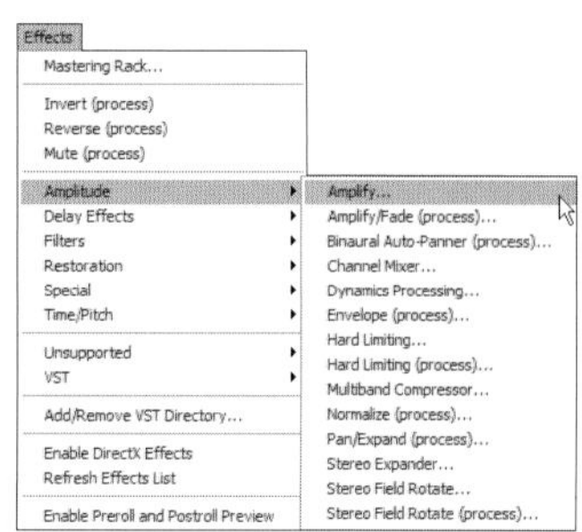

Figure 12.13 With your file open in Audition, select Amplify from Audition's Effects menu.

3. With the replacement audio file open in Audition, choose Effects > Amplitude > Amplify from Audition (**Figure 12.13**). In the resulting VST Plugin - Amplify dialog, add an 8.1 dB gain adjustment (**Figure 12.14**). Click OK and watch the waveform amplify within Audition. Select File > Save to save the effect settings into the file, then switch back to Premiere Pro (**Figure 12.15**).

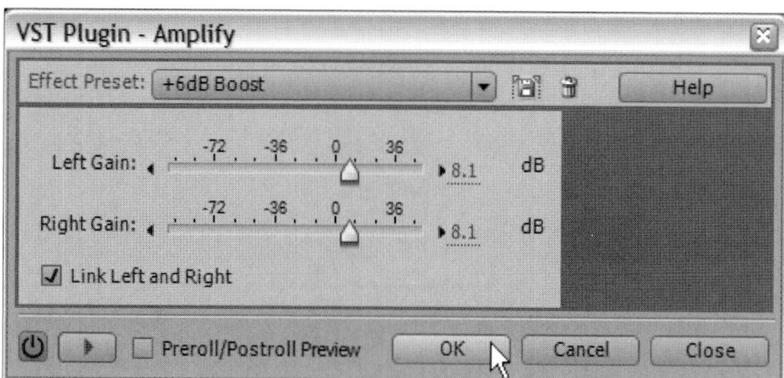

Figure 12.14 In the Amplify dialog, make your gain adjustments to your audio file.

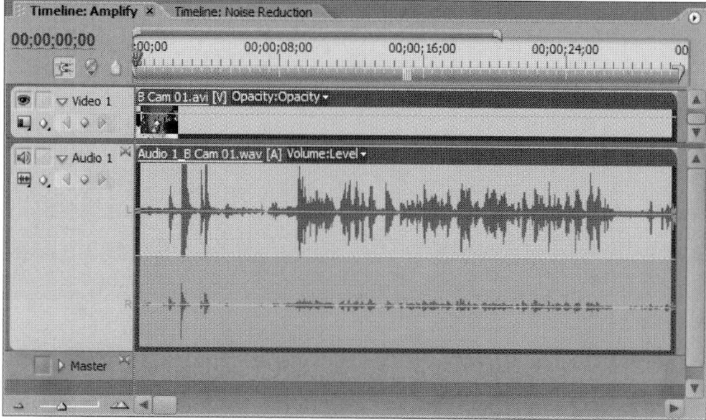

Figure 12.15 After you apply and save the Amplify effect in Audition, the PEK file associated with the audio clip updates and Premiere Pro displays the modified waveform. Compare this waveform to that in Figure 12.13, and you can see the clear benefit of using this workflow to enhance your audio.

Although your gain adjustment settings will differ from file to file, the steps are the same. With the file open in Audition, you quickly can apply an Amplify effect to the file to increase the gain of the audio. This effect updates the audio of the file, thus causing the waveform to expand. Saving the effect adjustment writes the changes into the file. When Premiere is opened, the snapshot of the audio waveform information (PEK file) updates and the waveform expands to display the changes.

This lesson is very simple, but you can use it time and again to create more robust audio waveforms for use inside of Premiere Pro. The next short lesson builds on this project and shows you how to reduce excess noise from files.

Noise Reduction

One audio effect that is sorely missing in Premiere Pro is a simple straightforward noise reduction tool. Audition, being the solid audio editing application that it is, has excellent Noise Reduction, Hiss Reduction, and Click/Pop Removal effects. For a quick example of how to reduce the noise in a file, follow these steps:

1. In Premiere Pro, open the Edit_in_Audition.prproj project file from the APPST2 Lesson Files/Chapter 12 folder.
2. Open the sequence Noise Reduction. Right-click on the file in the timeline, and choose Edit in Adobe Audition from the menu. Again, Premiere Pro renders and replaces the audio and then opens the file inside of Audition.
3. Play the audio in Audition to find a section of the file that yields only the noise that needs to be removed, such as the silent section near the end of the file. Click and drag within the audio waveform to select this section (**Figure 12.16**).

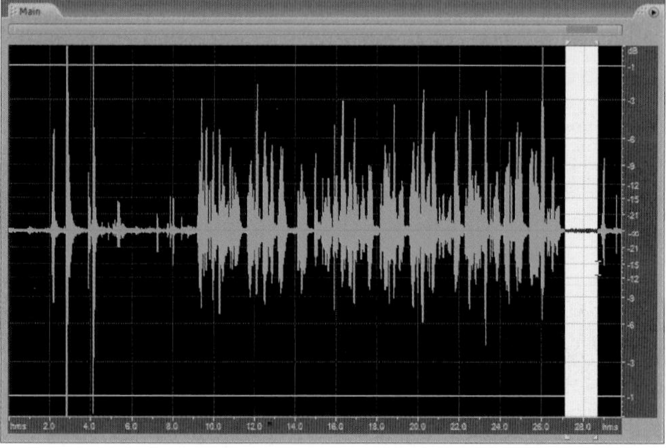

Figure 12.16 To properly reduce the noise in a file, you have to manually find a section of the file that has the noise without any other sounds. Click and drag to select an appropriate small segment from which Audition can capture a noise profile.

To remove noise, hisses, clicks, or pops, you need first to identify and select a portion of the file where you can hear the unwanted noise and nothing else. Then you're ready to open the Noise Reduction effect.

4. Choose Effects > Restoration > Noise Reduction. In the resulting dialog, click Capture Profile in the top corner. Click Select Entire File, then click OK (**Figures 12.17a** through **d**). Save the adjustment you just made, and switch back to Premiere Pro to play the fixed audio.

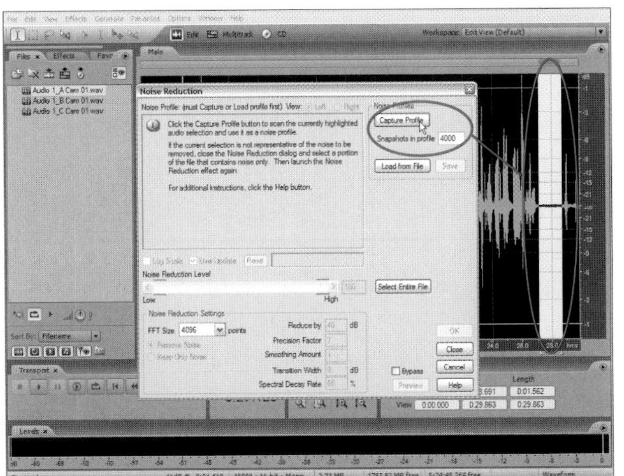

Figures 12.17a through d The profile Audition creates will reference the selection of audio beneath the dialog (a). Once the profile is captured, it displays graphically in the Noise Reduction dialog (b). Clicking Select Entire File (c) processes the effect to be processed on the entire clip, not just the previously selected short area. Look at the final waveform's amplitude (d); you can see it is completely flat in sections where it previously had a low but audible amount of sound.

a

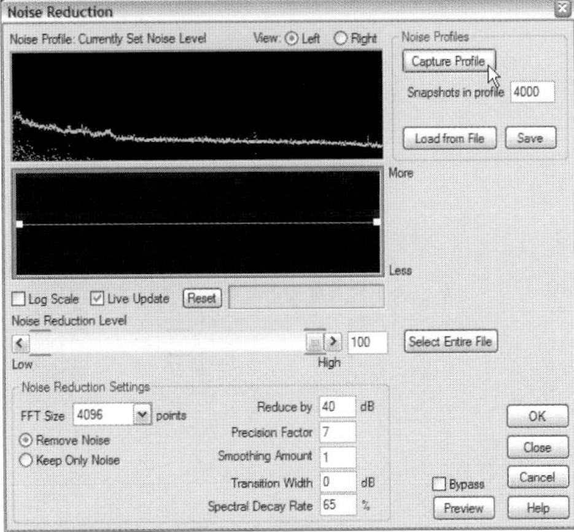

b

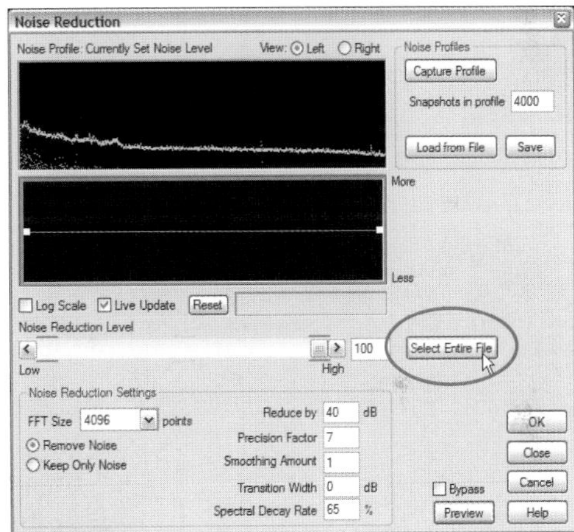

c

d

If you do not have Adobe Audition 2.0 (or choose not to install the tryout version of the book's disc) you can simply open the Project Edit_in_Audition_FINISH.prproj file from the APPST2 Lesson Files/ Chapter 12 folder and compare the FINISH sequence audio to that of the original.

By capturing a noise profile of the selected area, Audition intelligently identifies the audio that should be there and the "noise" that shouldn't. Clicking Select Entire File applies the Noise Reduction profile to the entire clip so that the effect removes the noise from the entire file, not just the section you captured as the profile.

In my opinion, Noise Reduction and the other restoration effects make Adobe Audition 2.0 a necessity for your video editing system. It's not too difficult to learn how to run these simple effects that can clean up clips beyond what's possible in most audio and video applications. Audition's restoration features are second to none, and with Premiere Pro 2.0's Edit in Adobe Audition feature, they are easy to access and apply to any editing workflow.

After Effects and Dynamic Link

As I mentioned earlier, Adobe Dynamic Link provides tighter integration between Premiere Pro and After Effects for Production Studio owners, allowing you to create an After Effects composition with a placeholder inside of Premiere Pro that updates dynamically as you update the composition. In former versions you had to copy and paste from Premiere Pro to After Effects or vice versa. Now you can import an After Effects composition directly into Premiere Pro and have it appear as a clip in your Project panel. Because the general steps of using Dynamic Link to create or import composition are the same no matter what the content of the composition, this lesson is a generic step-by-step that highlights the important moments of the workflow.

Only Adobe Production Studio provides access to the Dynamic Link feature inside Premiere Pro. It will not help you if you purchased Premiere Pro and After Effects as stand-alone programs.

1. Open a Premiere Pro project to which you wish to add an After Effects composition. I chose the Sample Project so I could add some animated text.
2. With your project open, choose File > Adobe Dynamic Link > New After Effects Composition (**Figure 12.18**) from Premiere Pro. Give the After Effects file a name, such as Text Animation.

Figure 12.18 From the File menu of Premiere Pro 2.0 (with the Production Studio installed), you can create an After Effects composition by selecting File > Adobe Dynamic Link > New After Effects Composition.

To create a Dynamic Link composition, simply select the option from the File menu. When creating a composition you must first name the project, then After Effects launches with a new comp open that is linked back to your Premiere Pro project. The name of the comp will include your project's name as well as the phrase "Linked Comp 01." The number increments for every Dynamic Link comp you create.

3. In After Effects, select Workspace: Text from the Workspace drop-down menu in the top-right corner of the interface. Right-click on the tab of the Effects & Presets panel and from the right-click menu choose Browse Presets. In Bridge, double-click on the Text folder in the content area, double-click Fill and Stroke, then double-click on Pulse Orange.ffx (see **Figures 12.19a** and **b**). Reopen After Effects and double-click the newly created Text layer in the comp (see **Figure 12.20**) and type the phrase "Saleen S7" (see **Figure 12.21**).

4. Click and select the Text layer in the Timeline panel and press the P key to open the Position settings. Assign

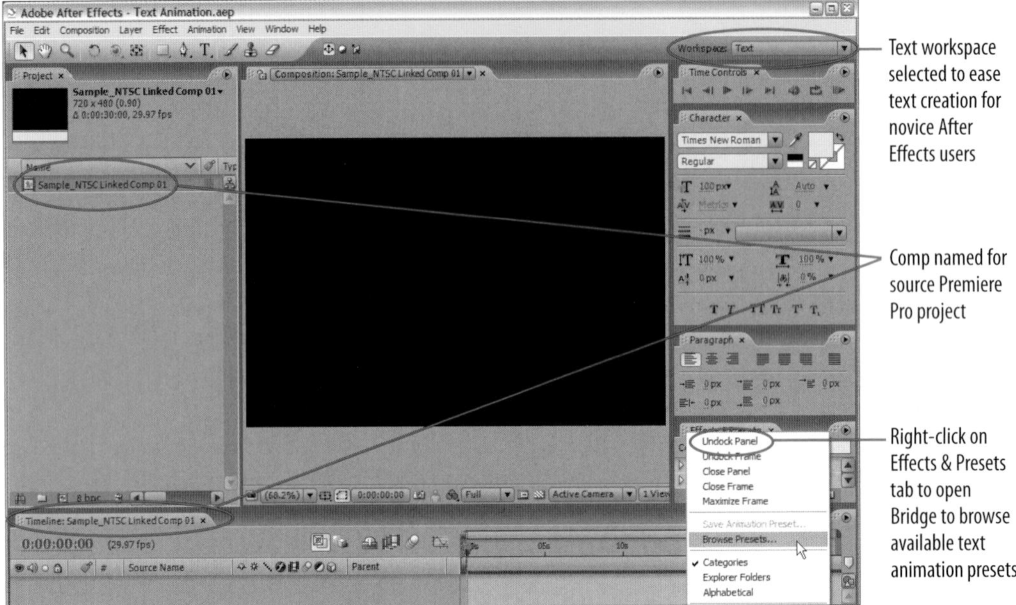

a

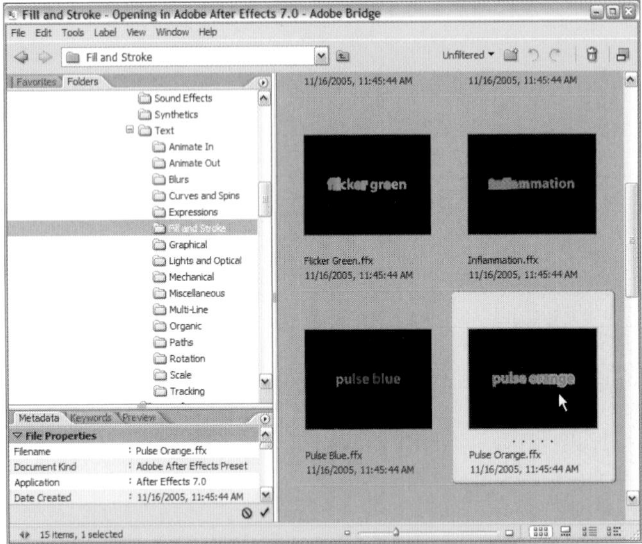

b

Figures 12.19a and b With After Effects open and the Text workspace active, you have all the panels necessary for doing text animations (a). Right-clicking on the Effects & Presets tab opens Bridge from which you double-click on the text effect preset that you want to apply, in this case Pulse Orange.ffx (b).

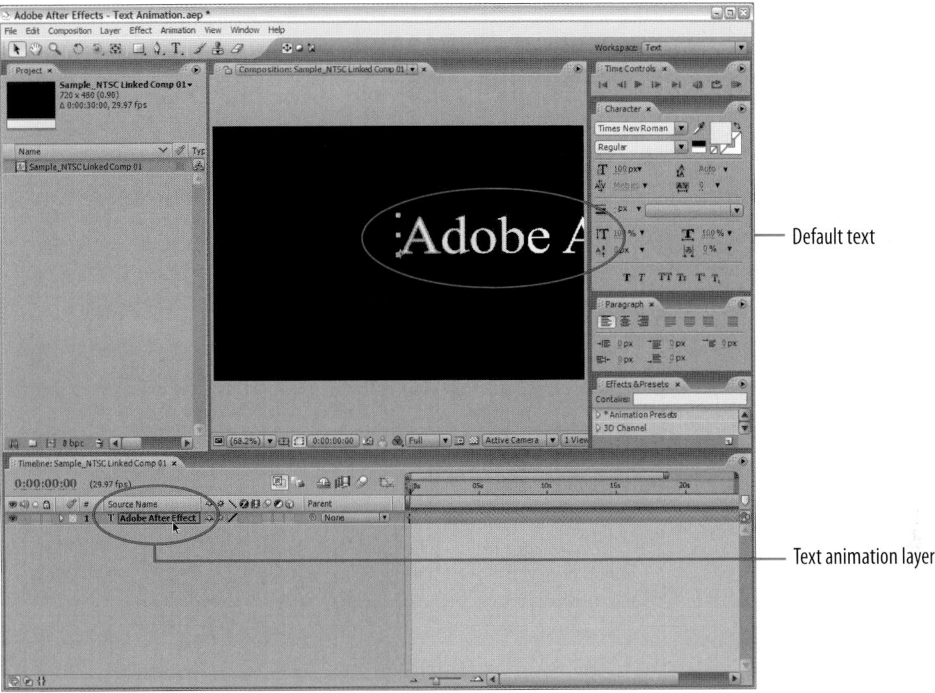

Figure 12.20 When you double-click on a text animation preset, by default it applies itself as a text layer in the currently open comp.

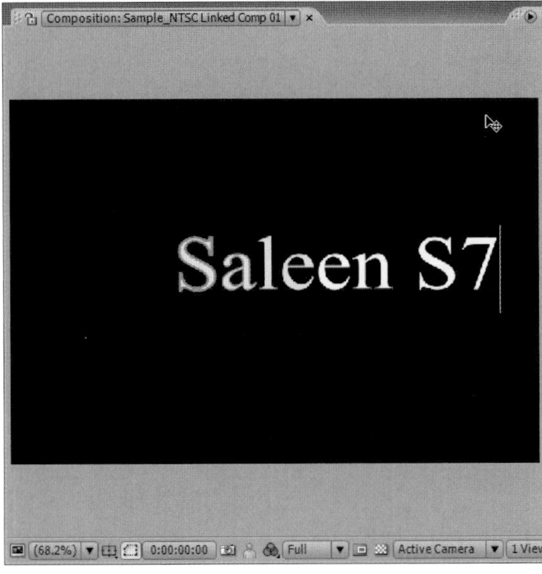

Figure 12.21 Double-clicking on this text layer selects the text and allows you to immediately change the characters by retyping whatever you want. When you finish typing, click back in the blank space of your Timeline panel.

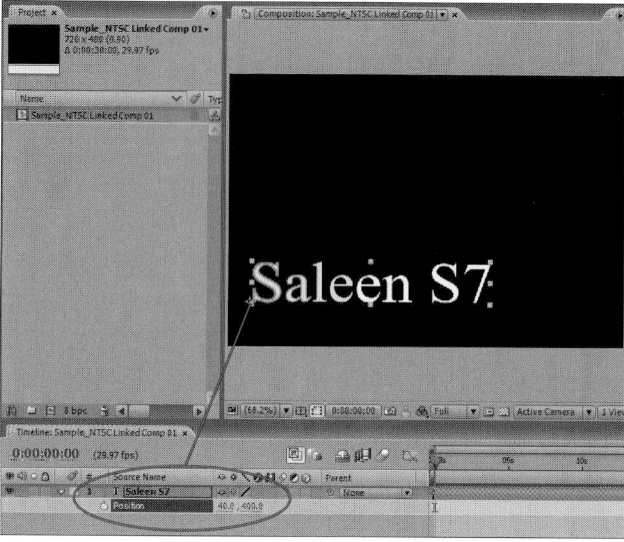

Figure 12.22 Selecting the Text layer Saleen S7 in the Timeline panel and pressing the P key reveals the position settings associated with the Text layer. Modifying the value repositions the text into a more desirable location.

the value 40.0, 400.0, press Enter (**Figure 12.22**), and then press Ctrl+S to save the After Effects project.

You quickly repositioned the text into the lower-left corner of the frame, then saved the project to ensure that the adjusted composition will reveal through Dynamic Link exactly as you set it up once After Effects is closed.

5. Toggle back to and open Premiere Pro. In the Project panel you should see a file named in the form PREMIERE PROJECT NAME+Linked Comp 01/AFTER EFFECTS PROJECT NAME. In this case, the name is Sample_NTSC Linked Comp 01/Text Animation.aep. Drag and drop this file directly onto the Video 2 track at the beginning of the timeline and trim the clip so that it ends at 04;00 in the sequence. With the Timeline panel active, press the Home key and then press the spacebar (**Figure 12.23**).

When creating a Dynamic Link composition, Premiere Pro creates a project item that directly references the Dynamic Link composition from After Effects. The Dynamic Link clip is in essence a placeholder for the After Effects comp. When the After Effects comp updates, the Premiere Pro Dynamic Link file updates to reflect those changes. You can edit and manipulate the Dynamic Link clip as you would any other clip in Premiere Pro. To make this example more fluid you could add a Dissolve

NOTES

Bridge is also the hub for previewing and selecting presets and templates for use in Adobe After Effects. When you double-click a preset it is loaded into the open comp. Double-clicking on the Text layer allows you to quickly select and then change the letters to customize them for your project. After you finish typing, be sure you switch back to the Selection tool or click off the Composition panel or in the blank space of the Timeline panel.

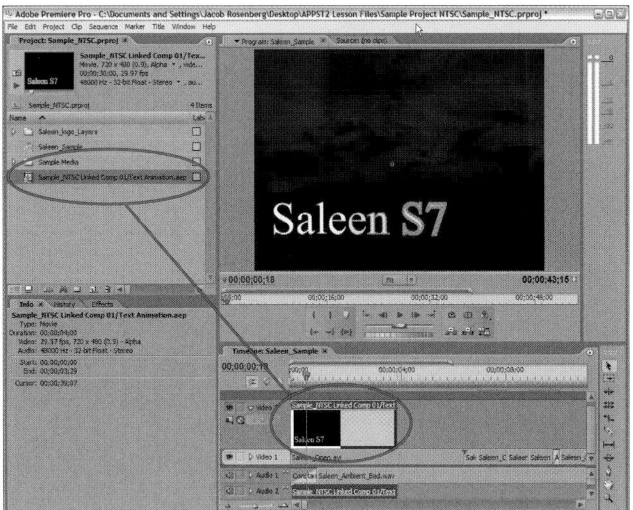

Figure 12.23 Here you can see the icon and Project panel item created by the Dynamic Link feature. With the file added to the timeline, you can see that the animated text created with the comp in After Effects appears inside of Premiere Pro's Program Monitor. Because the Text Animation file is built as text with an alpha channel, the Sample Project's video plays underneath the animated title.

Transition to the beginning and end of the clip in the timeline after you trim the clip to the proper duration.

This lesson serves as a teaser for what you can do with Dynamic Link. A second Dynamic Link feature enables you to import an existing composition from a previously created After Effects project. To do this:

1. Select File > Adobe Dynamic Link > Import After Effects Composition.
2. In the Import Composition dialog, navigate to the After Effects project that holds the composition you want to import: APPST2 Lesson Files\Chapter 12\Text Animation.aep (**Figure 12.24**).
3. Select the composition to import into Premiere Pro using Dynamic Link.

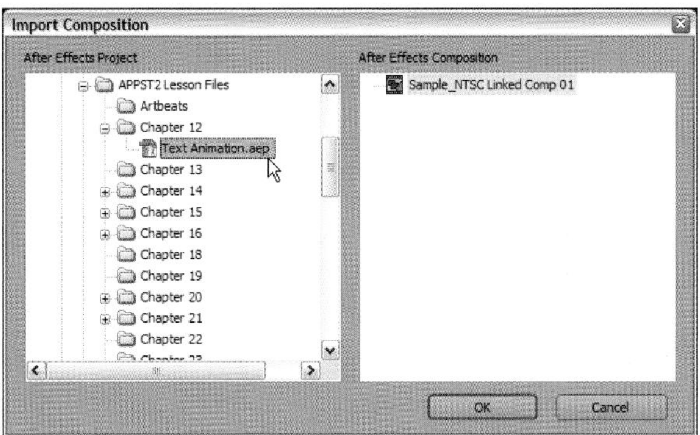

Figure 12.24 If you want to import an existing After Effects composition into a Premiere Pro project using Dynamic Link, select File > Adobe Dynamic Link > Import After Effects Composition, then navigate to the desired After Effects project file in the Import Composition dialog. Finally, select the composition you want to open inside of Premiere Pro.

Things to Remember

Although Production Studio might be beyond some budgets, it does offer a number of very valuable features not available otherwise, such as Adobe Dynamic Link. When using Dynamic Link, remember to save your After Effects project as you work. Dynamic Link always references the current status of the composition; however, if you close the hosting After Effects project without saving your modifications, Premiere Pro will reference the last saved version once the project is closed.

In my opinion, one of Premiere Pro 2.0's most valuable integration features is the Edit in Adobe Audition function. Ttaking what you learned in this chapter and honing your technique can help you clean up and strengthen your audio far beyond what is possible using Premiere Pro's audio editing tools. I would encourage you to add Audition 2.0 to your editing system; you'll be pleased with the results.

If you take the time to add metadata to your files, then Bridge can truly open up more potential in better arranging and organizing your projects and system.

Leaving Bridge open while you work in the various applications can make the file import process much more visually satisfying when trying to locate a questionable file that doesn't stick out to you in a text-based list.

This chapter concludes the first section of the book, which established the fundamental techniques and expectations you need to use Premiere Pro most efficiently. From here you will explore advanced techniques with step-by-step lessons geared toward giving you more control over your editing experience with Premiere Pro. The next section focuses on graphics editing, still image manipulation, and custom DVD authoring.

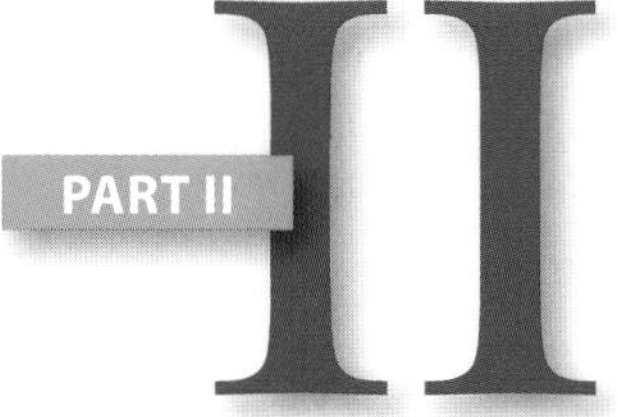

PART II

Advanced Graphics and Titling

13

Working with Photoshop Files: Nesting and Animating

An excellent feature of Adobe Premiere Pro 2.0 is its ability to import a layered Photoshop file. Importing all those layers, however, can significantly increase the number of files in your final sequence.

To reap the benefit of this feature without the added cost, use nesting. *Nesting* is the process of consolidating multiple files into a single sequence that represents the entire group. Not only is nesting a powerful way of minimizing clutter in sequences, it is also an efficient way to group clips for better control of effect placement.

In this chapter, you will learn how to nest groups of layers to add motion and effects to individual layers without altering the integrity of the original Photoshop file. The first lesson will teach basic nesting by creating a graphic opening for a photo montage. You will then apply motion and some transitions to the elements of that nested sequence in the second lesson.

Progressive Projects for Photo Montages

To continue the trend of forward thinking with this new version of Premiere Pro 2.0, this nesting lesson also demonstrates a feature that benefits still-image montages destined for distribution on DVD: 24p support. To take advantage of DVD player technology, you will create the montage in a DV 24p project setting. Because the photo montage will be still images only with no video clips, you can safely use a progressive frame rate for your project settings; DVDs read progressive frame rate encoded files automatically. Building a project progressively reduces any interlace anomalies, such as flickering or shaking artifacts, that can appear when you pan and enlarge images in an interlaced environment.

The photo montage itself is the subject of Chapter 14, "Working with Stills: Motion and Advanced Keyframing."

To import a single layer from a Photoshop file, set Import As to Footage and select the layer you want to import from the Choose Layer drop-down menu.

If you have a DV device connected to your computer, Premiere Pro will interlace the progressive project using one of two conversion methods to get the 24p frame rate to your DV device's 29.97 frame rate. To specify the method of conversion, click the Output button in the Program Monitor, select the Playback Settings listing (**Figure 13.1**), and in the resulting dialog choose either Repeat Frame or Interlaced Frame. For the example, I'll use Interlaced Frame because it doesn't repeat any frames. Instead, it breaks the progressive frames into interlaced frames. Premiere Pro will play the Progressive footage progressively on your desktop and encode it progressively to a DVD when you export it.

Now that you understand the benefits of working with 24p settings for photo montages, get ready to try some nesting techniques that draw on the flexibility of using layered Photoshop files with Premiere Pro.

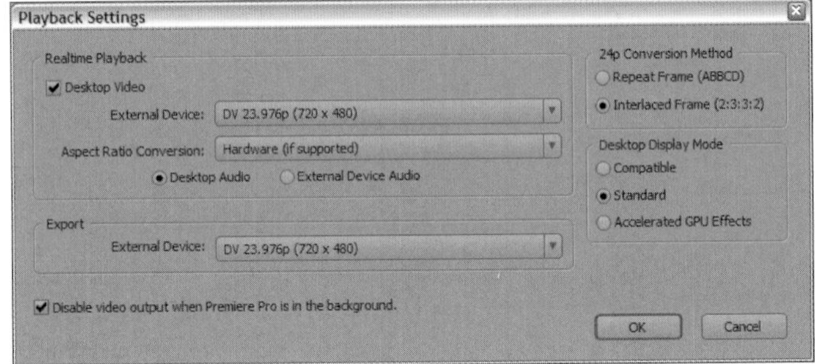

Figure 13.1 In the Playback Settings dialog, you can choose how you want a progressive project converted to interlaced when the video is sent out the DV port. The two 24p Conversion Methods are Repeat Frame and Interlaced Frame.

Nesting Sequences

Using nesting techniques, you can create effects that are much easier to control and adjust. Here, you will import a nine-layer Photoshop file and reduce it down to four sequence files, each consisting of grouped layers.

The Photoshop file for the example project maps three cities in Italy and will become the intro to a photo montage.

Each of the city's names will fade in and enlarge, then the scene will cut to photographs of the named city. To adjust the different city names separately, you will need to nest specific cities together. This lesson preps the framework for the files so that you can create the desired effect with a greater amount of control in the next lesson.

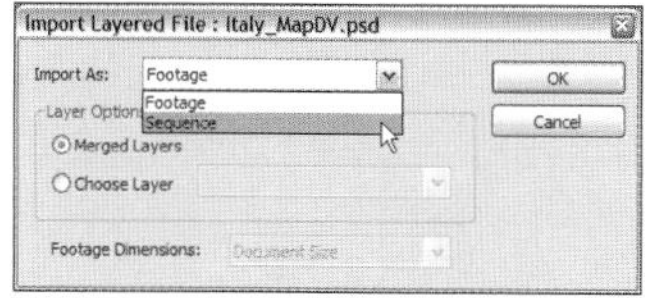

Figure 13.2 When you open a Photoshop file, you can import single layers or the entire document as a flattened still (Footage) or import all of the layers as a sequence.

1. Open the Nest_Start.prproj file from the APPST2 Lesson Files/Chapter 13 folder. Select File > Import, and open Italy_MapDV.psd from the same folder. From the resulting Import Layered File dialog, select Sequence from the Import As drop-down menu, and click OK (**Figure 13.2**).

   This step imports the Photoshop file as a unique sequence that properly reflects the Photoshop document's stacking order. Each layer becomes a separate still in its own track (**Figures 13.3** and **13.4**). Transfer modes, such as Darken, Difference, and Exclusion, are not supported when importing into Premiere Pro.

Figure 13.3 The original document in Photoshop. Notice the name of each layer and the order in which the layers are stacked.

Figure 13.4 Importing the layered Photoshop file into Premiere Pro creates this sequence. Notice that the stacking order and layer names duplicate those of the original and that the image looks the same in the Program Monitor as it did in Photoshop. Also notice that the track names match the layers as well.

When you import, Premiere creates a new folder: Italy_MapDV. Inside are nine still images and a single sequence. Each still image reflects an individual layer from the Photoshop file. The sequence, named exactly for the Photoshop file, contains all the stills stacked above each other in the same order as the original Photoshop file. These nine files make up the image that displays in the Program Monitor when you scrub over their timeline position.

2. Select Project > Projects Settings > Default Sequence. Set Video Tracks to 2 and Audio Master to Stereo with 1 Stereo Track. Click OK to close out of this dialog, then create five new sequences and name them: Rome, Florence, Portofino, Italy Map, and Map Comp.

   Adjusting the default sequence value lets you quickly create sequences with a specific track number. The five unique sequences you created later will house, respectively, the three city layers, the map layers, and the final composition of the four sequences.

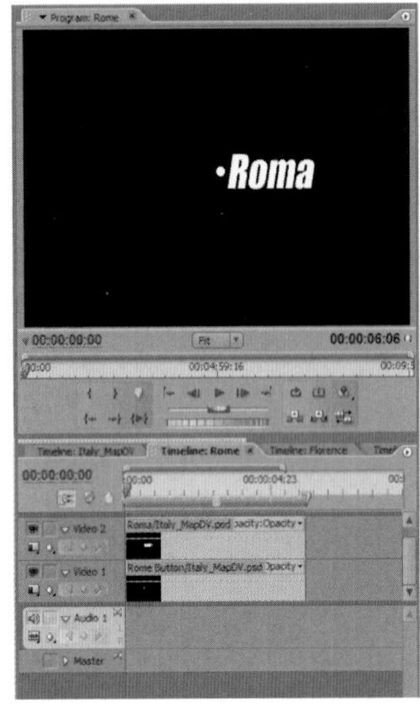

Figure 13.5 With the Edit Line over the two tracks, the Program Monitor displays the result of the two Rome layers, the name and the button. Because the layers were created in Photoshop, the black space around the letters is attributed to the alpha channel; this means that it is transparent and will key out when you place it on top of other content.

3. Click on the Rome tab in the Timeline panel to open the Rome sequence. Open the Italy_MapDV folder, and drag and drop the Rome Button/Italy_MapDV.psd file onto the Video 1 track of the Rome sequence. Drag and drop the Roma/Italy_MapDV.psd file onto the Video 2 track directly above the instance on Video 1 (**Figure 13.5**). Open the Florence sequence. Drag and drop the Florence Button/Italy_MapDV.psd file to Video 1 and Firenze/Italy_MapDV.psd to Video 2. Finally, open the Portofino sequence, then drag and drop the Button layer to Video 1 and the Name layer to Video 2.

   Because you want to control the city name and its button independently, both layers need to be nested into their own sequence. Putting the button on Video 1 and city name on Video 2 ensures that the city name remains on top of the button when it is resized or repositioned. Each single city sequence now reflects the result of the two layers inside of it.

4. Click the Italy Map tab in the Timeline pane to open the sequence. Drag and drop the Pattern Fill/

Italy_MapDV.psd to Video 1. Drag and drop the Color Layer/Italy_MapDV.psd to Video 2 directly on top of the file on Video 1. Drag and drop the Outline/Italy_MapDV.psd file into the gray space above Video 2, snapping to the head of the timeline directly on top of the files below. This is known as the drop zone.

As you did for the city names, here you created a single sequence to display the map layers. Because there were only two tracks available for adding content, you created a third by dragging and dropping to the empty gray space above Video 2.

Although you won't be applying an effect to the Map layers, one file will be easier to manage than three in the final composition.

5. Click on the Map Comp tab in the Timeline pane to open the Map Comp sequence. Locate the five sequences you created in the Project pane. Hold down the Ctrl key, and double-click on the Italy Map sequence in the Project pane to load it in the Source Monitor. Toggle the Take Audio/Video button to Video Only. Drag and drop the Source Monitor sequence into the Video 1 track of the Map Comp sequence **(Figure 13.6)**.

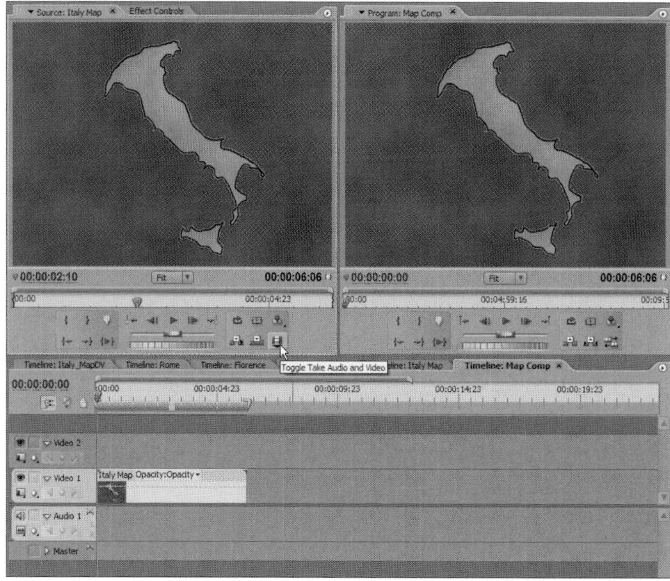

Figure 13.6 The Italy Map sequence was opened as if it were a clip in the Source Monitor by holding down Ctrl and double-clicking on the icon for it in the Project pane. When Take Audio/Video is set to Video Only the result of the drag and drop to the timeline is a single video clip on the Video 1 track. Notice that the clip name is the same as the name of the sequence that it represents. Double-clicking on this clip, which is now a *nested sequence*, in Video 1 opens the Italy Map sequence in the Timeline pane.

Because you are not going to use any of the audio tracks from the individual sequences, you turned off their audio before nesting them into the final composition. Nesting the Italy Map on Video 1 ensured that the map is beneath all the other layers. Now you can finish nesting the rest of the sequences.

6. Open the three remaining city sequences in the Source Monitor, turn off their audio, and add them to the Map Comp sequence with Florence on Video 2, Portofino on Video 3, and Rome on Video 4 (**Figure 13.7**).

Figure 13.7 The final result of your nesting work. Here you can see all four of the nested sequences stacked one on top of the other with the result displayed in the Program Monitor. Notice how the icon for the nested sequence in the Timeline pane displays a snapshot of the content of the sequence. Even when nesting, the alpha channel for the files in the city name sequences is preserved and used to display the city names on top of each other and the map.

TIP

To open the source sequence for any nested sequence, simply double-click on the nested sequence; the source sequence opens inside the Timeline pane. Alternately, you can target the video track that holds the nested sequence, and with the Edit Line positioned over the nested sequence that you want to open, press Shift+T. This action is called Match Frame.

If you want to open a nested sequence in the Source Monitor, just Ctrl+double-click on the nested sequence.

Compared to the original nine-layer sequence, the Map Comp sequence is now quite manageable with fewer files, revealing the benefits of nesting. Say you want to fade up the Rome name and Rome button. In the original sequence, you would have dropped transitions on both files, whereas in the nested sequence you can drop a transition on only the single nested sequence for Rome. If you want to create a motion path for the Rome Name and Button layers, instead of creating the same path twice, you could apply the motion path to the nested sequence. To look at the final results I came up with, open Nest_Finish.prproj in the APPST2 Lesson Files/Chapter 13 folder.

All of the work in this first lesson builds the proper framework and structure from which you can independently adjust groups of layers without affecting the entire document. To take this even further, you can open any of your nested sequences and apply effects to the individual tracks in the sequence. Any effect applied to the contents of the nested sequence will be revealed any place the sequence is nested. This next lesson demonstrates the power and benefits of this feature.

Adding Effects to Nested Sequences

With all the layers properly nested into separate sequences, you're ready to try applying effects to the nested sequence material. For this lesson, you will be fading in and enlarging the Rome name, alluding to the fact that the Rome photo montage will appear next.

Figure 13.8 Using the Pen tool, you can adjust individual keyframes or constant values for displayed effects in all audio and video tracks. Adjusting a constant effect value yields a small line with two arrows next to the Pen tool's icon. Here, the adjustment reduces the Opacity of the entire clip to a constant 50% value. In Premiere Pro 2.0, Show Keyframes is the default track display.

1. Open Nest_Effects_Start.prproj from the APPST2 Lesson Files/Chapter 13 folder. Open the Map Comp sequence in the Timeline pane, and click on the Florence clip in the Video 2 track. Press the P key to activate the Pen tool. With the Pen tool, click on the Opacity line for the Florence clip and drag downward so that Opacity is 50% (**Figure 13.8**).

   Instead of using the Effect Controls panel in this step, you displayed and adjusted keyframes in the Timeline panel. Setting Opacity to 50% made the entire Florence name clip somewhat transparent. Next, you will assign a simple fade out of the Opacity setting.

2. Position the Edit Line at 02;00 in the timeline. In the Video 2 track header, press the Add Keyframe button to add a keyframe handle to the current position

(**Figure 13.9**). Move the Edit Line to 03;00 in the timeline, and add another keyframe. With the Pen tool selected, click and drag the second keyframe to the bottom of the track, making Opacity 0%.

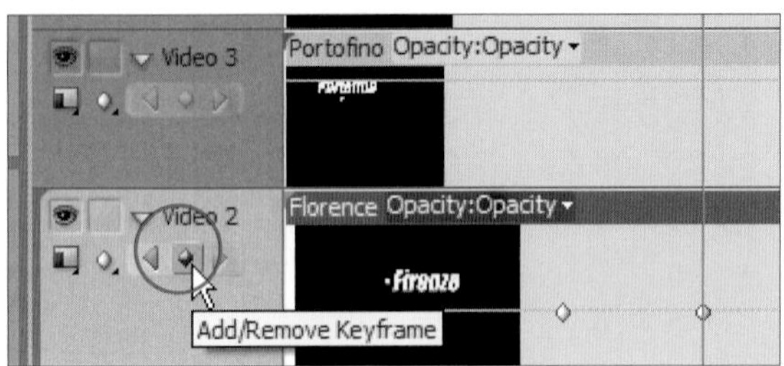

Figure 13.9 To add a keyframe to the current Edit Line position, simply press the Add/Remove Keyframe button in the track header. Clicking the same button when the Edit Line is on top of a keyframe removes that keyframe.

This step introduced a method for creating a custom opacity fade: You created two keyframes to anchor the starting (50%) and ending (0%) Opacity values of the fade. Now the clip starts at 50% Opacity for two seconds and has a one-second fade out to 0%. Because you want all the city names to start opaque and fade together, in the next step you will copy the opacity keyframes from the Florence clip into the other city clips.

3. Using the Pen tool, hold down the Shift key and click each of the opacity keyframes that you created. With both keyframes selected (yellow), right-click on one of the two and select Continuous Bezier from the menu that appears (**Figures 13.10a** and **b**).

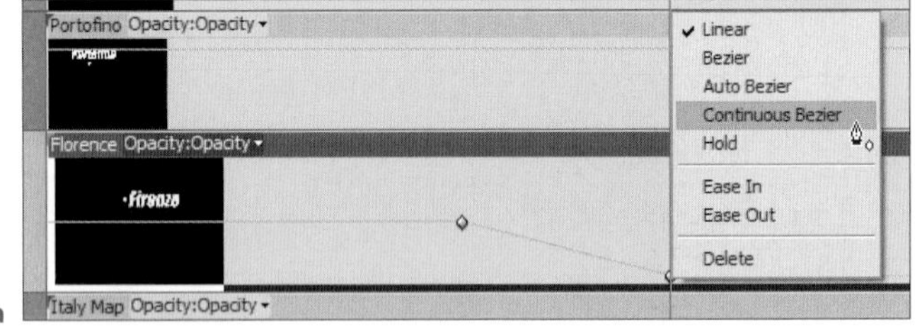

a

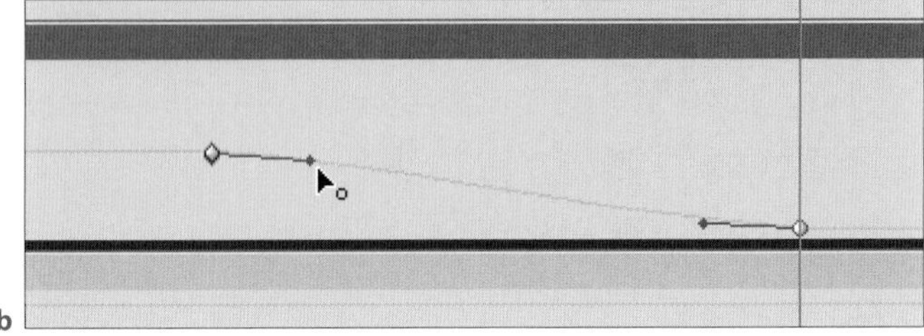

b

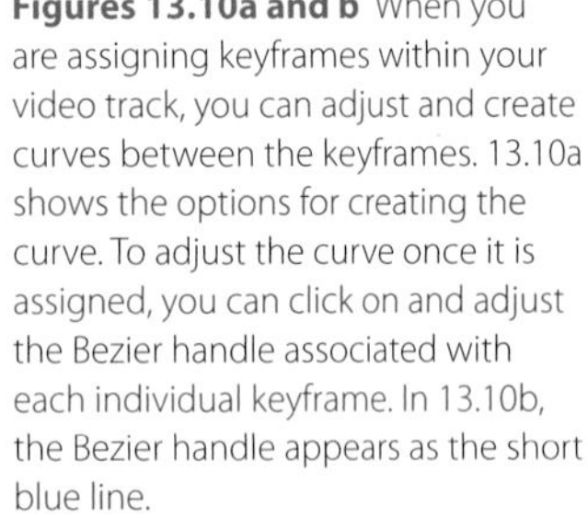

Figures 13.10a and b When you are assigning keyframes within your video track, you can adjust and create curves between the keyframes. 13.10a shows the options for creating the curve. To adjust the curve once it is assigned, you can click on and adjust the Bezier handle associated with each individual keyframe. In 13.10b, the Bezier handle appears as the short blue line.

When you first created the keyframes to assign the fade, a straight line joined the two. This would be considered a Linear relationship between the two keyframes. To create a smooth fade from one to the other, you assigned Continuous Bezier. If you want a smooth curve between multiple keyframes, you can select all the keyframes that you want to adjust the line for and select Continuous Bezier.

4. Open the Effect Controls Panel in your workspace, and click on the Florence clip in the Map Comp sequence if it isn't already selected. Right-click on the Opacity listing in the Effect Controls panel, and choose Copy (**Figures 13.11a** and **b**). Select the both the Portofino clip and Rome clip in the Map Comp sequence, and press CTRL+V on your keyboard to paste the selected opacity settings onto the two selected clips.

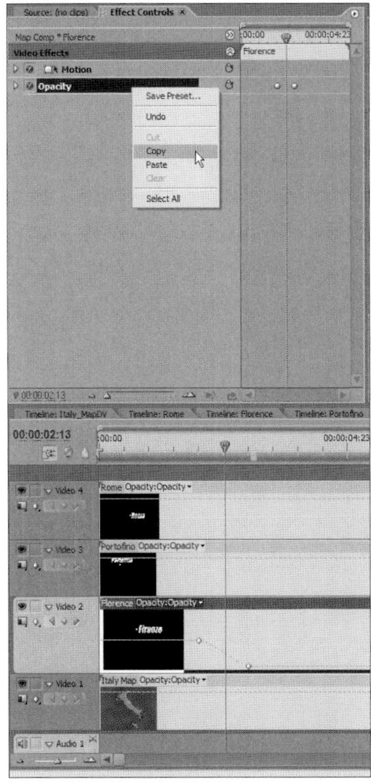

a

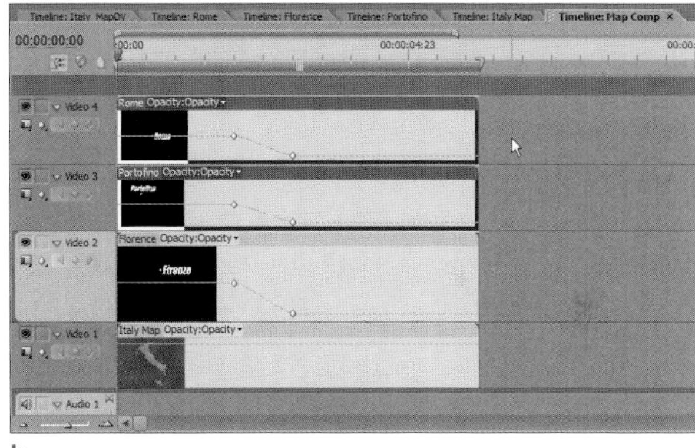

b

Figures 13.11a and b Select the Florence clip in the Timeline panel to display its effect parameters in the Effect Controls panel. By selecting an individual effect listing, Opacity in this case, you can right-click and copy the entire effect to your clipboard (a). Selecting other clips in the timeline, you can paste the Opacity selection directly onto them (b).

Copying and pasting effect listings in the Effect Controls panel is a quick way to apply the same effect and keyframes to multiple clips. Keep in mind that you would have done about three times more work if the sequences had not been nested.

Although you originally made the opacity adjustments in the timeline, you can view and manipulate the entire effect parameters for each individual clip in the Effect Controls panel. Anytime a clip is selected, you can view its effect parameters in the Effect Controls panel.

5. With the same workspace layout, select the Rome clip in the timeline. Position the Edit Line at 03;00. In the Effect Controls panel, twirl down the Opacity listing and change the value of the current Opacity keyframe to 100% (**Figure 13.12**).

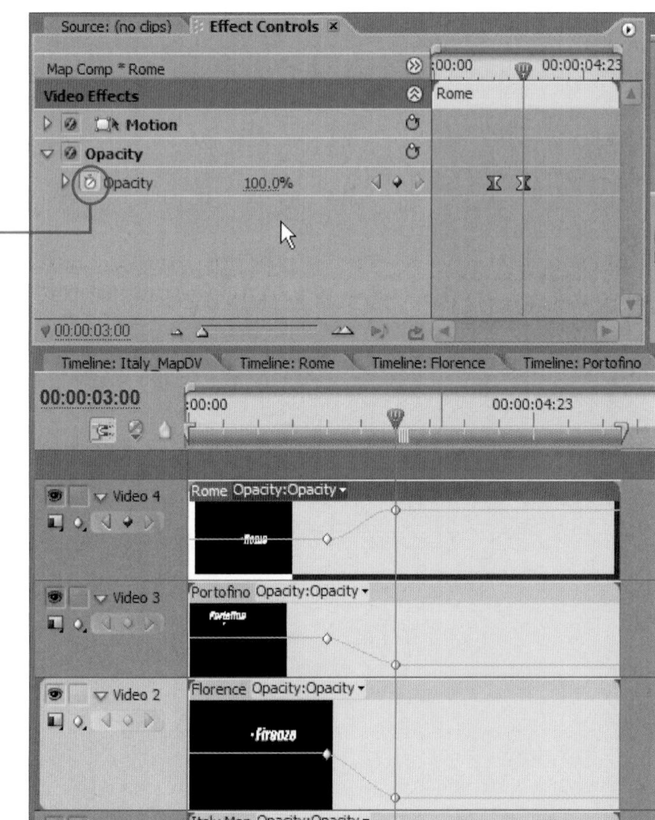

Figure 13.12 With the Rome clip selected, you can view its keyframes in the Effect Controls panel. Here, the Edit Line is positioned on top of the second Opacity keyframe, which was previously set to 0%. Notice how the Add/Remove Keyframe button is darkened, indicating you are positioned on a keyframe. Twirling down the Opacity listing you can manually assign a new and exact Opacity value for this keyframe. Adjusting Opacity to 100% changes the fade out to a fade in. Also notice that Toggle Animation stopwatch is active, signifying that there are keyframes assigned to the effect. Notice how the fade ramps up in the timeline below.

You can easily modify keyframes directly in the Effect Controls pane. Here you changed Opacity to create a fade in for the Rome clip. (You'll need it in the next chapter when you build the Rome photo montage.) Next, you will apply a gradual size increase that occurs as the word "Rome" fades in.

When you want to adjust an exact keyframe, the Edit Line must be positioned directly on top of it. To make sure you are on top of an exact keyframe, use the Go to Next/Previous Keyframe buttons for the keyframed effect's listing.

6. Double-click on the nested Rome clip in the Map Comp sequence to open it in its own Timeline panel. Select Roma/Italy_MapDV.psd on the Video 2 track. In the Effect Controls panel, twirl down the Motion listing. Position the Edit Line at 02;00. Click the Toggle Animation button on for Scale. Reposition the Edit Line to 05;00. Adjust the Scale value to 175.0. Marquee select both of the keyframes you just added, right-click on one, and select Continuous Bezier from the context menu (**Figures 13.13a**, **b**, and **c**). Press Enter to preview your results. Finally, click on the Map Comp sequence tab in the Timeline panel, and press Enter to preview the results of the entire nested sequence.

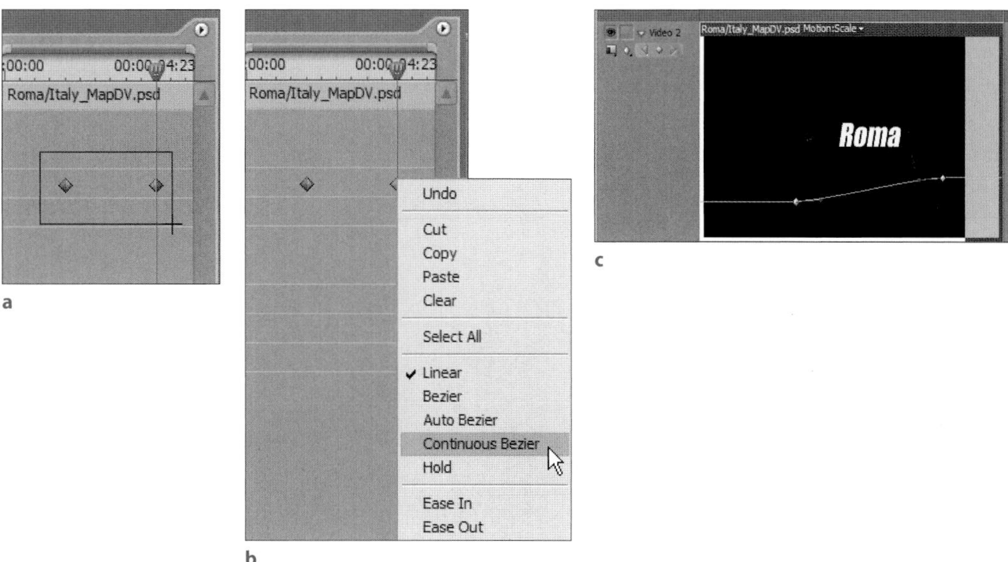

Figures 13.13a, b, and c You can marquee select two Scale keyframes (a), and set the Continuous Bezier option for interpolating a curved line between them (b). The resulting curved value for Scale appears in the video track (c) when displaying keyframes for Motion:Scale. The result is a smooth scaling increase from 100% to 175%.

To emphasize only the city name, you navigated into the original Rome sequence and applied a Scale adjustment to the city name layer only. Turning on Toggle Animation assigns a keyframe at the current Edit Line position with the current value for the parameter being animated. In this case, 100% Scale was assigned at the 2;00 keyframe. With keyframe animation turned on, if you reposition the Edit Line and modify an effect parameter, Premiere will create a new keyframe to reflect the adjustment. Here, a keyframe for 175% Scale was created at 5;00. You also made sure that the Scale was a smooth curved value between 100% and 175% by assigning a Continuous Bezier to the keyframes.

This step articulates the power and control of nesting. The result of the two keyframes is a dynamic scaling of the single layer from 100% to 175%. Because this sequence is nested into the Map Comp, the scaling adjustments are seen along with the Opacity adjustment made to the nested sequence itself.

7. Create a new sequence and name it Photo Montage. Holding the Ctrl key, double-click on the Map Comp sequence from the Project pane to open it in the Source Monitor. (If you click Play, Premiere will play the Sequence in the monitor.) Toggle Take Audio/Video to Take Video Only. Drag and drop the Map Comp sequence into Video 1. With the Edit Line positioned at the head of the timeline, press Ctrl+D (**Figure 13.14**). Now you are ready for the next chapter, where you will easily incorporate these graphics with your photo montage.

   Here's to redundancy! This step nested the Map Comp sequence inside a new sequence, which you will use in the next chapter to build your final photo montage. If any changes need to be made to the Map Comp, you can tweak any of the nested sequence settings in the Map Comp sequence or the individual layers in the original city name or map image sequences.

Figure 13.14 Compared to the original nine layers, this final nested sequence is much easier to manage. Because this nested sequence references numerous sequences and source files with specific settings, the results show through in the current nested view.

By properly nesting the Map Comp into the Photo Montage sequence, any and all changes to the sequences and layers it references will be revealed in the final nested instance. To see my final results, open the file Nest_Effects_Finish.prproj from the APPST2 Lesson Files/Chapter 13 folder.

As you can see, using a nested structure has definite advantages. By separating individual layers and sequences, and thus controlling them separately, you can more easily modify and change any of the nested elements. So, not only can you easily apply changes to an entire sequence in one step, you can also quickly adjust any single element. From reducing clutter to controlling separate layers, there are numerous uses for nesting.

Things to Remember

Premiere Pro works hand-in-hand with Adobe Photoshop's layering capabilities, enabling you to import Photoshop files with each layer in a separate sequence.

Using the nesting technique, you then can group specific layers in one sequence to apply effects to the entire group. If you want to vary the effect within the group, you just simply go into the original nested sequence and adjust the layer/track directly. Throughout the course of this book, you will see the nesting concept referenced again and again; in many instances, nesting is a highly practical and valuable technique.

In the next chapter, you will create a photo montage, integrating a still image sequence with the map sequence that you just created. Using custom presets, you will add your own motion adjustments to create beautiful and precise image pans to your still image files.

CHAPTER

14

Working with Stills: Motion and Advanced Keyframing

With the release of Premiere Pro 1.0, the ability to preserve the overall quality of still images was increased dramatically. Instead of resampling and reducing the resolution of imported still files, Premiere Pro now processes the full resolution of the still files, rendering the final result to your output video settings.

In former Premiere versions and in competitive nonlinear editors, when you imported a 1600 × 1200 still image, the still was automatically resized to 720 × 480 or your project dimensions. If you wanted to zoom in on the image, you were no longer zooming in on your 1600 × 1200 image; instead you were zooming in the resized 720 × 480, which yielded lesser quality results. With Premiere Pro 1.0, this was no longer a worry. With Premiere Pro 2.0, the same resolution maximizing behavior remains; however, now you can automatically resize an image to your project dimensions.

This chapter aims to help you understand how to properly prep your images, import individual stills or groups of images with ease, and then create smooth and dynamic image pans like those Ken Burns used in *The Civil War* and *Baseball*. Along the way, you'll learn some good guidelines for working with still images, as well as how to save the image pans as reusable custom effect presets. You will also investigate some new features of the Effect Controls panel, such as the Value and Velocity graphs.

Importing, Image Size, and Auto-Scaling

Print and video images inherently have different requirements: Video has a set screen resolution of 72 dots per inch (dpi) and a standard frame size of 720 × 486 (NTSC), while much higher dpi counts and image sizes are often used for printing. In past versions of Premiere, importing still images with these larger resolutions resulted in a compromise where the image was converted to a smaller size and this resulted in a loss of image quality when you wanted to enlarge or pan the image. Premiere Pro, however, takes a new approach that accurately processes stills and preserves their true resolution while still offering you an alternate method for quick resize adjustments. In Premiere Pro 2.0 you have a choice: Do you want to add stills to the timeline at their original full size and zoom or pan on their entire resolution, or do you want Premiere Pro to scale them automatically to fit in the video frame? When Premiere Pro 2.0 auto-scales an image, it will re-rasterize your still at your project's frame size. In other words, Premiere Pro internally creates a reference file for your still that is the size of your project's frame and no longer relies on the information in your original large-sized image.

How do you know which method to choose? It's very simple: If you want to zoom in on or pan on an image, do not turn on Auto-Scaling. If you are going to use still images as static shots, turn on Auto-Scaling. When working with oversized images that you intend to pan or zoom on, make sure the horizontal width is at least 1000 pixels for landscape-oriented stills, and the vertical height is at least 1000 for portrait images. If you plan on zooming up to 200%, then make sure the still is at least double the size of a standard video frame.

PAR: Square Pixels vs. Non-Square Pixels

A video frame, like all computer graphics, is made up of pixels. Most pixels are exact 1:1 squares, meaning they have a 1:1 *pixel aspect ratio* (PAR). The pixels that make up an NTSC DV video frame, however, are 1:0.9 and, thus, non-square.

The easiest way to see the results of how square pixels are distorted in DV space is to create a still image of a perfectly round circle in Photoshop with square pixels. When you import the file into Premiere Pro and add it to a DV sequence, the PAR for DV shifts the circle to become an oval.

Photoshop CS2 can work with and tag images properly for non-square pixels. Premiere Pro can recognize the tag and preserves the integrity of the image when it is imported so that there is no distortion. If you are prepping images in Photoshop and you want to use them in a DV project, use the Non-Square Pixel for DV (720 × 480) setting when creating your still.

If you want to create a square pixel document in Photoshop for use with an NTSC DV project and you want to retain the integrity of the image when you bring it into Premiere Pro, you should save the image at 720 × 534. When Premiere Pro imports the image and incorporates it into the timeline, the shift of the PAR is compensated for by the additional 154 extra pixels.

Auto-Scaling

If you don't plan any zooms or pans, try Premiere Pro's automatic scaling. When this option is on and you import a still image at a frame size of 1600 × 1200, Premiere Pro then automatically resizes the image so that it fits snug within your project's video frame. If you wanted to zoom back into the image at a later point, you can turn off the auto-scaling for that individual still and just animate the Motion/Scale effect listing. In Premiere Pro 1.5, the Auto-Scaling feature made a physical modification to the scale of a still in the Effect Controls panel; that way, you could reset the Scale properties to get the still back to its full resolution. In Premiere Pro 2.0, the Auto-Scaling feature does not use the Effect Controls panel; it simply re-rasterizes the still and lists the scale as 100%.

In this lesson, you'll examine the benefits of both approaches, as well as learn how to assign a default duration to all still images that you import.

When opening the different projects for each lesson, keep in mind that you will sometimes have to locate certain files associated with the project. For example, if Premiere prompts you to locate Italy_MapDV.psd, you can find the file in the Chapter 13 Lesson Files folder on the book's disc.

For this lesson, you are building the Montage in a DV 24p project so that when you pan and animate the still images you do not have the potential for revealing any interlacing artifacts. If you are building a photo-only montage that does not contain any other video and it will be burned to DVD, using a progressive frame rate project is your best bet for good results. Because you are still using DV as the format, the pixel aspect ratio of 0.9 should be considered for graphics and imported elements that have square pixel aspect ratios.

1. Open Still_Import_Start.prproj from the APPST2 Lesson Files/Chapter 14 folder.

   This lesson starts where you left off in the last chapter, adding a photo montage to the opening graphic you created.

2. Create a new bin in your Project panel, and name it Rome Stills. Create a new sequence within this bin (one video track and one stereo audio track), and give it the same name.

   Continuing to emphasize the idea of nesting, you are structuring this project so that all the individual elements are contained within their own sequences. Because you want the final photo montage to be accessible as a single clip, you will assemble all the Rome stills in a sequence of the same name.

3. From the Edit menu, select Preferences > General. In the General Preferences pane, change Default Duration to 144 frames. At the bottom of the pane make sure the check box for Default Scale to Frame Size is checked, and click OK. Click on the Rome Stills bin in the Project panel. Press Ctrl+I to access the Import dialog. From the Rome subfolder in the APPST2 Lesson Files/Chapter 14 folder, select Rome06.jpg and Rome11.jpg, and click Open. In the Project panel, click on the images to view their properties (**Figure 14.1**).

   Because still images can be an infinite duration, assigning a default duration for all imported stills streamlines your workflow, especially if you are importing several images. You assigned the Default Duration for these two stills to be 144 frames (6 seconds at 24 fps), because they are the first and last images of the montage. Later, you will fade the montage in and out; therefore, you will need some extra frames to play with. Secondly, you imported these images scaled to your current project's frame size; take note of this as we'll get to that in a few more steps.

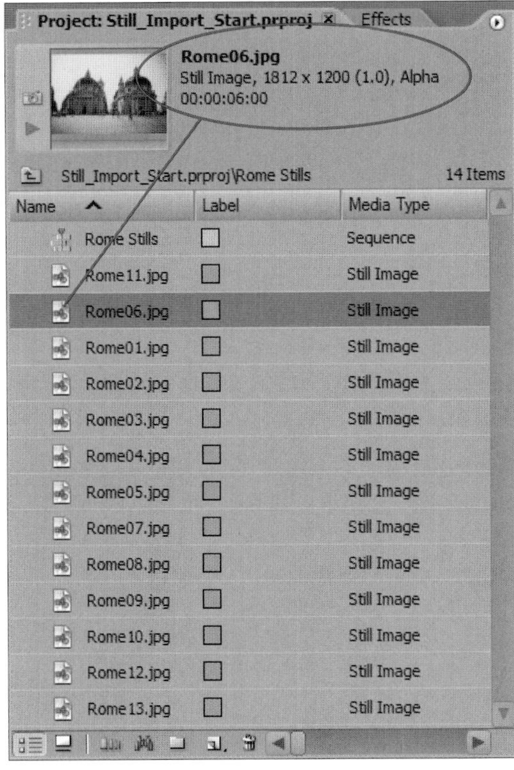

Figure 14.1 Clicking on a file in the Project panel reveals its properties in the Project Preview area. Here you can see the frame size for the imported image, its pixel aspect ratio (PAR), whether the image contains an alpha channel, and its assigned duration.

4. Choose Edit > Preferences > Still Image, and set Default Duration to 120 frames (5 seconds) and turn off the check box for Scaling. Import the remaining files in the folder (select all except Rome06 and Rome11). Click on the newly imported stills individually, and view their properties in the Project Preview area to see their change in duration.

   The second batch of imported stills does not need extra frames for transitions, so you lowered Default Duration to 120. Now the Project Preview area reports the stills are only five seconds long.

5. In the Project panel, select Rome11.jpg and Rome01.jpg and add them onto Video 1 track at the head of the timeline. Open the Effect Controls panel and expand the Motion effect listing (**Figures 14.2** and **14.3**).

Figure 14.2 When Default Scale to Frame Size is checked, Premiere Pro 2.0 resizes your still so that it fits exactly within the boundaries of your project's frame size. Notice that Rome11.jpg fits within the 720 × 480 frame and more importantly, the scale listed in the Effect Controls panel is 100%. Because the Pixel Aspect ratio for the still is 1.0, the image does not quite have a 4 × 3 aspect ratio; this is why there are small black bars (letterbox) at the top and bottom of the frame. Now take a look at Rome01.jpg and Figure 14.3.

Figure 14.3 Because you turned off the Default Scale for the import of Rome01.jpg, when you add the still to the timeline it displays at full resolution. Here, the scale of the Program Monitor is at 25% and the wireframe surrounding the monitor frame shows the entire dimensions of the Rome01.jpg in the timeline.

When you have the Default Scale to Frame Size preference checked, Premiere Pro automatically resizes the imported still so that the entire image fits within the confines of the 720 × 480 video frame. When a still is imported with such a preference active, this is the expected behavior. When you turn off the option, the still imports at its full resolution, which may or may not exceed the current project frame size.

If you imported an image or a group of images with the check box on, you can easily turn the resizing off so that you can animate the original dimensions of the file.

6. Right-click on the timeline instance of the clip Rome11.jpg. From the right-click menu, turn off the checked item: Scale to Frame Size (**Figures 14.4a** and **b**). Right-click on the Rome01.jpg, and activate the listing for Scale to Frame size.

a

b

Figures 14.4a and b Whether you import a previously scaled file or you want to automatically scale the still to the default frame size, results are only a right-click away. Here you can see the Rome11.jpg is auto-scaled. Deactivate the Scale to Frame Size menu listing (a) to get these results (b).

Whether you import a Photoshop file, create a new title, or create a color matte, these items are considered stills and adhere to the Default Duration value you set in your Still Images preferences. When you open a layered Photoshop file as a sequence, all the layers that make up the sequence adhere to the same default duration.

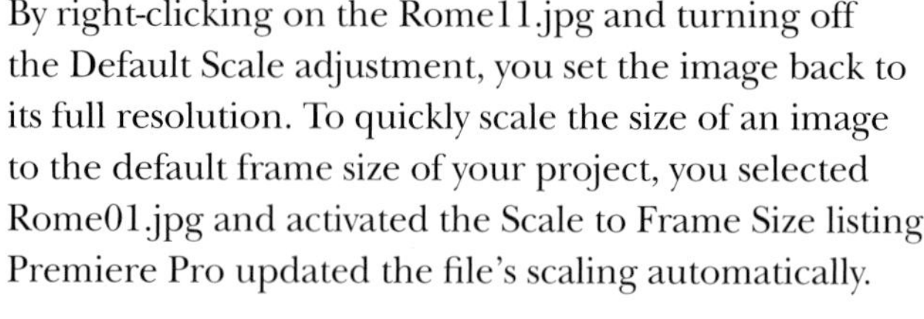

By right-clicking on the Rome11.jpg and turning off the Default Scale adjustment, you set the image back to its full resolution. To quickly scale the size of an image to the default frame size of your project, you selected Rome01.jpg and activated the Scale to Frame Size listing. Premiere Pro updated the file's scaling automatically.

The nice thing about the menu listing is that it works with multiple stills selected. This means you can have auto-scale on or off for multiple images at the same time. Also consider auto-scaling when using video clips that are larger that your current project's dimensions.

NOTES

Take note that when you import a still that does not have a 4 × 3 aspect ratio, such as 1280 × 720, when the file is automatically scaled to fit the 720 × 480 frame, it yields empty space where the aspect ratio is different. The example image would have empty black space at the top and bottom of the image, much like a letterbox for a widescreen film transferred to video. If you don't want the black space, simply adjust the scale to find the right size.

This lesson laid a foundation of basic settings for importing stills. You learned when and why to turn on Default Scaling as well as how to better control default durations of your still images. In the next lesson, you will build on these skills and learn to use Premiere Pro's Automate to Sequence feature.

Automate to Sequence

The Automate to Sequence feature allows you to select a group of files from the Project panel and add them to the timeline. You can add them sequentially or in a custom order, and even instruct Premiere to place transitions between the clips automatically.

TIP

Because it is very easy to map keyboard shortcuts to menu commands, you can open the Edit Keyboard Customization dialog and assign the keyboard shortcut Alt+G for the Application > Edit > Preferences > General menu listing. This way you can alter General preferences with a quick keystroke. Additionally, assign Alt+S for the Application > Clip > Video Options > Scale to Frame Size feature so that it is only a keyboard shortcut away from applying or un-applying a default scale adjustment to any clip.

In this short lesson, you will use Automate to Sequence to create the skeleton for your photo montage by quickly adding a group of stills to the timeline.

1. Open Automate_Start.prproj from the APPST2 Lesson Files/Chapter 14 folder. Expand your Project panel so that you can see all the files and columns, then rearrange the column order to read: Comment/Good/Video Info. For every vertical (portrait) image, click the Good check box (**Figure 14.5**).

   First, to see whether an image is vertical or not you will either have to turn on the thumbnail view from the Project panel's wing menu, or click through every still. Second, you can either re-arrange the columns by dragging the columns physically in the Project panel's layout or through the Edit Columns dialog in the wing menu.

Because a folder full of still images can take up a lot of screen real estate when scrolling through and selecting images, you can rearrange and use specific columns to tag files and quickly adjust their order. Checking the Good box gives you the option of seeing which images are desirable (in this case, desirable means vertically aligned) if the file thumbnail is turned off.

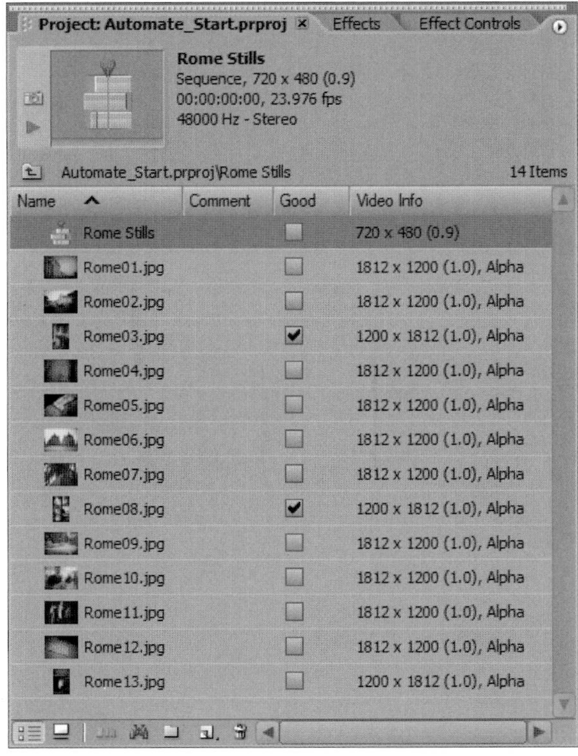

Figure 14.5 Drag a column by its heading to change its position in the Project panel. The column order will persist when you open other bins in your project. You can add or remove columns by checking or unchecking the boxes associated with the columns in the Edit Columns dialog, accessed from the Project panel wing menu.

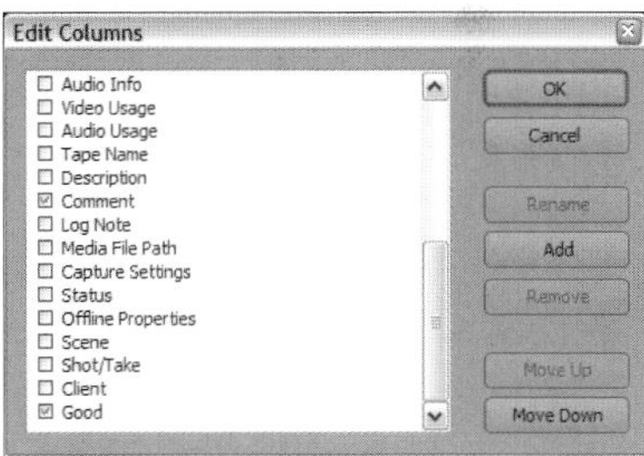

2. Double-click the Comment column for Rome06.jpg, and enter a 01. Enter a 02 in the Comment column for Rome01.jpg. Enter a 13 in the Comment column for Rome11.jpg. Enter random values for the rest of the images so that 01 through 13 are used in the Comments field. Click on the Comment column header to change the sort order to ascending (the arrow points

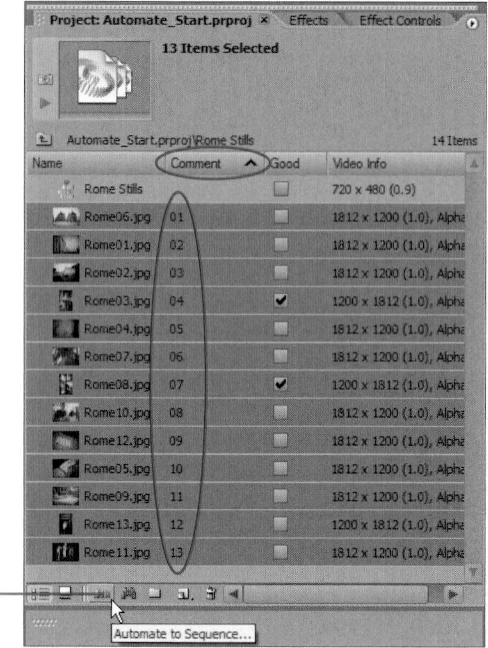

Figure 14.6 With metadata entered into the Comment column and the sort order ascending, all the images with empty comments appear before the images with data added. This enables you to select the remaining files you need to add in the order that they were named. With the files selected, the button for Automate to Sequence becomes active.

up). Select all the images, but do not select the Rome Stills sequence (**Figure 14.6**).

You can enter alpha/numeric data in the Comment column, then sort based on that data. Here you used the technique to group the images in numeric order that differed from their originally named file ordering. Next, the Automate to Sequence feature will send your files to the timeline based on the sort or selection order you define.

3. With the 11 stills selected in the Project panel, click the Automate to Sequence button. In the Automate to Sequence dialog, make the following settings and click OK (**Figure 14.7**):

   Ordering: **Sort Order**
   Placement: **Sequentially**
   Method: **Overlay Edit**
   Clip Overlap: **24 Frames**
   Apply Default Video Transition: **On**

   First you need to tell Premiere where to automatically add your stills, and then you tell the program how to

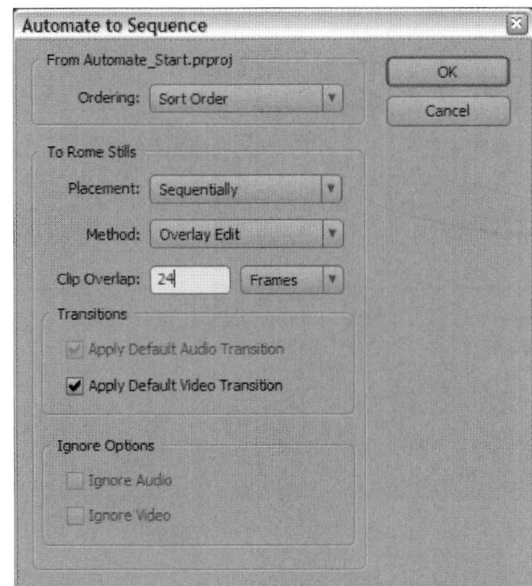

Figure 14.7 The Automate to Sequence dialog tells you the origin of the clips being added, as well as the name of sequence to which Premiere will add them. The most visible benefit of the Automate to Sequence feature is the ability to add audio and video transitions to every cut in the sequence. Notice how all the clips are added to the sequence with no gaps and transitions at the cut points.

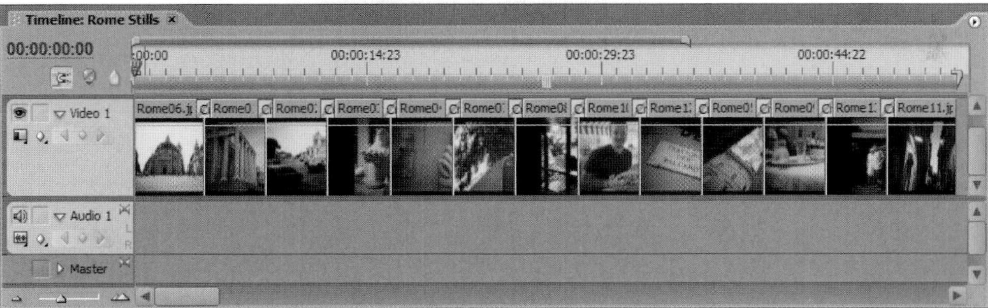

add them. In the Automate to Sequence dialog, you then tell Premiere to add the images sequentially based on their sort method, using an Overlay edit, with a 24-frame overlap duration for the transitions. Because of the current default transition setting, Premiere will add cross dissolves (unless you have personally assigned a different default video transition).

When assigning the Clip Overlap value, remember that the value is not added to the existing stills, but used from their default duration. For each of these five-second stills, Premiere would use one second for its dissolve in and one second for its dissolve out, leaving three seconds as its unobstructed display time.

4. For the final step, with Video 1 targeted, position the Edit Line at head of the sequence (press Home on your keyboard) and press Ctrl+D to add a default transition

that fades in at the beginning of your sequence. Go to the end of the sequence (press End on your keyboard) and press Ctrl+D to add a default fade out.

Although Automate to Sequence places transitions between the files it is adding, it does not apply transitions to the clips at the cuts in which the edit occurred. To streamline the entire sequence, you put transitions at the head and tail. Now you are ready to add some motion.

The Automate to Sequence feature offers a means of quickly getting your edit into shape. Because I had scaling turned off when I created this project, all the stills were added to the timeline at 100% in the original frame size. In the next lesson, you will adjust those settings and add clean motion and scaling effects to create fluid image pans and zooms with your still images.

Image Panning and Creating Custom Effect Presets

Incorporating motion can make the difference between a boring photo montage and one that holds your attention. The first step to address this was assigning a short duration to each image: five seconds. The next step to packing more of a punch with your montage is animating the motion of the images. By slowly revealing elements of the picture or focusing on a particular area of the photograph, still images become dynamic and thus come to life. To add some life into the Rome montage, you will add some crisp and clean motion effects to scale and pan on the stills. Specifically, in this lesson you will create four motion settings that incorporate keyframe animation. You will also learn how to save these motion settings as custom effect presets for use on other projects.

1. Open Still_Effects_Start.prproj from the APPST2 Lesson Files/Chapter 14 folder. Using the Effects Workspace, select the first still (Rome06.jpg) in the Timeline panel. Press the Home key and position the Edit Line at 00:00:02:00. In the Effect Controls panel,

click the Motion effect listing to turn on direct manipulation. Adjust the clip's Anchor Point to be 906.0 × 800.0. Check the box for Uniform Scale, and increase Scale Height to 125. Turn keyframing on for both Scale and Position by clicking their respective Toggle Animation buttons (**Figure 14.8**).

Figure 14.8 Select the Rome06.jpg clip to view its effect properties in the Effect Controls panel. Based on the position of the Edit Line, you can add animated keyframes for any of the effect parameters that have Toggle Animation (the stopwatch icon) turned on. By adjusting the anchor point you have assigned where your scale and position adjustments will originate from.

Once you turn direct manipulation on, you can see the various handles associated with the selected clip. The center cross reflects the anchor point, which is like a thumbtack through the image. Just as a piece of paper moves around the point where it's tacked, your moves are based on the image's anchor point. For example, as you scale the image out, the zoom will originate from the anchor point, assigned here in the bottom center of the image. Although direct manipulation offers a lot of adjustment points, you can only modify the anchor point from its field in the Effect Controls panel.

To dynamically scale and move the image, you assigned two keyframes near the beginning of the clip (Edit Line position 00:00:02:00). Because you have transitions at every cut point in the edit, the best way of creating images pans is to define the In and Out pan points in the center of the clip away from the transitions and then move the keyframes to the beginning and end of the clip respectively. To properly animate the keyframe settings in the next step, you will need to reposition the Edit Line and modify the value of the keyframes.

2. With the Timeline panel active, press Page Down to advance the Edit Line to the cut point of the next clip. With the Rome06 file still selected in the Effect Controls panel, enter 360 × 333 for Position and 45 for Scale. Premiere creates two keyframes. Shift-click or marquee select these two keyframes, and drag them to the very end of the selected clip (**Figures 14.9a** and **b**). Marquee select the first two keyframes and slide them to the absolute beginning of the clip. Press the Home key, and click Play to preview the image zoom that you just created.

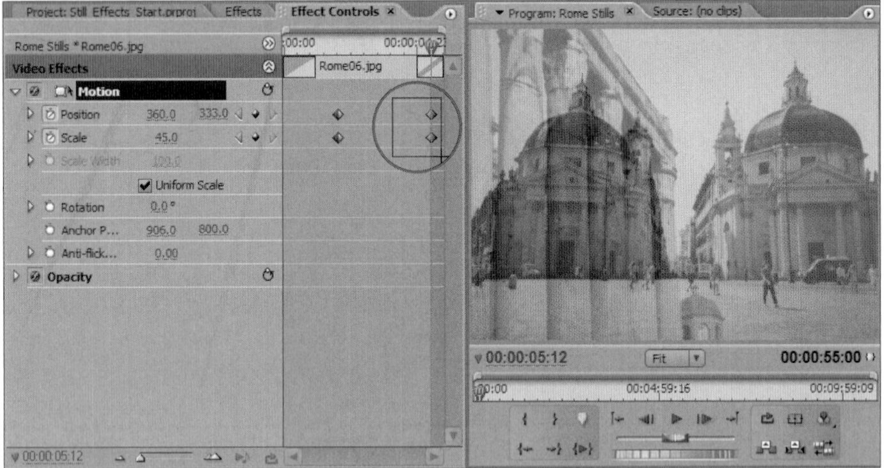

a

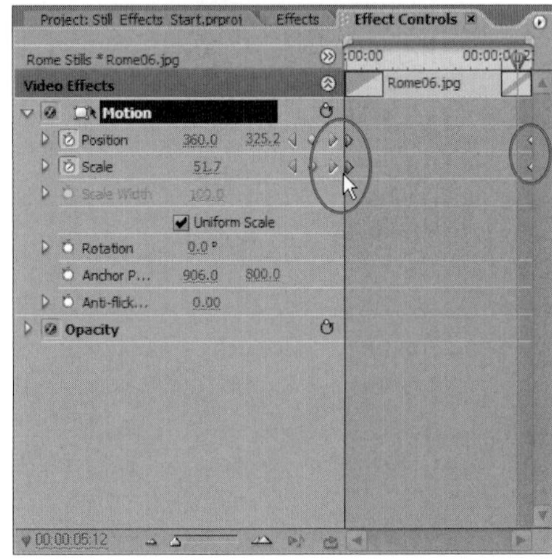

b

Figures 14.9a and b The final Position and Scale keyframes are at the center cut point between the two clips (a). By Shift-selecting both of the end keyframes and dragging them so that they are tucked a bit under the right edge at the very end of the clip (b), you are ensuring that the effect will be animated throughout the entire transition. By moving the two start keyframes to the beginning of the clip, the animation will begin as the transition fades in.

Because the end of the Rome06 clip instance is covered by a transition, you cannot see its last frame. The final frame of Rome06 has completely dissolved into the file Rome01. By navigating to the cut point, which is nearly the end of the clip, you can see Rome06 in relation to the shot that will next appear, as well as see your adjusted effect values and create two keyframes.

You can then select the keyframes and drag them to their final position at the end of the timeline view for the Rome06.jpg. By creating the first two keyframes in the visible area of the beginning of the clip, you did the same thing as selecting them and moving them underneath the transition at the beginning of the timeline. The result of this first animation is very clean: a simple zoom that emphasizes the idea of motion from the beginning to the end of the clip.

3. With the Rome06.jpg file still selected and active in the Effect Controls panel, right-click on its Motion listing and select Save Preset. Rename the preset Rome Zoom Out 01. Click Scale for Type, and add the brief description "Horizontal Zoom Out, Position and Scale KF" (**Figure 14.10**).

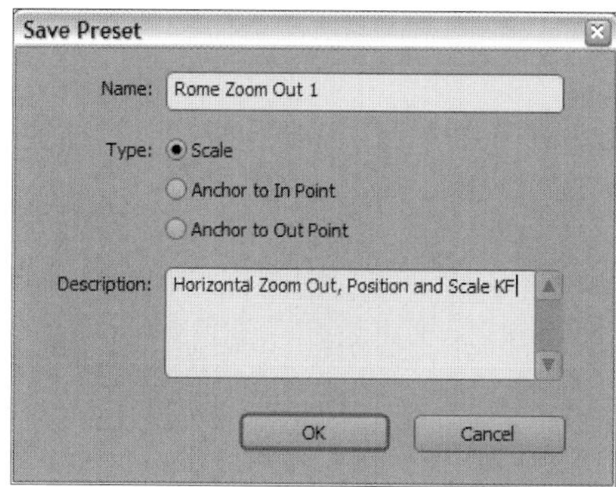

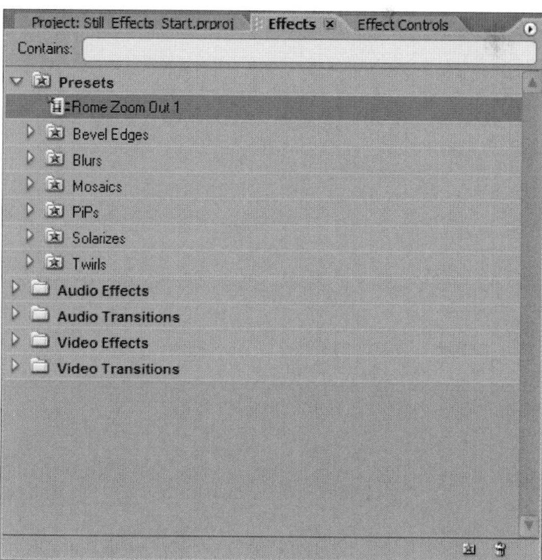

Figure 14.10 You can save effect settings as individual custom presets to be reused at any time. The custom effect preset shows up in the Presets folder in the Effects panel.

Remember, when Toggle Animation is on for an effect, moving the Edit Line to a new position and adjusting any of the effect's parameters adds a new keyframe with the new values.

Saving the effect as a custom preset enables you to reuse it for the other stills in this sequence and beyond. Because this effect has a start and end keyframe, you chose Scale as the type of preset. Choosing Scale allows you to apply an effect to a new clip of different duration. Scale applies the effect proportionally across the duration of the clip; a shorter clip means a faster effect. Anchor to In Point keeps the exact timing and pacing of the animation but starts it at the clip's In point. Anchor to Out Point keeps the exact timing and pacing of the animation, but it starts at a calculated time and ends exactly at the Out point.

4. With the Rome06.jpg file still selected and the Effect Controls panel active, twirl down the listing for Scale. Click on the first keyframe for Scale. Grab the handle for the first velocity keyframe and drag it to the left and slightly downwards (**Figures 14.11a** through **d**).

   This step took advantage of the new Velocity graph controls in Premiere Pro 2.0. The Velocity graph dictates the velocity at which the effect parameter is processed to get from one keyframe to another. Although you'll certainly want more feedback from the controls, let's review what you did. Upon first glance at the Velocity graph, you could see that it contained a constant value; to smooth the zoom out, you converted the constant value into a curved value that gently ramps from beginning to end.

   First you selected the first keyframe for Scale; doing so activated the handle for the Velocity keyframe value. By pulling on the handle and dragging it up or down you dynamically adjusted the value of the velocity in the form of a curved ramp. By dragging outwards you lengthened the slope of the ramp, thus making the desired velocity ramp more gradual. By dragging down the handle you increased the start value of the velocity. Because the scale is zooming outwards, the velocity is a negative value. Whether you are zooming in or out, to speed up the velocity you should increase the numeric value; -100 and 100 are both fast velocity values, -100 for a Zoom out and 100 for a Zoom in.

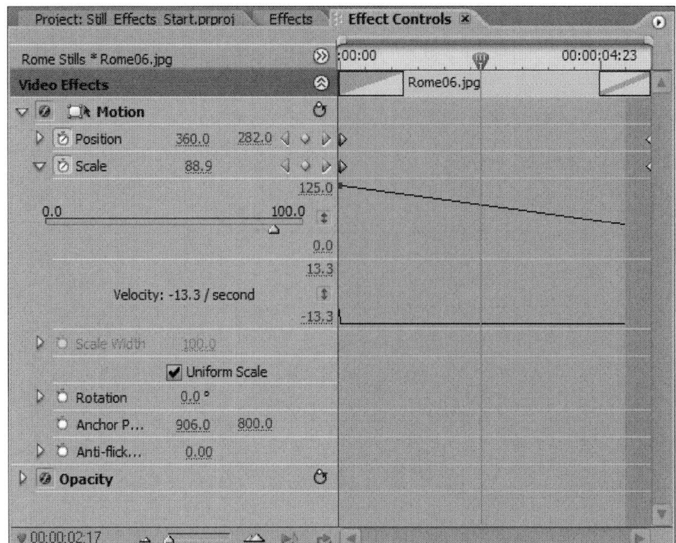

a

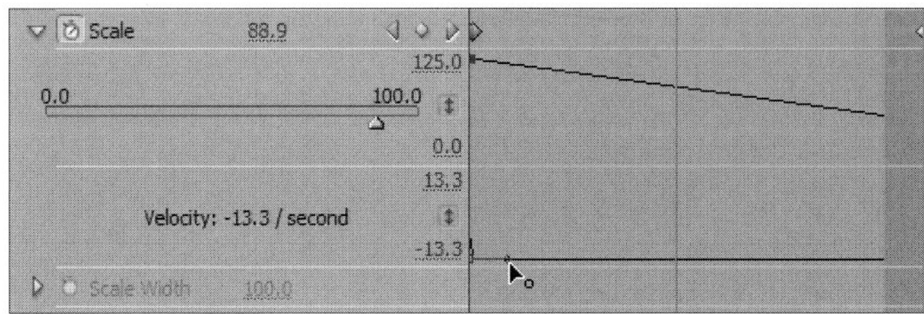

b

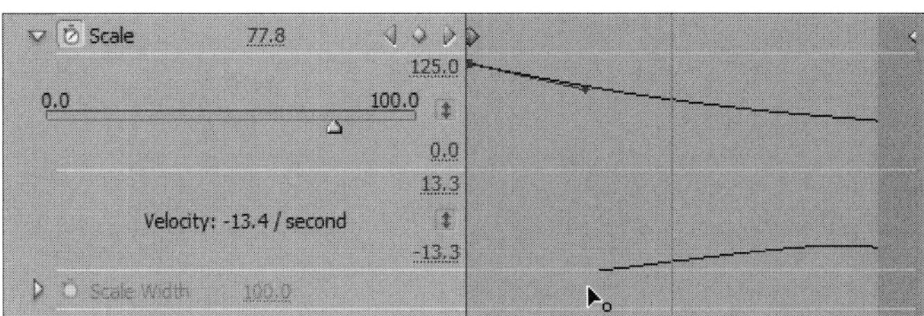

c

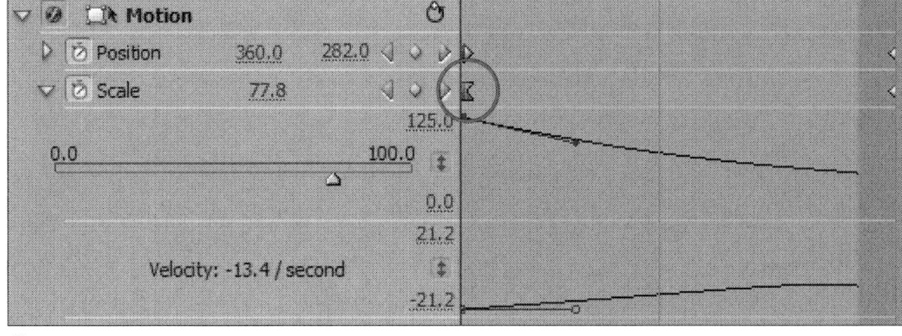

d

Figures 14.11a through d The velocity graph begins with a constant value (a). Once the first keyframe for scale is selected the handle to adjust the velocity keyframe is available for adjustment (b). Positioning your mouse near the handle allows you to adjust it dynamically. Dragging inwards, outwards, up, and down adjusts the curve for velocity (c and d).

5. Select the second clip in the Rome01 Sequence. Position the Edit Line at 6:00. Activate direct manipulation for the Motion of this clip. Set Anchor Point to 0.0×1200.0, and Position to 0.0 × 480.0 (**Figure 14.12**). Turn on keyframing (Toggle Animation) for Scale and Position. Reposition the Edit Line at 8;00. Adjust the Position to –97 × 480 and Scale to 41. Select both keyframe groups, and reposition the right keyframes at the head of the clip and left keyframes at the tail. Right-click on the second keyframe for scale and choose Ease In from the submenu.

   For the second clip, you anchored the image in the lower-left corner and then repositioned it so that the image scaled with a slight panning move from the lower-left corner outward. Because both sides of this clip have transitions, you created your start and end position keyframe groups in the center of the clip and then dragged each group outward to its corresponding edge.

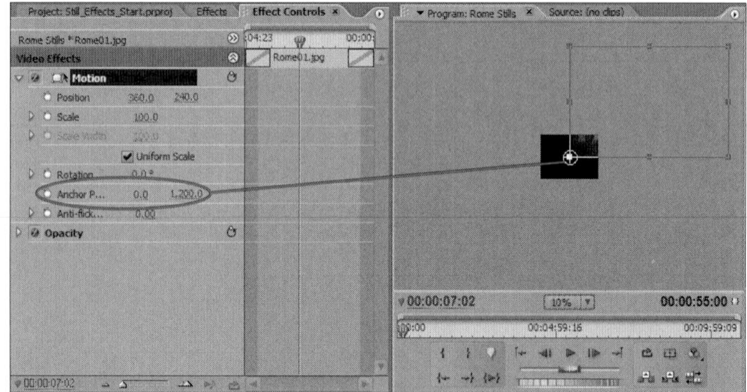

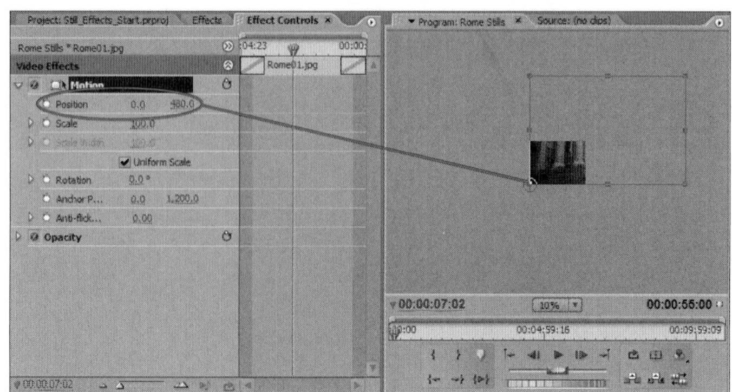

Figure 14.12 By changing the anchor point, you originated all motion adjustments from the bottom-left corner of the still file. By changing the position of the still to reside at 0 × 480, you tucked that left corner of the image in the left corner of the video frame.

Twirl down the Scale effect parameter, and look at the Velocity graph. Notice that by choosing to ease in to the second Scale keyframe you created a curve that reduces the velocity from the first to second keyframe in the form of a smooth upwards ramp. Also notice that because the first and last keyframes are tucked beneath transitions and other clip material, you cannot see the Velocity keyframe point. This is why using the right-click temporal interpolation menu can be very quick and easy to adjust the velocity going into or out of keyframe handles.

6. With the Ease In applied, right-click and save this effect as a custom preset with Type set to Scale and name it Rome Zoom Out Anchored LL. In the Description, note that the effect was created for a horizontal clip. Position the Edit Line at the head of the timeline, and play back the two clips to see your results.

If you create a zoom-in effect and want to quickly make the effect zoom out, simply swap the position of the Scale keyframes. Because the individual keyframes have a specific effect value embedded in them, adjusting their position preserves their original settings.

7. Select the third clip in the timeline, Rome02. For this clip, a simple Scale adjustment will do. Position the Edit Line at 11:00. Set Scale to 44.0 and Position to 412.0 × 240.0. Click on the Toggle Animation button for Scale. Reposition this keyframe at the end of the clip instance in the Effect Controls panel. With the clip still selected, reposition the Edit Line before the current keyframes in the Effect Controls panel (approximately 10:00). Adjust Scale Height to 110. Marquee select the two Scale keyframes and choose Continuous Bezier (see **Figure 14.13**). Position the keyframes at the beginning and end of the clip instance. Save this effect as a custom preset named Rome Zoom Out 2. In the Save Preset dialog, choose Scale and add a description specifying a horizontal image.

   Resizing this image helped you find the optimum scale at which you could see the entire image. With Scale at 44, the frame was slightly shifted so you readjusted the position of the clip. Because this is a simple zoom out, you only animated the keyframes for scale. Instead of using Ease In for one of the keyframes, you selected both and chose Continuous Bezier. If you twirl down

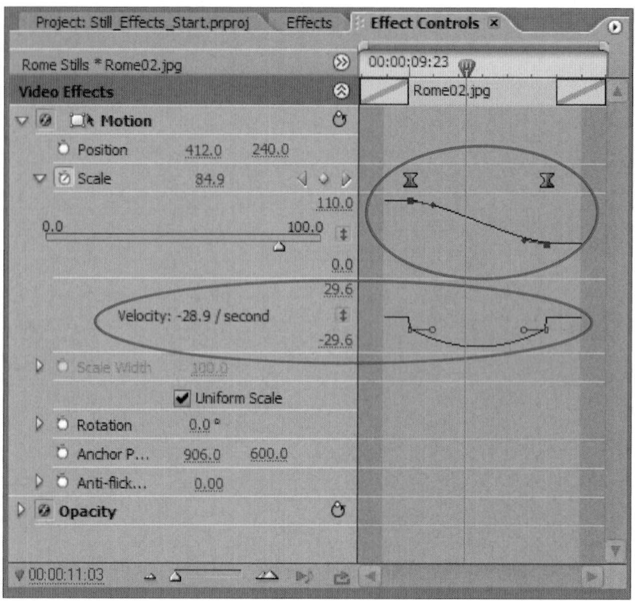

Figure 14.13 The Value graph shows a smooth Scale adjustment that goes from 110% to 44%. Below this, the Velocity graph shows a nice smooth curve where the Scale velocity start slow and speeds up, then slows down again as it reaches the second keyframe.

the Scale parameter in the Effect Controls you would see a Velocity graph that reflected a smooth acceleration out of the first keyframe and then a smooth acceleration into the second one.

8. Select the fourth clip, Rome03.jpg. Position the Edit Line at approximately 15:00. Expand the Motion settings and click on the Motion effect name to activate direct manipulation. In the Program Monitor, adjust the zoom view to a percentage value that reveals the entire wireframe for the selected image (**Figure 14.14**).

   To create the vertical pan of this image, you will need to resize the image to fit snugly to the edge of your video frame. In order to later resize and reposition it, here you activate direct manipulation to display the wireframe for the entire image. With direct manipulation turned on, you can click on the handles in the Program Monitor panel to resize or reposition the image.

9. Grab the side handle of the wireframe, and drag it inward to scale the width to 54 (**Figure 14.15**). Grab in the center of the image, and drag upward so that the bottom of the image is in the frame (**Figure 14.16**). A

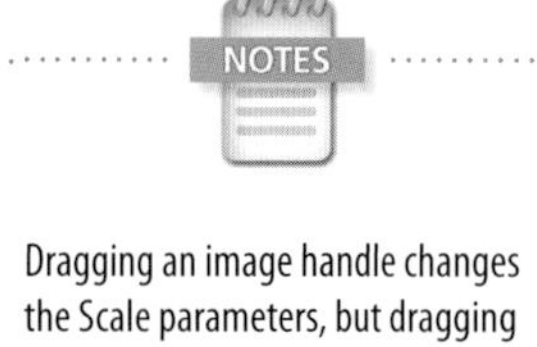

Dragging an image handle changes the Scale parameters, but dragging the entire image changes the Position parameters.

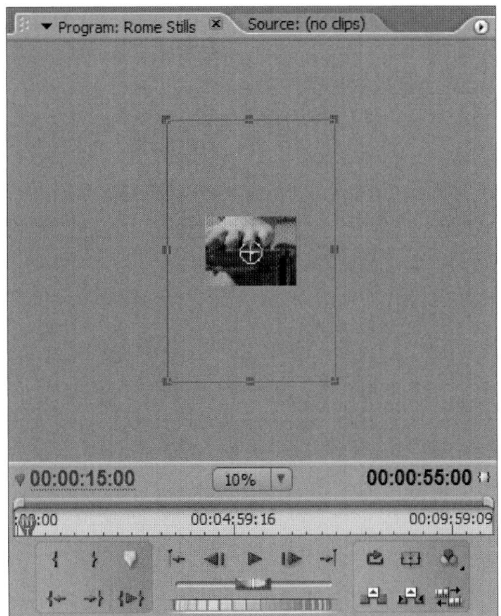

Figure 14.14 To see an entire vertical image larger than the frame, activate direct manipulation and reduce the size of the Program Monitor zoom. Now you can adjust and manipulate the image by dragging it in the Program Monitor panel, which now references the full frame dimensions.

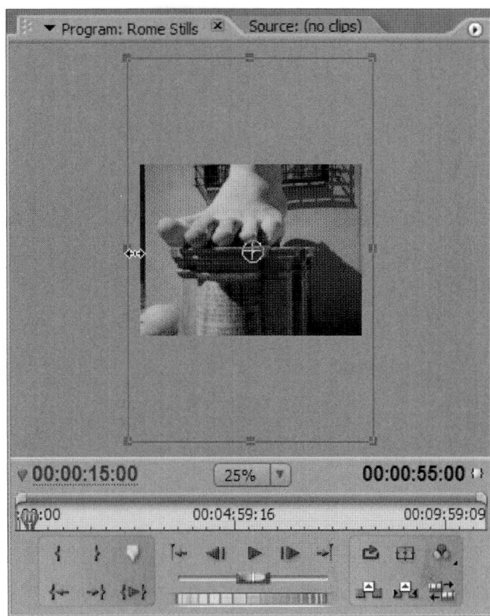

Figure 14.15 Grab and move any of the eight image handles to scale the image. Because this clip has Uniform Scale turned on, adjusting the horizontal handles adjusts both horizontal and vertical scale values.

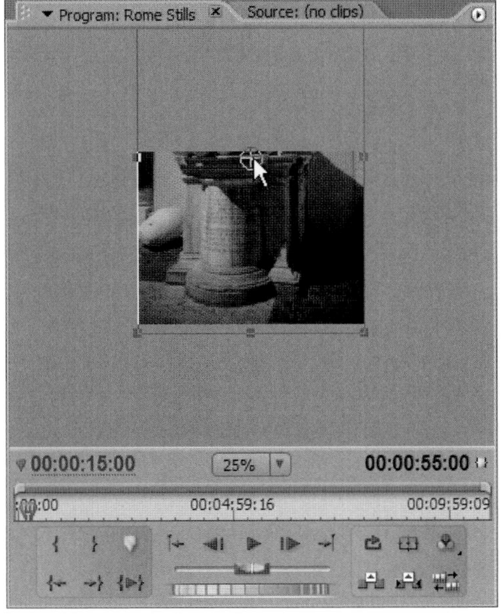

Figure 14.16 Hold down the Shift key when repositioning the center position to lock the alternate position coordinate. Here, holding Shift while you drag downward locks the horizontal position of 360.

Position value of 360 × 40.0 should be perfect. Turn on keyframing (Toggle Animation) for Position only.

After finding the image's proper scale and position, you assigned a keyframe for Scale to achieve a vertical pan from the bottom of the image to its top. In the next step, you'll find the end keyframe.

10. With clip Rome03 still selected and direct manipulation active, reposition the Edit Line to 17:00. In the Effect Controls panel, adjust the Position value to 360 × 480 (**Figure 14.17**). Move the respective keyframes to the head and tail of the selected clip. Select the second Scale keyframe, right-click on it, and choose Ease In. Save this Motion effect as a custom preset named Rome Vert Pan Up, and click Scale for Type.

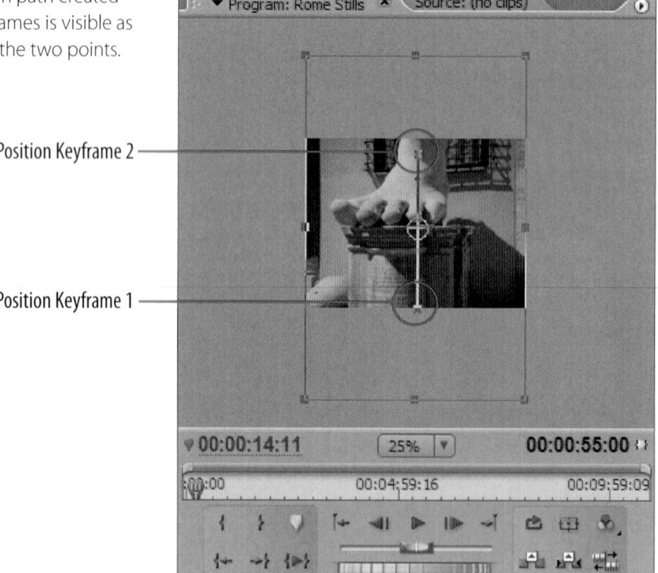

Figure 14.17 The motion path created by the two Position keyframes is visible as the dotted line between the two points.

Modifying the vertical Position value revealed the motion path for the selected clip. Because you modified the Position value, Premiere created a new keyframe at the current frame. Notice that when direct manipulation is turned on, all path adjustments and keyframe positions are visible.

11. Drag and drop the Rome Zoom Out 01 custom effect preset onto the last clip in the sequence, Rome11.jpg. Extend the tail of this clip by 1 second. With Rome11.jpg selected, open the Effect Controls panel to reveal the keyframe properties. Position the Edit Line in the middle of the clip at 52:00. Selecting each group of start and end keyframes, swap their position to reverse the effect. In the Scale effect listing, click the Go to Next Keyframe button if the Edit Line is before the last keyframe of the scale effect. If the Edit Line is past the last keyframe, click the Go to Previous Keyframe button to snap the Edit Line to the last Scale keyframe. Adjust the Scale value to 100 (**Figure 14.18**).

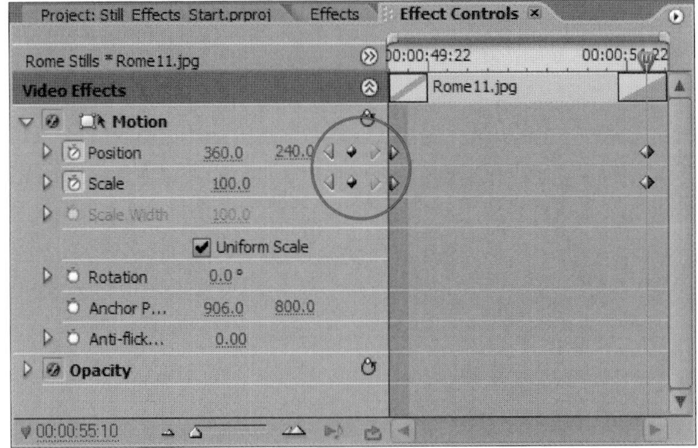

Figure 14.18 Clicking on the Go to Next Keyframe button for the Scale parameter snapped the Edit Line to the last Scale keyframe. Because there are no more keyframes to the right of the current keyframe, the Go to Next Keyframe button is now dimmed. When the Edit Line is positioned over a keyframe, you can adjust parameter settings for that keyframe. To delete the keyframe, click the Add/Remove Keyframe button.

Once you apply a custom effect preset to a selected clip, you can then easily modify the assigned keyframe values. If you apply an effect and do not see all the keyframes, you might have to extend the duration of the clip to see the rightmost keyframes. In all cases, keyframes are applied at the cut point of a clip, in this case, in the middle of the transition when Rome13.jpg dissolves into Rome11.jpg. This means that the end keyframes are about 12 keyframes past the end of the previous out-point of Rome11.jpg. I don't make the rules as to why Premiere does this, I just know to warn you about it.

To perfectly position the Edit Line on a keyframe, use the Go to Next or Go to Previous Keyframe buttons for the desired effect in the Effect Controls panel. After

If you can't get enough of this photo montage example, the Premiere Pro video training series from Total Training goes into great depth about creating additional motion effects, as well as adding music to the montage. My "Tips & Tricks" series covers more photo montage effects.

you swapped the positions of the beginning and ending keyframes you had to be exactly on top of a keyframe to adjust its value. It is a good practice to always use the Go to Next/Previous Keyframe buttons, because if you are off by even one frame, a new keyframe will be created and it may cause undesirable effects.

12. Using the workflow you just learned, create your own custom motion settings, or add and modify your newly created custom presets to the remaining images in the sequence. To take a shortcut to the final step, simply open Still_Effects_Finish.prproj from the APPST2 Lesson Files/Chapter 14 folder and examine the remaining effects that I applied.

13. From the Map Files folder, open the Photo Montage sequence in the Timeline panel, click in the timeline and press End. The Edit Line repositions to the end of the Map Comp nest. Press Ctrl+D to add a Default Transition at the end of the clip. From the Rome Stills folder, drag and drop the Rome Stills at the end of the Map Comp clip (**Figure 14.19**). Press Enter to render the work area and view the final, full-resolution version of the montage.

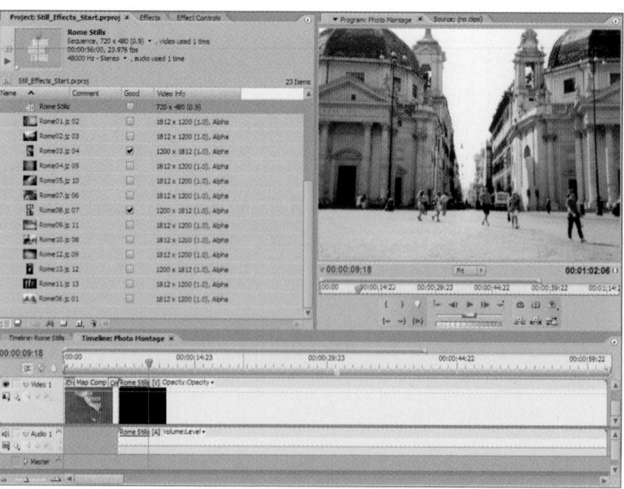

Figure 14.19 Here you have the nested Map Comp from the last chapter and as the Rome graphic alludes, you cut to the sequence you just created; the photo montage of Rome.

For the last step, you nested the Rome Stills sequence into the Photo Montage sequence. Dropping a cross dissolve after the Rome graphic scales up creates a simple transition into the Rome photo montage. Because you had a transition at the beginning and end of the montage, the sequence fades in and out.

You'll take this project further in Chapter 16, "Custom DVD Design," creating a custom DVD with markers and buttons that reference the different photo montages of Italy.

This lesson lays the ground work for Motion effects, but there is a lot left to cover. With the foundation established and a handful of presets, you should be able to tweak, adjust, and then come up with your own version of the perfect image pan or zoom presets.

Things to Remember

When working with stills, proper management of the imported image's resolution and frame size is vital. It's best to work with images at an equal high resolution; that way they can share effect presets easily. If you plan on zooming at levels between 150% and 200%, be sure that the frame size of your image is at least double that of your video frame; a 720 × 480 video frame, for example, would need a 1440 × 960 picture frame.

Because you can't range select and adjust the duration of an entire group of stills, you will want to adjust your default still duration value before you import groups of stills. Your chosen duration value is will be assigned to your images when they are imported.

After you import your images, you still have resizing options. When adding stills to your sequence, remember that you can you can instruct Premiere to automatically resize them to fit entirely within the video frame, just remember that if you decide to animate them, you should turn the Default Scale off.

One thing I didn't cover in this chapter, because it wasn't necessary, was the Anti-Flicker filter in the Motion effect. This filter should be applied (by increasing its value) if you find that any of your image pans and zooms yield undesirable flickering or shimmering from the image. Simply increase the Anti-Flicker filter to reduce the presence of any flicker.

Finally, consider using custom effect presets. You can create and reuse effect presets to your heart's content. You can also export and import presets to and from other Premiere Pro systems. All of the presets that were created for this lesson can be imported individually. Just choose Import Preset from the Effects panel wing menu, and select the presets from the APPST2 Lesson Files/Chapter 14/Custom Presets folder, and use them as much as you like.

The next chapter switches gears a bit. You will explore the more advanced features of the Titler to quickly and efficiently create your own custom titles, styles, and templates.

CHAPTER

15

Advanced Titling: Styles and Templates

The Titler combines the power to create unique, attractive titles with the ability to save the style and design of the title's text and objects. With the Titler, you can create and save custom personalized titles and templates that you then can use over and over for multiple projects. Creating custom templates allows you to quickly load a title and update its text to reflect what is unique in its current application. If you produce your own videos, for example, you have the option to streamline and customize the titles that appear in your videos to incorporate custom logos or specific font styles.

While Chapter 10 taught you the basics of creating titles with the Titler, this chapter focuses on creating styles—the way text appears, creating custom templates, modifying pre-made templates, and finally, creating a custom credit roll that can be saved as a template.

Aside from a new layout, the most powerful new Titler features are the ability to leave the Titler open while using the application and the saving of newly created titles directly into the project you are using (rather than as an individual file). Don't worry, you can still save titles out to disk and open existing titles without any hiccups. Because of the new default saving method, however, templates become an even more powerful storage area for the titles you use and create.

To kick off this chapter you will first create a geometric object with a custom style, and then you will create custom text that fits into the object. The result will be a lower-third title template that you can use for future projects. Along the way, you will learn about all the properties that make up the style of the text or object.

Creating a Style from an Object

The easiest way to understand style properties is to apply them to an object.

1. Open Title_Style_Start.prproj from the APPST2 Lesson Files/Chapter 15 folder.
2. Choose Title > New Title > Default Still or press F9 to open the Titler. Name the title Style. Rearrange the frames of the Titler to match the layout in **Figure 15.1**. (To learn how to do this, view the Titler_Workout.wmv video tutorial located on the book's DVD.) Then, go to Window > Workspace > Save Workspace, and name this workspace Title Workspace.

On the book's disc, I include a helpful video clip that guides you through the same Titler panel setup depicted here. Open the Titler_Workout.wmv file, located in the Video Tutorials folder. When the file loads in Windows Media Player, press Alt+Enter to play it back at full-screen size.

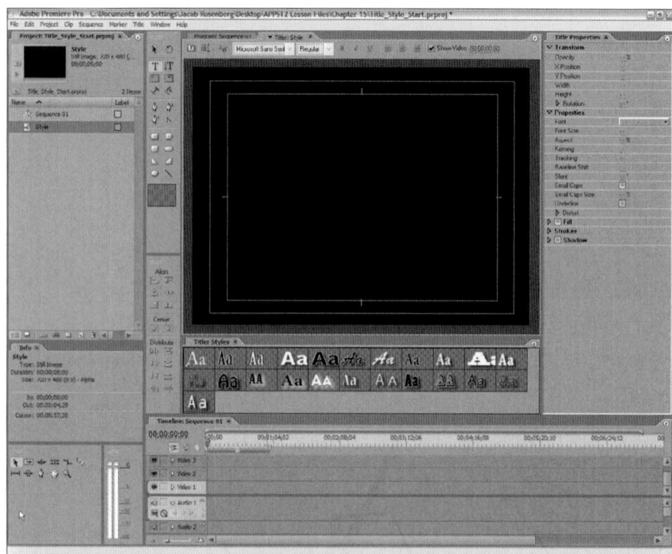

Figure 15.1 When you've finished rearranging your Titler workspace (see the video tutorial on the book's disc), it should look like this.

With Premiere Pro 2.0 you can create a still, roll, or crawl title directly from the Title menu or with a keyboard shortcut. Because the titles are getting saved into the project file itself, when you create a new title, you must assign a name to it to begin working with it.

Version 2.0's new frame- and panel-based interface also makes the Titler customizable with your workspace layout. Although moving all these panels around may seem awkward, refer to Figures 15.1c through j to help get your workspace prepared for title work. By saving this workspace, you can now easily switch from any current workspace to this custom workspace, which is efficient for creating titles.

If you are having too much trouble with this step (and believe me, it can get confusing), you can copy the APPST2 Lesson Files/Chapter 15/Title Layout file into your c:\Documents and Settings\username\My Documents\Adobe\Premiere Pro\2.0\Layouts folder. Quit and restart Premiere Pro. The title workspace should now appear in your Workspace menu. Keep in mind that my desktop resolution is 1280 × 1024.

3. From the Tool panel, select the Rounded Rectangle tool and create a rectangle in the center of your Title panel. Readjust only the Width and Height in the Transform Values to be 325 and 80, respectively (**Figure 15.2**).

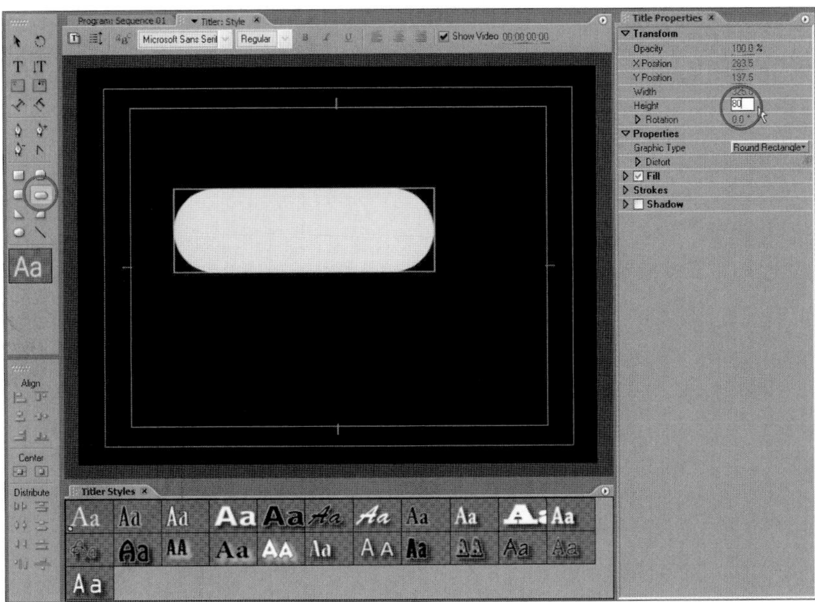

Figure 15.2 To create an object, click and drag using the object creation tool of your choice; I used the Rounded Rectangle tool. When using the object creation tool, the range of your drag determines the size of the object. If you want your object to have an exact width and height, be sure the object is selected (as pictured) and adjust the two parameters in the Titler's Transform section. Notice Width is manually set to 325 and Height to 80.

For this title, you need a simple, but striking object that can be centered in the lower third of the frame and fit text. With a little bit of distortion, you will alter the dimensions of this object to look more stylish.

4. With the new object selected, twirl down the Properties listing in the Title Properties panel, and then twirl down Distort. Assign 20% to X and 30% to Y (**Figure 15.3**).

   The Distort values pinch the selected object on its X and Y axes. To distort the opposite direction, use a negative Distort value.

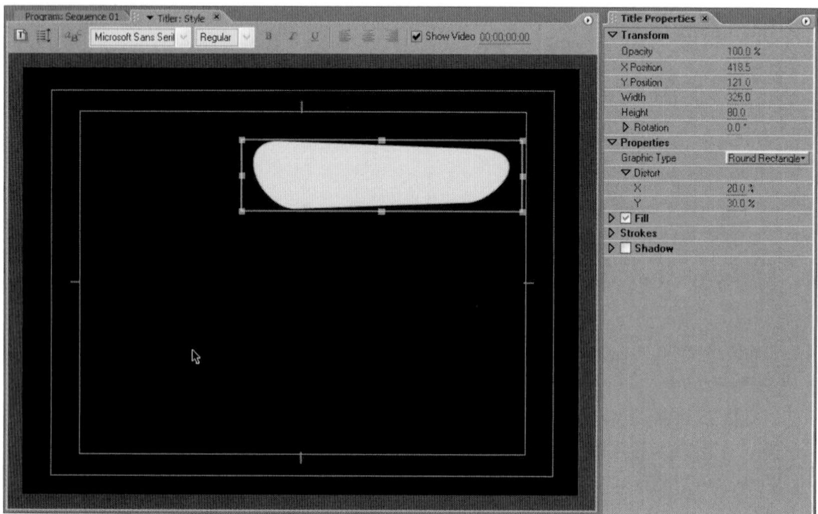

Figure 15.3 With the object selected, you can further adjust its properties in the Title Properties panel. Adjusting the Properties/Distort settings give the current object an obtuse shape.

5. With the object still selected, in the Title Properties panel make sure the Fill check box is checked and twirl down the Fill listing. For Fill Type, select 4 Color Gradient. Click on the upper-left square of the Gradient display so that it is punched out and selected. Click the color swatch next to Color Stop Color to open the Color Picker (**Figure 15.4**). Select the values R0, G138, B0, and click OK. Click to select the lower-right square of the gradient, and assign that position the same color value.

   The Fill listing determines the coloring that fills your selected text or object. Of the several choices in the drop-down menu, I think the 4 Color Gradient offers a good method of creating a professional-looking title with more color depth.

Your 4 Color Gradient is now diagonally green from northwest to southeast and diagonally white from northeast to southwest. For this step, you just assigned a basic color for the object. You can easily change the color for your subsequent projects.

6. Click the Sheen check box, and twirl down the Sheen listing. Click the Color Picker, and assign a darker green (R0, G102, B0). Click OK. Set Size to 35, and leave Angle at 90 degrees (**Figure 15.5**).

A *sheen* is essentially a line that appears in the fill coloring of your object. Using the Size, Angle, and Offset parameters, you can position that line wherever you want within the boundaries of the object. While you based your initial object coloring on a green value, the sheen is dark green, so that when applied it almost looks like the color starts dark in the center and in two corners it gets a little bit lighter. If you are using a different color than green, the guideline is for the gradient to have the base color and the sheen to be the same color, only darker.

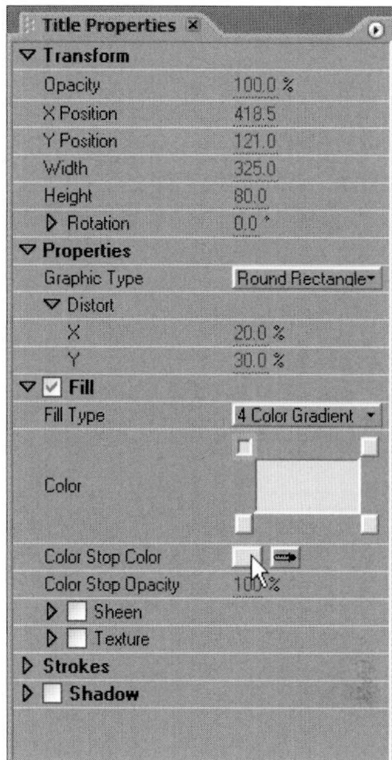

Figure 15.4 When you assign colors to a gradient, you must first click the color box for the position that you want to assign. The selected position will look like it's punched out. To assign a specific color to that position, click the Color Picker box shown here beneath the mouse. Additionally, you can assign color using the eyedropper, which allows you to pick a color from any region of the desktop. This is very helpful for picking a color that is a part of your video frame, but may be difficult to identify in the Color Picker.

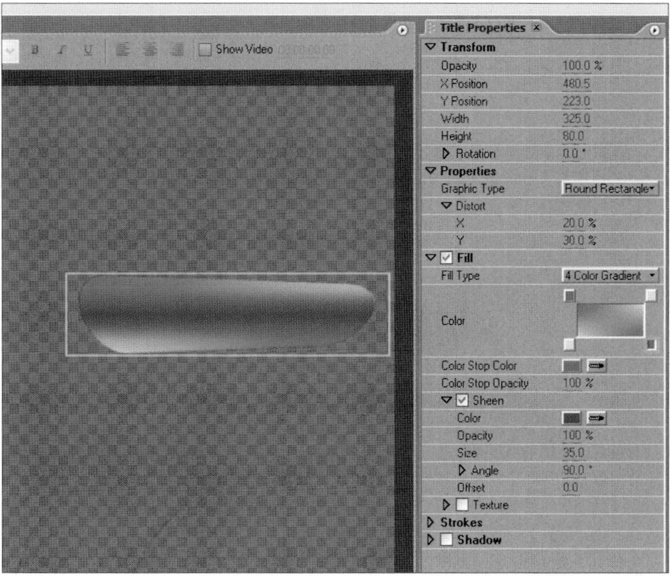

Figure 15.5 Sheens are an integral part of adding subtle depth, gloss, and elegance to a title object. In this image, you can see how much better the object's coloring looks with the dark green sheen through the center of the object; this gives more depth to the green color and allows the white to be more subtle.

Inner strokes are lines that trace the inner contours of the object or text and that stack and expand inward. *Outer strokes* are outlines that begin on the edge of the object and grow outward as their size increases.

7. Twirl up the Fill listing, then twirl down the Stroke listing. Click the Add button next to Outer Strokes, and twirl down the Outer Strokes listing. Twirl down the newly checked Outer Strokes listing, and assign the following values:

   Type: **Edge** — Fill Type: **Solid**
   Size: **4** — Color: **R0, G60, B0**

   The guideline for the first outer stroke color was an even darker green than the fill's sheen. In the same way that the fill can have its own sheen, individual strokes can have a sheen applied to them. For this lesson, the combination of multiple outer strokes with different sheens creates a great-looking object.

8. Click the Sheen check box for the first Outer Stroke, and twirl down the Sheen listing. Enter the following values, then twirl up the Outer Stroke listing (**Figure 15.6**):

   Color: **R229, G255, B196**
   Size: **25**
   Angle: **260**

   For the first outer stroke sheen, you chose a light green/yellow color that is closer to the corner white

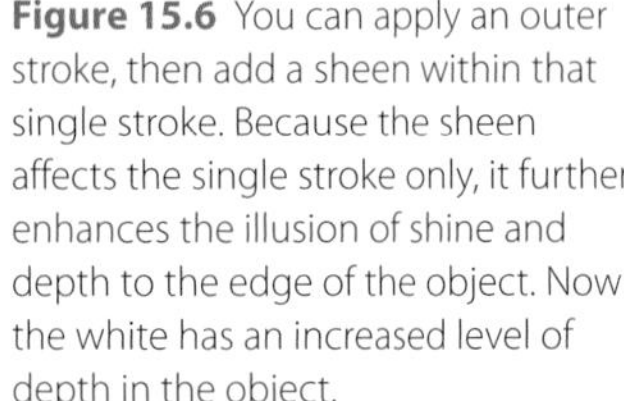
Figure 15.6 You can apply an outer stroke, then add a sheen within that single stroke. Because the sheen affects the single stroke only, it further enhances the illusion of shine and depth to the edge of the object. Now the white has an increased level of depth in the object.

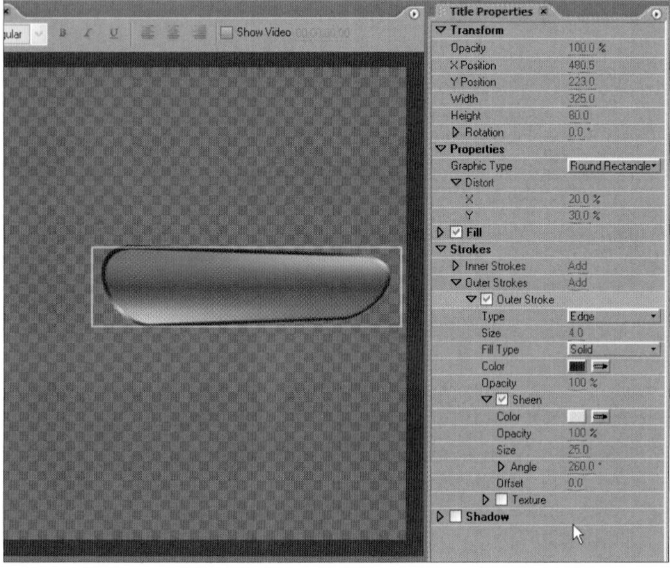

than the corner green. Adjusting its angle, you positioned the sheen near the curves of the object. This positioning gives the illusion of added dimension to the object. The slight change in color makes a distinction between the fill and the stroke. To add the finishing touches on the object, add another outer stroke.

9. Add a second outer stroke, and assign the values:

   Type: **Edge**
   Size: **4**
   Fill Type: **Solid**
   Color: **Default Black**
   Opacity: **100%**

10. Click the Sheen check box to add a sheen. Assign the values:

    Color: **Default White**
    Opacity: **100%**
    Size: **40**
    Angle: **100**
    Offset: **0.0**

    Each additional stroke is applied to the edge of the previous stroke, not the edge of the initial object. For this step, you added a final black outer stroke and used the same sheen technique to give it the appearance of depth (**Figure 15.7**). The black outer stroke gives the object a definitive outer edge and completes its design.

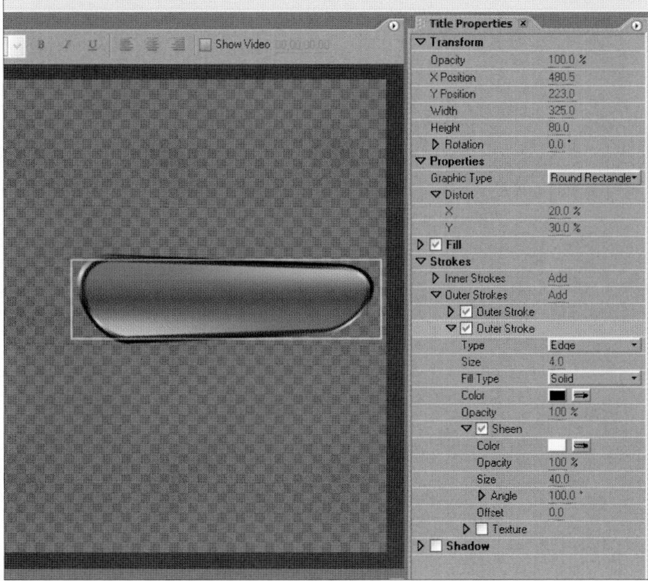

Figure 15.7 With two outer strokes, each with a slightly different sheen color and sheen position, you can easily create the illusion of depth for any object created in the Titler. Here, the edge looks metallic, as if there was light shining on it.

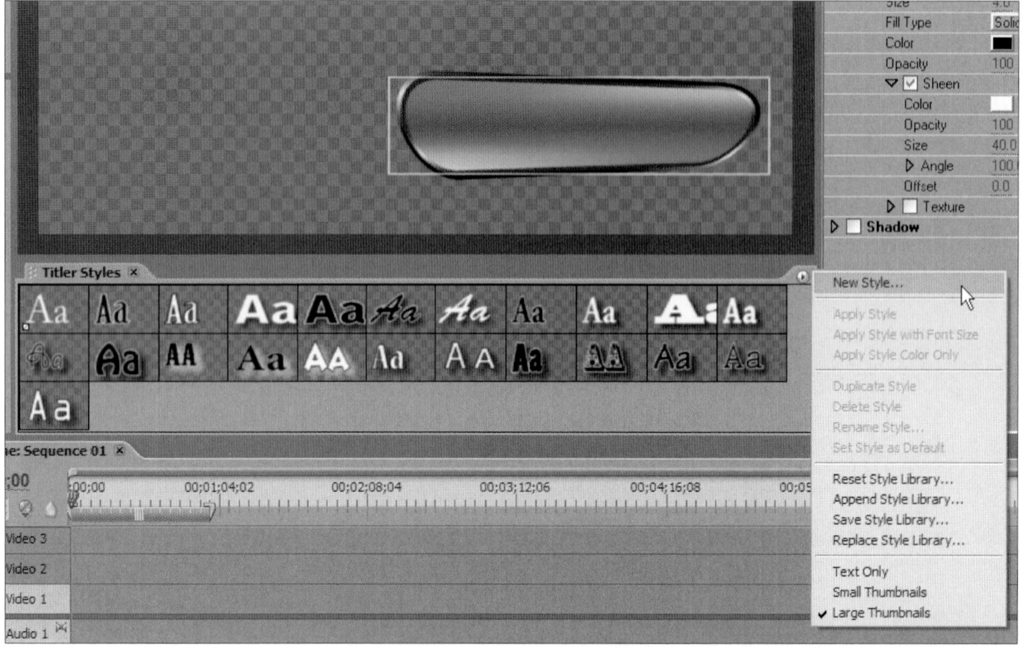

a

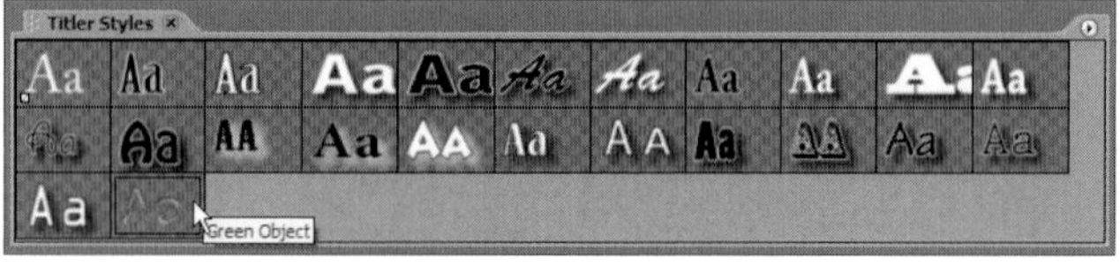

b

Figures 15.8a and b With an object selected, creating a new style automatically saves the current properties of the selection as a custom style setting (a). Once a new style has been created, it becomes available for reuse in your Titler Styles panel (b). Clicking on an object, then clicking on a Titler Style panel swatch, assigns those style properties to the object.

11. With the object selected, click the Titler Styles panel wing menu and select New Style. Name the style Green Object. Click OK (**Figures 15.8a** and **b**).

    In your Titler Styles panel, Premiere Pro creates a new swatch that reflects the entire object style properties for the object you just created. Whenever you create a new style, the style will be added as the last swatch in the Titler Styles panel.

12. Select the Rectangle tool, and create a new object in your Title window. With the new object created and selected, click the last thumbnail that you just added in the Styles palette.

By creating a thumbnail for the object style properties, you now have the ability to apply custom styles to multiple, different types of objects or text.

The final and most important element of this lesson is to emphasize the ease in which you can save and apply a customized style. Using this workflow, you can create your own title elements and save them for future work so that you don't waste time repeating the same design steps. If you modify your design on a new object, you can create a new style from that object by selecting it and then accessing the Styles panel wing menu and choosing New Style.

To see some final title objects, open the file Title_Style_Finish.prproj and open the Objects title. You'll be able to see how I adjusted individual parameters, increasing the fill sheen for certain objects and shifting the position and size of the stroke sheen in other objects. To further understand the technique of creating attractive and effective object styles, open any of the title templates and select an object element. Its style properties will be active and easy for you to browse in the Object Style palette.

Creating a Custom Text Style and Saving a Custom Template

Creating a custom text style is quite similar to creating a custom object style. The main difference is that working with text enables you to define several additional text-specific parameters as well. You'll investigate adding styles to text in the steps that follow. By the end of the lesson, you will combine the text with the object you created earlier to produce a good-looking, lower-third title template.

To change styles for text, select the text element and click the new style swatch. Premiere updates the text with the style of the selected swatch. To update a text element's fill, strokes, and shadow properties, but not its text properties, hold down the Ctrl key while you click another style swatch. With the Ctrl key held down, the original text properties remain intact but the fill, strokes, and shadow update.

1. Open the project file Text_Style_Start.prproj from the APPST2 Lesson Files/Chapter 15 folder. Double-click on the Style title file in the Project panel to open the title. If you are not already using our custom Title Workspace, follow the layout hints in Step 1 of the previous lesson.
2. Using the Type tool, click in the title frame and enter:

   First Lastname

   Use upper- and lowercase as shown. From the top of the Titler panel, select Myriad from the font drop-down menu and then Bold from the menu to its right (see **Figure 15.9a**). In the Title Properties panel, change Properties > Font Size to 40. Click the check box for Small Caps and change the Small Caps Size to 80% (see **Figure 15.9b**).

a

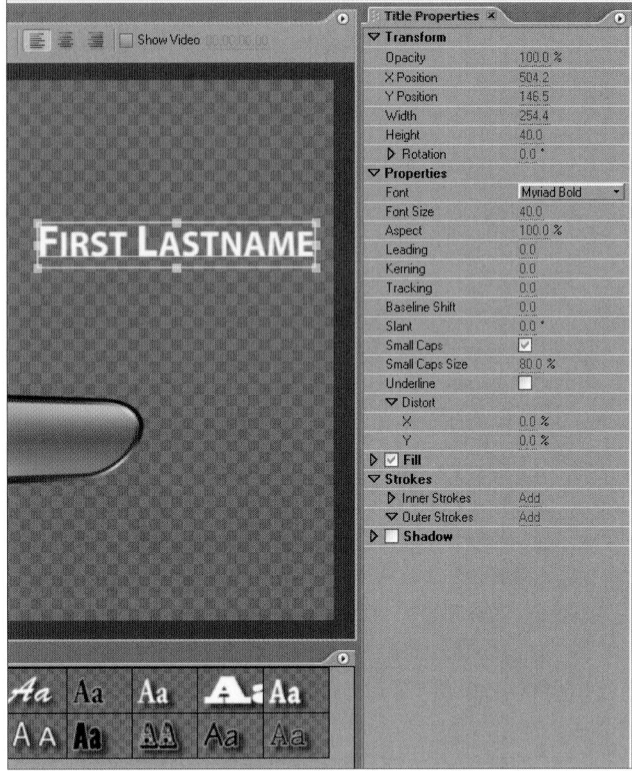

b

Figures 15.9a and b With the Font browser built into the Titler panel, it's easy to see what any font looks like (a). With a text element selected, consult the Title Properties area to see and adjust its font name, font size, Small Caps status, and Small Caps Size (b).

With text selected, you can change the displayed font from the drop-down menu at the top of the Titler panel. This menu, new in 2.0, shows you a preview of the font, as well as its name. If the font has associated bold, italics, or other font-specific properties, you can activate and select them from the drop-down menu to the right of the Font menu. Adjusting the size of the text was necessary to fit it into your object. Turning on Small Caps switches every character into capital letters. Adjusting the Small Caps Size enables you to preserve the relationship of the upper- and lowercase letters by reducing the size of the letters originally typed in lowercase. The choice to turn on Small Caps was strictly a creative decision for the design of this title template.

Premiere Pro supports TrueType font sizes. When you use a TrueType font in Photoshop with a size of 38, the same font at the same size will be exactly the same in Premiere Pro. In previous versions, the Titler's font sizes were a bit bigger. The titles you created in version 1.0 of Premiere Pro should automatically convert to a new size when you open them in 1.5 or 2.0 so as to not appear different.

3. In the Title Properties panel, twirl up the Properties listing, and twirl down the Fill listing. For the selected text, assign 4 Color Gradient as the Fill Type. Assign the following color values for the gradient (**Figure 15.10**):

Top Left corner box: **R255, G255, B191**
Top Right: **R255, G255, B148**
Bottom Left: **R247, G247, B89**
Bottom Right: **R242, G223, B78**

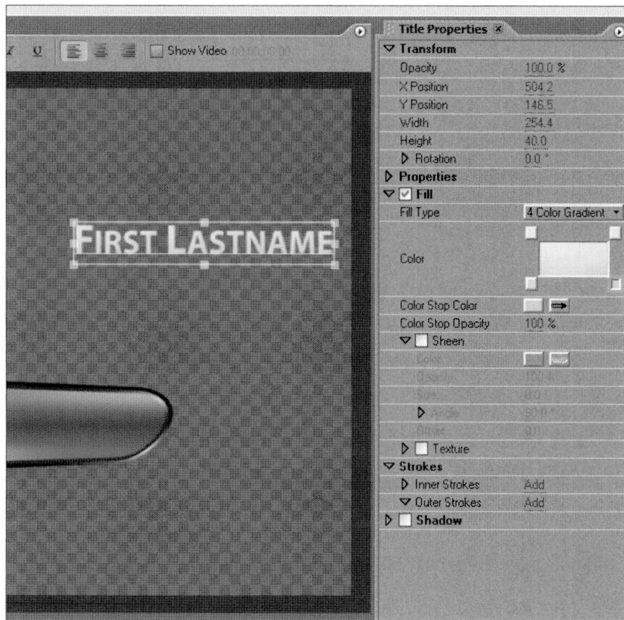

Figure 15.10 For the 4 Color Gradient fill of the text, the yellow's intensity increases over the course of the gradient. Using yellow for text is recommended in certain titles, because pure white can tend to be too bright. This light, subtle yellow color will be easy to read on top of the object's green gradient.

Instead of having two colors in this gradient as you did for the object, you set each corner of the gradient to gradually increase the intensity of yellow.

4. Twirl up the Fill listing, and twirl down the Stroke listing. Add one outer stroke, and assign the values:

   Type: **Edge** Color: **Default Black**
   Size: **14** Opacity: **100%**
   Fill Type: **Solid**

5. Click the Sheen check box for the outer stroke, and enter the values:

   Color: **R255, G255, B168** Size: **60**
   Opacity: **60%** Angle: **65**

   As you learned with the object, adding a sheen can create a subtle illusion of physical depth. For the first stroke, you added a sheen similar in color to the fill color. At first glance, this sheen looked far too strong, but once you reduced its opacity, it blended in with the stroke. When you close the text style by adding another black outer stroke, it will look great.

6. Twirl up the current outer stroke, and click Add to create a second outer stroke. Twirl down the second Outer Stroke listing, and assign the values:

   Type: **Edge** Color: **Default Black**
   Size: **14** Opacity: **100%**
   Fill Type: **Solid**

   Adding the second outer stroke gives a final outline that properly defines the visible text.

7. Twirl up the Outer Strokes listing, then click the Shadow check box and twirl down the Shadow listing. Enter the following Shadow values:

   Color: **Default Black** Distance: **10**
   Opacity: **50%** Size: **0**
   Angle: **122** Spread: **35**

   While Opacity controls the transparency of the shadow, Spread gently increases its size and things out the emphasis of the color. For this adjustment, you want a shadow that is reasonably close to the text with a spread that still emphasizes the shape of the text (**Figure 15.11**).

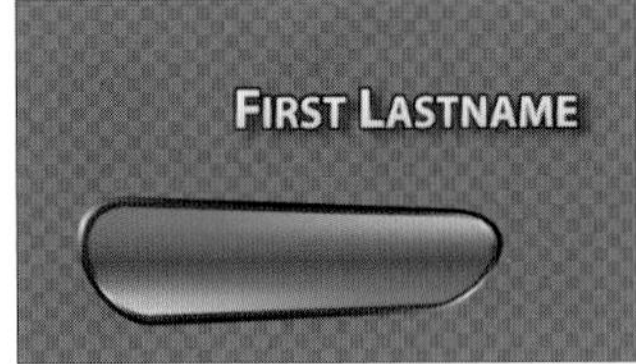

Figure 15.11 The result of your style adjustments is a very clean-looking text element that will stand out on top of another object.

8. With the text selected in the Titler panel, click on the wing menu of the Styles Panel and select New Style. Name the new style Custom Yellow Text, and click OK.

   Saving and preserving a custom style for text works the same as for an object.

9. Using the Selection tool, choose the text and object (Shift-click each, or drag and marquee select them both). With both selected, click the Alignment button for Horizontal Center, then click the Alignment button for Vertical Center. With the objects still selected on top of each other, click the Horizontal Center button then finally right-click again Position > Lower Third (**Figures 15.12a**, **b**, and **c** and **Figure 15.13**).

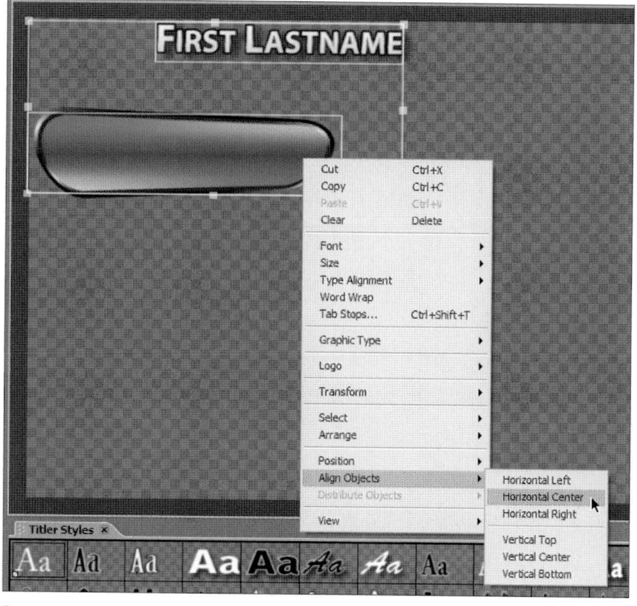

a

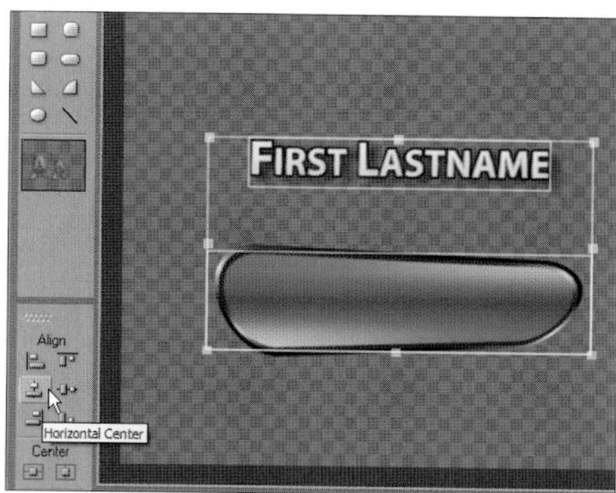

b

c

Figures 15.12a, b, and c Right-clicking within the boundaries of multiple selected objects allows you to access the Align Objects context menu (a). Choosing Horizontal Center yields the same results from the menu as it would by clicking the icon in the Align panel. First the elements are aligned horizontally centered (b), then finally vertically centered so that they fit exactly within each other (c).

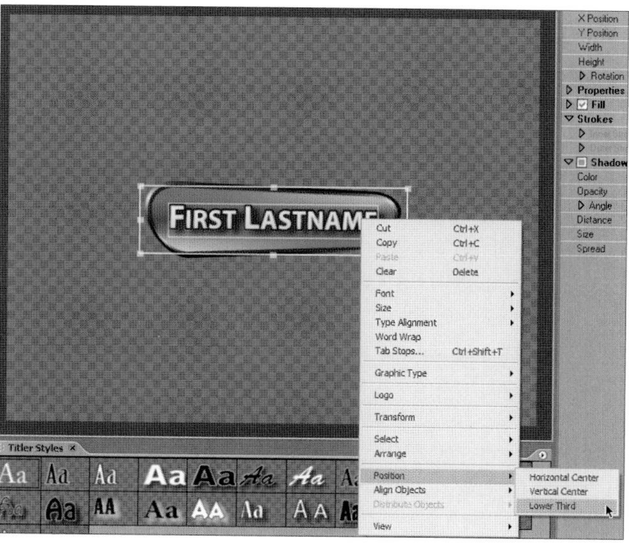

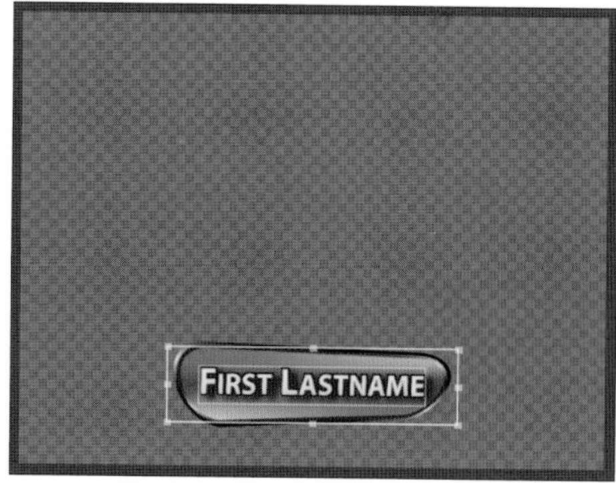

Figure 15.13 Once the elements are placed perfectly together, you can reposition them to the proper location on the screen by accessing the position shortcuts from the right-click or Title > Position menu.

You centered the two elements horizontally first so that the text was in the horizontal center of the object. Aligning them to the vertical center then ensures the text will fit properly inside the absolute center of the object.

Next, you centered the selection horizontally so that it appeared in the absolute center of the frame, then you repositioned it to the lower-third region for later use as a title template to introduce people in your video (**Figures 15.14a** and **b**).

Figures 15.14a and b When you position the Selection tool on top of an area that only the object occupies, Premiere surrounds the object in a transparent box (a). Clicking when the transparent box appears selects the element that the box surrounds (b).

10. Select Title > Templates (**Figure 15.15**) or press Ctrl+J to access the Templates dialog. From the File menu, choose Save As and name this file Merged Styles.

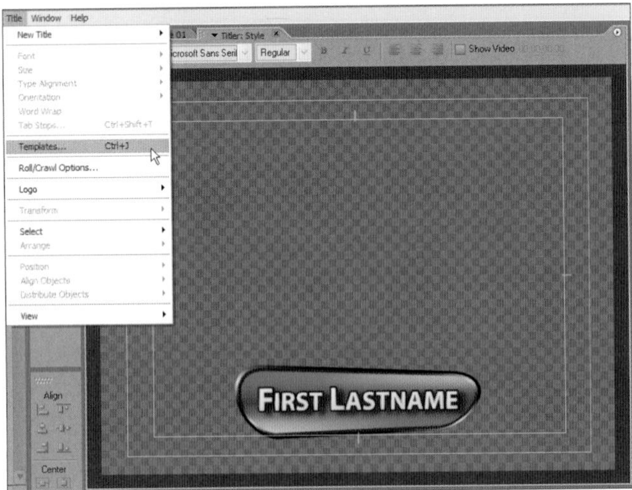

Figure 15.15 Unlike earlier versions, Premiere Pro 2.0 does not have a Templates button in the Titler layout; remember to use the Ctrl+J keyboard shortcut of the Title menu listing.

Creating your own template is quite simple. From any open title you can save a custom template comprised of all the title's elements and their properties. After you save a title as a custom template, that title file resides in the Custom Template folder managed by Premiere Pro—even if you delete the project title on which the template was based. You then can load the title anytime you want by accessing your templates and choosing the custom template, as opposed to importing an exported title file.

11. In the Template dialog's wing menu, select Save Style as Template (**Figure 15.16**), and type Custom Lower Third for the name when prompted. Click OK.

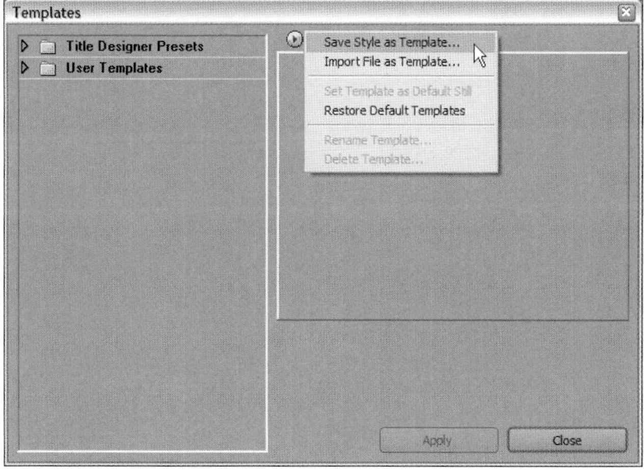

Figure 15.16 Premiere Pro inserts the name of your title in the Save as Template wing menu option. Remember that when you save your open title as a template, Premiere duplicates the title's entire state and layer ordering when making the template.

When you save your current title as a template, you can assign it a custom name. Premiere saves the newly created template into the User Templates folder.

12. With the Templates window still open, twirl down the User Templates listing and select Custom Lower Third

Because you can create still, roll, and crawl titles through a menu command, you can save a default template for each of these title types. When you save a roll as a template, you will have the option to set the roll as a default roll template.

(**Figure 15.17**). Click on the wing menu to view your options (**Figure 15.18**). Select Set Template as Default Still. Close the Templates window.

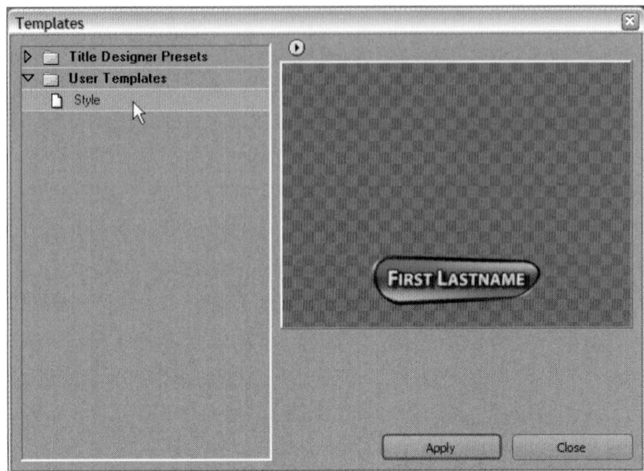

Figure 15.17 Selecting an item in the User Templates listing shows the preview image at right.

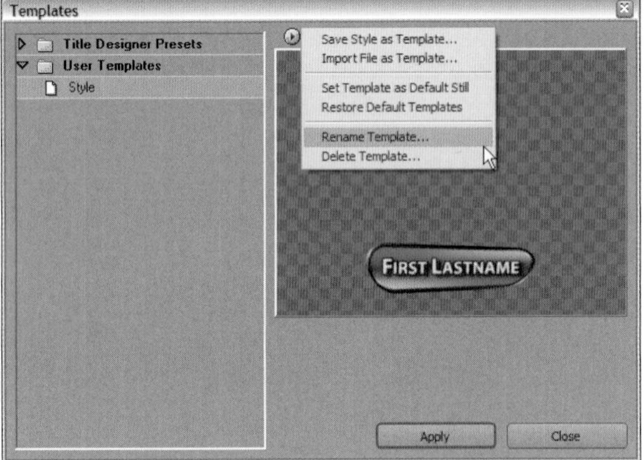

Figure 15.18 A few additional options are available from the wing menu when a template is selected. Note you can now choose Set Template as Default Still, Rename Template, or Delete Template.

After creating your own custom template, you can change its name, delete it, or assign the selected template to be your default title template. Premiere Pro automatically loads the default title template into the Titler's drawing area when you create a new title.

13. Select File > New > Title.

When you open a new title, Premiere Pro automatically loads your default title template. Because you set your lower-third template as the default, you can easily create any number of titles in this format: Just open a new title, enter the appropriate text, and save the title with a unique name. To turn off the modified default title template, open the Template dialog and select Restore Default Template from the wing menu.

Using the foundation from creating an object style, you applied a similar method to the text with some slight variations. Because text letters vary in shape, the sheen technique for adding depth might not always be appropriate; some letters might not have the proper angles for the sheen to work on. To get around this, reduce the sheen's opacity to produce a more subtle effect. By the same token, instead of two diagonal colors in the four-color gradient, you focused on gradually emphasizing one color. This way the letters, which consist of all shapes, have the same general color tone. Once again, the end result was a new style in your Styles Library that you can use again and again in future projects. This lesson also illustrated how easy it is to create custom templates and how they can expedite and streamline your title creation workflow.

More Template Timesavers

Some of the most practical and simple aspects of the Titler are its template functions. As you can deduce from the last step of the previous lesson, templates are ready-made titles with text and objects that you can replace and modify on a project-by-project basis, without altering the original. You can build your own custom title templates as we just did, modify the templates included with the Titler, or use the built-in designs as is.

For the second half of the chapter, you will modify a ready-made template and resave it as a custom template and then create a credit roll template, which is very valuable for most production work.

These lessons rely on such basic title functions as selecting, moving, and modifying the properties of existing objects in the title template. The final lesson goes a bit further, exploring Tab Stops, Roll/Crawl Options, and Properties settings for text.

Adding Logos and Modifying Pre-Made Templates

When you want help refining the style and eloquence of your titles, the best place to look is the Templates dialog. You very easily can load one of the more than 100 built-in templates, then alter its elements to suit your project needs. In this lesson, which assumes you're putting together a DVD of a baby's first birthday, you'll learn how to alter a template and save the adjustments as a new template.

You will open one of the templates in the Celebrations folder and add a picture to personalize the title. Just in case your family has a baby boom, you will save the modified template as a custom template. An important element of this lesson is incorporating pictures or graphic file elements to your title document: You will explore adding a logo as well as using an image for a fill texture.

NOTES

Premiere Pro can insert a logo or a texture, but what's the difference? A *logo* is the type of identifying graphic for which people and companies pay a lot of money. They are very client-oriented, professional graphics that are meant to be used as delivered. The logo tools manage the size and aspect ratios of logos, providing minimal support for altering them artistically. *Textures*, on the other hand, are all about the art and adding mood, depth, and feeling to your graphics and titles.

So, if you want to preserve the aspect ratio of a graphic, you can insert it as a logo and reduce the adjustments that can be applied to the image. If you want to blend the graphic with other title elements, then insert it as a texture.

1. Open the Template_Start.prproj file from the APPST2 Lesson Files/Chapter 15 folder. Be sure you are using the workspace layout defined in the first lesson of this chapter. BdayBoy.jpg, which is located in the same folder, is the primary image (logo) that you will incorporate into the title template.

2. Select File > New > Title or press F9 to open a new title. Name it Baby_Template. Press Ctrl+J on your keyboard and in the Templates dialog, go to Title Designer Presets > General > Baby Boy > Baby Boy Low3. Click Apply to load the template.

   Once the template is loaded, you can modify and manipulate any of the title elements without affecting the original template. For this template, you want to replace the image of the rattle with a picture of the baby boy. There are two ways of doing this; I want to show you the most efficient method.

3. Using the Selection tool, select the rattle graphic in the lower-left corner and twirl down the Properties in the Title Properties panel. The Logo Bitmap should display a small version of the rattle graphic. Click within the

boundaries of this graphic (**Figure 15.19**). From the Choose a Texture Image dialog, choose the BdayBoy.jpg file from the APPST2 Lesson Files/Chapter 15 folder.

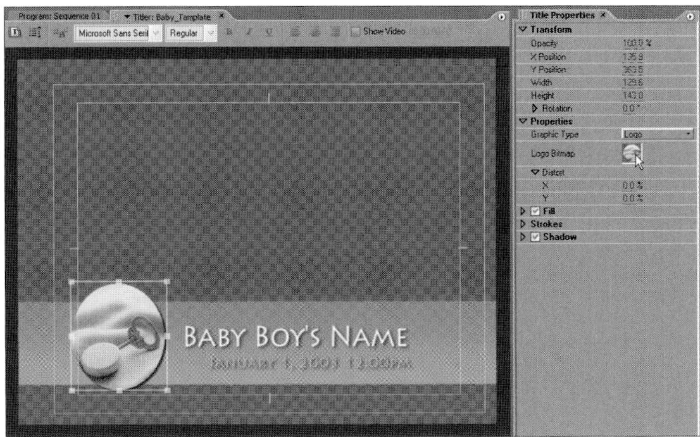

Figure 15.19 With a logo selected from your title, you can see the dimension of the logo in Transform area; this logo is 129.6 × 143. In the Properties area you can see a preview of the selected logo. Clicking on that logo allows you to replace the current logo with a new one, preserving the exact dimensions of the original.

When a logo is selected in your title, you can quickly replace it by clicking on the Logo Bitmap icon in the Properties area of the Title Properties panel. Using this technique replaces the current logo with the new logo using the exact dimension and sizing that the previous logo had.

An alternate method for this same task would be to right-click within the boundary of your Titler panel and select Logo > Insert Logo. This inserts the Logo at its full size, and then you must manually resize it to get it to the proper dimensions.

Note that because the rattle was not the same aspect ratio as the BdayBoy logo, there is a slight distortion to the image.

4. With the Logo of the boy still selected, turn off the Shadow setting in the Title Properties panel, twirl down

and expand Strokes, and then expand Outer Strokes. Add an outer stroke with the settings (**Figure 15.20**):

Type: **Depth**
Size: **9**
Angle: **315**
Fill Type: **Solid**
Color: **Black**
Opacity: **70%**

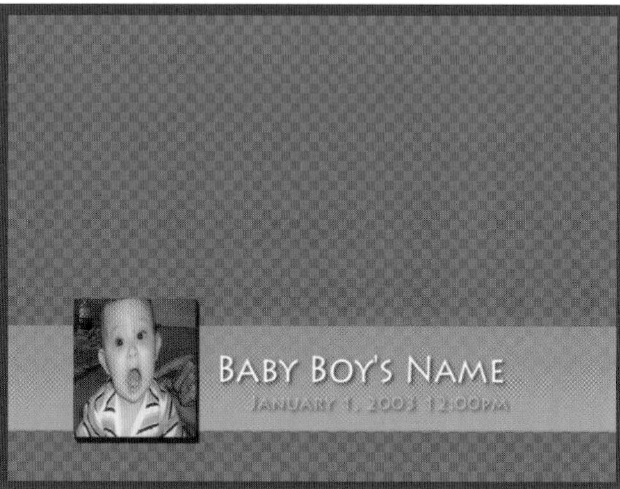

Figure 15.20 The rattle logo image was replaced with a new image, and its properties were adjusted because the new logo is a rectangle and not an oval.

Because you replaced the rattle logo, the properties of the object itself are still intact. Because the rattle was a circle and this is a square, you turned off the shadow and instead, added a stroke.

You now have a custom picture in your template, but say you would prefer it in an oval like the rattle graphic. The primary limitation of using the Logo feature is that the original shape and dimensions of the file will be adhered to in the title. If the picture is a square, you can't just change it to a circle. This is good when you are bringing in corporate logos that should not be adjusted or distorted; you can, however, work around this limitation by assigning a logo or graphic to fill an object.

5. Right-click on the baby picture, and clear the file from the title. Press the E key to select the Ellipse tool, and make a circle in the bottom-left corner of the title frame. Click the default style swatch in the first position of the Titler Styles panel to give the object a default white fill. The circle should be approximately 140 × 140.

Instead of using the square image of the baby, you created a circular object in which you will use the baby picture as a texture fill.

6. With the newly created circle selected, twirl down the Fill listing in the Title Properties panel. Check the box for Texture, and twirl it down. Click in the blank gray box to the right of the word "Texture," and select the BdayBoy.jpg file from the Choose a Texture Image dialog box. Click Open (**Figure 15.21**).

   To add a picture, graphic, or grayscale texture to any object, activate the Texture Fill and select your desired texture file. With the texture in place, you can modify it a number of ways.

Figure 15.21 No matter what type of object you create, you can fill it not only with gradients and colors, but also with textures or graphic images. Here you can see the selected texture in a small preview area and the circle now filled with the image of the boy.

7. Continuing in the Title Properties panel, twirl down Fill, then Texture, then Scaling, and set Object X and Object Y both to Face from the drop-down menus. Set Horizontal and Vertical to 110%. Next, twirl down Alignment, and set Object X and Object Y both to Face. Change X Offset to 2.0 and Y Offset to -1.0.

   When you are working with a texture fill, you need to keep in mind some scaling and alignment rules for the texture that is filling the object. In terms of scaling, Clipped Face and Face resize the graphic to fit within the boundaries of the object it is filling. Texture uses the graphic's default size as the dimensions of the fill image. You then scaled the texture to make it a little larger within the oval.

If you reduced the size of the texture to be smaller than the boundaries of the object shape, the Tile check boxes allow the image to tile vertically and horizontally in order to fill the object. Without tile, there would be black space around the image where it did not fill the object.

Once the image is scaled and placed within the boundaries of the object, Alignment lets you offset or slightly nudge the image horizontally or vertically. Here, shifting the image a bit to the left centered it within the object.

When the Alignment Rule X is set to Left, the texture locks to the left edge and it grows to the right. Offsetting the X value by 2 moves that left edge a value of 2 to the left; it is offset. Rule Y is set to Top, this means it is locked to the top edge and grows downward. With a Y Offset of -1, you pull the image one pixel toward the top. In order for no black space to appear in the area above the image where it was pushed down, tiling is turned on. Tiling repeats the texture from all edges.

8. Add an inner stroke to the selected object:

   Type: **Edge**
   Size: **6.0**
   Fill Type: **Solid**
   Color: **White**
   Opacity: **100%**

9. Add a shadow with the settings (**Figure 15.22**):

   Color: **Black**
   Opacity: **40%**
   Angle: **135**
   Distance: **9**
   Size: **1**
   Spread: **33**

Figure 15.22 The new graphic is now unified with the other elements to match color and shadowing with a far better look and feel than the square image that you originally inserted. If a general logo insert doesn't give you the result you want, consider using an image as a texture within a custom object instead.

The small inner stroke and shadow unify the look of the added object with the look of the title's other objects. Now that the title is complete, you can save it as a template for continued use.

10. Finally, select and change each of the text elements in the title (Baby Boy's Name and January 1, 2003 12:00 PM) to information relevant to your project. If you like, you now can open the Templates dialog, select Save <Baby_Template> as Template from the wing menu, and name the template. I saved it as New_Baby_Template.

I encourage you to use your own graphics and images in the titles that you create and templates that you modify. Although logos have less flexibility and adjustment qualities (for good reason), you can always add an image or graphic into your title as a texture fill. Design-wise, if you don't feel like you have a good sense of how a title should look, simply load a template and modify it to suit your needs.

Creating a Custom Credit Roll Template

To provide you with more experience working with text and moving titles, the final lesson of this chapter will guide you through creating your own custom credit roll. Although your font taste and spacing may deviate from the example, the most important things to learn are the basic settings and adjustments needed for a simple, clean credit roll. With that in mind, you will focus on text spacing and tab stops.

1. Open Rolling_Title_Start.prproj from the APPST2 Lesson Files/Chapter 15 folder. From the Title menu, select Title > New Title > Default Roll. Name the title Credit Roll. Select the Area Type tool from the Tool panel, then click and drag from the top-left corner of the inner title-safe boundary down and to the right just out of frame with the right side of the tool on the edge of the right title-safe boundary (see **Figure 15.23**).

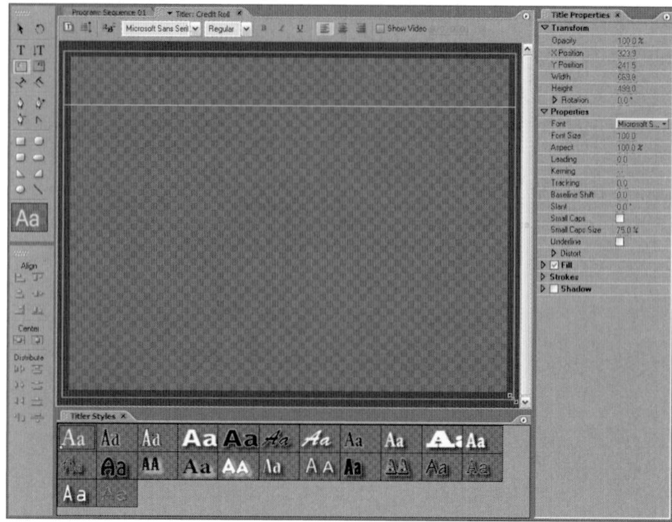

Figure 15.23 Because you want to roll from above the top of the frame to below the bottom of the frame, you want your text square to be larger than the inner frame in the Titler drawing area.

This first step shows you a new feature for 2.0: the ability to automatically create a rolling credit from a menu, as opposed to selecting the option from the Titler panel itself. The rest of the step defines the area in which the rolling text will be written and roll from. The area you defined is the absolute boundary in which your text can roll. By defining the top and bottom of the area text to be outside the visible frame (as delineated by the title-safe boundaries), you ensured that your credit will roll up and then out as if it came from below the image and disappeared above the image. If you instead created a square that fit inside the title-safe boundary, the rolling text would appear rolling up in the lower-third portion of the frame and disappear as it reached the upper-third portion of the frame.

2. Go to the wing menu of the Titler panel and turn on Tab Markers. Either select Title > Tab Stops or press Ctrl+Shift+T to open the Tab Stops dialog. Click in the white space above the ruler bar to add a tab stop. Position the tab stop so that it rests in the center of the drawing area on top of the center hash mark in the title-safe boundary. Click the Centered Tab button to make this tab a center justified tab stop. Add a second tab stop just to the right of the left edge, and click the Left Justified button. Add a third and final tab stop just

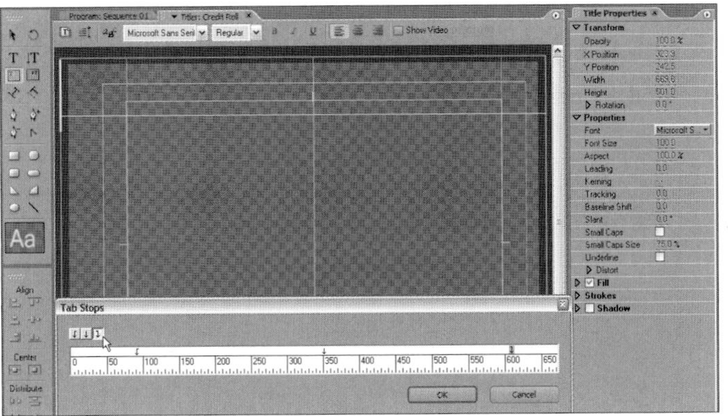

Figure 15.24 Each of the tab stops has an associated justification for the text that is assigned to it. Each tab stop directly corresponds with the yellow tab stop lines in the Titler. The center tab stop is center justified, the left tab is left justified, and the selected right tab stop is right justified.

to the left of the right edge, and click the Right Justified button. Click OK (**Figure 15.24**).

When you tab to the stops you set, the text you add will assume the right, left, or center justification that the tab stop represents. Try adding some text to see how it looks.

3. Select the Type tool, and press the Tab key twice to navigate to the center tab stop. Type the word "Group." In the Title Properties panel, twirl down Properties and set Courier New > Bold for Font. Set Font Size to 30 and Leading to 8.2. Back in the drawing area, press Enter to create a new line. Press the Tab key once, and type the word "Position." Press the Tab key twice, and type First Lastname. Select the second line of text from the word "Position" to "Lastname." As shown in **Figure 15.25**, set:

   Font Size: **21.8**
   Leading: **8.2%** T
   Tracking: **–5**

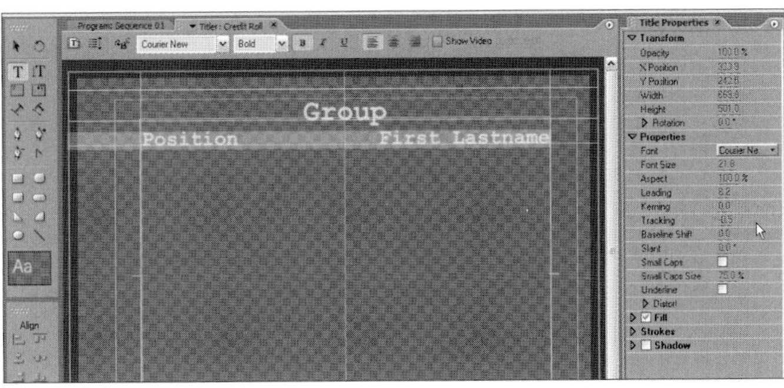

Figure 15.25 By selecting a group of words, you can alter the font size and all the styles properties of the selection separate from that of the other text in the square.

First, you center the main heading for the group of credits to follow. You could change the word "Group" to "Cast" later, for example, if the first section of credits is for the cast of your project. The second line of text creates two listings, one for the cast position and the other for the individual's name. The second line's reduced font size enables more text to fit, and the reduced tracking tightens the space between each letter on a uniform scale. Reducing the leading closes the overall space between the first and second line.

4. With the second line of text still selected, press Ctrl+C to copy it. Click after the letter "e" in Lastname in the second line, and position the cursor at the end of the text on the right tab stop. Press Enter to create a new line. Paste the text onto the second line (Ctrl+V). Repeat this step twice more to create four listing lines. Select these four lines, and reduce their leading to 6.

   Notice that instead of pasting at the first tab stop, you paste at the left edge of the square. The selection for the text recognizes that the first word has a tab stop value of 1 and the second set of words has a tab stop value of 3, so Premiere pastes them accordingly.

5. With the Type tool still selected and the cursor blinking after the last Lastname, press Ctrl+A to select all the text. Copy it (Ctrl+C), deselect the text by clicking after the last Lastname, and then press Enter three times to create three lines of spacing. Paste (Ctrl+V) the text at the current cursor position. Press Enter three more times, and paste again. To extend the Roll area lower than currently assigned, grab the bottom of the Text area and drag it downward to elongate the roll text area (**Figure 15.26**).

   Although the last copied text group is technically off-screen, you can still scroll down through the text and modify the information by dragging the Text area downward allowing you to scroll even further. In these five steps, you created a custom credit roll with groups of text that you can fill on a project-by-project basis. Now it's time to assign the Roll/Crawl Options and save the template.

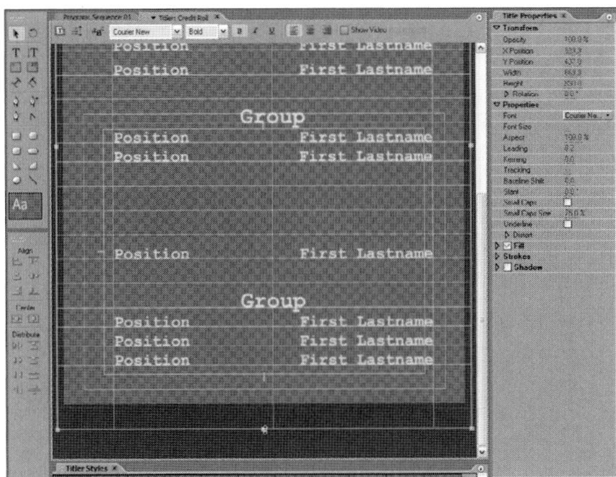

Figure 15.26 To lengthen the roll area, grab the bottom of the text area and manually drag it downward to reveal any text beneath it. Once you have dragged it down, you can scroll with the scroll bar on the right side of the Titler panel to see all the text.

6. From the Title menu, select Roll/Crawl Options. In the resulting dialog, click the check boxes for Start Off Screen and End Off Screen. Click OK. Click the Templates button to open the Templates dialog. From the wing menu, select Save < Credit Roll > as Custom Template. Name the title Custom Roll, and click OK.

   Choosing to start and end your title off screen means that even if you have text at the top of the frame, your titles will start blank and roll the text of your title into frame, then end by rolling the text completely out of frame. The Ease-In and Ease-Out settings slow the title when it first rolls in and when the title ends and rolls out.

The speed of a rolling or crawling title depends on the duration you assign to the title when it is added to the timeline. When added to the timeline, the title file must complete from top to bottom or side to side within the duration it is assigned. If you have 200 lines of text in a rolling title and the title has a duration of only five seconds, for example, the text will fly by in order to get from the top to the bottom in that amount of time. To slow a rolling or crawling title, extend its duration; decrease its duration to speed it up.

To see the title I came up with and how different durations affect the speed at which the title rolls, open Rolling_Title_Finished.prproj from the APPST2 Lesson Files/Chapter 15 folder. You can take a number of clues and tips from this lesson and switch them to customize your tabs stops, font, font size, and line spacing to create your own custom credit template or title with text.

Things to Remember

This chapter certainly covered a lot, from custom objects to custom text, to templates and rolling titles. With text and objects, the fundamental things to remember are that objects and text have the exact same fill, stroke, and shadow properties, the only differences being the text parameters for text elements and the differing geometric shapes for the object elements. If you happen to create a unique text style that you want to add to an object, you can create an object and apply that same style to the object. The object will not convert to text; it will just assume the fill, stroke, and shadow properties of the applied style. The same rules apply when applying an object style to text, except for the fact that object styles will use the default text parameters.

Filling and coloring the elements is by far the most important attribute of the titling process (aside from your choice of fonts for the text). Although the example used strokes of single solid colors, you can fill a stroke with a four-color gradient just as you can an object or text. If at any point while you experiment, you want to save the current style, simply create a new style with the element selected in the Title window.

As for templates, all the clues to making an attractive title reside in the physical properties of the title templates that you like best. If you find a particular template that you really like, simply click on the individual elements that make up the title and scour over all of the settings in the Title Properties panel, especially the Properties twirl down. With an object selected you can see the technique used for filling, adding strokes, and creating more depth to the elements in the title. You can find an object with a sheen, for example, and click the sheen off to see the difference. The more you investigate, the more you'll understand why your favorite templates look the way they do.

Remember, too, that you can change specific text properties of individual text elements in a large group of text. If you want every line to have different leading, fonts, and tracking, for example, select each line and make the adjustments on a line-by-line basis.

Fiddle with the Titler whenever you have spare time; in 2.0, you'll find a ton of new templates for both HD and DV. You'll find that you very easily can create customized templates that will save you time on many later projects. On the other hand, if you create a unique title for a project, consider saving the title as a template. You never know when it will come in handy.

CHAPTER

16

Custom DVD Design

As discussed in Chapter 11, "DVD Basics," Premiere Pro 2.0 supports both the creation of auto-play DVDs as well as customizable menu-based DVDs. This chapter provides a complete workflow for creating a customized menu-based DVD from the Italy map and pictures that you have been working with throughout this section.

You'll start by loading a template into which you will assign relevant Scene markers. You will add and modify the scenes, then continue customizing the background of the DVD menus as well as add your own custom music loop. The chapter completes with the burning of the DVD.

DVD Templates and Scene Marking

Premiere Pro 2.0 comes with a selection of DVD templates that you can assign to any sequence intended for DVD authoring. To load a template for a particular sequence, open the DVD Layout panel and choose the Change the Template option. Let's begin working with our project to make this happen.

1. Open APPST2 Lesson Files/Chapter 16/Custom_DVD01.prproj. Before you start working on this project make sure that your layout looks like **Figure 16.1**.

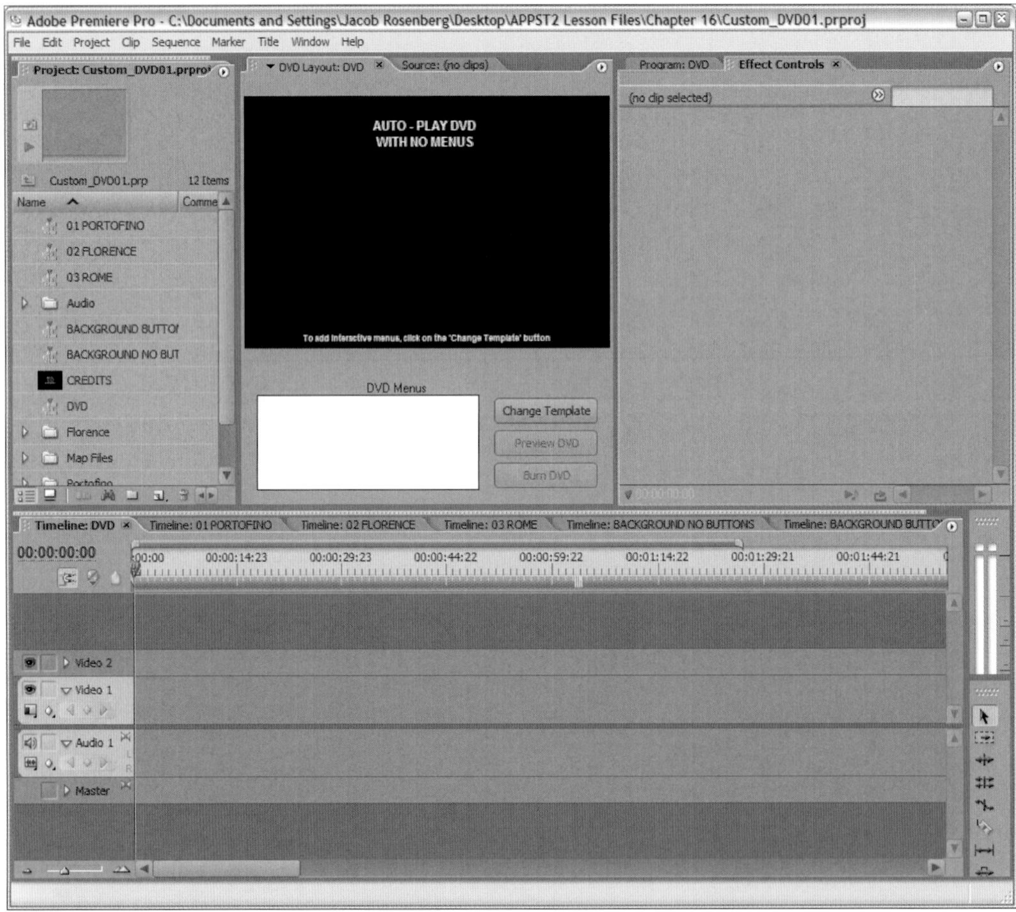

Figure 16.1 Your Project panel, DVD Layout panel, Effect Controls panel, and Timeline panel should be visible in your layout to make the DVD building process more efficient.

I went ahead and added the two remaining photo montages (Portofino and Florence) to complete the Italy photo montage with three complete picture sequences. Each sequence follows the same editorial structure as the Rome sequence created in Chapter 14, "Working with Stills: Motion and Advanced Keyframing."

2. Make sure the DVD sequence is open in the Timeline panel. In the DVD Layout panel, the loaded sequence should be DVD. From the Project panel, drag and drop the 01 PORTOFINO, 02 FLORENCE, and 03 ROME sequences to the DVD sequence in the Timeline panel. Make them adjacent to each other with no gaps and in their numbered order (**Figure 16.2**).

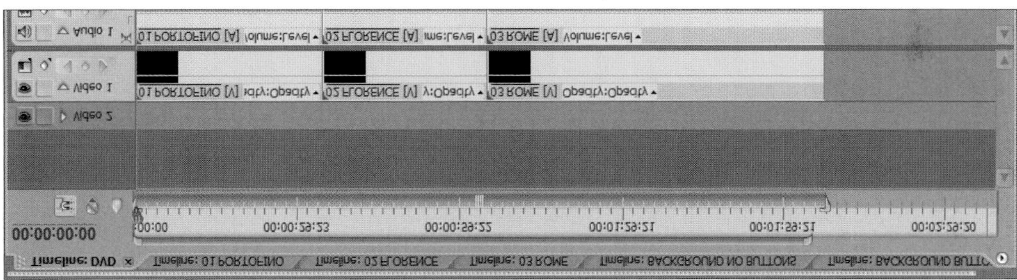

Figure 16.2 Here you quickly laid down the three sequences that make up your photo montage. Nesting each location sequence allowed you to define their boundaries much more efficiently and simplifies the process of defining scenes for the DVD.

Each location is identified in the Project panel by a single sequence that is then nested into the master DVD sequence. Laying down the three location sequences establishes the entire photo montage. Having each location defined by a single nested clip eases the process of defining scenes for your DVD menu. The entire DVD sequence is now the Play All movie track for your DVD, while each of the nested sequences becomes a scene from that movie.

3. With the DVD sequence active in the DVD Layout panel, click the Change Template button. In the DVD Templates dialog, click the button for Apply a Template for a DVD with Menus. From the Theme drop-down menu select Entertainment. Click on the Film Main

Menu template (**Figure 16.3**), and click OK. When the Missing DVD Markers dialog appears asking if you'd like Premiere to create DVD markers automatically (**Figure 16.4**), click Yes. In the Automatically Set DVD Scene Markers dialog, make sure that At Each Scene is checked and click OK (**Figure 16.5**).

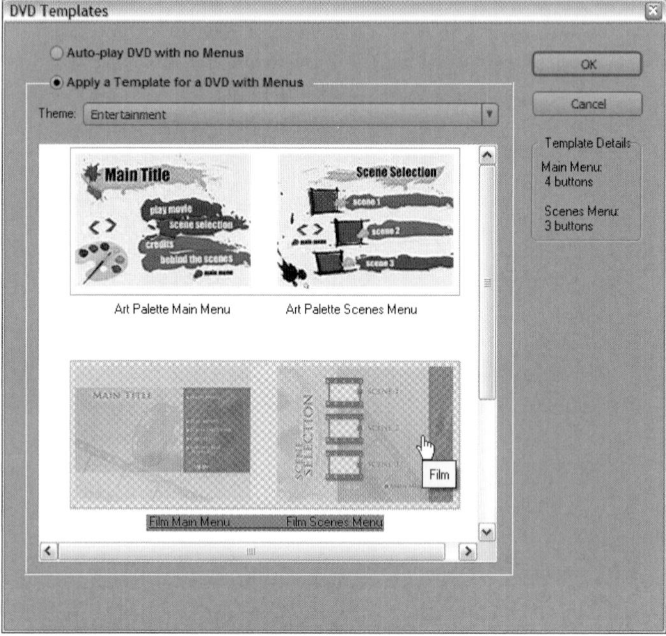

Figure 16.3 First, select a template to use for the DVD. Here, I've chosen Film Main Menu. Click OK.

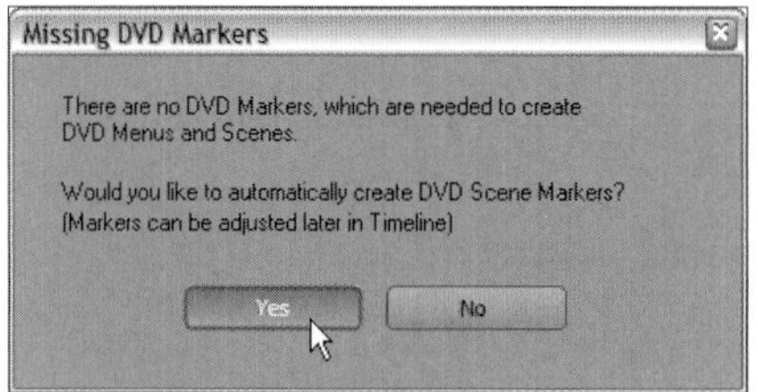

Figure 16.4 A dialog then appears stating that no DVD markers exist in the DVD sequence. To add markers automatically, click Yes.

Figure 16.5 In the final dialog, you choose to have markers automatically added at every scene cut point in your sequence. A scene cut point is defined as an edit.

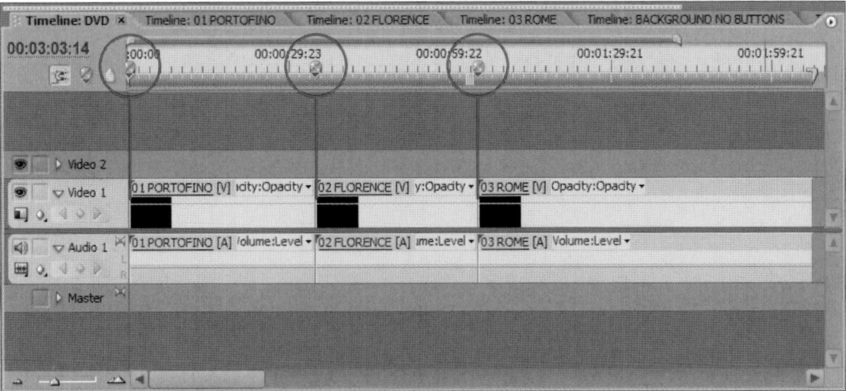

Figure 16.6 Here is the timeline showing three cut points, one for each of the three nested sequences.

With your DVD sequence open in the Timeline panel, the DVD Layout panel also hosts the DVD layout information for the sequence (**Figure 16.6**). Because the default DVD mode for sequences is Auto-play no template is loaded. To apply a template to the active sequence and begin working on menu structure and layout, you selected Change Template.

After you select the template, Premiere looks for DVD markers to populate the template's Scenes menu. If the DVD sequence has no Scene markers, Premiere Pro will create them for you automatically. In step 2, you nested the three location sequences creating three distinct edit points: the start of the sequence with the first location, the cut from the first to second sequence, and the cut from the second sequence to the third. When Premiere analyzes your sequence, any cut in the timeline is defined as a scene point. Choosing to apply a marker at each scene applies a Scene marker to every cut in your sequence. The resulting DVD menu has one Main menu and one Scenes menu with three scenes. If you were to build a DVD with more than three scenes, additional Scenes menus would automatically be created to accommodate the total number of scenes. By default the Film template displays a maximum of three scenes in its Scenes menu. Into the DVD Layout panel, click between

When you plan to customize a template, consider the layout and text of the template as opposed to the exact image contents of it. For the example, I liked the Film template's simple text formatting and its Scenes menu structure, which shows thumbnails with text written horizontally to the right from the thumbnail.

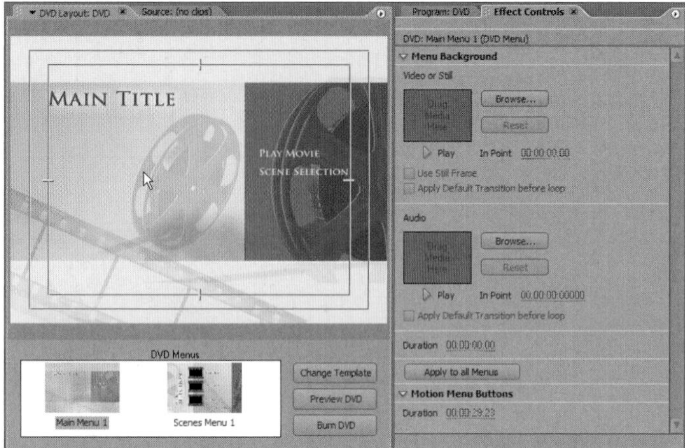

a

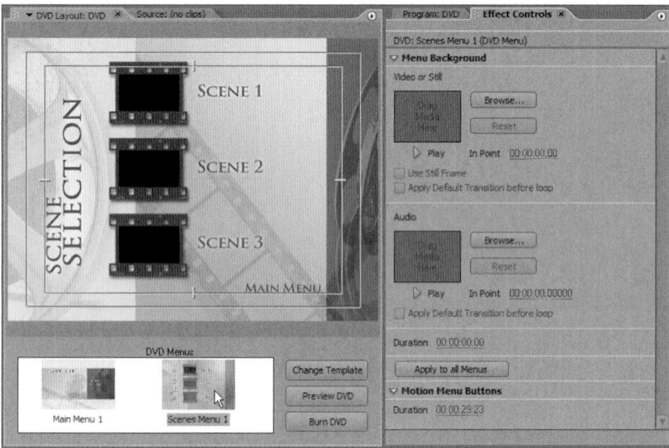

b

Figures 16.7a and b With the DVD Layout panel and Effect Controls panel both open, you can see the layout for the Main menu (a) and the Scenes menu (b), which has three scenes that you can access.

Main Menu 1 (**Figure 16.7a**) and Scenes Menu 1 (**Figure 16.7b**) to see the structure of the DVD you are building.

4. In the DVD sequence, double-click on the first DVD scene marker at the beginning of the sequence. Type Portofino into the Name field (**Figure 16.8a**), then click Next. Type Florence in the Name field for DVD marker 2 of 3, click Next, type Rome in the final marker's Name field, and click OK. Click on Scenes Menu 1 in your DVD Layout panel (**Figure 16.8b**).

   By opening the markers and adding the name that corresponds with the nested sequence beneath the markers you now have a scenes menu that accurately

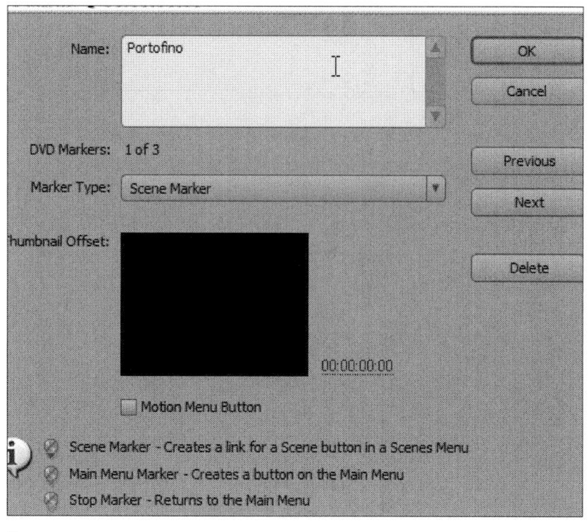

a

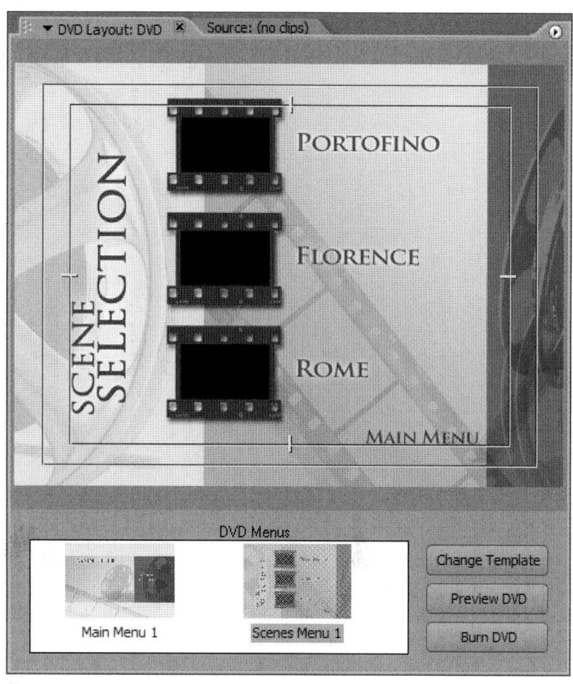

b

Figures 16.8a and b To modify the name of a Scene marker, double-click on the physical marker in the Timeline panel and enter the name in the Name field (a). After step 4 all three markers are named for the montage to which they link (b).

reflects the scene names to which links lead. This is the first true customization step.

5. Activate the DVD sequence in the Timeline panel and press the End key on your keyboard. With the Edit Line aligned to the end of the 03 ROME clip, click the Set DVD Marker button below the Timecode field of the Timeline panel (**Figure 16.9a**). In the resulting DVD Marker dialog box set the Marker Type to Stop Marker, and click OK (**Figure 16.9b**). In the DVD Layout panel, click the Preview DVD button and navigate the menu structure clicking the links you created to familiarize yourself with what leads where.

   The Play Movie command in the Main menu of your DVD layout plays from the beginning of the DVD sequence to the end of the last clip in the sequence. Adding a Stop marker at the end of the 03 ROME clip forces Play Movie to end at that point. (In the next lesson you are going to add another clip to the sequence that serves as an additional track on the DVD.)

a

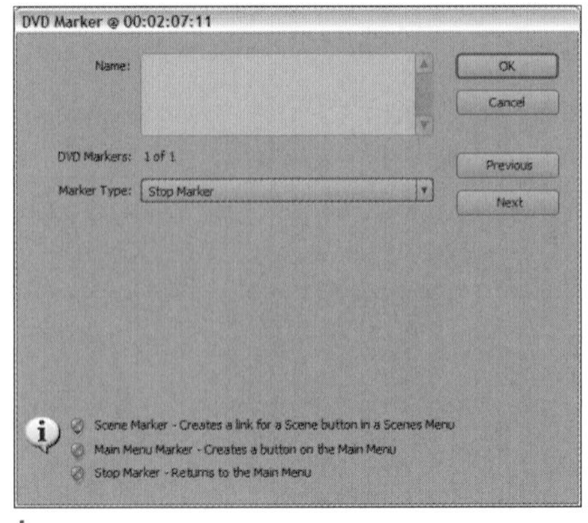

b

Figures 16.9a and b Click the Set DVD Marker button to access the DVD Marker dialog (a). Because the Edit Line is at the end of the sequence's final clip, you assign a Stop marker to signify the end of the sequence (b).

Navigating your DVD in preview mode simulates the user experience. Clicking Play Movie plays the entire sequence in one play. Clicking on Scene Selection accesses the Scenes menu and then clicking on the individual scene names start playback from that scene.

Having assembled your sequence and loaded a template, you are well on your way to customizing and burning a DVD. In the next short lesson you will customize the thumbnail image for each scene and add a second movie track to the Main menu.

NOTES

To start this lesson you can either continue with the project you are currently working with or open the project Custom_DVD02.prproj from the APPST2 Lesson Files/Chapter 16 folder.

Animating Thumbnails and Adding a New Movie

Let's take the DVD design a step further by adding a credits movie to the Main menu and turning on the thumbnail images for each scene so that you can see a reference image from it.

1. With the Custom_DVD02.prproj project open, be sure that the DVD sequence is open in the Timeline panel and that the DVD Layout panel displays the same sequence. Click the Scenes Menu 1 icon on the DVD Menus section of the DVD Layout panel. Click once on the Portofino text, and open your Effect Controls panel (**Figure 16.10a**). In the Poster Frame area of the Effect Controls panel for the Portofino button, click the Play button and then stop playback around 15;00 (**Figure 16.10b**).

   To customize the links (also referred to as buttons) on the Scenes Menu 1 page, you clicked on the scene you

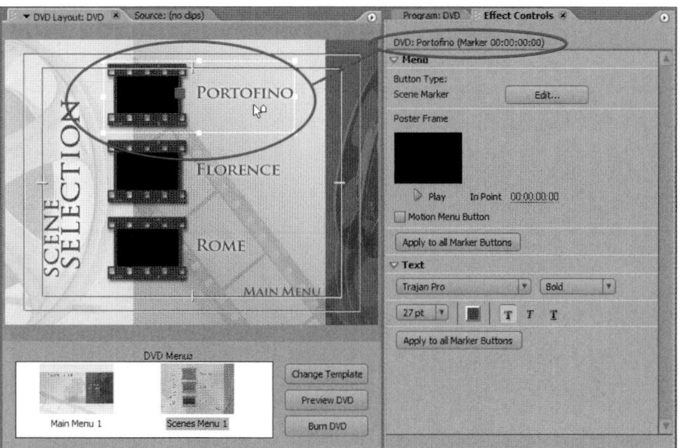

a

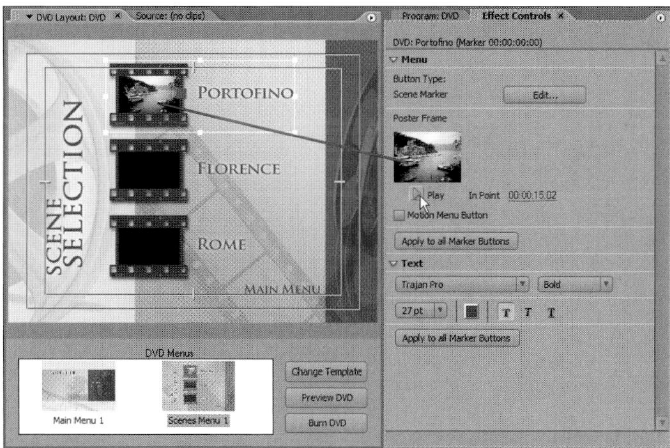

b

Figures 16.10a and b With the Portofino text selected, the Effect Controls panel shows the properties associated with that button. Although you have the option of making the thumbnail play live video (Motion Menu button), by playing back the Poster Frame and stopping it at a specific point (b), you can define the frame on which you stop (In point) as the Poster Frame inside the thumbnail of the Portofino button.

wanted to adjust and opened the Effect Controls to see the properties that could be modified. Because this template contained a Scenes menu with both text and a thumbnail as a single button, you can update the image in the thumbnail by playing back the video that the Scene button links to and stopping it at an exact frame. The frames at around 15;00 are indicative of Portofino and serve as a perfect Poster Frame for the thumbnail. To make the thumbnail for Portofino live video from the montage, click the Motion Menu Button check box and define the In point from which you want the live video to start.

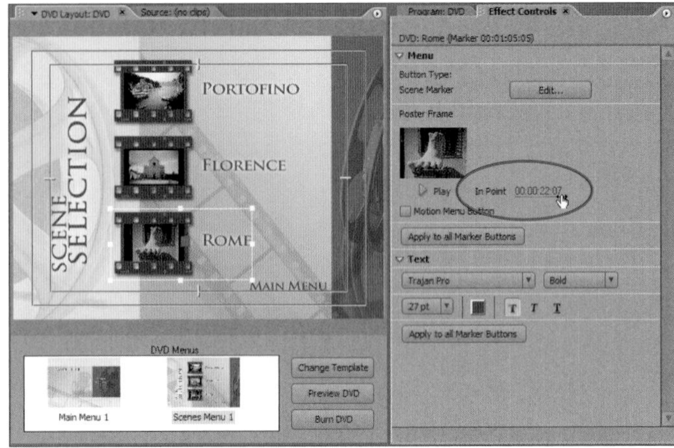

Figure 16.11 You can click and drag the In Point value to modify it or enter a specific value. Modifying each menu button's Poster Frame further customizes your DVD.

2. Select the Florence button in the Scenes Menu 1 menu. In the Effect Controls panel click on the In Point hot-text value, type 1522, then press Enter. Select the Rome button and type 2207 in the In Point field (**Figure 16.11**).

   Clicking once on the In Point field allows you to manually enter a value for the In point. Clicking and dragging enables you to scrub to the value you want as the Poster Frame. The benefit of scrubbing is that you see the video in the Poster Frame update dynamically.

3. With the DVD sequence active in the Timeline panel, drag and drop the CREDITS title from the Project panel after the 03 ROME clip; leave some blank space between the last clip and the CREDITS title. Press the End key to snap the Edit Line to the end of the CREDITS clip. With Video 1 targeted, press Ctrl+D to assign your default transition to the tail of the clip. Press Page Up to snap to the beginning of the CREDITS clip and press Ctrl+D to assign a default transition to the head of the clip. With the Edit Line at the head of the clip, click the Set DVD Marker button and modify the Marker Type to Main Menu Marker. In the Name field, type "...Credits" and click OK. In the DVD Layout panel, click the icon for Main Menu 1 in the DVD Menus area (**Figure 16.12**).

   Adding more than one movie file to your custom DVD is quite easy; you just add the files to your sequence and

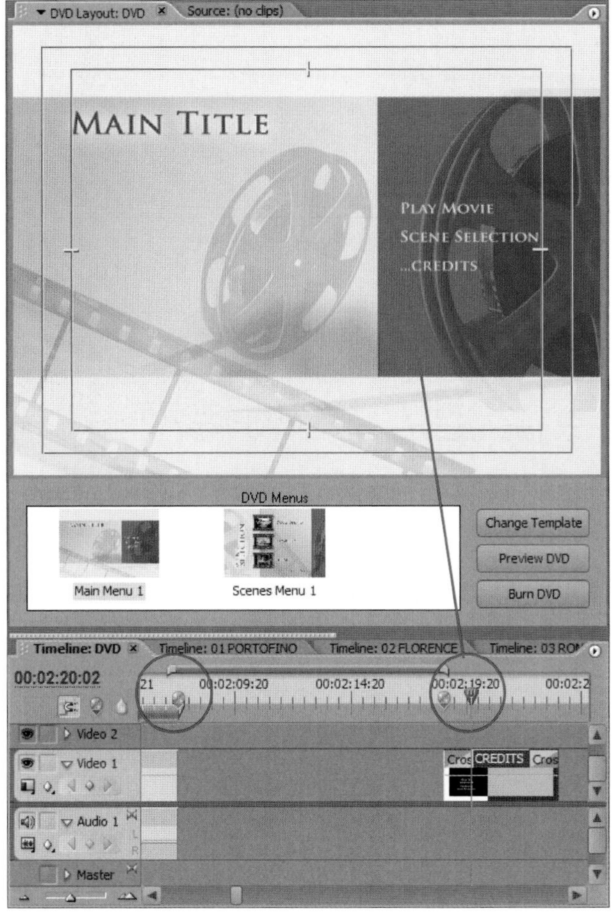

Figure 16.12 With the DVD Layout panel displaying the Main Menu 1 menu you can see the newly added "...Credits" button that links directly to the clip instance below in the DVD sequence. Notice that the Main Menu marker assigned to the beginning of the CREDITS title is green. Each DVD marker is signified by a different color: Red for Stop marker, Blue for Scene marker, and Green for Main Menu marker.

assign a DVD marker to the beginning of the content. If you assigned a Scene marker then you would be able to play back the movie by accessing it through one of the Scenes menus. By assigning a Main Menu marker to the file you get access to the movie through the Main menu. Each DVD template has a defined number of buttons that can be added to the Main menu; the Film template has a limit of four.

By assigning a transition at the beginning and end of the CREDITS title, when the button to play the movie is clicked, the screen will go black and fade into the credits and then fade back out when it gets to the end of the clip.

If you intended to add more clips to your timeline after the CREDITS clip, to make sure that the Credits button played only the Credits clip you would need to add another Stop marker at the end of the CREDITS clip instance.

4. Right-click on the CREDITS clip in the DVD sequence and access the Speed/Duration settings. Reassign the Duration value to 10;00. In the Project panel open the Audio folder and double-click on the file TheCoast_s.mp3. Assign an Out point to the clip at 10;00 and drop it directly beneath the CREDITS clip in the timeline. Open the DVD Layout panel and preview the DVD to see and hear the accessing of the ...Credits movie.

In the last step of this lesson you added some audio beneath the CREDITS clip so that audio and video played when the movie was accessed. This task also sets you up for some more customizations in the chapter's final lesson.

Customizing Your DVD Menus

It's time to complete the DVD customization by modifying the visual and audible elements of the menus. Updating a menu background and adding an audio soundtrack to a menu is easy to do, but you need physical files in your Project panel in order to do it. This final lesson (before you burn your DVD) reveals a method in which to customize any DVD with alternative project files and relevant project elements, providing the finishing touch to a custom menu-based DVD.

This lesson is will teach you how to incorporate elements of your existing project in your DVD's menu layout. Because the photo montage is about Italy and you have a sequence with a map of Italy, you will incorporate two flavors of the map as a background graphic for the Main menu and Scenes menu, respectively. For each menu, you will reposition and resize the links/buttons and add a looping soundtrack to complete the menu. Let's start with modifying the backgrounds.

1. Open the BACKGROUND NO BUTTONS sequence in the Timeline panel. With the sequence active, select File > Export > Export Frame. Use the default Windows Bitmap Settings as your file type for exporting and let Premiere assign the default name to the file. Open the BACKGROUND BUTTONS sequence and choose Export Frame again using the same settings (**Figures 16.13a** and **b**).

   Background elements for menus can be still images or a video clip. Because you couldn't use a sequence as a background for a menu, you exported a frame from the sequence as a still. The Main menu now shows the map of Italy to provide the flavor for the DVD.

For this lesson you can continue on your current project or open the Custom_DVD03.prproj project from the APPST2 Lesson Files/Chapter 16 folder. Either way, be sure that your Project panel, DVD Layout panel, Effect Controls panel, and Timeline panel (with the DVD sequence active) are all a part of your current workspace.

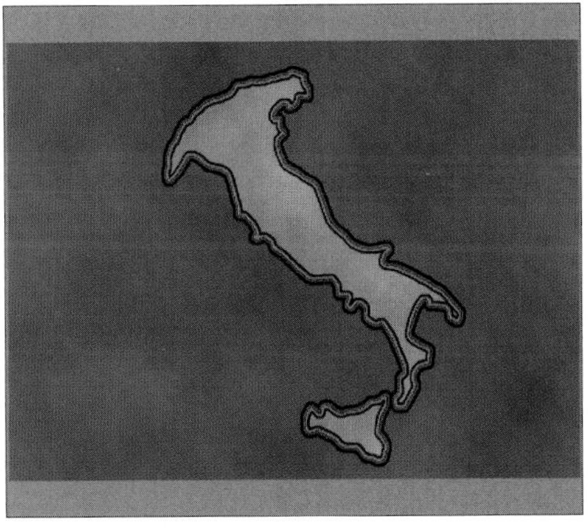

a

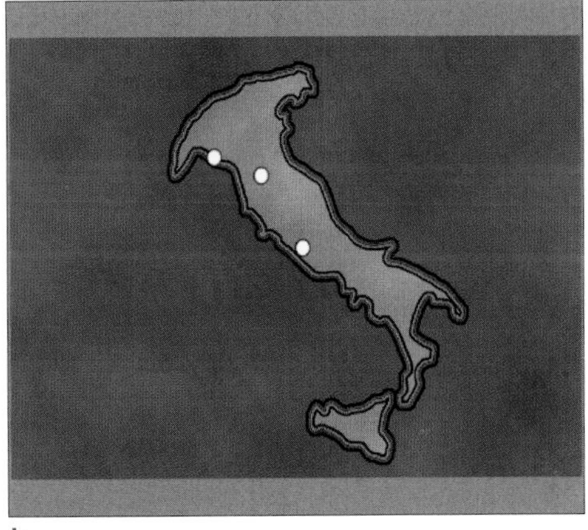

b

Figures 16.13a and b By exporting a single frame from each of the sequences you created a physical file that can replace the background of each menu. The first image of the map without buttons (a) will serve as the Main menu background, and the image with buttons (b) will be used for the Scenes menu.

2. Open the DVD sequence in the Timeline panel and in the DVD Layout panel click the Main Menu 1 icon in the DVD Menus area. From the Project panel, drag and drop the BACKGROUND NO BUTTONS.bmp file directly into the center of the DVD Layout panel (see **Figure 16.14a**). Click the icon for the Scenes Menu 1 in the DVD Menus area of the DVD Layout panel. Open the Effect Controls panel and be sure that the Menu Background properties are revealed. Finally, drag and drop the BACKGROUND BUTTONS.bmp file into

Figures 16.14a, b, and c You can drag and drop the still file directly into the center of the active Main menu in the DVD Layout panel (a), or you can drag and drop the still from the Project panel into the Background placeholder of the Effect Controls panel for the selected menu (b). In either case, the still becomes the background element of the Main menu (c).

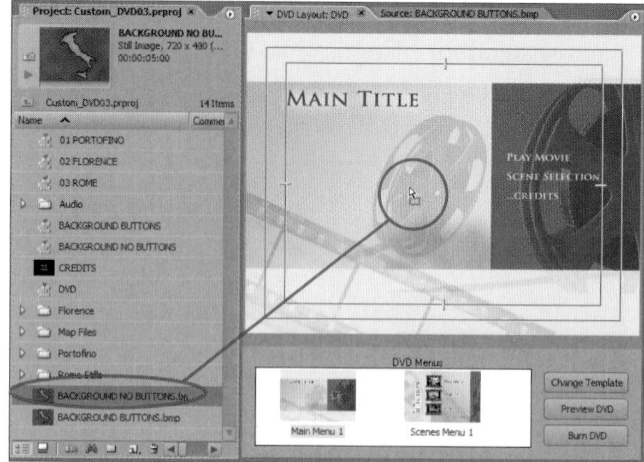

a Drag and drop into the active panel

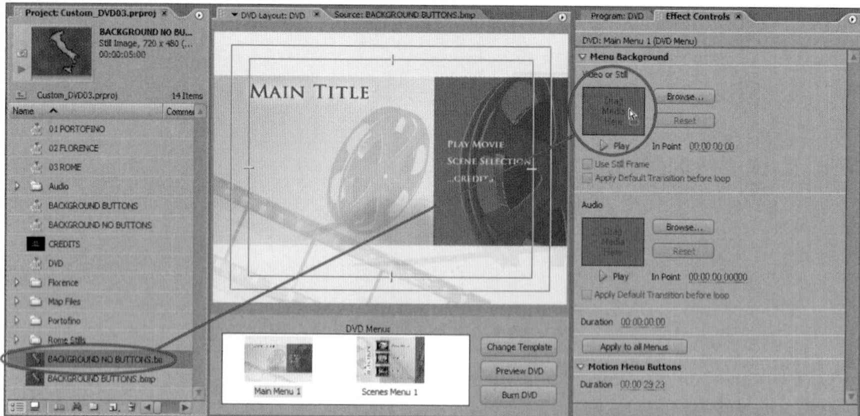

b Drag and drop into the menu background for the selected menu in the DVD Layout panel

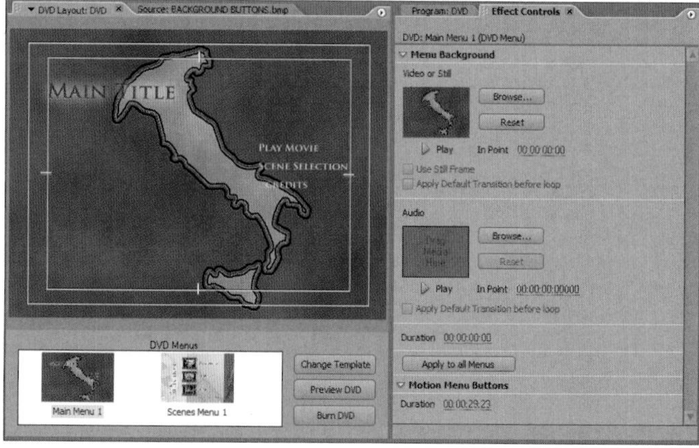

c

the center of the box below the video or still text that says Drag Media Here.

Although both actions achieved the same result, this step revealed two ways of updating a background. If you wanted the background element to be video instead, simply drag and drop a video file using either method technique.

Now it's time to alter the text and buttons a bit further to put the finishing touches on the two menus. To adjust a Scene button's text and color properties you select the button and modify the properties in the Effect Controls panel. To adjust a button's physical position, you simply click on it and drag it to a new place. We'll modify a few text elements together, then I will leave you to do the remaining buttons.

3. With the Main Menu 1 active in the DVD Layout panel, double-click on the phrase "Main Title" and change the text to Italy Trip 2003 (**Figure 16.15a**). Drag the updated text element to a lower region of the frame so that it does not overlap with the Italy graphic (**Figure 16.15b**). With the text still selected, click on the color

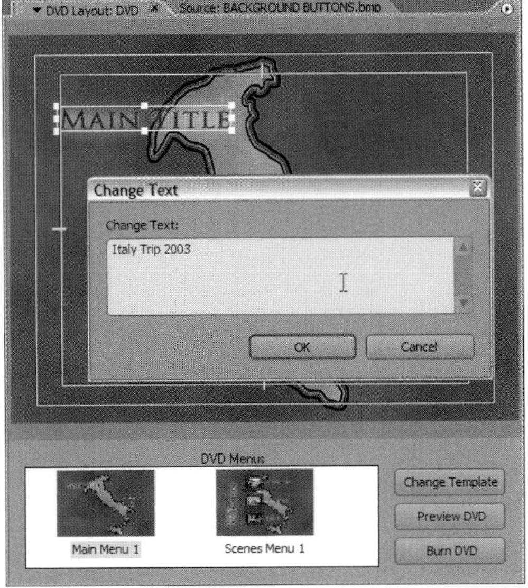

a

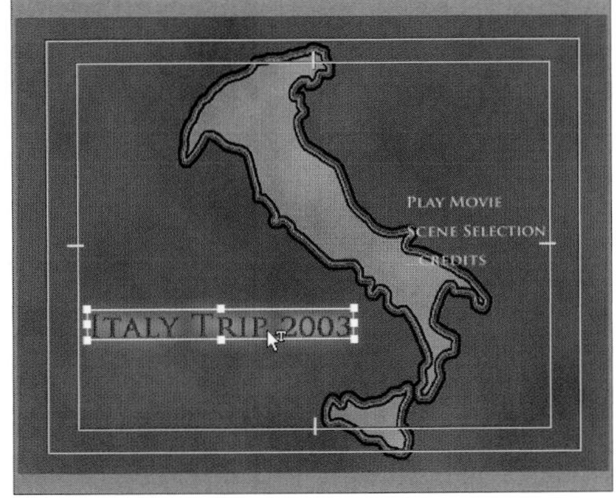

b

Figures 16.15a through b To change a button's text, double-click on the text in the menu and modify it in the Change Text dialog (a). To reposition a button or text element, simply drag and drop as you would in the Titler (b).

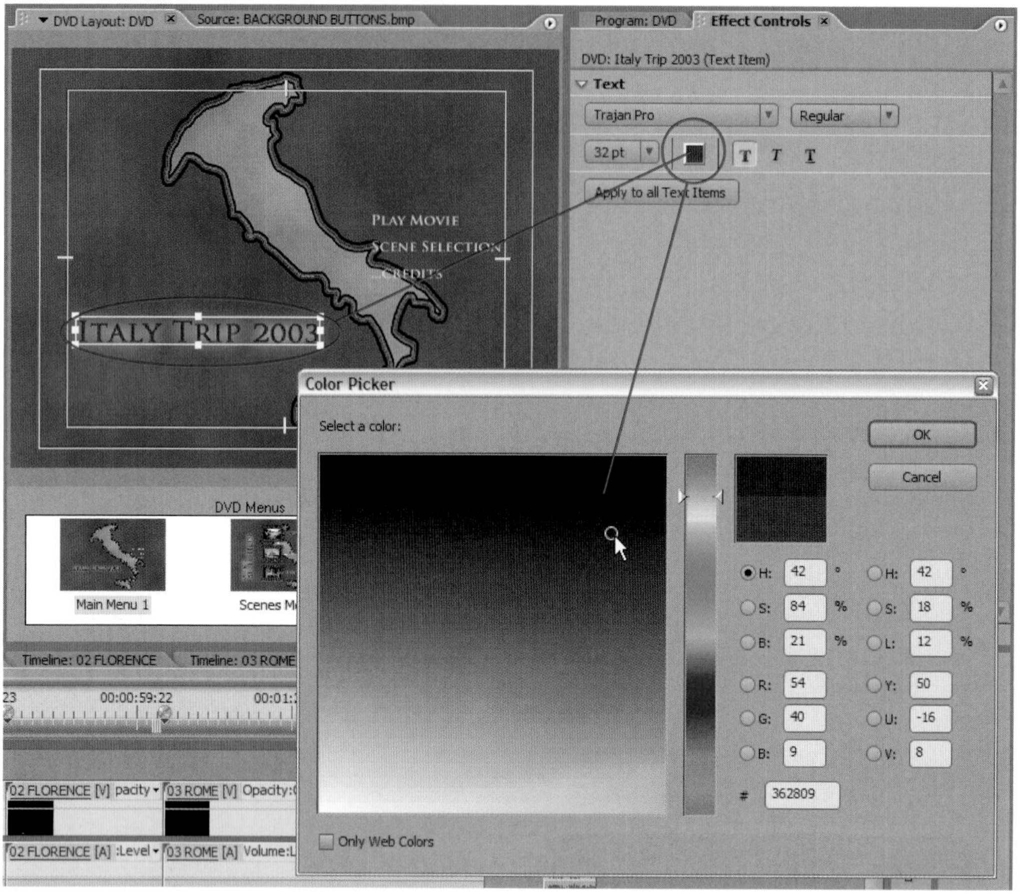

c

d

Figures 16.15c through d To modify the properties of the selected text, open the Effect Controls panel and reassign the values to your liking. To change text color, select the text, click the color swatch in the Effect Controls panel, and pick a new color (c). 16.15d shows the results of all these changes.

swatch for the text in the Effects Controls panel (**Figure 16.15c**) and make the primary color darker. Drag the other text elements and better position them in the frame to match **Figure 16.15d**. Because the Main Title text element was not a button, double-clicking opened the Change Text dialog. If it were a button, double-clicking would have opened the DVD marker associated with the button as you saw earlier in the chapter. With the text selected, the physical properties of the text are revealed in the Effect Controls panel, making it easy to change text color or many other attributes. The easiest way to customize a menu is to keep your Effect Controls panel open and right next to the DVD Layout panel so you can quickly select the element to modify and change its settings immediately.

4. Click the icon for the Scenes Menu 1 in the DVD Menus area of the DVD Layout panel. Click on the Portofino button and drag its lower-right corner in toward the upper left to shrink it (**Figure 16.16a**). Reposition the reduced button to just above the button for its real location on the map (**Figure 16.16b**). Resize and reposition the remaining buttons in the menu (**Figure 16.16c**), then change each button's text color to black. In the cases where the text still overlaps Italy on the map, double-click on the text and add a few spaces before the start of the word in the Name field of the DVD Marker dialog (see **Figures 16.17a, b,** and **c**).

   Because you cannot assign or change a button thumbnail to an exact size as you can text, you needed to drag the button dimension in the proper direction to

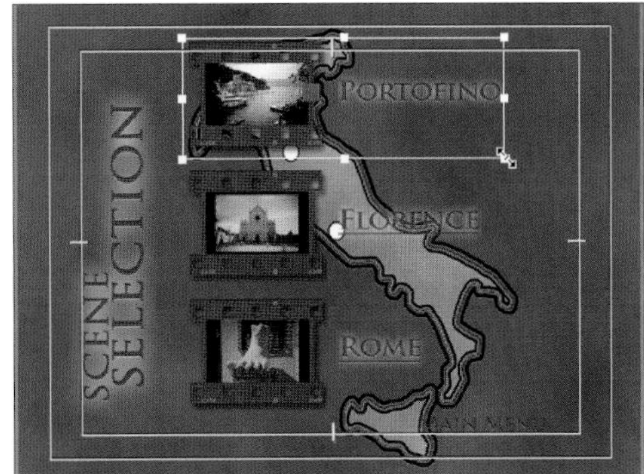

a

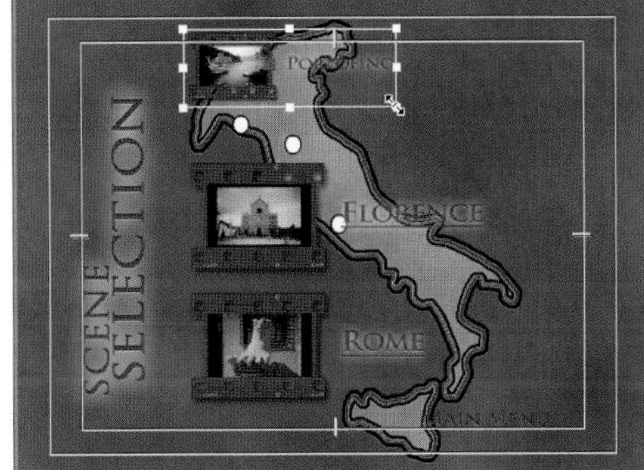

b

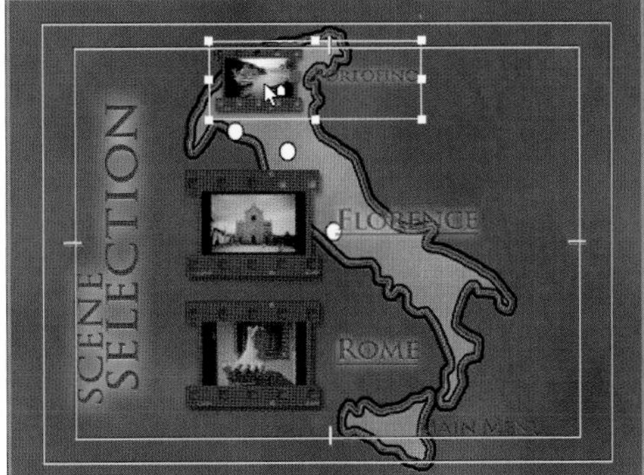

c

Figures 16.16a, b, and c Select a button and you can resize it in the DVD Layout panel just as you would in the Titler (a). Although you can resize the text again to make it bigger through the Effect Controls panel, the only way to reduce the size of the thumbnail is by dragging its boundaries in (b). 16.13c shows all the buttons resized and repositioned.

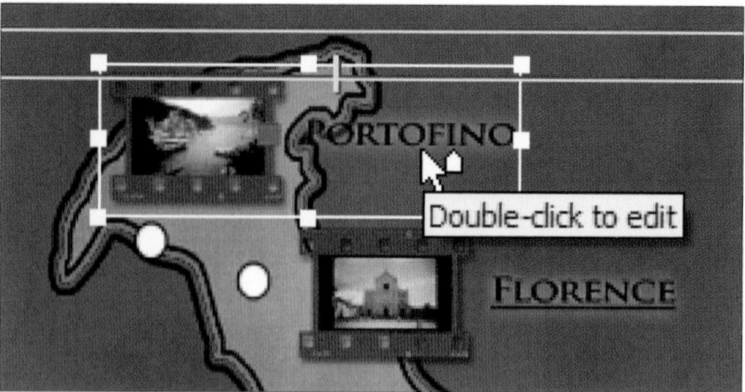

a

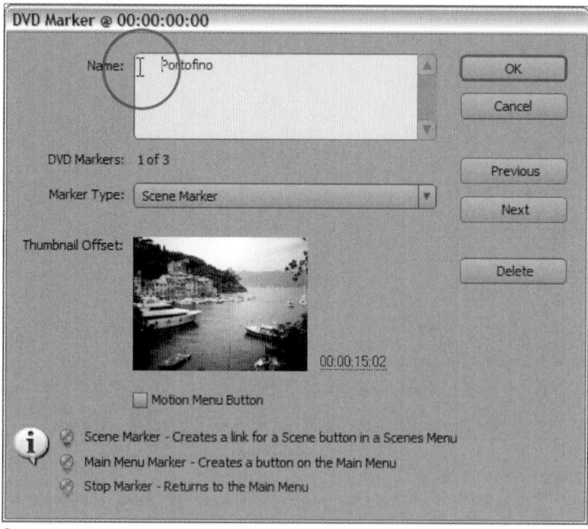

b

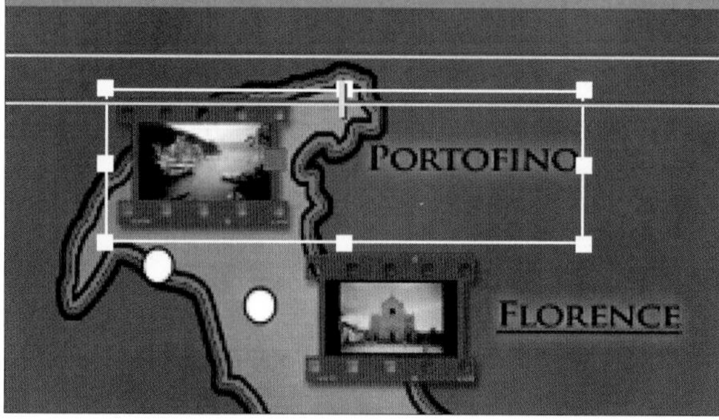

c

Figures 16.17a, b, and c Initially, the text overlaps Italy on the map (a). Double-click on the text to bring up the DVD Marker dialog where you can add five or six spaces before the word "Portofino" (b) to add more space between the thumbnail and the text (c).

change its overall size. Then you were able to increase the size of the text without changing the size of the thumbnail.

5. Open the DVD sequence in the Timeline panel and select the TheCoast_s.mp3 file beneath the CREDITS title. While holding down the Ctrl key, use the Selection tool (V) to click on the yellow volume fade line in the center of the clip and create four keyframes (**Figure 16.18a**). Clicking on the first and last keyframes individually, drag each to the bottom of the clip as in **Figure 16.18b**. With this file still selected, choose Clip > Audio Options > Render and Replace. Double-click on the created clip Audio 1_TheCoast_s.wav in the Audio folder of the Project panel and play it in the Source Monitor. Open the DVD Layout panel and select each of the menus. Drag and drop the newly created audio file directly into the DVD Layout panel as you did the stills earlier in this lesson (see **Figures 16.19a** and **b**). Click Preview DVD and navigate your DVD to see how it sounds and what it looks like.

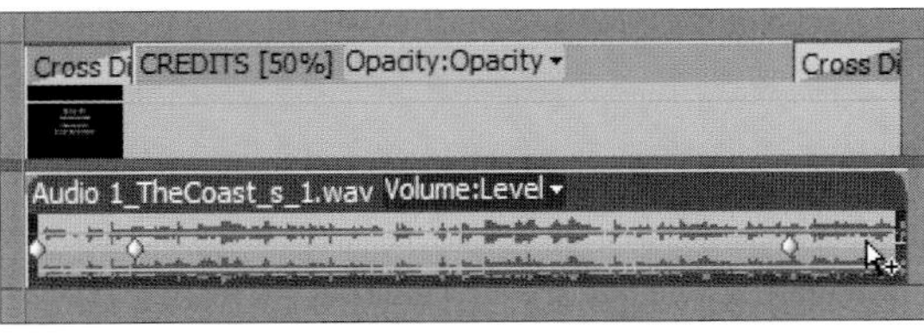

a

b

c

Figures 16.18a, b, and c To create a custom volume fade for the audio file in the timeline, you need to create four Volume keyframe handles by holding down the Ctrl key and clicking four times on the yellow volume fade bar in the audio file (a and b). Drag the first and last keyframes to the bottom of the clip so that the volume level fades up at the beginning and back down at the end (c).

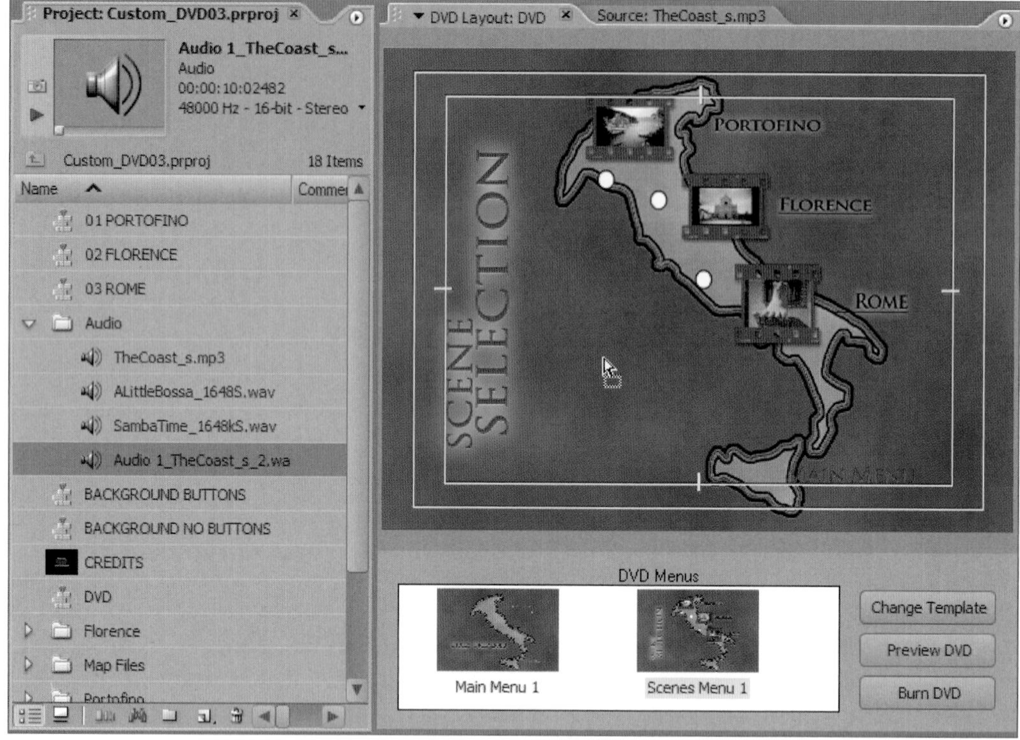

a

b

Figures 16.19a and b After creating a custom audio file with a fade in and out, simply drag and drop it onto the menus that you want the audio to play in when they are open (a). As you did with the stills, you can also drag the audio file directly into the Audio portion of the Menu Background properties in the Effect Controls panel (b).

Although this lengthy step alluded to some audio tinkering you will master later in the book, in essence you used the Render and Replace command to create a customized audio file that appears in your Project panel and can be used as a background audio loop for your menu.

You first adjusted the volume levels of the file in the timeline so that it fades up to full volume and then back down. The Render and Replace command takes the selected audio from the timeline and makes a new clip that has the volume fades written into the file. This is a physical file that is written to disk and populates your Project panel. Because the file exists as a unique clip it can be dragged and dropped onto any of your DVD menus to serve as the Audio portion of the Menu Background.

Because you can't use the audio or video from a project sequence to populate the background of a menu, you exported a still frame to serve as the image background and used the Render and Replace command to create loop-able short audio file to serve as the sound background.

That's it! Your DVD is customized and ready to burn.

Burning to Disc

If you are happy with your customized DVD Layout, it's time to burn to disc or write the DVD out to files. If you have been using one project for this chapter, you can complete it in this lesson, or you can open the Custom_DV04_FINISH.prproj project from the APPST2 Lesson Files/Chapter 16 folder.

1. With your DVD Layout completely customized for the active DVD sequence, click on the Burn DVD button in the DVD Layout panel.
2. In the resulting dialog, set the Burn to button to Disc and name the disc Italy Montage.

In the final step of the Burning to Disc lesson you changed the N Frames value from 15 to 12 in the Adobe Media Encoder. Due to a glitch in the software, you will always have to change the N Frames value when encoding a progressive frame project. If Adobe addresses this glitch in a future release of the software, check the Read Me file to see if this issue has been resolved. If you still have issues, even with the N Frames adjustment, import the progressive project into a new interlaced project and export to DVD from the new project.

3. In the Encoding area, click the Settings button and choose NTSC Progressive 4:3 High Quality 7Mb CBR 1 Pass from the Preset drop-down menu in the Adobe Media Encoder (top right). In the Basic Video settings set the Frame Rate to 23.976, and in the GOP settings set the N Frames value to 12. Click OK in the bottom right of the Encoder to get back to the Burn DVD dialog, then click that dialog's Burn button to execute the burn to disc.

   As Chapter 11 explained, when you click the Burn DVD button in the DVD Layout panel and access the Encoding settings, the Adobe Media Encoder opens with settings already in place for authoring DVDs. Because you are authoring a 24p DV project (the project settings for the montage) you chose the NTSC Progressive 4:3 presets and adjusted the frame rate to 24p (23.976). Because the DVD content is quite short you chose the High Quality 7Mb CBR 1 Pass flavor of the presets.

Congratulations. You got through a detailed chapter that revealed a specific workflow to help you author a consistently themed DVD directly from the timeline.

Things to Remember

DVD customization is all about details; let's review the most important ones. A menu-based DVD can reference the contents of one sequence only. How it references the content in either the Main menu or Scenes menu is entirely based on how you assign DVD markers to the contents of the sequence. When played from the Scenes menu or Main menu, a clip or segment plays from the marked start point until the end of the sequence unless a Stop marker is detected.

Every selected template has a default maximum number of Main Menu buttons and Scenes Menu buttons. If you plan on customizing the background and elements of a specific template, your choice of the template should be based on the layout, the font styling, and the number of buttons allowed for the respective menus.

To modify the text of a button or text element, you need to double-click on the text to alter it. Double-clicking a button that references a Scene marker or Main Menu marker brings up the DVD Marker dialog associated with that button, and to change the name you simply need to modify the information in the Name field. Double-clicking a simple text element in your menu reveals the straightforward Change Text dialog into which you type the new text.

To change the size of menu buttons, you select the button and drag its boundaries in or out.

Finally, remember that the Effect Controls panel goes hand in hand with modifying DVD menus. If you want to replace the background of a menu or add audio to a menu, make sure you select the menu itself and not any of the button elements that way the background properties of the menu reveal themselves in the Effect Controls panel. If you want to change the button properties of a menu, select the menu, then select the button you want to adjust and its properties will open in the Effect Controls panel.

This chapter concludes the graphics and titling section of the book. The next section, "Advanced Audio Techniques" will guide you through the entire process of recording, editing, adding effects to, and mixing audio using Premiere Pro 2.0.

I've created a small tutorial reviewing the more subtle yet important things to remember when working on DVDs with Premiere Pro 2.0. Check out the DVD_Tips.wmv tutorial, located in the Video Tutorials Folder on the book's DVD. When the file loads in Windows Media Player, press Alt+Enter.

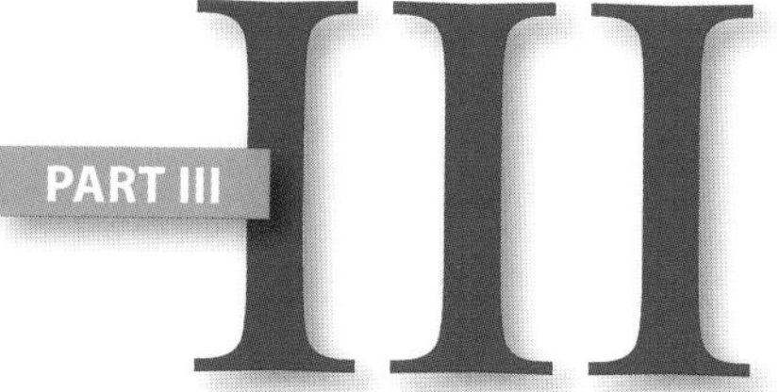

Advanced Audio Techniques

CHAPTER

17

Using Your Audio Hardware

As you know by now, Premiere Pro has some powerful and professional audio features. To make the most of them, however, you may need to customize your audio hardware and its parameters. For example, upgrading your system's default audio hardware with a third-party audio interface can provide better recording quality, more accurate playback acoustics, and a dynamic 5.1 surround mix environment. If a new audio interface isn't in your budget, a high-quality microphone can help you get the most from your existing system when recording. Of course, no matter what hardware you have, proper parameter settings can make or break your projects.

This chapter covers a lot of ground to help you understand a handful of facets relating to setting up, recording, and playing back the best quality audio possible. Whether you are using an additional audio interface or not, many system settings and Premiere settings can help you maximize the quality of the audio coming in and playing out.

Audio Interfaces

Most base-level audio cards that come with Windows systems record in from the microphone port (usually a 1/8" stereo plug) at 16 bits, stereo at a sample rate of 44kHz. They usually play back to the speaker port (another 1/8" stereo plug) at 16 bits, stereo, 44kHz. These settings are fine for most, if not all, general usage.

To capture at a higher bit depth and sample rate, however, say at 24 bits and 96kHz, then you need to invest in a more robust audio card, also called an *audio interface*. Capturing and working at higher rates increases the quality and detail of the sound you are recording and playing. To accurately work in and play back 5.1 surround sound audio, you will also need to add an additional *audio interface*. Default stereo devices have only two speaker outputs (two channels); to accurately play surround sound sequences you need an interface

Developed by Steinberg for its VST product line, ASIO (Audio Stream Input Output) is an audio communication standard that can access one or more devices (interfaces) to record or play audio through. The benefit of the ASIO communication method is that there is an immediate response when playing or recording high-quality audio. By supporting ASIO devices, Premiere Pro assumes the features of high-quality and instantaneous audio recording and playback with a ton of professional devices (interfaces).

For my laptop system, the default audio interface is the Sigma Tel-C Major Audio. For surround sound playback, I use an ASIO-certified Emagic A26 interface, which has two input ports and six output ports. If I connect the six output ports to the six speakers that make up a surround sound system—left, center, right, surround left, surround right, and LFE (low frequency)—I can properly play back from Premiere Pro in surround sound. On top of that, the device gives me the opportunity to record at a bit depth of 16 or 24 bits and a sample rate of 44, 48, or 96kHz.

M-Audio has an excellent line of FireWire interfaces that support ASIO. You can use them confidently with both laptop and desktop PCs, and they are highly portable. M-Audio also has very reasonably priced surround sound ASIO PCI interfaces.

with six separate output channels (**Figure 17.1**). Because Premiere Pro supports ASIO devices, however, making the jump to a more powerful interface is quite easy.

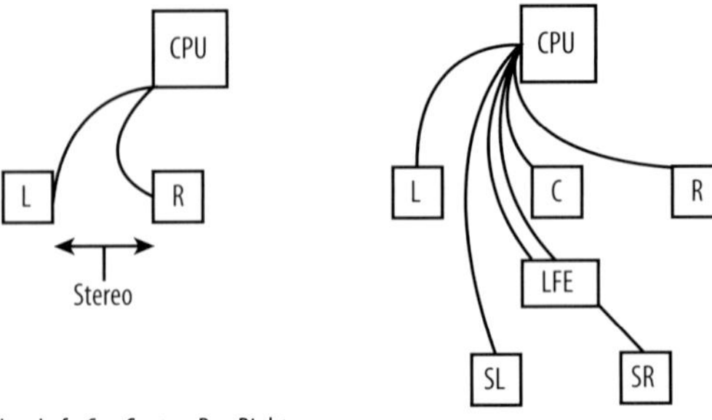

Figure 17.1 The standard stereo speaker setup (left) has a left speaker and right speaker that can connect to the default stereo output of your computer. To support six surround sound speakers (right), you need an audio interface with six output channels, each routed to the proper speaker.

If you want surround sound playback, be sure to pick up an interface with at least six output ports. In general, get a card that supports at least 16-bit, 48kHz recording and playback. Of course, 24-bit, 96kHz would be optimum.

For desktop PCs, most ASIO devices will be a PCI card installed inside your machine. The back of the PCI card may feature plugs where you can insert your speaker and microphone cable or it may have a breakout box. Sometimes called a rat tail, or B.O.B, it connects to the card on one end and has female insertion points for speakers and microphones on the other.

To upgrade a laptop PC, you'll need to purchase an external audio interface that connects via a USB or FireWire cable. These breakout boxes may come with various numbers of input or output ports. If you want true 5.1 support, be sure your new interface has at least six outputs.

After your new audio interface is installed, you'll need to set its properties. The exact process and options depend on your card, but at a minimum you'll probably have to set the sample rate. **Figure 17.2** shows the Device Options dialog for my eMagic A26.

If you are using the native supported Xena HD capture card, which supports ASIO playback, you can select it as your Audio Input and Output interface.

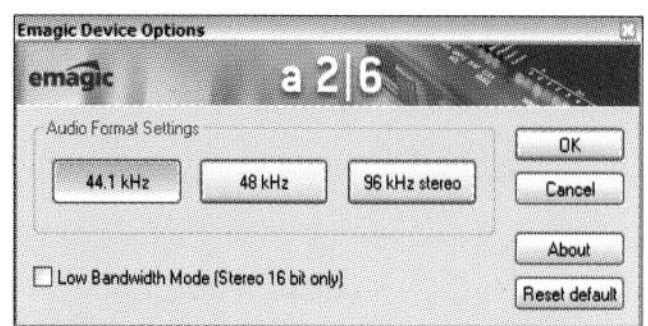

Figure 17.2 After installation, be sure to adjust the proprietary settings for your additional audio interface. Your Device Options dialog may differ from mine shown here.

Adjusting Audio Settings

No matter which audio interface you use, when you set up your system to record, you need to verify that the input volume level for your microphone is at the proper level. Additionally, when you play back to your speakers, you need to make sure that the speaker output volume is also adequate. For both of these adjustments, go to the Windows XP Sounds and Audio Devices Control Panel (Control Panels > Sounds, Speech, and Audio Devices > Sounds and Audio Devices) (**Figure 17.3**). The tabs you'll use most are:

- **Volume.** For setting your device volume level
- **Audio.** For specifying input and output device levels
- **Voice.** For helping to get your voice recording levels to the right point
- **Hardware.** For verifying and troubleshooting issues with audio in your system

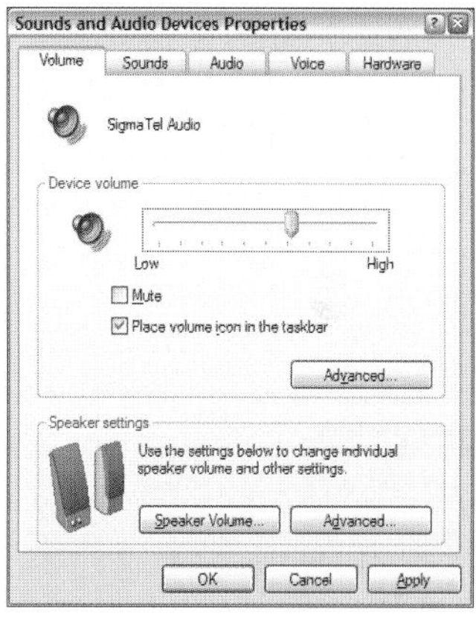

Figure 17.3 From the Sounds and Audio Devices Properties Control Panel, you can access all your system settings associated with audio input, output, and attached hardware.

In each tab, be sure to select the device for which you are adjusting settings—your default card or ASIO interface (**Figure 17.4**).

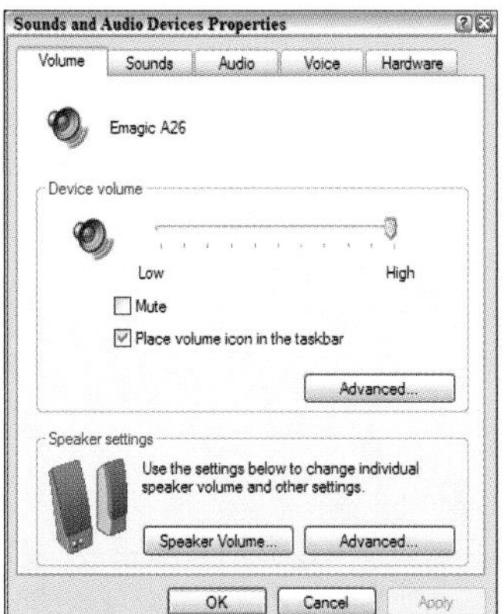

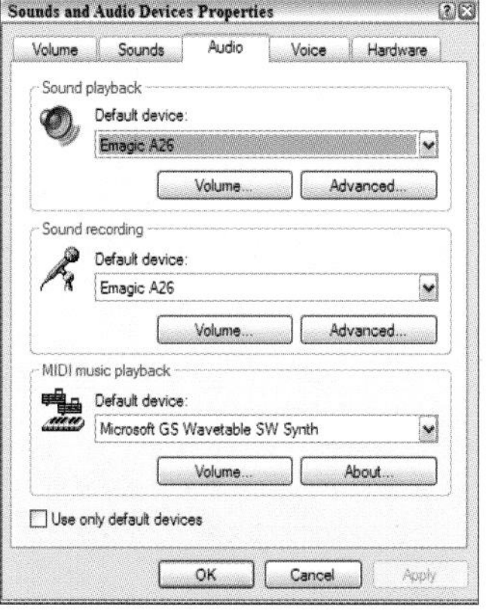

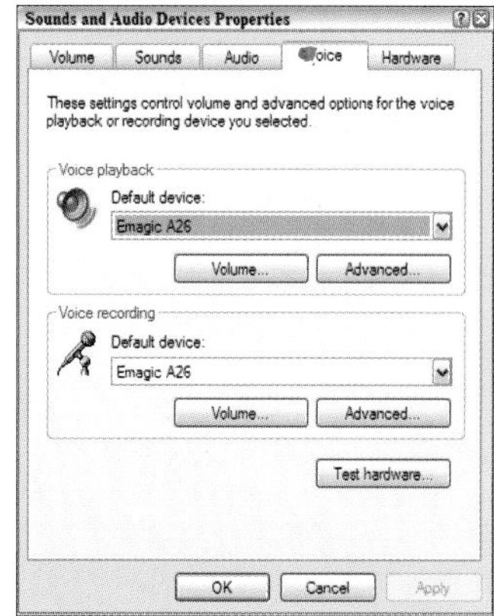

Figure 17.4 Notice how in each tab I have selected my ASIO device, the Emagic A26. When switching from the default device to your secondary audio device, be sure to click Apply so that your changes update the system settings.

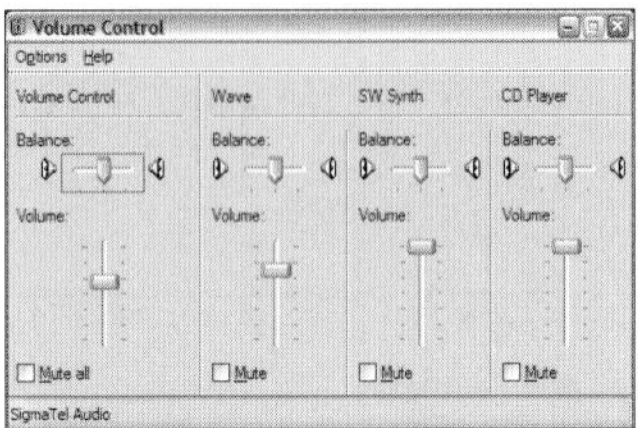

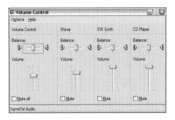

Figure 17.5 In the Volume Control dialog, you can see and assign volume levels for the devices or interfaces on your system. Be sure the Volume Control fader is not muted, because it adjusts the overall system volume.

The Volume Tab

The Volume tab allows you to control the *overall* output volume for your system (Figure 17.3). Clicking Advanced opens the Volume Control dialog where you can adjust the output volume for *individual* components of your system (**Figure 17.5**). If you are not hearing any audio when you play back, the Volume Control dialog is the first place to troubleshoot and check that your levels are properly set.

The Audio Tab

The Audio tab is the control area where you can switch between devices for different tasks (**Figure 17.6**). If you want to play back through your ASIO interface and record using your default interface, for example, use the drop-down menus to assign Sound Playback to the ASIO device and Sound Recording to your default device.

Clicking the Volume in the Sound Playback area opens the Volume Control under the appropriate slider: CD Player, Microphone, or Phone Line (**Figure 17.7**).

Click the Advanced button under the Microphone Volume slider to access the Advanced Controls for Microphone panel to fine-tune the incoming audio (**Figure 17.8**). When

Figure 17.6 The Audio tab offers you drop-down menus for selecting which device you are using for playback, recording, and MIDI playback.

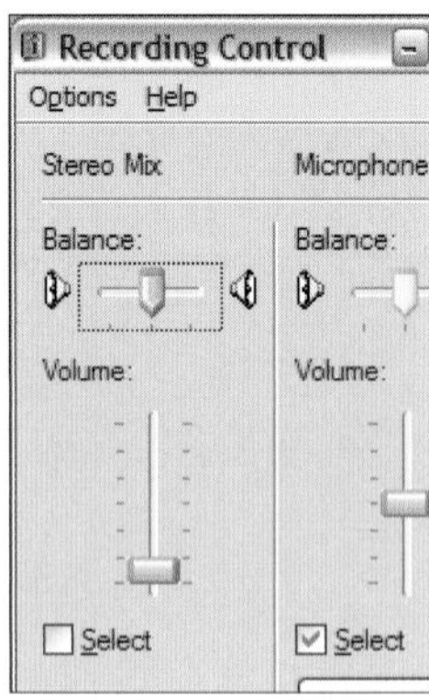

Figure 17.7 The Recording Control dialog allows you to adjust your recordi-ng volume. In this image, I selected the Microphone as the input device.

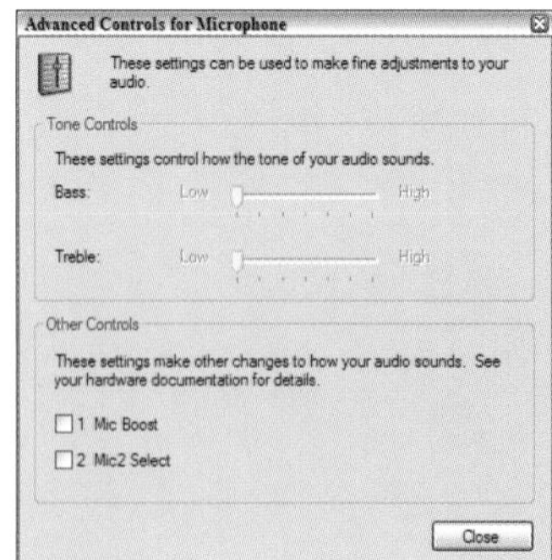

Figure 17.8 The Advanced Controls for Microphone allow you to adjust settings associated with the Microphone input. If your incoming signal is too low, you can click the 1 Mic Boost check box to gain-step the incoming signal so that it is stronger.

your microphone needs an additional boost, click the Mic Boost check box. These settings will vary from system to system and microphone to microphone, so you may have to fiddle with it to get the best level.

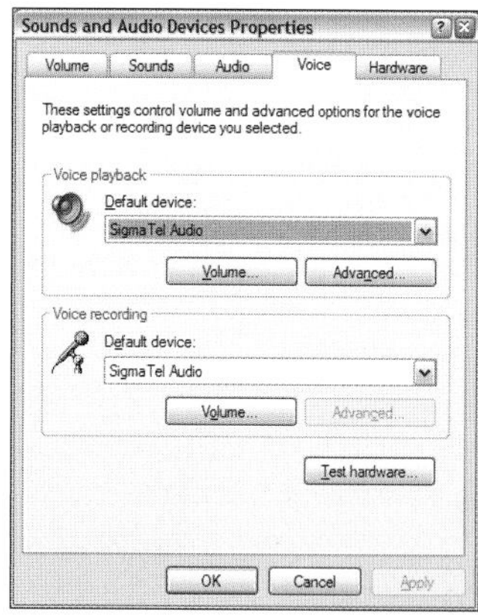

Figure 17.9 You can change your selected playback and recording device from the Voice tab. If you want to record from a secondary audio interface, select it from the Default Device drop-down menu under Voice Recording. If you are having difficulty configuring your microphone, click the Test Hardware button to run the hardware wizard, which walks you through steps to verify that your input and output for recording is configured.

The Voice Tab

The Voice tab verifies the input and output device for voice recording (**Figure 17.9**). If you are having trouble configuring and optimizing your recording and playback levels, you can click Test Hardware to use the Sound Hardware test wizard. Before you do, make sure your microphone is properly plugged in and you have speakers or headphones for listening. The wizard asks you to speak aloud and then analyzes the results to make adjustments to your volume settings.

The Hardware Tab

From the Hardware tab, you can view, select, and analyze the status of your connected devices and drivers (**Figure 17.10**). If you have a problem playing back with an additional audio interface, select the card from the Devices list to see if it is functioning properly. With the device selected, click Properties to reveal General, Properties, and Driver

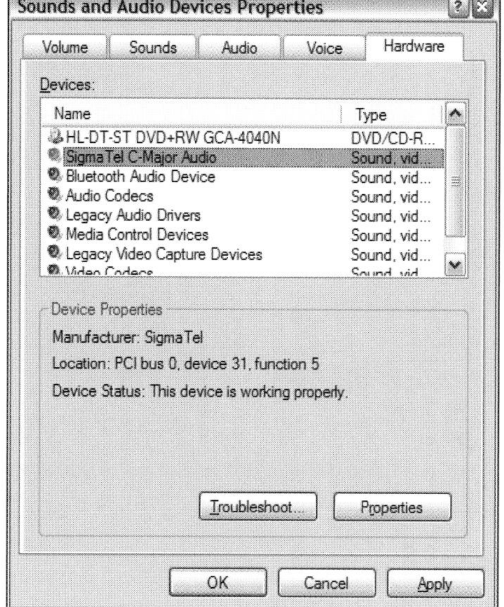

Figure 17.10 If you are experiencing trouble with sound from any attached device, you can click the Hardware tab to access a list of the sound devices associated with your system. With a device selected, click Troubleshoot or Properties to get more information and to troubleshoot the status of the device.

information. Additionally, you can run a troubleshooting wizard to help identify any current problems with your hardware devices.

Premiere's Audio Hardware Preferences

Once you get inside of Premiere Pro, you need to assign some additional audio hardware settings to map output channels and customize your ASIO device. Even if you are using your default audio device, it is helpful to understand what these controls do and how to adjust them.

Premiere Pro 2.0 offers two Audio Hardware specific preferences: Audio Hardware and Audio Output Mapping.

Audio Hardware and ASIO Settings

To designate your input and output device, head over to your Audio Hardware Preferences (Edit > Preferences > Audio Hardware). This preference dictates which audio device is used to drive sound playback (**Figure 17.11**). The default device setting, Premiere Pro Windows Sound, uses your internal audio hardware. If you have any additional ASIO-supported devices installed, you'll also see listings for

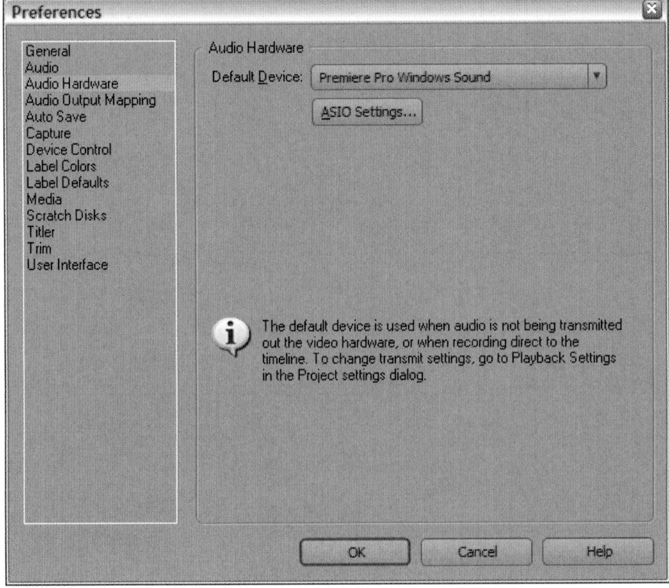

Figure 17.11 The Audio Hardware preference allows you to choose exactly which audio device to transmit your audio through when running Premiere Pro 2.0. If you are editing and transmitting DV or HDV or using external video hardware, these settings are overridden by the project's hardware settings. You can default back to these settings by changing your playback settings to the Desktop Only for Audio.

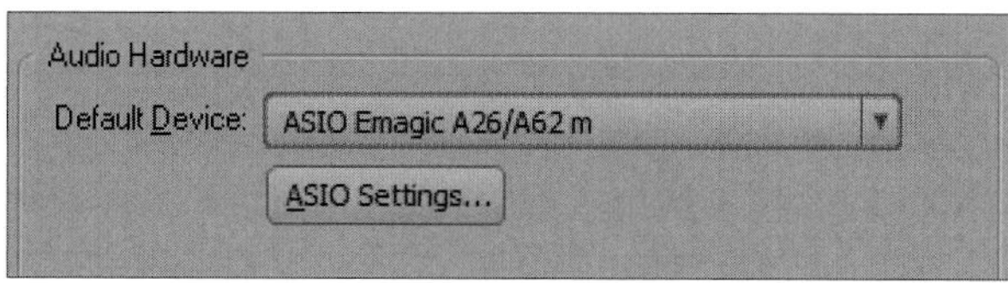

a

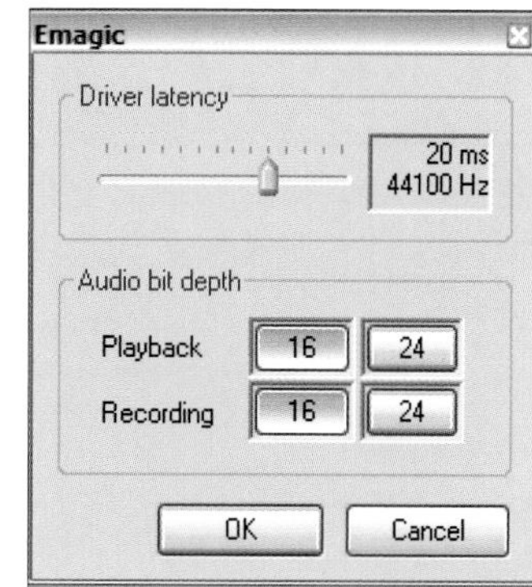

b

Figures 17.12a and b When you have a secondary interface installed, you can select it as your default device (a). With the device loaded, clicking the ASIO Settings button brings up a dialog that will be specific to the installed device (b) and will dictate its playback and recording parameters. In this case, this is the ASIO dialog is for an Emagic A26.

each device. Click the ASIO button for a listing to see its specific ASIO settings.

For example, **Figures 17.12 and b** shows the dialog for my Emagic device. The Driver Latency setting increases or decreases the latency period for playback with the device. The latency value is milliseconds over the assigned sample rate. Here the card is assigned to play at 44.1kHz. Increasing Driver Latency produces improved performance, because it allows the device a bit more time for processing. Decreasing the setting demands more from the device. The remaining fields toggle the card's playback and recording bit depths: 16 or 24 bits. Increasing the bit depth for input enhances the quality of audio being recorded.

Audio Output Mapping

The Audio Output Mapping preference (Edit > Preferences > Audio Output Mapping) reveals all the output channels associated with the available output devices, some of which (such as DV) are not listed in the Audio Hardware preferences. The Audio Output Mapping preference allows you to manually modify the routing of your audio channels. For example, for the Premiere Pro Windows Sound device, the mapping will list the channels associated with the device selected in Audio Hardware. The mapping now shows the two Sigma Tel channels for re-mapping. Dragging the left and right speaker icons from one channel to the other swaps which channel plays the left and which channel plays the right.

When you select a six-channel ASIO device for output, the ist gets more crowded. **Figure 17.13** shows the output mapping of the two stereo sigma channels. To route the channels for my 5.1 surround system, it is just a matter of matching the icons for the channels to where the speakers are plugged in (**Figure 17.14**). For example, the LFE is plugged into output port number 6, so the LFE icon in the output channel mappings should be in output 6.

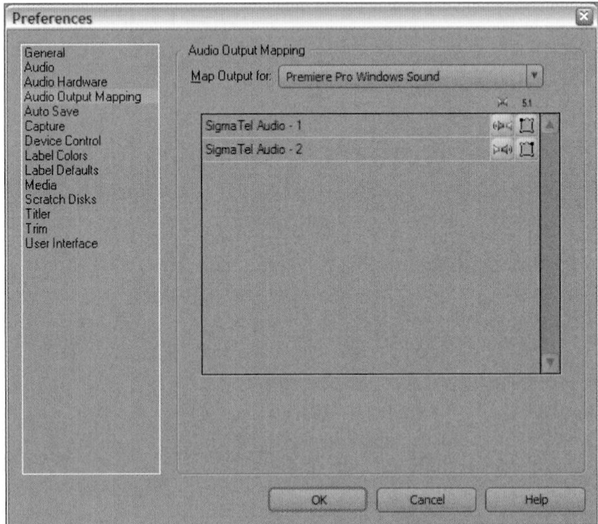

Figure 17.13 In the Audio Output Mapping preference, drag the speaker icons to assign them to an output channel.

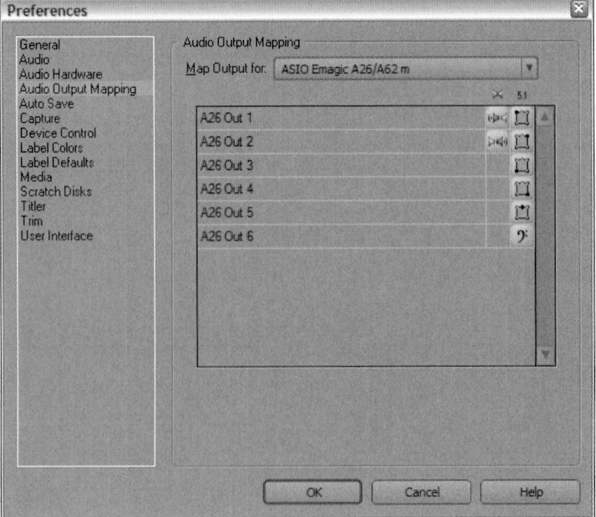

Figure 17.14 The Audio Output Mapping for an interface with six output channels contains icons for every speaker of a 5.1 surround system. The icon with the ear and the colon is for the LFE.

Input: Picking a Microphone

You configured and adjusted your input, but what about your input device? In many audio recording situations, the size of the input jack and type of audio card are not nearly as important as the microphone that you are using. If you have a good microphone and recording settings of at least 16 bit, stereo, 44kHz, then you should achieve an adequate recording. (Keep in mind that the standard for CD audio is 16 bit, 44.1kHz, but DV is 16 bit 48kHz.) To pick a good microphone, you need to consider a few factors.

Power and Pre-Amps

Some microphones, called *active microphones*, use batteries in their bodies to give them power, other mics require a separate device to provide power, and a third group requires no additional power, only a pre-amp to amplify the mic's signal.

Microphones requiring separate power are known as *phantom microphones* or *condensers*. They must be plugged into a port that not only takes in their signal, but also provides power. If the input port of your audio card does not provide phantom power for your microphone, then you must purchase a phantom power box that accepts the microphone input on one side, provides it power, and connects to your recording device with the powered signal on the other side. When you purchase or order your microphone, be sure to identify whether it is phantom or self-powering. Higher quality and expensive microphones commonly require either phantom power or a pre-amp.

Microphones that don't need power may, however, require a *pre-amp*, which is a small box that acts as a go-between from your microphone to your recording device. The microphone plugs into the pre-amp, which plugs into the recording device. The benefit of having a pre-amp is that it can *gain stage*, or boost, the incoming signal from the mic to give you a stronger incoming audio level. Some phantom boxes also come with a built-in pre-amp. Using the pre-amp's dial, you can increase or decrease the strength of the signal coming out of the microphone. Conveniently, the 1/8" stereo jack on your default Windows audio card has a built-in pre-amp, making it easy to use basic webcam voice microphones and other basic microphones without having to worry about any additional devices.

Microphone Classifications

The next factor to consider when shopping for a microphone is which type will be best for your projects. Microphones are specified in three groups:

- **Dynamic microphones.** The type of mics that you typically see on a desk at a press conference or near the drums of a rock concert. Shaped like ice cream cones, they are very durable, are self-powered, and can handle a very high range of noise, from loud crashes to whispers. These mics are usually not too expensive (around $100) and are perfect for the home recording of voiceovers. Dynamic mics that don't require power are commonly referred to as *passive*.
- **Condenser microphones.** Typically either phantom or battery-powered microphones. They have a better range and clarity level than dynamic mics; they also respond better to different frequencies. Condenser microphones break down into further categories, but for now it is important simply to know that condenser microphones are useful for recording professional voiceover content or the voice of a singer.
- **Ribbon microphones.** Very expensive and very delicate microphones that cannot handle high sound pressure levels (loud noises) well. Like dynamic mics, they do not require additional power. Ribbon microphones are perfect for recording ambient noises and natural sounds, because the character of the metallic ribbon's response to sound produces very warm, natural recordings. Related to ribbon microphones are PZMs (pressure zone microphone). Typically flat, plate-like devices, PZMs are omnidirectional microphones that can be placed on a wall to record the sounds and ambient atmosphere of an entire room. If you need to record atmospheres and ambient noises for a film or other project, you could rent a ribbon microphone.

Each type of microphone can either be omni-directional or uni-directional. For *omni-directional* mics, the field of recording sound comes from all in one focused direction and sounds that do not fall within the pickup pattern are rejected. In other words, the recording comes from one specific direction. Uni-directional microphones vary in their degree of sensitivity much like the angle and diameter of a spotlight (**Figure 17.15**).

For example, *shotgun* microphones are uni-directional microphones that are always pointed toward the mouth of the character who is speaking. On film sets, you see these microphones being held on a long stick (*boom*) above the actors' heads during filming. The boom operator is the person who gets the microphone close enough to record, but out of the view of what's being filmed. The real benefit of the shotgun mic is that it captures the actor's voice only, while rejecting most of the production sound and noise coming from behind or above.

Depending on your budget and intended use, you can explore a simple dynamic directional mic or a condenser mic for recording live audio.

Directional Microphones

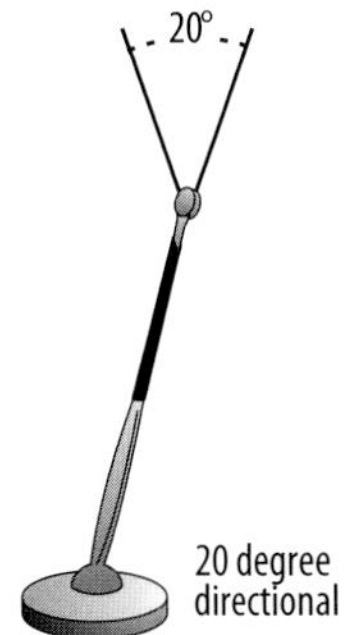

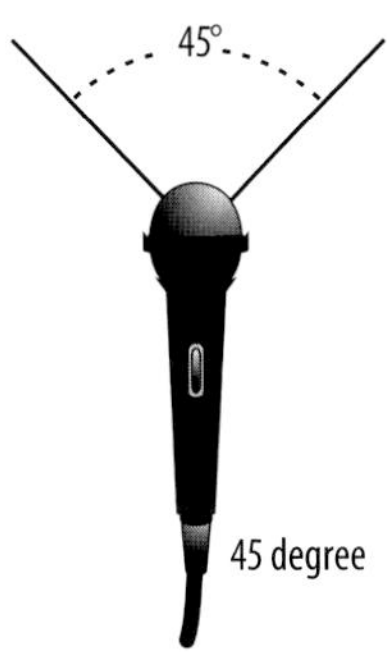

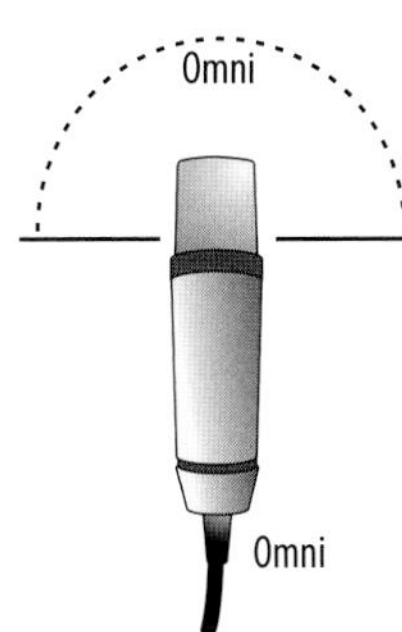

Figure 17.15 Common for film production, 20-degree directional mics (top) are pointed directly at the mouth of a character so as to not pick up other sounds. A 45-degree mic (middle) picks up sounds from a wider range. Omni-directional mics (bottom) are useful for picking up a full range of natural sounds coming from all directions.

Recording Live Audio

When recording from your default audio microphone jack or from the inputs on your additional audio device, you use the Premiere Pro Audio Mixer to determine which inputs to record from. These inputs directly relate to what was selected in your Audio Hardware Preferences.

Choosing an Input

Depending on which input/output device you have selected in Premiere Pro's Audio Hardware Preferences, you can easily choose which input channel to record from in the Audio Mixer. Select the track you wish to record into by clicking the Microphone Record toggle button. With the button on, you can select the recording input channel from the drop-down menu above the button (see **Figure 17.16**).

When recording, the track type that you are recording into is a critical choice (**Figure 17.17**). If you activate a stereo track for recording, Premiere creates a stereo file; activating a mono track results in a mono file. For a live voiceover recording, for example, recording a single channel, mono file is best, because you can mix down and pan your voiceover in a stereo or surround sequence later.

Live Level Adjustments

With your track selected, put the Audio Mixer into record mode by clicking the red record circle in the bottom of the Mixer window. Once you begin recording, you can either increase or reduce the incoming audio's volume by moving the Track Volume slider up or down (**Figure 17.18**). Of course, after you finish recording you can normalize the audio file so that it achieves its optimum volume. Getting a solid recording the first time around, however, is very important.

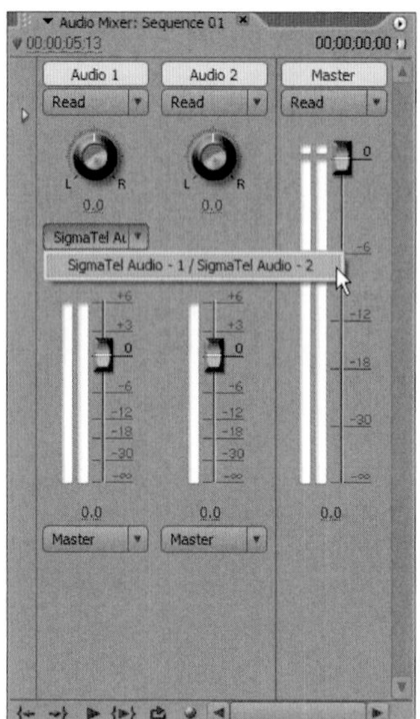

Figure 17.16 Turn on a track for recording, then use the drop-down menu in that track's Audio Mixer column to specify an input port for recording. Using the default stereo input from my default Windows Audio setting, I get to record both channels into my stereo track.

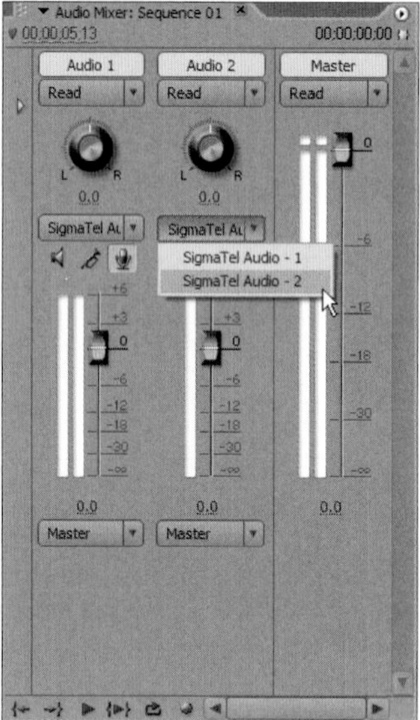

Figure 17.17 Using the same default Audio setting, notice how Audio 2, which is mono, allows me to select either channel 1 or channel 2. Although the input still may be stereo, you can record only mono (single channel) into a mono track.

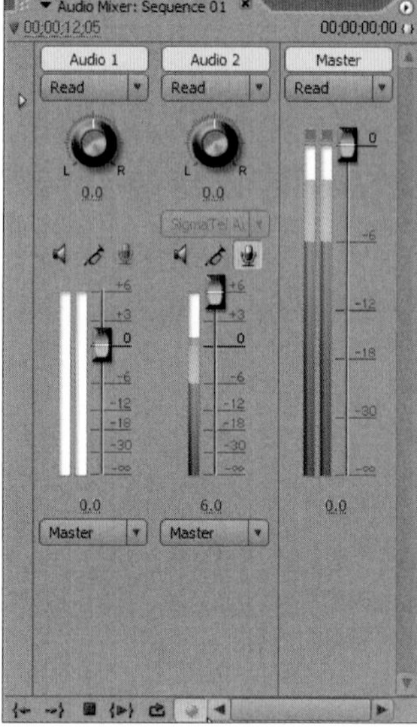

Figure 17.18 When you raise the slider above 0dB, you boost or add gain to the incoming signal, making the audio louder.

To further adjust or change the levels coming into your microphone port, you can revisit the Advanced Controls for Microphone dialog in your Windows XP Sound Control Panel (Figure 17.8).

Output: Speakers and Headphones

As you play back and mix your audio, you can listen to it with speakers and headphones. You can connect as many speakers as you need, or, you can purchase six-channel surround sound headphones (although they aren't quite the best way to properly listen to a 5.1 mix in surround sound).

If you are serious about your audio work in Premiere Pro, I recommend using both speakers and headphones, because of the amount of low and high frequency noise that can go undetected with most speakers, especially small computer speakers. Having big snug headphones wrapped around your ears completely immerses you in the world of sound, and when you work with sound it should be all consuming. A good pair of headphones that reduces or blocks out external noises is worth a few extra dollars. As for speakers, dollar amount still equals quality and that goes double for surround sound systems. Expensive speakers are likely to have a better dynamic ability to accurately play a higher range of frequencies.

To hear anything through either, however, you need to make sure all your levels are set up properly.

Mixing and Monitoring

As you remember, you can set the overall system volume level that is routed to the speakers on your system. It is always a good idea to keep this volume on the higher side and to reduce the volume on the individual speakers if it is too loud.

Although Premiere Pro's mixer accurately displays the exact dB level of your audio while it plays, if the sound output volume of your system is too low, you may not be able to distinguish distorted or garbled audio. If the volume is not loud enough, you also won't be able to hear the clicks, pops, and other noises that need to be removed.

Keep in mind that adjustments to the volume sliders in the Audio Mixer affect the mixdown. Adjustments to the sound out, headphone out, or speaker volume from the audio card will affect the loudness at which you hear the audio from Premiere Pro.

Things to Remember

There are a number of points to take away from this chapter regarding setting up, recording in, and playing out audio with Premiere Pro.

When setting up, use the Sound and Audio Devices Properties to adjust the incoming and outgoing volume levels for the default audio and additional audio interfaces with your system. If you are trying to use a 5.1 multi-channel surround sound system, be sure the interface supports ASIO and be sure you have properly mapped your speakers in the Audio Output Mapping preference. To access additional settings proprietary to the device, click the ASIO settings button with the default device set to the device in your Audio Hardware preference.

If you are doing voiceovers for home videos and your own projects, there is no need to shell out $1000 for a condenser microphone. A dynamic microphone from your local music store (or the web) is totally reasonable. When purchasing your microphone, check if it requires a pre-amp. If it does, see if you can get the mic with a 1/8" plug adapter; that way you can use the pre-amp of your default audio device.

If you want to record higher quality audio or have a specific task in mind, research the condenser or ribbon options. At the end of the day, if you only need to record a few things, you can always rent a good microphone and return it once your work is complete. Again, verify the pre-amp, phantom, and battery power needs for each microphone.

When listening to your audio, have the best and worst scenarios readily available. For example, I have a television with a mono speaker as my worst listening environment. On the flip side, a sensitive pair of big snug headphones allows me to block out all other sound and focus on the audio. For the best in speakers, I have surround speakers properly placed and positioned so that the sound is accurately distributed. At the end of the day, not all of us can afford a sound-tight room and precise JBL speakers, but given the portability of Premiere Pro, you could achieve a decent amount of work at home then bring your project into a professional studio to finish the job.

Finally, one last thing my mentor always said was that the audio coming out of your system can only be as good as the audio coming into it. Meaning, if you have a poor quality recording, there's a lot you can do to fix it, but it will never compare to a crisp, clear, and full-bodied original recording.

In the next chapter, you will dive into recording an actual voiceover. In later chapters, you will cut it up, clean it up, and then fix it up to make it sound as good as possible.

CHAPTER

18

Recording and Editing a Voiceover

Whether you are creating a commercial for broadcast or a video for your family, voiceover narration can add a substantial amount of context and information to your piece.

This chapter will walk you through setting up your project for recording a voiceover, properly setting your input levels, arranging your sequence to better suit a recording environment, and the actual recording itself. In the second half of the chapter, you will edit your voiceover, cut it up, add subtle transitions, and remove unwanted breaths. For both these lessons, you'll add a voiceover file to the sample project that originally came with Premiere Pro 1.5.

Two Schools for Voiceover

Traditionally, there are two schools for voiceover work. School One is to write your script first, edit the voiceover, and then add the video where it needs to be placed. School Two is to edit the video first and then narrate and add your voiceover to color the video. Neither is right or wrong, but sometimes one approach is better suited to your material than the other. What's most important in your project? Audio and text are the foundations for School One (script first, video second), whereas video and visuals are the foundations for School Two (video editing first, narration second).

If I am working on a family video, photo montage, or DVD commentary, I edit the clips first, then narrate and add the voiceover while I watch it play back—School Two. If I am editing a commercial or putting together a project with a defined length, I follow School One. I record and edit the voiceover first to ensure that I am at the proper length, then I edit the video and make small adjustments to the voiceover where it's necessary to make words hit at exact moments. If a piece needs to convey certain verbal messages, slogans, or descriptions, it's important to write, record, and edit the entire voiceover so that you know it fits within the duration you have for your completed edit. You can always slide the words' positions after you know they fit.

When I edited the sample project for Adobe, I tried to make a short and simple montage of clips integrated with transitions on two tracks each for audio and video, as well as an animated Photoshop file to highlight that feature. For this audio section, you will treat the montage as if it were a car commercial.

To reduce the preparatory video editing steps, you'll use the completed sample project and follow School Two this time. To help you out, I have put together a brief script that echoes the visual emphasis of the edit. Time to get started.

Recording Preparations

To begin recording a voiceover, you have to have a sequence open and available to record into.

1. Open the Recording_Start project from APPST2 Lesson Files/Chapter 18 folder. To load the project properly, link to the media in the APPST2 Lesson Files/Sample Project NTSC folder when prompted.

   When opening the Recording_Start.prproj file, you need to link the files in this project to the same files.

2. Right-click in the track header of the open sequence, and select Add Tracks. In the resulting Add Tracks dialog, make the following settings in the Audio Tracks area:

   Add: **1**
   Placement: **Before First Track**
   Track Type: **Mono**

   Click OK to accept (**Figure 18.1**). Right-click in the track header of the newly created Audio 1 track, and select Rename. After the text highlights, change the track name to VO (for voiceover).

   Because you want the voiceover to be a single-channel file, you select Mono for Track Type. By specifying Before First Track for Placement, you ensure Premiere creates the track before the current track (the music track). I typically put my music track at the very bottom of my sound mix with the other tracks above. I also rename the track something specific to the content that will be in the track. Labeling your voiceover track VO enables you to easily verify what's in the track when your mixer is open and you can't see the physical content of the track.

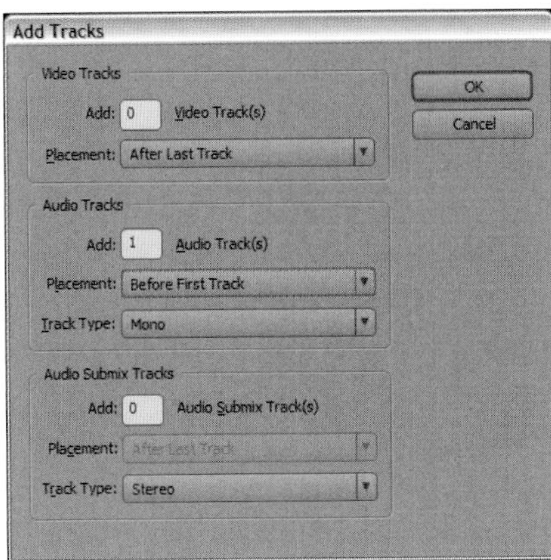

Figure 18.1 In the Add Tracks dialog, you can add three separate track types in one action, Video, Audio, and Audio Submix. For this lesson, you need to add just one mono track.

3. To better equip the timeline for recording the voiceover, create a new Universal Countdown Leader (UCL) and insert it before the current material in the timeline (**Figure 18.2**). After adding the UCL, hold down the Alt key and select only the audio portion of the UCL. Press Delete to delete its audio from the sequence.

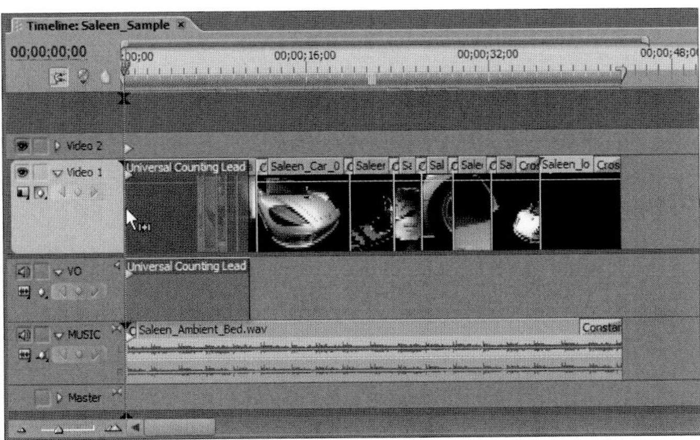

Figure 18.2 Holding down the Ctrl key toggles you into Insert editing mode, thus rippling the current media on all tracks to the right to make room for the inserted UCL file. Holding down Ctrl+Shift enables you to insert and ripple the content onto only the tracks where the edited media is added.

Because your voiceover recording begins at the moment you play back your sequence from the mixer in record mode, it is good to have a few seconds (or more) of

If you are having trouble configuring your device, consult Chapter 17, "Using Your Audio Hardware," to review the setup process.

pre-roll time to step back from the computer and begin your voiceover at the start of your edit. Adding a UCL to the timeline is a trick that buys you that time.

4. Select Edit > Preferences > Audio Hardware. In the Audio Hardware Preferences, verify the Input/Output device that you are using to record your audio. Your choices will be the Premiere Pro Windows Sound or any additional audio interface installed on your system. Click the ASIO button to verify the input you have selected.

   This step verifies which device you are using to capture your audio. If you have a two-channel ASIO device, for example, you can select that device from the drop- down menu and then record from the inputs on the device. For the default Windows setting, you will most likely be recording from your 1/8" microphone input jack.

5. From your Window menu, select Workspace > Audio. The Audio Mixer will open; double-check that it is expanded to show the full mixer. From the Audio Mixer's wing menu, choose Meter Input(s) Only.

   Adjusting your workspace is a quick and simple way to have access to certain windows. The Audio Workspace always has the Audio Mixer open in its layout. Selecting the Meter Input(s) Only option puts the mixer into a mode that displays the dB volume level of any incoming signal.

6. In the Audio Mixer, click the Microphone Toggle button in the VO track to enable the track for recording. From the drop-down menu above the icon, select the appropriate input channel (**Figure 18.3**).

   This step ensures you will be able to view and record the levels coming in from your microphone input during recording.

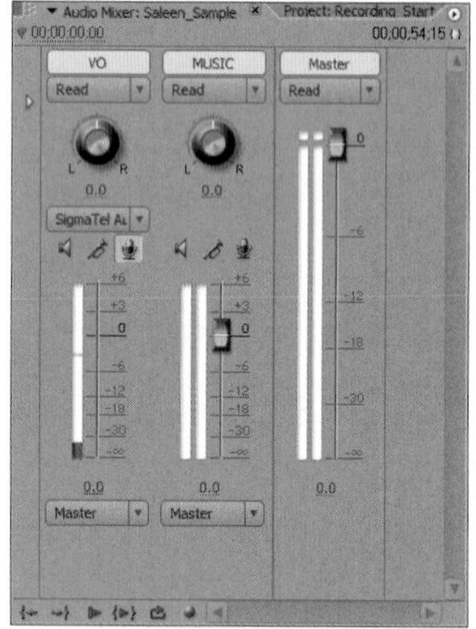

Figure 18.3 The mixer is set to monitor inputs only and the VO track is enabled for recording with an input channel selected. Notice how the VU meters register about –30dB of sound coming from my plugged-in microphone. Also notice the small yellow limiter line that indicates the loudest sound coming from the input device. As long as this line does not register above 0dB in the red, your levels are not too loud.

Because there's more to recording quality than the input line, give some thought now to your recording environment.

Room Acoustics

Where you record can have a big effect on your results. Although not all of us can afford to soundproof a room to eliminate echo and reverberation, you can do a few simple things to reduce and diminish potential unwanted noises.

Be sure that you are not recording near any appliances that produce a low-frequency hum (a refrigerator or certain light fixtures on dimmers). Although you can remove these hums with the Notch filter, avoiding them makes for one less element of noise. Similarly, placing your microphone near the computer potentially can pick up the noises of your computer and nearby devices.

Try not to stand in the center of the room. Recording from a corner with your back to the wall can reduce some immediate reverberation from your voice. Particularly if you have a dynamic directional mic pointing toward you and the corner, you won't have such a dramatic echo coming from behind.

Remember, too, that carpets absorb sound, whereas hardwood floors echo it.

At the end of the day, a little noise isn't the end of the world. Feedback, static, and poor volume levels (either too high or too low) can be far more damaging to your recording.

Recording Your Voice

Having prepped your timeline and set it up for recording, it's time to click Record and lay down your voice track. For this series of steps, make sure that your voice registers at a healthy level and does not peak or exceed the 0dB ceiling.

1. Practice speaking the voiceover script (see the sidebar "Sample Voiceover Script") into the microphone at a normal room speaking level. Be sure that you see your VU meters responding to your vocal level as you are speaking.

   As you speak into the microphone, the volume level coming from the microphone input should never exceed the dark black 0dB line. You will want to be somewhere between –12dB and just above –6dB.

   Find the optimum distance and relative position that the microphone should be from your mouth so that your voice is not too loud or too soft. After you are comfortable with your practice, move on to the next step. If

Sample Project Voiceover Script

"A dream comes to life. The Saleen S7 is a breathtaking sports car that blurs the line between science and art. From its sleek aerodynamic shape to its luxurious interior, the S7 is the premiere sports car for the twenty-first century. Built from the most solid materials and weighing under 2000 pounds, the Saleen S7 is truly a dream come true."

Disclaimer:

"This voiceover is not intended to endorse or represent Saleen and should only be used for instructional purposes. Thank You."

Troubleshooting Your Input Levels

From Windows, open the Sounds and Audio Devices Properties Control Panel. Select the Audio tab, and click the Volume button for Sound Recording. In the Recording Control Panel, be sure that Microphone is the selected Recording Device and that its volume level isn't too low (**Figure 18.4a** and **b**).

As discussed in the previous chapter, you can set and configure your input and output levels in this Control Panel as well as raise the volume level of your microphone.

If you are using a pre-amp with your mic, you can adjust the amp level to make your voice louder or softer. As you speak and adjust your amp, the levels will update live in the Audio Mixer window.

you still have low levels, refer to the notes below and/or see the previous chapter "Using Your Audio Hardware" and refer to the "Adjusting Audio Settings" sections.

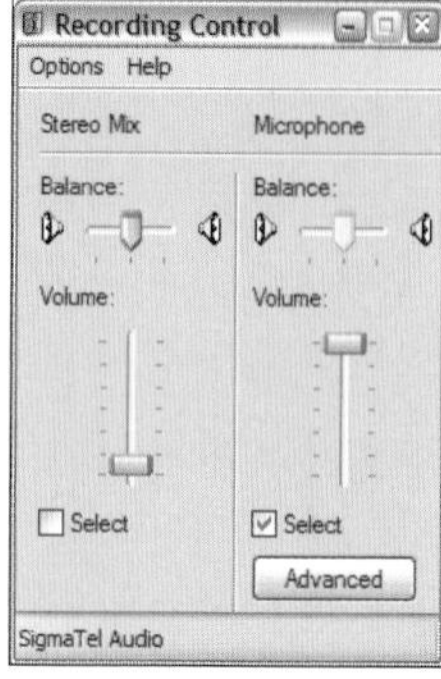

a

Advanced Controls for Microphone

These settings can be used to make fine adjustments to your audio.

Tone Controls

These settings control how the tone of your audio sounds.

Bass: Low High

Treble: Low High

Other Controls

These settings make other changes to how your audio sounds. See your hardware documentation for details.

1 Microphone Boost

Close

b

Figures 18.4a and b In the Recording Control dialog box (a), note that Select is checked under Microphone, indicating that your mic is the incoming device. Clicking the Advanced button then opens an additional dialog (b) where you can add a boost to the incoming levels from your microphone.

2. With the volume input level set and your rehearsal complete, click the Solo Track button (the horn button) in the VO track of the Audio Mixer (**Figure 18.5**).

   Clicking the Solo Track button mutes the Music track so that the music does not play back as you record. Regardless of whether you turn on Meter Input(s) Only, you will want to solo whichever track you are recording into at the time.

Figure 18.5 Clicking the Solo Track button automatically mutes the other tracks in the sequence so that the only audio you hear is that of the specified track.

3. Select the Timeline panel, and press the Home key to position the CTI at the head of the timeline. In the Audio Mixer, click the red Record button to arm the Audio Mixer for recording. When you are ready to record, click Play.

   There is maybe a one-second latency from the moment you click Play until the moment that recording begins. As soon as you see the timecode numbers moving in the Program Monitor, whatever sound that is coming into the microphone will be recording into a file onto the VO track. You can also verify this by watching the VU meters spike up and down when you speak into the microphone. If you do not see the spike while recording is engaged, check your connection and audio device set up.

   In terms of timing, once you see the number 3 countdown cut to black in the UCL, you have two seconds before your edit begins.

Figure 18.6 Notice how the newly created file is named with the track name, then a number: VO_107. Also notice how the file is added not only to the track in which it was recorded, but also into the Project panel.

After you are done recording, your timeline should look something like the one in **Figure 18.6**.

4. Once you record a take you are happy with, double-click the audio file from the Timeline panel to open it in the Source Monitor. With the Source Monitor active and the clip selected, choose File > Export > Audio. In the Export Audio dialog, rename the file something specific so that it is easy to identify. I used the name Saleen_VO.wav. If you have multiple takes, then you could name the first file Saleen_VO_01.wav and increment each take. In the Export Audio dialog, click Settings and from the General Settings, make sure that the file type is Windows Waveform and that you are exporting the entire clip. From the Audio Settings,

make sure the file is uncompressed with a Sample Rate of 48000Hz, 16 bit, mono. A 1 frame interleave is fine.

Whew! It sounds like a lot, but because the auto-naming format for audio recording isn't specific as to project and other attributes that you might want to add, it's important to save a version of the file to disk with a name you decide. The original file, VO_10.wav, will also be saved to your disk, and it will reside in the scratch disk location that you specified for captured audio (Edit > Preferences > Scratch Disks > Captured Audio). If you recorded a stereo track, then be sure that Stereo instead of Mono is selected when you export. It's always good to double-check your export settings before you save your file.

Additionally, if you recorded multiple takes in a single pass, you could mark In and Out points in the Source Monitor for the section of the clip that you want to export and choose the Export Range: IN to OUT from Audio Export General Settings. This exports the In and Out range as an individual file when exporting.

5. The final step for the lesson is necessary only if you feel you need to record your voiceover again. If that's the case, with the Timeline panel active, press the Home key and repeat steps 3 and 4.

   Although you will be overwriting the current file in the track with every new recording pass, you will not be deleting the overwritten files from your project.

Well, you've done it: You've gotten audio out of your mouth and into your timeline!

With the foundation built for recording a voiceover, you should have no problem adding a voiceover track to any sequence. Your only problems to solve will be configuring your volume and finding the right microphone and mic settings. For most of my voiceover work—roughing in tracks for later replacement—a simple PC microphone is fine. If you are doing voiceovers for DVD movies or for slideshows, however, I recommend putting the extra effort into getting a decent microphone and recording in a quiet environment.

For monitoring a voiceover while recording, I recommend using headphones or turning the volume of your speakers off. Any additional noise picked up by the microphone can loop back into the recording. This is called *feedback*. Greater intensities of feedback can occur if the signal you are recording is played out of the speakers and picked up again by the microphone that is recording. Feedback starts low and then quickly crescendos into piercingly loud audio that will make even the toughest punk rockers cry.

Because Premiere Pro allows you to play back your timeline as you record your voiceover narration, the first thing to do is render the sequence's preview files so that there are no playback hiccups. Once the files are rendered, any red render bars should now be green.

Now that you have successfully recorded your voiceover narration, you can do a lot to the file to clean it up and get it flowing and sounding better than the original recording. For the second half of this chapter you will edit the voice-over you recorded to match the flow of the video. You will add transitions to the head and tail of each clip so that there are no abrupt or excess noises. Finally, you will learn a technique for removing unwanted breaths or noises in the spaces between words.

Cutting Your Voiceover

Editing the voiceover file is the first step to getting it into shape. Once you normalize the volume level, you will cut the voiceover into smaller pieces and adjust the timing with the flow of the video. By spacing out the words and sentences you will create timing that is different than in the original recording.

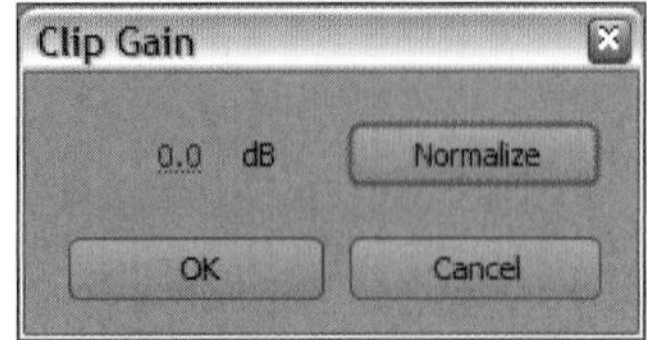

Figure 18.7 When you normalize the master file selected in the Project panel, all subsequent instances and uses from the master clip will use the adjusted Gain value. The first and most important step before cutting up your file is to Normalize its volume level.

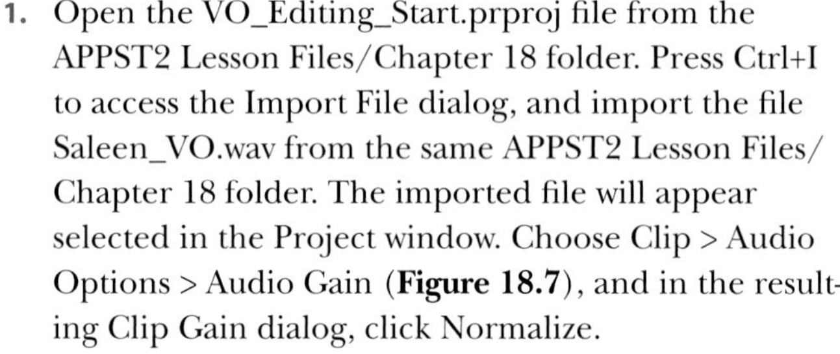

1. Open the VO_Editing_Start.prproj file from the APPST2 Lesson Files/Chapter 18 folder. Press Ctrl+I to access the Import File dialog, and import the file Saleen_VO.wav from the same APPST2 Lesson Files/Chapter 18 folder. The imported file will appear selected in the Project window. Choose Clip > Audio Options > Audio Gain (**Figure 18.7**), and in the resulting Clip Gain dialog, click Normalize.

   This voiceover file does not require any gain adjustments, and the result from Normalize is 0dB. This is because the pre-amp that I used for recording properly adjusted the incoming signal so that the levels were as strong as possible without exceeding the ceiling. I strongly recommend always starting your workflow with normalization of the audio, because you may often have a less than perfectly recorded file.

2. Double-click the Saleen_VO.wav file in the Project panel to open it in the Source Monitor. Adjust the viewing area bar so that you are zoomed into the details of the file (**Figures 18.8a** and **b**).

To begin cutting up the voiceover file, you want to be zoomed in tight enough to the source material so that your In and Out points don't include a lot of extraneous material.

The next step is to edit out all the mistakes and empty spaces between the important words and phrases that will make up your final voiceover edit. I'll walk you through cutting up the first element and then identify the rest of the cuts for you to finish later.

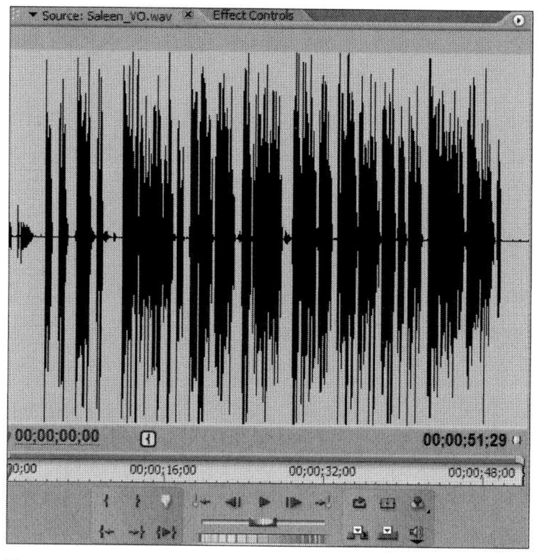

a

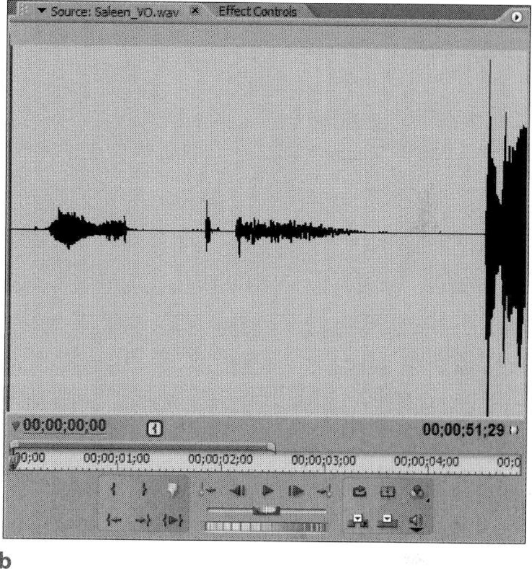

b

Figures 18.8a and b The clip as it is first revealed in its entirety (a) and with the viewing area bar reduced to zoom in tighter on the open clip (b). When editing audio, not only can you use the viewing area bar to zoom in, but you can also toggle your display to audio units so that you can zoom to the subframe level.

3. Make sure you are displaying video frames in your Source Monitor and not audio units. Click to select the current frame's timecode value in the lower-left corner of the Source Monitor, type the value 412, and press Enter. Your CTI should snap to the timecode value of 04;12, just before the first phrase, "A Dream." Press I to mark an In point. Select the current frame timecode value again, type 511, and press Enter. Your CTI should snap to 05;11, which is right after the phrase "A Dream." Press O to set an Out point. Click and drag the In/Out instance from the Source Monitor, releasing

Figure 18.9 By creating a small In/Out instance from the master clip, you have a unique clip that contains only the duration specified from the Source Monitor. Because Snapping is on, if you drag the subclip near any of the numbered markers, you can automatically snap to their position and release the subclip in that place. Notice that because you are dropping the subclip using no modification keys, the Overlay icon displays and no elements of the timeline are shifted when you release the clip. Finally, notice how the Snapping line has an arrow pointing up at the top of the timeline, this indicates that it is snapping to a timeline marker.

it onto the VO track at the 0 numbered marker in the timeline (**Figure 18.9**).

You identified a section of the audio file and determined precise In and Out points so that there was no extra material. Once you made your selection, you added the clip into a predetermined position in the sequence.

4. To make the next subclip, simply create a new In/Out instance and drag the subclip to the next marker position in the timeline. Table 18.1 lists the remaining In/Out instances and the phrases that each contains. After you have cut each up, your edit should look something like **Figure 18.10.**

Table 18.1: Voiceover In/Out Instances for Cutting

Timecode Range	Phrase	Marker Number
05;21–6;29	"Comes to life."	1
11;26–18;02	"The Saleen S7…art."	2
18;16–20;27	"From its sleek aerodynamic shape…"	3
21;01–23;02	"To its luxurious interior…"	4
28;17–32;21	"The S7 is…century."	5
33;03–41;18	"Built…dream come true."	6
42;00–49;09	"This…Thank you."	7

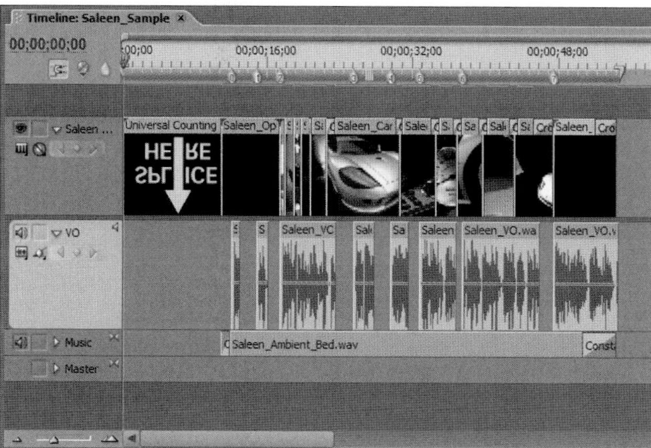

Figure 18.10 The markers make an easy guide for placing each subclip, but feel free to take some liberties if you want to change their position. Remember that if you do want to move the clips within a small range, you can toggle off Snapping ("S") so that every slight move doesn't snap to the next potential snapping point.

Once the pieces of the voiceover are separated, you can put certain elements farther apart or closer together. It's up to you to feel the rhythm and flow, deciding where exactly everything should line up. Because there is a music track, don't worry too much about the dead air between clips.

5. Open Edit > Preferences > General, and assign a value of 0.15 seconds for your Audio Transition Default Duration. Click in the VO track header to make sure that track is targeted (the track header will become dark gray). With no clips selected, press the Home key to snap the CTI to the beginning of the timeline. Press the Page Down key until your CTI is snapped to the head of your first voiceover subclip. Press Ctrl+Shift+D to add a default transition to the head of the subclip. Press Page Down to snap the CTI to the tail of the first subclip,

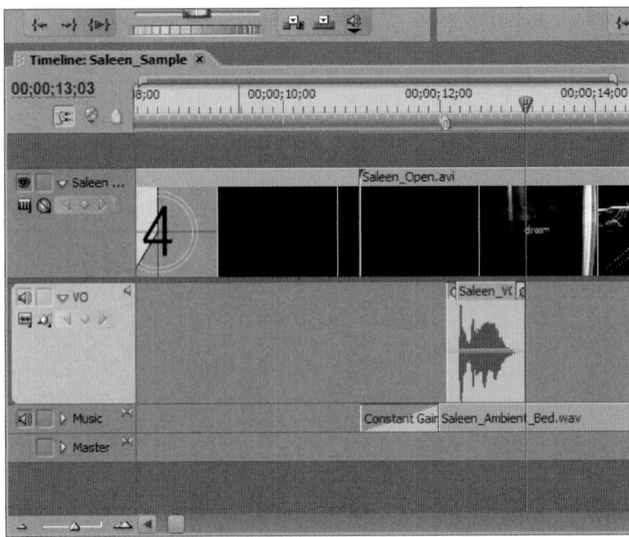

Figure 18.11 A one-sided transition was added to both the head and tail, creating a smooth volume fade from the empty space of the timeline to the audio of the subclip and then back to the empty space of the timeline. If your audio levels pop up in volume while you play the cuts of your inserted subclips, you can add transitions at the head and tail of each subclip to smooth the increase in volume.

and press Ctrl+Shift+D to place a default transition at its tail. Your first clip should look like **Figure 18.11**.

It may be necessary to zoom into your timeline to see the placed transitions because their size is 15/100ths of a second. You can vary the size of the transition to create a longer or shorter fade in and out.

Once you have placed your transitions, your edit should be in perfect shape to continue with the adjustments.

Speed Adjustments and Pitch Shifting

For the final disclaimer that is placed underneath the Saleen logo at the end of the edit, try picking up the pace, much like those rapid-fire disclaimers on certain television commercials.

To do this, select the clip you want to adjust in the timeline and press Ctrl+R (or choose Clip > Speed/Duration) to open the Speed/Duration dialog. In this dialog, adjust the speed of the clip to 120% and click the check box for Maintain Pitch. When you choose to maintain pitch, Premiere Pro dynamically adjusts the pitch of the sped-up audio so that it does not sound squeaky like a mouse but instead like a normal voice. The result is audio that is sped up to reduce its duration but without a distorted high-pitched sound.

Using this method in Premiere Pro, you can achieve the effect, but with some audible artifacts such as the slight echo effect. Listen to the file Disclaimer_PP_120.wav as an example (APPST2 Lesson Files/Chapter 18). Notice that although I was able to increase the speed and maintain a pretty similar vocal pitch, the file still has a slight electronic feel.

For comparison, I loaded the same file into Adobe Audition and used its Speed and Pitch tools to make an even faster speed adjustment while preserving the pitch. Listen to the file Disclaimer_AUD_170.wav (APPST2 Lesson Files/ Chapter 18) versus the Premiere processed Disclaimer_ PP_170.wav to hear the dramatic difference in quality.

As you can see—or hear—it is possible to expand or reduce the size of individual clips while keeping the proper pitch and sound of the voiceover intact. Although Premiere Pro has excellent audio processing capabilities, consider using Adobe Audition to take things to the next level.

Breath Removal

Some expendable elements that you can edit out of recorded speech are the subtle breaths and empty spaces between words. Particularly with voiceover narration, you don't want to hear any room tone or breaths between words and phrases. The effect is better when the only vocal sound comes when words are spoken; the rest of the track should be empty. Because your music will fill in the blanks, you want your voiceover to be as solid as possible for the elements that you want to hear. You can fine-tune and hone the audio a bit more with this technique for quick removal of smaller breaths or noises.

If you do not hear audio when you scrub, be sure that you have Play Audio While Scrubbing checked in your Preferences > Audio dialog.

Although Adobe Audition has excellent automated breath removal filters, I want to show you how to use volume keyframe editing in Premiere Pro to accomplish the same result. This technique will give you the skills to clean things yourself and help you further understand how to use of keyframes.

1. Open the file Breath_Removal_Start.prproj from the APPST2 Lesson Files/Chapter 18 folder. The second to last clip of voiceover, positioned at Marker 6, starts

with the words "built from the most." At approximately 41;25 in the sequence between the words "pounds" and "the Saleen," there is a little breath that you can easily clip out using the following keyframe adjustment method.

2. Click the Toggle Track Output button for your Music track to turn the speaker off. In your VO track, select Show Clip Volume from your Show Keyframes drop-down list.

   Because you turned off the output of the Music track, the only sound you'll hear while playing back will be the VO track. By setting Show Keyframes in the VO track to Show Clip Volume, you activate the visual display and interface for directly adjusting the volume of the individual subclip instances.

3. Move your CTI to 41;18 in the timeline. Switch your timeline counter to Audio Units from the Timeline panel wing menu, and zoom into your timeline at the current position. With your speaker or, preferably, headphone volume turned up, scrub the Edit Line between the end of the "sss" sound and the beginning of the "thhhh" sound—approximately 41:27000 to 41:44000 (**Figure 18.12**).

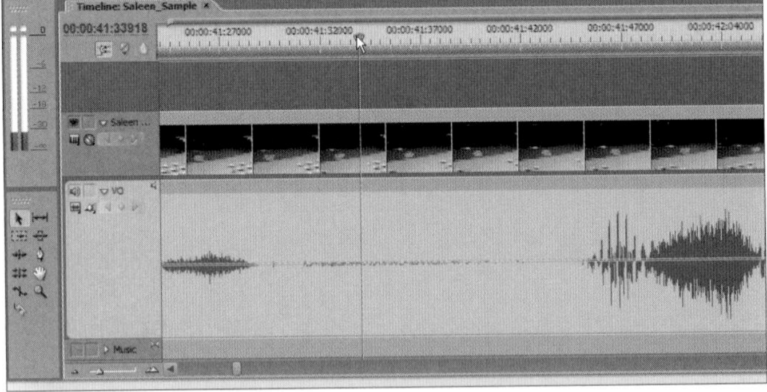

Figure 18.12 Notice that the breath does register a small waveform value where the Edit Line is scrubbing. Also, notice how even while scrubbing, the VU meters properly display the dB levels for the area being scrubbed. For this section, the volume level is about –30dB. Although this is not a particularly loud breath, it does register. By keyframing the overall volume levels in the section where the breath exists, you can easily get it out of your final edit.

   Because of the subframe sample level display, it is quick and easy to display your subframe waveform and scrub at the subframe level. By doing this, you can have greater accuracy in isolating and then removing unwanted sound elements.

4. With the Timeline panel active, press the P key to change your cursor into the Pen tool. Using the Pen tool, hold down the Ctrl key and add four keyframes starting from the end of the "sss" sound and ending at the beginning of the "thhh" sound (**Figure 18.13**).

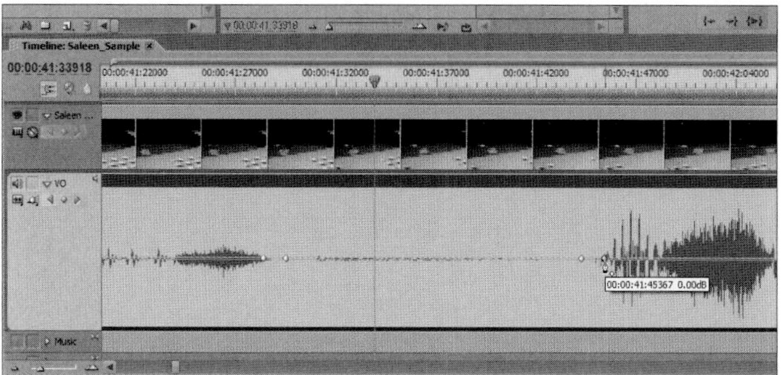

Figure 18.13 I have strategically placed the keyframes close together on each side. The first keyframe is placed at the end of the "ssss" sound with an accompanying keyframe just after. The fourth keyframe is created at the beginning of the "thhh" sound with an accompanying keyframe just before.

The Pen tool is your tool for adding, selecting, and adjusting keyframes. Holding down the Ctrl key toggles the Pen tool into a mode in which every click adds a new keyframe handle. The orange line displays the clip volume level, and now that you have added keyframes to that line you can adjust its value dynamically.

5. Continuing with the Pen tool, click and drag down the volume line between the two inner keyframes so that the volume line reads –oodB (**Figure 18.14**).

By dragging the center line down between the two inner keyframes, you have created a dip in the volume level of the subclip. The outer keyframe handles become the anchor points for the current volume level. The inner keyframe handles become the anchor points for the muted volume level.

Figure 18.14 When the Pen tool is held between two equal keyframe handles, it displays a horizontal bar with upward and downward pointing arrows. The function of the tool in this circumstance is to move the entire value between the two handles up or down in unison. Because it affects only the value between two handles, the outer keyframe handles preserve their current value. The inner two are adjusted to whatever you determine, in this case, 0dB or no volume.

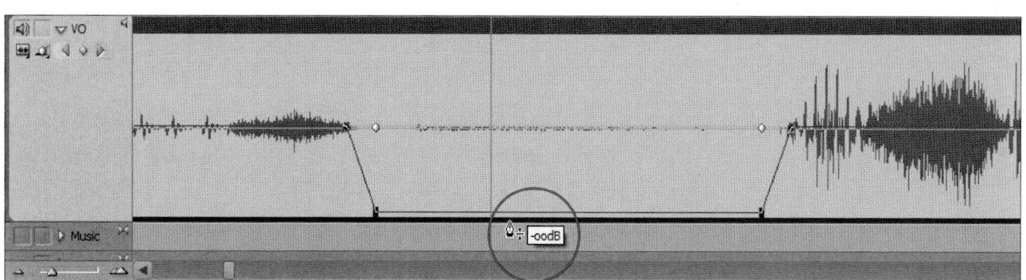

With your adjustment, the volume is at its normal level of 0dB until the end of the "ssss" sound. After the first keyframe handle, the volume fades down to –oodB, which is essentially muted. The volume remains muted until it hits the next –oodB keyframe handle, from which point the volume fades back up to the normal –0dB.

6. Click on the second keyframe with the Pen tool, and move it slightly closer to the first keyframe by gently dragging it left. This should make the line between the first two keyframes steeper. Click and drag the third keyframe closer to the fourth to make that angle steeper as well.

   By moving the keyframes closer together, you are causing the fade between volume levels to occur faster and less noticeably.

7. With the Pen tool still active, click and marquee select all four keyframes (**Figures 18.15a**, **b**, and **c**). Right-click on one of the keyframes, and select Continuous Bezier from the drop-down menu.

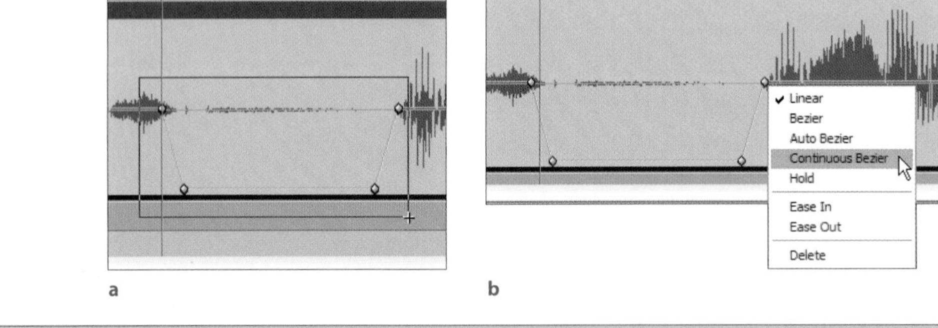

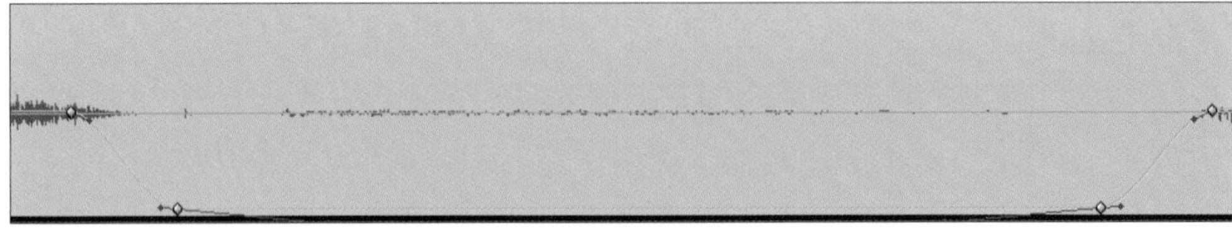

Figures 18.15a, b, and c By clicking and dragging over the keyframes, you can select them all (a). After the keyframes are selected (yellow), you can right-click on any of them and change the straight lines that connect them into Continuous Bezier curved lines (b). The result of the curved line connecting the keyframes is subtle but effective (c). Notice the Blue keyframe handles that can be adjusted to change the curve.

By choosing Continuous Bezier for the keyframe interpolation, you created smooth volume curves, as opposed to straight linear lines. Now, the audio smoothly fades out, then smoothly fades back up.

8. Using the Pen tool, and with the keyframes still selected (**Figure 18.16**), press Ctrl+C to copy the selected keyframes.

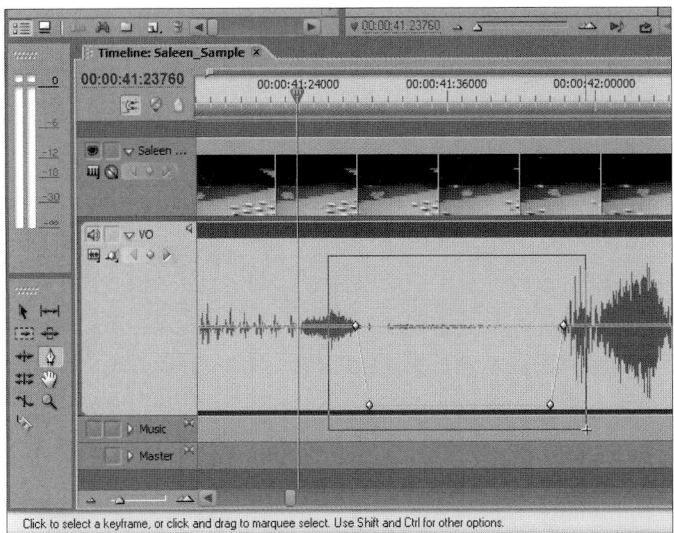

Figure 18.16 Just as in the last step, the Pen tool can range-select a group of keyframes. While pressing the mouse button, drag the Pen tool past a group of keyframes. The selected keyframes turn yellow. Pressing Ctrl+C copies the selected keyframe values and spatial positioning to your clipboard. You can then paste those exact keyframe values into the clip volume level of another subclip.

9. Position the Edit Line at 51:05000 (approximately), and click within the clip boundary of the Disclaimer subclip to select that clip in the timeline. Press Ctrl+V to paste the copied keyframes into the Disclaimer subclip, starting from the current Edit Line position.

   Notice that the keyframes are copied exactly into the new clip adhering to their copied parameters. From this point, all you need to do is use the Pen tool to range-select one side of the pasted keyframes and adjust them in unison.

10. Zoom into your timeline at approximately 51:22000. With the Pen tool, range-select the two right keyframes and slide them left so that the last keyframe lines up with the first spikes of the waveform (see **Figure 18.17**).

To copy and paste keyframes from one clip to another, the clip that the keyframes are being pasted into must be selected. Keyframes always are pasted starting from the position of the Edit Line.

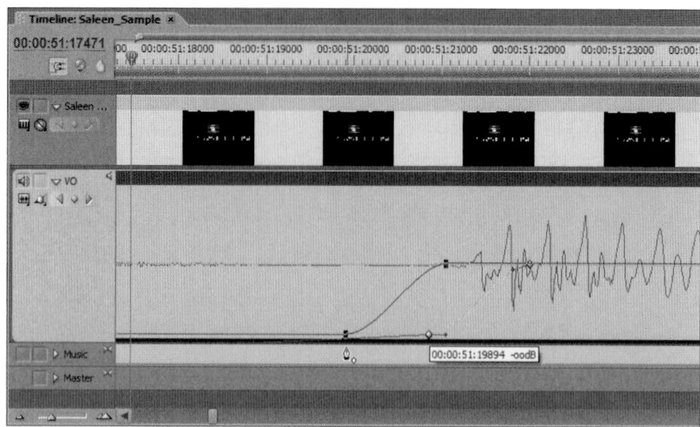

Figure 18.17 If you use audio units to zoom into the waveform, you can easily see where specific sounds begin. Because the end keyframes already have the smooth fade applied, all you need to do is range-select the two keyframes and slide them left accordingly. This picture was taken "in action," and the darkened keyframes reflect the new position to which the two keyframes are being moved. The tool tells you the exact timeline position of the first of the two shifted keyframes.

You have now created a very simple keyframed volume adjustment that mutes a portion of your clip's volume between two points. Using the copy and paste function, you can apply and easily adjust keyframes to remove any unwanted small breathes and sounds.

This technique is very powerful because once you create the first four keyframes with their volume adjustment, all you have to do is copy and paste them into a new position to reuse them.

Things to Remember

For voiceovers, record in stereo only if you are certain that is exactly what you need. The disadvantage of a stereo voiceover is that your voice may not be equally balanced between the left and right channels. A mono voiceover file, when added to a stereo or surround sound sequence, will have an equal value on all channels. Furthermore, you have greater control adjusting or panning from left to right with a mono file.

No matter which type you choose, I recommend that you listen to your voiceover after recording it and decide whether you want to keep it or not. If it's a keeper, export it and rename it. If you want to record again, overwrite the file in the timeline and keep at it.

The other important things to remember from these lessons are the simple facts about the value of clean sound without any unwanted noises. Although some audio work seems a bit tedious and highly detail oriented, I have been quite inspired by the depths in which Premiere Pro allows access to make important adjustments.

Zooming in to the sample level and assigning keyframes to precise positions in order to remove small noises and breaths is invaluable to a professional workflow. Although there are many filters and effects that can do this for you, by creating one keyframed breath removal instance, you can copy, paste, and slightly adjust the keyframes to accommodate any other removal in the volume of any clip in any sequence in your project. Although these keyframe lessons were geared towards audio, the Pen tool and Bezier handles apply universally to keyframe techniques in Premiere Pro, as does copying and pasting any selected keyframes.

Although this chapter shined a bit of a light onto Adobe Audition for professional processing and adjustments to your audio files, Premiere Pro has a number of very effective professional filters to help make your audio sound better. In the next chapter, we will explore a number of those filters as you learn about clip-based and track-based audio effects.

CHAPTER

19

Audio Clip and Track Effects

Recordings rarely come out perfect, but Premiere Pro offers some help. Several audio clip effect and track effect filters can help you clean up and further refine the sound of your recording. For example, you can use EQ, Pitch Shift, Reverb, and Delay to boost parts of your sound and adjust it, giving it more spatial and tonal personality.

In this chapter, you will apply clip and track effects to refine and add personality to the voiceover narration you recorded in Chapter 18. Clip-based effects alter an individual clip, while track-based effects alter an entire track, affecting all the clips contained in that track. By exploring both clip and track effects, you will understand the proper use for each while becoming more comfortable with using the Audio Mixer.

Applying Clip Effects

Once you have your voiceover, you can start playing with different effects as a means of creating a richer, more vibrant, and better sounding file.

For this lesson, you will use several effects to increase the quality and strength of the voiceover track's sound and tone. The most dramatic and effective adjustments can be done with the EQ effect, but you will get to that in a minute. The basic idea is to refine the sound into something better and clearer than what you began with.

1. Open Clip_FX_Start.prproj from the APPST2 Lesson Files/Chapter 19 folder. Be sure to link to the appropriate Sample Project video files and to link Saleen_VO.wav from the same folder that the project originates. Once the project opens, notice where I have already placed the Effect Controls panel and Effects panel. Activate both of these panels so that they are at the front of their respective frames. Position your Edit Line near timeline marker 2. If you like this workspace you can save it and reuse it for other projects.

Premiere Pro supports its own and third-party VST plug-ins. VST plug-ins are professional quality plug-ins that offer a wide variety of processing functionality. Common plug-ins for adjusting a voiceover file range from EQ to Pitch, Reverb, and Delay; occasionally there are other effects, but you can get a better taste for those in a book that covers working with audio. Additionally, note that you can clip out unwanted noises and frequencies using a Noise Gate in the Compressor effect. For this project, however, the results are far too dramatic and unnecessary.

Because the subclips in the VO track are mono, remember to drag and drop mono effects onto each of the subclips to which you want to apply effects. For stereo tracks and clips, use the stereo effects, and use 5.1 surround effects for 5.1 clips.

When working with audio effects in particular, I recommend increasing the size of your Effect Controls panel, as the VST plug-in controls have custom controls that can be quite large.

In the timeline, identify the audio clip instance that begins at timeline marker 2. This is the clip that you will be applying your effects to.

2. In the Effects panel, select Audio Effects > Mono > EQ. Drag and drop this effect onto the clip at timeline marker 2 in the VO track. Click on the subclip to activate its properties in the Effect Controls panel. Twirl down the EQ effect listing in the Effect Controls panel, and then twirl down Custom Setup to reveal the EQ interface (**Figure 19.1**).

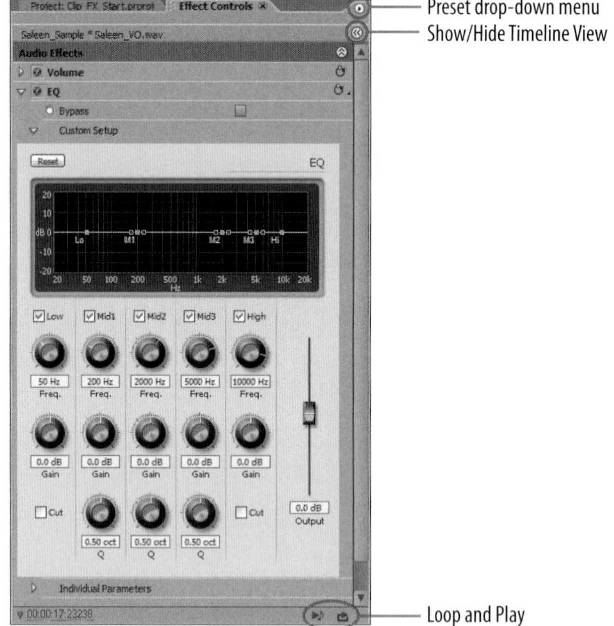

Figure 19.1 If you cannot see the entire custom setup dialog, click the Show/Hide Timeline View arrow at the top right of the panel to hide the Timeline view. The EQ effect dialog houses five frequency ranges: Low, Mid1, Mid2, Mid3, and High. Each column has a correlating grid position, so that while you manually adjust the exact value, you have a visual representation of the adjustments being made. The Output volume slider increases or decreases the gain of the overall audio being processed by the EQ. Also, notice the Loop and Play Audio buttons in the lower-right corner of the Effect Controls panel. The Preset drop-down menu enables you to access presets associated with the effect; choosing Default would essentially reset the effect.

The EQ plug-in is a frequency equalizer, which enables you to add or reduce volume gain levels within specific frequency ranges. If you had a loud low-frequency hum, for example, you could lower the gain in that low-frequency area as a means of reducing the overall presence of the hum. To get a good idea as to the type of adjustments the EQ can make, click on the Preset drop-down menu in the upper-right corner of the effect listing in the Effect Controls panel where the Reset button is located (Figure 19.1). Notice the adjustments that each preset makes to the controls in the interface.

To hear the kind of drastic adjustments you can make using the EQ, try twirling the Gain knob for the high-frequency from one end to the other while the audio loops.

In the next step, you'll make an EQ adjustment to help reduce some low-frequency noise and then to increase some of the high-frequency elements to make the voice sound a bit more crisp.

3. In the EQ custom setup, check the Low-frequency check box and set the frequency to 37Hz. Click the Cut check box. Adjust the following frequencies:

   Mid1: **Reduce Gain by –3 to –5.0dB in the 250 to 325Hz frequency**

   Mid2: **Reduce Gain by –3.0dB in the 1250 to 1500Hz frequency**

   Mid3: **Increase Gain by 1 to 3dB in the 3200 to 3700Hz frequency**

   High: **Increase Gain by 2 to 4dB in the 7500 to 9000Hz frequency**

   For comparison, **Figure 19.2** shows the exact settings that I used. For the next step, you can put playback into a looping mode so that you can do live adjustments to the effect while the audio continues to play back.

4. With the clip still selected, activate the Loop button in the lower-right corner of the Effect Controls panel, and then click the Play Audio button to its left.

   When you are setting and previewing audio effects using the Effect Controls panel, clicking the Loop and Play Audio (Play only the audio for this clip) buttons loops the entire selected clip instance until you click

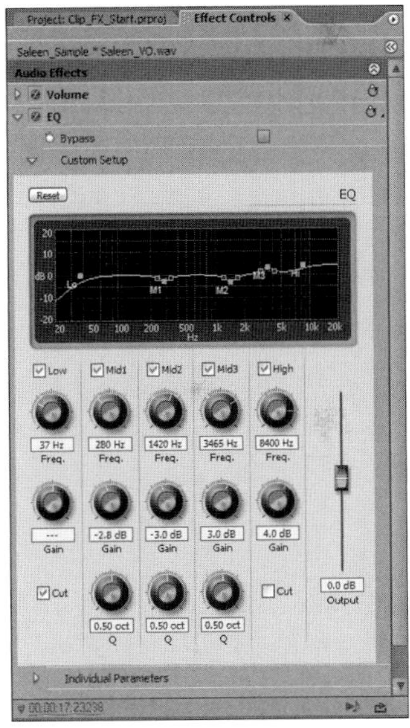

Figure 19.2 Cutting the low-frequency at 37Hz, as shown here, means nothing below 37Hz will be heard. Depending on the amount of low-frequency noise in your voiceover, you can cut your Low accordingly. The rest of the levels reflect a subtle but calculated adjustment. You can use the five listed adjustment ranges as potential choices to explore with your own voiceover file.

Stop. The power of looping is that your audio plays continuously while being updated with the live effect adjustments that you apply.

Having adjusted the EQ, it's time to add some more noticeable effects to help change the vocal tone. Perhaps you are not entirely satisfied with the tone or pitch of the voice; in the next step you will make a slight adjustment using the PitchShifter.

5. Collapse the EQ effect listing in the Effect Controls panel. Grab the Mono PitchShifter effect, and drop it into the Effect Controls panel below the EQ effect listing. Twirl down the PitchShifter and its Custom Setup. Set the Pitch to –1 Semi-t and the Fine to 30 cents; click off the check box for Formant Preserve. Click Play Audio to hear your adjustment. **Figure 19.3** explores the PitchShifter knobs and settings.

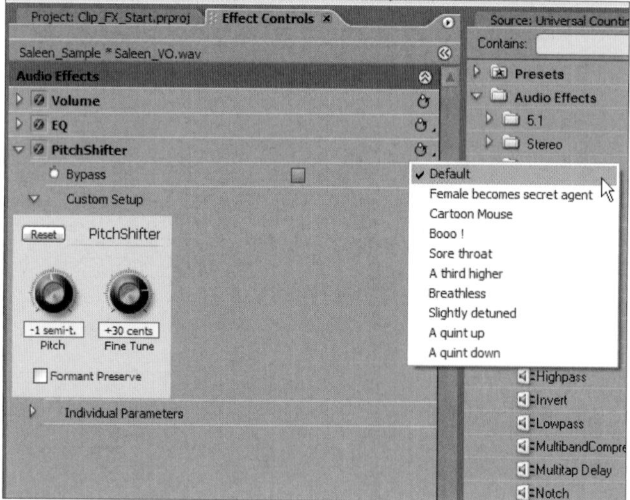

Figure 19.3 The PitchShifter has presets you can load and apply to achieve specific sound adjustments. Pitch adjusts the pitch; positive values go higher and negative values go lower. Fine Tune determines the detail of tuning in the adjustment for Pitch. The higher the Fine Tune setting, the better the Pitch adjustment. The Formant Preserve check box enables you to turn on or off the preserving of formants from shifting. When formants shift, the sound will become more cartoonish. An excellent way to illustrate this is to play the Cartoon Mouse preset, then turn on Formant Preserve and play it again. If you turn on Formant Preserve you will be avoiding pitch shifts that sound dramatically different from the original pitch.

The PitchShifter is a VST plug-in that dynamically increases or reduces the pitch of the audio being processed. Reducing the pitch value makes the voice sound as if it is speaking slower and deeper, while increasing the pitch makes the voice sound more high pitched and like a chipmunk. Using the PitchShifter to make slight adjustments can result in a more masculine or feminine sounding voice. Increasing Fine Tune helps increase the quality and precision of the pitch adjustment, and decreasing Fine Tune reduces it. When the formants in your audio clip shift, the pitch of the audio radically changes. Turning on Formant Preserve attempts to preserve the Formants so the pitch stays the same. When you speed up an audio clip and want the pitch to be the same, Formant Preserve is activated. Remember in the last chapter that when you sped the disclaimer up and preserved pitch in Premiere Pro, it yielded an unwanted echo. This echo is a direct artifact of the formant preserve that Premiere Pro uses. Audition has a better formant preserve.

TIP

You can expand or collapse all your effect listings and their individual parameters by holding down the ALT key and either twirling down (to expand) or twirling up (to collapse) an effect.

Now that you have added a slight Pitch effect and cleaned up the file using the EQ, it's time to add some spatial properties to the voiceover.

6. Collapse the PitchShifter effect listing in the Effect Controls panel, and click off its Effect toggle. Drag and drop the Mono Reverb Effect into the Effect Controls panel below the PitchShifter listing. Twirl down the Reverb listing, then twirl down its Custom Setup to reveal its interface.

   In the language of reverb there are two words that you need to know: bright and dark. *Bright* indicates more of an echo; *dark* is less of an echo. If you imagine the reverb sound of different rooms, bright would be wooden or marble floors; dark would be carpeted floors. Reverb refers to the reverberation of sound off of the walls and floors. The reverb is based on the size of the room, the distance you stand from the walls, and the brightness or darkness of the room. See **Figures 19.4**, **19.5**, and **19.6** to understand the visual difference between two different sounding rooms.

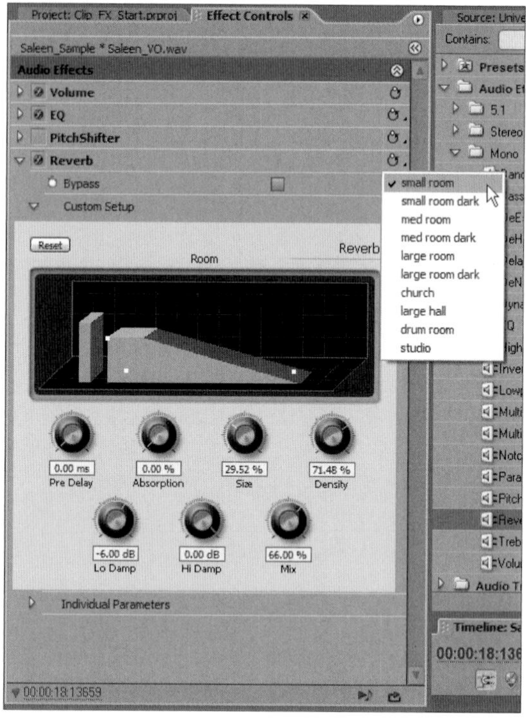

Figure 19.4 Click the Reverb Preset button to switch between different Reverb presets. This image shows what the Reverb interface looks like when it simulates a small room. Because the room is small, there is no Pre Delay for the sound. This preset is also bright and has an echo quality because there is also no absorption.

Figure 19.5 By contrast, this is the Reverb interface that simulates a small room, dark. Notice the increase in the Absorption, Density, and Hi Damp values. Also notice that the size of the room and the mix changed.

Figure 19.6 This preset shows the reverb qualities of the Church preset. Notice the drastic change in Pre Delay and Size; these two greatly increase the presence of the echo. The Absorption also has an increased value so the echo doesn't linger too noticeably. If you turn the Absorption back to 0, you can hear the "ssss" noises and other small sounds linger longer as the voice speaks.

Two effect choices offer somewhat similar processing results: Reverb and Delays. A reverb adds spatial properties to your sound, whereas a delay adds depth and strength. A large sounding reverb can make your voice sound as if it was recorded in a cathedral. A very minor 20 millisecond delay can make your voice immediately sound stronger. Delays of 0.02 or 0.04 seconds are typical in radio advertisements; think: "Sunday, Sunday, Sunday at the Monster Truck extravaganza!"

The Reverb interface attempts to display a room and the potential echo reverb properties. Imagine the sound originating from the left rectangle and into the right reverb object. The longer the object (pulling from the left white control point), the less absorption and the brighter the sound. This is why adjusting absorption adjusts the length of the object. The farther the object is from the rectangle, the greater the delay and the more apparent the echo. Clicking from the center of the object and dragging it to the right creates a more present echo. Finally, in terms of physical adjustments, the third and top-right white control point allows you to adjust and determine the height of the object. The height directly relates with the mix, and the taller the object, the more affected the sound will become.

7. Using these three basic properties, play around with the reverb by manipulating the different control points and then listening to your results. To fine-tune your results, you can reduce or increase the Size, Density, and Hi/Lo Damp settings. Use the Loop Playback button to get immediate feedback on your adjustments.

8. Set the reverb values as follows:

   Pre-Delay: **0.00**
   Absorption: **83.5**
   Size: **59**
   Density: **27.5**
   Lo Damp: **–15**
   Hi Damp: **–15** Mix: **7**

   Although these settings are subtle, the voiceover has no need for a dramatic reverb. Add just enough to give it some personality and to give the voice a slight spatial quality. Remember, after you finish with your effects, you will mix the music, so some of these adjustments will sound better when mixed with the music.

9. Collapse the Reverb effect listing, click it off, and drag in the Mono Delay effect into the Effect Controls panel just above the Reverb listing below the PitchShifter. Expand the Delay effect and its three expandable settings: Delay, Feedback, and Mix. Set:

   Delay: **0.02 seconds**
   Feedback: **+/–15%**
   Mix: **+/–35%**

   As mentioned earlier, delays can be very effective for enhancing the vocal presence. There is a very fine line, however, between a minor delay and an overly exaggerated doubling-up of sound. That difference is about 40 milliseconds.

   By placing the Delay above the Reverb effect you would be delaying the result of the EQ and PitchShifter; that delayed result would then be processed by the Reverb. Because you don't want to double up and delay the Reverb result, you place the effects in the order in which you want them processed.

Essentially, all the Delay effect is doing is doubling up the audio with a slight offset delay. The Delay value allows you to set the amount of time that exists between the original audio and its delay. For most voiceover work, a value between 0.01 and 0.06 seconds is effective; anything above that sounds like the echoing voice on the loudspeaker at the motor speedway.

The Feedback setting takes the delayed audio and signal and simulates the feedback of that signal on top of itself. Experimenting with Feedback can create a much more techno-cyber effect.

Finally, the Mix setting allows you to adjust the mix emphasis between the originating sound (0%) and the delayed sound (100%). A Mix setting of 50% has an equal emphasis on the original sound and the delay.

10. Collapse Delay, and turn off its toggle. Turn on the Toggle Audio buttons for the EQ, PitchShifter, and Reverb; these are the effects that you want to process together. Holding down the Ctrl key, click and select these three effect listings in the Effect Controls panel. Press Ctrl+C to copy these three effects.

    Delay was added merely to illustrate the effect; it is too much for the tone of this commercial.

11. In the timeline, Shift-click the seven other subclip instances that do not have any added effect settings. (Be sure that the clip from which you copied the effects is not selected.) Press Ctrl+V to paste the copied effects onto each selected clip.

    The result is that the other selected clips now have the same individual audio clip effect settings as the original adjusted subclip. This is one technique for creating a unique stack of effects and sharing them with a group of clips.

In Premiere Pro, there's often two routes to the same goal. Next you'll use the Audio Mixer and its effect interface to achieve the same result with less copying and pasting.

When you select and copy effect listings from the Effect Controls panel into your clipboard, you can then paste the effects into the Effect Controls panel of individual or multiple selected clips of the same format—audio effects to audio clips, video effects to video clips.

Also, you can save any assigned effect as its own custom preset; this workflow was covered in the second half of Chapter 14, "Working with Stills."

Render and Replace

After you apply audio clip or speed effects, Premiere Pro must render audio files before playing back your timeline. While rendering, the application processes the audio files with effects by creating preview files. Premiere then uses these preview files to play the effects accurately.

You can choose to permanently process a file with effects or speed adjustments applied. Select the file in the timeline, in this case the sped up disclaimer, and choose Clip > Audio Options > Render and Replace.

Premiere Pro then automatically creates a unique clip that is the same duration and has the same effects as the selected clip and saves that file to your disk. Next, Premiere Pro immediately replaces your original file with the newly created processed file.

This entire process is beneficial for exporting a single effect-enhanced audio file from your sequence. It also is helpful when you apply speed changes to a master clip, cut it up numerous times, and then add audio effects. To reduce the overall processing time, you can render and replace a clip, and then apply the effects on top of the replaced version.

Exporting and Consolidating Your Voiceover Track

After you apply your clip effects to all the clips in the VO track, you have the option to export and consolidate the edited voiceover with effects into a unique processed file. You later can archive the file or pass it off as a deliverable to send to a client who wants to hear the audio only.

To do this, you need to turn off the sound for the Music track by clicking off the speaker in that track's track header area. With the timeline active and the speaker off for the Music track but on for the VO track, choose File > Export > Audio.

In the resulting dialog, verify the Windows WAV format 48kHz, 16 bit mono file format settings. Name the file Saleen_VO_Final_FX.wav. At this point, you can use this one processed audio file as opposed to its smaller pieces.

Applying Track-Based Effects

Clip-based effects are excellent to use when individual clips need alternate adjustments and differing effects. If you need to apply a range of effects to an entire track full of clips, however, track-based effects are an intuitive solution.

Because track effects have the same parameters as their clip-based cousins, this lesson will spend less time on what to tweak and more time on how to interact with and apply track effects. You will do that in the expanded Audio Mixer.

1. Open the Track_FX_Start.prproj file from the APPST2 Lesson Files/Chapter 19 folder, and review the edit. Activate the Audio Mixer Panel from the rightmost frame in the workspace.

   I suggest you rework your workspace layout, so that the Audio Mixer, Timeline, and Monitor panels are at a reasonable size for your workspace. Choosing the Window > Workspace > Audio Workspace resizes the panels accordingly so that you can see the Monitor panel, Timeline panel, and full Audio Mixer.

2. In the Effects area of the VO track of the Audio Mixer, click the top empty effects drop-down menu and select EQ from the listed effects. Double-click the EQ listing to open the effect interface (**Figures 19.7a** and **b**).

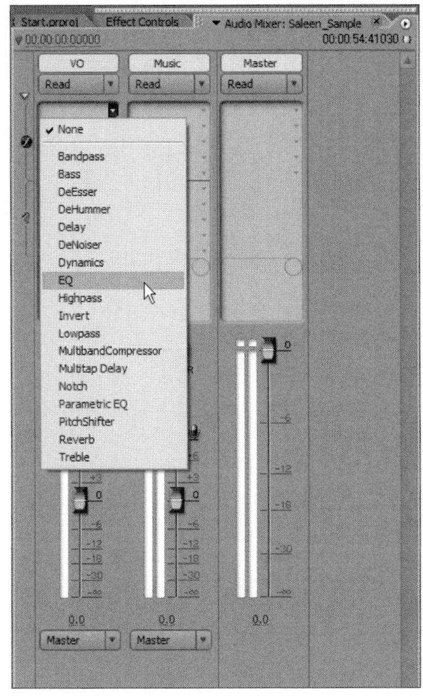

a

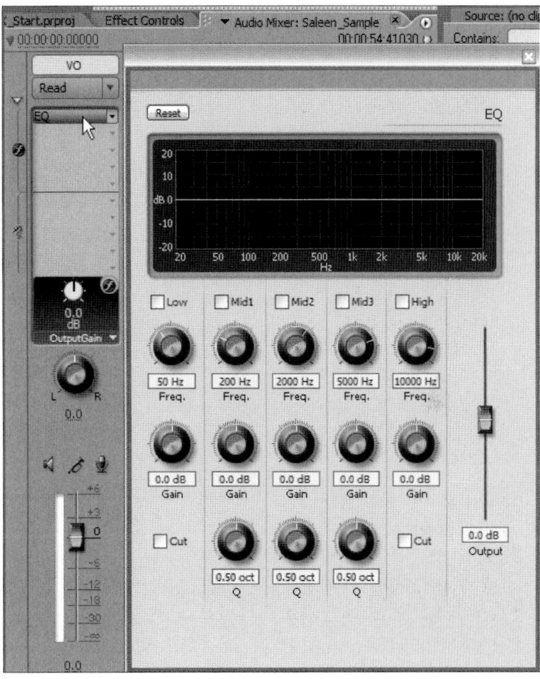

b

Figures 19.7a and b The top expanded area of each audio track in the Audio Mixer is known as the Effects area. Clicking on a blank field yields a drop-down menu with effects that you can activate and select for the track (a). Double-clicking on the effect listing opens its associated dialog box (b).

Instead of dragging and dropping as for clip effects, you simply select the desired track effect from the menu listing in the Effects area. You can have up to five effects per track. Notice the interface for the EQ matches the interface you learned from the EQ clip effects custom setup.

3. Check the Low-frequency check box, and set the frequency to 37Hz. Click the Cut check box. Assign the following EQ values:

   Mid1: **Reduce Gain by –3 to –5.0dB in the 250 to 325Hz frequency**

   Mid2: **Reduce Gain by –3.0dB in the 1250 to 1500Hz frequency**

   Mid3: **Increase Gain by 1 to 3dB in the 3200 to 3700Hz frequency**

   High: **Increase Gain by 2 to 4dB in the 7500 to 9000Hz frequency**

   For each selected effect in the Audio Mixer, there is a small knob and adjustment area at the bottom of the Effects/Sends area. If you want to make adjustments without opening the EQ interface window, select each knob from the drop-down at the bottom of the Effects/Sends area. With a specific parameter selected, the knob updates its value. In **Figure 19.8**, adjusting the knob for Output Gain achieves the same result as adjusting the Output slider in the EQ interface.

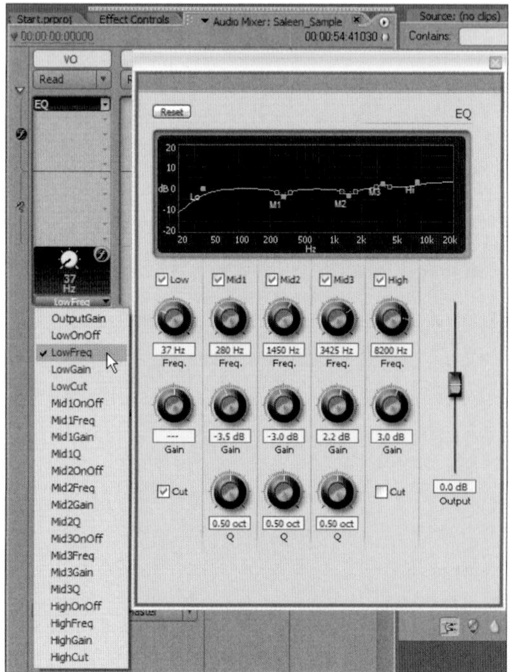

Figure 19.8 With the EQ effect active in the mixer for the VO track, a knob wheel and drop-down menu at the bottom of the track listing yield access to each individual effect parameter for the selected effect. In this case, the knob is set to Low-frequency, so its value reads 37Hz, which is the same as the Effect dialog to the right.

4. Select PitchShifter from the empty effect listing below the EQ track effect. Instead of double-clicking to open the effect interface, set the following values for the parameters in the adjustment area:

   Semitone: **–1**
   FineTune: **+30 cents**
   Formant Preserve: **Twist left to turn off**

   Although you can enter values in the adjustment area for the selected effect parameter, it is sometimes difficult to use the knob when trying to enter precise values. In that case, you can open the effect interface and enter the information in the selected parameter using your keyboard.

5. From the empty effect listing below PitchShifter, click and select Reverb from the drop-down list. Double-click on the Reverb effect to open its interface and enter the following values:

   Pre-Delay: **0.00**
   Absorption: **83.5**
   Size: **59**
   Density: **27.5**
   Lo Damp: **–15**
   Hi Damp: **–15**
   Mix: **7**

6. Play back your sequence so that you can hear the voiceover with effects and music at the same time. Click the Solo Horn toggle for the VO track, and play back the timeline to hear only the voiceover.

   Like the Effect Controls panel, the Audio Mixer has looping and playback buttons. Clicking Loop and then Play puts the mixer into a looping mode that continues until you click Stop. To loop an individual section of the sequence, place an In point at the beginning of the section you want to loop and an Out point at the end of the section you want to loop. With sequence In and Out points assigned, Premiere loops between the assigned In and Out points.

7. In the timeline, go to the VO track header and switch the timeline keyframe display drop-down list to Track Keyframes. Click the Track Effect drop-down menu to reveal the effect display options (Select PitchShifter > Pitch (**Figure 19.9**).

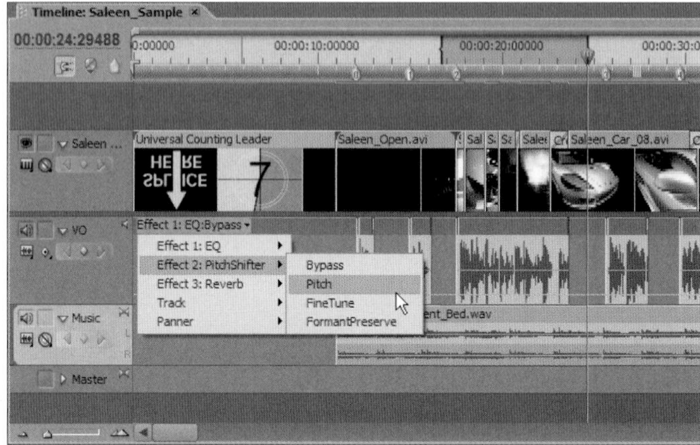

Figure 19.9 Setting your track display to Track Keyframes puts the track display into a mode in which you can add and manipulate keyframe values for specific effect parameters. The Effect drop-down menu for the track will be at the beginning of the track and it will list all the associated track effects and their parameters. Selecting a specific parameter updates the track display with its keyframe settings.

The same way you used keyframes to adjust the clip volume to remove breaths in Chapter 18, "Recording and Editing a Voiceover," you can also adjust exact track effect values using keyframes. To use keyframes to adjust a track effect, select the effect you want to adjust when the track is in Show Track Keyframes mode.

8. Position the Edit Line just before timeline marker 7. Press P to change your cursor to the Pen tool. Press Ctrl, and create two new keyframe handles just before the start of the voiceover clip at the marker. Click and drag the second keyframe handle upward so that the right end of the tool tip window reveals a value of 5 semitones as opposed to the current –1 (**Figure 19.10**).

   Although the 5 semitones are a bit high pitched, you can use the Pen tool to grab the 5 semitone line and uniformly reduce it down to 1 semitone. Because you have anchored the previous –1 semitone value with the first keyframe, the spatial positioning and height of the second keyframe dictates the speed of increase and point at which the exact new semitone value is reached. As you can see, you have timing control within a track for adjusting the applied track effects.

Figure 19.10 When displaying track effect parameters, the height positioning of keyframes within the track reflects an increase (upward) or decrease (downward) in the value for the selected parameter. In this case, you change the pitch such that it will increase from –1 semitones to 5 semitones. The voice will sound a bit more cartoonish and mouse-like. Notice the tool tip reveals the current position of the keyframe and the value of the effect parameter being adjusted.

9. Switch your Track Keyframe Display to Show Track Volume, and using the Pen tool, drag the track volume down somewhere between –3 and –4dB. Switching over to the Audio Mixer, click and drag the hot-text box below the Track Volume fader so that its value is –2.0dB.

   Notice how after you adjusted your track volume in the physical track, the Track Volume fader in the Audio Mixer updated to reflect the same settings and vice-versa (**Figure 19.11**).

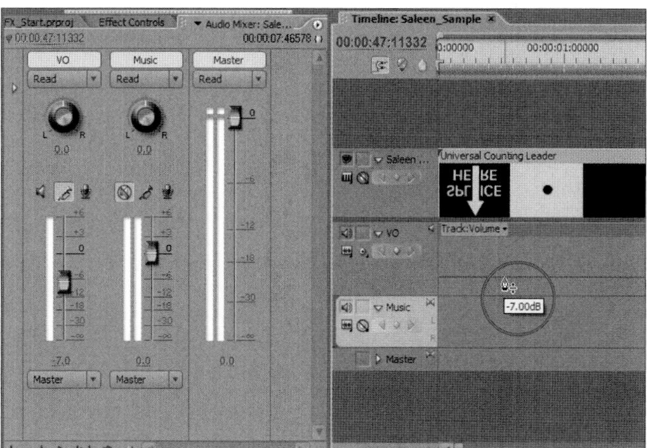

Figure 19.11 If you want to keyframe adjust track-based volume adjustments, you can do so with the Pen tool. You can monitor and readjust those settings using the volume fader for the track you want to adjust in the Audio Mixer. Notice how the volume being set with the Pen tool in the timeline matches the volume displayed for that track in the Audio Mixer: –7dB.

   This step shows that you can work in different areas of the application to get similar results. If you like working with keyframes, you can do so. If you want a precise value, however, you can literally enter the value to the fader in the mixer. To dynamically mix the levels up and down with the fader (automation) while playing back, you'll have to wait for the next chapter.

10. Click off the Solo Horn for your VO track (if it is still active), and listen to your voiceover and music together.

    In general, the voiceover sounds better with the music behind it. This is usually the case, and often you will have to mix the two to find the perfect value, which is exactly what you will do in the next chapter.

Using track effects was certainly a faster and more efficient method for adding effects to a cut-up voiceover file. Using this basic workflow, you can add or reduce track effects to achieve a result that works best for the audio file that you have. Although you dabbled a tiny bit in adjusting track effect keyframes here, the next chapter will dive much deeper into mixing your audio tracks.

Things to Remember

Adobe Audition is far superior and focused in filtering and audio effects processing. You can reference the Audition integration lession in Chapter 12 to understand how much farther you can take your audio files with Audition.

To enhance the sound of a voiceover narration, try using EQ, Reverb, PitchShifter, and, if appropriate, Delay. With each of these effects, you can save and load your own custom presets or try a few of the presets provided as a means of exploring the various possible adjustments to be made. A lot of what goes into making a voiceover file sound better is finding a few detailed effects or a particular pattern of effects to apply. Once you do this a couple of times, you will have a pretty good idea of where to go and what to adjust the next time around.

I hope this lesson gave you a little epiphany regarding audio effects—not only how to organize audio within tracks, but also how to decide when to use a clip effect or a track effect.

The next step in the sound process is to integrate the voiceover track with the music track, which you'll tackle in the next chapter. Chapter 20 will cover *automation*, the live mixing of the volume levels between the voiceover and music track.

CHAPTER

20

Mixing Your Audio

Creating a sound mix could possibly be the most difficult production task to put down onto paper. Mixing sound is based on nuance, tiny details, and a feeling you get (or don't get) while you are watching pieces of your project come together. Premiere Pro offers two powerful features to help you with this process: submixing and automation.

In this chapter, you will learn how to use submixing to share common effects and arrange sound elements in your sequence. You will also investigate using automation techniques for live mixing and adjusting of the audio in your sequence. Because so much of sound mixing is in the hearing, I encourage you, after reading, to practice and hone your mixing technique with your own material.

Creating Your Mix

To create a good sound mix with some layered effects, you are going to add a few sound effects files into the overall mix with the voiceover and music you have been working on in the last few chapters.

1. Open the Submix_Start.prproj from the APPST2 Lesson Files/Chapter 20 folder. You'll notice that the workspace I used for this project has a healthy size for the height of the timeline and height and width of the Audio Mixer. You can organize your workspace so that you have a good amount of space for a tall timeline and a wide Audio Mixer.

   When mixing audio, be sure to allocate enough space for the Audio Mixer and the audio track portion of your timeline. In my default workspace for this project, I collapsed one video and two audio tracks that weren't going to be manipulated during the lesson.

2. Choose File > Import, browse to APPST2 Lesson Files/ Chapter 20/SFX, and click Import Folder. You will be importing all the files contained in this folder if you choose the Import Folder option. Once the folder is imported, double-click and open the SFX subfolder in the Project window. For each clip in the Project panel, choose Clip > Audio Options > Audio Gain, then click Normalize in the resulting dialog. Adjust the Gain value hot-text field based on these recommendations for the following clips:

   Chains: **6.6dB**
   Clank: **0.9dB**
   Drill: **12.2dB**
   Electric Motor: **7.7dB**
   Fairy Dust: **8.0dB**
   WaterCrash: **–1.2dB**

   First, you import the desired files, then you get their individual Gain levels up so that you have a nice strong signal. The Chains file has one instance where the audio exceeds 0dB, so Premiere recommends you normalize it at 0dB. Because you are not going to use a section that is too loud, you will still want to bring up the Gain to 6.6dB.

3. Toggle the Track Output off for both the VO track and the Music track. Drag and drop the WaterCrash.mp3 file into the gray area below the audio tracks to create a new track for the clip. Position it at timeline marker 1 (**Figure 20.1**). Right-click in the new track's header area, and rename the track FX Smoke.

   By turning off the other audio tracks, you can focus solely on the new effect's sound and position. I previously identified this clip position, but as you proceed, you can take liberties shifting it to better suit the edit. Once you rename the track, if the entire track name does not display, you can drag the right edge of the track header to the right to make it wider.

TIP

When performing menu-based actions that are difficult to navigate to, you can set the menu command to a quick keyboard shortcut. To assign a Keyboard shortcut to Audio Gain go to Edit > Keyboard Customization. In the resulting dialog, select Application from the drop-down menu, twirl down Clip > Audio Options, and then click on Audio Gain to highlight it. Click in the blank Short Cut column to the right and hold down Shift+G on your keyboard. If Shift+G is not being used by any other shortcut, then you have just assigned it to be used to be the shortcut for Audio Gain. Click OK.

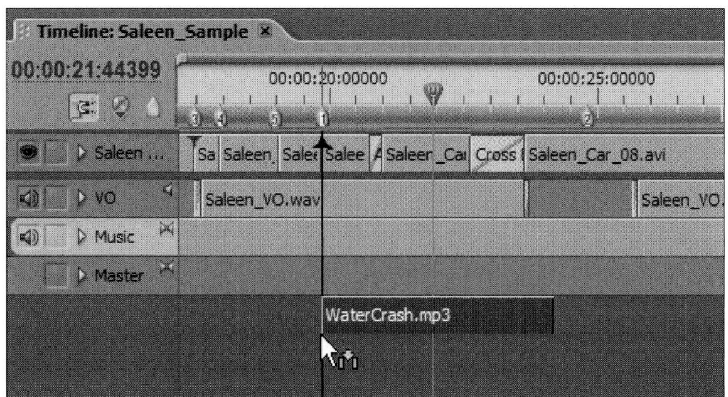

Figure 20.1 With Snapping turned on in the timeline, you can drag an added file into the timeline and still position it exactly where you want it to be placed when the new track is created. The upward snapping arrow indicates snapping to the marker position.

4. Add an effect to the WaterCrash clip. Open the Effects panel, and from the Audio Effects/Stereo folder, drag and drop the EQ effect onto the WaterCrash.mp3 instance in the timeline. Select the clip instance in the timeline, and open the Effect Controls panel. From the Custom Setup for the EQ effect listing, activate all five frequencies and enter the following values:

   Low: **52Hz**, **–20dB**
   Cut Off Mid1: **91Hz**, **10.2dB**
   Mid2: **775Hz**, **6.8dB**
   Mid3: **918Hz**, **7.2dB**
   High: **3801Hz**, **–20dB**,
   Cut Off Output: **–6.6dB**

   You will be doing track mixing later, but at times like this a clip effect does the job quickly and easily. The sound of the water crashing needs to resemble a sound that emphasizes the car passing through the cloud of smoke. Although this is slightly exaggerated by the water sound, it does the trick once the EQ has been tweaked.

   For this step, the goal was to take a sound that resembles the idea being explored and then manipulate it with a filter or two, to get it sounding more appropriate. With the EQ effect, the WaterCrash clip no longer sounds like water, taking on a new personality instead. Setting the Output level in the EQ Custom Setup reduces the overall volume of the clip instance, so there's not much more tinkering to do.

If your Effect Controls panel is cutting the custom setup in half, remember you can expand the panel to display the effect settings only by clicking the top-right double arrow to hide the Timeline view. Once it displays the double arrows pointing left, the same button can be clicked to get the Timeline view back.

5. Drag and drop the Fairydust_2.wav file into a new track at timeline marker 2. Rename the new track FX Fairy. Right-click on the Fairydust_2 instance in the timeline, and select Speed/Duration. Slow down the speed of the clip to 80%, and click Maintain Pitch. With the Fairydust_2 clip instance in the timeline selected, choose Clip > Audio Options > Render and Replace (**Figure 20.2**).

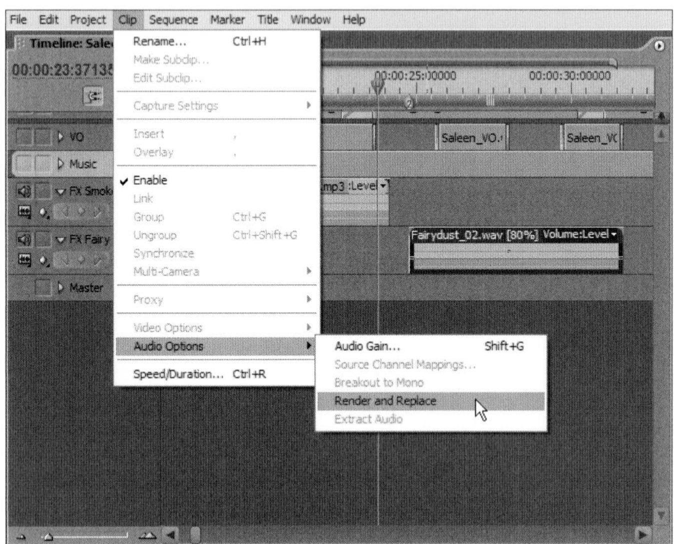

Figure 20.2 With the Fairydust_2 clip selected after the speed change has been applied, choosing Render and Replace processes the speed change of the clip and creates a new clip instance that does not require processing.

Because you are going to apply an effect on top of the Fairydust_2 clip after you have adjusted its speed, every time you want to play back and preview with effect adjustments you will have to render the audio. By selecting to render and replace the speed-changed Fairydust_2 clip, you are creating a new clip instance that is processed already at the adjusted speed. This means that applying and adjusting effects to the replaced clip will be played back in real time.

Notice that the visual waveform information in the clip was enhanced as well, because the previous Audio Gain setting you assigned to the Fairydust_2 file is getting rendered along with the speed change. Because Premiere Pro does not update the waveform when you make a gain adjustment, you may want to consider using Render and Replace to get more waveform information from gained files.

6. Apply the stereo Delay effect to the new replaced FX Fairy_Fairydust_02.wav in the timeline. Use the default setting, adjusting only the Feedback to 50%. Delay should be 1.000 seconds and Mix 50%.

   Adding the Delay effect further enhances and alters the fairy dust effect. While it seems a bit too loud and a bit obtuse, you will shape its panning and fading in the next lesson.

7. Right-click in the track header area, and add four mono tracks and one mono submix track. Rename the mono tracks FX Shop1, FX Shop2, FX Shop3, FX Shop4, and rename the submix track Sub Shop. Next, follow **Table 20.1** to add the clips into the proper positions. Your sequence should look similar to **Figure 20.3**.

Table 20.1: Mono Tracks to Add

Track	File	In Point	Out Point	Timeline Marker
FX Shop1	Chains.wav	02;17	03;09	3 FX
Shop2	Electric_Motor.wav	04;00	04;28	4 FX
Shop3	Clank.wav	01;02	02;04	4 FX
Shop4	Drill.wav	04;13	05;08	5

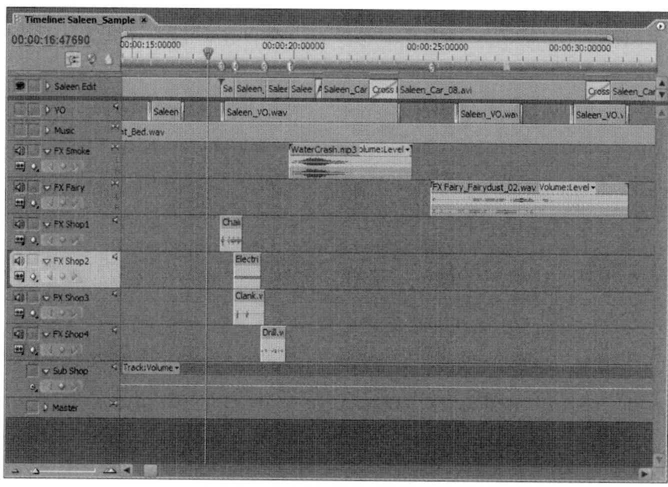

Figure 20.3 Both the Fairydust and WaterCrash clips display the purple clip effect line, which means effects are applied to those individual clips. At the marker positions 3, 4, and 5 the FX Shop tracks clearly display the stacked effects that make up some ambient shop noises.

Sending tracks to a submix track is a very easy way of ganging together clips with effects and controlling them with one easy slider.

Although you may take a few liberties with shifting the In and Out points and placement of the subclips, it is first important to label all the tracks in your audio mix so that when you work in the Audio Mixer you can easily distinguish between the tracks. Because there are four sound effects placed in close proximity, it is wise to keep each sound effect on a different track, not only for spatial position, but in terms of mixing flexibility. By having each effect on its own track, you have greater control and fewer adjustments if each track accommodates one specific effect type. This is obviously the case with the voiceover file cut up on its own track.

Here's a tip on how to quickly preview and loop specific sections of your timeline with the Audio Mixer: Create two timeline In and Out points, one at the beginning of the area you want to preview and one at the end. (Position the Edit Line, and press I to set the In point, then reposition and press O for an Out point.) Click the Loop button in the Audio Mixer, and then click Play. Because you have a defined timeline In/Out instance, looping will occur within those boundaries. When tweaking track effects in their effect interface, you can get live looping playback of your adjustments when you are in this mode.

8. Expand your Audio Mixer so that you can see the Effects/Sends area. In each of the four new Mono FX tracks, click in the top blank drop-down menu in the Sends area and select Sub Shop from the list that appears (**Figure 20.4**).

   This step redirects the processing of the new Mono tracks through the submix track. Now if you apply one effect to the Sub Shop Submix track, all the Mono FX tracks will be processed with that effect.

Figure 20.4 The bottom half of the Effects and Sends area of the Audio Mixer allows you to send the signal from one track to be processed by another track. Using the drop-down menu, you can send to a submix track (such as Sub Shop, chosen here) or your Master track, or you can create a new submix track.

9. In the Sub Shop submix track, apply the track-based Reverb effect. Right-click on the Reverb effect listing, and select the Church preset. In each of the FX Shop tracks, set the Send Volume value to 0.00dB (**Figure 20.5**).

Figure 20.5 Increasing or decreasing the Send Volume affects the overall level of the track volume being processed by the submix track. If you want one track to be a bit lower in the mix, for example, reduce the Send Volume. Keep in mind, the default Send Volume is always –oodB when you first send a track to a submix track; you must manually adjust each track to your desired volume. The tool tip calls out the value for the send parameter.

Because all four FX Shop tracks are being sent to the submix Sub Shop track, they will be processed with whatever effects are applied to the Sub Shop track. The volume level of the individual tracks will be based on the value of the Send Volume in each of the sent tracks. To give the sound effects a good spatial sound (as if they occurred in a large bright car shop), you can select the Church preset. Once all of the tracks are being sent with a solid volume level, the group of clips takes on a new shape in the mix.

10. For each FX Shop track, make the following volume adjustment below each of the associated Volume faders:

FX Shop1: **–3.7dB**
FX Shop2: **–3.4dB**
FX Shop3: **0.6dB**
FX Shop4: **–2.8dB**

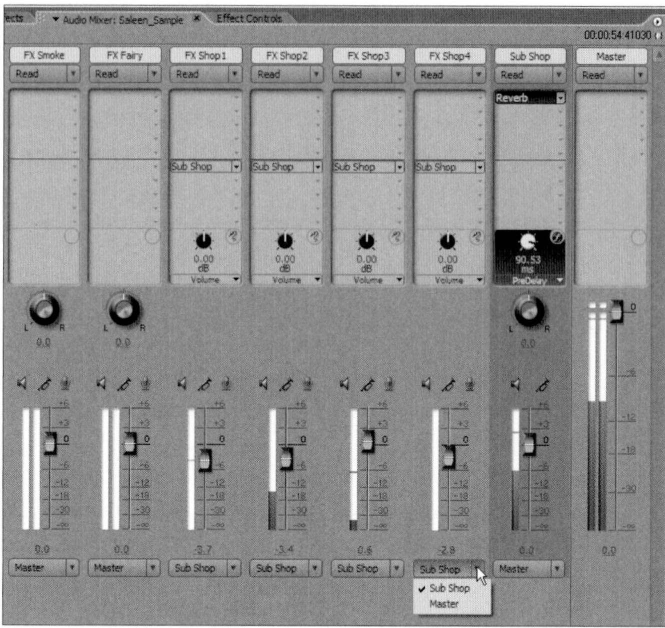

Figure 20.6 The VU meter lines reflect the ceiling of the audio being played back. As you can see, the audio is under the 0dB mark in the master mixer and the color is in the safe green range. (Yellow indicates safe but loud audio; red is too loud.) Assigning the Output controls for each of the Shop effect tracks to the submix track allows you to control their panning properties and overall volume with one slider and one panning knob instead of four sliders and four panning knobs.

Then, in each of the FX Shop tracks, change their Output controls from Master to Sub Shop (**Figure 20.6**).

By first adjusting the track volume for each track you mix the volume level for the track to find its optimum volume, in this case ensuring that each track does not exceed or come too close to the 0dB ceiling. By assigning the Stem (Track Output Assignment) controls to the Sub Shop you are then enabling the submix track to control the volume and panning properties of all four Shop tracks in unison. After you get your individual clips to the exact dB level that you want, you can then easily begin mixing all of the individual tracks with one volume slider and panning knob. The technical term for this is *stemming*.

11. Toggle on the Track Output Audio for your VO and Music tracks. Play back the sequence to get a sense of the volume adjustments that will be necessary in the next lesson.

By sending certain tracks to be processed and controlled by the submix track, you have the ability to position and place clips on top of each other while still allowing the clips to have the same effect processing. An additional advantage is that within the submix paradigm, you can still boost or tweak each sent track individually to further add depth to the mix. If you want to increase the volume of an individual element, you can adjust the gain of that individual track with its Volume slider. If you want to add an EQ effect to one of the tracks, you can apply that effect within the track. The resulting audio from the track-plus-effect will be processed by whatever track it is sent to with whatever effects are applied to the track.

A good way to think about Sends and submixing is to visualize an effects track that does not contain clips or media, just effects. Using a Send, you can send a physical track with content to use the effects of the submix track. Depending on how much volume from the physical track you send, the sound of the track will either be low and subtle or loud and obvious.

Automation and Live Mixing

Another option for mixing your sequence is using the four Automation modes—Read, Write, Touch, and Latch—which save live track adjustments as keyframes into the track being adjusted.

Every track-based volume adjustment, left or right pan, or effect change, such as increasing the pre-delay of a Reverb, can be seen visually in the form of assigned keyframes in the adjusted track. Instead of using the Pen tool and manipulating keyframe handles, you can use Automation to adjust the knobs, sliders, and interface controls live, while translating those adjustments into track-based keyframes.

In this lesson, you will create a track volume adjustment using Read Automation mode, then investigate the other modes. You will also make a panning adjustment using the Pen tool, then create another using automation. Although I can give you plenty of step-by-step instructions for automation, the important part of this next lesson is to understand the basic foundation and expected behavior with automation so you can use it dynamically to explore it further.

1. Open the Automation_Start.prproj file from the APPST2 Lesson Files/Chapter 20 folder.

   All of the files for this project are in the primary Chapter 20 folder and its SFX subfolder.

2. Expand the VO track, and turn on the track display for Show Track Volume. In the full Audio Mixer, solo the VO track by clicking the Solo Horn above its Volume fader. Click Play to play back the timeline while you monitor the sound level registering in the master VU meter. Using the Volume slider in the VO track of the Audio Mixer, raise and lower the volume to get the master VU meter registering a peak halfway between 0dB and –6dB. The level that I found to be about right is –1.7dB for the VO track volume; set the Volume fader to –1.7dB. Notice that the VO track is in Read Automation mode.

   Get a feel for making live adjustments and knowing where to look to see how much effect your adjustment is making to the sequence's VO track. It's a good idea to monitor the sound work in this section with headphones or good speakers.

   As noted in the last chapter, when adjusting track volume in the Audio Mixer the displayed track volume line in the timeline will match the value set in the mixer.

3. Collapse the VO track, and click the Lock icon in the track header to lock it. Expand the Music track. Set the Track Display to Show Track Volume. With the Timeline window active and no clips selected, press the Home key to get the Edit Line back to the head of the sequence. Click the Solo Horn for the Music track so that you can hear both the Music and VO only. Set the Automation mode of the Music track to Touch. Position the Volume fader at –oodB, activate the Timeline panel, press the Home key, and then press the spacebar to play. While the timeline plays back, click and drag the Volume fader for the music up and down between –oodB and 0dB. Continue holding the mouse down as you adjust the volume so that you can hear it fading in and out. Once you get near the end of the disclaimer, release the mouse and let playback stop at the end of the sequence.

Touch Automation writes keyframes on the parameters that you are adjusting while you play back. Unique to *Touch mode* is that whenever you click off your mouse and release the parameter you were adjusting, the parameter automatically goes back to its start position. In this case, you started the volume at –oodB, so when you released the mouse during the disclaimer it dropped from the current volume position down to –oodB. This is called *Automatch*. When you release a knob or fader in Touch mode it automatically shifts back to its start position. You can dictate the amount of time it takes to Automatch in the Edit > Preferences > Audio > Automatch Time field (see **Figures 20.7a**, **b**, and **c**).

4. Press the Home key, and then click Play to play back the timeline with your new fade adjustment. Watch the Music Volume fader in the Audio Mixer. Once the timeline finishes playing back, press Ctrl+Z to undo the volume adjustments you previously applied.

   If you watch the Music track's Volume fader in the Audio Mixer, you will see its position automatically update and move in accordance with the adjustments you defined in the previous step. Notice how your Volume fader now *automatically* adjusts over the course of playing back, and you can see the moving fader live during playback. In Automation mode, you essentially can create a mixing road map for the mixer to follow automatically.

5. Switch the Automation mode to Latch in the Audio Mixer for the Music track. Set the Volume fader to –oodB. Press the Home key to get to the head of your sequence, and click Play in the Audio Mixer. While the timeline plays, adjust the Volume fader so that you fade your music up as the music comes in. After you have faded it up, you can release the mouse. When the Disclaimer comes on, slowly click and drag the Volume fader back down to –oodB.

   Latch mode is different from Touch mode in that when you click off the fader, it will latch onto its current position until you click and drag to modify it again. If you

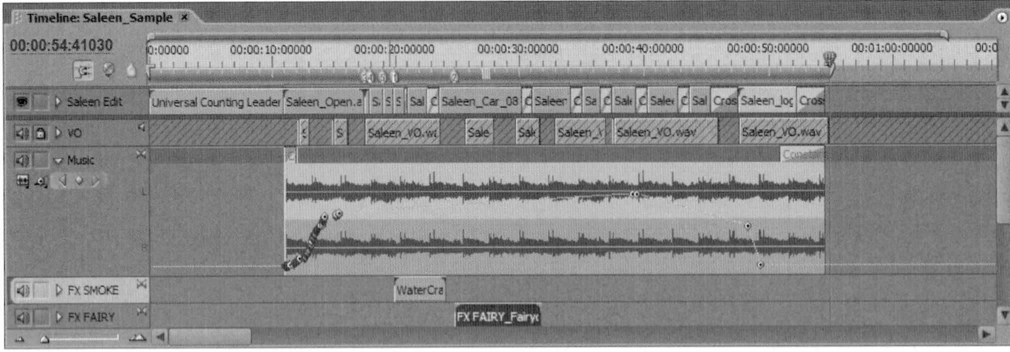

a

b

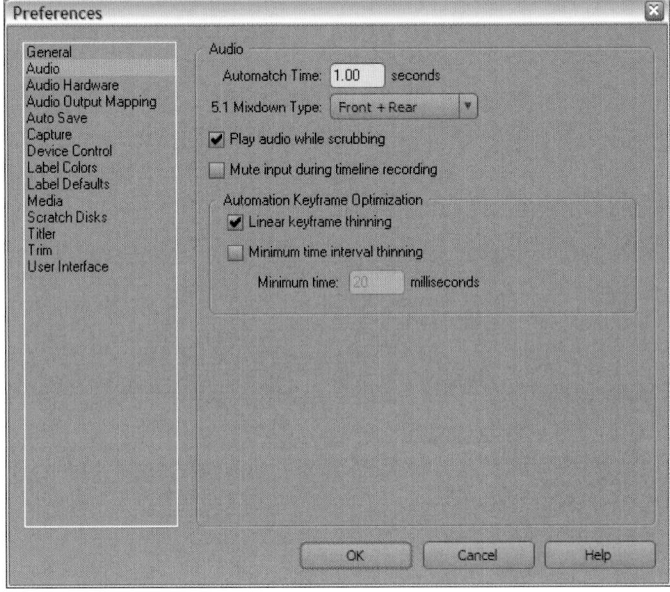

c

Figures 20.7a, b, and c After you play back your timeline and adjust a track in either Write, Touch, or Latch Automation mode, you will have keyframes written into the automated track that reflect the live adjustments you made. Here, the volume keyframes reflect the fading up, leveling off, and fading out at the end (a). Although these keyframes could be assigned manually with the Pen tool, automation assigns them automatically based on the dynamic value you are assigning in the mixer. The Touch mode you select (b) remembers the control values for the track being adjusted. As long as you hold down the mouse while adjusting, it will modify those values. Once you release the mouse, Touch mode automatically resets each value to its original state (Automatch).

don't have a steady hand, but want to fade up your volume, keep it level, then fade it back down, Latch mode is your best bet for manual adjusting.

6. Using either Latch or Touch mode with the Music track, automate the volume level so that the music has a good presence beneath the voiceover. Once you are finished, lock the Music track and then click the Solo Horn for the FX Smoke track, so you can hear all three tracks together.

7. Position your Edit Line at approximately 17;00000 in the timeline, and press the I key. Move the Edit Line to 24;37000, and press the O key. Leave the FX Smoke track in Read mode. Click Loop in the Audio Mixer, and then click Play. While the In/Out instance plays, adjust the volume level for the FX Smoke track so that the sound effect is present, but not overwhelming (**Figure 20.8**). The volume I found to be perfect was –3.0dB.

Figure 20.8 This In/Out instance is looping while the audio level is being adjusted. Read mode allows for the setting of a static track level, whereas Latch and Touch mode write keyframes for any adjustment made. If you were in Write mode, every time you looped, Premiere would update the keyframes with the adjusted values. In Latch and Touch, once you release the mouse button and looping reengages, you will not overwrite the previous assigned automation.

This is a perfect example of how well looping supports the tweaking and finding of adjustment levels. Because Read mode just updates the volume on a static level, you can keep sliding the fader up and down to find the sweet spot. Additionally if you pad your In and Out points around the area you want to adjust, you have ample pre-roll and post-roll time to start and end your effect, then listen, and try again if you decide.

As you remember from Chapter 18, "Recording and Editing a Voiceover," you can use the Pen tool to group/marquee select and move groups or sections of keyframes. If you have automated a fade that starts too late, you can use the Pen tool to grab the group of keyframes that make up the fade and drag them left so that they start earlier.

8. Collapse and lock the FX Smoke track. Click the Solo button for the FX Fairy track. Expand the FX Fairy track in the timeline. Create a new In point at 24;00000 and

an Out point at 32;46000. Using the same technique of adjusting the volume in Read mode, find the right volume level for the Fairy effect. I used –5.1 dB. Instead of automating a fade for the end of the clip, add the Audio Transition Constant Power at the tail of the clip to fade it out. I gave the transition a duration of 1 second.

After setting the proper volume for this track, you quickly slapped on a transition to accommodate a quick one second fade out. Now the Fairy FX audio plays and then fades out seamlessly.

9. In the track header for the FX Fairy track, change the Keyframe Display to Show Track Keyframes. From the Track drop-down menu, select to show the keyframes for Panning > Balance (**Figure 20.9**). In the Audio Mixer, twist the Panning knob for the FX Fairy track all the way to the right. Using Latch or Touch mode, click Play and slowly pan the knob from its full right position to a full left position while the Fairy Dust effect plays.

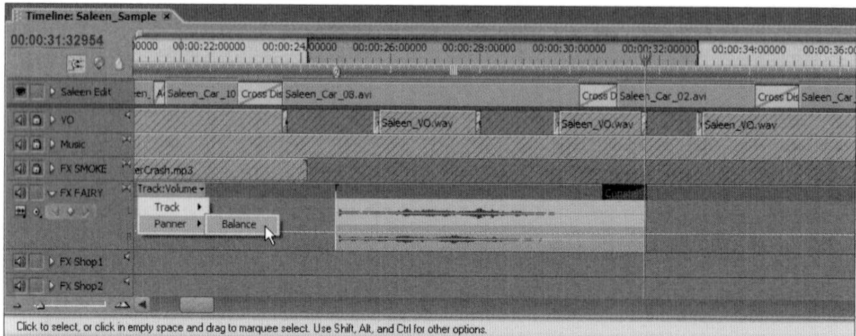

Figure 20.9 Depending on the display mode, if there are multiple keyframe parameters to view, you will be able to pick them individually from the selected track's drop-down menu. Using the Pen tool, you can also remove, add, or modify automation keyframes once you are displaying them.

If your mixer is still in Loop mode, you can let the loop reengage to hear your adjustment. If you don't like it, then wait for the loop to reengage again and click and adjust the pan for another pass.

What you have done here is adjusted the panning of the sound so that it "moves" with the image of the car on the screen.

10. Collapse and lock the FX Fairy track. Solo each of the FX Shop tracks. Using this lesson's technique, set timeline In and Out points around the Shop Sound effects and adjust their overall volume by sliding the Volume fader in the Sub Shop submix track. If you want their volume level to have a static adjustment, use Read mode. To keyframe or have an automated volume fade, use either Latch or Touch mode.

    Because you are stemming the output of each track to the fade and pan controls of the submix Sub Shop track, you don't have to adjust each track's Volume fader individually. In the last lesson, you preset each level within the group, and you now can bring the entire group up or down accordingly for your final mix. I used –11.4dB for the Sub Shop track's Volume fader level.

After you make all of these adjustments, clear your timeline In and Out points, turn up your speakers, and listen to what you have mixed. If you want to see my finished result, open the Automation_Finish.prproj file from the APPST Lesson Files/Chapter 20 folder. If you encounter any stuttering playback, be sure to press Enter to render any necessary preview files.

Write Mode Automation

Write mode is a bit different from Read, Latch, and Touch. In *Write mode*, every parameter is overwritten during automation, even parameters you are not adjusting. The safe way of using Write mode is to lock any track you don't want adjusted. Even then you will need to mind which parameters are being set. If you do have any existing automation on, for example on the panning properties of a track, and you are adjusting volume in Write mode, the pan automation will be overwritten by the value from the pan knob despite the fact that you are adjusting volume only. Because it can be very destructive to your mix, I don't recommend using Write mode, unless you are familiar with its behavior. The only time to use Write mode is if you want to delete all the automation on a specific track; in that case, lock all the other tracks, set the current track parameters to the exact values you want, and overwrite it in one pass.

Things to Remember

Although exact sound effects serve an exact purpose, there may be instances where one sound can substitute for another. In the case of the wave crashing file, a few adjustments in the EQ reshaped that file into something that worked perfectly for the car appearing through the mist.

Another important technique is the choice of creating and naming individual tracks to be used for specific clips. To have better control over your final sound mix, use individual unique tracks for specific sound effects and sound elements. In a narrative film scene, every character would have a dedicated dialogue track and foley track. The ambient noise would be on its own track, as would natural noises and specific sound effects. By isolating specific noises on their own tracks, you are creating a much easier final mix process. As revealed through the last two chapters, track-based mixing and effects are much easier to use and manipulate than clip effects. This becomes especially true with 5.1 surround sound mixing and having all your unique sounds on their own tracks, enabling a quick and painless conversion from mono or stereo into 5.1 surround.

In terms of mixing, get in the habit of using the VU meters to gauge the safe range of the audio levels you are playing back. You don't want to see anything registering red either in the individual track meters or the Master VU meters. While automation is very cool to use, sometimes the Pen tool easily does the trick to apply a simple fade or pan adjustment. You can also ensure that no damage comes to any mixed track by locking it after you have finished work on it.

In the next chapter you will learn about 5.1 surround sound mixing, specifically how to perform a surround sound mix within Premiere Pro, and then export it from your system. You will also see a new feature that allows you to open your audio files and edit them directly within Adobe Audition 2.0.

CHAPTER

21

5.1 Surround Sound Mixing

This short chapter builds on the stereo mixing foundation established in the previous chapter and introduces four more channels. Although Premiere Pro can handle 5.1 surround sound mixing easily, your task will be smoother if you learn a few techniques first.

The four short lessons in this chapter will give you the experience you need to effectively mix a 5.1 project. You will convert a stereo mix into a 5.1 mix, automate your surround sound mix, export your project into a file format that supports 5.1 audio, and learn how to ensure that your audio hardware properly plays back the six channels that make up your 5.1 surround sound mix.

Although a surround sound speaker system isn't essential to convert from stereo to surround sound, I recommend you have one. If you do not have the speakers and hardware to support six channels of audio, however, you can also reference the Audio Mixer to monitor the sound being played back. When you get down to it, mixing in 5.1 is similar to mixing stereo audio—you just have four more speakers to pan to. Let's give it a try.

Converting a Stereo Mix to 5.1 Surround

In the previous chapter's two-channel stereo project, you learned about mixing and automation to spatially distribute the sound so it came from either the left or right speaker. Two-channel stereo audio is fundamentally based on a left and right speaker, while 5.1 surround sound, also referred to as six-channel audio, is based on distributing sound to six speakers. Three speakers face the person listening: left, center, and right. Two are typically behind the listener: surround left and surround right. The sixth, LFE, is a low-frequency speaker that completes the surround environment by providing the deep bass. The LFE is typically in the front center on the floor.

For more on configuring a surround sound speaker system, see Chapter 17, "Using Your Audio Hardware."

Converting a stereo project to 5.1 is as easy as copying and pasting. To start this lesson, open the Project Surround_Convert_START.prproj from the APPST2 Lesson Files/Chapter 21 folder (**Figure 21.1**). To provide a project with the depth to properly articulate 5.1 mixing, this project file has 18 audio tracks all filled with sound elements from the final scene of my short film *Bleach*. You'll find the files for this project in the Chapter 21 and Chapter 26 folders.

Figure 21.1 Take a close look at the Surround_Convert _START project and its workspace. Notice how the Project panel and Audio Mixer panel are docked into the same frame, which is tall enough to accommodate the expanded mixer. Also notice how the timeline with all of its audio tracks is tall enough to display them. Because the Program Monitor and Effect Controls panel are less important, they have been reduced in overall size.

1. In the bottom of the Project panel, click the New Item button and select Sequence to create a new sequence. Name the sequence Bleach Edit 5.1. Set the number of video tracks to 1. Set the Audio Master to 5.1 and the number of stereo tracks to 1 with 0 for Mono, 5.1, and Submix Tracks (**Figures 21.2a** and **b**).

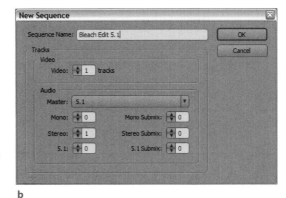

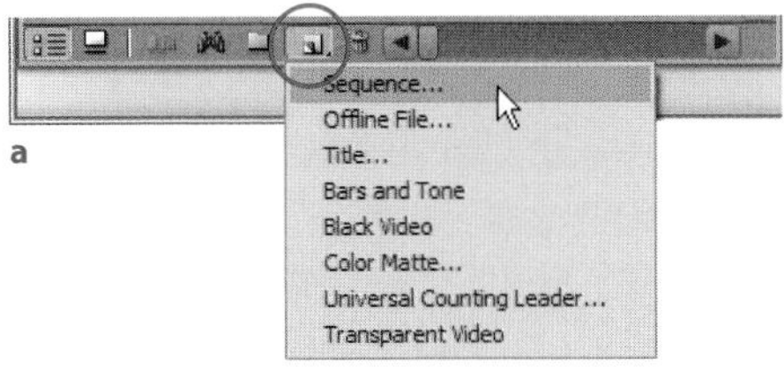

Figures 21.2a and b Clicking the New Item button at the bottom of the Project panel allows you to create a new sequence (a). Inside the New Sequence dialog box, you name the sequence and set its audio Master Track to 5.1 with one stereo track (b).

This first step simply creates a 5.1 surround sound project. Remember that you can have any type of audio track inside of any type of audio master project. When performing 5.1 surround sound mixing, the sequence Master Track setting needs to be 5.1. With a 5.1 Master Track setting, all the tracks in the sequence can be spatially mixed down within 5.1 space.

2. Double-click on the file Bleach Edit Stereo in the Project panel to make sure that the sequence is open in the Timeline panel. With the Sequence activated, press Ctrl+A to select the entire contents of the sequence, then press Ctrl+C to copy the selected content (see **Figures 21.3a** and **b**). Double-click on the file Bleach Edit 5.1 in the Project panel to open it in the Timeline panel, then press Ctrl+V on your keyboard to paste the selected material into the newly opened sequence. Realign the vertical positioning of the tracks to make sure you can view them all in the open space of the Timeline panel (see **Figure 21.3c**).

   In this step you physically copied all the material from one sequence and pasted it into another. The sequences are similar; you can adjust them, however, to make them virtually the same (see **Figure 21.4**).

Congratulations. You just converted a stereo sequence into a 5.1 sequence. Simple, eh? Of course, if you want to exactly duplicate the source sequence, you still have to manually rename each of the tracks in the 5.1 project. Notice that when you copied and pasted, the Paste command added the

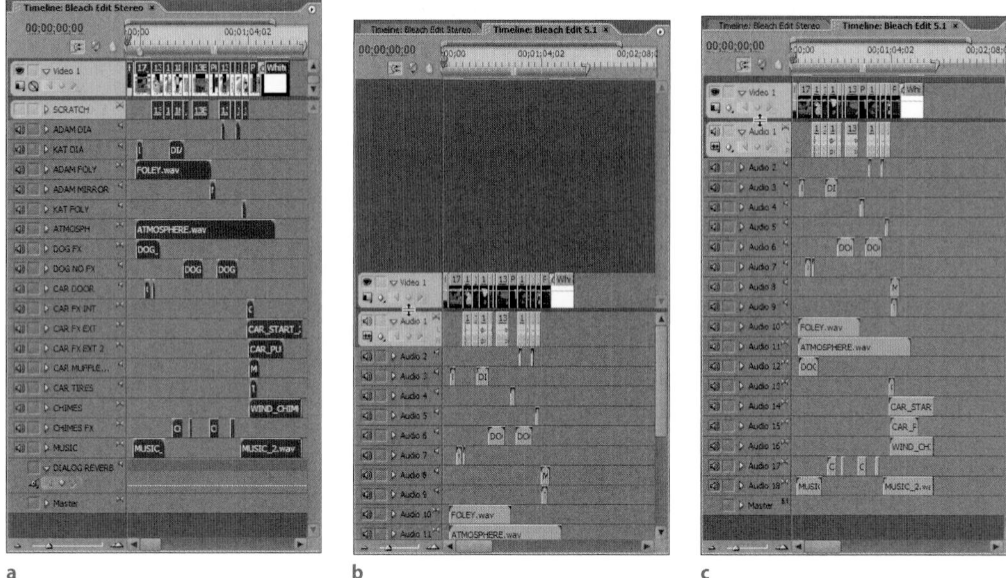

Figures 21.3a, b, and c To start, you selected all the files in the stereo sequence and copied them to your clipboard (a). Next, you opened a surround sound project and pasted the copied clips directly into it (b). Because the new sequence does not have the same vertical track shift, you dragged the dividing line between the Video and Audio tracks upward to reveal all the audio tracks (c).

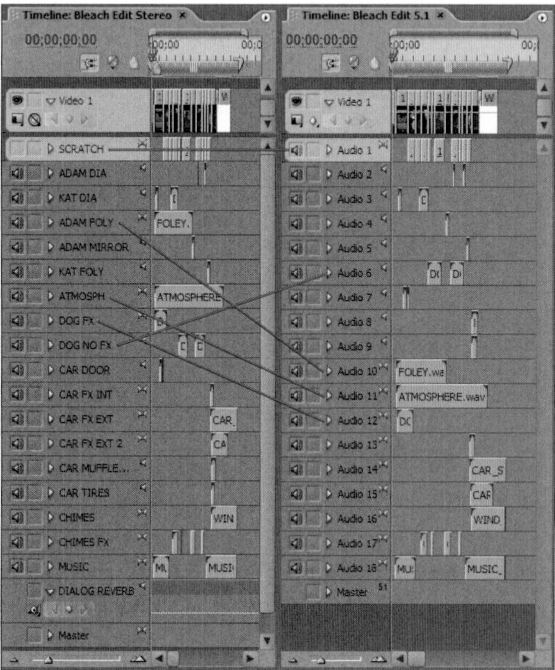

Figure 21.4 For this image, I split the current timeline frame in half, placing the two sequences side by side. When copying and pasting in this manner, you will find that the track types copy in groups. Because the first track being pasted was stereo, the scratch track copied it into exactly the same position. The remaining tracks then copied in descending groups, mono and then stereo. The stereo sequence does not have the source tracks grouped by type, so you will have to rename the tracks manually after you convert your sequence. But don't worry; I will do that for you in the next lesson.

tracks in groups. If the 5.1 sequence had 18 created tracks, each matching the stereo sequence's stack order, then the copied and pasted sequence will match the original. I have gone ahead and renamed the tracks so you can start remixing in the next lesson.

Automation and Mixing in 5.1

In the previous chapter, you positioned the playback head in the timeline, toggled a specific track to a desired Automation mode in the Audio Mixer panel, clicked play and panned the audio of the track dynamically as you watched the video playback. Automation in a surround sound project is exactly the same; you simply have more speaker choices for panning. Continuing to use the *Bleach* project, you can now experiment with surround sound automation to change the spatial properties of the audio mix.

Using mono (single channel) audio as source material for the sound mix allows you to more accurately distribute the sounds within your surround sound environment. Think of a mono track as a thin line; if you point the line at a precise point, hitting that point is relatively easy. Now imagine a stereo track as a line that is twice as thick; if you point it at the same point, the outer edges of the stereo track will expand slightly beyond the point. Likewise, with mono audio elements it is easier to control your mixing and your mix will yield better results.

Using some of the mono sound effects in the scene, let's quickly pan the audio and remix it in 5.1 surround sound. For this lesson, you'll need the Surround_Mix_START.prproj project in the APPST2 Lesson Files/Chapter 21 folder. Be sure that your workspace layout includes an expanded Audio Mixer, Timeline panel, and Program Monitor.

1. Watch the entire sequence and take note of sound effects and the potential for modifying their spatial property. In the timeline, pay close attention to the audio tracks ADAM MIRROR and CAR DOOR.

   You should hear that the sound design is generally in order. The atmosphere is there and all the necessary sound effects are in the scene from the keys jingling as the car engine is turned on to the creaking of the side mirror as the character adjusts it. In the next step, you are going to make a static adjustment of the side mirror track so that the audio comes from the front right speaker.

2. In the Audio Mixer panel, reveal the ADAM MIRROR track. Below the Volume fader of the track find the square with three dots along the top, two on the bottom and a small circle (called the *puck*) in the middle. This square reflects your 5.1 speaker configuration, and the puck dictates where the sound is panned. In the 5.1 Panner area of the track (**Figure 21.5a, b,** and **c**), drag the panning puck to the front right speaker (top-right corner). Play the sequence back and notice from where the sound originates.

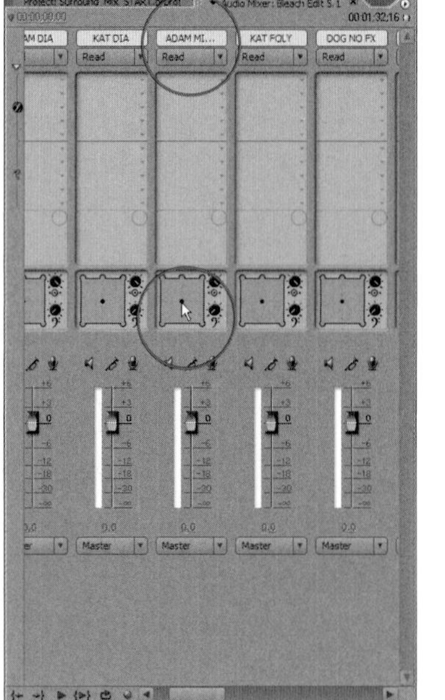

a

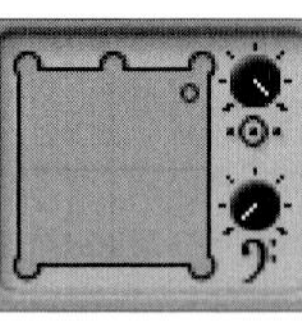

b

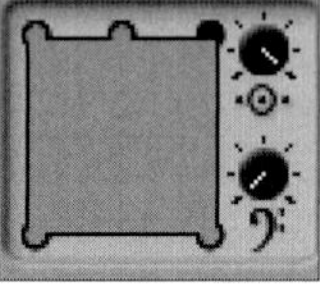

c

Figure 21.5 You begin with the Audio Mixer and the ADAM MIRROR track set to Read mode (a). Notice the surround sound panning area in the middle of the track. The puck in the center represents where the sound plays from in your mix. By default all panning in 5.1 is in the center and plays equally on the stereo (left and right) speakers in the front and back. Clicking and dragging the puck to the top right (b and c), you pan the track to the front-right speaker.

Although a stereo sequence reveals left/right panning capabilities, any track in a 5.1 sequence reveals 5.1 panning capabilities. Because the visual image for the sound effect shows the side mirror being on the passenger side of the car, you dragged the panning puck into the top-right corner of the 5.1 Panner to place all the audio for the panned track into that speaker.

The benefit of creating an audio mix with so many tracks is that it eases the process of mixing. Being able to isolate sound elements gives you faster and more accurate control over your mix. With no other sound effects on the ADAM MIRROR track and the Automation mode set to Read, you quickly panned the track to the speaker destination that matched the visual. If there were other effects on this track that didn't have the same visual location, you would have to keyframe the panning (also known as Automate).

3. In the Audio Mixer panel, set the Automation mode for the CAR DOOR track to Latch. Press the Home key on your keyboard and position the panning puck in the upper-right corner of the 5.1 Panner; however, do not stick it entirely in the top-right speaker (**Figure 21.6**). Play the timeline. As the first video shot completes (the actor opens the door), click and drag the puck down and to the lower right so that when the door closes in the next shot the puck is in the lower-left region. Press Home again, and play the sequence to hear and see your results.

a

Figure 21.6 Setting the Automation mode to Latch allows you to place the puck in any region of the Panner where it will remain until you manually drag it to a new position. After you drag it and move the mouse off, it stays in that new position. For the first door open moment, the puck is in the top-right corner, but not completely tucked into a speaker. For the door close, the puck is moved to the lowerright, which is accurate to the character's interpretation of where the sound is coming from.

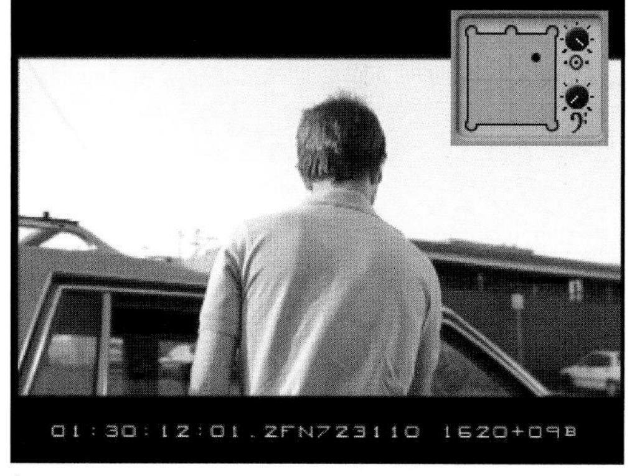

b

c

> At the beginning of the sequence when the actor opens the car door, the door is oriented in the front area of the frame and on the right side of the car. In the next shot, the door closes in the back right (as oriented to the actor). To have the sound effects reflect the spatial properties of the shots, you use the automation features to start the puck in the front right, then drag it to the back right. Because the track is made up of two sound effects and not one continuous track, you do not hear the sound panning from the front to the back speakers.

Mixing and automating in 5.1 is just as straightforward as these quick steps. Keep in mind, however, that the ease of mixing will be based on the complexity and breakdown of the tracks and effects in your sequence.

You can continue to automate and mix other effects, such as the ADAM FOLY track panning the sound to match the actor walking into frame and sitting down in the car. You can also adjust the panning of the car effects as the car drives away. I have gone ahead and applied a few more pans to the final project that are referenced in the remaining lessons. To look at the panning properties, play around the entire sequence with the Audio Mixer open.

Audio mixing is an organic and feedback-based (audible feedback) experience. Once you understand how the tools work, you may want to play around to find and achieve the results you desire.

Exporting and Playing 5.1 Audio

Having created the full 5.1 audio mix for your scene, you're ready to get the audio off of your system and out to other people. Consider this scene as a short clip you want to distribute on the Web retaining the full 5.1 surround sound mix. The first lesson in this last section explores the type of audio file formats that support six channels and what you need to remember about encoding into those formats. The final lesson overviews your Audio Hardware preferences so you can ensure that your six-channel audio plays properly on your system. Let's start by exporting the 5.1 audio.

Exporting 5.1 Audio

With your project converted and remixed in 5.1 surround sound, your next step is to actually export the file into a relevant viewing format. Premiere Pro supports two file formats for six-channel audio export: MPEG2-DVD (using the SurCode for Dolby Digital codec) and Windows Media. Windows Media actually supports up to eight channels of audio using the latest Windows Media Professional audio codec. If you are exporting 5.1 audio for DVD authoring, you can use the SurCode for Dolby Digital codec; three free trial uses come with Premiere Pro, and then you must purchase a full license. Because Windows Media is free and the most accessible format with which to author 5.1 sound, this lesson offers a quick overview of the presets, settings, and check boxes relevant for creating a surround sound Windows Media file.

1. Open the project file Surround_Export_START.prproj from the APPST2 Lesson Files/Chapter 21 folder. Open the Bleach Edit 5.1 sequence in the Timeline panel. With the sequence active, select File > Export > Adobe Media Encoder.

   To access the audio format that encodes six- and eight-channel audio, you need to use the Adobe Media Encoder. The Export > Export Movie or Export Audio commands will not give you access to the Windows Media codec that you need.

2. In the Adobe Media Encoder, select Windows Media from the Export Settings > Format drop-down menu (see **Figure 21.7**). Choose the preset labeled WM9 NTSC 1024K download. Click the Audio tab, click the Audio Codec drop-down menu, and select Windows Media Audio 9.1 Professional. From the Basic Audio Settings > Audio Format drop-down menu select the preset labeled 192 kbps, 48kHz, 5.1 channel, 16 bit (A/V) CBR (see **Figure 21.8**).

   Using Windows Media as your format in the Adobe Media Encoder, the Windows Media Audio 9.1 Professional Audio Codec is my preferred codec when encoding more than two channels of audio. Although

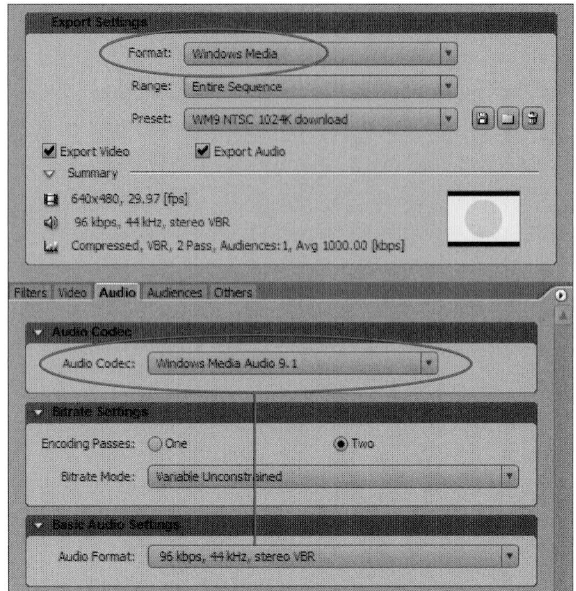

Figure 21.7 The Adobe Media Encoder is set to Windows Media. With the 1024K preset selected, you can see Audio Codec is set to Windows Media Audio 9.1. The Basic Audio Settings reveal Stereo as the Audio Format setting.

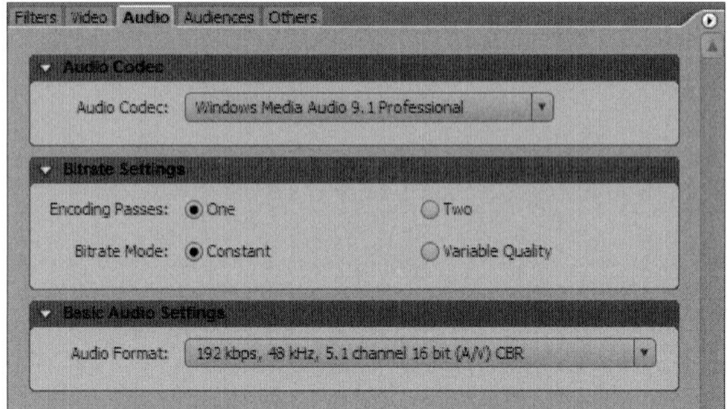

Figure 21.8 With the Windows Media Audio 9.1 Professional codec selected, you can choose presets that support two, six, or eight channels of audio.

the Windows Media Audio 9.1 Lossless codec supports two- and six-channel audio, the Professional audio codec gives you a ton of presets.

For this step, you chose a bitrate (192 kbps) that was not too high, but also not too low. This keeps your quality at a good level but does not make your overall file size too big. The rest of the preset dictated that the audio remained at its original 16 bit, 48 kHz. In general, the NTSC 1024K preset gives you decent quality video without a high data rate at a 640×480 frame size, which will be just fine for full-screen desktop computer playback. The video settings of the preset matched that of the source sequence, but the audio portion was the most important component and the flavor of audio preset should be based on the type of encode you are doing (audio only or audio and video) and the projected size of the file.

3. Go to the Source/Output side of the encoder, and click on Source. Crop the Left and Right values to 7 with Top and Bottom cropped to 68. Click on Output, then click Deinterlace and Scale to Fit. In the Export Settings area of the Encoder, click the Video tab and change Basic Video Settings > Frame Size to 640×346. Click the OK button in the Encoder to name and then render out your file. (If you do not wish to render out the file, you can simply open the Bleach Edit 5.1.wmv file in the APPST2 Lesson Files/Chapter 21 folder.)

   Because the content of the scene that you want to encode is smaller than the full frame, you cropped the file to the letterboxed frame size of the video. Because the clip is going to play back on computer monitors and not on televisions, you clicked the Deinterlace button to merge the fields for the encode. Finally you adjusted the frame size so that the cropped video clip was encoded exactly at the dimensions to which the video was cropped.

The Audio Format presets are very direct and easy to navigate, but Premiere Pro has a lot of them. If you are exporting audio and video (sequences or clips) with the encoder, use one of the (A/V) presets. This ensures that sync between audio and video does not drift and is frame-accurate during playback. Often when encoding into various codecs, sections of the playback might drift out of sync or audio may not play accurately to the video frame.

If you performed this type of workflow and wanted to encode only 5.1 audio from the timeline, you would uncheck the Video check box in the Export Settings area of the Adobe Media Encoder. The resulting audio-only file would have the extension .wma (Windows Media Audio) as opposed to .wmv (Windows Media Video).

This short lesson illustrates just how easy it is to export six-channel audio into a common file format. To watch this file prospective users need only Windows Media 9 or later installed on their system. If they have stereo speakers, the file will play in stereo. If they have 5.1 speakers, they will experience the audio exactly as you mixed it in Premiere Pro.

Playing 5.1 Audio

Although visually monitoring your 5.1 audio is pretty easy (keep the Audio Mixer panel open to review the panning properties of each track), this last quick lesson guides you through the Audio Output Mapping preference, which enables you to verify that your surround sound audio is playing back as you expect.

This lesson applies to anyone who has an attached USB, FireWire, or PCI-based audio interface. My eMagic USB audio interface will serve as the hardware example for this lesson.

1. With a 5.1 surround sound sequence or stereo sequence open, go to Edit > Preferences > Audio Hardware. In that preference, select the Audio device that you wish to use as your default device from the Default Device drop-down menu.

   On my system, for example, I chose the ASIO eMagic A26/A62m device from the drop-down menu. Selecting the device engages Premiere Pro to play back audio using that device. If you do not have a device with up to six output channels you will not be able to listen to 5.1 surround sound audio in its true surround environment.

2. Click on the Audio Output Mapping preference and check that the Map Output For drop-down menu matches the selection from the previous preference. In the Audio Output Mapping preference, also make sure that the speaker configuration displayed below the drop-down menu matches the routing of the speakers on your system (**Figure 21.9**).

   To accurately play back surround sound audio you need to make sure that the channel mappings of your audio interface match that of Premiere Pro. As seen in Figure 21.9 each of the six channels has a surround sound speaker assigned to it. The icon for the speaker in the Audio Output Mapping preference should match the physical position of the speaker connected to the output channel. For example, Output 1 in Figure 21.9 points toward the Left Stereo speaker icon in the dialog. At home or in your office, Output 1 should be connected to the left stereo speaker of your computer. If Output 2 is connected to your physical left stereo speaker, you can drag the icon for Left Stereo in the

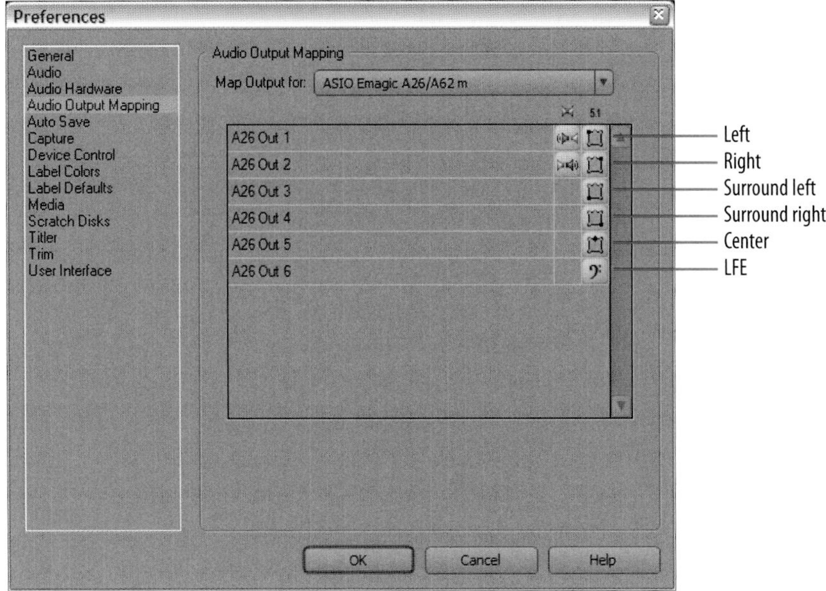

Figure 21.9 If you have an audio interface with six channels, you can easily configure it to properly play 5.1 surround sound audio. When connecting your speakers to your audio device, make sure the intended position of each speaker matches the output channel being mapped to in the Audio Output Mappings preference. Here, the Output 6 port on the audio interface should connect to the LFE (the bass unit) of the surround sound speaker system.

Audio Output Mapping preference down one track to reside in line with Output 2 instead of Output 1.

If you can't adjust the routing of your physical output ports on your audio interface, you can quickly reroute the mapping of the 5.1 speakers within the Audio Output Mapping preference to match that of your physical speakers.

You need just two steps to properly monitor and play back surround sound audio with Premiere Pro 2.0. The first step is having a 5.1 audio interface that supports six channels of playback, and the second is to create a 5.1 surround project. Although the first step in not an absolute requirement, you will, of course, have the best and most accurate results when you have a 5.1 playback setup to monitor your 5.1 mix.

Things to Remember

When converting a stereo project to a 5.1 surround sound project, remember that track-based effects are not preserved when you copy and paste between the two sequences.

Keep in mind that any project can be converted and remixed in 5.1; you just need to be exporting the audio into a format that supports six channels of audio. If you are creating a Windows Media file for the Web, although it increases the overall file size, 5.1 mixing fits right into the Windows Media file format.

To play back 5.1 audio through an added audio interface, your audio hardware must support at least six output channels. When setting up your surround sound system, make sure your speaker configuration matches the speaker distribution in your Audio Output Mappings preference.

This chapter concludes the audio techniques portion of the book. The next section covers such advanced effect techniques as green screen keying, color correction adjustments, and track matte examples, plus a lot more helpful tips and tricks for getting more out of the effects that come with Premiere Pro 2.0.

Advanced Effect Techniques

CHAPTER

22

New Color Correction Tools: Fast Color Corrector

One of Premiere Pro's biggest leaps forward in 2.0 is its handling of color space and color correction tools. Premiere Pro 2.0 has a Video Effects folder that contains a Color Correction subfolder. There you'll find such new effects as Fast Color Corrector, Luma Corrector, Luma Curve, RGB Color Corrector, RGB Curves, Three-Way Color Corrector, and Video Limiter. This chapter focuses exclusively on the Fast Color Corrector effect, while the next chapter will concentrate on the Three-Way Color Corrector. Before diving into these effects, however, you need to understand some color correction basics so you can better appreciate the use of each color correction effect. The four principal components of color correction are luminance and chrominance; red, green, and blue (RGB) channels; HSL; and tonal ranges.

Luminance and Chrominance

From every video frame you can extract two types of image data: luminance (luma) and chrominance (chroma). *Luma* data measures the brightness levels of your image, while *chroma* data measures the color values of your image. Think of it this way: Luma equals brightness, and chroma equals color. To conform your video to television broadcast standards, you need to be sure its luma and chroma levels are within broadcast-safe limits. When you are performing color corrections to your image and are concerned about broadcast-safe levels, you can set Monitor Output modes to track luma levels, chroma levels, or both at the same time. Simply click the Output Mode button in the Program Monitor and select the appropriate mode: Vectorscope to measure chroma or YC Wavefrom to measure

Figures 22.1a and b How does the composite output of this video frame in the Program Monitor stack up (a)? Toggle the Output drop-down menu to Vect/YC Wave/YCbCr Parade to view the luminance (YC Waveform), chrominance (Vectorscope), and channel values (YCbCr Parade) in one Output mode.

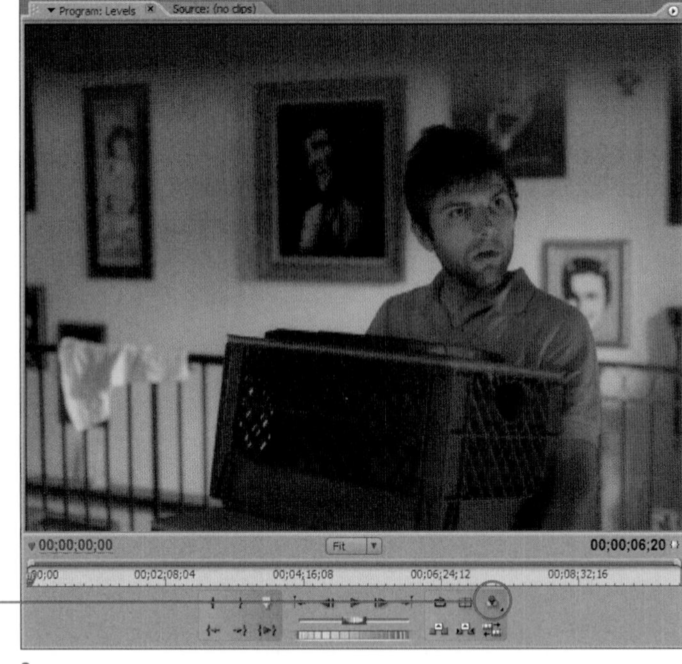

Output mode set to Composite

a

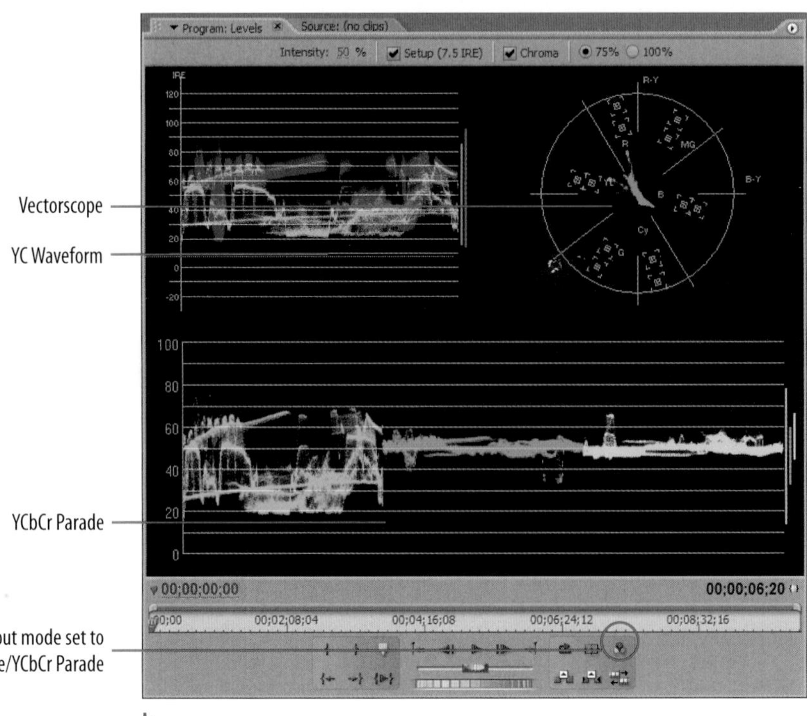

Vectorscope

YC Waveform

YCbCr Parade

Output mode set to Vect/YC Wave/YCbCr Parade

b

luma see (**Figures 22.1a** and **b**). When you are done, you can toggle your Output mode back to Composite Video. I often refer to these Output modes to see color corrections applied to the clips and understand how they affect the luma or chroma levels.

As you might expect, the Luma Corrector effect adjusts the lightness and darkness information of your clip. If you wish to make deep or subtle brightness adjustments to your image, head for the Luma Corrector. The Luma Curves effect makes the same brightness adjustments but from a curve-controlled interface. If you are comfortable with curves then I recommend using Luma Curves, otherwise stick with Luma Corrector.

Found in Premiere Pro's Video Effects/Color Correction folder, the Video Limiter effect is a one-click effect that auto-adjusts any illegal values in your video. You can drag and drop it onto any video clip in the timeline.

RGB Color Channels

In addition to monitoring your video's luma and chroma levels, you must consider the three *color channels* that mix together to make the frame: red, green, and blue (RGB). Video color correction is inherently tied to these three color channels. Setting the Program Monitor's Output drop-down menu to RGB Parade lets you monitor the values.

Toggle your Output mode to RGB Parade before you color correct so that you can see which color channel has the most emphasis in the image. Knowing the dominant color channel can expedite the color correction process by giving you some inkling of the correction you want to apply. For example, if your image looks too warm and upon analysis you find that the red channel is quite dominant, you may want to color correct specifically within the red channel to lower its brightness and saturation, or you could increase the value of the blue channel to "cool" off the image. For a cool image with lots of blue, you can increase the red channel a bit to "warm" it (see **Figures 22.2a** and **b**). As you then make corrections, take note of how the channels increase or decrease in height or thickness in RGB Parade.

Of course all of these corrections are not as simple as I am describing, but the essence is exactly how it reads. With Premiere Pro 2.0 there are RGB color channel correction tools that can do this type of job quite easily.

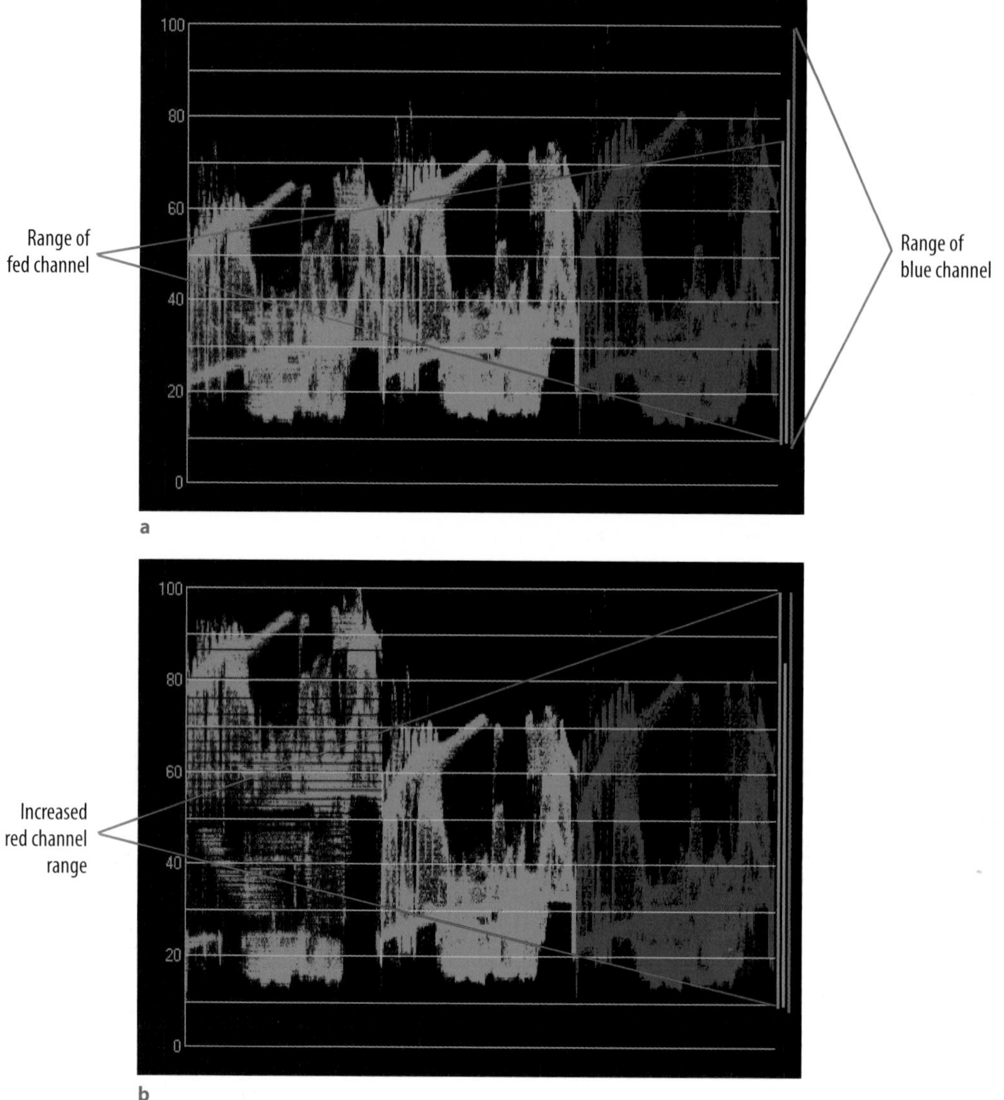

Figures 22.2a and b By monitoring your footage in RGB Parade Output mode you can see the strength of each color channel in the image (a). Checking the height of the line on the right of the panel, you can see the color data here shows that the blue channel has the most strength. After you make a color correction to the red channel, the RGB Parade display updates with the results (b); notice that the red channel has increased amplitude.

To make color correction adjustments specific to the color channels of the image, you should be using either the RGB Color Corrector or the RGB Curves effect. Both of these effects have deep adjustment capabilities that can offer very subtle and practical results.

Tonal Ranges

A third method of viewing your image enables you to determine how best to adjust the image using your color correction tools: viewing the *tonal range* of your image. Tonal range is made up of three parts: *highlights* (brightest components), *shadows* (darkest components), and *midtones* (what's in between). Using the Premiere color correction tools it is very easy to look at the tonal range of your image, quickly understand which portion of your image falls into which tonal range, and then make exact adjustments (**Figure 22.3**).

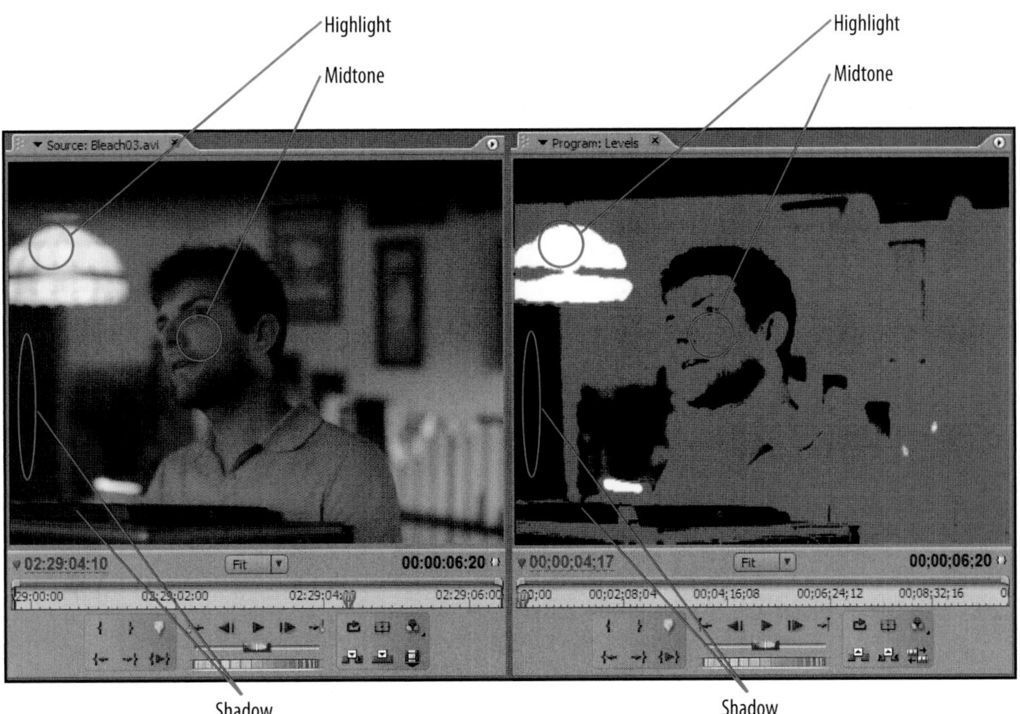

Figure 22.3 The left frame shows the clip as it plays; the Program Monitor displays the same frame with its tonal range being revealed. Highlights appear as white, midtones as gray, and shadows as black.

Say you want to cool off the flesh tones of your character's face. Analyzing the tonal range you determine that the character's face is a midtone. Using color correction tools you then selectively add blue to the midtone range only. The technical term for color correcting these three tonal ranges is *three-way* or *three-point color correction.* The Three-Way Color Corrector effect offers you full access to the individual tonal ranges as well as the entire image. The Fast Color Corrector can make adjustments to the entire image only. For quick color adjustments Fast is the effect to use; for more detailed corrections use the Three-Way effect.

Chapter 23, "Advanced Color Correction: Three-Way Color Corrector," will teach you how to dynamically redefine the tonal range of your image to more precisely control the corrections being made within the tonal ranges.

HSL: Hue, Saturation, and Lightness

The controls for making corrections with the Fast Color Corrector and Three-Way Color Corrector are commonly referred to as *HSL controls* or *HSL offsets.* HSL stands for hue, saturation, and lightness. Hue and saturation are color values (chroma) and lightness deals with your brightness (luma) value.

The HSL controls for color correction usually consist of a color wheel to define the color correction (chroma), a slider bar to increase or decrease the saturation of that color, and brightness and contrast controls to define the lightness (luma). Take a look at the Fast Color Corrector to see how Premiere Pro implements these controls.

The top half of the Fast Color Corrector deals with the physical color correction that you are applying; in **Figure 22.4** the color being applied is pink-blue. As you click and drag within the color wheel to define the color you wish to apply, the sliders beneath the wheel update to reveal exact coordinates and values. Each color you select is defined by an exact Hue Angle, Balance Magnitude, Balance Gain, and Balance Angle. After you find the desired color, use the sliders to adjust that color within the same selected range. The Input Level settings at the bottom of the effect allow you to determine where black, gray, and white fall in your image. The Output Level settings allow you to remap the black and white levels to adjust the brightness further.

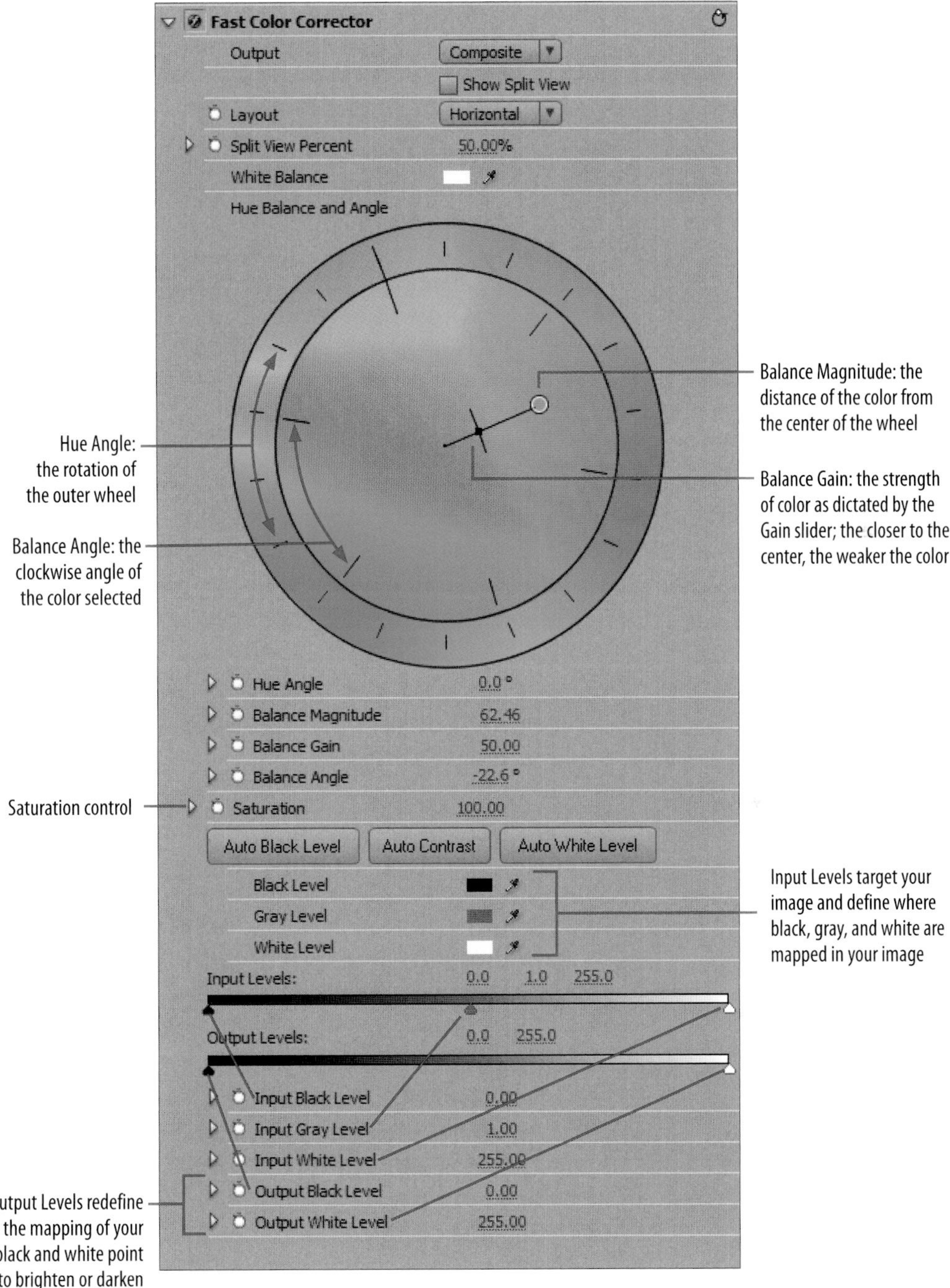

Figure 22.4 The top half of the Fast Color Corrector effects deals with the color that you are applying as a correction. Once you find the color that you like, you can use the sliders to adjust the color within the same selected range.

Let's review: Adjusting the Hue Angle gives you a specific color. Adjusting Saturation increases or decreases the richness of selected color. Adjusting Brightness and Contrast adjusts the strength of the selected color. Once you learn how to manipulate these controls for the Fast Color Corrector, you'll be able to move on to the Three-Way Color Corrector easily. The basic controls are the same, with just a few extras added to handle changes to individual tonal ranges. So, let's get right to it and start using the Fast Color Corrector for a number of practical adjustments.

Using The Fast Color Corrector

Because the Fast Color Corrector adjusts only the master tonal range (all three ranges combined) of your image, it is useful when you want to white balance your shots or make one quick overall adjustment. The first of this chapter's two lessons will cover how to use the Fast Color Corrector to white balance your shots. The second lesson explains how to use the Fast Color Corrector effect to adjust the levels of your shot to make it brighter or darker.

White Balancing

When filming someone on location, on a set, or even outdoors, the color temperature of the light that fills the location can often add a color cast to your recorded image. Although the human eye does not detect these color casts as easily, video cameras and film cameras always record them. When filmed, fluorescent lights have a tendency to add light green or light blue color casts to your image. If you were to hold a pure white piece of paper up to the camera under fluorescent lights, the paper would not appear as pure white on video; instead it would be bright blue/white or bright green/white.

The term "white balancing" refers to a color adjustment of the image's white value so that the color-tinged paper on tape returns to the pure white that your eye saw on the location. White balancing removes the color cast by allowing you to target a portion of the image that should be pure white and making a color correction adjustment back to pure white. By sampling information from the white area, this color correction removes the identified color cast from the entire image.

Most cameras offer an Auto White Balance control that allows you to point at a white object and click a button to apply an automatic white balance, but I find this setting to do more harm than good. Cameras also frequently have additional white balance settings for either outdoor or indoor lighting. I recommend choosing one of these settings depending on whether you're indoors or outdoors, instead of using your camera's Auto White Balance control. In either setting, I record a few seconds of a white card that I will reference back in the editing room. After capturing the footage, I then properly white balance my shots using either the Fast Color Corrector or Three-Way Color Corrector effects.

In general when recording you want to stay away from a fluctuation in color. Setting the camera's balance to Sunlight/Outdoor or Electric Light/Indoor at least puts your camera into a consistent mode when shooting outside or in a studio, meaning any effect your camera imparts to footage will be consistent across the board rather than fluctuating each time you auto-balance a new shot. After you set your camera to the proper mode, I also recommend filming a white card in every location to have that pure white reference. Simply hold up a pure white card (or piece of paper) in front of the camera in the direct path of the light at your location. (You can refer to my white card technique in the clips in Chapter 27, "Advanced Editing: The New Multi-Cam Workflow.")

If you didn't have a white card to balance with at your shoot, there are other techniques for white balancing using the Fast Color Corrector. Give it a try by using the Fast_Color01_Start.prproj project in the APPST2 Lesson Files/Chapter 22 folder. Make sure that your workspace allows for a large frame with your Program Monitor and another large frame for your Effects Controls panel. You can customize the one my project already uses if you like.

Figure 22.5 The layout includes the Effect Controls panel, Timeline panel, and Program Monitor. With the first Bleach01.avi file selected in the Timeline panel, its Effect properties are revealed in the Effect Controls panel. To expand the horizontal size of the Effect listings, click the Show/Hide Timeline button.

1. With the Fast_Color01_Start project open, open the White Balance sequence in the Timeline panel. Open your Effect panel and twirl down Video Effects/Color Correction. From the Color Correction folder, drag and drop the Fast Color Correction effect onto the first Bleach01.avi (**Figure 22.5**) in the timeline. Click on this instance of Bleach01.avi, open your Effect Controls panel, and expand the Fast Color Corrector effect listing. At the top of the Effect Controls panel, click the Show/Hide Timeline button to expand the Effects area and hide the timeline.

   This first step is very direct; you navigate to the color correction effect folder, then drag and drop the desired effect onto the first clip in the white balance sequence. To adjust the Fast Color Corrector effect, you selected the clip and then opened the Effects Controls panel to see the effect properties. Because you aren't going to keyframe any effect adjustments in the timeline area of the Effect Controls panel, you click the Show/Hide

TIP

When you hold down the Ctrl key and click on a color with an eyedropper, you sample a five-pixel radius to determine the color you are picking, as opposed to the one pixel that the eyedropper targets without the modifier key. Very often, the color difference between single pixels can be drastic and although you might think you are targeting a specific color, you are not. Holding down Ctrl ensures a more accurate color selection.

Timeline button to give the Color Corrector effect more screen real estate to display in.

2. In the Effect Controls panel for the Fast Color Corrector effect, click on the White Balance eyedropper. Drag the eyedropper over to the counter top in the lower center of the video frame in the Program Monitor (**Figures 22.6a** and **b**). Hold down the Ctrl key and click once on the counter.

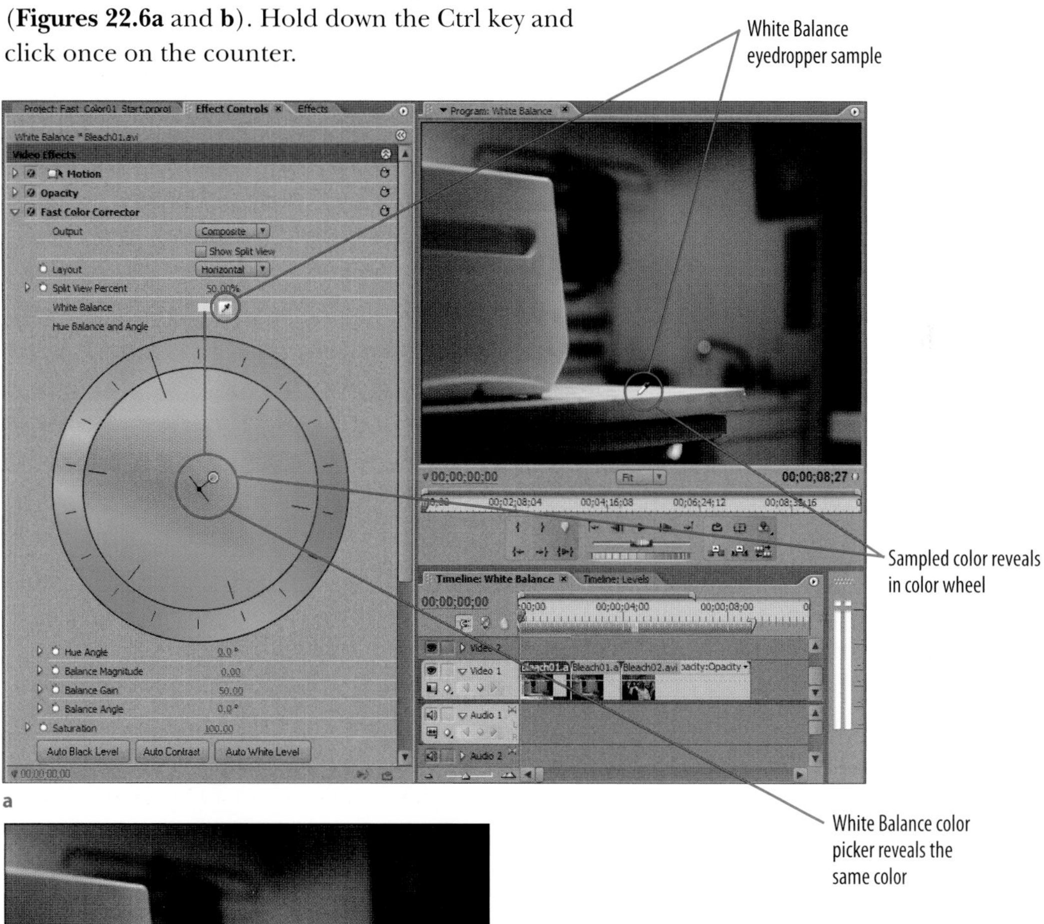

b

Figures 22.6a and b The White Balance eyedropper samples color from the counter top (a). Meanwhile, the color wheel updates to define the color selected as does the color picker next to the White Balance eyedropper. The results of this selection (b) reveal a frame with the green color cast removed.

To white balance a clip you need to find a frame in which the unwanted color cast is clearly visible. In the first frame of the Bleach01.avi you can clearly see that the entire image has a greenish tint. You can identify the green tint in the countertop in the center of the frame. Knowing that the countertop should be white, you clicked on the White Balance eyedropper and dragged it over to click on the countertop area of the image. Holding down the Ctrl key toggled the eyedropper from a one-pixel selection radius to a five-pixel selection radius. Because the White Balance feature is an automatic adjustment, the Fast Color Corrector adjusted the clip to remove the green color cast. In essence the White Balance feature is taking the light green color and shifting it so that it is pure white instead of light green. White balancing is exactly that simple.

3. Now try another white balance technique on the same clip that assumes you don't have a white card reference from which to sample. Drag and drop the Fast Color Corrector effect onto the second Bleach01.avi file in the White Balance sequence. Select the clip and press the Page Down key to advance the playback head to the beginning of this clip, then expand the Fast Color Corrector effect in the Effect Controls panel. Click on the White Balance eyedropper and instead of sampling from the counter, hold down the Ctrl key, sample from the side of the toaster oven (**Figure 22.7**), and click on the sampled region.

   Although you did not have a pure white reference point, you found a region of the image that wasn't brightly colored and should be considered white. You sampled from the side of the white toaster (which had a green tint after being filmed), and the Fast Color Corrector yielded the same results by analyzing the sampled color (in this case a midtone green) and removing the greenish tint until the sample color became a white midtone. Based on the results of this step, all you need to do to white balance a shot is sample the color from a region of the image that should be considered any shade of white. The lighter the color, the more accurate your results will be.

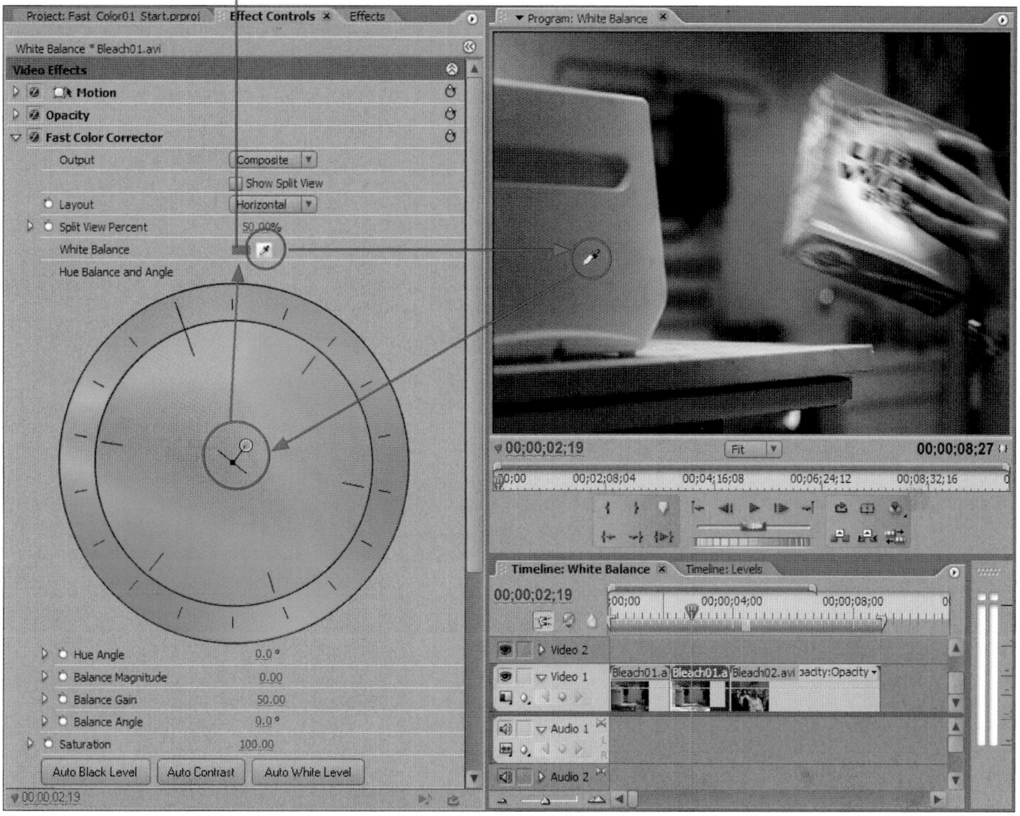

Notice the sample color is darker than in Figure 22.6a

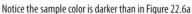

Figure 22.7 If you do not have a bright colored or pure white area to sample, you can still sample from a region that has the tint you want removed. The Fast Color Corrector will adjust the brightest color from the selected color to pure white. In this case, sampling the side of the toaster (although even a darker green), yielded the same results.

4. Drag and drop the Fast Color Corrector to the Bleach02.avi and apply your own white balance adjustment (**Figure 22.8**) based on one of the shirts from one of the men in the frame.

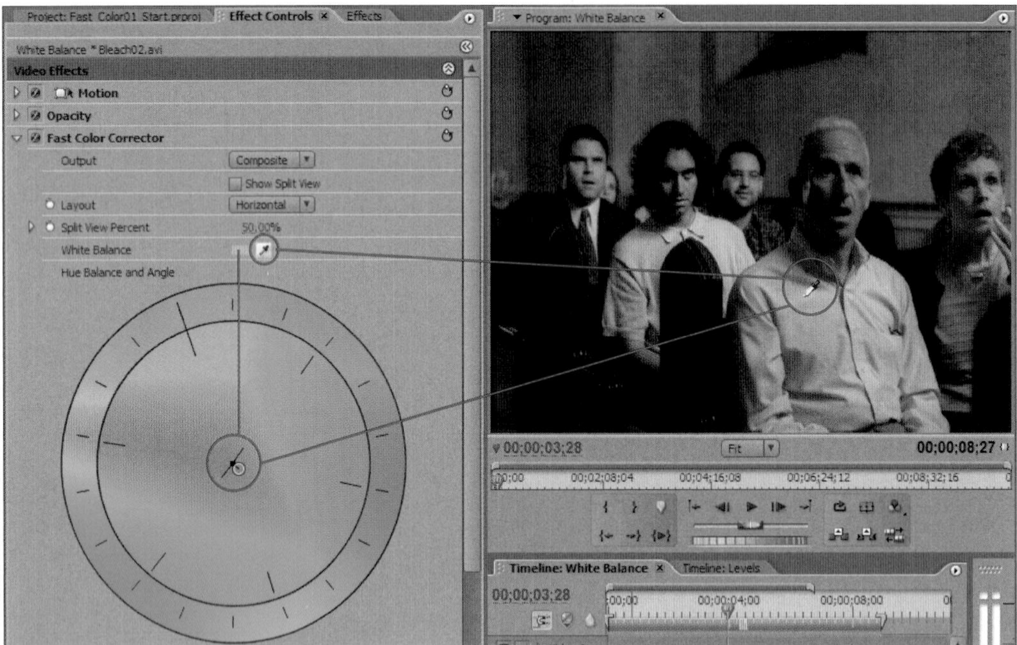

Figure 22.8 This image has a warm tint to it already. If I sample the old man's beige shirt for white balancing, look how cool the image gets. In the case of this shot, the color is already just right and unnecessary to adjust. The white balance adjustment took the warmth right out of the image by shifting the light beige to pure white.

I put this last clip into the sequence because I think it already has a good warm visual tone. The same way the first steps showed the cool green cast shift to white, this last step shows you how you can sample from a warm beige cast and cool off the image. For this clip, the cooling was too much but based on the sample it yielded expected results. Sometimes you need to see an adjustment that goes too far before you can understand how much is enough.

This lesson showed you exactly how to white balance your shots so that the color information shifted away from any tinting or color casts added by the camera. To see my results from this lesson, open the White Balance sequence in the Fast_Color02_Start.prproj from the APPST2 Lesson Files/Chapter 22 folder.

If you have a series of clips all shot in the same location with the same camera and same settings, you can white balance one of the shots with the Fast Color Corrector, then copy and paste the effect onto the other clips in the series.

Level Adjustments

White balance adjustments provide a good foundation to build on. The same Fast Color Corrector effect can quickly adjust the black and white levels of a clip to better control its brightness and contrast.

1. Open the Fast_Color02_Start.prproj project from the APPST2 Lesson Files/Chapter 22 folder. With the project open, open the Levels sequence and apply the Fast Color Corrector to the Bleach03.avi file. Be sure that your layout matches or is similar to that of **Figure 22.9**. In the Reference Monitor panel set the Output mode to YC Waveform.

Figure 22.9 The Fast Color Corrector effect is applied to the Bleach03.avi file in the timeline. The workspace reveals a Program Monitor on the top right and next to it, the Reference Monitor. Using a Reference Monitor while you color correct is essential for viewing the video's signal data, which updates as you make adjustments. Setting the Reference Monitor to YC Waveform enables you to view the luminance value of the video image while you manipulate it.

Setting the Reference Monitor's output mode to YC Waveform enables you to view the results of the Fast Color Corrector in the Program Monitor while viewing the luminance value of the results in the Reference Monitor. In YC Waveform mode, the Reference Monitor displays a scale that goes from -20 to 120 with increments of 10 denoted by horizontal lines. Illegal waveform values are above 100 (brightest) and below 7.5 (darkest, which is identified by dotted line). Check that the luminance adjustments result in values within this range (**Figure 22.10**).

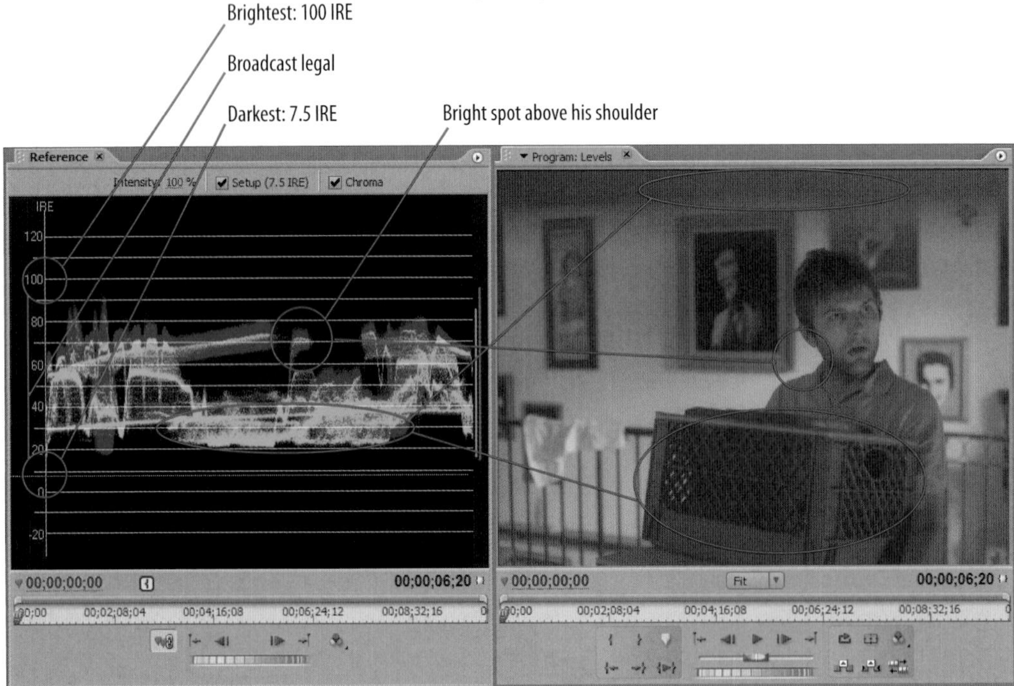

Figure 22.10 A waveform monitor measures the IRE values (luminance) of your video signal. Readouts higher on the scale reflect bright portions of your image, and readouts near the bottom reflect dark portions. The waveform represents the image from left to right as your frame does except it collapses all of the luminance value onto the scale. Here you can see that the darkened top of the frame and darkened crate both reveal low values on the waveform. The brighter white wall that appears behind the actor, however, should show up in somewhat of the same shape as it is in the frame.

Looking at the waveform values for the Bleach03.avi file you should be able to see that the image could be lighter in some parts and darker in others and still be legal. If you use the Auto Levels buttons, the Fast Color Corrector will achieve these adjustments for you.

2. Select the Bleach03.avi file from the sequence so that its effect properties are active in the Effect Controls panel. Twirl down the Fast Color Corrector effect. Click the Auto Black Level button (**Figures 22.11a** and **b**).

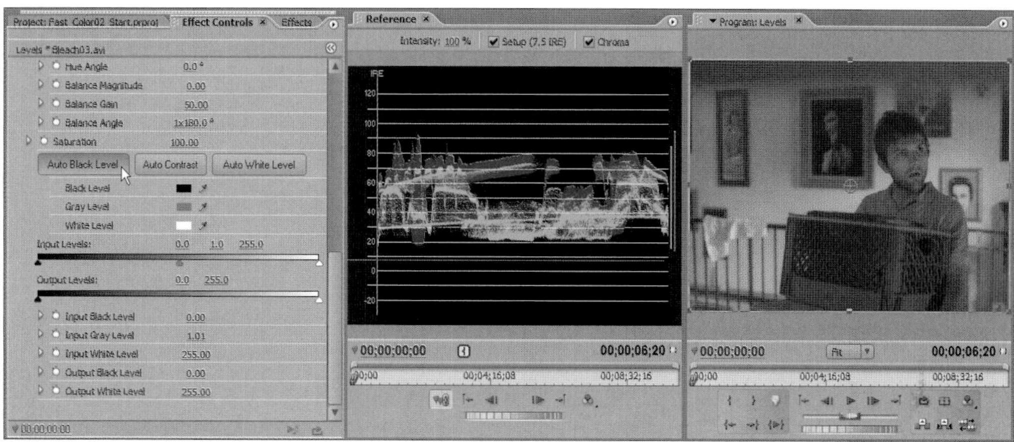

a

b

Figures 22.11a and b The darkest portion of the selected clip registers at about 21 IRE in the waveform display (a). Clicking the Auto Black Level button automatically adjusts the darkest information already in file to be true black (b).

Auto Black Levels shifts the levels of the image so that the darkest portions move to the lowest legal IRE value (7.5), becoming true black for video. The result, as seen in Figure 21.11b, is that black portions of your image are richer.

3. Now try the same operation for the clip's whites: Click the Auto White Level button (**Figures 22.12a** and **b**). Click in the farthest right Input Levels hot-text box and change the value from 204 to 212.

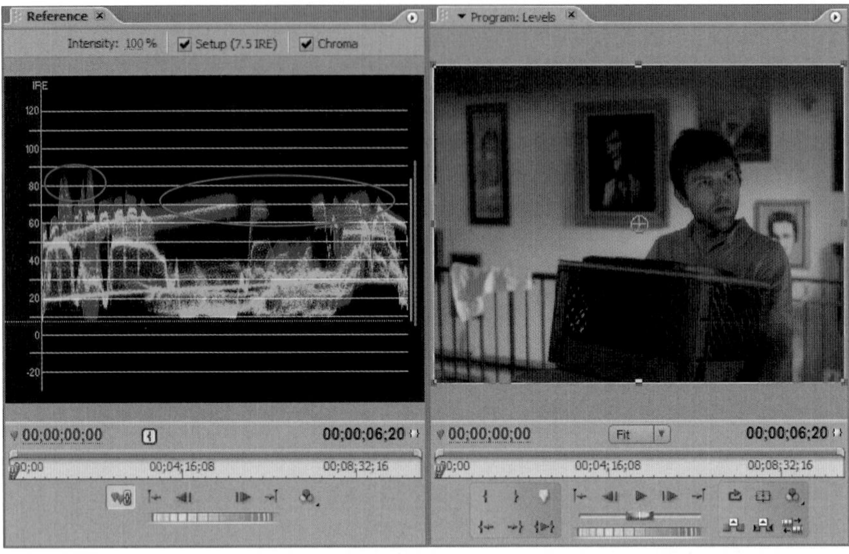

a

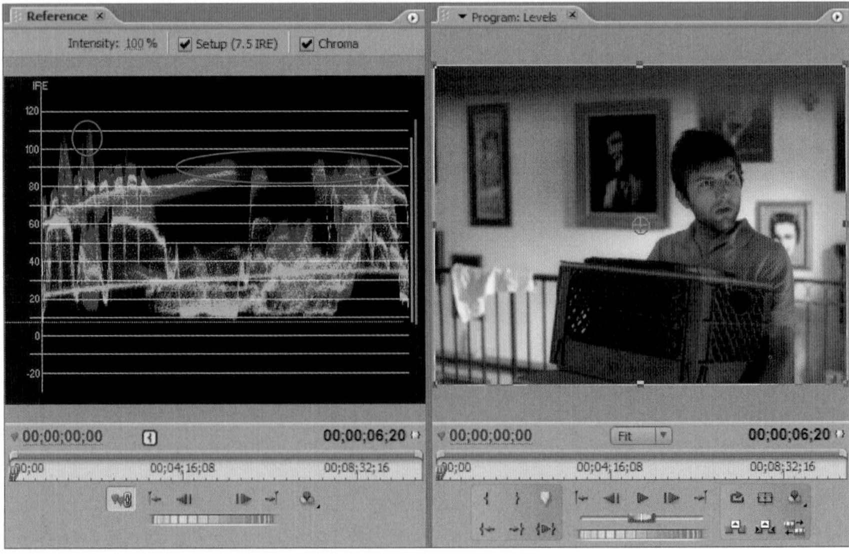

b

Figures 22.12a and b Compare the starting state of the waveform and image (a) with the result of activating Auto White Level (b). The clip becomes brighter with more defined contrast. Auto White Levels shifts the levels of the clip's brightest point so that the overall scale of the white increases, as evidenced by the feedback and shift in the waveform monitor.

The Auto White Levels effect analyzes an image and adjusts the brightest white it finds to become pure white. Unfortunately Auto White Levels does not constrain its results to only legal values. Because of this, you manually modified the White Input Level so that the brightest value was legal.

4. To put the finishing touches on this clip, adjust the white balance to take some of the coolness out of it. With the Bleach03.avi clip still selected, click the White Balance eyedropper. With the White Balance eyedropper, hold down the Ctrl key and click on the white wall to sample its color information (**Figures 22.13a**).

a

b

Figures 22.13a and b Sample your white balance from this section of the wall (a). Compare the levels-adjusted and white-balanced clip in the Program Monitor with the original clip in the Source Monitor (b). With a basic understanding of the effects and a few clicks you can achieve excellent results with the Fast Color Corrector.

> After redefining the black and white levels to strengthen the image, you quickly removed the soft blue color cast using the white balance technique from the previous lesson. The results as seen in **Figure 22.13b** prove just how crisp you can make an image and how simple using the color correction tools can be.

The end result of color correction is not the same for every project but the goal should be: to create through the manipulation of color a better-looking image. Whether performing straightforward color balancing to remove a color cast or using the Auto Levels buttons to give your black-and-white image components more strength and better definition, your eye and your taste dictate how far you take the image in any of these directions. When I am doing any professional job I hire a color correction artist and pay a hefty rate to get results beyond my abilities. Knowing a few things about color, watching over a colorist's shoulder, and doing my own color corrections on side projects, however, increases my ability to create a better image than was originally shot.

I've given you the keys; now hop into the Fast Color Corrector and try exploiting these clips further to test the color correction effects. The next chapter will introduce more clips and an even more powerful effect called Secondary Color Correction.

Things to Remember

For simple white balancing, brightness, and master color casts the Fast Color Corrector is the proper tool for the job. Using the White Balance eyedropper of the Fast Color Corrector effect, you can quickly assign a white balance adjustment to any clip in the timeline with just a few clicks. Using the Auto Black Level and Auto White Level buttons you can increase and redefine the white and black points of your image so that the brightest value of your image becomes pure white and the darkest, pure black.

Although color correction can be daunting, familiarize yourself with the subject the best you can so that you can increase your skills. Much as learning a few key features of Audition can help you improve your overall sound quality dramatically, learning how to use the color correction effects to their full potential can increase your projects' overall picture quality dramatically.

When applying color correction effects, one way of learning how video responds to the corrections is to view the various Output modes (Waveform, Vectorscope, and Parade) that monitor the color and lightness data of your image. Using a Reference Monitor that is set to YC Waveform enables you to monitor the video results of your color adjustments in the Program Monitor and signal results (remember, YC Waveform equals luminance) in your Reference Monitor.

Remember, if you intend on doing any individual color corrections for specific tonal ranges, such as highlights, midtones, or shadows, you need to use the Three-Way Color Corrector for that added level of depth. The next chapter shows you how to use the Three-Way Color Corrector for traditional color correction and for secondary color corrections. Secondary color corrections are a way in which you target one color range (not tonal range) and apply a color adjustment to that range. For example, if you wanted a certain shade of red to be more prominent in your image, the Secondary Color Correction effect would define that shade of red and allow you to apply a correction to only the selected color. It's brand new for 2.0, and it's very cool to play with.

To take effects work and color correction techniques a step further, take a look at the Nesting_FX.wmv turorial, located in the Video Tutorials folder on the book's DVD. Not only does this clip demonstrate the nesting technique, it also calls out a specific workflow that allows for a lot of control when trying to apply a single color correction to a large number of clips. When the file loads in Windows Media Player, press Alt+Enter to play it back at full-screen size.

CHAPTER

23

Advanced Color Correction: Three-Way Color Corrector

Building on the foundation of the Fast Color Corrector, the Three-Way Color Corrector can adjust color values not only for an entire image, but also within the three tonal ranges of your video image: shadows, midtones, and highlights. Adjusting within individual tonal ranges enables you to add very subtle and effective color shifts in order to change the look of your image. The Three-Way Color Corrector also enables you to select an exact color range and apply corrections selectively to that range, a process called *secondary color correction.*

This chapter's three lessons will guide you through the Three-Way Color Corrector effect and show off a few tricks. First, you'll learn how to white balance, adjust your tonal ranges, and then apply a selective color cast to the adjusted tonal range. The second lesson focuses on how to create and manipulate a secondary color correction, while the final lesson demonstrates how to take the Secondary Color Correction effect beyond the typical application: You'll add color to only a select portion of a color image that was converted to black and white.

Before you jump into the lessons, you should first take a deeper look at the Three-Way Color Corrector's workings.

The Three-Way Color Corrector

In the process of finishing any project, there comes a time when you need to change the coloring of your images so that either there is consistency or a specific look is achieved. To really change the dynamics of an image you need to chisel away at the color, brightness, contrast, and overall elements that make up that image. Although the Fast Color Corrector can offer a quick and simple adjustment, the Three-Way Color Corrector gives you a lot more tools and controls to make subtle or dramatic changes.

For example, with the Fast Color Corrector you can white balance an image and auto-adjust black and white levels. With the Three-Way Color Corrector you can white balance (highlights), gray balance (midtones), and black balance (shadows) with just a few eyedropper clicks (**Figure 23.1**).

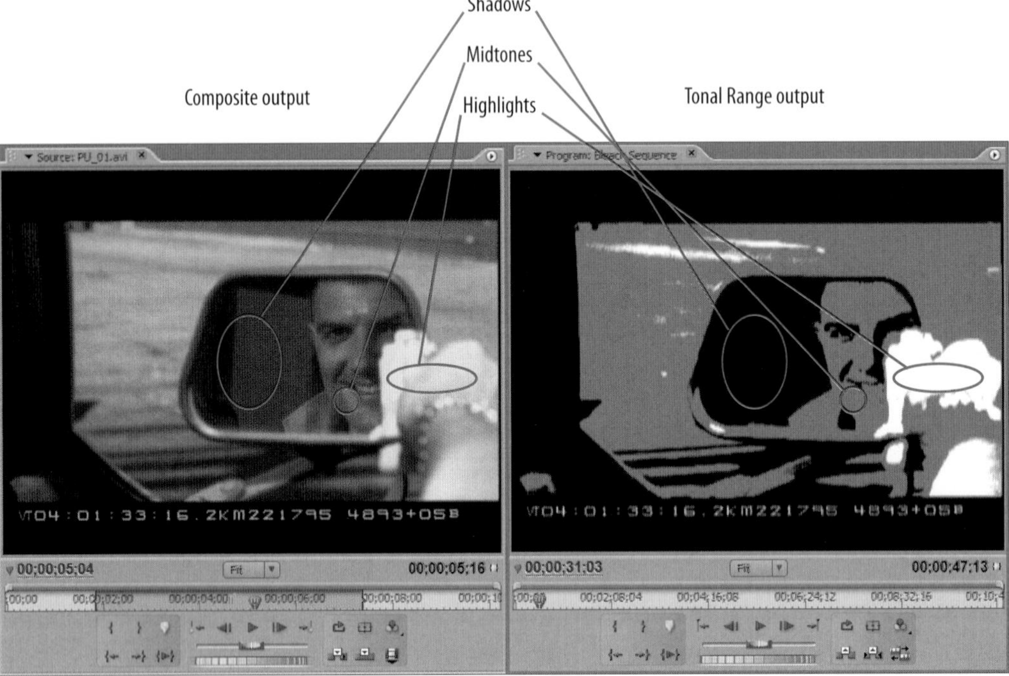

Figure 23.1 Compare the source video in Composite mode (left) with the same frame viewed in the Tonal Range Output mode (right). Notice that the grayscale tonal range image has three colors: black, gray, and white. Black represents the shadow tonal range, gray the midtone, and white the highlight. This image is on the darker side primarily made up of shadows and midtones. Because of the tonal range emphasis, color corrections made to the midtone range will be more prominent.

As you remember, to white balance an image with a color cast you target a color value in your image that you know to be pure white. The color correction tool then shifts the colors in the image to make that targeted color pure white. The same rules apply for gray and black balancing. With the Three-Way Color Corrector, when you gray balance you are targeting a color in your image that you know to be neutral gray but might not appear that way. By clicking on that color, the Three-Way Color Corrector shifts the midtones color so that the targeted value becomes neutral gray. For shadows, you click on a portion of your image that you know to be pure black; the effect then shifts the colors in the shadows from their current value to pure black. The Three-Way Color Corrector makes these shifts by using the tonal range color wheels (**Figure 23.2**) to add a slight color cast to each tonal range in order to achieve the desired color balance. Once you have balanced your image, you can further adjust the color casts and refine more settings to take your look further. That's the theory; now take a look at how to put these adjustments into practice.

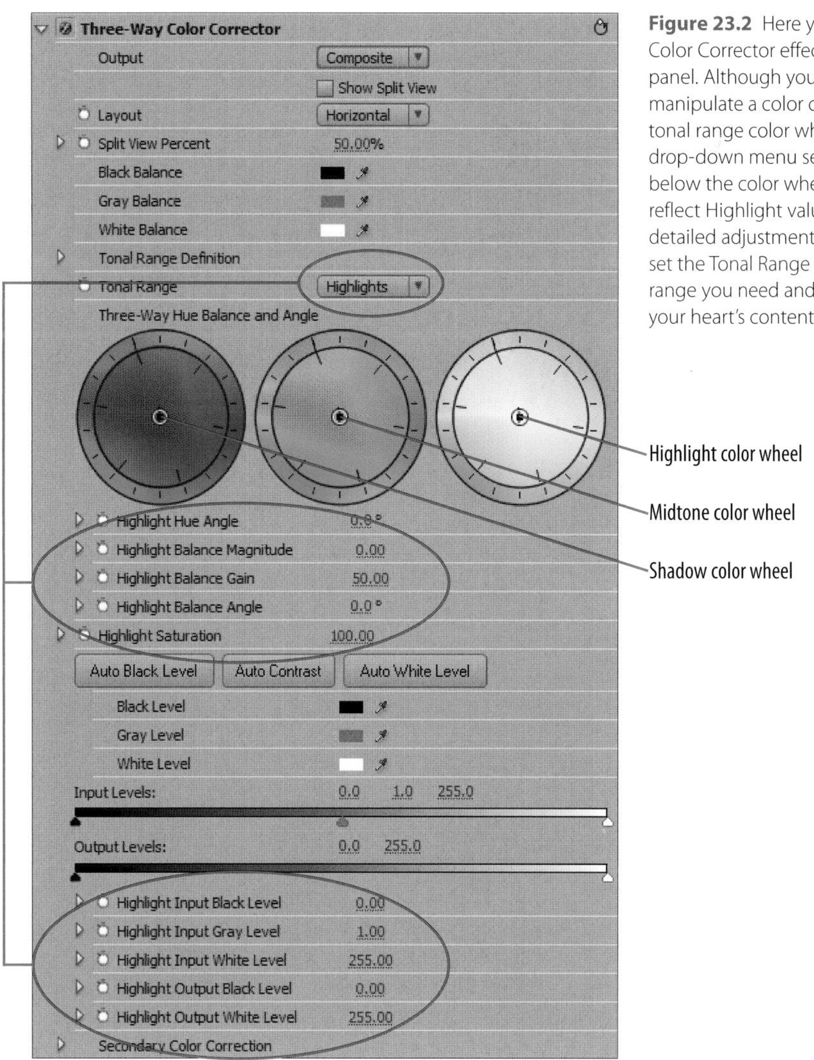

Figure 23.2 Here you have the full Three-Way Color Corrector effect from the Effect Controls panel. Although you can actively add and manipulate a color cast using any of the three tonal range color wheels, with the Tonal Range drop-down menu set to Highlights, the settings below the color wheels and in the Levels area reflect Highlight values only. To accurately make detailed adjustments to individual tonal ranges, set the Tonal Range drop-down menu to the range you need and then tweak the values to your heart's content.

White Balancing and Custom Looks

In this first lesson you will learn to balance all three of the tonal ranges and then add and adjust a color cast in one tonal range. You will prepare a scene from my short film *Bleach*, giving select shots a specific look that contrasts the rest of the scene.

NOTES

You will notice that this project yields red render bars above the Bleach sequence. Because this chapter focuses on secondary color correction with an uncompressed SD/SDI video clip, I chose to import the DV version of the Bleach sequence and open it in this project which is set to Uncompressed SD.

Open the 3way_Color1.prproj project file from the APPST2 Lesson Files/Chapter 23 folder. As you review the scene, notice the overall cool look (meaning lots of light blues and greens) and washed-out flesh tones of the actors. You will apply color correction to the point of view (POV) shots that reveal the male actor's perspective. Without spoiling the film, suffice to say that there needs to be a contrast between the establishing shots (him in the car) and the POV shots: The actor sits living and breathing in the cool blue environment of the car, but the world through his eyes is much warmer and more vibrant.

Using an SD/SDI project instead of a DV project allows for less compression when rendering out your effects. If you intend on exporting to DVD or even creating a higher-quality, uncompressed rendering of a DV project, you can import a DV project into an SD/SDI project and process all your titles and effects uncompressed as opposed to DV compressed.

1. Be sure that your workspace has a healthy-size frame devoted to your Effect Controls panel, because the Three-Way Color Corrector is easier to use with more space. You can either modify the workspace that the project adheres to or activate Window > Workspaces > Color Correction. Open the Bleach sequence in the Timeline panel. From the Effects panel, navigate to Video Effects/Color Correction, then drag and drop the Three-Way Color Corrector onto the Orange shaded clip 03 in the Bleach sequence. Position the timeline Edit Line at 00;00;13;19 to reveal the clip in the Program Monitor. Click on the 03 clip in the timeline, open your Effect Controls panel, and finally expand the Three-Way Color Corrector effect listing to view its parameters.
2. In the Three-Way Color Corrector effect listing, click on the White Balance eyedropper; then, holding down the Ctrl key, click on the rearview mirror outside of the car (**Figure 23.3**).

   By clicking the White Balance eyedropper you target the highlight area of the image. With the Tonal Range drop-down menu set to Highlights, the effect values for the Highlights color wheel are visible beneath the wheel. Using the individual effect values for the Highlights color cast, you can fine-tune the color correction beyond your initial selection.

Each color wheel is a circle, and technically, each of the 360 degrees on that circle is a unique color value. Colors at their lightest points reside in the center of the circle, and on the outer edge colors are at their darkest. Once you target a precise angle you can adjust the Balance Magnitude to select a lighter or darker iteration of that angle's color. Lower values are closer to the circle's center, while higher values are closer to the outer edge. Adjusting the Balance Gain then allows you to dynamically adjust the overall emphasis of that color as it casts onto your image. The higher the gain, the more prominent the color casts appears.

Figure 23.3 With the White Balance eyedropper selected, clicking on the bright white in the rearview mirror adds a slight color cast to the highlight tonal range so that the bright white that is targeted shifts to pure white. Notice that with Tonal Range set to Highlight, the values beneath the color wheels reflect the exact color values to the color cast being applied. Balance Angle tells you the actual color that is being selected, and Balance Magnitude tells you how far into that color on the brightness scale you are going. A value of 0 would be the absolute center of the wheel and 100 would be the outer edge. Because the white in the rearview mirror is almost true white, a very light cast is applied.

3. Click on the eyedropper for Gray Balance, and while holding down the Ctrl key, click on the window in the top right of the frame (**Figure 23.4a**). Click on the eyedropper for Black Balance, and holding down the Ctrl key, click on the dark area of the car door (**Figure 23.4b**).

a

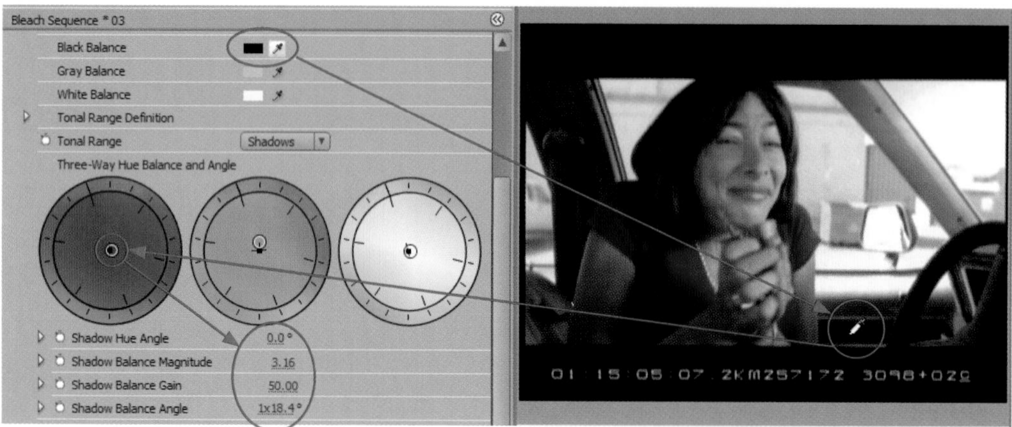

b

Figures 23.4a and b Target a region for your Gray Balance (a) and Black Balance (b) values. The Tonal Range drop-down menu will reveal the exact color values associated with the targeted color.

The gray balance is probably the most noticeable and drastic selection of the three balance points. Because the cool blue/green color is not that visible in the black and white (shadows and highlights) areas of the image, you will get the best results in the gray/midtone range. You can easily click on a color that emphasizes the color cast that you want to remove. By clicking on the teal-colored window panel of the car, you told the color corrector to rebalance the image so that this color was more neutral. The result, although not as obvious in the location of the panel you selected (the brighter blue is actually in the highlight tonal range), is obvious in the rest of the image (**Figures 23.5a** and **b**).

a

b

Figures 23.5a and b Compare the frame before three-way balancing (a) and after (b), in which the flesh tones appear warmer and there is slightly more contrast in the image. The Three-Way Color Corrector enables you to make subtle but effective image corrections like these.

4. Having established a more balanced image, try pushing the look further. In the Three-Way Color Corrector, click the check box for Show Split View and set the Layout value to Vertical. In the Tonal Range drop-down menu, select Midtones. After making these settings

Figure 23.6 Here you can see the original image unaffected on the right side of the split and the further adjusted midtone results on the left. Balance Angle shifts to a different warmer color (more orange); Balance Magnitude slides up the scale toward the outer edge, taking a darker version of that color, and the Balance Gain then adds the overall emphasis of the color onto the image.

below the color wheels, clear the Show Split View check box (**Figure 23.6**):

Midtone Balance Angle: **1x240.0**
Midtone Balance Magnitude: **50.0**
Midtone Balance Gain: **45.00**

Although the settings you adjusted may have seemed out of order, I wanted to guide you through the process so you could see more clearly how each slider affected the overall color parameters. First, you changed the Midtone Balance Angle, which effectively targeted a different, warmer color (Orange/Red) than what was targeted by the gray balancing. Next, you increased the Midtone Balance Magnitude to select a darker version of that color. Finally, you backed down the Gain so that the emphasis of the color cast onto the image was slightly reduced. Doing all of this with the Split view active allowed you to see how much you altered the coloring of the image.

With Split view off, look at the right side of the actress's hair and take in the general warm look of the image. The next step will further adjust that.

- Change the Output drop-down listing to Tonal Range and expand the Tonal Range Definition parameter. Set:

  Shadow Threshold: **81** Highlight Threshold: **205**
  Shadow Softness: **35** Highlight Softness: **34**

  Switch the Output drop-down back to Composite, and collapse the Tonal Range Definition settings (**Figures 23.7a** through **d**).

a More warmth

Figures 23.7a through d Compare the correction from the end of step 4 (a) and the tonal range definition of that image (b). Notice how the black, gray, and white colors do not fade from one to another, rather they are more blocky in the regions they define. Now consider the results of step 5's adjustments to the image's tonal range (c and d). After adjusting the tonal range definition, you modified and softened the transitions from black to gray and from white to gray, which reduced the emphasis of the midtone color cast to both the highlight and shadow areas of the image.

b Original tonal range

c Redefined less warmth

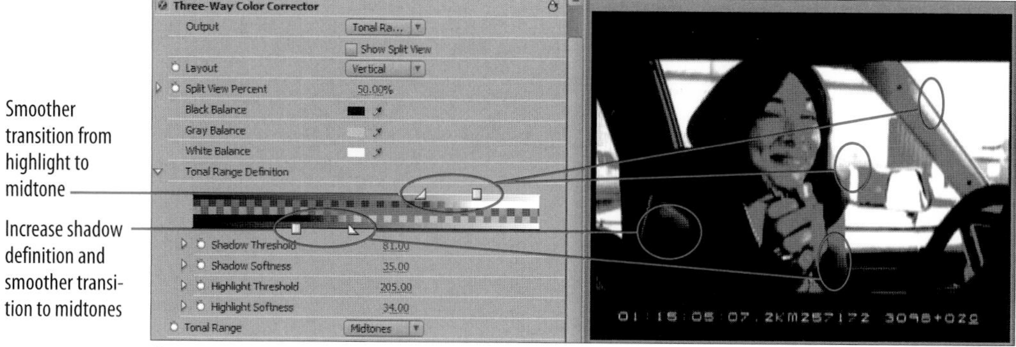

d

Understanding Tonal Range Definition

The tonal range of your image has a default value that you can see when you toggle the effect Output to Tonal Range. In this mode you can view which regions of the image are shadows, midtones, and highlights. When you adjust the Tonal Range Definition settings you are not altering the image itself, you are actually altering the mapping of the tonal ranges. Remapping or rather redefining the tonal ranges, affects the way in which shadow, midtone, and highlight corrections apply to the image.

Increasing the Shadow Threshold associates more of the image with the shadow range, removing some of the midtone emphasis from it. By decreasing the Highlight Threshold, you associate more of the bright colors of the image with the highlight tonal range. Adjusting each tonal range's softness level creates a smoother transition from shadow to midtone and from midtone to highlight. In essence, the Tonal Range Definition controls allow you to broaden or narrow each tonal range of your image; the effects applied within those ranges obviously will be more prominent (broadened tonal range) or more subtle (narrower tonal range). If you never apply a three-way color correction but do redefine your tonal range, the image will look no different.

In this step you reduced the width of the midtone range and created a smoother transition from shadows to midtones and from midtones to highlights. The result is a more controlled application of the warm color cast to the midtone.

6. Set the Tonal Range to Shadows and then scroll down to the Input/Output area of the Three-Way Color Corrector. Set the Shadow Input Black Level to 25.00. Change the Tonal Range to Master, and set the Master Input White Level to 220.00.

   Toggling the Tonal Range to Shadows switched all the effect parameters to adjust only within the shadow tonal range. On the Levels scale, 0 is pure black and 255 is pure white; all of the levels of brightness and darkness exist within that 0 to 255 scale. By increasing the Shadow Input Black Level to 25, you have made all of the darker values in the shadow range from 0 to 25 be adjusted to 0 (black). The visual result is that the darker portion of your image has more contrast getting to pure black. The midtones and highlights retain the same level mappings as they started with.

   At the end of the step, instead of adjusting the White Level in only the highlights, you selected Master for Tonal Range, which technically selects your entire image (all three tonal ranges together). Scaling the value of the Master Input White Level increased the contrast for all the white levels in your image (shadows, midtones, highlights), making the transition to pure white shorter and allowing more of the brighter white values to be recognized and processed as pure white. The levels from 220 to 255 are all interpreted as 255. If you compare this image to the original image you can see how much work these few steps have accomplished (**Figures 23.8a** and **b**).

7. With clip 03 selected in the Bleach sequence, click on the Three-Way Color Corrector listing in the Effect Controls panel and press Ctrl+C to copy your selection. Back in the Bleach sequence, click on clip 05, then holding down the Shift key select clip 08 and clip 10.

a Before

b After

Figures 23.8a and b Compared to what you started with (a) the completed image (b) has more contrast, crushed blacks, warm flesh tones, and "pop." All of this was possible through subtle and precise effect adjustments.

Press Ctrl+V to paste the copied effect onto these three selected clips. Press the Home key and the spacebar to play your timeline and preview the results.

In the Effect Controls panel, you selected the primary look that you created and then copied it to the other clips in the sequence that needed the same treatment. If you want to push the look further for any of the other clips, you can select the individual clips and adjust the Three-Way Color Corrector in the Effect Controls panel.

Using the Three-Way Color Corrector you can refine, tune, and dramatically adjust any clip that you edit in Premiere Pro 2.0. By isolating and making adjustments within redefinable tonal ranges you have full control over creating any type of look. Color correction is a mood and practicality oriented art. Cinematographers can spend hours and hours in a color correction suite, tweaking their images far further than any book could lead you. At the end of the day, it is a matter of trying to create your own look that fits with the mood and tone that you envision. Starting with the Fast Color Corrector to white balance or add a quick color cast, then adding the Three-Way Color Corrector on top of that to take it further, you will be well on your way to developing a more practical approach to cleaning up your images.

The Three-Way Color Corrector still has more to offer, however, as you'll see in the next two short lessons, which explore using the Secondary Color Correction effect.

Secondary Color Correction

Say you shot some outdoor video on location or around town. When you filmed, the sky was nice and blue, no clouds, just perfect. But, wait. When you got back to the editing room and watched the video, the sky wasn't the blue you thought it was! In fact, it was light blue and washed out. This scenario is a perfect example of how secondary color correction can be valuable to almost any editor. To increase the saturation of blue in the sky, you need to go into your image and adjust only in the color that makes up the sky: blue. Using the Secondary Color Correction tool in the Three-Way Color Corrector, you can do just that.

Create a Secondary Correction

Using the Three-Way Color Corrector for tonal range and color cast adjustments is just fine; however, if you twirl down the very last effect parameter in the Three-Way Color Corrector effect, you switch the effect into a whole different mode: Secondary Color Correction. For this lesson, open the 3way_Color2.prproj project file in the APPST2 Lesson Files/Chapter 23 folder. Continue using either the Color Correction workspace or your own custom workspace that has a large Program Monitor and Effect Controls panel.

For this secondary correction you are going to target the dark red shirt that the actress is wearing and make it much more rich and vibrant. With the Three-Way Color Corrector, after you target a secondary color, all the controls of the effect are devoted to only adjusting the targeted color. Let's begin.

1. With the 3way_Color2.prproj project open, make sure the Secondary sequence is active in the Timeline panel. Apply the Three-Way Color Corrector effect to the Bleach04.avi file in the timeline. Advance the Edit Line to 00;25 in the timeline, then adjust the Program Monitor zoom to 150% and reposition the viewing area so that you can clearly see the girl in the red shirt (**Figure 23.9**). Open the Effect Controls panel, expand the Three-Way Color Corrector effect, and then twirl down the Secondary Color Correction effect parameters.

Figure 23.9 The Program Monitor is zoomed in to view at 150% with the viewing area repositioned to view the actress in the right corner of the frame. With the Three-Way Color Corrector and Secondary Color Correction listings expanded, you can easily target and define your secondary color.

You will be using the eyedroppers at the top of the Secondary Color Correction settings to define the secondary color for selection. Having the image enlarged in the Program Monitor gives you more area to target your color.

2. Click on the leftmost Secondary Color Correction eyedropper next to the color picker. Holding down the Ctrl key, click on the red color of the actress's shirt to make a selection (see **Figure 23.10**).

   Clicking the first eyedropper defines the center color point of your Secondary Color Correction. As you remember, holding down the Ctrl key gives you a broader color sample in order to make a more accurate color selection. You have targeted the T-shirt's red as your secondary. Because that red has different shades, you

Figure 23.10 Clicking with the first eyedropper on the T-shirt's red selects that tone of red to be your secondary color selection. After you target your color center, you can then add colors to the selection and tweak the settings beneath the eyedroppers to further refine the secondary. With the secondary defined, use the color wheels and Three-Way controls to adjust it.

need to refine your secondary, add more shades of red to it, and make sure you are selecting the entire T-shirt.

3. Scroll up to the top of the Three-Way Color Corrector and change the output mode to Mask. Scroll back down to the Secondary section and click the eyedropper with the plus sign beneath it. Hold down the Ctrl key and click on a darker red region of the T-shirt (**Figures 23.11a** through **f**). Click on the plus sign eyedropper again and click on another region of the T-shirt that is not covered in white when the Mask output mode reappears.

Toggling the Output to Mask allows you to see your secondary selection. When performing secondary color corrections you are targeting a color range and applying a color adjustment to that range. The effect creates a mask through which it applies the color adjustments. When you look at the Mask Output mode, anything that is black is completely transparent, which in the case of the secondary means that it is not selected as the secondary color. The portions of the mask that are pure white are the portions that will have

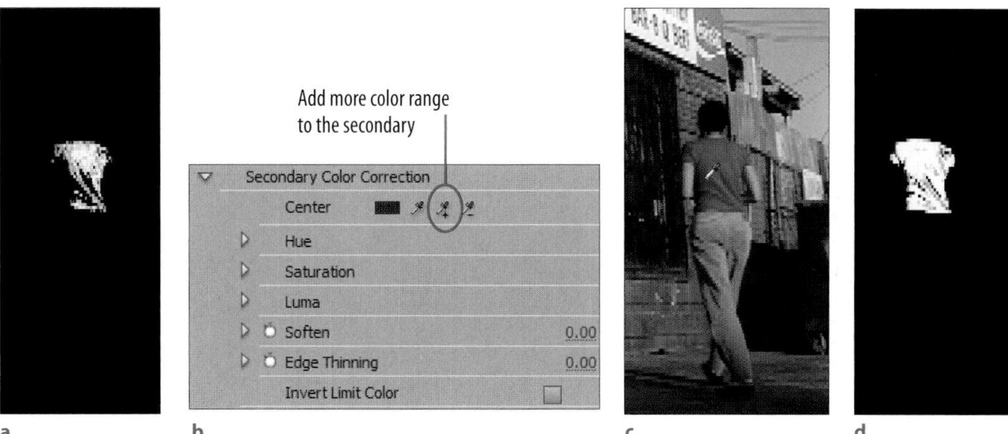

Figures 23.11a through f When you apply secondary color corrections, the Mask Output mode lets you see which portion of your image is defined as the secondary selection (a). Any white or gray colors in the Mask view is considered your secondary selection. The first image shows the initial selection of the red shirt in Mask view. To increase the range of red color being selected, you must add to the secondary color using the Add eyedropper (b). Once you click the Add eyedropper, the Mask output toggles off in order for you to click on and select the color you wish to add (c). Once you click, the mask view updates (d), and in this case more of the shirt is selected. Clicking the eyedropper and selecting a different region of the red T-shirt (e), yields a secondary selection that covers most if not all of the T-shirt (f).

the color adjustments applied to it. Gray areas of the mask are portions that will partially adjust. The goal of using the Mask Output mode is to be able to construct a pure white selection of the color range that you want to be your entire secondary. By clicking the Add Color (plus sign) eyedropper on the darker shades of red in the T-shirt, you are adding to the secondary color range.

4. With the Three-Way Color Corrector effect still outputting in Mask mode, twirl down the Secondary Color Correction effect listings for Hue, Saturation, and

Luma (**Figures 23.12a and b**). For Soften enter 1.5, then enter the values in Table 23.1

Table 23.1 Secondary Color Correction Settings

	Hue	Saturation	Luma
Start Threshold	40	15	0
Start Softness	5	2	0
End Threshold	53	38	43
End Softness	5	4	3

When selecting and defining your secondary color, each of the settings will vary; your goal, however, should be the same. You want to adjust each of the above effect values so that you create a pure white selection of *only* the intended secondary selection—in this case, the shirt's dark red color.

Hue allows you to broaden or narrow the actual color of your selection; Saturation allows you to pick the width of the color's strength. Notice that for the selected red, the defined area of Saturation (designated by the gradient scale below the parameter's name) is within the darker region of the scale; this means that a less saturated range of red is being defined as the secondary. The Luma range then targets the brightness of the selected color range that should be attributed to the secondary. Increase the Luma's End Threshold to say 60 or 70, and the secondary will select the brighter red values in the image.

With the Hue, Saturation, and Luma defined, the final step to making the secondary apply smoothly onto your image is to increase its Soften value. So far, I have never used a Soften value higher than 5.

5. Switch the Three-Way Color Corrector's Output mode to Composite. Toggle the Tonal Range drop-down to Master, and enter:

   Master Hue Angle: **0.0**
   Master Balance Magnitude: **78**
   Master Balance Gain: **70**
   Master Balance Angle: **-115**

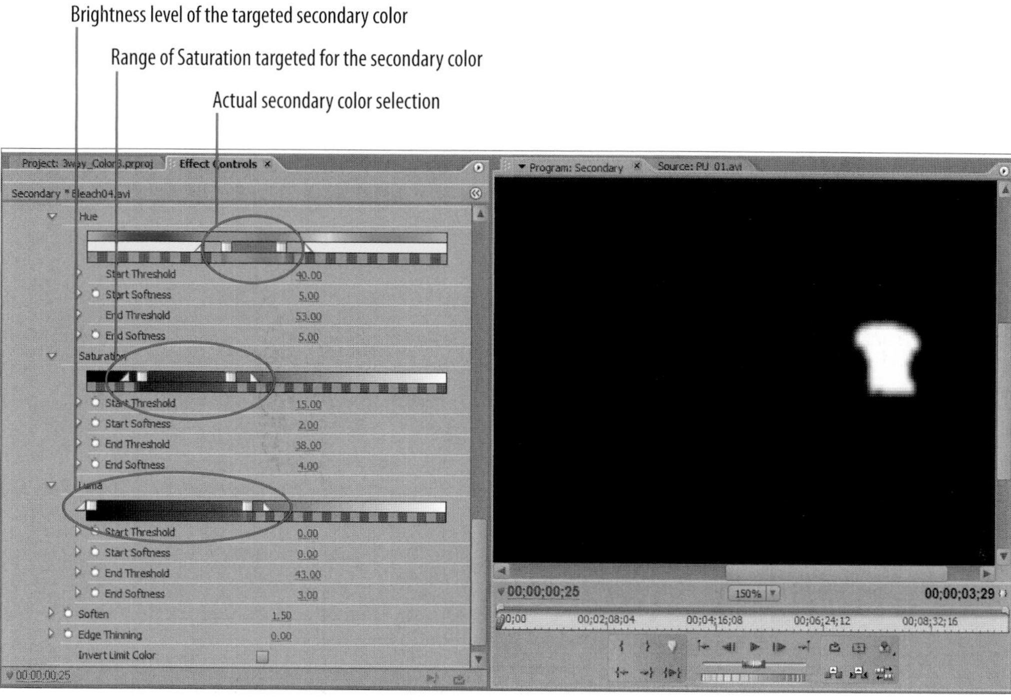

a

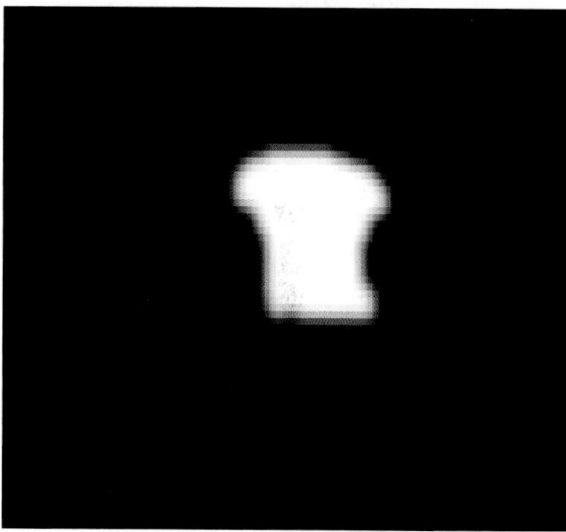

b

Figures 23.12a and b Based on the adjustments made to the Hue, Saturation, and Luma settings (a), you perfectly defined your secondary selection of the red shirt (the mask is all white). Slightly adjusting the Soften value allowed the edges of the mask to smoothen. Here, the entire shirt is selected, it is pure white and it has a soft edge (b). Hue defines the actual range of the secondary selection. Saturation complements this by determining the actual saturation values the secondary selects. Luma then defines the brightness levels of the color that is targeted. To see the effectiveness of your Hue, Saturation, and Luma adjustments, compare Figure 23.11f to Figure 23.12b.

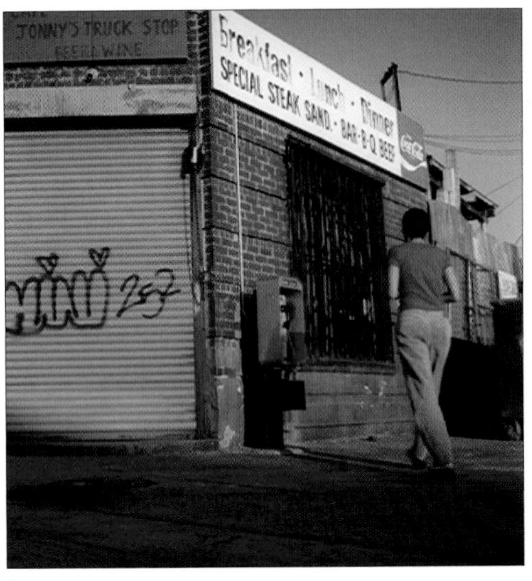

a

b

Figures 23.13a and b Although the red in this secondary is a bit exaggerated, the effect is quite obvious when you compare the original (a) and the secondary result (b).

To see your results versus the original clip state, toggle on and off the Three-Way Color Corrector effect listing in the Effect Controls panel (**Figures 23.13a** and **b**).

With your secondary defined and softened, you finally applied a color cast to the selection. Because your mask covered the red of the T-shirt only, this red was magnified when you added a Master color cast (a brighter red color) to the secondary selection. If you were to analyze the tonal range of the image you would find that the T-shirt has both midtones and shadows within its boundaries. Selecting the Master tonal range you were able to apply the color cast evenly between the tonal ranges defined in the T-shirt. Congratulations! You achieved a fairly complex effect process in a few steps.

Although the technical settings, sliders, and values may seem daunting, the basics of Secondary Color Correction should not. Let's review: First you target the primary color you want to correct; this color is your center. Switching to the Mask Output mode you can see your selection in a simple black-and-white view; your goal now is to get the exact color you want to select to become pure white and the rest of the image pure black. Using the Add Color eyedropper, you click on closely associated colors to expand the range of the secondary color selection. After defining the color, you refine the Hue, Saturation, and Luma settings while the Mask Output mode is still active. Once you have your secondary color all white with the mask you soften its edge and switch back to the Composite Output mode. From here, you use the Three-Way Color Corrector to add a color cast, brighten, darken, or tweak any way you like; just keep in mind that your effect tweaks will apply to only the area defined by your secondary selection.

Practice will help your technique. Let's now finish this chapter by adding a slight twist to the usage of the Mask Output mode and Secondary Color Correction.

Using Your Secondary as a Track Matte

Track mattes are the subject of the next chapter; however, I can't pass up the opportunity to show you a very neat trick with Secondary Color Correction and the Track Matte Key effect. For this lesson, I have organized a timeline that is already set up for you to quickly adjust. You will convert the secondary image to black and white and add your secondary red selection as the only color.

This final lesson is results-oriented, meaning that I am not going to explain too much about exactly what the tools are doing; I am just going to walk you through the steps so that you arrive at a very cool final destination. Chapter 24, "Track Mattes and PiPs," explains the Track Matte Key effect in its entirety. Read it, then return to this chapter and review this lesson to understand exactly what the Track Matte Key effect is doing.

1. Open the project 3way_Color3.prproj from the APPST2 Lesson Files/Chapter 23 folder. Open the Secondary Track Matte sequence and note the three video layers all holding the same clips placed one on top of the other. Position the Edit Line at 01;00 in the timeline. Apply the Black and White effect (Video Effects panel: Video Effects/Image Control/Black and White) to the clip on Video 1. Apply the Fast Color Corrector effect to the clip on Video 2, then apply the Track Matte Key effect (Video

Effects panel: Video Effects/Keying/Track Matte Key) to the same clip. Notice that the Three-Way Color Corrector is already applied to the clip on Video 3 and it is using the same Secondary correction you applied in the last lesson. Open the Effect Controls panel.

The Black and White video effect on Video 1 will serve as your primary image, which is now black-and-white. Because you are using the Track Matte Key effect to key your secondary color, you applied the Track Matte Key effect to the clip on Video 2 beneath Video 3. To adjust the color of the T-shirt, which will be the only color in the image, you applied the Fast Color Corrector to the clip on Video 2.

2. Select the clip on Video 3. In the Effect Controls panel expand the Three-Way Color Corrector effect and toggle the Output mode to Mask. Turn off the Track Output of Video 3 by clicking off the eyeball in its track header. Select the clip in Video 2 and expand the Track Matte Key Effect listing. Set Matte to Video 3 and Composite Using to Matte Luma. Expand the Fast Color Corrector for the same clip and pick any color on the color wheel to change the T-shirt color and have it reveal through the track matte (**Figure 23.14**).

Although the steps are very straightforward, the results you achieve with this exact layout and workflow are consistent whenever you want to achieve this type effect. Before you move on to investigate the Track Matte Key effect in the next chapter, you should understand one critical detail: When you apply the Track Matte Key to a video clip it allows the video of that clip to appear inside of a mask or alpha channel from any track above it. By toggling the Three-Way Color Corrector to Mask you created a black-and-white mask image for the video to punch through. Choosing Composite, using Matte Luma with the Track Matte Key, allowed the video from Video 2 to key through the white (luminance) displayed from the Corrector on Video 3. Turning off the Video 3 track is just part of the workflow. Because the clip on Video 3 is exactly the same, when the color of Video 2 punches through the luma matte it is exactly on top of itself, achieving the colorized effect.

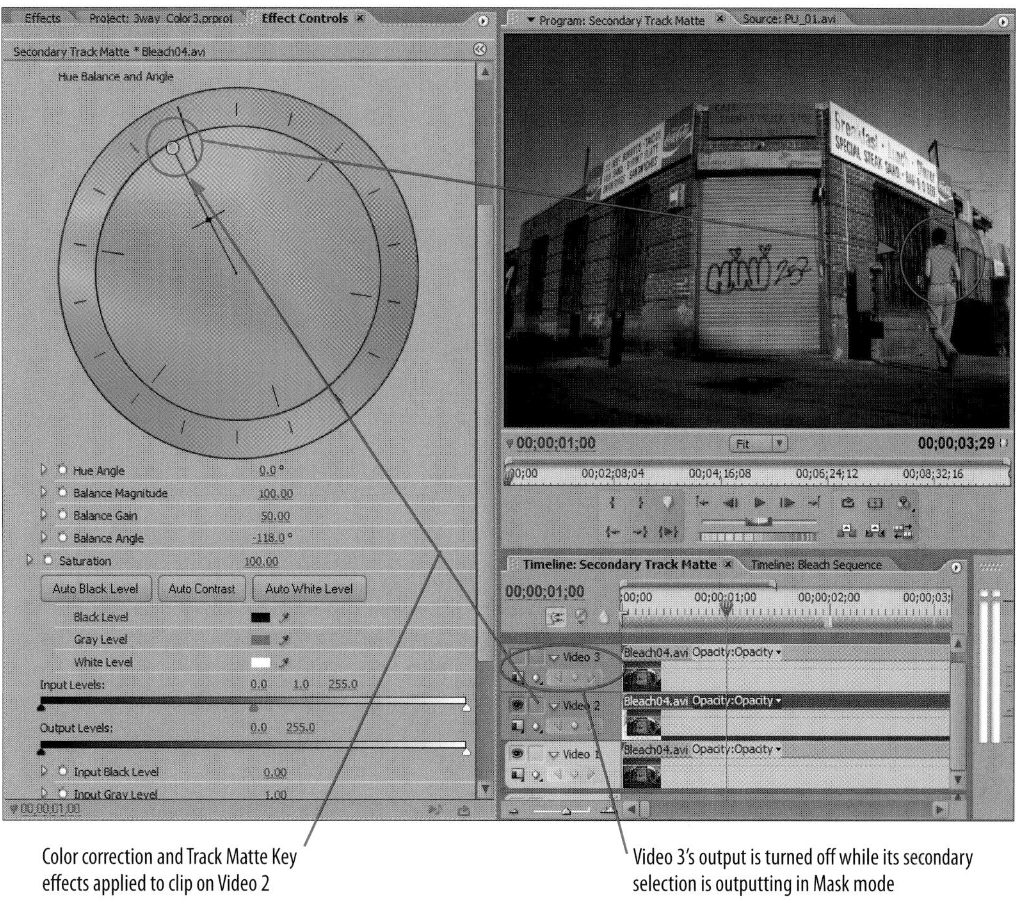

Figure 23.14 With the Fast Color Corrector picking a bright red color, the T-shirt takes on that color as it is processed with the Track Matte Key.

I think this trick is quite cool. Although it doesn't apply to a ton of situations, if you use it frugally, it could provide a great effect here and there. The main thing that this lesson aimed to provide was a different way of looking at some of the tools used in the application. Here the Three-Way Color Corrector is left in an Output mode that is supposed to provide the user with feedback as opposed to being a literal effect. By looking at the Output mode as a way of creating defined luma mattes, you can use the data quite efficiently with the Track Matte Key effect to create something not normally possible with Premiere Pro.

For powerful examples of what you can do with the Track Matte key and color correction, take a look at the Color_Matte.wmv tutorial, located in the Video Tutorials folder on the book's disc. When the file loads in Windows Media Player, press Alt + Enter to play it back at full-screen size.

Things to Remember

It sounds obvious, but one of the most important things to remember when using the Three-Way Color Corrector effect is what exactly you are using it for. If you are making a secondary color correction, then all the color casts (offsets) and level controls apply only to the secondary selection. If you are white balancing or applying offsets, then the moment you start to adjust and select a secondary those adjustments go away and you are working with only the secondary selected. For standard three-way corrections don't touch the Secondary Color Correction effect unless you aim to use it.

If you plan on doing secondary corrections, you can use the Fast Color Corrector to white balance your shots, then apply the Three-Way Color Corrector on top of it to make your secondary color correction. When defining your secondary the easiest way to build and select it is in the Mask Output mode of the Three-Way effect. Once you have defined your secondary always apply a little bit of softness to the edges of the mask to remove the possibility of pixilated artifacts or pixilated edges being rendered.

As you can with all effects, you can save any three-way correction as an effect preset that you can apply to multiple clips. In the next chapter I will reveal two cool effect techniques: track mattes (which you got a nice taste of) and picture-in-pictures (also known as PiPs).

CHAPTER

24

Track Mattes and PiPs

This chapter shows you how to work with two types of effects: Track Matte Key, which has been updated for 2.0, and PiPs (picture-in-picture), which remain the same as in previous versions of Premiere Pro. After examining the new workflow for Track Matte Key, you'll review PIP techniques.

The uses for a picture-in-picture effect are fairly obvious from its name, but what about track mattes? Say you want a video clip to play in the letters of your title. You know it will look very cool—but you don't know how to do it. Look to Premiere Pro's built-in keying effects for the answer: Composite the title and video together with the Track Matte Key effect. Keying effects are a way to combine, or *composite*, elements of multiple images into one final image. Basically, you stack images on top of each other, then you identify specific elements of the top image to cut out using a *matte* or *key* so that images beneath can show through. The Track Matte Key effect uses an image's alpha channel or luma (white) information to delineate the matte elements.

For the example, you would place the title in one video track and the video file in another. Next, apply the Track Matte Key effect to the movie clip, choosing the title to be the matte that you would like to key through.

In Premiere Pro 2.0, revisions to the workflow for creating track mattes have made this process easier and better than ever before. After having played with the new effect for quite some time, I have also found a way to combine track mattes with color correction effects to make even more defined color correction adjustments.

The first track matte lesson teaches the basics by showing you how to create a static track matte. The second track matte lesson goes a big step further and shows you how to combine matte with color-corrected video clips to create better color correction adjustments.

Creating a Static Track Matte

To demonstrate the most effective and clean use for track mattes, this first lesson shows you how to key a video clip through the text of a static title element. To fully integrate the video with the entire look of the title, you will then add a second title element on top of the stacked layers. The sequence nesting technique will ensure that you later can drag and drop the elements as a single clip instance into other sequences. **Figure 24.1** shows the final result you're aiming for.

Figure 24.1 The fruits of your labor will be a nice clean title element that includes full motion video punching through the letters of the title.

1. Open the project Static_Matte_Start.prproj from the APPST2 Lesson Files/Chapter 24 folder from the accompanying DVD. Double-click to open both the Title_Fill (**Figure 24.2**) and Title_Stroke (**Figure 24.3**) files in the Titler.

   The media for the project can be found in the APPST2 Lesson Files/Artbeats folder. The titles are embedded into the project, but have physical copies in the APPST2 Lesson Files/Chapter 24 folder.

Because Title_Fill will be the matte, it is basic text filled as pure white, with no outer strokes or any other elements. After you assign the Track Matte Key to this title, the video will composite through the center of each letter. Title_Stroke has an outer stroke, but Fill turned off. Because Title_Stroke has no fill, when you drop it on top of Title_Fill, the video will show through within the stroke to create a complete, integrated look.

Figure 24.2 You'll use Title_Fill for the track matte. It's plain text with a pure white fill and no shadows, strokes, or sheens. To composite properly using the Track Matte Key effect, you want only simple graphic elements such as this.

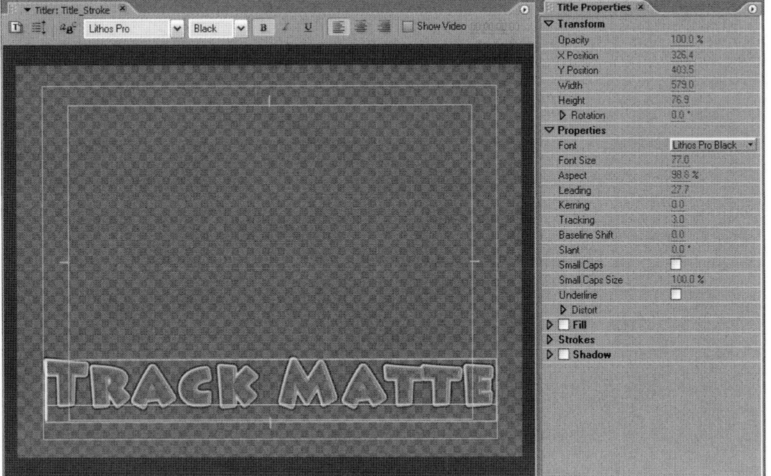

Figure 24.3 Title_Stroke has Fill turned off and only full color outer strokes, which you will want in the final composite of the title.

2. Drop Title_Fill onto the Video 2 track (**Figure 24.4**) of the Matte Basics sequence. Drop LIL124.avi directly below the title on the Video 1 track (**Figure 24.5**). Add a few clip instances back to back, and extend the title so that the title covers the clips for at least 10 seconds.

Figure 24.4 Place Title_Fill (your Track Matte source) on the Video 2 track.

When assigning the Track Matte Key effect, you will want the video to be on a track below the matte graphic. Below these layers, you can place whatever video or other material you want to play underneath the track matte elements. For this example, you are building your matte in a separate sequence so that you can nest it and treat it as an individual clip for use with other sequences.

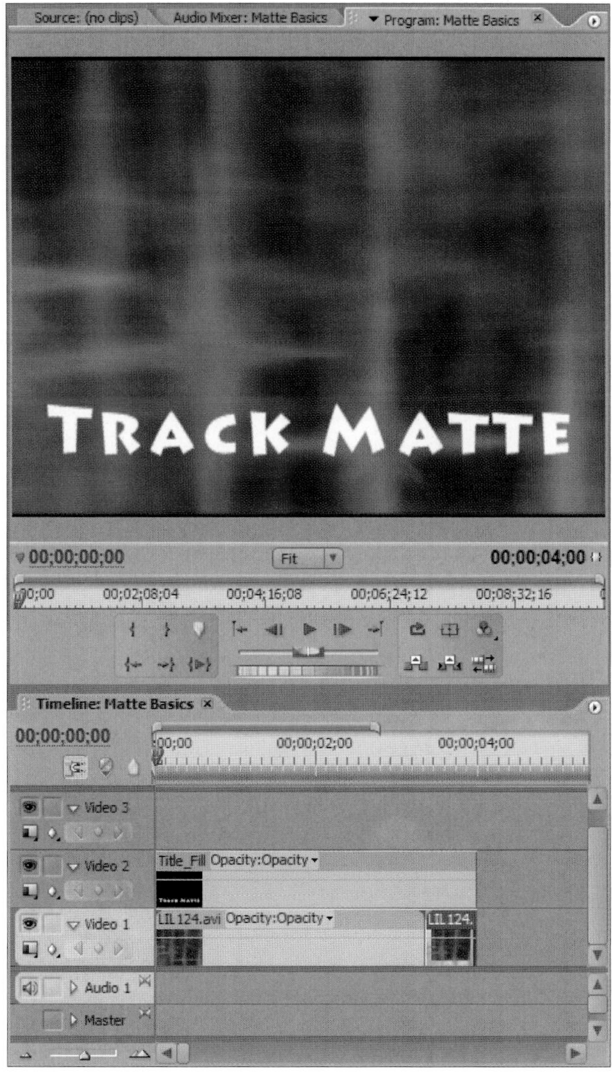

Figure 24.5 When you drop the video clip onto Video 1, you can see the video clip through the transparency (empty space) of the title. The fill for the title is white, so it is easy to see over the video.

To create your own title elements like the examples, design your full color final title (Title_Stroke) first, then save it as another title (Title_Fill). Turn off Fill in the stroke title. In the fill title, set Fill to pure white and turn off all the strokes. Because one is a copy of the other, size, position, and spacing will match exactly.

3. From the Effects panel's Video Effects/Keying folder, drag and drop the Track Matte Key effect onto the first video clip in Video 1. Select the video clip, and activate the Effect Controls panel so that you can view the effect properties. Twirl down the Track Matte Key effect listing, set Matte to Video 2, and set Composite Using to Matte Alpha (default value), as shown in **Figure 24.6**.

Figure 24.6 With the proper settings in the Track Matte Key effect listing (left), the video composites perfectly through the text of the title. Because the Track Matte effect has been applied using Video 2 as its source, it automatically uses the alpha information as the matte source and disables the video overlay of the graphic. This is a new workflow in Premiere Pro 2.0.

To get the proper matte results, you have to specify which video track you want the Track Matte Key effect to composite through. Here you assigned Video 2, which contains the title. By compositing with the Matte Alpha option, the title's alpha channel becomes a transparent matte and the video punches through the text. When using the Track Matte Key effect with titles, you can safely assume that all drawn objects in a title are treated as alpha, while the background/empty area is completely transparent. This means that when you apply the Track Matte Key effect to key through the alpha of a title, it keys through the object area, in this case the text.

When you use the Track Matte Key effect you can composite using either the alpha or the luma information. Choosing Matte Alpha composites through the alpha information of the image, making the alpha channel completely transparent and keyed through. Compositing using Matte Luma enables you to punch through the pure white areas of the image regardless of the alpha channel information, but the surrounding alpha area also punches through. You will use the Matte Luma function in the next lesson.

4. Copy and paste the Track Matte Key effect from the first instance of the LIL124.avi clip in Video 1 to the other two instances. Right-click on the Track Matte Key effect listing in the Effect Controls panel for the first instance, and select Copy. Select the second clip, right-click in the Effect Controls panel, and select Paste from the drop-down menu. Paste in the selected Effect Controls panel for the third clip.

   To copy and paste the effect settings from one clip to the next, you copied the adjusted effect from the first clip and then pasted it directly into the Effect Controls panel for the other two.

5. Drop the Title_Stroke file onto the Video 3 track directly above the content on the tracks below. Press Enter to render your sequence and view your results (**Figure 24.7**).

Figure 24.7 Because the two titles are duplicates with alternate Fill settings, the video composited through Title_Fill appears perfectly inside Title_Stroke for a very clean effect.

Dropping Title_Stroke on top of the two video layers completes the look of the title. So that you can use this title sequence as a single clip instance for later projects, however, you will need to nest it.

6. Open the Nest sequence tab in the timeline to open the sequence with the nature clip on Video 1. Drag and drop the icon for the Matte Basics sequence in the Project panel onto the Video 2 track. For a finishing touch, apply the Drop Shadow effect (Video Effects/ Perspective) onto the Track Matte clip on Video 2. In

the Effect Controls panel, twirl down Drop Shadow and set (**Figure 24.8**):

Shadow Color: **White**
Opacity: **75**
Direction: **115**
Distance: **8**
Softness: **30**
Shadow Only: **Off**

Figure 24.8 By nesting the entire track matte, you can now apply effects, such as this Drop Shadow, to the entire nested clip as opposed to every layer of the original.

The Drop Shadow effect would have affected the initial composite of the track matte if you'd applied it to either of the title elements. By nesting the Track Matte sequence as an individual clip, you were able to apply Drop Shadow as a clip effect to give the finished title some depth.

By applying the Track Matte Key effect to your basic title elements and then adding more effects to the nested sequence, you can create a pretty compelling graphic image. Consider using this technique for creating lower-third backgrounds or objects for use in a DVD menu.

Luma Track Mattes with Color Correction

I am very excited about this new lesson. Prior to 2.0, you were never able to easily apply a color correction effect to a specific defined region of your image in Premiere Pro. In a professional color correction session this type of effect is called *power windows*. A power window defines a region of your image and within that region applies a precise color adjustment. Thanks to upgrades to the Track Matte Key effect, this new workflow is possible in Premiere Pro.

To demonstrate this, you will create luma mattes in the Titler to define the regions of the your image to which you want to apply your color correction. Your final result will be a stylized color correction of a specific shot from Bleach (**Figure 24.9**). Using a color correction adjustment, you will darken the area around the box of bleach to make the box visually stick out in the frame.

Figure 24.9 The image in the Source Monitor shows the original clip. The image to the right in the Program Monitor shows the luma matte result. In Premiere Pro 2.0, you can easily animate or move your luma matte by adding motion to the graphic used as the matte.

1. Open the project Luma_Mattes_Start.prproj in the APPST2 Lesson Files/Chapter 24 folder. Drag the Bleach_Box file from the Project panel onto Video 1 in the panel. Drag the file again directly above itself onto Video 2 (**Figure 24.10**).

   To control the region of the luma matte and color correction applied, you need to place the clip you want to adjust directly on top of itself using two video tracks. This is the secret step that enables you to apply a color correction effect to the clip instance on Video 2 using a regional luma matte from Video 3.

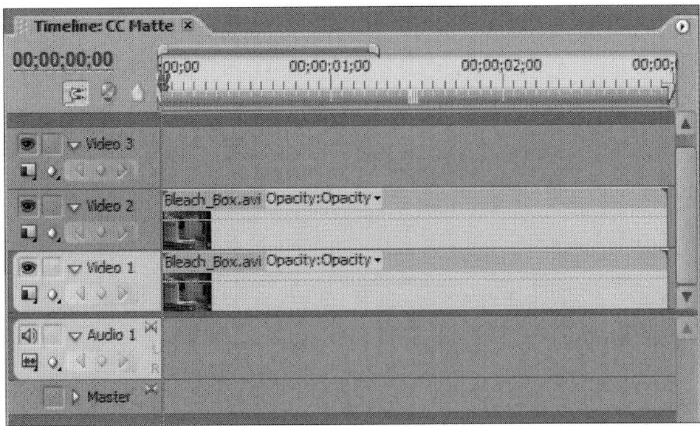

Figure 24.10 The only cumbersome part of this workflow is that in order to do luma matte color correction effects, you need to place the corrected clip on top of itself. If you plan on animating the corrected result, you will want to nest the stack of clips into your final sequence.

2. In the Effects panel, go to the Color Correction subfolder within Video Effects. Drag and drop the Luma Corrector on top of the Bleach_Box instance on Video 2. With the clip selected, open the Effect Controls panel and enter the following settings for the Luma Corrector (**Figure 24.11**):

   Tonal Range: **Master**
   Brightness: **0**
   Contrast: **0**
   Contrast Level: **0**
   Gamma: **.8**
   Pedestal: **-.08**
   Gain: **.8**

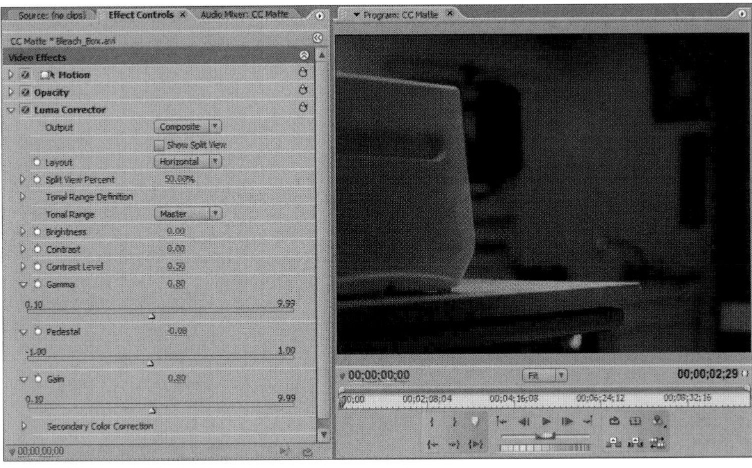

Figure 24.11 The Luma Corrector is the tool you use if you want to quickly increase or decrease the brightness and contrast of your clip. For this effect, you have darkened the video quite drastically.

The Luma Corrector is your quick and simple color correction effect that allows you to adjust all the parameters associated with brightness and contrast. By reducing the Gamma, Pedestal, and Gain you have effectively pulled down all the primary brightness levels of the image, decreasing the highest bright points and making them darker. This luma correction reflects the look that you want applied to the matte region.

3. Press F9 on your keyboard to open the Titler, and name your new title Color Matte. With the Titler open, click the Show Video check box and position the Edit Line at 00;00;01;00. Using the Default Pure White style, select the Rectangle tool from the Titler Tools panel and make a rectangle that covers the entire frame. Twirl down the Fill properties and set the Fill Type to Radial Gradient. Click on the left color square and reduce its Opacity to 0%. Grab the right color square and slowly drag it closer to the left one so that the circle in the center has a smooth gradient edge and it encircles the Bleach Box (**Figures 24.12a** and **b**).

   In this step, you created your luma matte. You filled the image with a pure white rectangle, then changed its fill to Radial Gradient so that you could effectively punch a hole through the center of the rectangle. By assigning a 0% opacity level to the first color square, which reflects the center of the radial gradient, you created a pure white gradient that smoothly transitions to completely transparent. Sliding the color squares left reduces the size of the radial center. Sliding the color squares closer together shortens the gradient that connects the two. The trick here is to first define the size of the center circle with the left color square, then slowly drag the right color square left to find the perfect gradient amount that connects the two.

   When doing luma mattes for color corrections you should always use gradients with opacity adjustments as your object file. You should also keep the gradient as smooth as possible when it transitions from white to transparent.

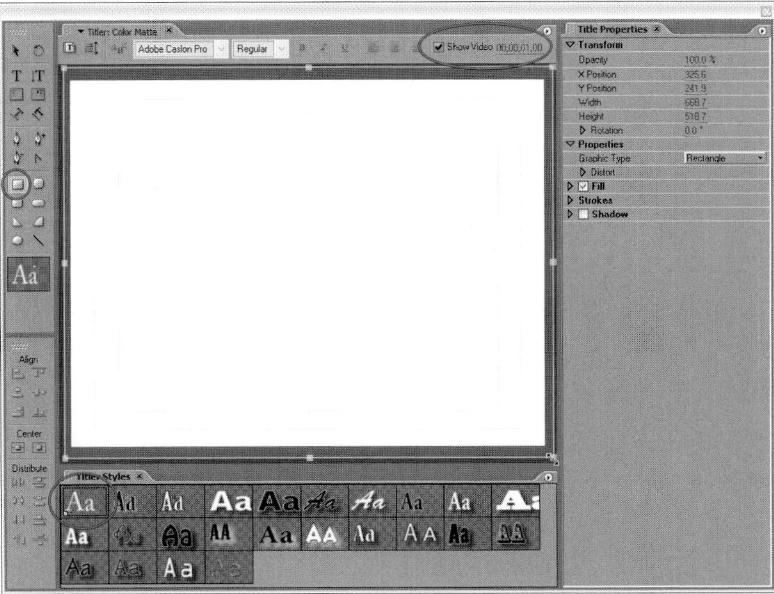

a

b

Second color square
First color square

Figures 24.12a and b First, you need to select the Rectangle tool and create a rectangle that covers your frame (a). Clicking on the first style in the Titler Styles panel ensures that the rectangle is filled with pure white. Then you apply a Radial Gradient fill to the rectangle (b). By assigning the first color square to be 0% Opacity you ensure that its color point becomes completely transparent. By pulling the second color square closer to the first you are reducing the length of the gradient that connects the two color squares. Because they are both white and the center is transparent, the result is a gradient that dithers into complete transparency.

4. Drop the Color Matte Title onto Video 3. In the Effects panel, go to the Keying subfolder of Video Effects. Drag and drop the Track Matte Key effect onto the Bleach_Box clip on Video 2 (**Figures 24.13a** and **b**). With the clip selected, set the Track Matte Key effect parameters to

   Matte: **Video 3**
   Composite Using: **Matte Luma**

a

b

Figures 24.13a and b 24.13a shows your final result with the specified Track Matte Key settings. Notice that with Video 1 turned off in the timeline (b), you can see exactly what is being keyed using your custom title as a luma matte. This reinforces how important it is to have a smooth gradient that helps with the transition between the color corrected matte portion of your image (Video 2 and 3) and the original colored image (Video 1).

This last step used the created title as a luma matte to key the color-corrected Bleach_Box clip through. The length of the gradient that transitions the pure white outer region to the transparent center region is what ultimately sells the effectiveness of this technique. If the gradient is too short, the line of distinction between the original clip and the corrected clip will be very obvious. To see this for yourself, simply open the Color Matte title and drag the second color square (right) to the left so that it is immediately next to first color square. As with the previous lesson, if you want to integrate this color-corrected clip into a master sequence, nest this sequence directly into the master. If you want to adjust the color correction effect, simply select the clip on Video 2 and continue adjusting its effect properties.

To take this lesson a step further, experiment with using gradient fills and 0% opacity values on one of the two color squares. In the case of the Radial Gradient, giving the second color square (left) 0% opacity would make your luma matte element a circle. With a white circle, you could apply a color correction adjustment to only someone's face. You could also add some motion to the title in the sequence and track color corrections with the movement of someone's face. To see an example of this, check out the Luma_Mattes_Finish.prproj project.

Although still in the world of effects, the next section of this chapter switches gears slightly to focus on creating a clean and simple picture-in-picture effect and template.

Creating a Good Picture-in-Picture

A picture-in-picture effect (PiP) is quite easy to achieve in Premiere Pro: Drop a clip in the timeline on one video track, then drop a second clip above it on another track. Resize the top clip to make it smaller, add a drop shadow, and quickly you've created a simple PiP. The result is a small video clip on top of another full-size clip. This effect is useful when you are trying to put more information on the screen or when you want to reference a video clip that someone on screen is talking about. The best and most common PiP examples play every night on the news.

To help your PiP image stand out from the image it's covering, however, you need more than a basic drop shadow.

You need a frame. In this chapter, you will learn the Adobe Title Designer settings that make up a great-looking frame, then you will marry the title and the video to build a simple, clean picture-in-picture effect. You will then learn how to transform your settings into custom presets that can be used for multiple PiP effects.

Building a Custom Frame

The most common question I hear about Premiere picture-in-picture effects is how to create a strong border or edge for the image that is overlaid on the other clips.

Using effects only on a clip, you might add a Bevel Edge and a soft Edge Feather, but this typical look doesn't frame the PiP image well or make it stand out.

Using the Titler, I discovered a picture perfect way of creating a custom frame that you can resize and adjust to look different every time you use it. Here's how:

1. Open PiP_Start.prproj from the APPST2 Lesson Files/ Chapter 24 folder. Press F9 to open the Titler, name the title PiP Frame, and create a rectangle in the center of the Titler's drawing area by selecting the Rectangle tool. Drag from the upper-left corner down to the lower right, trying to stay in the safe-area boxes. To ensure the resolution and position of the rectangle are correct for this lesson, assign it the following values in the Title Properties panel (**Figure 24.14**):

Opacity: **100%**	Width: **648**
X Position: **324** Y	Height: **480**
Position: **240**	Rotation: **0.0**

   You now have a title that fits to the exact edge of the frame. Using what you learned about inner strokes in Chapter 15, "Advanced Titling: Styles and Templates," you next can create an inner stroke that grows inward from the outer edge to help build a border or frame for your PiP effect.

2. In the Title Styles panel, click off the check box for Fill. Twirl down Stroke, and add one inner stroke.

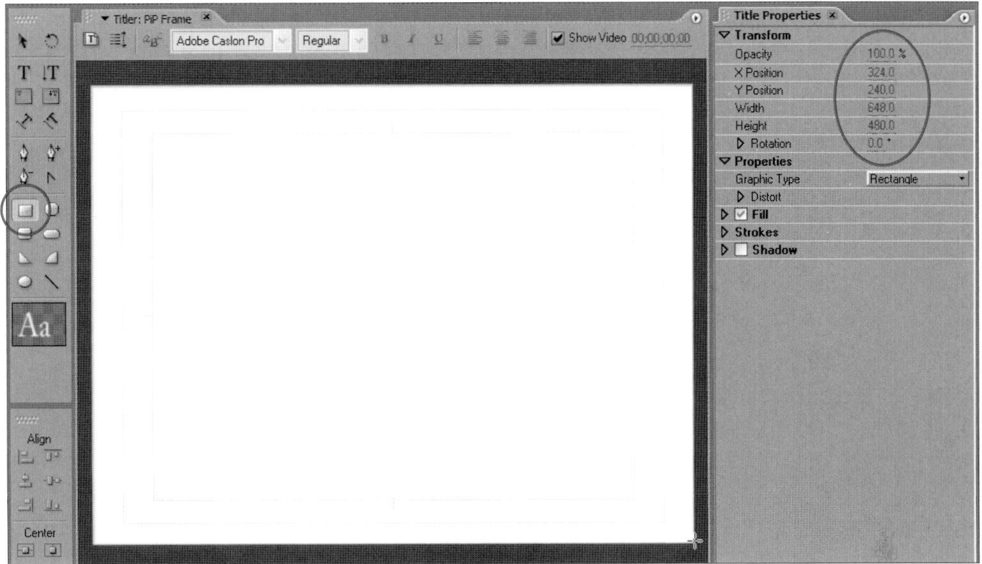

Figure 24.14 The rectangle fits exactly to the edge of the title frame, because the Titler window size is not 720×480, but 648×480. For this lesson, that actual size is important to remember.

By making the fill of the rectangle empty, you can see directly through the center of the title. The inner stroke provides an "outline" that is bound to the edge of the frame and will expand inward, always locking to the edge of the frame when you increase its size. Next, you'll give that inner stroke a personality to transform it into a beautiful frame, or at least a good-looking frame.

3. Assign the following settings to the inner stroke:

   Type: **Edge**
   Size: **40**
   Fill Type: **Bevel**
   Highlight Color: **47,35,100 (HSB, Golden color #FFECA6)**
   Highlight Opacity: **100**
   Shadow Color: **47,35,69 (HSB, Brown color #B0A272)**

   Using a Bevel fill for the inner stroke gives the appearance of a more three-dimensional stroke, one that stands out a bit more. Although I used a skin tone type of color, you can use your own color choices to customize the frame. The highlight color should be a bright color, and the shadow should be a darker setting of the same color. Notice how the H (Hue) and S (Saturation) values are the same; you just decrease the B (Brightness) value to make an exact color darker.

4. Click the Lit check box (**Figure 24.15**), then click on the Tube check box (**Figure 24.16**). Click off the Lit check box (**Figure 24.17**).

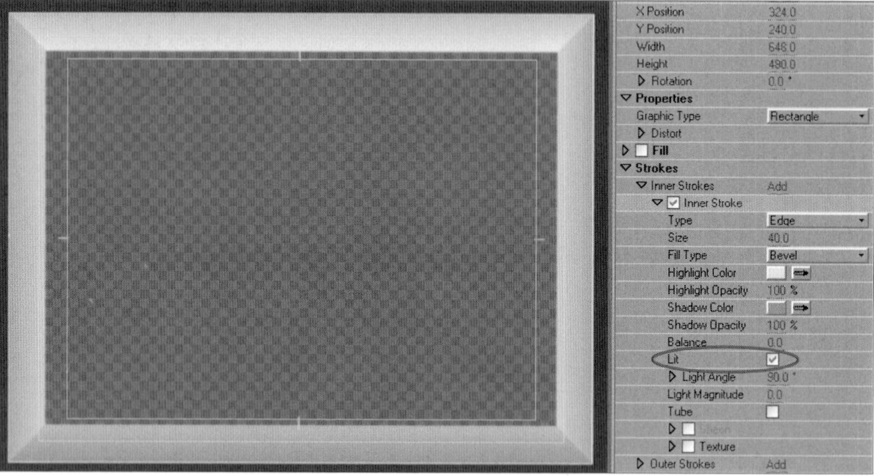

Figure 24.15 With only Lit checked the result is a typically angled-looking flat frame. Changing the Light Angle adjusts the direction the light comes from, while altering Light Magnitude affects the strength and presence of the light.

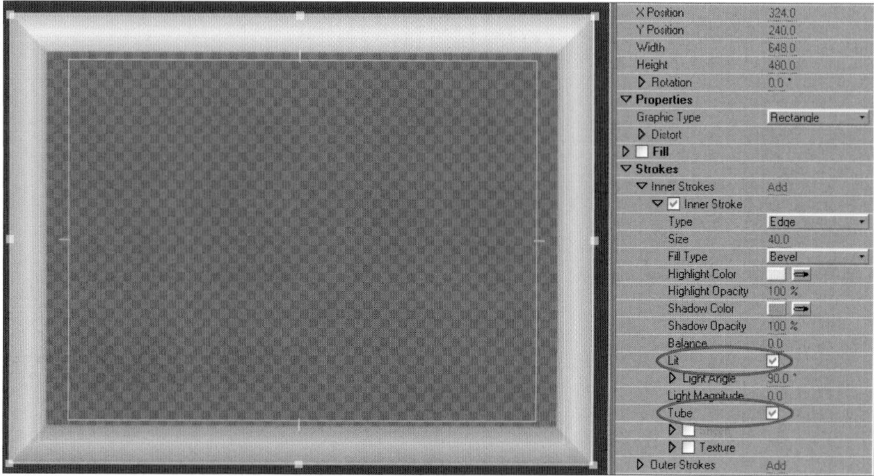

Figure 24.16 With both Lit and Tube checked, the result is a rounded bevel edge with a gentle lighting effect. Increasing Light Magnitude adds even more emphasis to this effect.

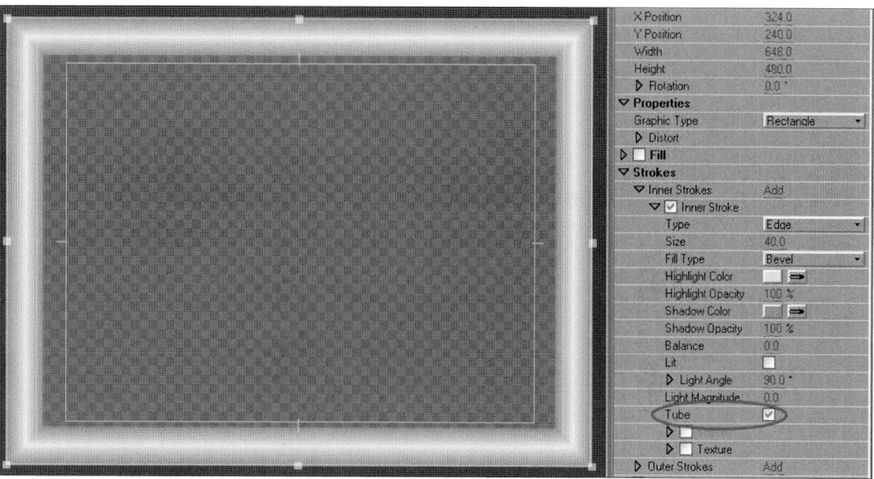

Figure 24.17 Turning off Lit and checking Tube creates a simple rounded frame rim with the light shadowing bleeding off to the sides of the edges.

The Lit check box engages an effect that assumes a light source is shining down on the edge and provides a more three-dimensional look. The light source comes from whatever angle you like; you can increase or decrease the magnitude to heighten or lessen the effect. When checked, Tube makes the bevel edge rounded; turn it off for a flat edge. Lit and Tube offer a good selection of options for creating an attractive PiP frame.

5. With the Titler open, press Ctrl+J to access the Templates dialog. From the wing menu of the Templates dialog, select Save PiP_Frame as Template. Name the template the same as the title, PiP Frame, then click OK.

   By saving your new title as a custom template, you can use it time and again with any project. Because of what you learned about modifying templates in Chapter 15, you can quickly load this PIP Frame template and change its color and lighting properties to make it unique and appropriate for any subsequent projects.

This PiP frame technique is quite simple and straightforward, offering excellent results that you can customize as you like. Additionally, you can increase or reduce the size of the stroke depending on how much emphasis you want to give the frame and its image. You can continue with this project for the next lesson.

Nesting Your PiP

To make your PiP files easier to manage you can add your custom title frame to the video file and nest the two elements in their own sequence. You will then be able to use the frame and video file synonymously as one file. With the two files nested, you can more easily explore additional effect settings to help complete the look and position of your PiP.

TIP

Because the title picture frame is using an inner stroke, it is technically cropping inward onto the video clip that it surrounds. You can adjust the size of the stroke to reduce the size of the frame, or you can reduce the size of the video clip on Video 1 so that it fits inside the inner edge of the inner stroke. To reduce the size of the video clip on Video 1, select it and in the Effect Controls panel's Motion listing, reduce Scale to the appropriate size.

1. Open PiP_Nest_Start.prproj from the APPST2 Lesson Files/Chapter 24 folder.

   The video file for this project is in the APPST2 Lesson Files/Chapter 27 folder and the WA114.avi file is located in the APPST2 Lesson Files/Artbeats folder.

2. Drag and drop the file A Cam 01.avi to the Video 1 track in PiP Sequence. Drag and drop PiP Frame to the Video 2 track, covering the clip. Extend the duration of the title to cover the entire clip beneath it (**Figure 24.18**). Preview the results in your Program Monitor.

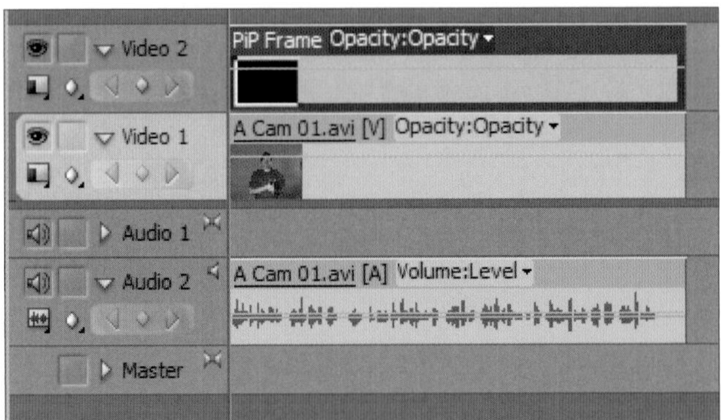

Figure 24.18 When you are nesting your title and video clip, keep the duration of the title equal to the duration of the video clip it is covering, unless you want the border to disappear.

   Because the title frame is bound to the exact edge of the video frame, placing the title above the PiP video file is all you need to do to merge the picture frame with the video clip. Now that these two elements are merged into one sequence, you can develop the final look of the PiP.

3. Open the Master Sequence and drag and drop the WA114.avi clip to Video 1 six times in a row. Drag and drop the PiP Sequence to Video 2. Press the \ key to

snap the zoom of your sequence to completely contain the added clips (**Figure 24.19**).

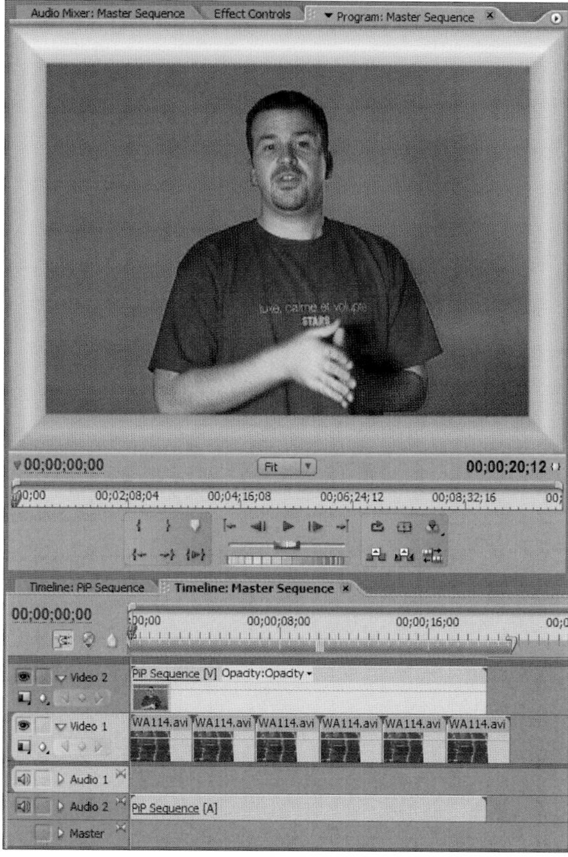

Figure 24.19 By nesting the title and video element into one sequence (PiP Sequence), you can now drag and drop the sequence file as if it were an individual clip. The Artbeats graphic on Video 1 serves as the background under the PiP image.

Because you have married the title border with the video clip, you can now treat them as a single clip by dragging and dropping the host sequence. For the PiP to appear on top of the background video element, the PiP sequence must be placed on Video 2 above the background on Video 1. With the two files stacked in the proper hierarchy, you can reduce the scale, change the position, and then add a nice drop shadow effect to give the appearance that the PiP is on top of the other video.

4. Turn on the Safe Margins in the Program Monitor. Select the PiP Seqeuence clip on Video 2, and open the Effect Controls panel. Open the Motion effect, and reduce the

Scale to 40%. Click on the PiP Sequence clip, and in the Program Monitor physically reposition the clip in the upper-right area of the frame (**Figure 24.20**). My final position was 530×123.

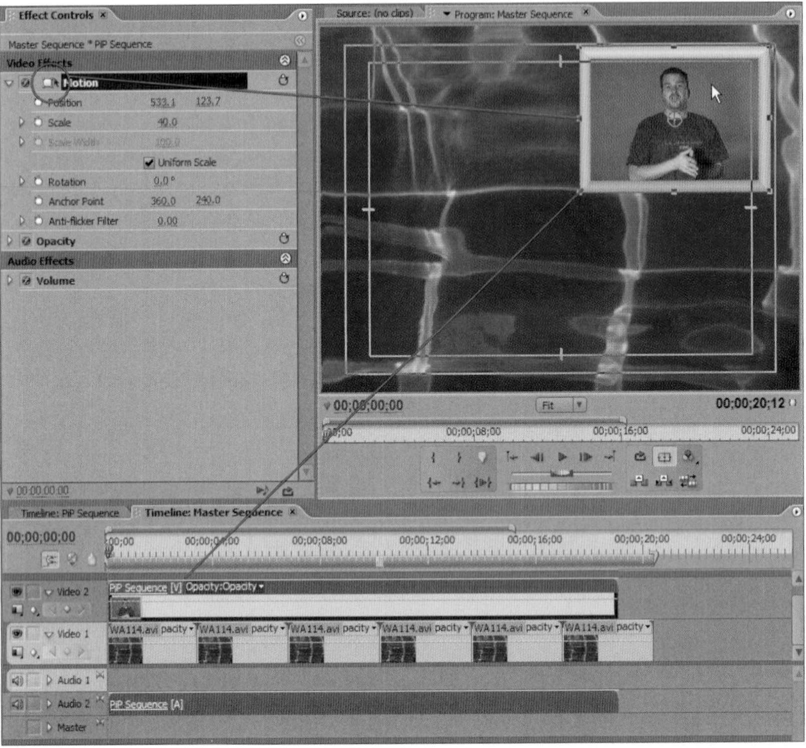

Figure 24.20 With the PiP Sequence selected in the timeline, if you click on the clip in the Program Monitor you have direct manipulation automatically activated. For any effect displaying the Direct Manipulation square next to its name, you can click and make adjustments directly inside the Program Monitor panel. For the PiP effect, you dragged the selected clip to the upper-right frame region.

Turning on Safe Margins enables you to see the title- and action-safe areas of your frame. By positioning the PiP on the line of the title-safe margin, you are ensuring that the entire clip will be visible on a standard television. Placement and scale of your PiP is entirely up to you. I recommend 40% as the half size and 25% as a small size.

5. From the Effects panel, drag and drop the Drop Shadow effect from the Video Effects/Perspective folder onto the clip PiP Sequence in the Video 2 track

of your Master Sequence. In the Effect Controls panel, assign these Drop Shadow effect settings:

Color: **Default Black**
Opacity: **45**
Direction: **135**
Distance: **40**
Softness: **40**

A drop shadow gives a sense of depth to the composition. The direction and settings of the shadow are entirely up to you. I chose a simple and subtle lower-right falling shadow. The shadow is not too dramatic, yet it still gives off the appearance that the PiP is floating on top of the video that it covers.

6. For the final step, target Video 2 by clicking its track header or holding Ctrl while pressing the + key. Target the Audio 2 track by clicking its track header or pressing Ctrl+Shift++. With both Video 2 and Audio 2 targeted, press the Home key, then Ctrl+D, then Ctrl+Shift+D. Press Page Down so that the Edit Line snaps the end of the A Cam PiP, Ctrl+D, and Ctrl+Shift+D again (**Figure 24.21**). Press Enter to render your sequence and see the final results.

   By targeting Video 2 and Audio 2, you activated each track to receive keyboard editing commands. After you pressed Home to snap the Edit Line to the head of the timeline, you added video and audio default transitions to the clips on those tracks. Page Down advanced you

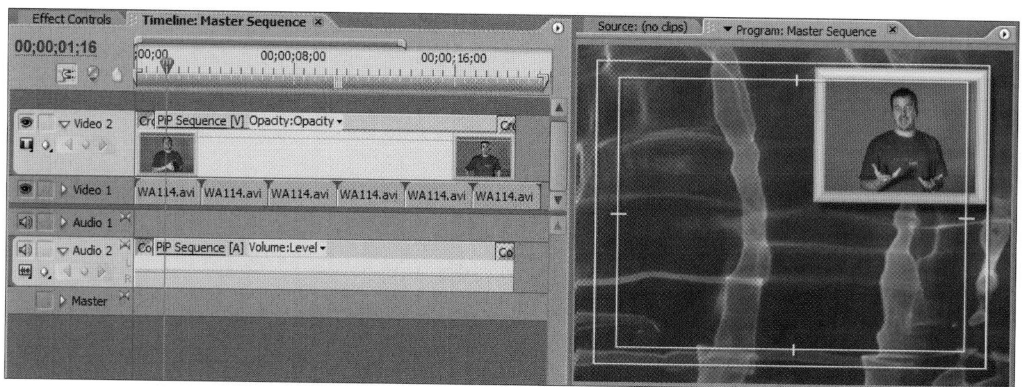

Figure 24.21 On Video 2, you can see the purple effect line signifying that effects have been added to the clip. Also, the one-sided dissolve transitions appear at the head and tail of the clip. Having applied all the effects and transitions to this clip, you can move it up to another track or down the timeline to a different position without reassigning effects or reapplying transitions. The integrity of the clip with effects will remain unchanged until you manually adjust it.

to the next edit point, which got you to the end of the same clip. Here you added two more default transitions. The end result is an attractive PiP effect that fades in and out to the upper right with a nice drop shadow for added depth.

With the files nested, making refinements is easy. If you want to add any effects or color correction to the video in the PiP, simply adjust the original file in the nested sequence. If you want the title border to be thicker, open the title and adjust the size of the inner stroke. Once you save the adjustment to the title, all instances where the title is used will update to reflect its saved state.

While you're in the mood to make adjustments, take a look at some of the custom PiP presets that came with Adobe Premiere Pro 2.0. You can easily customize them for your projects.

Using Custom Effect Presets

Part of my contribution to the previous 1.5 version of Premiere Pro was to create a bunch of custom effect presets that you can quickly apply to clips in the timeline for immediate results.

This final lesson shows you how to use the custom effect presets to quickly create and enhance a PiP effect—a moving PiP. For this effect, the PiP will spin in to hold in the upper-right corner. As the clip finishes, the PiP will spin out and off to the right. Three custom presets make this easy: Drop Shadow LR, PiP 25% UR Spin In, and PiP 25% UR Scale Out.

When using the PiP custom presets, take note of the abbreviations UR (upper right), UL (upper left), LR (lower right), and LL (lower left). The effects are organized by the start or end position, so all UR effects either start or end in the same upper-right position.

Because of how Premiere Pro handles effect settings, however, you can't just add the three effects to the same clip at once. To accommodate two separate motion adjustments, you must razor the clip into two pieces.

1. Open PiP_Presets_Start.prproj from the APPST2 Lesson Files/Chapter 24 folder.

   This project starts midway through the last lesson, just before you assigned the PiP effects.

2. From the Custom Presets/PiPs/25% PiPs/25% UR folder drag and drop the PiP 25% UR preset onto the PiP Sequence clip on Video 2 in the sequence.

Here you dragged and dropped a custom effect preset onto a clip in your sequence. The clip automatically updated with the settings of the preset; in this case Scale resized to 25% and Position updated to the upper-right picture-in-picture location.

3. Press the C key to access the Razor tool. Make incisions at 2;00 and at 17;00 in the PiP Sequence clip.

   With the clip split into three pieces, you can apply two different keyframed presets to begin and then end your PiP effect.

4. Drag and drop the PiP 25% UR Spin In custom effect preset from the Presets/PiP/25% PiP/25% UR preset folder onto the first instance of the A Cam Pip clip. Drag and drop PiP 25% UR Scale Out from the same folder onto the third instance of the same clip (**Figures 24.22** and **24.23**). Press Enter to preview your results.

   Having properly split the clip into three pieces, you can't see the seam when you play back the shots, although the division is clear in the timeline. Each clip accommodates a different move, and the result is a

All Custom presets have a default duration of one second. Any preset displaying the word "In" anchors its first keyframe to the first frame of the clip it applies to. Any preset displaying the word "Out" anchors its last keyframe to the last frame of the clip it applies to.

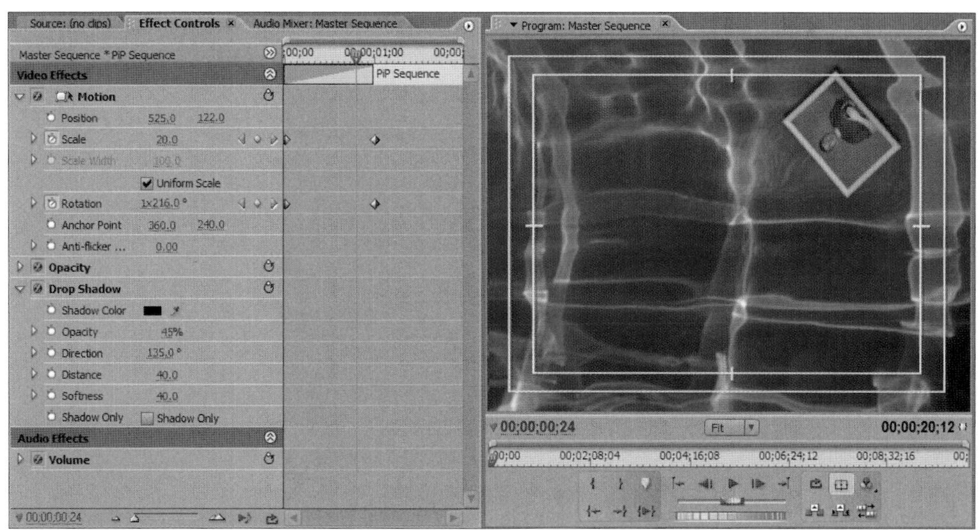

Figure 24.22 In the Effect Controls panel, two scale keyframes represent the scale in so that the PiP zooms into position. At the same time, two rotation keyframes represent two full rotations from the first keyframe to the second. If you want to slow the scaling, just slide the second keyframe to the right. If you want to increase the number of rotations, position the Edit Line on top of the second rotation keyframe and increase the number of rotations from 2 to 4.

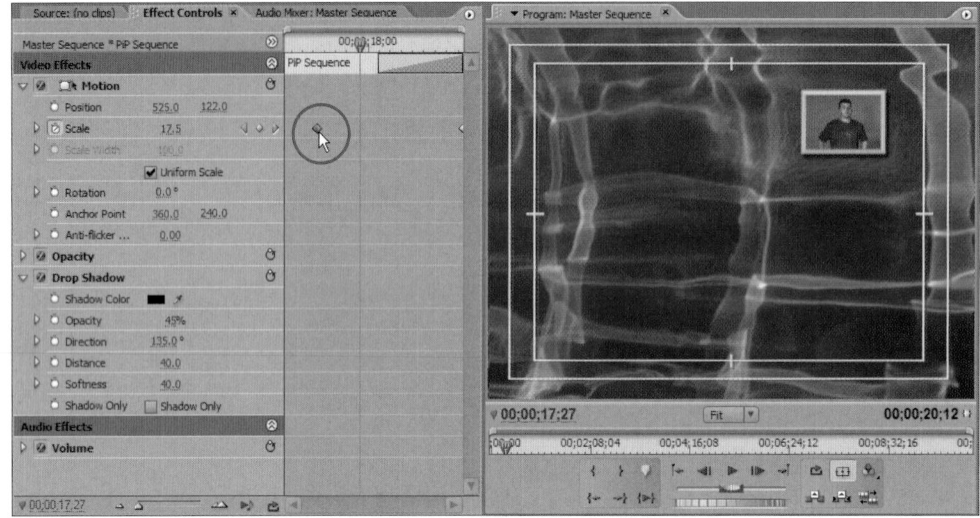

Figure 24.23 The last clip has two scale keyframes that represent the clip scaling from its current 25% down to 0%. If you want to slow the scale, just move the first Scale keyframe to the left.

more dynamic PiP effect. The next step will show you how to adjust the keyframes created from the preset, in case you decide to adjust timing of the effect.

5. Select the first instance of the PiP Sequence clip in the timeline, and open the Effect Controls panel displaying the Timeline view. Marquee select the second two keyframes for scale and rotation (**Figure 24.24a**). With both keyframes selected, move them to the right to move their position closer to the end of the clip (**Figure 24.24b**).

   By either marquee selecting or holding down the Shift key and clicking multiple keyframes, you can select and move multiple keyframes in unison. To deselect the keyframes, click off of them.

You cannot see literal time positioning when moving keyframes, but you can reposition the Edit Line to give you an idea as to the time value of the adjustment you are making.

6. Holding down the Shift key, select all three pieces of the split clip. Right-click on the selection, and choose Group from the context menu. To ensure that these three clips remain together, joined as a seamless trio, you grouped them. Grouping the clips creates a hard link that binds them together, enabling you to physically drag them to another track or timeline position while they are locked together. If you want to update or modify individual effect or keyframe settings, you must right-click and select Ungroup to get the individual clip effect parameters back.

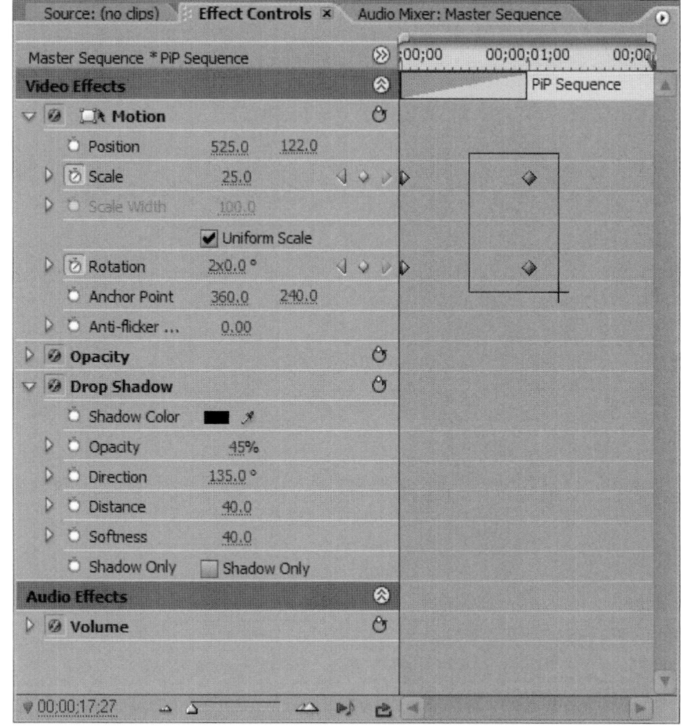

a

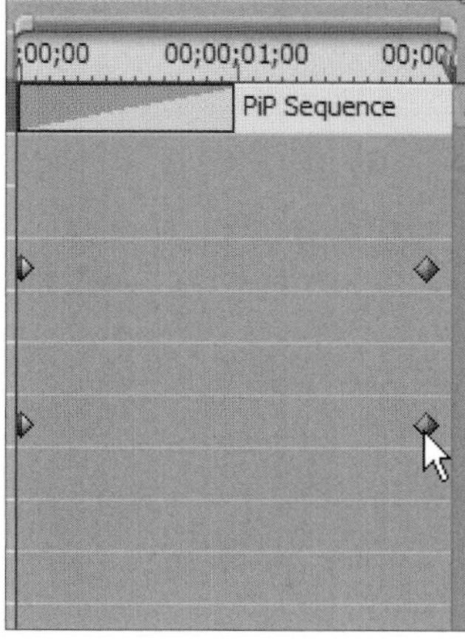

b

Figures 24.24a and b Marquee select the separate keyframes in the Timeline view of the Effect Controls panel (a). Once the two keyframes are selected, you can quickly drag them to a new position to adjust their timing (b). Now the scale and rotation are a little slower.

Presets are great for streamlining effect building. The lessons from the second half of this chapter should help you not only to use the custom PiP presets to their highest potential, but also to create an attractive PiP easily. Keep in mind that all your clips with anchored In or Out custom presets should have a duration of a least one second to ensure all the keyframes can be displayed. If you want to add multiple keyframed presets to one clip, remember to split the clip before you apply the In and Out presets.

Things to Remember

We started with the Track Matte Key, a revised powerful effect in Premiere Pro's arsenal. Because you can use alpha channel information to matte out elements, there is no resolution compromise when you output and render your final results.

When creating your track matte graphic elements, remember that the Matte Luma setting of Composite Using composites through pure white and can be used with gradients fading to complete transparency to have a smooth matte key. If you want to key through the black information of a clip without an alpha, check the Reverse option to composite through the black using luma. With Matte Alpha, Premiere Pro composites through the nontransparent alpha channel information of your media. With titles and Photoshop files, their empty space is not considered the alpha channel; instead the graphic and object within the frame will be attributed to the alpha channel.

Using the method of double-laying clips, you can use Track Matte Key effects to create powerful color correction and image effect. If you haven't yet read Chapter 23, "Advanced Color Correction: Three-Way Color Corrector," check out the Secondary Color Corrector effect used in conjunction with the Track Matte effect.

Finishing with custom PiPs. you learned that with a few simple steps you can use the Titler to create an adjustable border that adds a great look to your PiP effects. To change the emphasis of the frame size around your PiP, adjust the size of the inner stroke in your title frame. To change the shape and look of the frame itself, play with the Lit and Tube options to toggle between a flat frame and a rounded one. As for the colors, you can specify them on a project-by-project basis by loading the frame you build from the Templates dialog.

Adding a slight drop shadow helps give the PiP a greater feeling of depth on top of the image that it covers. You can even add a slight edge feather if you want to soften up the edges a bit.

Finally, using the custom PiP presets can save you a lot of time if you apply them properly. If you intend on using two keyframed effect presets, remember to split the clip in half before adding any of the keyframed presets.

Having one custom title frame and all the custom presets should make your life much easier when it comes to creating a good-looking PiP effect.

In the next chapter, you'll complete your look at advanced effects by learning how to properly shoot and key out green screen material.;

25

Green/Blue Screen Keying

As you learned in the last chapter, keying involves replacing elements of one image with those of another. Green and blue screen keying keys out the green and blue information from one image, making it transparent so other images can show through. Using green and blue screen keying techniques, you can make a person appear in different locations or environments. In the *Lord of the Rings* films and the last remake of *King Kong*, for example, green screen tarps were hung up around actors and blue screen sets were constructed to enable full flexibility for incorporating computer-generated background elements in hundreds of shots.

In this chapter, you will learn how to set up and light a green/blue screen shoot, as well as how to key out the recorded green/blue elements in Premiere Pro. The first lesson provides an overview of setting up your shoot and of the tools you can use to make green/blue screen keying much easier and more accurate. The second lesson takes some imperfect green screen elements from Chapter 27's live multi-cam shoot and shows you how to key out the green screen to introduce different backgrounds for the material. You also will use Garbage Mattes to clip sections of your image, removing excess material in a single action. Finally, you'll investigate using the new Secondary Color Correction effect in the Three-Way Color Corrector to clean up and strengthen your green screen for better keying results.

To get things started, let me first give you some tips about the fundamentals for setting up a good-looking green screen shoot.

Setting Up Your Green/Blue Screen Shoot

From the screen itself to properly placing your lights, here's what you should consider when setting up a green screen shoot.

A *cyclorama* is a stage with walls that smoothly curve into the floor, instead of meeting it perpendicularly (**Figure 25.1**). Because of this slightly curved transition, no harsh shadows get caught in the angle of the wall hitting the floor. Cycloramas painted white give the appearance of an infinite background, as in George Lucas' film *THX-1138* where characters wandered aimlessly, lost in an empty, sterile pure white world.

Ultimatte, a company that is synonymous with green/blue screen compositing, offers several plug-ins that assist with green screen post-production work as well. For a complete list of Ultimatte plug-ins and hardware acceleration products

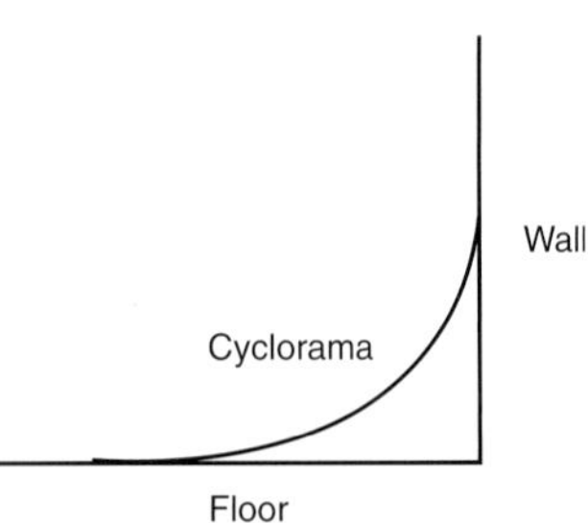

Figure 25.1 Where a regular wall meets the floor, a shadow hits the floor and also hits the wall in a slightly disjointed fashion. With a cyclorama, you cannot see where the floor ends and the wall begins, and the shadow appears as one continuous shadow.

Any place where you can rent lighting or grip equipment you can likely pick up a big roll of thick green screen paper. The rolls are typically six to ten feet wide, and you can hang them from the ceiling and unroll them to reveal a flat, pure green background. I used this type of green screen for the example material. If you want more space and more room to move around, you might consider renting a stage that has a cyclorama painted the proper green color, which is technically called Ultimatte Green.

Your screen is hung; now you need lights. **Figure 25.2** illustrates proper lighting for the subject and green screen in medium to close-up shots. Do the best with the resources you have; even the lighting for the example footage wasn't perfect. Premiere Pro and other tools can help you later.

Position your subject far enough from the green screen that the shadows created from the lights on the subject do not cast on it. Keep an even light source on the green screen itself (L1 in Figure 25.2), producing an even tone rather than various shades of green. An evenly lit green screen background can be more effectively keyed out. If the light is severely angled and very close to the screen, you'll see color shades and a noticeable bright spot. If a green screen is lit too brightly or the subject is too close to the screen, you risk the green color reflecting off the screen and spilling onto the subject. The spill color, which could end up on clothes or the side of your subject's face, is the same color as the screen; when you key the screen, the spill area will be keyed out as well.

Pointing one light directly at your subject produces a flat effect. Instead, place at least two lights at or slightly above head height, pointing downward on the subject (L3 and L4 in Figure 25.2). Of these two lights, one light should be half as bright as the other. With each light coming from a different angle, the lighting has some mild depth.

To create a clear distinction between the background green screen and the foreground subject, you need a back light. This third light (L2 in Figure 25.2) should be small, bright, and narrowly focused at an angle so that it hits the back of your subject's head and shoulders (**Figure 25.3**). In terms of exposure, the background green should be equal to the exposure of the foreground subject. The back light should be brighter so that it is visible above the lighting of the other elements. With your subject well lit, both front and back, you can more easily get an exact edge to your subject, meaning it will integrate better with whatever is keyed into the green screen. With your lighting set up, you're ready to find the right camera angle and start recording.

If you can't avoid the green screen reflecting on your subject during the shoot, you can try the Spill Suppression feature of Adobe After Effects to remove the green tone in post-production.

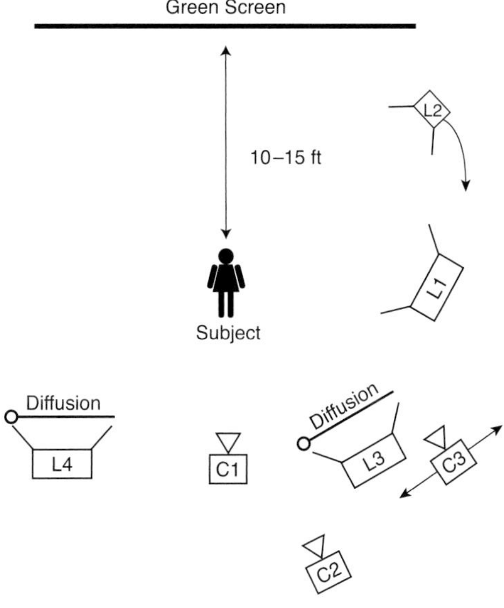

Figure 25.2 In this overhead shot, cameras are marked as C1 through C3 and lights as L1 through L4. Note the distance between the subject and the green screen. Also notice that both the green screen and the subject are lit from a host of angles.

Figure 25.3 In the aerial view, you can see that the back light (L2) is pointed at an angle at which it can spread light over the entire back of the subject without pointing directly into any of the shooting cameras. In the head-on camera view, the outline to the subject shows the result of the light.

Green/Blue Screen Keying and Premiere Pro

Premiere Pro has adequate green/blue screen keying tools, but does not have a wide range of controls for fine-tuning the key, which is a hot topic. Because the primary Green Screen Key lacks these extra controls, for this lesson you will use the secondary color correction functionality of the Three-Way Color Corrector to enhance the green screen, making it easier to key. If you don't have After Effects, you can still get keying work done in Premiere Pro; however, if you have the Production version of After Effects, it comes

If you have the budget, you might consider some new alternatives to hanging a literal green screen. In the last couple of years, there have been some great breakthroughs that aid the green/blue screen process.

For example, Reflecmedia's LiteRing enables you to create a sharp blue or green screen by using a small ring of light and a reflective gray screen. The LiteRing fits around the lens of your camera and emits a blue or green light. A custom fabric screen reflects this light directly back into the lens of the camera. Although the screen appears gray to the naked eye, the blue or green color can be seen perfectly and evenly through the camera's lens. One advantage to using this technology is that you need to light only your subject, and you don't have to worry about lighting the screen. With the LiteRing around the lens, the technology of the fabric takes care of a perfect-looking blue or green screen. The other advantage is that you will never have any reflective blue or green spillage onto your subject. For more information on LiteRing, see Reflecmedia's website at www.reflecmedia.com.

with the Keying tool, Keylight, which is one of the best in the business for doing green/blue screen key work.

In this lesson, you will separately key out each of the backgrounds from Chapter 27's multi-cam shoot. Once you have the proper key set, you will then use the Garbage Matte effect to remove some excess material from the frame of the cluttered B and C cameras. As you work, you quickly will understand why you must have a bright and strong green screen background to get good results in Premiere Pro. However, you will also learn just how powerful the secondary color correction tools are.

1. Open Key_Start.prproj from the APPST2 Lesson Files/Chapter 25 folder on the accompanying DVD. This project is a variation on the edit you will create in the forthcoming Chapter 27.

   The multi-cam media in the project can be found in the APPST2 Lesson Files/Chapter 27 folder. The remaining files can be found in the APPST2 Lesson Files/Artbeats folder.

2. Open the MultiCam Sequence in the Timeline panel, and review the stacked clips. Turning on and off the eye dropper for each video track, get acquainted with which shots are where and the green screen elements they contain (**Figure 25.4**). Drag and drop the Three-Way Color Corrector effect onto each of the A Cam 01, B Cam 01, and C Cam 01 clips. Finally, drag and drop the Green Screen Key effect onto the same clips (**Figure 25.5**).

   For successful green screen keying, the green screen material needs to be on a track above the background. Because each of these clips will be keyed against the RT113 Artbeats file, your sequence contains each clip stacked on top of the other with the RT113 file as the underlying background. To apply the proper setting for each clip, temporarily disable the output of the other Camera tracks.

   In this step you first applied the Three-Way Color Corrector effect. Keep in mind that effects process in descending order, so by placing the Three-Way Color

Corrector above the Green Screen Key you have the ability to color correct the clip and then process the Green Screen Key effect on the results of the color correction.

Figure 25.4 In this sequence you have a camera shoot with each camera angle shooting me in front of a green screen. Using the Multi-Cam tool you will cut between each camera in a later lesson. For this lesson, you'll turn on and off each individual layer to assign and apply its proper Green Screen and color correction settings.

Figure 25.5 With a Color Correction effect applied first, you have the ability to adjust the color properties of each clip to enhance the effectiveness of the Green Screen Key effect that is applied second. Here you can see that each clip does, in fact, key out some of the green when the effect is applied.

3. Turn off the Output of Video tracks 3 and 4 in the Timeline panel. Click on A Cam 01.avi clip in Video track 2. Switch your workspace to Window > Workspaces > Color Correction. In the Effect Controls panel, turn off the Green Screen Key effect listing. Twirl down the Three-Way Color Corrector effect and set the Output mode to Mask. Twirl down the Secondary Color Correction listing in the Three-Way Color Corrector effect.

NOTES

Effects applied in the Effect Controls panel are processed hierarchically; Premiere applies the top effect listed first, then applies the remaining effects on top of each other. In step 2, you applied the effects in the order in which they should be processed, the Three-Way Color Corrector effect is processed, before the Green Screen Key. This order ensures that the key will take advantage of the image adjustments made with the Three-Way Color Corrector.

In the Secondary section, click the eyedropper labeled Center (eyedropper only), and target the green of the green screen in the image (**Figure 25.6**). Click the eyedropper Add Color (the one with a + sign), and click the green areas of the screen that appear black in the mask view. After you make the mask white except for my body in the center (which should be black), set the Output mode back to composite.

As you learned in Chapter 23, "Advanced Color Correction: Three-Way Color Corrector," using the Secondary Color Corrector can be an excellent way to isolate and select an entire color value from your video. Here you set your output to Mask so that you could gauge your results as you went. After you target the Green as your Center Secondary color, you used the Mask view to

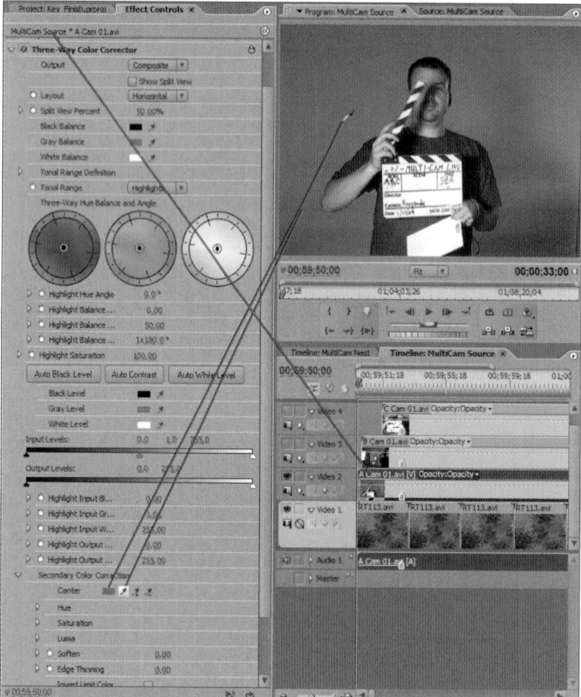

Figure 25.6 When you target a secondary color you want to set your output to mask. Pick the color that you want to be your Secondary selection, then with the Mask output mode active, use the Add Color eye dropper to select more shades and tones to associate with your Secondary selection. This sequence of images shows how you can look at the Mask view, click the Add Color eyedropper, then target a region that is not in the Secondary and have it added.

identify areas of Green that were not within the range of your Center selection. Using the Add Color eyedropper, you broadened the range of your Secondary selection so that the entire green screen behind me was White in the Mask view, which means it is selected.

4. In the Three-Way Color Corrector Effect for A Cam 01.avi, set the Tonal Range to Midtones. Enter the following values into their fields; do not change any fields that aren't specifically called out (**Figures 25.7a** and **b**):

   Midtone Balance Magnitude: **100**
   Midtone Balance Gain: **80**
   Midtone Balance Angle: **136**
   Midtone Output Black Level: **150**

   At the very bottom of the Secondary Color Correction twirl down, set the Soften value to 4.0.

   If you were to evaluate this image by setting the Output to Tonal Range, you would find that most of the image is gray and thus associated with the midtone range. Because the Secondary green selection is primarily midtone based, you selected the midtone range in which to modify the Secondary selection. By adjusting the Midtone color

a

Black output level increased
Compare the fluctuation of color tone in the original versus the affected areas with the Black output level increased.

b

Figures 25.7a and b With both images I have turned on the Split view so you can compare the original with the secondary adjusted results. In 25.7a, you see the selected Secondary region with a Midtone color offset applied, thus making the Secondary region more green. In 25.7b, the Midtone Output Black Level has been increased dramatically. Because you are only selecting and adjusting in the Secondary color selection, previously dark portions of the green Secondary become much brighter, thus reducing the tonal range of the green Secondary.

wheel to an extreme green value, you have strengthened the presence of green in your selection. This is the first step to making the Green Screen Key have an easier time of keying out the video more accurately. The second value you adjusted that made a big difference was setting the Output Black Level to a brighter value. Because your Secondary selection is very precise, you can make drastic tweaks without altering the image at large. By increasing the Output Black Level you reduced the tonal range within your Secondary selection, making the dark green become brighter and more of a flat overall value. The final adjustment was to slightly soften the Secondary selection so that the edges weren't so rough.

5. In the Effect Controls panel for the A Cam 01.avi file, twirl up the Three-Way Color Corrector listing, then turn on the Green Screen Key and twirl it down. If you want to see what your Three-Way Color Corrector did to help the default application of the key, toggle the Three-Way Color Corrector effect listing off. Turn the Effect listing back on, then apply the following settings to the Green Screen Key (**Figure 25.8**):

   Threshold: **40%**
   Cutoff: **18%**
   Smoothing: **High**

   Toggling between the original clip without the Three-Way Color Corrector adjusted and the affected clip, you can see how accurate the Green Screen Key effect will be when it is applied. Reducing Threshold makes the image even more transparent by reducing the strength of the green part of the overlaying image. Increasing Cutoff further defines what the effect keys by making sure that anything below the Cutoff value is not keyed. Adjusting both these sliders is not really an exact science, it is typically a matter of reducing Threshold to a point that looks good and then increasing Cutoff to make it look better. With both controls you can go too far, and the effect will be obviously wrong when that happens.

6. Using the same methodology to target the Secondary Green Region, mold it into place with the Three-Way

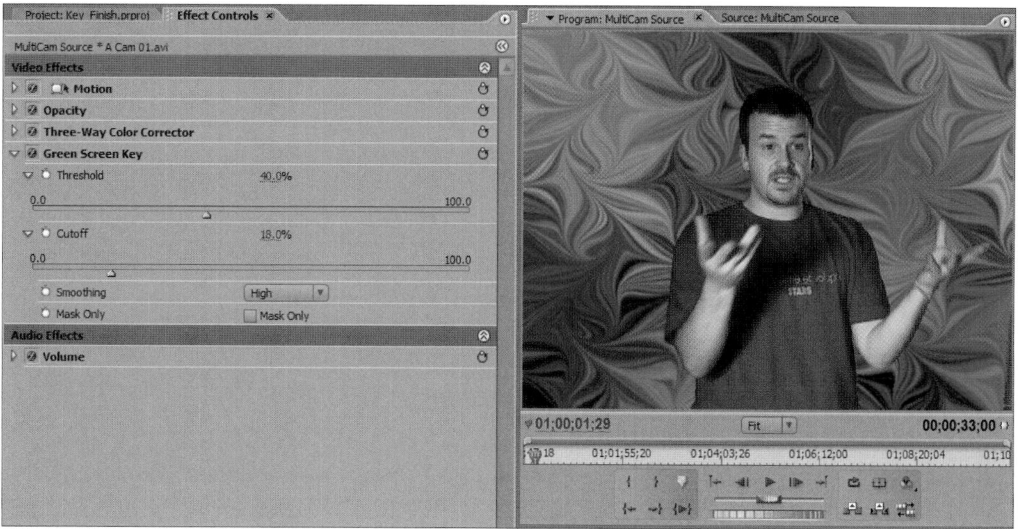

Figure 25.8 I chose this frame because my hands are in a typically dynamic state, here you can see that all the detailed work you did paid off. By creating a stronger green screen presence in the clip, you allowed the green screen to do a better job, isolating the green screen portion of the clip.

Color Corrector controls and then refine the Green Screen Key effect, giving your best shot to clean up B Cam 01.avi and C Cam 01.avi.

Although the last step might prove a bit too challenging, you can skip ahead to my finished project to see the results (APPST2 Lesson Files/Chapter 25/Key_Finish). Or you can import the Secondary Effect presets that I created and apply them to the appropriate clips and refine only the Green Screen Key settings. To import the Secondary Effect presets, right-click in the Effects panel and choose Import Preset, then import any of the A Cam 2nd, B Cam 2nd, or C Cam 2nd files from the same chapter folder. Remember to apply the Three-Way Color Corrector on top of the Green Screen Key and delete the current Three-Way Color Corrector effect that is applied if you decide not to do it (see **Figures 25.9a** and **b**).

Before you move on to the next lesson, whether you have applied the adjustment to the other effects or not, click on the MultiCam Nest sequence in the Timeline panel and take note that the keying results are preserved through the nesting process of doing

a

b

Figures 25.9a and b Compare my results with the B Cam01.avi clip (a) and the results with the C Cam 01.avi clip (b). In both instances the Secondary corrections definitely helped clean up and refine the raw green screen element.

a multi-cam edit. The Green Screen Key simply took the portion of the image that was green and made it transparent. The background video on Video 1 plays through the keyed-out portions of each clip instance in the multi-cam edit; therefore, instead of applying the key effect and Secondary in the MultiCam Nest sequence to every clip, you applied the effect to the source files, which carried the effect with them to the destination sequence.

Keying out the green screen at the source level of the multi-cam sequence makes you better appreciate the value of the nesting structure set up for you with this first lesson. Because the effects are applied to the entire source clips, you can update the nested sequence by making a quick alteration to the source. With your Green Screen Key effect assigned, you're ready to use the Garbage Matte effects to remove the extra elements from B and C cam clips.

Garbage Mattes

Eight- and Sixteen-Point Garbage Matte effects can be used to clean up and remove unnecessary elements that appear in a clip. Garbage Mattes are a way of cropping your image so that certain frame areas are cut entirely. Take a look.

1. Open Garbage_Start.prproj from APPST2 Lesson Files/ Chapter 25 folder. In your desktop workspace, be sure you have the Effect Controls panel and Effects panel open.

2. In the MultiCam Source sequence, turn off the Output for Video 2 and 4, then click and select the video clip on Video 3. Open the Effect Controls panel, and click the Effect Toggle button for Green Screen Key and Three-Way Color Corrector to temporarily turn the effects off. Position the Edit Line at 1;00;00;00. From the Effects/Video Effects/Keying folder, drag and drop the Sixteen-Point Garbage Matte effect on top of the selected clip. Reposition the Garbage Matte effect so that it is at the top of the Video Effects list. Click on the Sixteen-Point Garbage Matte effect listing in the Effect Controls panel (**Figure 25.10**).

   A bunch of elements need to be removed from the B camera shot. Because this shot is from a tripod and the camera remains stationary, you can safely crop out certain areas of the frame to remove the objects surrounding the subject. Turning off the Green Screen Key effect enables you to see clearly the definition of the objects surrounding the subject and to identify which need to be matted out. Turning off the Three-Way Color Corrector effect as well enables you to have a faster update in your Program Monitor.

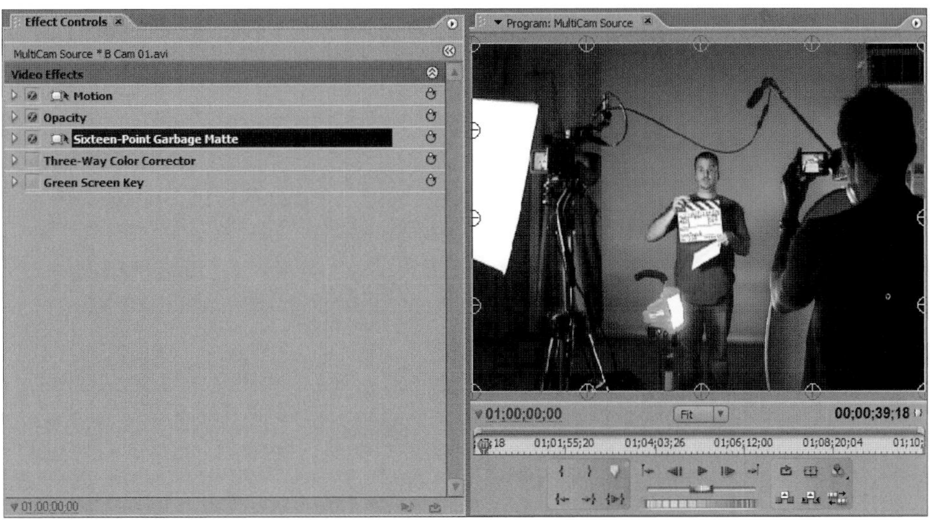

Figure 25.10 With both the Green Screen Key and Three-Way Color Corrector effects toggled off, you can see which elements need to be cropped out: the hanging microphone cord and the camera objects. Clicking on the Garbage Matte effect listing enables direct manipulation; you then can manually drag any of the visible handle points to a new position to crop the image.

Because direct manipulation is available for the Garbage Matte effects, clicking on the effect listing displays each of the 16 points that you can move and reposition to crop out extra elements.

3. Clicking on the various points for the Garbage Matte effect, drag each inward so that the wires, lights, cameras, and cameraman are cropped out (**Figure 25.11**).

Figure 25.11 With 16 points to manipulate, you can easily crop a cluttered frame. As the image is cropped, you can see the background clip beneath it appear in the cropped area.

A Garbage Matte enables you to crop an image so that you can easily erase and entirely remove whatever portions of the image reside outside the matte's boundary.

4. Increase your Program Monitor zoom to 150%. Select the Hand tool (H), and reposition the frame in the Program Monitor so that you can see the top of the subject's head. Press V to get back to the Selection tool, and be sure that the matte is cropping out the wire and not the top of the head (**Figures 25.12a** and **b**).

   Although the Program Monitor zoom is not used that often, this is a perfect example of when and where it is practical to zoom in and study your image to make sensitive adjustments.

5. Click off the Garbage Matte effect in the Effect Controls panel, and toggle on the Green Screen Key and Three-Way Color Corrector effects. Scrub through the sequence, and check out the results.

a

b

Figures 25.12a and b The Hand tool allows you to grab and reposition the image in the zoomed Program Monitor (a). At this level of magnification you have better feedback as to how much of an adjustment you can make. In 25.12b, because you are zoomed in, you can define the Garbage Matte so that it properly crops out the microphone cable.

The image is obviously much cleaner, and to see just how much the three-way correction helped the key, temporarily toggle off and on the Three-Way effect.

6. Toggle the track output for Video 3 off and turn on the output for Video 4. Select the C Cam 01.avi clip and try what you've learned by applying the Eight- or Sixteen-Point Garbage Matte.

   Study the full C Cam 01.avi clip and notice that it is a bit more difficult to matte, because the camera moves. Like all effects, however, the Garbage Mattes are keyframe-able, and you will need to use keyframes to remove the light that keeps appearing on the left side of the frame.

   Remember to assign keyframes before the move begins and then continue assigning them as the move progresses. To see my results, open the Garbage_Finish.prproj from the APPST2 Lesson Files/Chapter 25 folder and look in the Effect Controls panel for the C Cam 01.avi instance.

Using the Garbage Matte effects, you can quickly crop out areas of your image. Because there is a video clip beneath your clip with the Garbage Matte, as soon as you start making matte adjustments the clip elements are removed and the background shows through. By clipping out the extra pieces of the image, you can clearly see that the Green Screen Key effect did the trick you wanted it to.

If you have a perfect green screen key, then Premiere Pro can do the job just fine; however, if you have a troublesome or less than desirable green screen key, try using the Three-Way Color Corrector to enhance it. If that doesn't cut it, your next option is to take the project into Adobe After Effects. Adobe After Effects and its Keylight plug-in (available with the Production Bundle) can complement Premiere Pro by adjusting keys further without compromising the integrity of the original image.

Things to Remember

If you are in a studio and can't paint or hang your matte, you may want to explore Reflecmedia's LiteRing option, which I have found to be very reliable and effective. Using LiteRing also ensures that the power and brightness of your screen is consistent and easier to key out.

This chapter presented a common production scenario: The footage wasn't perfect and needed tweaking. Using the Three-Way Color Corrector you got the green screen element to be more uniform and easier to key out. If you think about what the Three-Way Color Corrector achieved, it should point you towards the visual qualities that your photographed green screen should have when you photograph it. A good green screen has a strong green color value that has little to no tonal range variation or shadowing in it. The color of the green screen should not reflect back and spill onto the shoulder and side of your subject. Premiere Pro doesn't have any tools to fix that color spill, but you can turn instead to After Effect's Keylight and it's powerful spill suppression tools. If you are serious about your green/blue screen work then I won't pull any punches: You're better off using the After Effects Production Bundle and Keylight; if budgeting and a learning curve has got you down, however, this chapter showed you the way within Premiere.

Beyond green/blue screen keying, Premiere Pro's Garbage Matte effects enable you to crop your image. Simply drag the handles to remove entire sections or areas of your image.

Whether you enhance your image from the get go by having a cleaner brighter key (LiteRing) or you use another tool for compositing (After Effects or Ultimatte), this chapter has outlined and exposed a number of issues involved in the shooting and post-production process working with green/blue screen material.

This concludes the Advanced Effect Techniques section and from here you'll get into advanced editing and professional workflows, all of which build upon the foundation and rhythm of work that has been established thus far.

Advanced Editing

26

Advanced Editing: Creating Your Cut

To explore how Premiere Pro's timeline editing tools behave in a real-world environment, you will edit a typically photographed film scene in this chapter. Specifically, you will piece together an initial edit, inserting and overlaying footage from my short film, *Bleach*. As I did for the original scene, you will then clean up and fine-tune the rough cut using the Ripple Edit, Rolling Edit, Slip, Slide, and Trim tools.

Your editing should always be motivated by the story and ideas being articulated in the scene you are cutting. The story and its various scenes are captured with numerous shots from multiple angles, each with a different emphasis or focus. The available shots for this example scene are a straightforward mix of actor shots (medium shots) and point-of-view shots (of the objects or people at which the actor is looking, commonly referred to as POVs). You will have the flexibility, for instance, to cut from a shot of the character looking at something to a shot of what the character sees. Whether you show the character or the character's point of view (POV) will be dictated by the scene's rhythm and tempo. Finding that rhythm is the essence of editing.

Assembling Your Edit

When initially editing a scene, first identify the shots and takes that you like most. When I am working with an editor on a film, for example, I make sure I know all of my footage and material inside and out. I identify which shots convey the right emotion and have the actors' best performances. My initial rough cut of a scene is a loose edit based on the original script that was photographed. I cut from one shot to the next feeling out the story

For more information on *Bleach*, go to www.bleachyoursoul.com or www.formikafilms.com.

being told and the performances given. In many cases, the rough cut of Scene B, for example, may need to be overhauled once I see it in juxtaposition to Scenes A, C, and D.

To successfully reflect a scene's mood and tempo, you need to understand not only what's happening in the scene, but also how it fits into the film's greater story. In the example scene from *Bleach*, the main character, Fulton (played by Adam Scott), has already gone into his friend Zach's house to deliver some stereo equipment and get some money. While his girlfriend Laura (played by Katrina Bronson) impatiently waits for him to emerge, Fulton's recent sobriety is challenged by an uncanny offer from his crazed friend. With a promise to clean the stains from his life, Fulton returns to Laura with the money and a surprising new perspective.

The scene that you are editing is supposed to reveal through the eyes of Fulton that the world he sees is not the same as the world others see him in. Cutting from the dirty environment that he occupies to his "cleaned up" point of view, you will establish a distinct difference between the real world and the bleached world of Fulton's mind.

The Rough Cut

Continuity is important in editing; you do not want to surprise or jar the audience when cutting from one shot to another. Cutting on the movement in one shot to the movement in another shot is a way of making the editing feel more fluid. This technique is referred to as *continuity editing*.

Note that this lesson's edit is purposefully loose without exact continuity, so that I can demonstrate techniques to fix and clean an edit in the next lesson.

The steps in this section will guide you through an initial rough edit, explaining a specific order for placing all of the scene's clips. You will use the Ctrl modifier key to toggle between inserting and overlaying the clips. In the next lesson, you will trim and fine-tune the edits to make the scene flow better. As you become more comfortable in Premiere Pro, you will combine these three processes into a single workflow. For now, however, concentrate on the rough cut only.

1. Open Editing_Start.prproj in the APPST2 Lesson Files/Chapter 26 folder. Watch all the source material in the Video Files folder to become familiar with the entire content of each clip.

   I can't emphasize enough that you need a good understanding of the scene's flow. After linking all of the material to the project (all associated clips are in the

Chapter 26 folder), open and look at 13E_TK01. This clip is a master shot that shows the entire scene from beginning to end. Watching it, you can see the basic structure of the scene and perhaps start sensing when you want to cut and to which shot. Looking at the rest of the shots, you can see the options and choices you have; these are your shot selections.

2. Open clip 13E_TK02. Mark an In point at 12;00 and an Out point at 22;00. Add the clip to the head of the timeline using an Overlay edit (drag and drop it into position). Open clip 13G_TK02, mark the In point at 10;00, and the Out point at 18;00. With Snapping turned on, drop the second clip so it snaps to the end of the first. Open clip 18E_TK01, and mark In and Out points at 1;18 and 3;20, respectively. Overlay this clip after the second shot. Open clip 13G_TK01, mark an In at 11;07 and an Out at 27;13, then drag the clip into position at the end of 18E_TK01. Your edit should look like **Figure 26.1**.

   Clip 13E_TK02 is the master shot that establishes the scene's setting: Fulton sits down in the car and looks to his left at Laura, who appears as she is in reality.

   The key to this scene is Fulton's altered point-of-view, so you cut from the master, establishing shot to a medium

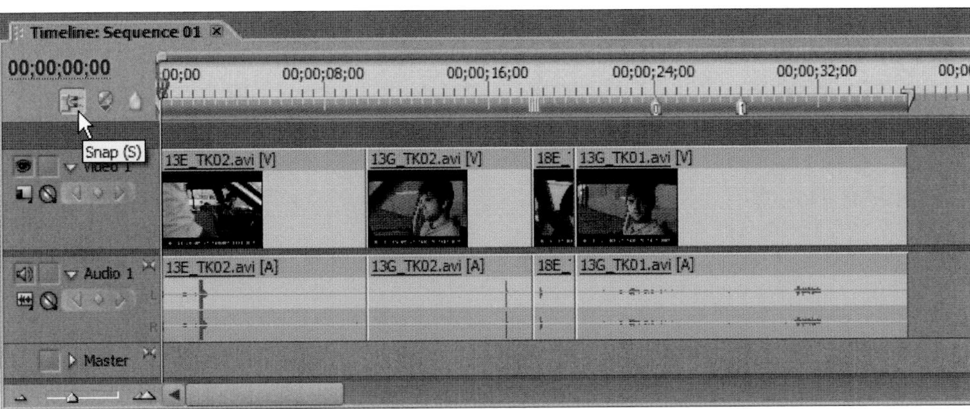

Figure 26.1 A first edit is not meant to flow perfectly from shot to shot. Once assembled, the shots and moments can be refined in a second pass. Here, the first four shots are placed back to back so that none of the material is edited out. Notice the Snap icon indicates Snapping is active (at top).

shot of Fulton turning his head to look at Laura. This edit works because the medium shot (13G_TK02) is of the character who is the focus of the scene and it continues the action of the scene. With the cut to the medium shot, you now see Fulton looking directly at Laura. He is clearly perplexed and responding to what he sees. His reaction in this medium shot motivates the next cut, which reveals his exact POV of Laura (18E_TK01).

To continue on with the scene and show him looking in the back seat, you edited in an alternate shot, 13G_TK01, in which he looks at Laura and then into the back seat.

3. Continue adding the necessary shots into the edit: Open clip PU_01 in the Source Monitor panel, mark an In point at 1;03 and an Out point at 8;03, and drop the clip at the end of 13G_TK01 (the fourth clip). Open a second instance of clip 13G_TK02 in the Source Monitor panel. (Do not double-click and open the instance already in the timeline.) Mark In and Out points at 29;13 and 42;26, respectively. Drop this down as the sixth clip. Finally, open a new instance of clip 13E_TK01, in the source side and mark an In at 47;17 and an Out at 51;13, and add it to the timeline as the seventh clip.

   From the fourth clip (13G_TK01) set in step 2, you cut to a POV shot of Fulton looking at himself in the side mirror (PU_01). You then cut back to the medium shot (13G_TK02), this time using a different take that has better eye contact and action that matches the previous shot. You finish the scene back on the master shot of the two characters seated in the car (13E_TK01).

4. So far, you have created a rough, shot-to-shot template and you still have to insert a few more shots (clips) into and between shots already in the edit. The same way you cut to the POV on Laura (18E_TK01) after the second shot, you now need to edit in the other POV shots in their proper places. **Table 26.1** lists markers for placing the remaining shots, as well as their In and Out points. To switch from the default Overlay mode, use the Ctrl key modifier while dragging and dropping for Insert edits. Your complete sequence should look like **Figure 26.2**.

Table 26.1: Shots and Edit Points

Shot	In Point	Out Point	Timeline Marker	Edit Type
18C_TK01	2;22	4;15	0	Overlay
18A_TK02	9;03	10;21	1	Insert
18E_TK01	4;15	10;25	2	Insert

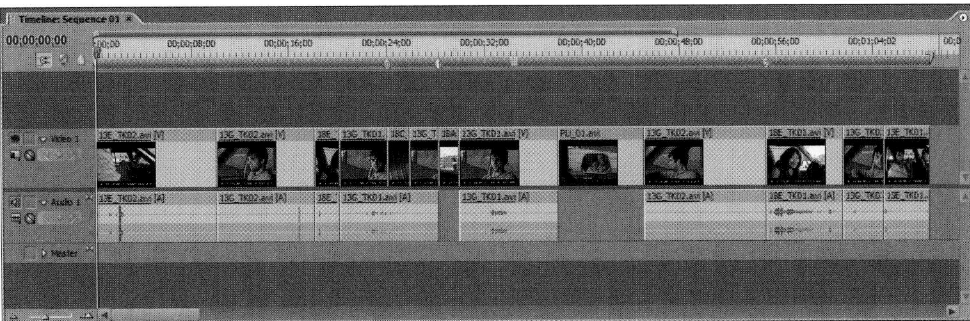

Figure 26.2 With all the shots in place, your rough cut is an exact copy of my initial cut of the scene for *Bleach*.

To follow the table, consider the example of inserting the second POV shot: Give 18A_TK02 an In point at 9;03 and an Out point at 10;21 in the Source panel. Insert it in the timeline at marker 1 by holding the Ctrl key while dragging it to the timeline. Holding the Ctrl key modifier switches from the default Overlay edit to an Insert edit.

You overlay the first shot on top of existing material because you want to preserve the timing of the moment, by not adding to it. By overlaying it you don't shift the placement or ripple any of the surrounding media. For the other two shots, you use Insert edits to add the material to the timeline and ripple the existing material right from the cut point, so that nothing is overwritten. Because the response time by the actor looking at each of the things in the car is not that long, you are extending those moments by inserting the Point of View shots and not overlaying them.

With all the pieces in place, pause and consider the scene you've made. Keep in mind the toggling of the edit modes (Insert/Overlay) that you used to piece the scene together, the snapping of clips, and the rhythm or flow of the scene.

Reflect and Reorganize

Play back the entire sequence to get a feel for the flow of the scene and the pacing of the cuts. I sat with this exact order of shots for this scene for a couple of months while we worked on the sound mix. Eventually, I decided it needed reworking, and re-edited the scene with a few very minor, but very effective changes. The next few steps reflect this re-editing and re-placement process. Using the Ctrl key to Extract and Insert edit, you will make a few simple changes to adjust and get the proper placement for the shots.

1. Right-click on clip 18A_TK02 at timeline marker 1, and select Ripple Delete.

   Because this clip was inserted into at timeline marker 1, ripple deleting the clip instance brings the separated shots back together by rippling the timeline media left to fill the gap that 18A occupied. If you scrub over the cut and observe the burned in timecode in the frame, you will see it flow continuously (**Figure 26.3**).

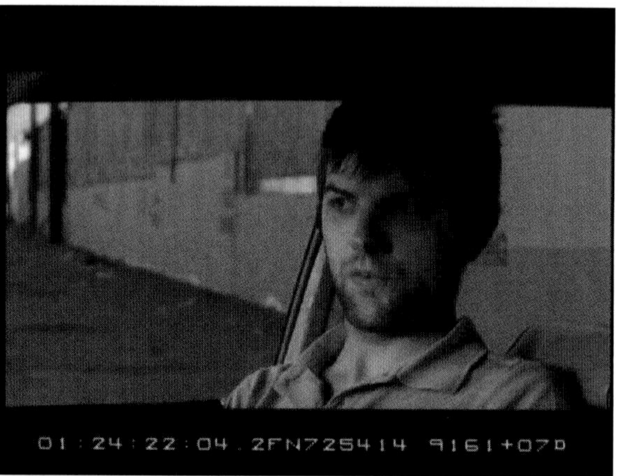

Figure 26.3 The numbers at the bottom of the video frame reflect timecode (left) and keycode (right). The timecode value is a window burn from the master Digibeta tapes onto which *Bleach* was transferred from film. The keycode numbers reflect the literal frame counting format from the original film negative. Using timecode and keycode you can find out where the shot originates on your video master and where the shot originates on your film negative.

   I removed this shot primarily because it seemed a bit overkill and unnecessary. I had already established that what he sees in the car is different from what is really in the car, so the shot of the dashboard was not as important as the shot of him looking around. In this case, more attention is given to Fulton and his realization that the car is different than at the beginning of the film.

2. Holding down the Ctrl key, grab (extract) the third clip in the sequence (18E_TK01), which is the first shot of Laura. Continuing to hold down the Ctrl key, insert the shot right before the second shot of Laura (18E_TK01) near timeline marker 2 (**Figures 26.4a** and **b**). Holding down the Ctrl key before selecting a clip puts the pointer tool in Extract mode. You may want to look at the figure before performing this edit.

a

b

Figures 26.4a and b Holding down the Ctrl key before you grab the first shot puts the Selection tool into Extract mode (a). Extract ripple deletes the selected clip from its current position when you drag it. Continuing to hold down Ctrl enables you to drop the shot at a new timeline position as an Insert edit (b).

3. Using the same technique, select the second, longer clip of Laura (18E_TK01, right next to the newly inserted shot), extract it, and then insert it at the cut that the previously moved clip occupied (**Figures 26.5a, b**, and **c**).

   In two moves, you swapped both shots and quickly changed the order of the edit. Swapping the two shots of Laura distinctly changed the rhythm and tone of

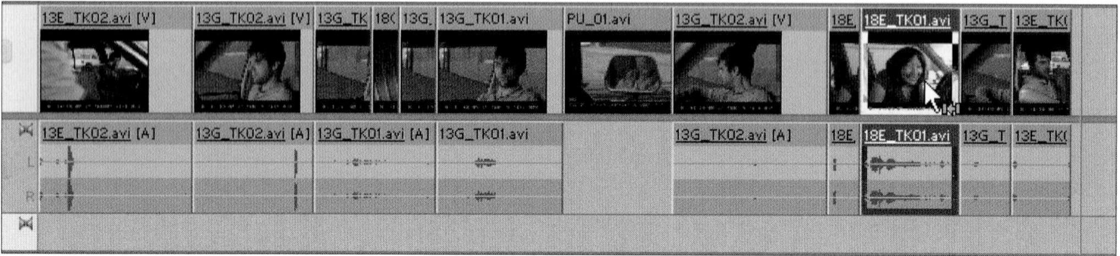

a

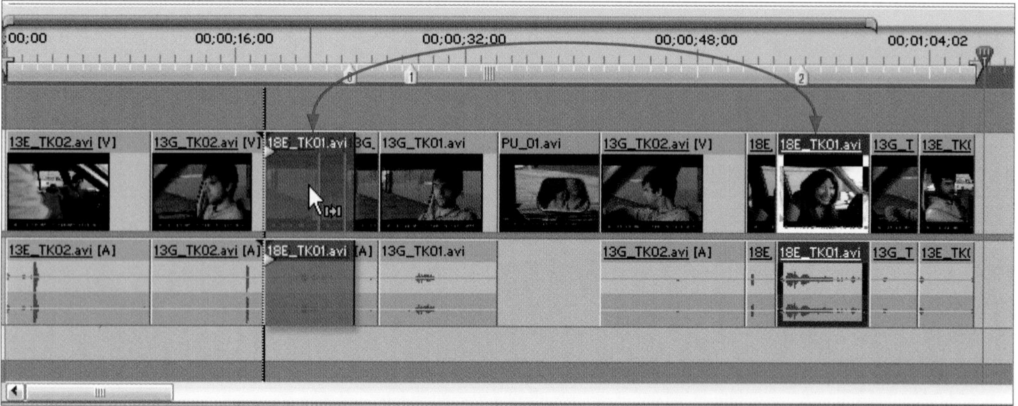

b

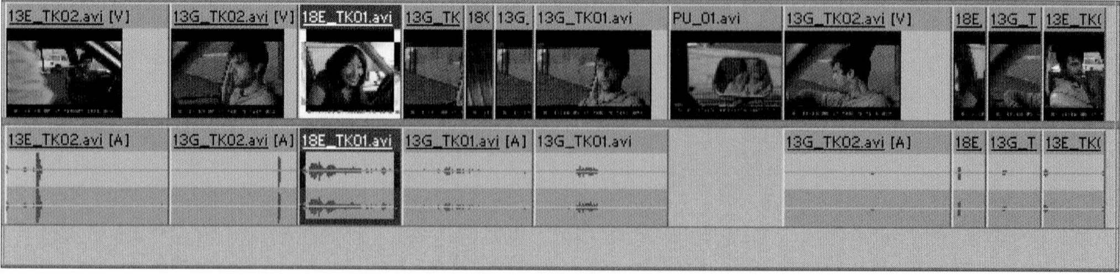

c

Figures 26.5a, b, and c The Extract tool icon appears next to the pointer as you Ctrl-grab the clip to move it (a). Continuing to hold the Ctrl key down, you are then in an Insert edit mode (b). Dropping the clip into the same position that the former clip (from Figure 26.4) occupied produces the revised cut (c).

the edit. In the former version, Fulton sat down and slowly took in the altered environment culminating in the dialog from Laura. In the adjusted version, Fulton is immediately engaged by Laura and her dialog. This image contradicts her portrayal throughout the film and the rest of the scene serves as a reassurance that the world Fulton perceives is truly different. In the last POV shot of Laura, she smiles at him in a manner affirming the fantasy. Two shots later, the audience sees a stark contrast to the POV images from Fulton's eyes and ends on a master shot of the two in the car.

With the adjustments made here, the sequence now reflects the final version of the film. Although the looseness of the edit still needs trimming, the basic scene structure is intact. The lesson establishes a workflow of finding the In and Out points in your source material, and then one by one editing the clips together. Using the Ctrl key, you can use the Insert, Overlay, Lift, and Extract edit functions to quickly add, replace, and shuffle the material of your edit. Now it's time to play with the tool box!

Trimming and Modifying Your Edit

Now that you have the pieces and structure in place, you need to clean up the edit and adjust the timing to fit the flow of the scene. In this lesson, you will establish continuity of action between shots to create a better rhythm.

1. Open the project Trim_Start.prproj from the APPST2 Lesson Files/Chapter 26 folder. Notice that I renamed the timeline instances of each clip so it is easier to identify the clips and cut points that you need to adjust. You will start at the beginning of the timeline and work your way right.

   Also, notice that I no longer have a frame for my Source Monitor, instead I have my Program Monitor and Trim panel in one large frame above the frame for the Timeline panel.

2. With Video 1 and Audio 1 targeted in the Timeline panel, press Ctrl+T to open the Trim panel. Press Page Down to advance the Edit Line to the cut between shots 1 and 2

(**Figure 26.6**). Place the cursor within the frame boundary for the outgoing shot on the left, click and drag to the left, trimming off –3;19 of material; the new Out point for the clip should be 18;12 (**Figure 26.7**). Using the Jog wheel below the incoming shot, jog to the right to move the In point to 11;19, which is a shift of +1;19 (**Figure 26.8**). Press Play Edit to preview the trim that you just made.

If your Trim panel is not open in your workspace, after you press Ctrl+T to open it, dock it in the frame with the Program Monitor.

To cut from shot 1 to shot 2 without the edit feeling too abrupt, you want to cut in the middle of action or movement that hopefully exists in both shots. You trimmed off the tail of the first shot and the head of the second shot so that as the character's head turns left you cut from one shot to the other. When you have a rough cut

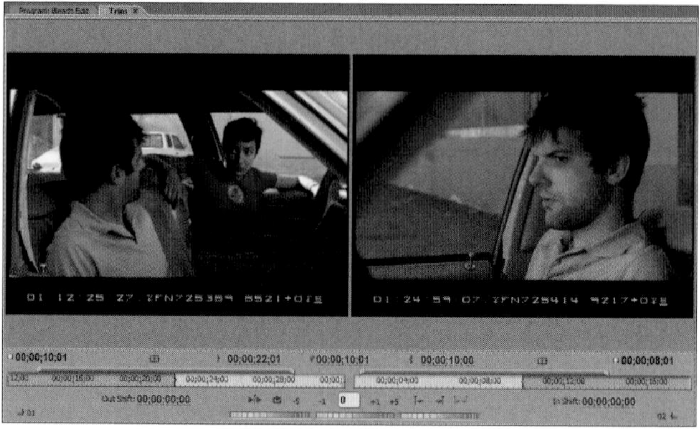

Figure 26.6 The Trim panel enables you to perform Ripple and Rolling edits on the cut points between material in your sequence. The left frame shows the outgoing shot, and the right frame, the incoming. Like the Ripple Edit tool in the timeline, the Trim panel enables you to grab the edge of a clip and drag it, but with greater clarity because of the frame size and detailed window feedback.

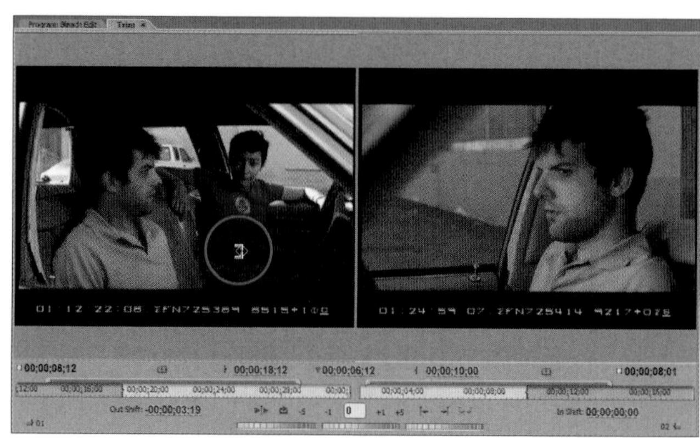

Figure 26.7 Holding the cursor inside the frame boundary puts the Trim panel into Ripple Edit mode. Clicking and dragging left inside the outgoing frame reduces the duration of the clip being trimmed. All the material to the right of the cut will be shifted left so that no gaps are created between the shots. Notice the out shift is –3;19, meaning 3 seconds and 19 frames have been trimmed off and the new Out point of the subclip in the timeline is 18;12.

Figure 26.8 The same way clicking and dragging within the frame enables you to perform a Ripple edit, jogging the wheel below either the outgoing or incoming shot achieves the same effect. Dragging to the right on the incoming shot trims off material from the head of the subclip in the timeline. Jogging the wheel to the left adds material to the head of the incoming shot. In both cases, a Ripple edit occurs either replacing the space created or pushing material right to make room for added content.

sketched out, it's very simple and easy to open the Trim panel, trim the Out and In points at each cut, preview the adjustments, then move on to the next cut.

3. With the Trim panel still open on the cut between shots 1 and 2, click in the gray space below the two frames and above the center counter so that the blue selection line runs below both images. Enter 9 in the text box above the center jog wheel. Press Enter, then press Play Edit to preview the adjustment (**Figure 26.9**). Activate the Program Monitor.

   With both clips selected, entering a value of 9 rolls the edit forward nine frames, so that the Out point from the outgoing shot is extended by nine frames and the In point from the incoming shot is reduced by the same number. Positive values roll the edit right, and negative

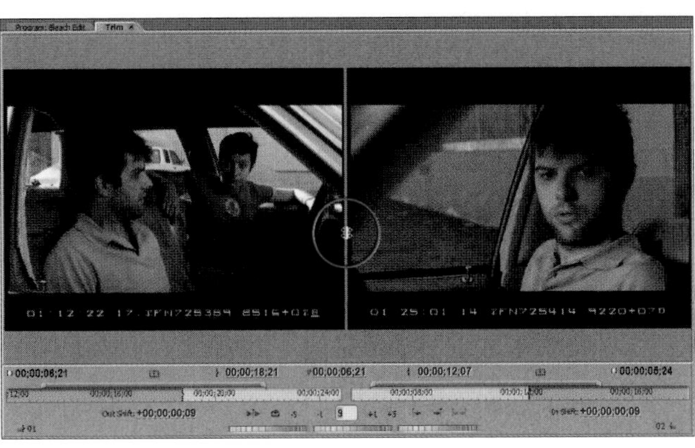

Figure 26.9 Holding the cursor in the gray space between the two frames reveals the Rolling Edit tool. If dragged to the right, the Rolling Edit tool synchronously extends the Out point of the outgoing shot and retracts the In point of the incoming shot. Dragging left extends the In point of the incoming shot and retracts the Out point of the outgoing shot. In both cases, there is no shifting or rippling of the timeline, only the edit rolls to reveal a new cut point between the shots. The center jog wheel is the one for rolling the edit. The empty text box above the center jog is for entering edit adjustment values (frames or samples). If you select the left frame, the entered value ripples the number of frames entered; the same applies if you choose the right frame. If you select both frames as pictured (note the blue underline under both images), the value entered rolls both clips.

TIP

The Trim panel is essentially a glorified Ripple and Rolling Edit tool that enables you to clearly see the frame you are trimming. Additionally, you have corresponding visual data about the entire range of the clip you are trimming, the number of frames you are trimming off or adding, and so forth. Although using the Ripple Edit tool in the timeline reveals a two-up display in the Program Monitor, the Trim panel can be as large as you like with a lot more detailed information.

A few rules about the Trim panel: To trim linked audio and video tracks together, both audio and video tracks need to be targeted in the track header area. To trim just video, target only the video track you want to trim. To trim just audio, target only the audio track you want to trim. If you happen to move the Edit Line off of a cut point in your sequence, the Trim panel will continue to display the previously loaded cut point.

values roll the edit left. In this trim adjustment, you rolled the cut point between shots 1 and 2 to a spot a bit more in the middle of the action for a more subtle cut.

4. Back in the timeline, make sure Snapping is turned on and move the Edit Line to 11;00. Hold down the Ctrl key to toggle the Selection tool to the Ripple Edit tool. Click and drag from the tail of clip 2 to the left, snapping the edit to the Edit Line (**Figure 26.10**). Move the Edit Line to 13;19, and holding down the CTRL key, ripple the In point of clip 3 so that it snaps to the Edit Line.

Figure 26.10 Holding down the Ctrl key turns the Selection tool into the Ripple Edit tool. Using the Edit Line as a guide to the new cut point's location, you can drag and snap the Out point of shot 2 to the Edit Line. When using the Ripple Edit tool, notice how the Program Monitor reveals the small two-up displays of the frame being trimmed (left) and the first frame of the next shot (right). A new feature for 2.0 is that the source clip's timecode displays in the overlay so you know exactly which frame you are cutting on.

Using the Ctrl key, rippling an edit point in the timeline is quite quick and simple. First, scrub through the clip in the timeline to find the moment at which you want the cut to occur, then use the Ripple Edit tool to trim off the tail or head of the clip that needs trimming. Because of timeline snapping, you can have exact precision as to where the cut occurs.

For this cut, Fulton looks at Laura and you will notice that his eyes size her up. After his eyes go from down to up is a perfect moment to cut. Although this cuts in the middle of Laura's dialog, you will use the Rolling Edit tool to roll the audio cut separate from the video cut.

5. Press the N key to switch the cursor to the Rolling Edit tool. Hold down the Alt key, and click in Audio Track 01 at the cut point of clips 2 and 3. Click and roll the cut left –3;02 (**Figures 26.11a** and **b**). Press the V key to switch back to the Selection tool, move the edit before the clip 2, and play back the adjustment you made.

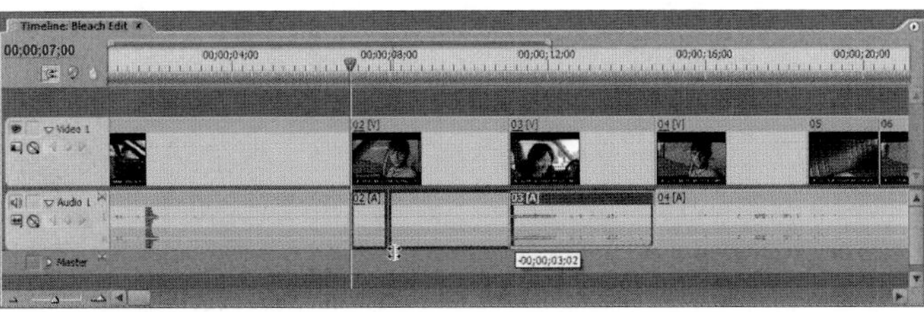

a

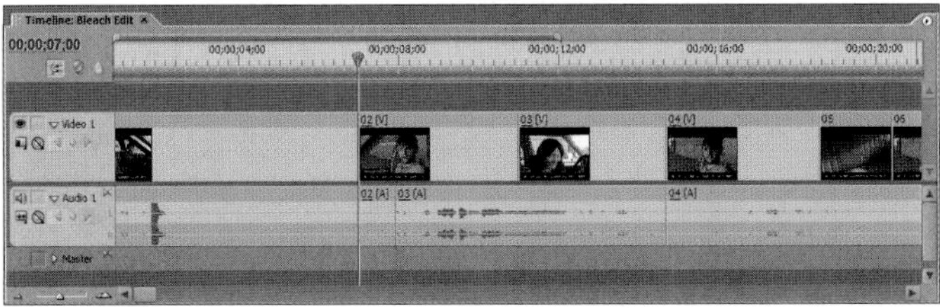

b

Figures 26.11a and b Holding down the Alt key allows you to temporarily break the link between the audio and video to select and adjust only one or the other. In this case, you are rolling only the audio edit between the two shots. When using the Rolling Edit tool, not only does the Program Monitor display your adjustments, but a new 2.0 tool tip tells you how far you have adjusted the cut (a). For this example, you needed to roll back –3 seconds and 2 frames. You can see that this was the perfect amount of time to allow for all of Laura's dialog (b).

The Alt key can be very useful when you want to trim and adjust the audio or video separately from each other. This can happen when you have an abrupt sound just before the end of a shot that is being used in your edit. Instead of trimming both the audio and video, you can try rolling the audio back a bit from the next shot in the sequence to cover the unwanted sound. In this case, you would want to be sure you had the extra material from the incoming shot to extend.

This edit is called a *J cut*, because the audio portion of shot 3 occurs before the video portion. An *L cut* is when the video cuts out before the audio cuts out. (These names are based on the shape of the letters, of course.)

The audio of Laura's voice further helps to motivate the cut to the POV of Fulton. Even though Adam's performance was not in response to Katrina speaking dialog, it looks as if he is quite taken by what he is seeing and hearing. I think it works very well.

6. Move the Edit Line to 14;04, and ripple the Out point of clip 3 to the Edit Line. Move the Edit Line to 15;07, and ripple the In point of clip 4 to the Edit Line. Move the Edit Line to 16;13, and press the U key to switch from the Selection tool to the Slide tool. Click and drag clip 5 left so that the left edge of the clip snaps to the Edit Line (**Figure 26.12**).

Figure 26.12 The Slide tool is essentially a double-sided tool for rolling edits. With it, you can select a clip and slide it left or right while retaining the clip's In and Out points. As you slide it left, you trim off frames from the adjacent clip to the left and reveal frames of the adjacent clip on the right. Notice how the four-up display in the Monitor window shows the In and Out frames from the selected clip smaller at the top. On the bottom, the large frames reveal the new Out point from the clip to its left and the new In point from the clip to its right. The tool tip in the timeline tells you how many frames you slid.

After adjusting the edit point for better timing between clips 3 and 4, you used the Slide tool to slide the entire clip 5 to the left. Now when Fulton looks to the back seat, the scene cuts directly to his POV shot. The Slide tool moves the entire selected clip, not just one edge. The Slide tool works very well when you have a clip that exists in the timeline for an exact duration and you want to adjust its position. The Slip tool, preserves the position of the selected clip, but modifies the content of the clip.

7. Press Y on your keyboard to select the Slip tool. Still working with clip 5, click and drag just slightly to the left for –10 frames (**Figure 26.13**). Release the mouse button, and play the section you just adjusted.

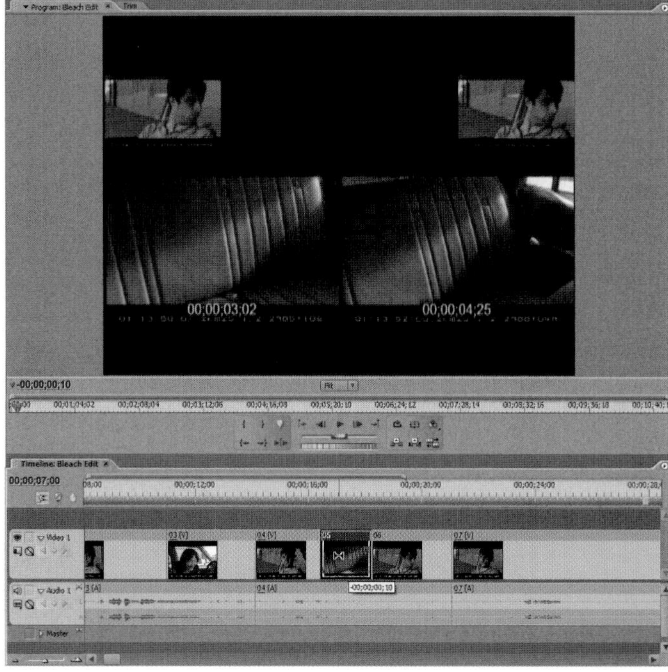

Figure 26.13 The Slip tool takes the defined edges of your edited clip in the timeline and slips the material left or right to reveal new content using the same duration and clip position. The four-up display shows the adjacent Out frame and In frame from left to right on the top with the updated slipped to In point on the bottom left and the slipped to Out point on the bottom right. The counter value in the bottom right corner displays the frame adjustment. Negative values equal slips left, and positive values slips right.

For this step, you slipped the clip material to reveal a different portion of the shot. The adjustment you made of –10 frames slipped the material up so that the beginning and end of clip 5 was ten frames later than before. This fit the head movements of the characters you were cutting from and to, much better. The Slip tool is very effective for updating the contents of a clip without disturbing the overall duration of the shot or affecting the surrounding media.

The Slide tool modifies the physical position of the clips being adjusted, but the Slip tool modifies just the material inside of the clip at its current timeline position.

The easiest way to visualize what the Slip tool does is to mark an In and Out point in a clip in the Source Monitor. The In and Out points have a specific duration, say one second. If you click in the center of the In/Out point markers in the Source Monitor, you can drag that In/Out duration to cover a different portion of the source clip. The Slip tool essentially does the same thing. As you drag left, you are slipping the content of the subclip left, revealing a later portion of the clip. If you drag right, you slip the clip material to the right, revealing an earlier portion of the clip.

8. Using the tools and techniques illustrated in this lesson, continue editing the sequence so that you have continuity of action and better timing for the rest of the cuts between the rest of the shots.

   To see what I came up with, open the Trim_Finished.prproj file from the APPST2 Lesson Files/Chapter 26 folder.

Despite the number of steps in this lesson, there are a great number of details and techniques to be extracted. Using the Ctrl key to quickly toggle from your Selection tool to the Ripple Edit tool is very intuitive. Using the Alt key to adjust only the audio or only the video of linked clips is another gem not to be forgotten. If at the end of the day, you find yourself struggling with the editing tools behavior, then you can use the Trim panel to help with a solid visual reference for Ripple and Rolling edits.

Keep in mind that you can make much more precise adjustments by zooming in to the timeline to increase the size of the frames.

Once you are comfortable with the editing tools and the ideas introduced in this chapter, I encourage you to stray from the lesson and explore a different version of the scene, trying to edit it in a slightly different manner with different timing or shot selection.

Things to Remember

At the end of the day, your content rules, so the more pre-planning and preparation you do before you shoot, the more secure the editing process can be. If you are unsure how to handle a scene, then take some risks and try some new ideas and shoot more than you need. Editing should serve the story, but should also reveal new ideas and new structure that may not have been anticipated before shooting. I see editing as possibly the single most important part of the filmmaking or videography process. In editing many problems can be solved and new options can be explored.

Once you understand which tool serves which purpose, editing efficiency simply becomes a matter of necessity. First you preview your material, then begin assembling it in a linear fashion. Using the Insert, Overlay, Extract, and Lift functions you can add or change the order. Moving a step further, use the timeline tools to make any small or large adjustment in relation to the accuracy and details of your edit. If you want a bit more control and details from your editing modifications, target specific tracks and use the Trim panel to adjust the cut point further.

When working with multiple scenes or different sections of a large project, I always find that the first and most important step is to roughly put together one scene in its own sequence. Instead of adding other scenes to the same sequence, make each new scene its own sequence with another sequence that is used to tie all the scenes together. The nesting of individual scenes reduces clutter and enables you to control and better manage the individual pieces of the project. For this workflow, I also make individual bins for each scene, with each holding the scene sequence and sub-bins containing all the footage for the scene.

In the next chapter, you will get your hands on some bona fide multi-cam material and edit a live three-camera shoot into a seamless sequence of shots.

CHAPTER

27

Advanced Editing: The New Multi-Cam Workflow

In the previous edition of this book, I dedicated two chapters to creating a custom workflow for multiple camera (multi-cam) editing. Premiere Pro 2.0 simplifies the process immensely, so this time the book offers this single chapter that contains a diverse range of examples and advice for honing your multi-cam editing technique.

When might you encounter multi-cam footage? Sporting events, the nightly news, music videos, and any shoot that has more than one camera shooting a single event simultaneously. To demonstrate the basic technique of the new multi-cam workflow, the first lesson walks you through editing a live three-camera shoot. In later lessons you'll explore alternate techniques while synchronizing and editing music video clips.

A successful multi-cam project requires attention to all phases of the production. How you set up your shoot, for example, affects your ability to synchronize the material from multiple cameras in post-production. This chapter will also provide shooting guidelines to ensure success. Let's get started with understanding synchronization, which serves as the basis for editing a multi-cam shoot.

Synchronization

The goal of a multiple-camera shoot is to record the same action from a variety of angles, getting different shots of the same moment. In a professional environment, such as a newsroom, multi-cam shoots are live and edited as they are shot. The command center of a multi-cam shoot is the *control room*, which houses a small screen for every camera and a *switcher*. The *live director* sits in the control room and calls out which cameras to cut to. The *live editors* then execute the edits on the switcher. Because the shoot is live, the cameras are automatically synchronized.

NOTES

If you are setting up a multi-cam shoot where some cameras are recording separate angles and cannot all identify the same image, you can use a camera flash bulb instead of a slate to create a sync point. Recording a slate relies on seeing the hinged clapper come together or hearing the clap; however, a flash bulb creates a short instantaneous burst of light that covers a very broad area. Because the moment of the actual flash can be isolated as a single frame of video, the frame of the flash occurring can be your sync point. After you recorded the sync point, keep all cameras recording until the shots are complete.

Without the luxury of multiple monitors and a live switcher, syncing your cameras requires a little more ingenuity: You need to first establish a clear *sync point* at which all of the cameras record the same thing before they record their individual shots. That sync point will be identified as the same moment in physical time, even though it exists at different tape positions in each camera that is recording.

An excellent way to establish a sync point for multiple camera shoots in which all cameras can record the same image is to clap a *slate*, like they do in the movies. This is the technique I used when recording the multi-cam footage for this chapter. First, you point every camera at the slate and start each camera recording. Clap the slate closed, and then continue recording with each camera until you have recorded *all* of the necessary material. After you establish the sync point, do *not* stop any of the cameras mid-shoot. If a camera does happen to stop, you must establish an intermediate sync point for that camera to be synchronized with the other cameras. Recording a new slate mark with the stopped camera and one of the already synchronized cameras, which continue recording, is usually enough.

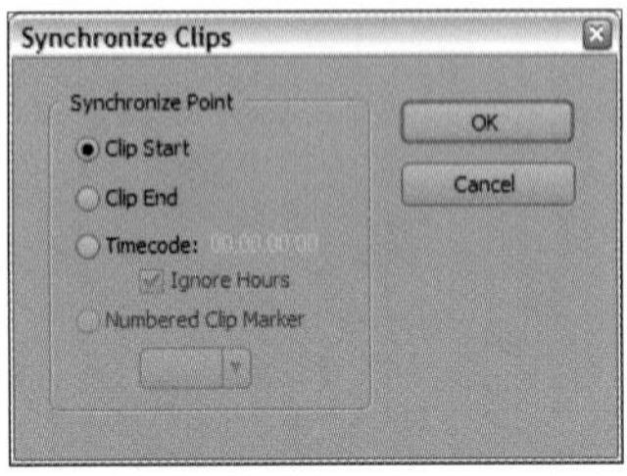

Figure 27.1 The new Synchronize Clips dialog speeds up the synchronization process by offering a choice of four sync methods. With at least two clips selected, you can synchronize them based on any of the parameters listed.

Once you get your footage into Premiere Pro, you'll use the Clip menu's new Synchronize feature, which enables you to synchronize your clips based on a variety of parameters (**Figure 27.1**). Jump into the first lesson and see how it works.

Editing a Multi-Cam Shoot

For this lesson you are going to open three video clips that comprise a multi-cam shoot. Because each camera produced a separate tape with different timecode, the resulting footage does not have a shared timecode value (**Figure 27.2**). Regardless of the timecode values of the individual clips, all the cameras do share one instance: the sync point (the slate clap). You will assign a Numbered marker to each slate clap and synchronize the clips in one quick step.

Although new, the entire multi-cam workflow is based on a fundamental concept that should be familiar: nesting At the workflow's most basic level, you place up to four clips in a "source" sequence, then nest that source sequence

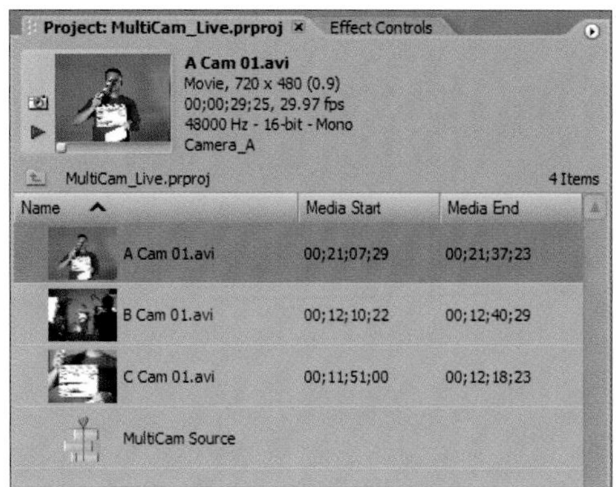

Figure 27.2 Each shot name is preceded by a letter—A, B, or C—that allows you to immediately distinguish between the shots (cameras). Notice how the Media Start timecode value for each shot is different; if the timecode was the same it would be easier to synchronize the clip.

into a new sequence. Using the new Multi-Camera Monitor you then execute edits on the nested sequence simulating the behavior of a switcher. This lesson serves as an overview of the workflow, focusing more on the features and behaviors of the Multi-Camera Monitor than on illustrating exactly when to cut between cameras.

NOTES

Before you embark on this lesson, you might find it valuable to watch the tutorial reviewing the new Multi-Cam workflow. To watch it, open the file Multicam_Workout.wmv, located in the Video Tutorials folder on the book's DVD. When the file loads in Windows Media Player, press Alt+Enter to play it back at full-screen size.

1. Open the Multi-Cam_Live.prproj project from the APPST2 Lesson Files/Chapter 27 folder.
2. In the Project panel you will see three clips, one for each camera of the multi-cam shoot. Double-click on A Cam 01.avi to open it in the Source Monitor. Scrub to 21;10;25 in the clip and right-click within the frame boundaries of the clip. Choose Set Clip Marker > Next Available Numbered (**Figure 27.3**). Double-click on B

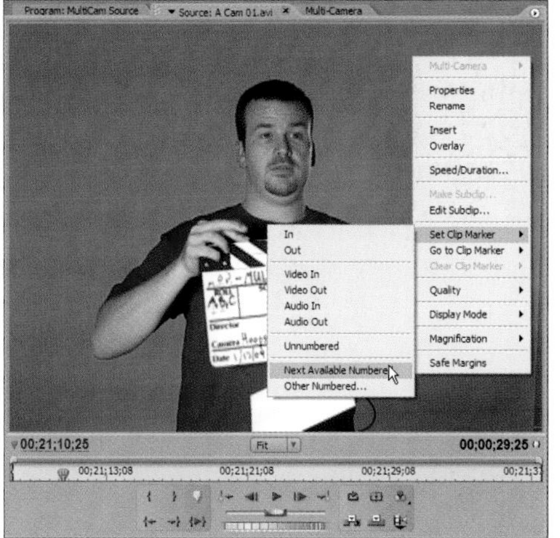

Figure 27.3 When you don't have matching timecode values to synchronize cameras you can create your own sync point and assign a Numbered marker to it: Right-click on the face of the clip in the Source Monitor and assign the Numbered marker.

Cam 01.avi to open it in the Source Monitor. Navigate to 12;13;10, right-click on the clip, and choose Set Clip Marker > Next Available Numbered. Finally, open C Cam 01.avi and assign a Numbered marker at frame 11;52;10.

Whenever you want to synchronize multiple cameras without the luxury of matching timecode, you need to scrub to the frame in each clip that reveals the slate clapping together (the sync point) and assign a Numbered marker to it. Premiere Pro automatically assigns the first marker in a clip the number "0." If you want another specific number instead, choose Set Clip Marker > Other Numbered and then type the number in the resulting dialog.

To use Premiere Pro 2.0's synchronization tools, you must use Numbered markers as opposed to unnumbered. This enables you to apply multiple markers with unique numbers that may be used for multiple sync points.

3. Open A Cam 01.avi from the tab menu of the Source Monitor then drag and drop the clip directly onto Video 1. Open and drop B Cam 01.avi onto Video 2. Open and drop C Cam 01.avi onto Video 3. With the Multi-Cam Source sequence active in the Timeline panel, press Ctrl+A to select the three clips. Right-click on the group and from the menu select Synchronize (**Figure 27.4a**). In the Synchronize Clips dialog click the button for Numbered Clip Marker, which designates the slate clap frame (the sync point), make sure the Numbered value below is set to 0, then click OK to realign the clips(**Figure 27.4b**).

Synchronization based on the Target track can be helpful when you want to align two clips, one of which you don't want to be moved. The Synchronize feature doesn't always have to be used for multi-cam scenarios and is available from either the right-click menu when more than two clips are selected in the timeline or from Clip > Synchronize when two or more clips are selected.

When you added the clips to individual tracks you should have noticed that each displayed an icon within the clip boundary signifying the 0 marker that you assigned. You chose to synchronize the clips based on this common marker, and Premiere Pro aligned the clips.

Notice how the clips on tracks 2 and 3 shifted to the right in to align with the position of the 0 marker on Video 1. Video 1 was the Target track when you executed the Synchronize command. When you synchronize clips, the clips in the non-targeted tracks dynamically shift so that they align with the sync point of the clip on the targeted track. I will refer to the clip on Video 1 as the *Guide track.*

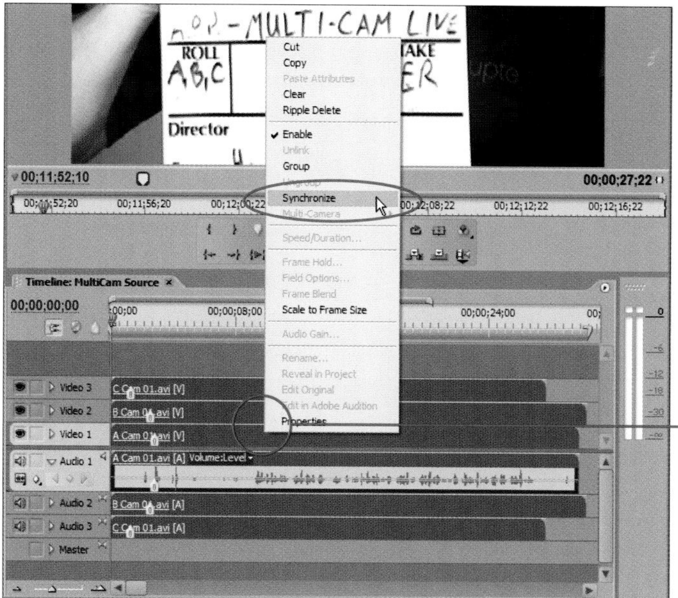

a

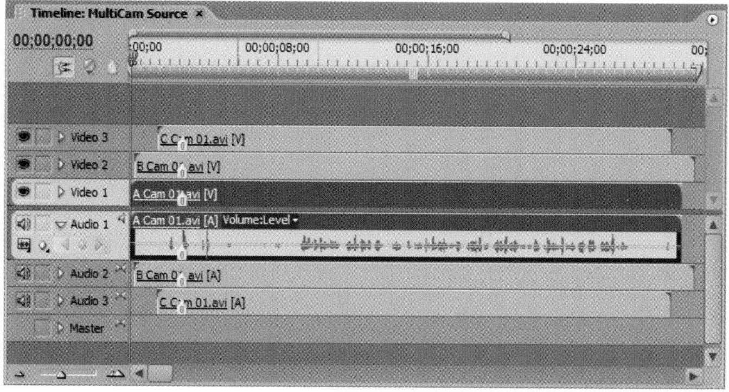

b

Figures 27.4a and b Select the clips you want to synchronize, right-click on them, and choose Synchronize from the menu (a). After setting the Numbered marker to 0 in the Synchronized Clips dialog, Premiere Pro then realigns the clips (b).

4. At the bottom of the Project panel click the New Item icon and create a new sequence. Name it Multi-Cam Edit and assign it one video track and one stereo track with Audio Master set to Stereo. The sequence will automatically open in the Timeline panel. From the Project panel, grab the icon for the Multi-Cam Source sequence and drop it onto Video 1 of the Multi-Cam Edit sequence. Press the / key to zoom into your timeline, then right-click on the nested Multi-Cam Source sequence and choose Multi-Camera > Enable (see **Figure 27.5**).

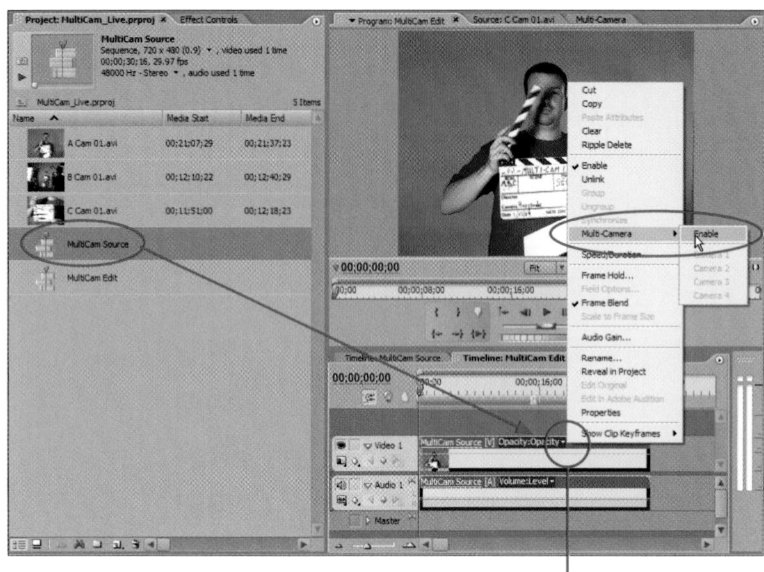

Figure 27.5 Here you can see the Multi-Cam Source sequence nested into the Multi-Cam Edit sequence. Keep in mind the Multi-Cam Source sequence has three synchronized tracks of video in it. Right-click on the Multi-Cam Source sequence and select Multi-Camera > Enable to effectively tag this nested sequence as eligible for editing using the new Multi-Camera Monitor.

Technically any sequence with more than one layer of video that is nested into another sequence can be enabled for multi-camera monitoring and editing. This means that when you open the Multi-Camera Monitor for the enabled sequence you have the ability to see up to four tracks of source content from the nested sequence.

Remember, to perform multi-cam edits using the new Multi-Camera Monitor you must use nesting. Here, you nested the Multi-Cam Source sequence, which is composed of three synchronized video tracks, into the Multi-Cam Edit sequence. Because the nested sequence is filled with multi-camera material synchronized and on separate tracks, you enabled the Multi-Cam Source sequence (now a nested clip) for multi-camera monitoring and editing.

5. From the wing menu of the Program Monitor select Multi-Camera Monitor (**Figure 27.6a**). Dock the Multi-Camera Monitor into your workspace so that you can see the Timeline panel and the Multi-Camera Monitor at the same time. I typically dock it into the same Frame as my Program Monitor (**Figure 27.6b**). It's time to edit! Click the Play button in the Multi-Camera Monitor and as the video plays press the 1 key on your keyboard (*not* on the numeric keypad). Let the clip keep playing, and after a moment or two, press the 2 key. Let the clip continue playing; then press the 3 key, and then finally press the spacebar to stop playback.

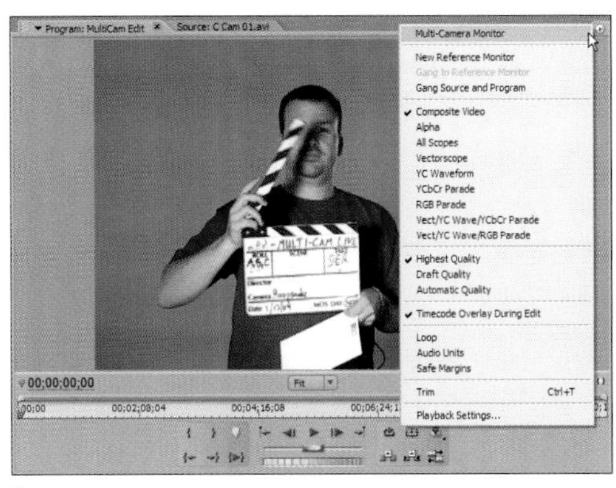

a

Source side

Preview side

b

Camera 1 = Video 1

Camera 2 = Video 2

Camera 3 = Video 3

Camera 4 = Video 4

Record

Figures 27.6a and b With the Multi-Cam Edit sequence active, clicking on the Multi-Camera Monitor listing from the wing menu (a) opens the Multi-Camera Monitor (b) which is a quad-view monitor that allows you to play back and execute multi-camera edits from up to four sources. Because the monitor is displaying the beginning of the nested clip, the only track that currently has video is Video 1, which is considered Camera 1 (top left).

As you most likely deduced, once the nested sequence was enabled for multi-camera monitoring, the Multi-Camera Monitor revealed the tracks of the Multi-Cam Source sequence in the left side of the Multi-Camera Monitor. As you play back, the clips play in the four-square quadrant. Because the clips were properly synchronized they play in unison (**Figure 27.7**). The

Figure 27.7 Because the clips were properly synchronized in the Source sequence, my gestures match in each of the quadrants showing video.

tracks of the nested sequence reveal themselves in the quadrant in a left-to-right, top-to-bottom fashion. Video 1 plays in the top left and should be referred to as Multi-Camera (MC) 1, Video 2 or MC 2 plays in the top right, Video 3 or MC 3 is in the bottom left, MC 4/Video 4 is in the bottom right. Because there is no Video 4 in this nested multi-cam sequence the fourth quadrant is empty. Since at the beginning of the sequence tracks 2 and 3 are empty, only MC 1 shows an image.

Once you engage playback and the Multi-Camera Monitor plays the nested sequence you can use the keyboard's 1, 2, 3, and 4 keys to execute a cut/take to the video track (MC) to which you want to switch. When you pressed 1 to "take" MC1, a red record square surrounded the activated quadrant and the preview side (right side) of the Multi-Camera Monitor displayed Video 1 in full frame. At the same time, an edit was performed in the timeline, slicing the nested sequence and updating it to reference the camera being switched to: MC1 (**Figure 27.8**). The moment you

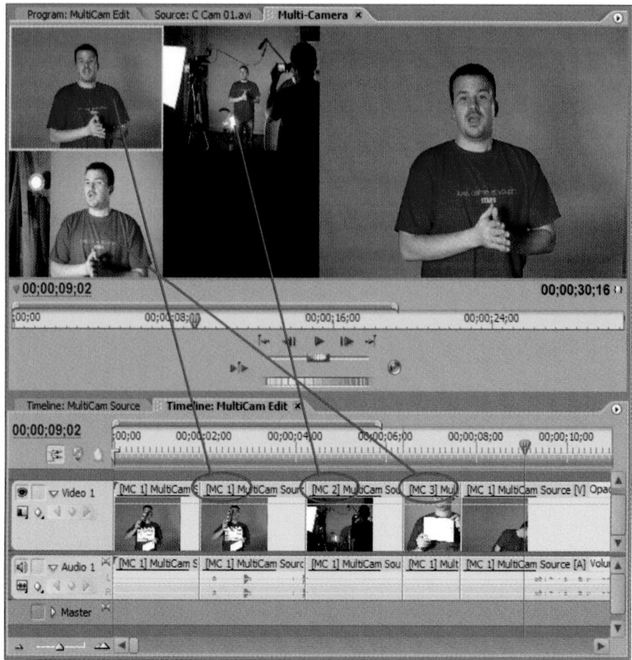

Figure 27.8 This timeline should be similar to yours at the end of step 4. Notice the prefix "[MC1]" Before the clip names. This was added because the default track for any multi-camera sequence is Video 1, which is referred to by the initials MC1. When you executed an edit by pressing 2, which is associated with Video 2 of the nested sequence, Premiere Pro performs a physical edit on the nested sequence. Because you are cut to a different track of the same nested sequence, its name updated to [MC2] Multi-Cam Source and the timeline displayed the thumbnail associated with Video 2 from that point.

pressed 2, the Multi-Camera Monitor executed another edit to the timeline (MC2) and in unison switched to display Video 2 in the Preview area. MC2 in the Source area took on a red border. Pressing 3 applied a cut in the timeline, which referenced MC3, and the Multi-Camera Monitor updated accordingly. Although the Multi-Camera Monitor continued playing during this process, updating the monitor quadrants and preview area along the way, the timeline did update until you stopped playback.

Now that you know the keyboard short cuts to switch between cameras, try clicking directly on the quadrants to switch cameras.

6. With the Edit Line in the same position as at the end of the last step, click Play in the Multi-Camera Monitor. As the video plays back, click directly onto the multi-camera quadrants: 1 (wait a few seconds), 2 (wait a few seconds), 3 (wait a few seconds), then click Stop. Position the Edit Line back at the beginning of the Multi-Camera Monitor's time viewing area, then click Play to watch the edit. This time, don't click on any quadrants. As the Monitor plays, pay attention to the yellow selection square in the camera area and the edits below in the timeline.

   Just as you can switch between cameras by pressing the number key associated with the Multi-Camera source, you can also click directly on the quadrant to which you wish to cut as the Monitor plays back. When you click on a camera/quadrant it is surrounded by a red square indicating it is the current shot being recorded to the timeline. By clicking on another camera or pressing one of the four camera buttons you can dynamically cut to the new selected camera, which creates a new edit in the timeline.

With the Multi-Cam Monitor open and a multi-cam-enabled clip active you can always get feedback as to which camera is being used at which time as you scrub or playback the timeline. A yellow border indicates the current camera during non-recording playback, while a red border indicates that you are recording your edits.

7. Position the Edit Line back at the beginning of the sequence and click Play in the active Multi-Camera Monitor. Press 3 immediately as the timeline plays back to take MC3. After the slate clap, press 1. After I put down the White Card press 2. As I verbally call out each

camera in the shots, press the buttons associated with them in unison: 1, 2, and 3. Press the spacebar to stop.

By having you execute an edit based on cutting to specific camera angles at exact times, this step shows one very important thing: When you play back a multi-camera sequence that has already been edited you can easily overwrite the edit by executing new camera decisions. This means that if you ever have a section of your multi-cam sequence that you want to redo, you can always just position the Edit Line over that section, click Play in the Multi-Camera Monitor, and try a different edit combination by clicking in the quadrants or pressing camera number keys. When you reach the end of the section you want to adjust, stop playback. If you click Play again and don't click any quadrants or press any camera keys, the edit will play as a preview in the Multi-Camera Monitor.

8. In the Timeline panel, position the Edit Line at 00;00;12;21. At this point in the timeline your Edit Line should either be on MC2 or MC1. Press the N key to switch your Selection tool to the Rolling Edit tool. Find the cut point of MC2 to MC1 and click on it with the Rolling Edit tool. Holding down the mouse, roll the cut point over to the Edit Line at 12;21 (**Figures 27.9a** and **b**), then release the mouse button. Position the Edit Line at 00;00;14;19 and using the same tool, drag the MC1-to-MC2 cut point to the Edit Line. Finally, position the Edit Line at 00;00;16;01 and roll the MC2-to-MC3 cut point to it. Press the V key to toggle back to the Selection tool.

   Rather than trimming material off the clips and altering the shots' synchronization, the Rolling Edit tool does not physically move the clips in the timeline. Instead it allows you to roll the cut point between two clips to a different moment in time. In any multi-camera scenario, always use the Rolling Edit tool when you want to modify the timing of the cuts between cameras. If you don't, you will throw off the synchronization established between the clips in their source sequence.

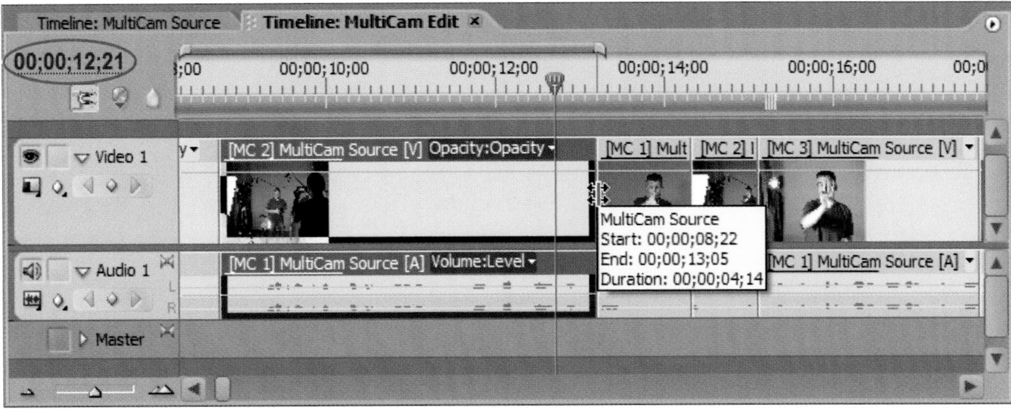

a

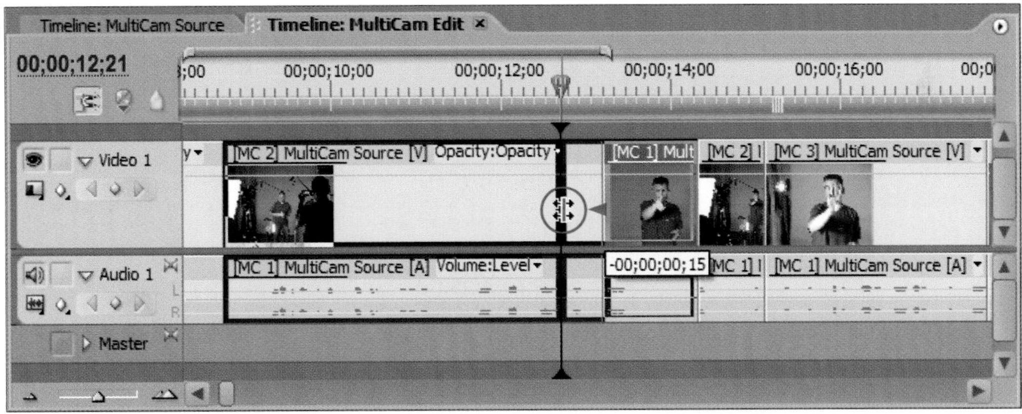

b

Figures 27.9a and b As you modify the cut point with the Rolling Edit tool (a), the clips don't physically move; the clips just cut earlier in time (b). Using the Edit Line to define the moment at which you want to new cut to occur allows you to have a physical "snapping" point to execute the edit easier.

9. Right-click on the MC2 instance before the 1,2,3 edit you executed in step 8 (just before 00;00;12;21). In the menu that appears, select Multi-Camera and from the submenu select Camera 3 (see **Figure 27.10a**). Press the Home key and play back your sequence to view the results (see **Figure 27.10b**).

   This final step revealed a helpful feature that allows you to quickly swap the camera angles in your edited sequence. If you ever have a multi-cam edit in which you want to swap one camera angle for another you

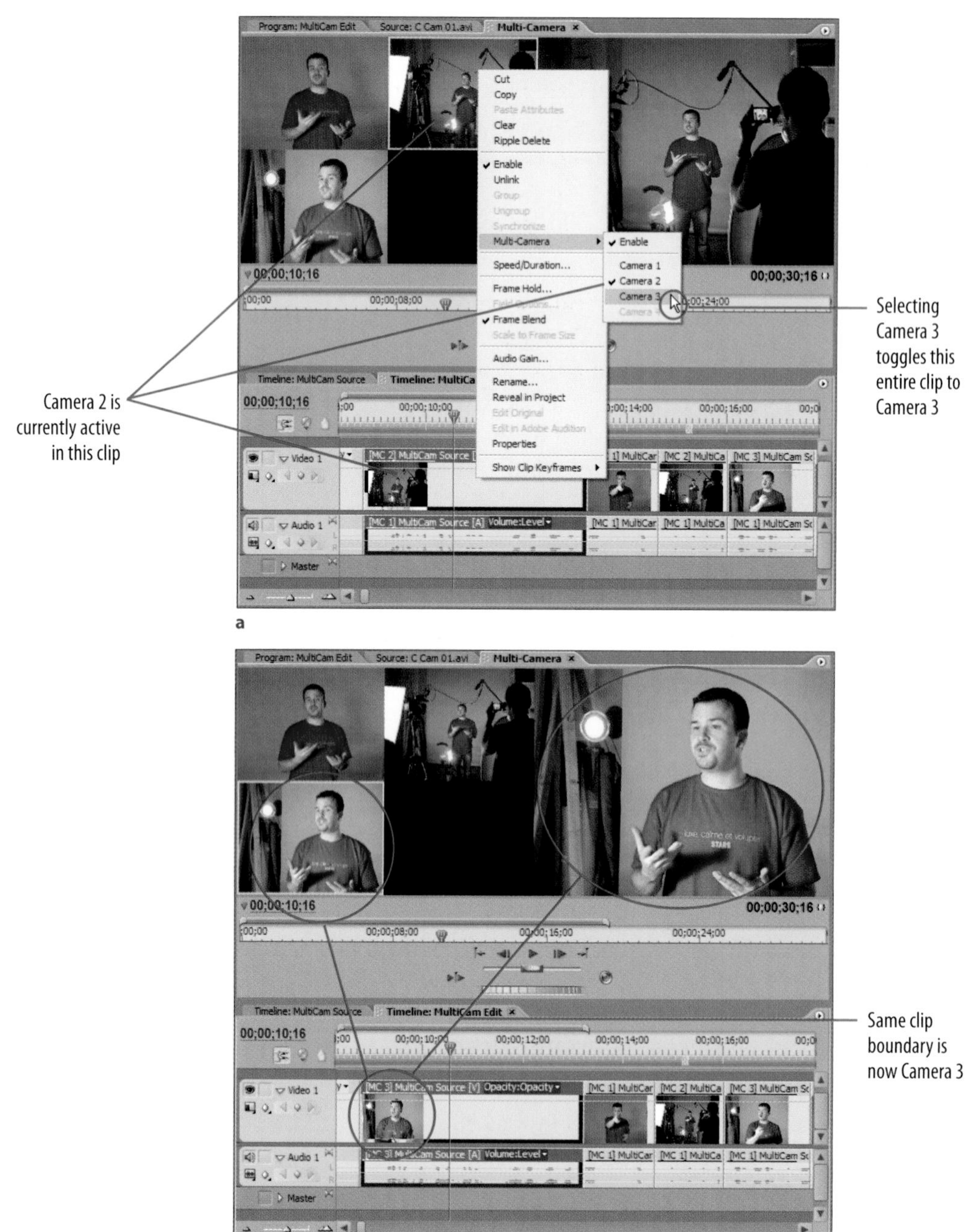

Figures 27.10a and b Right-click on any multi-camera clip to access the Multi-Camera menu, which indicates via a check mark which camera is active in the clip boundary (a). Choosing an alternate camera from the Multi-Camera menu updates the selected clip with that camera's footage within the same space allotted in the timeline (b). Notice that the MC2 clip updates to MC3 within the exact same clip boundary.

can right-click on the current clip instance (the one you want to update) and choose from any of the other three cameras in the Multi-Camera submenu. Selecting another camera updates the clip instance in the timeline, replacing it with the new camera you selected. Instead of updating the entire nested sequence, only the boundaries of the edited nested clip that you select are updated.

Learning the multi-cam workflow is really a matter of familiarizing yourself with the tools. This lesson established the basics of using the tools and is geared toward editing a specific three-camera type of shoot; it certainly doesn't address every type of question that could arise in your own specific project. With that in mind it's my goal to give you actual multi-camera material so that you can learn the technique and figure out the way in which you want to work so that it suits you best. The contents of this first lesson will be invaluable for that and I encourage you to try this lesson a few times if it doesn't click at first.

I'll next address the techniques for creating synchronization for clips with unified timecode or clips that require synchronization but have no slate to designate an exact sync point. These clips come from two music videos I directed back around the turn of the century.

Editing a Music Video

Synchronizing and editing music videos can be quite simple, especially when you think of them as multiple camera shoots. The only difference is that in a music video, you shoot the same song 30 times from 30 different angles, instead of shooting with 30 cameras at once.

Building on the foundation established in the first lesson, these next two lessons will show you how to synchronize alternate source material. In the chapter's first lesson, you will use the "eye match" method of synchronization, which involves matching a moment in the video clip when you can clearly make out the word the singer is singing with the same word being sung in the soundtrack. The second lesson matches moments with the assistance of a Smart Slate for a sound reference. A

Smart Slate is basically a slate with a digital readout that displays the timecode value of the music tape being used for playback during the music video.

Whichever method you choose for your own projects, by the end of the chapter you will be able to easily and efficiently create sync between your audio and video.

As you read through the next few pages, you'll find the YNK and IYM Media subfolders in the APPST2 Lesson Files/Chapter 27 folder on the disc.

Eye Matching

On a music video set, the band performing needs music to lip sync to while the film/video is recording, so that when you edit it together the band appears to be really singing the song. The most basic method of synchronizing video and audio is the eye match technique: Through sharp-eyed observation, you clearly identify a word being sung on the video clip and match that moment with the instant the same word is sung in the soundtrack. This technique is well suited for low-budget music videos shot on film and for synchronizing a videotaped performance with the original song. For the technique to work, you need to make sure that the sound being played back while you were filming the video is the same sound being used to synchronize the video in the editing room.

For the sake of this lesson, assume that you have captured the audio for your song off of a DAT (digital audio tape) or copied it from a CD. You also captured four clips that reflect four different shots. You, of course, know the lyrics to the song inside and out. This last point is very important for the eye match technique, because you need to be able to follow the song without having to consult the music and be able to clearly identify moments where specific words that are easy to spot are being sung. Believe me, after spending a day shooting one song, you will never forget the words!

1. Open the YNK_Start.prproj project file from the APPST 2 Lesson Files/Chapter 27 folder. With the Multi-Cam Source sequence open in the Timeline panel, open the YNK_Audio.wav from the Project panel in the Source Monitor. Navigate to 25;25 and right-click on the clip choosing Set Marker > Next Available Marker for that frame. Drag and drop the clip on the beginning of the timeline in Audio 1.

With the audio file open, the first step in the eye match technique is to identify a moment where the word being spoken has an obvious *plosive.* In this case, you identified the "ttt" sound as the artist says the word "towel," assigned the first available marker (0) to that exact frame, and dropped the marked clip into the timeline. The synchronization tool discussed in the last lesson can work on any type of file in the sequence, so the 0 marker of the audio file will become the sync point to which all of the video clips will sync.

2. From the Project panel open the YNK_Beach01.avi file in the Source window. Scrub the CTI to 16;06, and set the next available marker to that frame. Drag and drop the clip down into Video 1. Open YNK_Mall01.avi, and apply the next available marker at 15;20. Drop the clip into Video 2 of the timeline. Open YNK_Market02. avi, apply the next available marker at 17;10 and drop it onto Video 3. Open YNK_Store01.avi and apply the next available marker at 17;10 (yes, the same frame), then drop it onto Video 4 (**Figure 27.11**).

Figure 27.11 Here you can see the four takes for the one verse of the song, each on a separate track with a 0 Numbered marker specifying the same moment in time relative to the song being sung.

In this step you opened each of the shots and identified the exact frame in which the artist is making the sound that you marked in the audio file "towel." You applied the same Numbered marker to each of these shots and then added them to their own track in the timeline. Now it's time to sync them up.

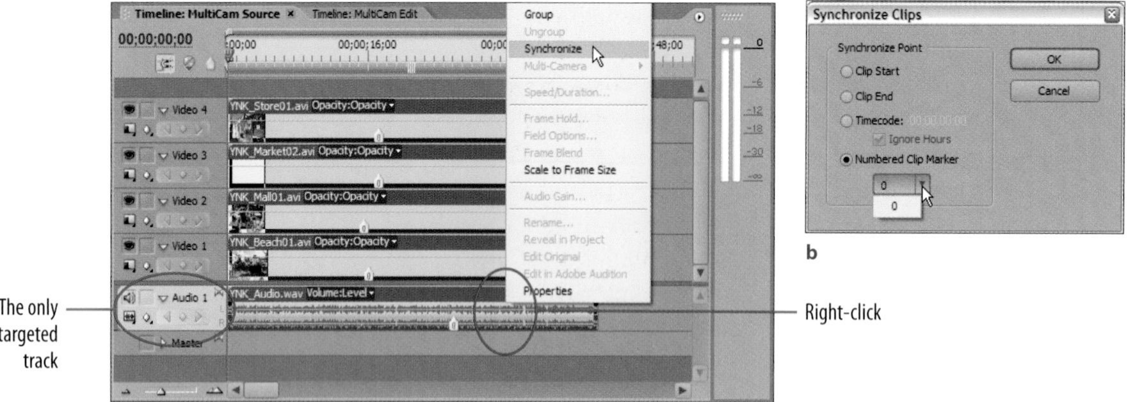

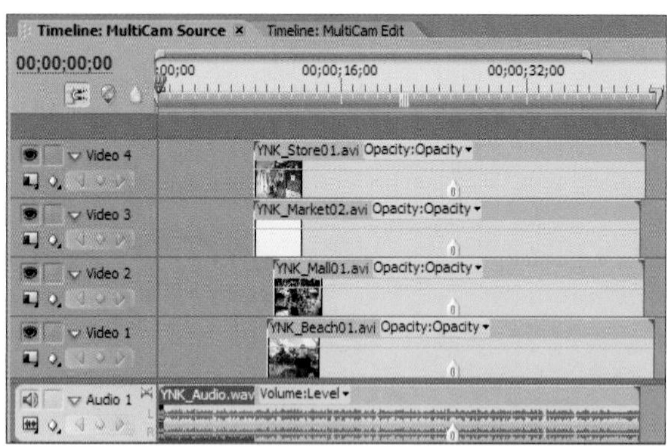

Figures 27.12a, b, and c The only track that is targeted is Audio 1 (a). Because Audio 1 and all the rest of the clips have a 0 Numbered marker for the same point in time, you select Numbered Clip Marker 0 in the Synchronize Clips dialog (b). All the video clips shift right to align with the Audio clip's sync point (c).

3. Click in the Track header for Video 1 so that it turns a darker gray and ensure that Audio 1 is the only targeted track and appears light gray (**Figure 27.12a**). Select all of the clips in the timeline and right-click on one of them. From the right-click menu select Synchronize. From the Synchronize Clips dialog select Numbered Marker 0 and click OK (**Figures 27.12b** and **c**).

   In this step you targeted only Audio 1, which holds your master sync point to which you want all the video clips to align. By targeting only Audio 1 and none of the other video tracks, when you executed the Synchronize Clips command the video clips shifted to the right to align themselves so that the 0 marker in each of the clips lined up with the 0 marker in the YNK_Audio.wav in Audio 1.

4. Your hard work of synchronizing the clips is done; now you just need to nest the sequence, enable it for Multi-Camera, and make your edit. Open the Multi-Cam Edit sequence in the Timeline panel. Drag and drop the Multi-Cam Source sequence from the Project panel into Video 1 of the Multi-Cam Edit sequence. Right-click on the nested clip sequence and from the menu that appears select Multi-Camera > Enable. With Multi-Camera enabled, open the Multi-Camera Monitor from the Program Monitor's wing menu, click Play, and edit away.

   This step finishes the process of composing and setting yourself up to finally start multi-camera editing. First you nested the source sequence, which is synchronized and holds all of your shots, into another sequence You then selected this new nested sequence and enabled it for multi-camera editing. Opening the Multi-Camera Monitor you can now dynamically switch and create your own edit of the video.

As this lesson demonstrates, you can assign a marker to an audio-only file and use it to synchronize video clips. Music videos shot on film yield this type of a workflow because film does not record audio. Instead, you have to synchronize the video to the audio in post. If you shoot your music video on a video format that does have audio on it, but the quality is bad, you can use this same workflow with a slight adjustment: Place a Numbered marker at the same point in each clip and in your master audio (Audio 1 in your Source sequence). Then turn the audio off for each source video clip and add the video clips to the timeline synchronizing them to the audio master track. The final lesson illustrates a scenario in which you might have a bit more money for a few extra on-set tools to ease the synchronization process.

Timecode Sync

Instead of recording your band's performance in its entirety and matching mouth movements to the music in post, what if you could simply queue up the DAT to the point of the song you want to film, play it back while the band performs that scene, and sync them up easily later in post? With the addition of one piece of equipment—a Smart Slate—you can.

Figure 27.13 Timecode from the DAT that provides the music for lip synching is sent via a transmitter to the Smart Slate. Film a few frames of the Smart Slate as the music plays from the DAT to show exactly which frame of the audio is playing at the exact moment being filmed. With this information, you can easily sync the video with the audio.

Because timecode dropness plays a role in this lesson, you might want to watch the Timecode_Review.wmv tutorial, located in the Video Tutorials folder on the book's DVD. When the file loads in Windows Media Player, press Alt + Enter to play it back at full-screen size.

Here's how it works: During a video shoot, the band's song comes from a DAT with pre-striped timecode. You cue up the DAT to the portion of the song you wish to film. Via a wireless adapter, the DAT transmits its timecode to a Smart Slate (**Figure 27.13**). You film the timecode value displayed back on the Smart Slate before or after the band performs that particular section. Because the timecode on the Smart Slate corresponds with the timecode of the DAT, you can easily marry the captured video and audio by reassigning the timecode of the video file to match the timecode displayed in the Smart Slate. This lesson will show you how. The primary difference from the last lesson is that the audio for this lesson comes with timecode assigned already and is married to a Master video track. Because the audio comes off a captured DAT tape, you will use the tape's prewritten timecode as the basis for synchronizing the clips in the sequence.

For this lesson, assume you have one video clip that was married to the source audio and its timecode. This one clip will serve as your master audio with the timecode matching what was recorded with the Smart Slate for each shot. Your goal is to quickly synchronize the shots so that you can start editing. You will use footage from the music video I directed titled, "If You Must" by Del tha Funky Homosapien. You have four full camera takes to work with. Once you complete the synchronization feel free to experiment with different versions of the edit using whatever timing you want.

1. To start this lesson, open the project IYM_Start.prproj from the APPST2 Lesson Files/Chapter 27 folder. Select the menu listing Project > Project Settings > General. In the dialog box that appears change Display Format to 30 fps Non Drop-Frame Timecode and click OK. Go to Edit > Preferences > Media and make sure the check box for Display Media Timecode in Source Frame Rate is off.

   Because the Timecode value of the Smart Slate and audio is original in a non-drop-frame format, you set your project to display timecode in all panels as non-drop-frame. To ensure that the DV clips being used in this project adhere to displaying this same frame rate you turned off the check box for them to display media timecode in the source frame rate.

2. Drag and drop the IYM_Master.avi file (located in Chapter 27's IYM Media subfolder on the DVD), into Video 1 of the Multi-Cam Source sequence. Double-click on the IYM_BBoys.avi file to open it in the Source Monitor. With the clip open and displaying its first frame, select File > Timecode. In the Timecode dialog, type in the exact numbers that display in the Smart Slate of the video clip (01024402) and then click OK. At first, the clip opens without timecode matching that of the Smart Slate (**Figure 27.14**). With the clip active in the Source Monitor, choose File > Timecode menu to bring up the Timecode dialog, enter a new timecode value to match the Smart Slate, then click OK (**Figure 27.15**). Premiere Pro then updates the timecode in the clip (**Figure 27.16**). Drag and drop the clip onto Video 2 of the Multi-Cam Source Sequence.

DV as a video format is inherently drop-frame so even with your project set to display in non-drop-frame, if the Media preference of Display Media Timecode in Source Frame Rate is turned on, the DV clips in your project will display drop-frame.

Figure 27.14 When you first open the clip, the Timecode and Smart Slate don't match.

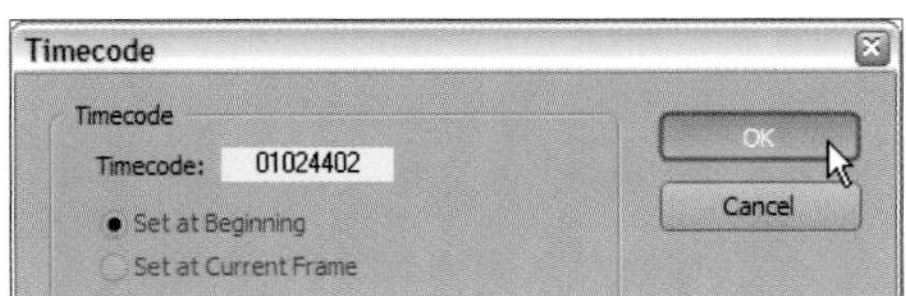

Figure 27.15 In the Timecode dialog, reassign a new Timecode value to match exactly what the Smart Slate displays.

Figure 27.16 Because the Edit Line was on the first frame, you can see that reassigning the timecode at the first frame was the only option to be selected. Once you clicked OK, Premiere Pro updates the clip's timecode.

This step is the nuts and bolts of the technique. You open a clip for which you want to reassign the timecode and you find a frame in which you can see the exact timecode value that you want to apply. In this case, the first frame of the clip has the Smart Slate displaying exactly the timecode value of the audio playing while the shot is being recorded. This audio timecode value is the same timecode that the IYM_MASTER.avi clip has assigned to it already.

With a clip either selected in the Project panel or active in the Source Monitor you can choose File > Timecode to access the Timecode dialog. Here you can reassign the timecode of any clip to update it to a new value. For this clip you updated it to have the same timecode as what displayed in the Smart Slate. Because you were on the first frame of video the Timecode dialog allowed you to choose Set at Beginning only. If your Smart Slate was 15 frames or 15 seconds into the clip, you would scrub to the frame revealing the timecode, access the dialog, enter the displayed timecode, and choose Set at Current Frame. Then you would apply a timecode adjustment so that the current frame in the Source Monitor updated to display exactly the value you entered in the dialog box. Adding the clip to the timeline provided your second multi-camera element.

In many instances multi-cam shoots will have different cameras with timecode that matches, except for the hours. If you think about it, Camera 1 sets its timecode to 01 hour, Camera 2 to 02, Camera 3 to 03, and Camera 4 to 04; when they start recording at the same time their minutes:seconds:frames line up but their hours are off. This makes it easy to distinguish between the cameras if you were looking at only the timecode. Clicking the check box to Ignore Hours is a feature designed for that type of workflow.

3. Open IYM_ChorusMaster.avi and reassign the first frame's timecode to the value displayed in the Smart Slate (01024114). Drop the clip onto Video 3. Open IYM_Crew.avi and reassign the first frame's timecode to be the value displayed in its Smart Slate (01024907). Drop it onto Video 4 of the timeline. Click in the Track Header of Video 1 to make sure it is light gray and the target video track. Press Ctrl+A to select all the clips, then right-click on the clips and choose Synchronize. In the Synchronize Clips dialog click on the button for Timecode and leave the value of 00:02:52:28 with Ignore Hours checked. Click OK (**Figure 27.17a, b,** and **c**). Now that the clips are aligned, feel free to nest the source sequence into the edit sequence, enable it for multi-camera, and practice your editing, creating your own cut of the end of the video.

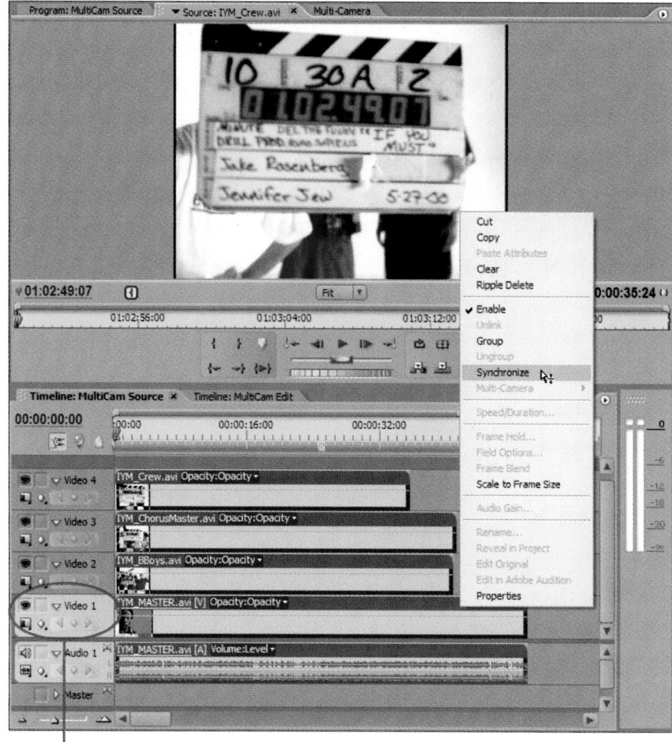

a

Regardless of whether an audio track is targeted, a video track overrides an audio track when synchronizing.

b

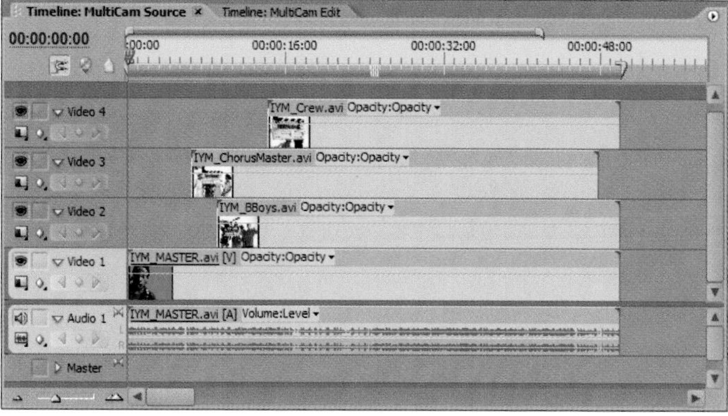

c

Figures 27.17a, b, and c To begin, drop all the clips into the timeline without synchronization (a). Targeting Video 1, which houses the Master Clip with the timecode reference matching the audio, choose the Synchronize menu listing. In the Synchronize dialog clicking on the Timecode button reveals the lowest timecode value that the selected clips all share in common (b). When you click OK with the default timecode value (c) all the clips align to have perfect synchronization as intended by the use of the Smart Slate.

For the final step you reassigned the Timecode value of the two remaining clips and added them to the timeline to complete your four-camera multi-camera clip limit. With all the clips in the timeline you first made sure that you targeted Video 1, which holds the reference timecode to which you want the other clips to synchronize. In the Synchronize Clips dialog you clicked Timecode. Because the clips share common timecode values, the lowest timecode value that is shared by all the clips is revealed as the default timecode to the right of the listing. Because each clip had the same 02 hour timecode value, leaving the check box for Ignore Hours checked was all right. Clicking OK realigned the clips so that Video 1 remained in place and all the above tracks shifted to accurately synchronize. In the synchronized timeline, when you scrub over the four video tracks each clip underneath the Edit Line will have exactly the same timecode as the clip above or below.

Continuing with the chapter's signature technique, you nested the source sequence, enabled it for multi-camera editing, and then hopefully kept experimenting and getting comfortable with multi-cam switching using the Multi-Camera Monitor.

Although this Smart Slate technique seems specific, it can be broadened to include multi-cam scenarios without Smart Slates in production. Because of the fact that you can reassign timecode to any frame, you could create your own custom timecode value to assign to sync points instead of using Numbered markers. If you applied a timecode value of 1;00;00;00 to the slate clap of each clip from the first lesson, you could synchronize them the same way; just use the Timecode feature in the Synchronize Clips dialog as opposed to Numbered markers.

Things to Remember

The biggest thing to remember about multi-cam shooting is to not stop any of your cameras until the shoot is complete. If a camera is stopped, you will lose your referenced sync point and have to create a new one for that camera. If you do stop one of your cameras, you must break the resulting clip up and create a second sync point for the new clip that starts after the initial sync point. Fortunately, with Premiere Pro 2.0 creating a second sync point is as easy as assigning two Numbered markers and using the Synchronize feature.

The workflow for shooting is

1. Start all cameras recording.
2. Use a slate or flash bulb to establish a sync point.
3. Continue recording material.
4. When all the material is complete, stop each camera.

The workflow for editing is

1. Create a source sequence and layer each camera on top of the other (up to four tracks).
2. Identify the sync point in each shot and assign the same Numbered marker to each clip at that point.
3. Select all the video tracks and right-click on the selection. Choose Synchronize and use the Numbered Clip Marker option assigned to the marker value you applied.
4. Nest the source sequence into a new sequence.
5. Right-click on the nested source sequence and choose Multi-Cam > Enable.
6. With the new sequence active open the Multi-Cam Monitor and start editing.
7. Adjust and modify edit points between shots in the sequence using the Rolling Edit tool.
8. Adjust and swap shots by right-clicking on any clip in your nested multi-cam sequence and selecting an alternate clip from the Multi-Cam menu.

This new workflow is very straightforward, and you now should be familiar enough with the tools and their behavior to get expected results. When using Numbered markers, custom timecode, or preassigned timecode values, remember that synchronization is always going to shift the clips that are not on the target track to align in the manner executed to the clip on the target track. If you want to synchronize to audio be sure that no video tracks are selected.

As for music videos when you are starting out, don't worry about having the Smart Slate or all the audio bells and whistles; just put as much money into the production of the video to make it look good as you can. There are easy ways to solve your audio and sync problems in post-production.

If you can shoot with synchronous timecode between all your cameras then it's very simple to align the shots in the timeline. If you have reference timecode that is visually shot but not recorded to tape, simply reassign the timecode to the clips and then synchronize them in the timeline.

If you are interested in viewing any of these videos in their entirety you can see them on my Web site at www.formikafilms.com.

Additional Chapters on DVD

Although this is the last page, it's not the end of the book.

Because Premiere Pro 2.0 has more features than will fit between these covers, on the DVD you'll find three bonus chapters that describe how professionals get things done. In these PDF files you'll learn to use the indispensable Adobe Clip Notes and Project Manager tools (Chapter 28), to encode into Flash, H.264, and Windows Media using the Adobe Media Encoder (Chapter 29), and to navigate the standards and settings for high-definition video (Chapter 30). If you want to stay ahead of your competition, pop in the DVD, head for the VI Professional Workflows folder, and keep reading.

Index

E

J

K

L

Q

R

S

T

U

V